D1180604

THE
SOVIET UNION
IN THE
THIRD WORLD:

THREAT TO
WORLD
PEACE?

THE SOVIET UNION IN THE THIRD WORLD: THREAT TO WORLD PEACE?

Joseph G. Whelan and Michael J. Dixon

PERGAMON-BRASSEY'S
International Defense Publishers, Inc.

Washington New York London Oxford
Beijing Frankfurt São Paulo Sydney Tokyo Toronto

Pergamon Press Offices:

U.S.A. (Editorial)	Pergamon-Brassey's International Defense Publishers, 1340 Old Chain Bridge Road, McLean, Virginia 22101
(Orders & Inquiries)	Pergamon Press, Maxwell House, Fairview Park, Elmsford, New York 10523, U.S.A.
U.K. (Editorial)	Brassey's Defence Publishers, Maxwell House, 74 Worship Street, London EC2A 2EN
(Orders & Enquiries)	Brassey's Defence Publishers, Headington Hill Hall, Oxford OX3 0BW, England
PEOPLE'S REPUBLIC OF CHINA	Pergamon Press, Qianmen Hotel, Beijing, People's Republic of China
FEDERAL REPUBLIC OF GERMANY	Pergamon Press, Hammerweg 6, D-6242 Kronberg-Taunus, Federal Republic of Germany
BRAZIL	Pergamon Editora, Rua Eça de Queiros, 346, CEP 04011, São Paulo, Brazil
AUSTRALIA	Pergamon Press (Aust.) Pty., P.O. Box 544, Potts Point, NSW 2011, Australia
JAPAN	Pergamon Press, 8th Floor, Matsuoka Central Building, 1-7-1 Nishishinjuku, Shinjuku, Tokyo 160, Japan
CANADA	Pergamon Press Canada, Suite 104, 150 Consumers Road, Willowdale, Ontario M2J 1P9, Canada

---

First printing 1986

Library of Congress Cataloging in Publication Data

Whelan, Joseph G.
  The Soviet Union in the Third World.

  1. Developing countries--Foreign relations--Soviet
Union. 2. Soviet Union--Foreign relations--Developing
countries. 3. World politics--1945-   . 4. Peace.
I. Dixon, Michael J. II. Title.
D888.S65W48   1986   327.470172'4   86-2382
ISBN 0-08-033999-9

*In order to make this volume available as economically and
as rapidly as possible, the authors' typescripts have been
reproduced in their original forms. This method
unfortunately has its typographical limitations but it is
hoped that they in no way distract the reader.*

Printed in the United States of America

To George Berdes and Bob Huber, staff consultants
of the House Foreign Affairs Committee,
who have an uncanny penchant for asking the basic question

PUBLISHER'S NOTE

Many concerned citizens fear that a nuclear conflict will not start directly between the two superpowers, but because of a smaller conflict as U.S. and Soviet interests clash in the Third World. It is because of the contribution of this U.S. government study to understanding these interests that we are pleased to publish this book and make it broadly available to an international audience.

This book covers critical issues that affect us all and is encyclopedic in its coverage of the Soviet Union's activities in the Third World. This book has four unique features: (1) a summary of past Soviet involvement in the Third World and a focus on key areas of conflict; (2) a global context that permits an analysis of the relationships between Soviet activities in all parts of the world; (3) a concentration on key regional issues of U.S. foreign policy; and (4) an assessment of possible future directions of Soviet policy, Soviet prospects, the implications for world peace, and the role of diplomacy and negotiations in avoiding conflict.

Pergamon-Brassey's International
Defense Publishers, Inc.
Washington, D.C.
May 1986

FOREWORD

This publication is the third in a series of studies published by the Committee on Foreign Affairs in cooperation with the Congressional Research Service of the Library of Congress on Soviet policy in the Third World. Since the last publication in 1981, Soviet policy has undergone some significant changes while still maintaining continuity in many of its basic objectives and their implementation.

The invasion of Afghanistan and the resultant Western response, the collapse of the SALT II agreement, the instability in Poland, and the lack of strong leadership during the 1980–85 period have produced a phase in Soviet Third World policy which has emphasized consolidation of past successes but also a marked hesitancy to take on the political and economic costs of obtaining major new friends and allies. Moreover, this publication documents a serious debate among Soviet officials and academic specialists concerned with Third World policy about the political and economic value of Soviet Third World successes, the relative strength of Western policy in the Third World, particularly concerning economic relations with the developing nations, and the questioning of the Soviet strategy of rapid industrialization as a model for Third World development.

This phase has also led to a strategy of greater attention to East-West questions such as arms control, proposals for confidence-building measures in Asia and the Persian Gulf, and the formulation of "rules of the game" for limiting superpower competition in the Third World. At the same time, the Soviet military buildup in Asia, the economic and military support for Cuba and its subversive activities in Africa and particularly Central America, and the continued occupation of Afghanistan demonstrate present unwillingness to alter fundamentally Soviet political, strategic, and ideological objectives in the Third World.

Preserving vital U.S. national security and foreign policy interests in the Third World areas while recognizing the possibilities for reducing confrontation with the Soviet Union that could lead to dangerous escalation remains a major challenge for U.S. foreign policy which will continue to confront Congress and the executive branch. This study will undoubtedly contribute to facing that challenge.

The material and findings herein are the views of the Congressional Research Service, in coordination with the committee staff.

The material and findings do not necessarily represent the views of the Committee on Foreign Affairs or its members.

DANTE B. FASCELL,
Chairman, Committee on Foreign Affairs.

ACKNOWLEDGMENTS

The authors wish to acknowledge with gratitude the assistance of the following colleagues in the Library of Congress Congressional Research Service, and the staff of the Committee on Foreign Affairs who reviewed this study in whole or in part, offered constructive criticism, and in some instances, particularly among the non-Soviet regional specialists, provided important bibliographic guidance: Francis T. Miko, Specialist in International Relations (Soviet Affairs); Stuart D. Goldman, Analyst in Soviet Affairs; William H. Cooper, Analyst in International Trade and Finance and a specialist in Soviet affairs; John P. Hardt, Senior Specialist in Soviet Economics; George D. Holliday, Specialist in International Trade and Finance and a specialist in Soviet affairs; Stanley J. Heginbotham, Chief, Foreign Affairs and National Defense Division, Senior Specialist in International Affairs, and specialist in Asian affairs and international development; Larry A. Niksch, Specialist in Asian Affairs; Richard P. Cronin, Specialist in Asian Affairs; Ruebens Medina, Chief, Hispanic Law Division, Law Library, Library of Congress; Nina M. Serafino, Analyst in Latin American Affairs; K. Larry Storrs, Analyst in Latin American Affairs; Steven R. Harper, Analyst in Latin American Affairs; Richard M. Preece, Specialist in International Relations (Middle Eastern affairs); Ellen B. Laipson, Specialist in Middle Eastern and North African Affairs; Raymond W. Copson, Specialist in International Relations (African affairs); Brenda M. Branaman, Analyst in Middle Eastern and African Affairs; James W. Robinson, Coordinator of Review and longtime specialist in international relations; James A. Sayler, a political scientist, writer, and senior reviewer in CRS' Review Section; and Robert T. Huber, staff consultant, Committee on Foreign Affairs, U.S. House of Representatives. Clerical support was provided by Linda S. Kline and Claudette C. Lytle.

SUMMARY OF THE STUDY

PART I—COMMITMENT IN PERSPECTIVE

Two previous studies prepared by the Congressional Research Service, published in 1977 and 1981 by the House Foreign Affairs Committee, suggest the following generalizations: (1) That the Soviet Union maintains a firm and active commitment to the Third World; and (2) that the Third World holds an important, perhaps even vital, place in the Soviet world view.

The principal purposes of this current study are to analyze Soviet activities in the Third World during 1980–85 and to determine whether these generalizations are still valid. The study, subdivided into six parts, is structured around four basic questions: Trends in the Soviet experience, the rationale and instrumentalities of Soviet policy, the meaning of its involvement, and the implications for U.S. foreign policy.

The limitations of the study derive from the magnitude of the Third World and from the diversity and complexity of Soviet policy. At best the study seeks only to suggest the main thrust and broad lines of Soviet Third World policy, concentrating on the non-Communist regions of Asia, the Middle East, Africa, and Latin America.

TRENDS, OBJECTIVES, AND INSTRUMENTALITIES OF SOVIET THIRD WORLD POLICY: A RETROSPECTIVE GLANCE

The Third World is a new source of international power and influence; it is a principal element in Soviet foreign policy. The importance of the Third World derives from its physical attributes, its political organization and activities, and its geopolitical and geostrategic potentialities. The Third World is a powerful force enabling it to apply pressure internationally. It has been and continues to be the focus of major and minor regional conflicts in the postcolonial era.

Soviet objectives in the Third World are ideological, political, economic, and strategic. The destinies of Third World countries are said to be linked ideologically to the Soviet Union, and an unchanging Soviet ideological objective is, therefore, to reinforce that linkage. The Soviets understand the great political value of the Third World in that it presents the opportunity and the instrumentality for expanding and globalizing Soviet influence and power. Economically, the Third World serves as a market for Soviet economic goods, military weapons, and a source for raw materials. Denial of resources, trade, and political support of the Third World to the West would weaken their "imperialist" adversary. The Soviets have strategic interests in the Third World, and the shift of their policy from traditional continentalism to globalism has placed a burden on strategic requirements. For these reasons the Third World is important in Soviet foreign policy and the composite of purposes suggest a surge toward globalism.

The Soviet Union has used multiple instruments for pursuing its multiple goals in the Third World: Economic aid and trade; military assistance and use of military power for political purposes; policies and actions that support Third World causes and interests while simultaneously serving those of the Soviet Union; and international radio broadcasting and cultural diplomacy. All instrumentalities are directed at the "national liberation zone," areas of strategic, economic and political importance in Asia, the Middle East, Africa, and Latin America. The transcending goal is to expand Soviet power and influence and to deny that of the United States, its allies, and China.

Soviet policy in the Third World has passed through four stages since 1945: One of hostility under Stalin; commitment and adventurism under Khrushchev; constraint and then expansionism under Brezhnev; and restraint and caution in the late Brezhnev and early Andropov era.

26TH SOVIET COMMUNIST PARTY CONGRESS: BREZHNEV'S REFLECTIONS ON THE THIRD WORLD

Brezhnev devoted a major part of his main report to the 26th Party Congress in February 1981 to the Third World. He emphasized successes in the national liberation movement at the expense of the former colonial powers, making a clear differentiation among the liberated countries. He reaffirmed the Soviet commitment to the Third World, citing such concrete evidence of support as treaties of friendship and cooperation, extensive Soviet economic, scientific, and technological cooperation, and military assistance on request.

In viewing the Third World within the larger context of international, East-West, and North-South relations, Brezhnev placed the Soviet Union squarely in the corner of the Third World and against the United States and the other "imperialist" powers. He made specific peace proposals bearing on Third World areas, designed to coincide with further Soviet policy interests. Brezhnev showed deference to the Third World countries, but only in a very general way. He reserved the highest praise for India which occupies "a major place" in Soviet relations with the liberated countries. In brief, Brezhnev seemed to have a good word for everyone in the Third World; he was out to win new friends, consolidate old friendships, and contribute to building a political environment in which Soviet policy could flourish.

Brezhnev reaffirmed the Soviet commitment to the Third World, but it is a commitment marked by caution and restraint, quite in contrast to his vigorously expressed triumphant views at the 25th Party Congress when Soviet expansionism was reaching a high point. This changing approach to the Third World suggests the possibility that the 1980's may not be the time for Soviet adverturism in the Third World, as exemplified by intervention in Angola and Ethiopia, but rather a time of greater restraint and caution—a time for backing off, recalling the carefully measured and rationalized commitment in the early Brezhnev years following the near decade of Khrushchev's often excessive adventurism.

ANDROPOV'S VIEWS ON THE THIRD WORLD

Continuity of policy was not broken when Andropov succeeded Brezhnev as Secretary General in November 1982, even to the most recent trend toward caution and restraint. Since assuming leadership, Andropov has concentrated primarily on East-West relations in his foreign policy speeches and other utterances and has given relatively short shrift to the Third World. He expressed Soviet sympathies for the LDC's, but only in general terms, and refrained from the verbal assertiveness apparent in Brezhnev's statements in the mid- and late 1970's. He acknowledged the dire economic conditions facing the Third World, but offered nothing more than moral support of the Soviet Union. Clearly, in the economic realm the word went out, as it had under Brezhnev, that the Third World must resolve its own problems and not necessarily look to the Soviet Union for assistance, particularly in areas where costs are not clearly matched by benefits. "Self-help" seems to be the watchword in current Soviet Third World policy. But low-cost targets of opportunity (e.g., Grenada) where political support and military assistance exact no great price would appear to be acceptable.

VIEWS OF SOVIET FOREIGN POLICY SPECIALISTS

Soviet specialists on the Third World have provided the leadership with a range of options upon which to build policy. Thus Soviet Third World policy in the 1980's may not necessarily reflect the whims and caprices of a particular leader (as in the case of Khrushchev), but rather rest upon serious study within the Marxist-Leninist context.

Marked differentiation in approaches to the Third World lies beneath the veneer of propaganda that conveys an apparent consensus in Soviet policy. Soviet foreign policy specialists differ in their analyses of the Soviet role in the Third World and sometimes offer radically different prescriptions to Soviet policymakers.

Soviet thought on approaches to the Third World is, therefore, by no means linear. The acknowledged complexity of Third World problems produces distinctive variations in the writings of Soviet scholars. Altogether they suggest creativity and intellectualism, but within accepted contextual dogma officially established rules and assumptions. Also, the commentaries by these specialists focus mainly on economic development in the Third World. Little or nothing is said about military assistance. And yet military aid, along with generous political support, as will be shown below, is a major component of Soviet involvement in the Third World. Unlike economic aid, it is a means for spreading Soviet influence and power "within the budget." And while questions may arise among Soviet leaders and scholars about the extent of commitment on the economic level, such reservations appear less often on the policy of military assistance.

PART II—THE SOVIETS IN ASIA: AN EXPANDING PRESENCE

SOVIET INVOLVEMENT IN ASIA

Russia is an Eurasian state with roots in both Europe and Asia. The Soviet Union shares the imperial legacy of the Czars whose expanding empire had absorbed vast territories in Asia. Beginning from its small Kievan base in the 9th to the 13th centuries, Russia was to expand beyond its European territories to Asia. European colonialism receded completely in Asia during the post-World War II period, except for the Soviet Union. By virtue of the continuous (and contiguous) expansion of its Asian territories, Russia accounts for more than one-third of Asia. Thus the Soviet Union is a European, Asian, and Pacific power. And territorial expansion has been and continues to be one of the most dynamic forces in Russian history.

GEOSTRATEGIC NEEDS, AMBITIONS, AND POLICY GOALS

As an Asian power the Soviet Union has geostrategic needs, ambitions, and goals in that part of the world. It has power, instrumentalities, and tactics for pursuing its ends. And it has pursued a policy that has taken on defensive (Brezhnev's peace offensive of 1981) and offensive (military buildup) characteristics.

The Soviet conflict with China, its military buildup in Asia, along with the Soviet invasion of Afghanistan and military involvement in Kampuchea as Vietnam's patron and mentor, have largely determined recent relationships between the Soviet Union and the countries of Asia. The effects of this buildup, particularly in naval and strategic forces, and the aggressive use of military power, have reverberated throughout the entire Asian Continent and have fundamentally and adversely impacted upon Soviet-American relations in Asia and the Western Pacific. In brief, the militarization of Soviet policy, notably the continuous military buildup since the early 1970's, has enabled the Soviets to establish an unprecedented military presence in Asia and the Western Pacific for the projection of its power and influence.

MAJOR TRENDS IN SOVIET ASIAN POLICY

Russia's military buildup has provided the kinetic energy for Soviet policy in Asia. This policy has contributed to shaping three major trends that were to affect Soviet political relations in the Third World area: (1) U.S. withdrawal, Soviet resurgence, and a U.S. recommitment in Asia; (2) the continuing negative impact on the countries of Asia of the Soviet Union's invasion of Afghanistan and its support for Vietnam's aggression in Kampuchea; and (3) an evolving stalemate and enduring paradox in a Soviet policy that proclaims peaceful intent but pursues an aggressive military course.

AFGHANISTAN: CATALYST AND STALEMATE

Afghanistan is a classic case of Soviet military aggression against a Third World country. The Soviet presence in Afghanistan acts as a continuing catalyst for arousing Asian's suspicions of Soviet purposes. The Soviets have achieved only a qualified military success there. Military analysts speak of a stalemate with a Soviet strategy geared to the long-term erosion of resistance and gradual strengthening of the Soviet hold on the country. Efforts to reach a political settlement with Pakistan on aspects of the problem through U.N. auspices have failed. Though stalemated on the military and diplomatic fronts, the Soviets have, nonetheless, managed to carry forward their program of Sovietization, meaning the reconstruction of Afghanistan along Soviet lines and possibly even its ultimate absorption into the U.S.S.R. as a Union republic. Mongolia is often cited as the interim model.

Thus far the Soviets have achieved some political, military, social, and economic gains in their occupation and continuing war in Afghanistan. They control the urban areas, leaving the countryside largely to the mujahidin "Freedom Fighters." But they are paying a high price. Prospects for the immediate future appear not to be particularly bright for either the Soviets or the mujahidin guerrillas. Stalemate best describes the prevailing condition.

CHINA: BARRIER TO EXPANDING SOVIET POWER

The aftershock of Russia's invasion of Afghanistan continues to reverberate throughout Northeast Asia. China, for a long time at odds with the Soviet Union, was visibly alarmed by this act of aggression. These fears were further heightened by Soviet support for Vietnam's military conquest of Kampuchea and by the general, and continuous, Soviet military buildup in the Far East. The militarization of the sino-Soviet border has added to growing tensions over the years. Soviet efforts to conciliate China have thus far failed, but the dialog goes on, though differences remain fundamental and, therefore, durable.

China's rivalry with the Russians extends beyond the Asian Continent to the Third World where for over two decades they have competed for influence. But Russia's aggressive policy in Asia has worked at cross purposes with its larger Third World policy: It has harmed Soviet ties with the Third World countries of ASEAN and unwittingly benefited the Chinese. For in its search for a counterweight to the Soviet presence in Indochina, ASEAN found China. Russia's aggressive Asian policy has also regenerated China's interest in competing more vigorously in the Third World.

REAWAKENING OF JAPAN

Soviet policy of expansion and military buildup in Asia has also had a profound impact on Japan. Arousing long suppressed Japanese anxieties for its security, this aggressive Soviet policy has accelerated the changing direction of Japanese policy from pacifism and isolationism to a greater involvement in international affairs, even to assuming a larger share of the defense burden for the Asian-Pacific region.

Soviet policy has been counterproductive in another way. It has deepened Japanese political and economic involvement in Southeast Asia, to the detriment of Soviet interests in that Third World area. As in the case of China, Russia's Asian policy and its aggressive behavior in the Far East have conjured up the reality of a

Soviet threat, spurred the building of an informal anti-Soviet coalition, created a new and more outgoing role for Japan in Asia, and adversely affected Russia's larger designs on the Third World countries of Southeast Asia.

Soviet policy in Asia has also worked at cross purposes in another way: It has alienated Japan, the only Asian country that could contribute considerably to the much needed development of Soviet resources in Siberia and the Soviet Far East.

STIFFENING ASEAN RESISTANCE TO SOVIET EXPANSION

Soviet policy objectives in Southeast Asia seem designed to satisfy much larger strategic needs for expanding Soviet power in Asia, the Pacific and the Middle East. Vital chokepoints, located in Southeast Asia through which sea traffic from Asia to the Middle East must pass, are prizes to be won in any contest for predominating influence in the Asian-Pacific region.

Filling the vacuum left by American withdrawal from Vietnam, the Soviets appear to have set their sights on expanding their influence throughout the Indochinese Peninsula, using Vietnam as their base and promoting a trend toward neutralism within the Asian nations. They seem bent on drawing the Communist states of Vietnam, Laos, and Kampuchea into the Soviet orbit. Their ultimate purpose appears to be the removal of resurgent U.S. influence from Southeast Asia; the isolation of China; and the creation of a new balance of power in Asia favorable to Moscow.

Russia's expansionist policy in Asia, particularly its support of Vietnam's invasion of Kampuchea, accelerated the unity of ASEAN and transformed its perception of the Soviet Union from one of "guarded reserve" to the belief that it was a "threat potential." ASEAN has reacted in a variety of ways to counter the perceived Soviet threat, such as increasing defense spending and staging joint exercises. Even the strategic role of Taiwan, overseeing the north-south traffic through the Formosan Strait and long considered an "outcast" in the international politics of the area, is apparently being reevaluated.

In sum, Soviet involvement has brought changes in the structuring of the international politics of Southeast Asia and the building of a loosely connected anti-Soviet coalition; it has denied the Soviet Union, therefore, a prime potential Third World target; but it has also created for the Soviets a formidable presence in Vietnam that has brought them substantial benefits (naval bases within easy range of critical Southeast Asian chokepoints), however, at heavy cost.

INDIA, CENTERPIECE OF SOVIET THIRD WORLD POLICY

The Soviet approach to India has differed remarkably from that of its approach to other Asian countries. India is a special case, an exception. Since the mid-1950's, India, a major force in the nonalignment movement, has been the centerpiece of Soviet policy in the Third World. Perceiving India as a "natural ally" in accordance with its ideological construct of "peaceful coexistence," the Soviets have persistently attempted to solidify their relationship with India by dispensing timely and valuable political support and equally valuable economic and military assistance.

India has it own interests to be achieved through the Soviet connection. These interests flow from the need for foreign assistance in internal economic development and from a perceived need for Soviet support in foreign policy. Specialists on Soviet-Indian relations speak of a "coincidence of interests," internal, regional, and strategic, that have bound both countries in a unique and mutually satisfying relationship.

The Soviet invasion of Afghanistan and Vietnamese occupation of Kampuchea have tested the Soviet-Indian relationship as nothing before. Afghanistan, particularly, has had the potential for disrupting the relationship. Most of the nonaligned Third World have voiced their opposition to the Soviet invasion. But India, following a cautious and equivocating policy, has refused to condemn the Soviets. But it has expressed disapproval; urged the withdrawal of military forces; and has quietly worked behind the scene to bring this about.

The Soviets have faced the major task of salvaging a damaged relationship. To accomplish this, they have exerted countervailing pressures on the diplomatic level (official visits by political and military leaders) and provided a substantial outpouring of economic and military aid.

The central issue in Soviet-Indian relations, viewed as a problem in Moscow's Third World policy, is the matter of influence. In brief, the Soviets have a strong presence in India; they have invested much resources, political, economic, anc military, to strengthen this relationship. However, in such key cases as the Afghan issue, arms transfers, and efforts to pressure India within the nonalignment movement, Soviet success has gone no further than what the Indians themselves have permitted. Conversely, the Indians have not been able to bring sufficient influence to bear on Moscow to fundamentally affect its policy in Afghanistan.

In the future, the Soviet presence in India will probably remain formidable, and Soviet economic and military assistance, along with key political support, the principal instruments of policy. Yet, India has succeeded in keeping its principles and interests in its relations with Moscow firmly intact. Thus Soviet influence in the future as in the past will no doubt have to be measured by what New Delhi perceives to be its own interests.

SOVIET INVOLVEMENT IN ASIA: ITS MEANING

This brief survey of the expanding Soviet presence in Asia from the perspective of its Third World policy suggests four broad generalizations that give meaning to the unfolding events and to the general direction of Soviet policy in the 1980's: (1) The Soviets have been inclined to take the military option in their approach to Asia, notwithstanding the sacrifice of potential, political and economic gains; (2) the militarization of Soviet policy has tended to polarize the international politics of Asia, creating a new balance of power and a "massive barrier" of nations opposing Soviet expansionism; (3) India, as the nation in between the major contending forces in Asia, more regionally directed and apparently unmindful of larger continental strategic considerations, is an exception to Russia's Asian policy, though the militarization of Soviet policy, notably in the Afghan and Kampuchean issues, has imposed serious limitations on Moscow's effectiveness in India; and (4) the extent of Soviet involvement in Asia in recent years suggests that the Soviet Union may be entering a new stage of expansion in the Asian-Pacific region. Accordingly, the Soviet commitment to the Asian part of the Third World continues to be essential, even vital, to its world view, and that commitment is firm and expanding. Yet, significant internal and external factors exist that can deter, perhaps even undermine, Soviet expansionism in Asia and elsewhere in the Third World. These factors can be summed up in the term, "the limits of imperial power."

Part III—The Soviet Union in the Middle East

The Soviet Union seeks to be a Middle East power and its role there has been either as a participant or a spoiler in the region's affairs. Despite the U.S.S.R.'s proximity to the region, the United States is still the more influential power, particularly in the Arab-Israeli and oil-producing spheres, and exerts strong constraints on the exercise of Soviet power. The Middle East has been an arena of superpower competition since World War II, during which time the United States has sought to contain Soviet expansionism. Competition with the United States greatly affects Soviet policy toward the Middle East, and is likely to increase in the future as long as the United States follows the principles of the Carter doctrine, enunciated in 1980 after the Soviet invasion of Afghanistan, to defend the Persian Gulf against foreign military challenges. Soviet calculations concerning the possiblity of U.S. involvement and the desire to avoid a military confrontation with the United States appear to be an overriding consideration in Soviet decisionmaking. At the same time, Moscow's policies are intended to reduce U.S. and Western influence in the Middle East and deny Washington military and security relationships with local states.

The Soviet Union has been excluded from Arab-Israeli negotiations; its recent involvement in this area of Mideast politics has been as a spoiler, attempting to undermine the successful follow-through of the Camp David treaty and seeking to block a resolution of the Lebanon conflict on U.S. terms, primarily through support for Syria. Recent U.S. and Western participation in the Lebanese peacekeeping force contributes to Moscow's viewing the competition in the Mideast as an East-West confrontation. Reagan administration policy toward Libya, viewing that country as a client state of the U.S.S.R. aided and encouraged by Moscow to destabilize pro-Western governments, further illustrates the superpower competition endemic to the region.

An indication of the importance of the Middle East to Soviet security is the amount of military aid it has provided. In 1981, the latest years for which reliable, official U.S. estimates are available, the Soviets signed military agreements valued at $3.5 billion with North African and Middle East states, equivalent to 58 percent of all military agreements signed with the Third World in that year. Eastern Europe signed arms agreements worth over $2 billion with

Mideast states in 1981, and only $20 million with other Third World countries. A similar share of Soviet military advisers in the Third World was located in the Mideast and North Africa, about 9,400 personnel or 58 percent of the total. In 1981, 76 percent of all Soviet and East European economic technicians abroad (or about 73,000) were in the Mideast and North Africa, most of whom were in Libya, Iraq, Algeria, and Syria. In the 28 years from 1954 to 1981, of the $34 billion in Soviet bloc aid extended to the Third World, nearly $17 billion—almost half—went to the Middle East (including Turkey).[1]

The Soviet Union probably will continue to stress past themes in its policies toward the Middle East. Moscow has found limited success with close relations with such client states as Syria and the People's Democratic Republic of (South) Yemen (PDRY), as well as friends like Libya and Iraq (where Soviet influence has generally diminished owing to the Iran-Iraq war and Soviet relations with Iran). The Soviets can probably by expected to nurture close ties, with arms transfers and economic aid, to these countries; however, major inroads will probably be limited to these countries. In the year since Yuri Andropov replaced Leonid Brezhnev as Soviet Communist Party leader in November 1982, Moscow has demonstrated a shift toward Iraq and away from Iran, most dramatically by the resumption of arms shipments to Iraq as well as with high-level official exchanges. Under Andropov, the Soviets reaffirmed their strong support for Syria with the delivery of sophisticated SAM–5 antiaircraft missiles in late 1982. The move has been interpreted as a signal to the United States that the U.S.S.R. intends to protect its interests in the Middle East.

Although relations have been poor since 1980, new opportunities may arise in Iran where Soviet maneuverings could capitalize on internal instability, ethnic unrest, the prolonged war with Iraq, and Iranian requirements for arms and perhaps greater economic assistance and trade from the Soviets. In 1983, Soviet-Iranian relations dipped to an all-time low, largely as a consequence of the crackdown by the Islamic Republic authorities on the Communist Tudeh Party and Iranian dissatisfaction with the U.S.S.R.'s pro-Iraqi tilt in late 1982. Although the Islamic Republic is fundamentally hostile toward Moscow, its foreign policy has oscillated between confrontation and coexistence with Moscow. Despite the presence of many Soviet bloc military and economic advisers in the country and increased trade with the U.S.S.R., Iran is not dependent on commerce with the Soviets. Moscow has been frustrated by Iranian actions on important issues such as Afghanistan and natural gas deliveries. Soviet involvement in Afghanistan, commitments in Eastern Europe, and logistical obstacles indicate that a Soviet invasion is not likely, barring a crisis of strategic proportions. Soviet leaders may be anticipating future instability in Iran followed by a government with pro-Soviet inclinations as their best option, rather than military interference in the country.

The focus of superpower rivalry in the Middle East has shifted from the Arab-Israeli zone since the fall of the Shah and the Soviet

---

[1] Figures derived from: U.S. Department of State. Soviet and East European Aid to the Third World, 1981. February 1983. Publication 9345, pp. 2 and 17–21.

invasion of Afghanistan to the Persian Gulf. There, Soviet policies might concentrate on rolling back U.S. military capabilities and undermining U.S. security ties to the conservative sheikdoms of the Arabian Peninsula, while preventing a long-term improvement in U.S.-Iranian relations. The Soviets have attempted to impress the Gulf states of its benign intentions. Moscow has tried to develop normal diplomatic relations, as well as encourage commerce and arms sales, with the conservative governments. A number of limited breakthroughs occurred in 1980–82 in Soviet relations with the states of the Arabian Peninsula. Kuwait, once inaccessible to the Soviets, concluded an agreement for arms from Moscow in 1980 and has stepped up trade with the Soviet bloc, including oil deliveries. Kuwait has also been critical of the U.S. military presence in the region and seeks to prohibit foreign military bases and rights in the region, a position supported by the Soviets. The United Arab Emirates has shown signs of opening up its relations with the Soviet bloc.

Jordan, a moderate, pro-Western monarchy, has received deliveries of $200 million in Soviet air defense equipment, representing a major achievement in the Arab-Israeli sphere for Soviet policies. Further south, while Soviet relations with the PDRY remain strong, South Yemen has apparently moderated its attitude toward its pro-Western neighbors, particularly Oman with whom it has at least temporarily improved relations. Nonetheless, the possibility of Soviet-PDRY subversion in North Yemen, Oman, and Saudi Arabia remains. The moderation of PDRY foreign policy, if it in fact develops, could aid Soviet efforts to improve ties with the Persian Gulf states and may indicate a Soviet willingness to moderate ideological considerations for short-term political gains. In North Yemen (the Yemen Arab Republic), where the Central Government has been waging an on-and-off civil war with leftist rebels aided by South Yemen, Soviet influence has increased with the delivery of vast amounts of arms and the presence of numerous East bloc military and economic advisers. By many accounts, the YAR's security is indebted to Soviet assistance despite U.S. and Saudi efforts to aid the Sana's Government and pry it loose from Soviet influence. With a strong presence in North Yemen and overwhelming control of the PDRY, the Soviet union may be in a position to pressure Saudi Arabia militarily and politically. Yemeni unification (with a resultant population approaching that of Saudi Arabia), long a source of speculation, is not an immediate goal of Soviet policy, although under more promising conditions future Soviet attitudes may change. The Soviets have so far successfully managed relations with both Yemens.

Although the Saudis continue to resist Soviet offers to establish diplomatic relations, in recent years, the two sides have hinted that there might be a possibility of exchanging embassies. However, Soviet relations with Riyadh may depend more on the state of Saudi-U.S. relations than anything else. There is no indication yet of direct Soviet successes in Saudi Arabia, but the Soviets may be encouraged by Saudi unwillingness to publicly sanction a U.S. military presence in the region despite the strengthening of U.S.-Saudi security ties and Saudi views on recent U.S. moves toward closer cooperation with Israel.

Although in the late Brezhnev years, the Soviet Union was excluded from negotiations toward a peaceful resolution of the Arab-Israeli confrontation, now that the peace process has extended beyond the Egyptian-Israeli phase, the Kremlin has based its policies on the expectation that U.S.-sponsored peace proposals and U.S. identification with Israel will serve broader Soviet interests in the Middle East. Moscow has often claimed that it is better able to represent the Arab cause in international efforts than the United States. The Soviets adopted a similar policy following the Israeli invasion of Lebanon, hoping that Arab opinion would turn against Western involvement resulting in a loss of U.S. and European influence in the region. At the time, the Kremlin chose not to come to the direct aid of the Palestinian Liberation Organization (PLO) or Syria, a decision that brought criticism upon Moscow as weak, indecisive, and unreliable. During 1983, however, the Soviets have demonstrated strong support for Syria and the PLO even though Syria has attempted to undermine the leadership of Yasir Arafat.

The U.S.S.R. continues to support the existence of the State of Israel but also demands in its peace formulas the creation of a Palestinian nation. Since the assassination of President Sadat in October 1981, Moscow and Egypt have moved toward normalizing relations. Egypt under President Mubarak is less anti-Soviet than under Sadat, though still committed to a close security relationship with the United States. Meanwhile, the Soviets have sharply stepped up arms shipments to Syria, completely replacing and exceeding inventories Syria possessed before the Lebanon war with Israel, including the delivery in late 1982 of long-range SAM-5 surface-to-air missiles, manned by Soviet technicians, never before available to Soviet client states.[2] Although Soviet and Syrian political objectives diverge on a number of important issues, the two nations developed a closer relationship in the years 1980–83 based primarily on military assistance and a diplomatic partnership.

PART IV—THE SOVIET UNION IN AFRICA: CONSOLIDATION OF GAINS

Soviet involvement in the Third World has been an important part of Soviet foreign policy since the 1950's. With the 1974 Portugese and Ethiopian revolutions, Africa assumed a larger role in Soviet calculations in the Third World because it presented Moscow a unique target of opportunity. Estimates of the importance of Africa to the U.S.S.R. and the success of Soviet policy in the region differ markedly. With the possible exception of the Horn, sub-Saharan Africa ranks low in Soviet strategic priorities and would be of little value in global or European conflicts. This paper examines Soviet policy in sub-Saharan Africa in the early years of the 1980's and attempts to assess its successes and failures with an eye toward future Soviet engagement in the continent.

The complexity of the African political scene makes any assessment of the Soviet Union's intentions there difficult. The nations of the continent have suffered the turmoil of decolonization, and they remain largely dependent on Western economic and technical as-

[2] U.S. House of Representatives. Committee on Foreign Affairs. Subcommittee on Europe and the Middle East. Hearings. (June 2, 1983) Developments in the Middle East, June 1983, pp. 9–10.

sistance and trade. Africa is impoverished, militarily weak, and politically, ethnically, and socially divided—all factors that encourage political crises that the Soviets can exploit to their advantage. Africa's vulnerabilities have invited Soviet involvement and successes, while such factors as political instability and economic necessity have also caused Soviet setbacks on the continent. In the 1960's and 1970's, for example, Soviet influence expanded into newly independent, avowedly socialist, anti-Western states such as Ghana, Guinea, Mali, Congo-Brazzaville, and Somalia. Soviet influence quickly evaporated when governments were overthrown, as in Mali and Ghana, or when nations reevaluated the need for closer Western connections, as in Somalia and Egypt. Africa's inherent instability and the independent views of Africa's leaders on the continent's own best interests may continue to bedevil Soviet policy and check Soviet advances.

In 1980, the Soviet position in Africa seemed strong. The Soviets had scored major gains in Africa when, in 1975 and 1976, they supported the massive intervention of Cuban forces in Angola, on the side of the MPLA faction, as Portugal withdrew. The Marxist government in newly independent Mozambique, another Portuguese colony, signed a treaty of friendship and cooperation with the Soviets in 1977. These advances were followed in 1977 and 1978 by Soviet and Cuban aid to revolutionary Ethiopia, which was at war with the U.S.S.R.'s former ally, Somalia. The U.S.S.R. appeared to have made important inroads into Africa and this elicited a strong U.S. reaction. The Soviets, many argued, had demonstrated their intention to exploit political crises in Africa for their own benefit.

The record of Soviet achievements now appears more ambiguous. The Soviet Union maintains a commitment to "socialist-oriented" governments in African countries such as Ethiopia, Angola, Mozambique, Congo, and Guinea-Bissau; but many of these countries continue to face domestic and foreign challenges to the consolidation of a Soviet-style government. Indeed, the U.S.S.R. has confronted resistance in Africa to its models of political and economic development. African nations have also recognized the limits of Soviet resources and the assistance it is willing to offer for development. Many of Moscow's allies are turning to the West for trade and economic aid, a trend that disturbs Soviet leaders. In southern Africa, the negotiation of security agreements between the Republic of South Africa and Angola and Mozambique in February 1984 represents a clear embarrassment for Soviet policies in the region. Moscow may wonder whether such arrangements indicate a turn in favor of diplomacy and pragmatism for the black frontline states arrayed against South Africa and a lessening of the viability of a militant resolution of the southern Africa problem.

Soviet achievements in one area often lead to setbacks elsewhere. For example, the Soviet switch to Ethiopia has apparently closed the door to better relations with Somalia and probably contributes to poor ties with the Sudan. Soviet-Libyan relations, which are uneven and difficult to manage for the Soviets, present obstacles to a rapprochement with Egypt and the Sudan. A Soviet presence in the region also invites close U.S. security arrangements with such countries as Somalia, Sudan, Kenya, and Zaire. Furthermore, past Soviet ties to such tyrants as Idi Amin of Uganda and Macias

Nguema of Equatorial Guinea, both now deposed, have discredited Moscow to some degree. Finally, the limited Soviet ability or willingness to contribute to the resolution of the hunger crisis now confronting much of Africa could restrain the growth of Soviet influence.

Soviet achievements in the late 1970's and early 1980's have been real, however. The Soviets have visibly succeeded in projecting their military and political power in African affairs and in reinforcing political behavior in their interests. The continuing presence of Cuban troops and large numbers of Soviet military advisers in Angola and Ethiopia, as well as in other nations in smaller numbers, attests to this impact. The Soviet military presence is also manifested in the increased number of naval visits, access to air facilities in a few countries, and the dramatic rise in the amounts of arms transferred to Africa (and to states not formerly recipients of Soviet-bloc weapons). Political interaction with African states has intensified; Moscow constantly seems to be hosting visiting African delegations of all levels and fostering party-to-party exchanges. East Germany, like Cuba, has become a close collaborator of the Soviet Union, dispatching technical, security, and ideological advisers to numerous African states. The number of radical, anti-Western African governments, whose foreign policy objectives often parallel Soviet goals, has risen. The Soviet engagement in Africa is important for U.S. and Western interests and its role must be evaluated when examining African affairs.

This text addresses Soviet influence, policies, and intentions in sub-Saharan Africa, primarily because a convenient distinction exists between Africa north and south of the Sahara. In a strategic sense, North Africa is related to southern European security and the Mediterranean. The region is also more closely tied to the politics of the Arab world and the Arab-Israeli conflict. Sub-Saharan Africa, on the other hand, has implications for Socialist development in the underdeveloped world (where the U.S.S.R. is more active in promoting Soviet-style government), for naval rivalry in the Indian Ocean, and for East-West competition in southern Africa. Soviet opportunities and involvement have expanded more rapidly in sub-Saharan Africa than in any other Third World region in the past 10 years.

The paper examines briefly Soviet achievements in Africa in the 1970's and how they affected Soviet policies in the early 1980's. Further, it attempts to assess the strategic importance of the region to Moscow and some of the interests that have induced the Soviets to invest military and political assets. The instruments of Soviet policy are important vehicles for expanding Soviet influence and for this reason Soviet economic assistance and military aid to African countries are assessed. Although Moscow's economic aid has been minimal, it has been successful in targeting a small number of African states for highly publicized aid programs. Nonetheless, increasing African demands for assistance cannot be met by the Soviet Union and may be a factor in decreasing future Soviet influence. In the past decade, Soviet military assistance has been dramatic, outstripping Western aid and in some cases perhaps effective in acquiring Soviet influence among important elites. Also significant has been Soviet cultural diplomacy (or propaganda) in

Africa which, according to some sources, is more active than else-where in the Third World.

Two regions of sub-Saharan Africa were investigated to assess Soviet achievements: The Horn (primarily Ethiopia) and southern Africa. In both cases, Soviet advances in the past decade have been great. However, Moscow now faces increasing difficulties in consolidating its position and presenting itself as a valuable partner in both regions. Ethiopia appears to present a model for Leninist political development in the Third World, but its economic straits are desperate and it is not yet clear how strong a hold ideology has on the Ethiopian leadership. Still, Ethiopia remains a staunch Soviet ally in the region. Southern Africa offers Moscow opportunities for demonstrating the U.S.S.R.'s commitment to Third World liberation, but in recent years it has been cut off from the negotiating process leading to Namibian (South-West Africa) independence. The rise of South Africa as a regional power is cause for considerable alarm in Moscow, particularly as Angola and Mozambique appear to have reassessed the value of the Soviet alliance.

Part V—Latin America in Soviet Third World Policy, Variations on Revolution and Traditionalism

THE VIEW FROM LATIN AMERICA

Latin America is a major configuration of power in world affairs. Yet only in recent years has it attracted Soviet attention. "Geographic fatalism"—meaning close proximity to the United States and thus geopolitically within its sphere of influence—had placed limitations on Soviet interests and activities.

Two developments in the post-World War II era changed the context of the Soviet role in Latin America and altered Latin American perceptions of the Soviet Union and its own role in international relations: The "multipolarization" of power in world politics, and the emergence of détente in East-West relations. Both developments held out the opportunity for Latin American countries to expand their relations with Moscow and play a larger and more independent role in world affairs.

A second major influence shaping the Latin American perspective is the anticolonial tradition in their history and the resulting resentment of U.S. hemispheric "hegemony." The Soviets have been able to exploit this negative attitude to their own political advantage, submerging their own culpabilities, such as, the conquest of Eastern Europe and the invasion of Afghanistan.

A vigorous revolutionary tradition also permeates the Latin American region that has affected its outlook. Three distinct traditions seem to have shaped Latin American views on politics and political philosophy: The Iberic-Latin tradition; democratic idealism fostered by the Enlightenment; and Marxist Socialism. Distressing political, social, and economic conditions—"anguishing conditions," it is said—have acted as a catalyst for revolution.

All of these influences appear to have had a maturing effect on Latin America. For not only has Latin America come to have its own distinctive hemispheric interests, but also the desire and often the wherewithal to seek and achieve those interests independently, bilaterally, or collectively. Latin Americans, like so many other Third World peoples, began to see new opportunities in a changing international environment, and when possible, they took them.

Thus, the view from Latin America has changed markedly in the three decades since the Soviets moved out into the Third World. No longer a dependency of the United States, it projects a different image, one of markedly greater confidence, maturity, and independence.

THE VIEW FROM THE UNITED STATES

The United States views Soviet encroachments into Latin America as a contending superpower determined to protect its vital national security interests and ultimately to reassert a historic position of power, but not predominance, in the Western Hemisphere.

Three elements seem to constitute the American perspective on Latin America: The historical, the geostrategic, and the regional. U.S. success in national expansion has been at the expense of Hispanic America. This historical experience left a residue of resentment mixed with envy among many Latin Americans. American hemispheric power evolved within the textual confines of the Monroe Doctrine that ruled out further European colonization and called the extension of the European system to the Western Hemisphere "as dangerous to our peace and safety."

Castro's revolution in Cuba during 1959–60 opened a new era in U.S.-hemispheric relations. For Cuba was to become an effective instrument and Castro a "point man" for Soviet policy not only in Latin America, but also in Africa and within the nonalignment movement.

The second element in the American perspective is the geostrategic; that is, the inclination to see the region, particularly vulnerable Central America and the Caribbean Basin, within the context of the Soviet-American global rivalry and specifically in terms of U.S. security requirements. Of particular concern to the United States is the security of vital sealanes of communications in the Atlantic, Caribbean, and Central American region from any Soviet threat.

In contrast to the geostrategic, the regionalist perspective, the third element in the American perspective, tends to go to the source. Regionalists seem more inclined to view Soviet involvement in the hemisphere from the Latin American side and look to the regional roots of the problem as a first priority. Unlike the geopoliticians who view the problem from an East-West perspective; that is, military weaponry, arms control, and defense strategy, the regionalists see it more clearly as a North-South problem, that is, one of regional development, human rights, and social questions. Both perspectives coexist, not necessarily peacefully, in the community of interested scholars, journalists, and specialists in the U.S. Government.

Thus, Americans view Latin America and Soviet involvement from many perspectives. They share a common historical experience with policies, a doctrine and its corollaries designed to expand, maintain, and protect American power in the Western Hemisphere. Adjustments have been made to suit changing times and requirements, at least until the introduction of Soviet power in the region. Since then, perceptions have mirrored the geopolitical needs of a superpower wanting to protect its global position and the regional needs of a hemisphere whose deprived and underdeveloped countries create fertile soil for revolution and Soviet-Cuban intervention. Though sharing a common history, Americans of the mid-1980's seem divided and thus uncertain on how best to address the current Soviet-Cuban challenge in Central America and the Caribbean Basin. This uncertainty and division can create opportunities for the expansion of Soviet influence in this Third World area.

THE VIEW FROM THE SOVIET UNION

Geographic, ideological, and geopolitical elements have constituted much of the Soviet view of Latin America. Until the Cuban Revolution, the Soviet Union had not paid much attention to the region. The doctrine of "geographic fatalism" seems to have been its guiding principle.

Marxist-Leninist ideology provides the larger philosophical construct within which the Soviets perceive Latin America. Latin America plays a key role in the fulfillment of the Soviet ideological view that the future belongs to socialism and that nations in the Third World are Russia's "natural allies" in seeking that end.

The geopolitical ingredient completes the triad of elements shaping the Soviet perception. Central to the Soviet worldview is the belief that the correlation of forces now favors the Socialist world and that world capitalism is in decline. From this view flows the belief that U.S. influence, even in its own "strategic backyard," Latin America, is on the wane. The Soviets have also come to value Latin America as playing an important role in international politics. Still, they are aware of the special importance Latin America has for the United States and the power that the United States can bring to bear.

The Soviets, therefore, seem to perceive Latin America from both the regional and geopolitical perspective. They are cognizant of the changing social structures of the nations and the force and appeal of revolution in such vulnerable areas as Central America. But their views are shaped by the concept of the changing correlation of world forces. This concept has significant geopolitical implications: It holds out the expectation of increased opportunities for spreading Soviet influence in the region; conversely, it recognizes the diminution of U.S. influence; and it acknowledges the growing independence of Latin America from U.S. hegemony—all of which have a fundamental effect on East-West relations since it has the potential for magnifying aggregate Soviet power and diminishing that of the United States.

The Soviets now view Latin America and deal with it essentially in three categories: Socialist Cuba, with its revolutionary ambitions in Latin America and elsewhere, and as a reliable Socialist ally internationally; the explosive Caribbean Basin and Central America where revolutionary ferment is intense and targets of opportunity are opening up; and finally, the settled, established governments of Mexico and much of South America where stability dictates the pursuit of traditional diplomacy.

Major trends in Soviet-Latin American affairs have followed roughly this three-part approach. Soviet objectives have also reflected the same categories of maintaining Socialist Cuba, seizing revolutionary opportunities in Central America and the Caribbean, and carrying on traditional diplomacy in Mexico and South America.

In pursuit of its objectives the Soviets have used instrumentalities differentiated by circumstance: Political, economic, and military. Soviet military assistance, a vital component of its Third World policy, has been the principal instrumentality for seeking its objectives in Latin America; trade and technical assistance, also important, seem to have been secondary.

CUBA, AN INSTRUMENT OF SOVIET POLICY

Socialist Cuba is an instrument of Soviet policy in Latin America and the Third World. Three points emerge in this relationship that bear directly on Soviet strategy: The ideological defects of Castro's revolution and its relevance to Soviet policy; the Soviet militarization of Cuba, transforming it into a disciplined and effective instrument of military power; and the use of this instrument in pursuing Soviet goals in Latin America and the Third World.

In using Cuba as an instrument of their foreign policy, particularly in the Third World, the Soviets have gradually escalated their support for Cuba, at least rhetorically, in its struggle with the United States. But in practice this support has been cautious and measured carefully in a calculus of risk and gain.

With Castro's experience as a model, the Soviets seem to have found the formula, having made the proper ideological adjustments, for allowing the transition of revolution-prone Third World countries from the inchoate state of "national liberation" to the rigidly structured socialism of the Soviet brand. The Soviets have also succeeded in militarizing Socialist Cuba, and they have also used Cuba, with mixed results, in pursuit of their own policy goals in relations with the United States, in Latin America, Africa, and elsewhere in the Third World.

Cuba and Castro have gained from this relationship. But the prominence of Cuba internationally is considerably compromised because it is due largely to Cuba's linkage with Soviet power and not something gained largely on its own. Cuban dependence on Moscow for its survival constricts its room for maneuver, making this an uneven relationship between a powerful patron and a willing, valued, but essentially weak client state. In this relationship, the Soviet Union still has the last word on matters that are important to it.

CENTRAL AMERICA AND THE CARIBBEAN: UPHEAVAL AND OPPORTUNITY

Political upheaval in Central America and the Caribbean in the 1970's created new, but initially unperceived, opportunities for Moscow. By 1979–80, this Third World region was considered to be "ripe for revolution." Cuba, a militarily strengthened regional power acting unilaterally and in concert with the Soviets, was to

become both the point man and instrument of Soviet policy. Qualified success thus far seems to have been achieved in Nicaragua,
though the ruling Sandinista regime faces serious economic problems and has a long way to go to establish any form of legitimacy
for their rule. But failure in Grenada was assured when U.S. troops
intervened in October 1983.

SOVIET UNION AND ARGENTINA: EMPHASIS ON TRADITIONALISM

Traditionalism, the third major category in the Soviet approach
to Latin America, is characterized by pragmatism and expediency.
Though fully cognizant of the various revolutionary movements in
the region, the Soviets have, nonetheless, placed greater importance in recent years on state-to-state relations than on revolutionary relationships. A case study is Argentina. Briefly, the Soviets
have carried on a fruitful economic relationship, despite mounting
trade deficits to Moscow's disadvantage. A mutuality of interests
has governed this relationship (Argentine grain and foodstuffs for
Soviet assistance in energy development); and nowhere is this
better demonstrated than in Soviet support for Argentina in the
Falkland war.

Many aspects of traditional diplomacy are, therefore, apparent in
Soviet relations with Argentina. State interests intersect at many
points, and both countries, notwithstanding basic differences in
social systems, have been guided by their national interests.

OPPORTUNITIES, RISKS, CONSTRAINTS, AND THE FUTURE

Soviet Third World policy in Latin America is an integral part of
its total Third World policy. It is a whole with many parts, and the
principles and policies, the instrumentalities and goals, institutional connections, and an enduring commitment appear to be only superficially different in Latin America from that of other Third
World areas in Asia, Africa, and the Middle East.

Revolutionary opportunism is a dominant characteristic, as indicated by the Soviet moves into Cuba, Grenada, and Nicaragua. Diplomatic traditionalism, as in Argentina, serves a useful short-term
Soviet purpose in Mexico and South America. But future Soviet-
American confrontations are always a danger, particularly in light
of Moscow's adventurous policy in Central America and the Caribbean. The Cuban missile crisis is the most accurate benchmark
against which to measure U.S. tolerance of Soviet military activities in Latin America; Grenada is another and the most recent.

The Soviets have made many gains in Latin America during the
past 5 years. They continue to maintain a strong presence in Cuba,
though at an enormous cost to an ailing Soviet economy. They
have succeeded in establishing a foothold in Nicaragua through
their active support of the Sandinista regime. They have gained in
their relationship with Argentina, but lost in their effort to convert
Grenada into a staging area for the future projection of Soviet
power.

The Soviets have had advantages, disadvantages, and constraints
in Latin America. Advantages are inherent in the central unified
control of the Soviet foreign policy process, the positive value of
ideology, and their freedom from any burden of responsibility for

past inequities in Latin America. Among the disadvantages and constraints are the serious limitations on Soviet foreign policy resources all across the board, notably their much troubled economy; the continuing validity of "geographic fatalism" despite so-called "breakthroughs" in Cuba and Nicaragua; and the sheer geographic size of Latin America, its philosophical roots in Western traditions that have generated the recent surge toward democracy, the predominance of Western cultural influences, the vast economic interconnections with the West—all act as a deterrent and constraint on the Soviets.

Soviet Third World policy in Latin America has far-reaching implications for both Latin America and the United States. The essence of these implications are the possibility of Soviet-American confrontations as the Soviets test American tolerance in their probes for expansionist opportunities and as the United States defends traditional interests in the Western Hemisphere. These confrontations, as in the Cuban missile crisis, could carry the worst case risk of war that neither the United States, the Soviet Union, nor even Latin America can escape.

As for the future, continuity in Soviet reliance on Cuba as an instrument of its Third World policy seems to be the more likely trend for some time to come. It also seems unlikely that the Soviets will break off their offensive in Central America, the region they judge to be most "ripe for revolution" and most vulnerable to diminishing U.S. influence and power regionally and globally. Diplomatic traditionalism in the stabler countries, from all appearances a reasonable success, seems unlikely to change.

Thus, developments in Soviet policy in the near future suggest little variation from its tripartite direction described in this study. Any change in course would seem to depend upon the impact of serious constraints and limitations on Soviet Third World policy, particularly the heavy demands on Soviet foreign policy resources, both military and diplomatic, and the overall burden of maintaining an empire stretching from Eastern Europe to Afghanistan and Cuba; the continuing loyalty of Socialist Cuba; the extent and effectiveness of U.S. counteraction against Soviet thrusts into Central America and the Caribbean; and the strength and effectiveness of a reconstituted inter-American system that is intended to collectively protect and preserve hemispheric interests and deter unacceptable and harmful Soviet encroachments into the Western Hemisphere.

PART VI—AND THE FUTURE?

Examination of Soviet involvement in the Third World since 1980, as recorded in the preceding five parts of this study, confirms the correctness of the generalizations set forth in the 1977 and 1981 studies published by the House Foreign Affairs Committee; namely, (1) that the Soviet Union maintains a firm and active commitment to the developing countries of the Third World; and (2) that the Third World holds an important, perhaps even vital, place in the Soviet world view of contemporay international relations. The Soviet commitment continues to be an enduring fact of international life affirmed by their words and their actions.

The Third World holds a central place in the Soviet view of contemporary international politics. Two elements, affecting Soviet Third World relations, make up this world view: The ideological connection between the Soviet Union and the Third World; and the underlying great power dynamics that normally operate in relations between nation-states without regard for time, place, or ideology. The unity of ideology with the great power dynamic creating the Soviet world view is a formula for unresolved conflict with the West. This idea together with the expansion of Russian power are realities of contemporary international life.

AN IMPERIAL BURDEN OR POLITICAL ASSET?

Great empires of the past have generally passed through various stages, from their inception and subsequent growth and expansion, to a period of success and prosperity, followed by decline and in some cases total disintegration and even extinction. By and large empires have taken on three forms, according to a recent study by Rand Corp: "internal empires," "contiguous empires," and "empires abroad." The Soviet Union falls into all three categories.

The question arises as to whether the imperial burden has not become too heavy for the Soviet Union to bear. It is now commonplace in the press, among Western government officials and scholars to consider the U.S.S.R. to be in something like Toynbee's degenerative stage of imperial "breakdown."

A review of Soviet activities in the Third World suggests that they have gained many political and strategic benefits from their Third World policy, notwithstanding the burden of empire they have assumed. It is impossible to balance total benefits and costs in such a global undertaking with anything but "impressionistic" judgments, particularly in measuring political assets, for in international politics there are political costs as well as benefits, equally unquantifiable. More precise judgments are possible for economic analyses and analogical comparisons with empires of the past as the Rand study has done.

The Soviets are aware that they are paying a high price for their efforts to maintain, consolidate, and expand their assets in the Third World, particularly in light of the added cost-producing economic problems besetting their "internal" empire at home and those troubling the "contiguous" empire within Eastern Europe. Soviet economists and Third World specialists have urged an easing of the economic burden and burden-sharing measures in the Third World. Their analyses have made a visible impact on recent Soviet leaders.

Soviet behavior in the 1980's suggests that the political and strategic benefits to be accrued in the Third World may be well worth the cost, for the Soviets have continued to seize "targets of opportunity" and expand upon them. Nor have the Soviets appeared to reduce but rather have continued to expand their political and military commitments in the Third World. In an impartial, objective weighing of imperial costs and benefits (though from the American perspective), Rand specialists conclude that from the Soviet view, in the aggregate the benefits of empire may amply justify the costs, and this suggests to these American specialists that Soviet efforts to expand are likely to continue.

At this juncture in the 1980's, the Soviets give the impression of having an empire in place and of pursuing a role in the Third World that is both an economic burden—but apparently thus far not an unbearable one—and a political and strategic asset. Whether the cautions of Soviet analysts who advise constraints on future commitments will influence Gorbachev's policies should be a matter of close U.S. attention.

IMPLICATIONS FOR U.S. FOREIGN POLICY

The Soviet Union has established a global presence, but its power is largely one-dimensional; that is, military, and accordingly lacks the sort of systemic ideological and socioeconomic appeal that could broaden and deepen its hold on allies and clients, making their relationship more lasting. The one-dimensional character of Soviet power and the adversarial philosophy underpinning and driving its foreign policy pose a challenge of the first magnitude to the U.S. world position.

Internationally, the Soviets have pursued a "strategy of disruption" by projecting power through military/political allies in Third World strife, while intimidating U.S. allies (as in the antinuclear movement). The Soviets have also sought to encourage trends hostile to U.S. interests in strategically vital areas of the Third World that have the greatest potential for affecting the global political-economic balance.

The U.S. response to Soviet thrusts into the Third World has turned full cycle since the publication of the first House Foreign Affairs Committee study on this subject in 1977. Then, the United States was caught up in the so-called "Vietnam syndrome" that virtually paralyzed policy, making difficult, if not impossible, a forceful reponse to Soviet and Cuban initiatives in Angola and Ethiopia. Restricted by this national mood of withdrawal from military and sometimes political involvement in far-off regions of the Third World, American policymakers seemed hard pressed to counter this and other Soviet challenges in the Third World. On the other hand, the United States did pursue an activist, internationalist policy as in concluding the Panama Treaty and Camp David Accords, and mounting a forthright human rights campaign internationally.

In a reversal of policy, brought on by the Soviet invasion of Afghanistan in 1979, the United States finds itself in the mid-1980's again on the political frontiers of the Third World, forcefully asserting a policy of global containment. The transcending reality of the mid-1980's is that the Soviet Union by its global military power has broken through the American policy of geographic containment first proclaimed in the Truman doctrine of 1947. In this progressive process, covering three decades, Soviet strategic and political purposes in the Third World have been clear; namely, to build an infrastructure to buttress its policy of expanding globalism. And for the West at this historical stage of transition from colonialism to interdependence in the Third World, the problem it faces has become equally clear; namely, how to reformulate its position in the Third World and adapt it to new conditions, doing so patiently and in a sustained incremental adjustment to preserve its vital interests now in contention with the Soviet Union.

Students of Soviet-American relations could now experience a sense of deja vu. Presently, the United States and the Soviet Union have undertaken what may well be far-reaching arms control negotiations in Geneva. Despite U.S. efforts to reach agreement in this critical arms control area through negotiations since 1982, the Soviet Union, while negotiating, has continued to test and probe opportunities in the Third World and intervene if necessary. The Caribbean and Central America have been prime target areas.

In the mid-1970's, virtually the same general situation had existed: The Soviet Union and the United States were negotiating SALT II that was concluded in June 1979; simultaneously, the Soviets intervened in Angola, Ethiopia, and elsewhere in the Third World. Brezhnev perceived no contradiction between détente based on arms control with Soviet support for "wars of national liberation" in the Third World.

In brief, the Soviets then as now seem to want it both ways; that is, nuclear stability in Europe and in East-West relations generally, but freedom to pursue Communist revolutionary goals in the Third World. Hence, the United States and its Western Allies face the same dilemma that perplexed them a decade ago; namely, how to resist multidirectional Soviet expansionism while simultaneously negotiating agreements to minimize the chances of nuclear war.

Other factors affecting the United States in pursuit of its policy of global containment are the limitations on its power and the difficulties in establishing a code of conduct for managing Soviet-American rivalry in the Third World.

Efforts to establish such a code have thus far failed. And given the power dynamics driving the Soviet-American rivalry and their incompatibly opposite ideological world views, the chances of establishing a workable code in the Third World seems very slight, except perhaps for selected areas of common interest and except in the long term. Perhaps the most that can be said is that arms control negotiations could at some point in the future contribute to an acceptable balance of power upon which an agreement could be concluded. And, as in SALT I, an arms control agreement negotiated on this basis could enhance prospects for establishing a code of conduct for the superpowers in the Third World.

THE THIRD WORLD IN THE SOVIET AND AMERICAN FUTURE

Perhaps the most important point in considering the Third World in the Soviet-American future is whether Soviet expansionism is a permanent or transitory feature of Soviet foreign policy. If it is permanent, then the Third World, the area most vulnerable to Soviet penetration, could become, as CIA Director William J. Casey foresees, "the principal U.S.-Soviet battleground for many years to come." If it is transitory, then it will cease to spur forceful counteraction by the United States and its allies, opening up an opportunity for establishing a greater range of harmony of interests in the absence of systematic, zero-sum conflict.

Russian expansionism is an historical reality, a fact of history given renewed stimulus in the Soviet period by its ideological and systemic commitment to global aggrandizement. Russian expansion has had three differentiated characteristics; namely, that of an "internal empire," "contiguous empire" in Eastern Europe and Mongolia; and an "empire abroad" in the Third World. What the Soviets seem to have in mind for a future world Socialist system are those characteristics that the Rand study would term an "empire abroad." Competition for and ultimately gaining influence over Third World countries rather than direct physical control, as in Eastern Europe, seems to be the principal characteristic of this expected relationship as, for example, that now existing with such Third World countries as Vietnam, North Korea, Cuba, Ethiopia, Syria, and, arguably, India.

Thus, if Soviet expansion leads to some form of world Socialist system allying the Soviet Union with the Third World, which they claim to be a natural historical development, it would seem more likely to be one that has evolved out of coalescing political interest among likeminded Third World Socialist states rather than a form of physical "domination" in the classic imperial sense.

Whether Soviet expansionism will continue can only be a matter of speculation. The historical record suggests, as the Rand study concludes, the likelihood of continuing Soviet efforts to expand their power, particularly when the political and strategic benefits of empire may amply justify the costs in the Soviet view. Yet in the long term the costs of empire could become too great, particularly if the socioeconomic problems now plaguing the Soviet Union are not corrected and the costs of Third World adventures grow. This and the awareness of failing to achieve cost-effectiveness could dictate some retrenchment.

ALTERNATIVE DIRECTIONS: MILITARISM OR GLOBAL INTERDEPENDENCE

Assuming that Soviet expansion into the Third World will continue at its present pace, the question arises as to which direction it may take. For the sake of analysis two hypothetical possible polar opposite directions are projected: One toward continuing militarization; the other toward achieving global interdependence, meaning a shared responsibility for solving global problems.

Whether the Soviets will take the path predominately toward militarism with all its serious consequences for Soviet security and world peace, or global interdependence through shared solutions to world problems can only be speculated. More likely they will opt for a mix of the two. This suggests an extension, more or less, of current Soviet policy with emphasis on maintaining military strength in order to preserve "equal security" with the United States, retain a hedge against U.S. superiority and protect the Soviet Union against perceived threats stemming therefrom. Sustained military strength also provides the Soviets with an instrument, albeit limited, for maintaining and expanding their influence in the Third World. It is also compatible with a pursuit of global interdependence, but perhaps only at a minimum level of activity as Soviet national interests may dictate.

What the United States does in the realm of international security will no doubt impact considerably upon the Soviet choice. The main focus of this study is on the Soviet Union, but the idea of alternative paths of militarism and global interdependence, hypothesized here for analytical purposes, applies also to the United States. The serious risks of militarism and the positive value of global interdependence have universal application.

Developments in both Soviet-American and international relations appear to be converging in the mid-1980's, bringing a choice of direction by both superpowers. The first step has already been taken with resumption of arms control negotiations in Geneva. Whether this first step will lead to consideration of larger issues of interdependence on the global agenda—establishing, for example, a code of conduct for the superpowers in the Third World—can at this juncture only be a hope and not an assured prospect.

THE THIRD WORLD IN THE CONTEXT OF CIVILIZATION

A review of the Soviet role in the Third World as presented in this study reinforces the prediction that the less developed countries "will be the principal U.S.-Soviet battleground for many years to come." Regional volatility and Soviet-American rivalry have created conditions that invite tensions and conflict.

A central idea, indeed the driving force, in the Soviet-American rivalry in the Third World, as seen from the West's perspective, is the matter of the Third World's future social organization. Simply stated, the power factor aside, the issue is the ideological struggle between the principles of Marxism-Leninism as interpreted and proselytized by the Soviet Union pitted against the principles of democratic capitalism advocated by the United States and democratic socialism, an acceptable compromise with Marxism based on political pluralism prevalent in Western Europe. (Of course, neither of the contesting forms may ultimately be accepted by the Third World nations who bring their own interest and perspectives to bear.) The Soviets enjoy certain advantages in the advocacy of their brand of socialism. But they have little to offer in the future social organization of the Third World beyond what their military power and military assistance can give and beyond providing an alternative source of political support in international politics.

In contrast, the United States, NATO Europe, and Japan—in brief, the industrialized democracies of the world—have much to offer the Third World, not only in the material and intellectual resources of their scientific-technological civilization, but, equally important, the organizing principles of pluralistic democracy. It is not surprising, therefore, that Third World countries turn to this source for support, sustenance, and ideas, for they have in the prospering countries of non-Communist Asia variously adaptable models for success in the modern world. Ironically, but realistically, even China now looks mainly to Japan and the industrialized West, not to Moscow (except for improving Soviet-built factories), for assistance in its current modernization drive. This appeal of the Western market economies to the Third World seems to represent perhaps another stage in the globalization of the ideas, values and knowledge of non-Communist Western civilization.

The industrialized democracies of the West and Japan, having achieved great things in the course of the evolving scientific-technological revolution, have the upper hand over the Soviets. Nonetheless, the struggle to influence the shape of future civilization in the Third World continues; and Soviet military power, Marxist-Leninist ideology aside, still remains a powerful force with which to contend. Were the ideological struggle resolved, the contest for power would still continue in a way that such contests have historically occurred between competing great powers.

DIPLOMACY AND NEGOTIATIONS: PROVIDING A MARGIN OF SURVIVAL

The future holds the answer to the final outcome of this contest. Perhaps all that can be certain in this relationship of uncertainties is the generally accepted and simple truth that only through diplomacy and negotiations will it be possible for the United States and the Soviet Union to manage their rivalry without placing mankind in jeopardy. Alexis de Toqueville predicted this Russian-American contest 150 years ago in his projection of the destinies of these dissimilar countries.

Whether the Russians and Americans can shift their rivalry in the Third World from its increasingly conflictual and militarized direction back toward less confrontational and more political and economic competition is a question of the greatest significance for all mankind; the latter course, as both recognize, improves prospects for world peace and survival. Power, properly and acceptably balanced, can offer at least some assurance of peace, but only when it is integrated into the process of diplomacy and negotiations. In such a unity, this assurance can be reasonably complete; for it is diplomacy and negotiations, properly used, that can provide the vital margin of survival. The resumption of negotiations in Geneva could be the first step in that direction.

CONTENTS

Part III—The Soviet Union and the Middle East

PART I—COMMITMENT IN PERSPECTIVE [1]

The achievements of the national liberation struggle of formerly oppressed peoples is yet more impressive evidence of how Lenin's ideas have come to life. More than 100 states in Asia, Africa, and Latin America, having liberated themselves from colonial and semicolonial dependence, are taking an ever more active part, as Lenin said, "in deciding the future of the whole world." Their anti-imperialist potential is also growing. Many of them, as Lenin foresaw, became involved "in the general spinning of the worldwide revolutionary movement." In these countries, the processes of social renewal are growing. Their peoples, struggling hard against imperialism and its accomplices, are persevering in cutting their way through to progress. The Soviet Union supports the just cause of the states that have liberated themselves and develops many-sided cooperation with them.

—Geidar A. Aliyev on "The Historical Correctness
of Ideas and Cause of Lenin," April 1985.

I. PURPOSES AND DESIGN, LIMITATIONS AND DEFINITIONS

A. PURPOSES AND DESIGN

The Congressional Research Service prepared two major studies on Soviet involvement in the Third World. They were published in 1977 and 1981 by the House Foreign Affairs Committee.[2] Both studies suggest the following generalizations: (1) that the Soviet Union maintains a firm and active commitment to the developing countries of the Third World; and (2) that the Third World holds an important, perhaps even vital, place in the Soviet worldview of international relations today.

The principal purposes of this current study are to analyze Soviet activities in the Third World during the years 1980–1985, and to determine whether these generalizations are still valid.

Four basic questions are addressed:

(1) What are the trends of the Soviet experience in the Third World during the years 1980–1985?

(2) Has the rationale for Soviet involvement in the Third World and the instrumentalities of their policy changed during that period?

(3) What is the meaning of Soviet involvement in the Third World; and

---

[1] Prepared by Joseph G. Whelan, Senior Specialist in International Affairs, Congressional Research Service. First published on Nov. 30, 1983, as CFS Report No. 83-2108.

[2] U.S. Congress. House. Committee on International Relations. The Soviet Union and the Third World: A Watershed in Great Power Policy? Prepared by Joseph G. Whelan, Senior Specialist in International Affairs, and William B. Inglee, Senior Research Assistant in Soviet and East European Affairs, Senior Specialists Division, Congressional Research Service, Library of Congress. 95th Cong., 1st sess. Wash., U.S. Govt. Print. Off., 1977, 186 p.

U.S. Congress. House. Committee on Foreign Affairs, Soviet Policy and United States Response in the Third World. Prepared by the Congressional Research Service, Library of Congress. 87th Cong., 1st sess. Wash., U.S. Govt. Print Off., 1981. 323 p. (Chapter II, "Soviet Policy and Involvement in the Third World," was prepared by Joseph G. Whelan, Senior Specialist in International Affairs, and William H. Cooper, Senior Research Assistant in Soviet and East European Affairs. The remainder of the study was prepared by the staff of the Foreign Affairs and National Defense Division.)

(4) What are the implications for U.S. foreign policy?

These questions establish the design of this study. Part I summarizes the trends, objectives, and instrumentalities of Soviet Third World policy as recorded in the previous CRS studies. The purpose here is to provide the base and give some perspective on what has occurred during the years under review. Also, the role of the Third World in the proceedings of the 26th Soviet Party Congress of 1981 is examined in an effort to track the possible direction of Soviet Third World policy in the 1980's. Specific attention is given to an analysis of Brezhnev's commentary on the Third World in his main report to the Congress. The views of Yuri Andropov, Brezhnev's successor, are also examined, as are the recent writings of Soviet specialists on the Third World. The views of Konstantin V. Chernenko and Mikhail S. Gorbachev, Andropov's successors, are examined in parts II, V, and VI.

Parts II through V record where possible the scattered evidence of Soviet regional involvement in Asia, the Middle East, Africa, and Latin America during 1980–1984. Each part includes where possible an examination of Soviet objectives, the instrumentalities of policy, an assessment of apparent successes and failures, and an estimate of possible prospects for the future.

The concluding Part VI, entitled, "And the Future?", contains some tentative generalizations drawn from an analysis of the four basic questions raised. In a very general way, Part VI responds to the query whether Soviet involvement in the Third World is an imperial or political asset. Estimates are made of overall Soviet successes and failures in the Third World during the period under review, the general prospects for the future, and the resources, particularly economic, for supporting Soviet Third World policy.

The implications of Soviet involvement in the Third World for U.S. foreign policy are examined in the final section of Part VI. Particular attention is given to the change in the U.S. approach to the Third World that has occurred since the Soviet invasion of Afghanistan in December 1979. The question of the future U.S. stake in the Third World is addressed in the context of defining U.S. national interests, dealing with the problem of Soviet incrementalism, and coping with the reality of interdependence.

Finally, part VI carries the narrative and analysis through April 1985. Particular attention is given to the unfolding crisis in Central America and to Gorbachev's views on the Soviet role in the Third World.

B. LIMITATIONS AND DEFINITIONS

1. MAGNITUDE OF THE THIRD WORLD

Severe limitations are placed upon any study of the Third World, and the most important are necessitated by its magnitude. To speak of the Third World is to speak virtually of a global diversity of power. For, excluding the developed world of the United States and Canada, Western Europe, Australia and Japan along with the Communist countries and other qualifying states, the Third World constitutes most of Asia, Africa, Latin America and Oceania. From a total of 70 in 1939, the number of nations in the world community have more than doubled to 157 in 1976 (and increased to 167 in 1983); the great concentration of newly independent nations lies in the Third World.[3]

2. DIVERSITY OF SOVIET POLICY

Diversity (and the complexity) of Soviet policy toward the Third World creates another limitation. Beyond the most generalized declarations (e.g., support for national liberation movements), Soviet policy-makers have not developed a single uniform policy toward the less developed countries (LDC's). Rather, they have continued increasingly to diversify their policies and actions, emphasizing through the mid-1970's relations with the Middle East and South Asia where their economic and strategic interests are far more important than areas more remote from the Soviet border. The invasion of Afghanistan added a new dimension to Soviet policy, contributing still further to its diversity.

The principal area of Soviet interests could, therefore, be described as a troubled crescent, extending from North Africa along the periphery of the Soviet Union though the Middle East, South and Southeast Asia. This area has been called, the "National Liberation Zone." Targets of opportunity, emerging since the mid-1970's, have attracted Soviet attention to Black Africa, the Caribbean and Central America, adding still further to the diversity of policy.

3. OBJECTIVE: PRESENT THE MAIN THRUST OF SOVIET POLICY

In light of these limitations perhaps the most that a brief study of this nature can hope to accomplish is to suggest that main thrust and broad lines of Soviet policy and activity in the Third World, recording these tendencies where possible with selected illustrative data.

C. DEFINITION OF TERMS

The terms "developing countries," "emerging countries," "less developed countries" (LDC's), and "Third World countries," are used interchangeably in this study. By and large they are to be construed to mean "less developed countries of the non-Communist world" in the CIA's report, "Communist Aid Activities in Non-Communist Less Developed Countries, 1978"—though excluding their reference to Malta, Portugal, and Spain in Europe.[4]

Such countries include the following: (1) all countries of Africa except the Republic of South Africa; (2) all countries of East Asia except Hong Kong and Japan; (3) all countries in Latin America except Cuba; and (4) all countries in the Middle East and South Asia, except Israel. Not included in this definition are the Communist states, many of which like Kampuchea, Laos, and Vietnam that became Communist in 1975, qualify as Third World countries.

---

[3] U.S. Dept. of State. Bureau of Intelligence and Research. Status of the World's Nations. Geographic Bulletin. Wash., U.S. Govt. Print. Off., 1976, p. 1. (Publication 8735). Up-to-date information was provided by the State Department.

[4] U.S. Central Intelligence Agency. National Foreign Assessment Center. Communist Aid Activities in Non-Communist Less Developed Countries, 1978: A Research Paper. Wash., Sept. 1979, p. vii. (Er 79–104120)

No attempt has been made in this study to differentiate the degree of development among the Third World countries. All are considered collectively as part of a chain of development extending from fairly primitive societies to those that are well advanced but not sufficiently to qualify as a developed country.

Generally Communist literature uses the term "socialism" to include not only the Communist countries but also Socialist oriented governments of the Third World and the so-called "forces of national liberation." Where possible in this study a distinction is made between the clearly Communist countries, as in the case of the Soviet Union, and Socialist oriented Third World countries like Burma, Algeria and Somalia. Use of the term "capitalist" (for example, to describe the United States and its Western allies) generally and collectively refers in Communist terminology to the non-Communist and non-Socialist oriented countries of the Third World.

II. TRENDS, OBJECTIVES, AND INSTRUMENTALITIES OF SOVIET THIRD WORLD POLICY: A RETROSPECTIVE GLANCE [1]

A. IMPORTANCE OF THE THIRD WORLD IN INTERNATIONAL AFFAIRS

1. U.S. REDISCOVERY OF THE THIRD WORLD: ENDURING SOVIET INTEREST

The United States has re-discovered the Third World. An over-simplification, no doubt, but it does best sum up the direction of American foreign policy since the Soviet invasion of Afghanistan in December 1979. The Soviet-American rivalry, viewed by Americans largely in a constricted European context for nearly a decade owing to Vietnam, has once again become globalized, and the Third World a center of attention. The catalyst of change was Afghanistan; the driving force was American fear of Soviet expansion into the oil-rich Middle East.

The Soviets discovered the Third World over 60 years ago, and its importance, its potentiality as a revolutionary ally, has never been lost upon them, particularly since the mid-1950's. A creation of powerful anti-colonial forces unleashed in the aftermath of World War II, the Third World has evolved today from a collection of individually weak underdeveloped states into a major component of international politics. Collectively, it is a new source of international power and influence; it is a principal element in Soviet foreign policy.[2]

---

[1] This section draws upon, HFAC, Soviet Union and the Third World, 1977, and HFAC, Soviet Policy and United States Response in the Third World, 1981.

[2] I. Zorina, a Soviet authority on the Third World, gives some insight into the value the Soviet Union places on the Third World and their awareness of its potentiality. In noting the quantitative indicators, Zorina calls attention to the fact that, "The number of independent states increased 2.4-fold between 1940 and 1981. Approximately three-fourths of them are developing countries with a population which exceeded 2.1 billion in 1981 and represents half of the world population. Therefore, colossal changes have taken place in the very geography of international politics." Zorina points out that "all of the conditions of the present era," notably the "competition and struggle" between the two social systems, communism and capitalism, "have created favorable opportunities for a more active foreign policy role for all of the developing states." The number of world centers where "important international political decisions" can be made has increased significantly, and they "are now located on all continents." Zorina turned to the United Nations to prove her point on the importance of the Third World. When created in 1945, membership of the Third World included only 19 countries in Latin America, 8 in Asia and 3 in Africa, and "even as a group these 30 states did not play an independent role in the United Nations (they were more likely to act as part of the pro-Western automatic majority)." By the beginning of the 1960's this situation changed. "After the 15th session of the General Assembly, at which time the young African states joined the United Nations en masse, anticolonial forces, including representatives of the socialist and developing countries, first gained an absolute majority, and by the beginning of the 1970's they had a qualified majority of two-thirds of the vote." To strengthen her argument, Zorina noted that representatives from the LDC's now occupy 39 percent of the U.N. administrative offices, including 42 percent of the highest positions." (Zorina, I. The Developing Countries in the Political Structure of Today's World. Morovaya Ekonomika I. Mezhdunarodnyye Otnosheniya in Rusian, no. 8, Aug. 1982, p. 80–91, in JPRS 8588, CSO: 1816/11.)

Karen Brutents, a deputy chief in the Central Committee's International Department and authority on the Third World, recently stated: "That part of the world which has managed to

Continued

2. PHYSICAL ATTRIBUTES OF THE THIRD WORLD

The importance of the Third World derives from its physical attributes, its political organization and activities, and its geopolitical and geostrategic potentialities.

Physiically, the Third World constitutes over two-thirds of the nations of the world; it occupies 40 percent of the globe's total landmass; it holds almost one-half of the world's total population. Raw material resources, vital to the existence and continued progress of the industrial states, can be found disproportionately, and abundantly, in the Third World, giving it under some circumstances, as the oil embargo of 1973 proved, enormous political leverage.

3. POTENTIAL FORCE FOR POLITICAL PRESSURE

The Third World has a will to organize as demonstrated by the Non-Alignment Movement, the Group of 77, the Organization of Petroleum Exporting Countries (OPEC), and the Organization of African Unity (OAU). It also has a will to act politically, and together. Terrorism, a formidable form of political pressure, has served a Third World purpose by dramatizing grievances and demands for redress.

The rise of the Islamic Movement in the context of the American hostage crisis in Iran during the late 1970's and the Soviet invasion of Afghanistan demonstrated anew that the Third World is a political force to be reckoned with. Most of the Muslim peoples of the world live in the Third World countries of Asia and Africa.

In all, the Third World, though differentiated as a political entity in form and content, represents a formidable potential force for exerting political pressure to achieve its chosen goals.

4. SOURCE OF CONFLICT

As the object of major and minor regional conflicts in the post-colonial era, the Third World has commanded the international limelight, for many of these conflicts had the potentialities for war on a wider international scale.

Such conflicts have involved greater and lesser powers in the anti-colonial struggle—the French in Algeria, the British in their far-flung dissolving colonial empire, the Portuguese in Angola. American participation in the Korean and Vietnamese wars and now the Soviet war in Afghanistan are special cases of superpower involvement in the Third World.

So-called "wars of national liberation," Soviet supported and sometimes directed, as those now enveloping Central America, is still another special case of regional conflict. Mini-wars, such as that taking place today between Iraq and Iran, has contributed immensely to the sense of interminable upheaval in the Third World.

---

wrest itself from the clutches of colonialism now numbers more than 100 states, in which more than half of the world's population lives. They possess huge resources and great potentials. These countries' sovereignty has strengthened, and their influence in world politics and economics is growing." (Brutents, Karen, Questions of Theory: The Soviet Union and the Liberated Countries. Pravda in Russian, Feb. 2, 1982, p. 4–5, in FBIS Daily Report: Soviet Union, v. 3, Feb. 2, 1982, p. CC6.)

All of these varieties of regional conflicts have disrupted regional peace, exacerbated international tensions and even endangered world peace by risking superpower confrontation.[3]

5. GEOPOLITICAL IMPORTANCE

And then there is the geopolitical factor. With many of the principal communication routes vital to the world's traffic adjoining or crossing its territory and with its abundance of resources vital to progress among the industrial nations, the Third World has become not only a political force to be reckoned with but a prime geopolitical target in the East-West rivalry.[4]

6. FOCUS OF SOVIET ACTIVITY

In brief, the Third World is an important configuration of power, a major component in the changing structure of international relations away from the pre-Twentieth Century Eurocentric system towards an evolving multi-polar system of the contemporary world. It cannot be ignored. and it is not ignored by the Soviets for whom it has been a principal component in their assessment of the correlation of world forces and an integral part of the Soviet ideological design of the world, past, present and future.

B. SOVIET OBJECTIVES IN THE THIRD WORLD

1. THE IDEOLOGICAL DIMENSION

Soviet objectives in the Third World are ideological, political, economic, and strategic.[5]

Ideologically, the Third World is central to the Soviet world outlook. This concept, dating back to Lenin who initially perceived the vulnerability of the West's colonial system calling it the "weakest link" in world capitalism, holds that the Third World is destined, at least in the contemporary era, to be a "natural ally" with the Soviet Union in the larger global struggle against capitalism. But

---

[3] The potentially explosive nature of the LDC's was demonstrated by David Wood in a study entitled, "Conflict in the Twentieth Century." (Adelphi Papers, June 1968, p. 19). He noted that the majority of conflicts during the post-1945 years to 1967 had taken place in Africa, the Middle East and Asia. He cited a list of 80 such conflicts. A larger number then followed on or had been associated with the breakup of colonial empires and the subsequent emergence of new states, often small, poor, and insecure. All but 8 of these 80 conflicts involved Third World participants on both sides. Since 1967, major wars have erupted in Nigeria, between India and Pakistan, in October 1973 between the Arabs and Israelis, in Lebanon since 1976, Indochina, in the Horn of Africa, Central America, and today, in Afghanistan, Iraq and Iran. The United States has been involved directly in many of these upheavals within the LDC's, most notably Southeast Asia (Vietnam, Cambodia, and Laos) and the Middle East, where today it finds itself deeply entangled. In many of these wars the Soviet Union, while not directly involved militarily, played an important role as supplier of military assistance. In Afghanistan, Soviet troops are directly engaged.

[4] Third World nations border on most of the world's important strategic straits, described in naval terminology as "chokepoints." Indonesia, Malaya, and Thailand surround the Straits of Malacca and Lombok; they connect the Indian Ocean with the South Seas, leading on to the Pacific Ocean and East Asia. This vital waterway controls sea communications from East Africa and the Middle East to East and North East Asia. Saudi Arabia, North and South Yemen, Ethiopia and Somalia surround the Strait of Bab-el Mandeb at the southern end of the Red Sea: Iran, Saudi Arabia, the Trucial Coast, and Oman border on the trait of Hormuz in the Persian Gulf—both straits are vital sea communications extending from the Middle East and East Africa. (Schumacher, Edward. Arms and the Third World: Threat to the Superpowers. The Washington Post, June 11, 1976, p. C.2.)

[5] For a recent analysis on Soviet objectives in the Third World, see, Donaldson, Robert H. The Soviet Union in the Third World. Current History, v. 81, Oct. 1982: 313–14.

in the longer term, Soviet ideologists regard it as an important component in a much larger international system that they envision, at least theoretically, for the distant future; namely, the creation of a Soviet socialist world state.[6]

In the historical transformation of world society the LDC's seem destined to play a key role. Meanwhile, in the immediate and practical short term the Soviets expect that the urgency of social and economic development will lead the LDC's over time to radical social change and to estabishing a close symbiotic relationship with Moscow. The destinies of Third World countries are thus ideologically linked to that of the Soviet Union. An unchanging Soviet ideological objective is to shape and strengthen that linkage in material forms.[7]

2. THE POLITICAL DIMENSION

Ideology along with the power realities is a central definer of the global parameters of Soviet action in foreign policy, and within those parameters the Third World, by its nature and history, attracts Soviet political participation. The Third World is politically important; it constitutes an impressive constellation of power and vulnerability; it presents political opportunities that the Soviets readily perceive. A prime factor in the Soviet calculation of the correlation of world forces, the Third World has become in Soviet eyes a prize to be won.[8]

For the Soviets the Third World has, therefore, great political value, great because it presents political opportunity and because it is the instrumentality for expanding and globalizing Soviet influence and power. The Third World enables the Soviet Union to magnify its great power role on the world scene as regional interests of the individual LDC's merge with Soviet global interests. The Third World connection sustains the Soviet compulsion to maintain its prestige and its status as a world power.

Conversely, the Soviets pursue the further political goal of denying Western and Chinese influence in the Third World. They seek to detach key LDC's from the so-called "capitalist-imperialist world system" and align them as potential allies in the "anti-imperialist struggle." In this process the Soviet Union is selective, mindful particularly of its strategic needs.[9]

3. THE ECONOMIC DIMENSION

The Third World has special economic importance for the Soviet Union: It has served as a market for Soviet economic goods, military weapons, supplies and equipment; it has provided a source for raw materials; it has created an opportunity for economic integration to the Soviet advantage—in all, it has served both political

---

[6] HFAC, Soviet Union and the Third World, 1977, p. 45–48. For a commentary from the Soviet perspective see, Ul'yanovskiy, R.A. The 20th Century and the National Liberation Movement. Naroidy Azii I Afriki, No. 2, 1980: 3–9, translated in, U.S.S.R. Report, Political and Sociological Affairs, No. 1052, JPRS 86193, Aug. 8, 1980: 19–27.

[7] HFAC, Soviet Union and the Third World, 1977, p. 45–47. For a commentary on Soviet expectations for the future, see, Goodman, Elliott R. The Soviet design for a World State. New York, Columbia University Press, 1960. 512 p.

[8] HFAC, Soviet Union and the Third World, 1977, p. 49.

[9] Ibid., p. 50.

and economic purposes by creating conduits for the inflow of materials, personnel, and ideas from the Soviet Union into the Third World.[10]

Hence, Soviet economic goals are fairly clear; namely, to satisfy Soviet economic needs through the Third World connection; to widen the breach of conflict between the Third World and the industrialized West and Japan; and in the long term to deny the latter vital markets, investment gains and especially raw material resources. In pursuing these goals the Soviets have emphasized to the LDC's a socialist tenet that they themselves have long preached internally; namely, that "true political independence" can only come when they win their economic independence.[11] Underlying this strategy is the Leninist ideological dictum that without exploitation of the LDC's the capitalist West must fall to internal societal class struggle.

The Soviets also put forward their brand of socialism as a model for economic development and building socialism. Despite its imperfections the Soviet model has appealed to many in the Third World, largely no doubt because of the Soviet Union's rapid success in achieving the stature of a great world power and because of political, economic and social realities and historical experience that have encouraged socialist oriented solutions.[12]

And finally Soviet economic and strategic interests in the Third World merge in Soviet offers to improve port facilities and develop commercial fishing under aid agreements that in time may evolve into a Soviet naval presence. Granting of air facilities serves the same dual economic and strategic interest.[13]

4. THE STRATEGIC DIMENSION

That areas in the Third World have great geopolitical importance for the Soviet Union is a commonly accepted truth. Size, population, and resources make the Third World a potentially immense configuration of power. But equally important for the developed countries of the West and Japan is the fact that many of the key strategic areas of the world, particularly straits, the "chokepoints" of ocean traffic, lie within the Third World. For example, the Persian Gulf, surrounded by LDC's varying in size and the largest single source of exported oil, is accessible only through the narrow Strait of Hormuz. Principal Soviet anchorages in the Mediterranean are also near "chokepoints" in the eastern Mediterranean and North Africa where the free flow of traffic could be interrupted in the event of war. LDC's rim that area of the Mediterranean.[14]

The Soviets thus have strategic interests in the Third World, and the shift of their policy from traditional continentalism to global-

---

[10] Ibid., p. 50–51. See also, Donaldson, Soviet Union in the Third World, p. 314–15.
[11] HFAC, Soviet Union and the Third World, 1977, p. 52.
[12] Ibid.
[13] Valkenier, Elizabeth Kridl. Soviet Economic Relations with Developing Nations. In, Kanet, Roger E., ed. The Soviet Union and Developing Nations. Baltimore, John Hopkins Press, 1974, chapter 8, p. 232.
[14] HFAC, Soviet Union and the Third World, 1977, p. 53–54. See also, map appended to this study entitled, "Soviet Involvement in the Third World: Economic and Military Aid; Naval Presence."

ism has placed a heavy burden on their strategic requirements. The principal instrument in this outward thrust has been the Soviet Navy, and the necessity of properly providing for its new mission has required the building of an elaborate and carefully selected infrastructure of overseas bases, port facilities, refueling stations, and so forth.[15]

5. SURGE TOWARD GLOBALISM

For many reasons, therefore, the Third World is important in Soviet foreign policy. Each element—ideological, political, economic, and strategic—is interrelated and integrated. The composite suggests one transcending idea; namely, a surge toward globalism.[16]

C. MULTIPLE INSTRUMENTS OF SOVIET THIRD WORLD POLICY SUMMARIZED

The Soviet Union has used multiple instruments in pursuit of multiple goals in the Third World: economic aid and trade; military assistance and the use of military power for political purposes; policies and political actions that support Third World causes and interests while simultaneously serving those of the Soviet Union; international radio broadcasting and cultural diplomacy. The foremost, and perhaps the most visible, instruments have been economic aid, trade, and, most important, military assistance. They have provided the initial point of penetration for the expanding arc of Soviet influence and power.[17]

The Soviet economic aid and military assistance program has been impressive. According to the CIA report on Communist aid to the non-Communist LDC's for the year 1979, Communist economic and military aid programs continued as "a major means of penetrating the military establishments and influencing the governments of key Third World countries." Communist arms sales rebounded from a five-year low in 1978 to $8.8 billion in 1979, and new economic aid commitments stood at $2.6 billion. Soviet sales of military hardware to the Third World increased to $8.4 billion in 1979, up from $2.5 billion in 1978. Soviet arms deliveries climbed to an all-time high of $6.6 billion. During the period 1954-1979, the Soviets extended economic and military assistance to 76 countries totalling $18 billion in economic aid and $47 billion in military aid. In addition, they trained 68,000 LDC nationals from 100 LDC's in

[15] Ibid.
[16] For commentaries on the Soviet worldview and their design for an international system, see, Thompson, W. Scott. Toward a Communist International System. Orbis, v. 20, Winter 1977: 841–55, and Nils H. Wessel. Soviet Views of Multipolarity and the Emerging Balance of Power. Orbis, Winter 1979: 785–813. For discussions of Soviet-American relations in the context of the Third World, see, America and Russia: The Rules of the Game. Foreign Affairs, v. 57, Spring 1979. Includes three articles: Donald Zagoria, Into the Breach: New Soviet Alliances in the Third World (p. 733–54); Robert Legvold, The Super Rivals: Conflict in the Third World (p. 755–78); and Richard J. Barnet, U.S.-Soviet Relations: The Need for a Comprehensive Approach (p. 779–95). See also two articles in Foreign Affairs, v. 56, Oct. 1977 under the heading, "On Power": William P. Bundy, Elements of Power (p. 1–26) and Robert Legvold, The Nature of Soviet Power p. 49–71).
[17] HFAC, Soviet Union and the Third World, 1977, p. 4–5.

Soviet academic institutions; another 33,000 in technical skills; and about 46,000 in military skills.[18]

The Soviets have also used trade as a mechanism for furthering their Third World policy.

Among the general characteristics of Soviet economic and military aid programs and of their trade relations with the Third World are the following: careful strategic targeting; the building of highly visible industrial projects (for example, the Bokaro and Bhilai steel mills in India); linkage to Soviet equipment purchases and joint projects; the extension of virtually no outright grants; rarely allowing disbursements through multilateral institutions and invariably directing them to the state sector; and particularly in military aid, easy credit terms, discounting, low purchase price and quick delivery.[19]

In the political sphere the Soviet Union has by various means of political support established a mutually identifiable policy connection with many countries of the Third World (for example, an "anti-imperialist" posture), their causes and interests. Conversely, by dramatizing an adversarial relationship, it has been able to turn this connection to advantage in its struggle against the United States, its allies and the Chinese, as in the case of Soviet support for the radical Arab cause.

Through the development of its navy, the Soviet Union has been able to use its sea power as an effective arm of diplomacy. By virtue of its power-in-being and the potentialities of its global reach in a sea denial naval strategy against the West, the Soviet Navy has become a force to be reckoned with.

Propaganda, notably through international broadcasting, has proved to be an effective political instrument. Finally, in cultural diplomacy the Soviets found an important instrumentality for expanding their beachhead of influence and power in the Third World.[20]

D. Direction of Soviet Activity in the Third World

1. SOVIET CRITERION FOR SUPPORT

Soviet aid and political energy have been carefully—and rationally—invested in areas of the Third World that clearly serve Soviet strategic and political interests. Undifferentiated aid to small LDC's having no significant impact on international politics—aid outside clear Soviet policy targetting—seems not to have fit into Soviet designs. Soviet leaders have felt no shared responsibility with the United States and the West for underdevelopment and poverty in the Third World: This is the West's burden; as the colonial-imperial powers, by Soviet reasoning; the West is responsible, not the Soviet Union.[21]

---

[18] CIA, Communist Aid Activities in Non-Communist LDCs 1979 and 1954–1979, Oct. 1980, p. iii, iv, 1 and 2.

[19] For a summary account of these general characteristics and a selective commentary on how they function in the Soviet context, see, HFAC, Soviet Union and the Third World, 1977, p. 60, 62, 66 and 70–71. For a discussion on the "sophisticated" use of Soviet foreign aid, see, Donaldson, Soviet Union in the Third World, p. 314–15.

[20] HFAC, Soviet Union and the Third World, 1977, p. 5.

[21] Ibid., p. 54–56.

2. THE "NATIONAL LIBERATION ZONE": TARGETS OF OPPORTUNITY

Soviet criterion for recipients of foreign aid and other favors is simple: Whoever serves Soviet strategic and political interests. In its perception of these interests the Soviet Union has concentrated on what is termed the "national liberation zone." This zone, as noted above, is shaped like a crescent and extends from North Africa, bordering on the strategically important Mediterranean, through the oil-rich Middle East and South Asia, whose countries are contiguous with the Soviet Union or, like India, constitute a counter-weight to China, and then on to Southeast Asia. Only in recent years have the Soviets directed a great deal of attention to sub-Sahara Black Africa as low risk opportunities open up there. Latin America has lain on the periphery of Soviet strategic interests and has been treated accordingly, though since the 1980's increased attention has been given to developing new prospects in Central America and the Caribbean.[22]

3. IMPORTANCE OF THE "NATIONAL LIBERATION ZONE"

From the Soviet view this "national liberation zone" is "supremely important," as Sen Gupta, a student of Soviet Third World policy, observed, because of the strategic raw materials and human resources that lie within it, the commercial and communications lifelines that intersect it, and the geographic reality that it is adjacent to the U.S.S.R. Within this zone most local regional conflicts of the postwar era have been fought—and are still being fought; and within it also are the leading contingents, the "vanguards" as the Soviets would say, of the national liberation struggle. In the Soviet perspective this "national liberation zone" provides the "main link" in the chain of the anti-imperialist struggle in the contemporary era. The outcome of the struggle is expected to lead to further retreats of the imperialist forces from the Third World.[23]

4. "NATIONAL LIBERATION ZONE" AS A SOVIET TARGET

Accordingly, the Soviet Union has targeted this "national liberation zone" for the bulk of its foreign aid and investment and much of its political energy. During the period 1954-72, the Soviet Union extended about $8.2 billion in economic aid to 44 LDC's. Nearly 75 percent of the total committed went to countries in the Middle East and South Asia. Afghanistan, Egypt, India, Iran, Iraq, and Turkey were allocated about 65 percent. During the period 1955-72, the Soviets extended about $8.5 billion in arms assistance. Some 90 percent went to 8 countries, all within the "national liberation zone"; about 70 percent was allocated to Egypt, India, Indonesia and Iraq.[24]

5. BUTTRESSING SOVIET GLOBALISM

The magnitude of aid allocated within the "national liberation zone" for Soviet strategic and political purposes has thus been for

---

[22] HFAC, Soviet Policy and United States Response in the Third World, 1981, p. 35–36.
[23] Ibid.
[24] Ibid.

midable. This commitment during the 1960's and early 1970's exceeded predictions about Soviet efforts to establish their presence and influence abroad.[25] The pattern persisted through the 1970's.[26] In retrospect, therefore, Soviet strategic and political purposes have been clear; namely, to build an infrastructure to buttress the Soviet policy of globalism.

And for the West at this historical stage of transition from colonialism to interdependence the problem it faces is equally clear; namely, how to adapt its position in the Third World under new conditions patiently and in sustained incremental adjustment in order to preserve its vital interests now in contention with the Soviet Union.

E. MAJOR TRENDS IN SOVIET THIRD WORLD POLICY, 1945–70'S

1. STALIN'S HOSTILITY TOWARD THE THIRD WORLD

Soviet policy in the Third World since 1945 has passed through four distinct stages: One of hostility under Stalin, commitment and adventurism under Khrushchev, constraint and then expansion under Brezhnev, and restraint and caution in the late Brezhnev and early Andropov era.

Stalin had not taken a creative approach to the Third World. He distrusted any alliance with the national bourgeoise; that is, the indigenous national leadership within the Third World, Nehru of India and Sukarno of Indonesia for example. And in the post-World War II period he failed to perceive the revolutionary implications of the rising spirit of nationalism in the colonies and the newly independent nations emerging from the collapsing Western imperial systems. Seeing the alignment of world forces from a purely Manichean view sharply drawn along antagonistic Communist and capitalist lines, Stalin dogmatically ruled out any alliance with the liberation movements in the Third World. The result was cold war with the West, Soviet revolutionary radicalism on all fronts, and eventually a Soviet Union isolated from the main currents of international life.[27]

2. COMMITMENT AND ADVENTURISM UNDER KHRUSHCHEV

a. *Emergence of peaceful coexistence*

Not until Khrushchev's rise to power was Stalin's doctrinal stance toward the Third World changed and a new formulation devised, with policies adopted accordingly. This new stance was designed to unite the Communist world community—or socialist community as the Soviets prefer—with the emerging LDC's and national liberation movements into a new and enduring correlation of forces. The Soviets have since insisted that this combination of power has tipped the balance of world power against world capitalism and to the advantage of world socialism. Within this new ideo-

---

[25] Valkenier, Soviet Economic Relations with Developing Nations, in Kanet, Soviet Union and Developing Nations, 231–34.

[26] CIA, Communist Aid Activities in Non-Communist LDCs 1979 and 1954–1979, Oct. 1980, p. iii, iv, 1 and 2.

[27] HFAC, Soviet Policy and United States Response in the Third World, 1981, p. 37.

logical construct, peaceful coexistence with the capitalist West could and would be pursued, and the way was thus cleared for a radical shift in Soviet policy. Khrushchev now openly courted the Third World; their national bourgeoise were selectively accepted as allies and their states as national democratic states; and Soviet policy moved from the stance of isolationist continentalism toward interventionist globalism.[28]

b. Characteristics of Khrushchev's approach

Khrushchev's approach in the Third World from the mid-1950's to his removal at the end of 1964 was characterized by political opportunism, adventurism, excessive propaganda, and exaggerated optimism. Soviet activity concentrated on South and Southeast Asia, the Middle East, Cuba and to a lesser extent Africa. The main instrument of political action was economic and military assistance. As a consummate political activist and traveling salesman for socialism, Khrushchev moved into all areas of international politics, vigorously and confidently proclaiming the virtues of socialism and voicing Soviet support for Third World causes against the West.[29]

c. Results of Khrushchev's policy

The results of Khrushchev's thrust into the Third World were a mixture of successes and failures. The Soviet Union established a strong global presence, extending from Cuba to Indonesia. The connection with the Third World was firmly established. The Soviet image was changed favorably in the Third World and its prestige enhanced globally. The Soviet Union was able to penetrate the LDC's with men, material, and ideas and accordingly impinged on what had once been a Western preserve. Soviet support for the nationalist movements in many LDC's had paid off, leading to a further weakening or elimination of Western economic and political influence in some areas.

But Khrushchev's failures appeared to cancel out, or at least balance off, some of his successes. His approach to the Third World was oversimplified, overoptimistic, and oversold. The primacy of politics and ideology over economics led to serious errors in judgment. The decline of Western influence was not always matched by the equivalent rise in that of the Soviet Union, for Third World nationalism was inner directed and only incidentally pro-Soviet. The impact of Soviet supported indigenous communist parties and their ideology—at least within the narrowly constructed Soviet definition—was minimal. Finally, many of the leftist regimes upon which Khrushchev depended lacked staying power. Brezhnev was to reap the whirlwind. In brief, Khrushchev had serious failures in the Third World, and these failures contributed to his removal from power.[30]

---

[28] Ibid.
[29] Ibid., p.37.
[30] HFAC, Soviet Union and the Third World, 1977, p. 26–30. See also, Schwartz, Morton. The U.S.S.R. and Leftist Regimes in Less-Developed Countries. Survey, No. 2, v. 19, Spring 1973:218.

3. CONSTRAINT AND EXPANSION UNDER BREZHNEV

a. Characteristics of Brezhnev's approach to mid-1970's

In contrast to Khrushchev, the approach of the Brezhnev successor regime to the Third World was highly rationalistic, realistic, pragmatic, and, until Angola in the mid-1970's, cautious. Priorities were reversed: Economics took precedence over politics; ideology took a back seat to economic rationalism. In ideology, Brezhnev did not abandon Khrushchev's conceptual formulations: He retained them as part of the ideological infrastructure of peaceful coexistence but changed their function to suit his pragmatic approach.

Initially, Third World priorities and expectations were lowered and interest declined as the primary focus of Soviet concerns shifted increasingly to problems involving the West and China. Still, the Soviet commitment to the Third World remained intact as Soviet economic and military assistance continued to be concentrated in the "national liberation zone." But now Africa became secondary in Soviet considerations, and Latin America received greater attention, in addition to the static commitment to Cuba, as new opportunities opened up in Chile and Peru.[31]

b. Costs and benefits

Brezhnev's Third World policy during the decade from 1964 to the mid-1970's yielded costs and benefits. He lost when a series of Soviet supported leaders in Africa and Asia were overthrown. Expulsion from Egypt in mid-1972 was a particularly serious blow to Soviet prestige and to its position in the Middle East. But Brezhnev accrued such benefits for the Soviet Union as affirming the Soviet presence in the Third World; introducing Soviet power in the Mediterranean, Persian Gulf, and Indian Ocean; successfully extending Soviet influence into the northern tier states of Iran and Turkey; and establishing a greater Soviet influence in South Asia than enjoyed by the West. Economic arrangements made with the Third World (for example, joint projects) also reinforced the Soviet connection and assured economic benefits for the Soviet Union.[32]

c. Expanding activities in mid-1970's

In the mid-1970's, the Soviets, seizing new opportunities at first in sub-Sahara Africa and ignoring the constraints implicit in the rules of detente, resumed the outward thrust initiated by Khrushchev. Some observers saw in the renewal of this outward thrust the emergence of a "new imperial phase" in Russian history. Involvement in Angola followed by a deeper and more serious involvement in the Horn of Africa gave the Soviets clear geostrategic advantages. And so it was perceived particularly by a United States then still caught up in the "Vietnam syndrome," inattentive to Brezhnev's thrusts in the Third World and overattentive to

---

[31] For a review of Brezhnev's activities up to the mid-1970's, see, HFAC, Soviet Policy and United States Response in the Third World, 1981, p. 38–39.
[32] Ibid., p. 39–40.

maintaining detente in Western Europe and in its bilateral relations with Moscow.[33]

In retrospect the collapse of the U.S. position in Vietnam in April 1975 proved to be a critical, if not decisive, event not only in Soviet-American relations but in Soviet Third World policy. This humiliating defeat exposed American weakness in and to the Third World; it revealed the limits of American power; it generated a new era of "withdrawal" in American foreign policy described popularly as the "Vietnam syndrome"—that is, "No more Vietnams"; it was a signal to the Soviets that the time was right for moving out and seizing new opportunities to expand their power and influence in the Third World; and finally, it doomed detente as understood by Americans in the Basic Principles of 1972. Professor Adam Ulan, a leading American specialist on Soviet expansionism, put it very succinctly, "Hanoi's victory was also Moscow's."[34]

d. Impact of Afghanistan crisis

(1) Reversal of U.S. policy

Direct Soviet military intervention in Afghanistan during December 1979 produced a great reversal in U.S. policy; but as the war ground down to an often brutal military occupation and sometimes fierce guerrilla fighting, it contributed to an evolving trend of restraint and caution in Soviet Third World policy.

For Americans, Afghanistan now seems to have been a "watershed event", as National Security Adviser Zbigniew Brzezinski had said: It derailed the SALT process, placing detente in jeopardy; it produced a radical shift in American public opinion, countering the "Vietnam syndrome," expanding the allowable limits of foreign involvement, and energizing a resurgence of U.S. military power; it marked the beginning of American reentry into the Third World, perhaps even a return to globalism.[35]

(2) Estrangement of Muslim world

Afghanistan also had a great impact on Soviet policy, particularly in the Third World. Relations with the United States still remain estranged, with little promise of a return to normalcy perhaps for some time. But more important, for the purposes of this study, many Muslim countries—and they constitute much of the Third World—also remain estranged and have yet to become wholly reconciled to this latest and continuing act of Soviet aggression.[36] Accordingly, continued Soviet occupation and suppression of Afghanistan, now going into its sixth year, stands as a barrier to the advance of Soviet policy in the Muslim Third World.

---

[33] Ibid., p. 40–41.
[34] Ulam, Adam B. Dangerous Relations: The Soviet Union in World Politics, 1970–1982. N.Y. Oxford University Press, 1983, p. 129–39.
[35] For a discussion of the impact of the Afghanistan crisis on Soviet-American relations, see, HFAC, Soviet Policy and United States Response in the Third World, 1981, p. 001–116. See also, U.S. Library of Congress. Congressional Research Service. Afghanistan: Soviet Invasion and U.S. Response. Afghanistan Task Force of the Foreign Affairs and National Defense Division. Washington, Jan. 10, 1980. 36 p. (Periodically updated.)
[36] HFAC, Soviet Policy and United States Response in the Third World, 1981, p. 106–08.

(3) Launching of Brezhnev's peace offensive

Clearly on the defensive internationally, Brezhnev launched a peace offensive at the 26th Soviet Party Congress in February 1981, suggesting a search for accommodation not only in East-West relatons but also with the Third World. The deeper underlying purpose of this peace offensive seemed to be directed toward moderating Soviet policy in the Third World and countering the outward thrust of U.S. policy.

Thus, Brezhnev's policy of expansionism in the Third World, like that of Khrushchev's, had run into serious trouble as a result of Afghanistan. By 1983, Soviet policy seemed directed towards backing off and dissolving the harmful consequences of its activities in Afghanistan and elsewhere within its imperial domain in an apparent diplomacy of accommodation. The point of departure was Brezhnev's report at the 26th Party Congress.

III. 26TH SOVIET COMMUNIST PARTY CONGRESS: BREZHNEV'S REFLECTIONS ON THE THIRD WORLD

A. TRANSCENDING THEMES

1. THIRD WORLD PRESENCE

Perhaps the most recent and most authoritative statement on Soviet attitudes toward the Third World is contained in Brezhnev's main report to the 26th Soviet Communist Party Congress on February 23, 1981. This report of nearly 15,000 words, authoritative and comprehensive, is a basic Soviet document giving their appraisal of the state-of-the-Soviet Union at that particular time in history.[1]

The audience was right for the occasion and no doubt receptive to Brezhnev's reflections on the Third World, for the Third World presence at this Congress of nearly 5,000 delegates was formidable. From a total of 123 delegations of Communist, Workers, Revolutionary Democratic and other parties and organizations representing 109 countries all over the world, more than 90 came from Third World countries in Asia, Africa and Latin America. In opening the Congress, Soviet Party leader Mikhail Suslov paid special tribute to those delegations, as he said, "of many revolutionary-democratic parties, of that great and influential detachment of forces of national liberation, of forces of national and social liberation." [2]

2. FOCUS ON THE THIRD WORLD

Brezhnev made an appraisal of the Soviet role in the Third World during the five years since the 25th Party Congress, candidly discussing Soviet policy, attitudes, intentions and activities, and linking the national liberation movements and other "progressive" Third World elements with Soviet foreign policy as a positive force in international relations. He focused on two aspects: first, the Third World in a strictly ideological-political sense, as part of world socialism and an ally of the Soviet Union and Socialist bloc against world capitalism; and second, the Third World in the context of international politics, that is, as a problem in international affairs, East-West relations and Soviet foreign policy—in brief, as a reality of international life.

---

[1] Brezhnev, Leonid I. Report of the CPSU Central Committee. Moscow Domestic Service in Russian, 0720 GMT, Feb. 23, 1981, in Foreign Broadcast Information Service (FBIS), Daily Report, Soviet Union. Proceedings of the 26th CPSU Congress, v. 1, Supplement 1, Feb. 24, 1981, p. 5–54.

[2] Ibid., p. 4.

B. Third World in the Ideological-Political Context

1. THIRD WORLD DIFFERENTIATED

At the outset Brezhnev identified as one of the major trends in contemporary world affairs, the "fresh victories" of the "revolutionary struggle of peoples." "The liquidation of colonial empires was effectively completed" in the 1970's, he said, narrowing the "sphere of imperialist domination in the world." [3] In his mind the promise of national liberation was thus being fulfilled.

For Brezhnev the Third World was a differentiated world. Countries liberating themselves "from the colonial yoke" have pursued diverse paths of development—some socialist, others capitalist oriented; some followers of an independent policy, others "are today still following in the wake of the policy of imperialism." In brief, the Third World presented "a fairly variegated picture." [4]

Nonetheless, the "main direction" of development among the progressive Socialist oriented states has "similar" characteristics:
—The gradual liquidation of "the positions of the imperialist monopolies, the local grande bourgeoisie and feudal lords, the curbing of the activities of foreign capital";
—Success in securing control of the "commanding heights" for the "people's state";
—The acceleration of the transition to the planned development of productive forces;
—The encouragement of the cooperative movement in the countryside;
—The growth of the role of the "working masses" in public life;
—The gradual reinforcement of the state apparatus with "national cadres dedicated to the people";
—The pursuit of an "anti-imperialist" foreign policy; and
—The growing strength of the "revolutionary parties reflecting the interests of the broad masses of the working people." [5]

2. SOVIET COMMITMENT TO THE THIRD WORLD REAFFIRMED

Such characteristics were positive signs to the General Secretary and further justification for the correctness of Soviet policy and ideology. Accordingly, he reaffirmed Russia's traditional commitment to the Non-Alignment Movement as "an important factor" in international relations and re-iterated Soviet support in its efforts to establish a "just" new international economic order on a "democratic basis and on the principles of equality." [6] "No one should doubt," Brezhnev said in a sweeping pledge to the Third World, that

the CPSU will continue to pursue consistently the development of cooperation between the U.S.S.R. and the liberated countries and the consolidation of the alliance between world socialism and the national-liberation movement. [7]

The Islamic movement was an integral part of this National Liberation Movement. Differentiating the positive from its negative

---

[3] Ibid., p. 5.
[4] Ibid., p. 9–10.
[5] Ibid.
[6] Ibid., p. 12.
[7] Ibid.

aspects, Brezhnev stated categorically that, "The liberation struggle can unfold under the banner of Islam." Despite its complications and contradictions, this movement, as in the case of Iran, was
essentially "anti-imperialist" and was thus in the battle for liberation.[8]

The National Liberation Movement was, moreover, untainted by
terrorism. Brezhnev defended the movement against charges from
"imperialist circles" that it was a "manifestation of terrorism."
Singling out the Untied States by implication, Brezhnev asserted
that such opponents of the "liberation struggle of the popular
masses" have "truly set themselves an unattainable goal—to place
a barrier in the path of progressive changes in the world and reas-
sume the power to decide the fates of peoples." [9]

3. CONCRETE EVIDENCE OF SOVIET COMMITMENT TO THE THIRD WORLD

a. Treaties of friendship and cooperation concluded

To buttress words with deeds and to demonstrate that Soviet
policy in the Third World was more than just an airy ideological
abstraction, Brezhnev gave concrete evidence of the Soviet commitment. Since the 25th Soviet Party Congress five years ago, the
Soviet Union had concluded treaties of friendship and cooperation
with Angola, Ethiopia, Mozambique, Afghanistan and the People's
Democratic Republic of Yemen. Such a treaty was recently concluded with Syria in the expectation that it "will serve well" the
cause of Soviet-Syrian friendship and of "achieving a just peace" in
the Middle East.[10]

b. Economic and scientific-technical cooperation

Broad economic, scientific and technological cooperation, "beneficial to both sides," was, moreover, developing with the "liberated
states." Construction of major economic projects in which the
Soviet Union participated constituted "a large place" in Soviet relations with the Third World. In recent years projects were completed, "several of major importance," that held "a leading place"
in the economy of the receiving country.[11]

Examples of such projects were the Ath-Thawrah hydropower
complex in Syria that produces more than 70 percent of the power
generated in the country; the second phase of the metallurgical
works in Algiers which has increased its capacity to 2 million tons
of steel; enterprises for extracting 2.5 million tons of bauxite in
Guinea; "and so on." [12]

Soviet economic aid was complemented by the training of
cadres—"engineers, technical workers, qualified workers, doctors
and teachers." Tens of thousands of Soviet specialists were "working selflessly" at "building sites in the countries of Asia and
Africa, in industry and agriculture, in hospitals, and education establishments." "They are worthy representatives of their great so-

---

[8] Ibid., p. 11.
[9] Ibid., p. 15.
[10] Ibid., p. 10.
[11] Ibid.
[12] Ibid.

cialist homeland," Brezhnev exclaimed. "We are proud of them and send them our cordial wishes for successes." [13]

c. Military assistance on request

Finally, the Soviet Union and its Socialist allies gave military assistance to the "liberated states" on request, as in the case of Angola and Ethiopia, in order to frustrate attempts from the outside to encourage "internal counterrevolution or aggression." Brezhnev reiterated what has become a stock Soviet policy position on aid to the Third World and a self-serving justification for Soviet military intervention when he declared quite ambiguously: "We are against exporting revolution but we cannot agree either with the export of counterrevolution." The military invasion of Afghanistan was justified on grounds of insuring Soviet security and the necessity of countering the "real undeclared war" that "imperialism unleashed . . . against the Afghan revolution."[14]

C. THE THIRD WORLD IN THE CONTEXT OF INTERNATIONAL AND EAST-WEST RELATIONS

1. IN DEFENSE OF THIRD WORLD INTERESTS

Brezhnev went to great lengths to defend what he perceived to be Third World interests. In describing the "intensive struggle of two trends in world politics," the Third World was placed securely on the side of the Soviet Union and the Socialist community. This "side of the angels," so to speak, pursued the foreign policy course of "curbing the arms race, strengthening peace and detente and the defense of the sovereign rights and freedom of peoples." In contrast, the other trend, manifested by the "forces of imperialism" led by the United States, opposed these policies and pursued a course toward "undermining detente, boosting the arms race, the policy of threats and interference in other people's affairs and the suppressison of the liberation struggle."[15]

Starting from this assumption, all else falls into place. The United States was sharply criticized for its expansionist policy in the Middle East, Africa and the Indian Ocean, claiming for itself the right of "domination and coercion" for other states and peoples, declaring the area, with its rich resources, to be "in the sphere of vital U.S. interests," and undertaking extensive military preparations in Diego Garcia, Oman, Kenya, Egypt—"What will be the next move?" Accordingly, American strategists, reaching out for NATO support,

would clearly like to involve in their military preparations scores of other states and enmesh the world in a spider's web of U.S. bases, airfields and arms depot.

To justify their military preparations, these "Washington strategists" "spread tales" about the "Soviet threat" to the oil resources and communications routes of the Near and Middle East. Such charges were "a deliberate fabrication" since its authors were well aware that the Soviet Union "has no intention of encroaching on

---

[13] Ibid.
[14] Ibid.
[15] Ibid., p. 5.

either of these things." It was "absurd" to think it possible "to defend the West's oil interests by turning this region into a powder magazine."[16]

2. PEACE PROPOSALS BEARING ON THIRD WORLD AREAS

On the positive side, Brezhnev proposed negotiations on a number of issues bearing directly on and appealing to the Third World. One such proposal concerned the extension of confidence-building measures contained in the Helsinki Agreements in Europe to the Far East (e.g. notification of troop movements, naval and air exercises). The Soviet Union was ready to hold specific talks with "all interested countries" in the Far East on such "measures of trust."[17]

The Soviet Union was, moreover, ready to negotiate an agreement on the Persian Gulf "as an independent problem." It was also prepared to participate in a settlement "of the situation around Afghanistan," provided that only the international and not the internal aspects of the Afghan problem were discussed.[18]

And finally, the Soviet Union was ready to withdraw its military forces from Afghanistan. But on the following two conditions: that the dispatch of "counter-revolutionary gangs" into Afghanistan be "completely stopped"; and that "reliable guarantees" be given in accords between Afghanistan and its neighbors insuring that "no new intervention" would take place.[19]

Whatever the specific motivations of Brezhnev for making these proposals, there seems little doubt that they served the general purposes of the peace offensive he launched in his report. For they clearly had an appeal to many people in these troubled areas of the Third World.

3. ATTENTIVENESS TO SPECIFIC THIRD WORLD AREAS

No doubt the Third World derived some gratification from the deference Brezhnev had shown to them in his report. Latin American countries such as Mexico, Brazil, Argentina, Venezuela and Peru were praised for their "considerably increased" role in the world arena. The "broadening of mutually useful links" between them and the Soviet Union was a source of "satisfaction," and the Soviet Union was, accordingly, "ready to develop their links even further."[20]

Cooperation with India continued to occupy "a major place" in Soviet relations with the "liberated countries" and would remain "one of the main directions of Soviet foreign policy." Ties with India, whose role in international relations was becoming more prominent, were "stronger," so that Soviet-Indian friendship was evolving into "a deep-rooted popular tradition."[21]

No obstacles were in the way of establishing "good cooperation" with Indonesia and the other member-states of the Association of

---

[16] Ibid., p. 15.
[17] Ibid., p.20.
[18] Ibid.
[19] Ibid.
[20] Ibid., p. 18.
[21] Ibid., p. 11.

Southeast Asian Nations (ASEAN) as well. Sympathetic Soviet concern for the new states of Africa, the Caribbean and Oceania was manifested by immediate recognition. The Soviet Union also looked with favor upon the liberation struggle in Namibia and South Africa, and on the birth of the Zimbabwe Republic. Here was evidence that "the rule of the old-style colonizers and racists is drawing to a close." [22]

And in the Middle East Brezhnev cautioned that the "fratricidal war" between Iraq and Iran was "absolutely senseless" and "very advantageous to imperialism." National interests of both states dictate that this war should be brought to an end. And finally he claimed for the Soviet Union a positive role in solving the Arab-Israeli problem, but on terms more favorable to their Arab clients. [23]

Brezhnev seemed to have a good word for everyone in the Third World. And so it should be, for he was out to win new friends, consolidate old friendships, and contribute to building a political environment in which Soviet policy could flourish.

D. Commitment Reaffirmed, But With Caution and Restraint

1. continuation of khrushchev's third world policy

Brezhnev reaffirmed the Soviet commitment to the the Third World. This is the central meaning of his report to the 26th Party Congress. But it is a commitment marked by caution and restraint.

Brezhnev's speech represents the continuation of Soviet Third World policy launched by Khrushchev in the mid-1950's. It represents a re-commitment to the forward strategy of globalism that Khrushchev had initiated and Brezhnev extended during his nearly 20-year reign.

Certain elements in the speech justify these generalizations and among them are:
- —The thematic definition of world forces, in keeping with the traditional Soviet ideological worldview that explicitly and implicitly links the Third World with the Soviet Union and the Socialist community, setting it apart from the "repressive" forces of "Western imperialism";
- —The re-statement of the adversarial relationship with the United States and its Western allies, a central tenet in Soviet thought, as it magnifies under the pressure of new problems emerging in the Third World;
- —Concentration on the National Liberation Zone, a persistent direction of Soviet policy, as a fertile area for political exploitation and expanding Soviet influence;
- —The enlarging area of Soviet involvement in international issues that bear on Third World concerns with the Soviets claiming to be spokesman for its interests in concert with its own;

---

[22] Ibid.
[23] Ibid.

—The singling out of specific Third World countries as examples
of political, economic and military benefits to be accrued from
close political association with the Soviet Union; and
—The forthright expression of Soviet concern for peace and
progress in the Third World, in defense of Third World interests.
On the surface the Soviet commitment was there, and it seemed
to be firm. But was it?

2. CHARACTERISTICS OF BREZHNEV'S COMMITMENT

a. 25th Party Congress: Recommitment to the Third World

(1) In a spirit of certainty, adventurism, and self-confidence

Brezhnev's commitment to the Third World was indeed firm, as
will be shown in the other parts of this study, but it was cautious
and restrained. And judging from the tone of the speech, very carefully measured. This was particularly evident when contrasted
with his report to the 25th Party Congress in February 1976.

That speech exuded a sense of boldness, arrogance, even hubris.
Triumphant in its references to the Third World, it seemed to reflect a spirit of adventurism and challenge to the United States
and the West. Soviet relations with the liberated or developing
countries, he said, "have expanded and become more lasting." The
political content of "our ties has become richer." In this area of
"radical social changes" socialism has continued to "strengthen
and expand." Despite difficulties, "profound progressive changes
are taking place" within the Third World; "the class struggle is intensifying"; its influence in world affairs has increased "appecia-
bly." Victories of the National Liberation Movement have opened
up "new horizons" (i.e., targets of opportunity) for countries gaining their independence. The "class struggle" of the working people
against oppression, monopolies, and exploitation was "gaining
strength." "The revolutionary-democratic, anti-imperialist movement" was assuming "even larger proportions," producing "a
worldwide revolutionary process." From that Party rostrum, sym-
bolizing the highest political authority in the Soviet state, Brezhnev pledged again the full support of the Soviet Union.[24]

Brezhnev neither doubted the superiority nor the historically assured destiny of communism; nor did he doubt the vigorous growth
of the revolutionary process as a continuing world reality and its
movement in the direction of communism. "The events of the past
few years," he said, presumably having in mind "the deepening
crisis of capitalism" and growing political disorders in the Third
World, confirmed with "new force that capitalism is a society without a future." Counterrevolution and international imperialism
(i.e., the forces of democracy, capitalism, and democratic socialism)
were forces "doomed to failure" and the "cause of freedom and the
cause of progress" (i.e., communism) were "invincible." [25]

---

[24] U.S. Congress. House. Committee on Foreign Affairs. Soviet Diplomacy and Negotiating Behavior: Emerging New Context for U.S. Diplomacy. Prepared by Joseph G. Whelan enior Specialist in International Affairs, Congressional Research Service, Library of Congress. Wash., U.S.
Govt. Print. Off., 1979, p. 432.
[25] Ibid., p. 434.

(2) Source of Brezhnev's confidence

The source of Brezhnev's confidence was a combination of two tendencies: the deepening, and successful, Soviet involvement in the Third World, in contrast to the growing uncertainty in the United States of its role and interests, brought on by the collapse of the U.S. position in Vietnam and its reverberations throughout the Third World.

New successes provided a positive background against which Brezhnev could project his thoughts on Soviet Third World policy. The Soviet Union was pushing outward into the Third World and its most striking gain in the mid-1970's was in Africa, particularly Angola. By 1977, Ethiopia was to fall under its influence, though at the price of a lost ally in Somalia.

In contrast, the United States was still caught up in the so-called "Vietnam syndrome"—meaning "never again" will the United States be involved in, or even risk, war in the Third World. Uncertain of its interests there, the United States had seemingly retreated to a state of timidity.

Moreover, detente in Europe and Soviet-American relations had given the Soviet Union stability in this its most crucial relationship. With that vital base of national interest secure, it could and did pursue an adventurist policy toward targets of opportunity in the Third World. For in Brezhnev's position there was no contradition between the pursuit of detente and supporting revolutionary change in the Third World.

b. 26th Party Congress: Uncertainty, vulnerability, defensiveness

(1) Setbacks in the Third World

How different the background was for Brezhnev's report to the 26th Party Congress. Much had changed. By that time the Soviet Union had suffered serious setbacks in the Third World. Military intervention in Afghanistan proved to be costly, far more so than the Soviets seem to have expected; and the cost continues to rise. Afghanistan produced a negative impact on the Third World, especially among the Islamic nations. Unresolved after a 3-year commitment of over 100,000 troops, the Afghan question has become "a monkey-on-the-back" of Soviet policymakers. Comparisons of the Soviet experience in Afghanistan with that of the United States in Vietnam have become increasingly credible.

Equally important, Afghanistan has proved to be something of a "watershed" in Soviet-American relations. Clearly, the "Vietnam syndrome" was reversed in American fears that were generated by the Soviet invasion. Since December 1979, the Soviet Union has had to face a United States determined to strengthen its defense and to assess its vital interests in the Third World with greater clarity and certainty.

Elsewhere in the Third World, the Soviet Union has lost out, as in Somalia, though compensated somewhat by gain of uncertain value in Ethiopia. And in the Far East its only asset, not entirely dependable, has been Vietnam. Taking a retrospective glance at Soviet involvement in the Third World, there are no assurances of success. Plagued by an instability fostered by problems of underdevelopment, the Third World offers great risks to the intruder. The historical record thus far is marked by many serious Soviet failures (and some successes). Experience has shown that the countries of the Third World pursue their own interests, not necessarily those of other nations.

Brezhnev had good reason, therefore, for caution and restraint in his Party Congress speech.

(2) Collapse of détente with the United States

Collapse of détente with the United States and deterioration of relations no doubt affected Brezhnev's assessment of Soviet policy in the Third World. No longer did the Soviet Union have a secure base for its relations with the West, a policy posture that gave it greater freedom of action of probe soft spots in the Third World.

Other problems emerged, compounding Brezhnev's assessment: A new arms race was threatening on the horizon; the Polish crisis of 1980–82 served as a reminder of potential instability in Europe and possible loss of control in Eastern Europe; and in early 1981 the Soviets had to face what Brezhnev called a "bellicose" Reagan Administration determined on re-building its military strength, on pursuing a forward foreign policy, especially in the Third World, and on balancing and ultimately containing Soviet power.

(3) Encirclement and vulnerability

Added to these woes were other foreign policy problems that conjured up in the minds of some Soviet observers the vision of the old Stalinist bugaboo, "encirclement." As explained by one Soviet analyst in justification for intervention in Afghanistan, the Soviet Union faced:

—A hostile China and Japan in the Far East, backed by U.S. power, an unsympathetic North Korea, and a growing regionalism among Southeast Asian states as a protective barrier against Soviet influence;
—In the Middle East and particularly along the Soviet border, further Islamic hostility;
—Unreliable allies in Eastern Europe; and,
—In Western Europe the growing strength of NATO similarly backed by U.S. military power.

The result: the resurrection of a new form of "encirclement" that induced a sense of defensiveness and vulnerability.

During the five years between the 25th and 26th Party Congresses, the international environment changed considerably, and by no means to the advantage of the Soviet Union. Brezhnev's speech suggests that the time had come for caution and restraint, not only in international relations generally but in the Third World in particular. Hence, the rationale for launching his "peace offensive" at the Congress, and for the visibly diminished commitment, at least in rhetoric, to the Third World.[26]

---

[26] For a survey and analysis of Brezhnev's peace offensive, see Whelan, Joseph G. Brezhnev's Peace Offensive, 1981: Propaganda Ploy or U.S. Negotiating Opportunity? Washington, Office of Senior Specialists, Congressional Research Service, Library of Congress, May 17, 1982, 129 p. (Report No. 82–96S).

3. BREZHNEV'S SPEECH, ITS MEANING FOR THE 1980'S: A TIME FOR BACKING OFF?

What this augurs for the 1980's is in the realm of prophecy. But it does suggest at least the possibility that this may not be the time for Soviet adventurism in the Third World as in Angola and Ethiopia, but rather a time for restraint in action—a time for backing off, perhaps going no further than a carefully measured and rationalized commitment as in the early Brezhnev years following the near decade of Khrushchev's excesses and adverturism. A clue that such may be the direction of Soviet Third World policy was Brezhnev's proposal in a speech on April 27, 1981, a month after the closing of the 26th Party Congress, for establishing certain "rules of the game" in the Third World.[27] His purpose was to avoid any superpower confrontation.

---

[27] This proposal is discussed in, Whelan, Brezhnev's Peace Offensive 1981, 1982, p. 24-26. For an analysis of the 26th Party Congress by Soviet specialists in the Congressional Research Service, see, the 26th Soviet Communist Party Congress. Washington, Office of Senior Specialists and Foreign Affairs and National Defense Division, Congressional Research Service, Library of Congress, Sept. 1, 1981, 71 p. (Report No. 81-203 F).

IV. ANDROPOV'S VIEWS ON THE THIRD WORLD

A. ANDROPOV'S APPROVAL OF BREZHNEV'S THIRD WORLD POLICY

On November 10, 1982, Brezhnev's near 20-year rule ended with his death. Yuri V. Andropov, former head of the KGB and long-time high-ranking Party functionary, became General Secretary.[1] What were his views on the Third World?

During the Brezhnev years Andropov's published views on the Third World conformed to official policy. And continuity of policy had not been broken. He consistently supported the National Liberation Movement, particularly when opposed by the West. Like Brezhnev, he argued that support for Third World clients was not inconsistent with detente in the West. And he defended established Soviet policy on the necessity of invading Afghanistan.[2]

B. ANDROPOV'S SPEECH AT THE PARTY PLENUM, NOVEMBER 22, 1982

1. GENERAL CONTINUITY IN FOREIGN POLICY

Andropov's first published comments on the Third World as General Secretary were made at the regular plenum of the CPSU Central Committee on November 22, 1982. In general, Andropov provided little information about specific policies the new leadership would be pursuing. No mention was made of Poland or Afghanistan, nor did he offer any initiatives toward the West. Themes were highlighted that suggest an inclination toward the more active diplomatic strategy already underway at the time of Brezhnev's death—a strategy that emphasized ties with China, the Communist bloc, and the non-aligned states as a counterweight to deteriorating U.S. relations.

2. PERFUNCTORY COMMENTS ON THE THIRD WORLD

But Andropov said little about Soviet policy in the Third World, nothing beyond the platitudes of the past that might suggest a clue to future policy:

The importance of the group of states which created the Nonaligned Movement is growing in international life. With many of them the Soviet Union has all-round friendly ties which benefit both sides and make for greater stability in the world. One example of this is the Soviet Union's relations with India. Solidarity with the

---

[1] For CRS material on the succession, see, Whelan, Joseph G. Soviet Successions from Lenin to Brezhnev: The Troubled Searh for Legitimacy. Washington, Office of Senior Specialists, Congressional Research Service, Library of Congress, Sept. 20, 1982, 92 p. (Report No. 82–152); CRS Audio Brief: AB50066, Soviet Succession by Francis Miko, Joseph Whelan and John Hardt, Dec. 1982; and Miko, Francis T. and Alexis Pogorelskin. Soviet Succession. Foreign Affairs and National Defense Division, Congressional Reserch Service, Library of Congress. Issue Brief 82090 (Updated), 9 p.

[2] For Andropov's views on a wide range of subjects, see, Collection of Speeches and Articles by Yu. V. Andropov. U.S.S.R. Report. Political and Sociological Affairs. JPRS, L/10971, Nov. 29, 1982.

states which have gained freedom from colonial oppression, with the peoples who are upholding their independence has been and remains one of the fundamental principles of Soviet foreign policy.[3]

It is significant that Andropov, like Brezhnev in his 26th Party Congress speech, singled out India for special attention. But it is also significant that nothing was said about the left-wing countries of "socialist orientation" traditionally favored by the Soviet Union. No special praise or pledges of support were forthcoming.

C. ANDROPOV'S SPEECH ON U.S.S.R. 60TH ANNIVERSARY, DECEMBER 21, 1982

1. STRESS ON ARMS REDUCTIONS

In a major speech on December 21, 1982, commemorating the 60th anniversary of the U.S.S.R., Andropov dealt selectively with outstanding domestic and foreign policy issues. On foreign policy he indicated that arms control would be a priority by devoting most of his comments to new Soviet proposals for arms reductions in Europe and related issues. Concern for relations with Europe and the United States now seemed to be taking precedence over the Third World, quite in contrast to Brezhnev's policy in the mid-1970's but in line with his views expressed at the 26th Party Congress.

2. THIRD WORLD POLICY DOWNPLAYED

As in the plenum speech Andropov said very little about Soviet policy in the Third World beyond the usual platitudes. He called attention to the economic problems facing the Third World but offered nothing more than Soviet moral support as a corrective. The LDC's were suffering from "growing pains," he said," adding rather reservedly that the Soviet people "wish them great success" in pursuit of their prosperity and progress and the preservation of their independence. In these efforts "We respect the non-aligned movement," Andropov continued, "whose policy of peace is making a useful contribution to international relations." He placed the Soviet Union "squarely and unswervingly" on the side of those fighting for freedom, independence and "the very survival of their peoples, those who are forced to rebuff aggressors or are threatened with aggression."[4]

Andropov's restatement of Soviet policy seemed at best to be no more than a formal routine pronouncement of stock policy positions. Third World countries, particularly those that are "Socialist oriented" and others who customarily look to the Soviet Union for support, could probably find little solace in Andropov's words. Detachment seemed to be the tone of his statement, suggesting perhaps an attitude that solutions to problems of the Third World lie more within themselves than with the Soviet Union. Or it may be

---

[3] Andropov Plenum Speech. Moscow, Tass in English, 1848 GMT, Nov. 22, 1982, in FBIS, Daily Report: Soviet Union, v. 3, Nov. 23, 1982, p. R8.
[4] Kremlin Meeting Marks U.S.S.R. 60th Anniversary: Andropov Speech. Moscow, Tass in English, 0820 GMT, Dec. 21, 1982, in FBIS, Daily Report: Soviet Union, v. 3, Dec. 21, 1982, p. P7. See also, New Times (Moscow), no. 52, 1982:8.

that Soviet policymakers themselves were reconsidering their Third World policy particularly the extent of their commitment.

D. THE PRAGUE DECLARATION OF THE WARSAW PACT, JANUARY 5, 1983

1. MODERATION ON THIRD WORLD ISSUES

Equally low-key towards the problems of the Third World was the Prague Declaration issued at the conclusion of the Warsaw Pact meeting on January 4–5, 1983.[5] This declaration echoed Andropov's moderate tone on Third World issues, rejecting bellicose anti-American rhetoric. It differed from declarations of the past by softpedaling proclamations of support for Third World clients and emphasizing concern over the broader international consequences of regional and local conflicts.

2. URGING CONTAINMENT OF THIRD WORLD CONFLICTS

a. *"Danger of local conflicts"*

An uncharacteristic amount of attention was devoted in the Prague Declaration to the "danger of local conflicts." Largely absent from previous declarations, this issue constituted a unifying thread in the current statement. The declaration warned of the "danger of local conflicts erupting into armed confrontation on a world wide scale," and it linked improvement of the "world situation" to the elimination of current conflicts in Asia, Africa and Latin America and to the "prevention" of new conflicts.

Special credit was given to the Nonalignment Movement for its "major contribution towards the elimination and prevention of crisis situations." Citing efforts to create "zones of peace and cooperation" in troubled Third World areas, the declaration emphasized the importance of peaceful political solutions:

It is necessary to use political means to achieve solutions to problems existing in the Caribbean and Southeast Asia, and to contribute towards stronger peace in Asia and the Pacific.[6]

b. *Revived interest in Brezhnev's "Code of Conduct"*

Warsaw Pact stress on resolving Third World conflicts is not new, but significantly its proposed solutions essentially amounted to a restatement of the ideas set forth in Brezhnev's "code of conduct" speech in April 1981. These ideas include renunciation of "spheres of influence," noninterference in the internal affairs of Third World states, and respect for the territorial integrity of Third World countries and the inviolability of their borders. The Prague Declaration also reiterated one of Brezhnev's last peace proposals by calling on NATO to join the Warsaw Pact in refraining from extending "the zone of action of their bloc to any part of the world, in particular the Persian Gulf."[7]

---

[5] Political Declaration of the Warsaw Treaty Member States. Moscow, Tass in English, 1025 GMT, Jan. 6, 1983, in FBIS, Daily Report, Soviet Union, v. 3, Jan. 6, 1983, p. BB3–BB16.
[6] Ibid., p. BB11.
[7] Ibid.

Brezhnev's "code of conduct" speech, as noted in the section above, came in the wake of the Afghanistan crisis and the newly elected Reagan Administration's pledge to link Soviet-American arms dialogue with Soviet restraint in the Third World. The speech, an important component of Brezhnev's peace offensive, suggests a new appreciation in the Soviet Union of the corrosive effects of Third World conflicts on East-West relations and the need for the superpowers to adopt a "code of conduct." The idea faded into oblivion as Soviet-American relations deteriorated during 1982, but the approach taken in the political declaration suggests that it may still be on the agenda of the Soviet leadership.

3. REDUCED EMPHASIS ON SOVIET THIRD WORLD COMMITMENTS

The reduced emphasis on Soviet commitments to the Third World reflected in the Prague Declaration is consistent with the pattern emerging somewhat fitfully since Brezhnev's 26th Party Congress speech and persistently pursued by Andropov. The declaration defined the economic issues facing the Third World in this clinical and detached way:

> The eradication of underdevelopment, the gradual narrowing of the gap between economic development levels and provision of conditions for the harmonious growth of international contracts in the economic, scientific and technological fields constitute one of the basic factors of economic stability and the improvement of the international political climate.[8]

The Soviet prescription for these problems went no further than to reiterate the position of the Warsaw Pact members in favor of,

> restructuring international economic relations on a fair and democratic basis, establishing a new international economic order, and ensuring the compelete sovereignty of countries in Asia, Africa, Latin America and Oceania over their natural resources.

The declaration called for early "global talks on major economic problems," seeming to carefully distance itself by adding, "in accordance with U.N. resolutions." As a further indication of apparent Soviet desire to shift attention to Third World problems towards the United Nations—and inferentially away from the Soviet Union—was the statement that the member states,

> advocate a greater role for the United Nations in international affairs as an important forum for pooling the efforts of states to promote peace and international security and to contribute to the solution of urgent world problems.[9]

4. SHIFT OF CONCERN FROM THIRD WORLD TO EAST-WEST RELATIONS

The reduced emphasis in the declaration on the Soviet bloc commitment to the Third World was consistent with Andropov's expressed views. Andropov concentrated primarily on East-West relations in his foreign policy speeches and gave relatively short shrift to the Third World. He expressed Soviet sympathies for the LDC's, but only in general terms; and he refrained from the verbal assertiveness apparent in Brezhnev's statements in the mid and late 1970's. His few remarks on the Third World did not mention the traditionally favored client states of the Soviet Union, singling out

---

[8] Ibid., p. BB12.
[9] Ibid.

only India for special praise. And while in his December 21st speech he acknowledged the dire economic conditions facing the Third World, still he offered nothing more than moral support from the Soviet Union.[10]

Thus, the Soviet leadership seemed to have set upon a course of restraint and caution in their policy towards the Third World, particularly in areas where costs may outweigh benefits. Low cost targets of opportunity (e.g. Grenada) where political support and military assistance exact no great price would appear to be acceptable but this opportunism did not extend to far-reaching economic aid. Significantly, Soviet foreign policy specialists on the Third World have provided the leadership with a range of options upon which to build policy. Soviet Third World policy of the 1980's does not necessarily reflect the whims and caprices of a particular leader (Khrushchev comes to mind), but rather rests upon what seems to be very serious scholarly study.

---

[10] Significantly, the Tass release reporting on the approval of the Politburo and the Presidium of the Supreme Soviet and Council of Ministers on the action taken by the Soviet delegation headed by Andropov failed to mention the Third World; all comment dealt by and large with East-West relations. (In the Politbureau of the CPSU Central Committee, the Presidium of the U.S.S.R. Supreme Soviet and the Council of Ministers of the U.S.S.R. Moscow, Tass in English, 0603, Jan. 8, 1983, in FBIS, Daily Report, Soviet Union, v. 3, Jan. 10, 1983, p. BB1–BB2).

An analysis by Sallie Wise, Soviet analyst with Radio Liberty, emphasizes that Andropov's policies in the Third World, apart from Afghanistan, may in part be determined by its relations with the West. Soviet influence in the Third World, she notes, "has recently been on the wane." Accordingly, "the U.S.S.R. might not stand to lose a great deal if it were to ease up on its support for insurgent movements in Latin America and Africa as a gesture to Western opinion." Wise adds that in a period of transition the new leaders, as a practical matter, "are almost certain to preoccupied by domestic affairs and by their most important foreign relationships and may not want to become overextended in parts of the world where the potential rewards are not so great." (Wise, Sallie. Soviet Foreign Policy After Brezhnev: Unfinished Business. RFE–RL, Radio Liberty Research, RL 458/82, Nov. 16, 1982, p. 4.)

V. VIEWS OF SOVIET FOREIGN POLICY SPECIALISTS

A. VALKENIER'S ANALYSIS OF THE SPECTRUM OF VIEWS

1. DIFFERENTIATION BENEATH VENEER OF UNIFORMITY

Marked differentiation in approaches to the Third World lies beneath the veneer of propaganda that conveys an apparent (and distorted) uniformity in Soviet policy. Soviet foreign policy specialists differ in their analyses of the Soviet role in the Third World and sometimes offer radically different prescriptions to Soviet policymakers.

Elizabeth Kridl Valkenier, an American authority on Soviet Third World policy at Columbia University's Harriman Institute for Advanced Study of the Soviet Union and author of a forthcoming book, "Soviet Union and the Third World: The Economic Bind," summarized the various views of Soviet scholars on the Third World under three general categories: "the conservative, tradition-bound ideologues" and "the forward-looking globalists" at the extreme ends of the spectrum, with the "skeptical realists" between those polar positions.[1]

2. "THE CONSERVATIVE, TRADITION-BOUND IDEOLOGUES"

According to Valkenier, there is "little agreement" among Soviet foreign policy specialists on the role of the LDC's in international politics and, therefore, as a problem in Soviet foreign policy. At the one extreme are the "conservative, tradition-bound ideologues." Their views, shared by most Americans as a guide to Soviet thinking on the Third World, can be reduced to the general proposition that Third World "grievances and animosities toward the West serve Soviet interests." They contend that Lenin's thesis on the "natural alliance" between the Soviet Union and the oppressed colonial peoples against the imperialist powers is as relevant in the post-colonial period of today as it was 65 years ago when first proclaimed.

These conservative ideologues, according to Valkenier, are "rarely starry-eyed Marxists" who hold that international solidarity obliges the socialist states to support the political and economic liberation of the LDC's. Rather they believe that the manipulation of Third World complaints and demands "well serves Soviet rivalry with the United States."[2]

---

[1] Valkenier, Elizabeth Kridl. Inside Russia: Globalist vs. Ideologues. The Christian Science Monitor, Dec. 24, 1982, p. 23.
[2] Ibid.

3. "THE FORWARD-LOOKING GLOBALISTS"

At the other end of the spectrum are the "forward-looking globalists." Only in the past two years has this group become vocal, according to Valkenier. Since the mid-1950's, when the Soviets first entered the Third World, the "entrenched ideologues" have held center stage.

The globalists look upon the problems of the LDC's in terms of "threats to international equilibrium and peace," Valkenier observes, not as a "useful lever for tilting the balance of forces in favor of the U.S.S.R." The growing gap between the LDC's and the advanced industrial states, they contend, has created "a sense of alienation," transforming the nationalism directed against the West into Third World chauvinism. All industrialized nations, whether socialist or capitalist, are looked upon with hostility by these "superheated" Third World nationalists.

Globalists, moreover, see the increased poverty in the LDC's as the cause of political and social unrest which by turns can lead to civil and international strife, and ultimately great power involvement. From the globalists' view the increase in military spending by Third World regimes aggravates the situation. Scarce resources are as a consequence diverted from pressing domestic needs, retarding development and contributing to "further destabilization and fanning local and larger conflagrations."

The globalists have not explicitly proposed an international "code of conduct" to reduce the possibility of great power confrontation on Third World related issues, Valkenier continues. But they frankly concede that the socialist community of nations does not have all the answers. What they urge, according to Valkenier, is "broad, constructive cooperation of all the advanced countries in solving the problems that create unrest in the LDCs—overpopulation, food shortages, and backwardness." Finally, the globalists look upon access to raw materials as another destablizing factor, and accordingly advocate global regulation "to assure the legitimate interests not only of the producing LDCs but also of all the consuming industrial states."[3]

4. "THE SKEPTICAL REALISTS"

From their centrist position between the extremes, the "skeptical realists" have been arguing since 1977–78, according to Valkenier, that "in effect, the LDCs behave like the proverbial calves that are suckled by two cows." Accordingly, they conclude that too close an identification of Soviet interests with those of the Third World is "counterproductive and far too expensive." According to their view, such close association "sours Russia's relations with the West, and it costs too much in economic aid."

The "skeptical realists" seek to "puncture the doctrinaire claims of the conservatives," Valkenier notes. The Soviet Union should maintain a "safer distance" from the Third World, they argue, conducting a Third World policy based on "careful cost-benefit analyses rather than an outdated ideology." Moreover, they point out

---

[3] Ibid.

that the colonial stage of imperialism is over and that the LDC's are not "helpless victims of exploitation who automatically gravitate toward the communist bloc," but, as Valkenier explains, "independent actors in international relations and on the world market." The policy implication of this view from the perspective of the "skeptical realists" is, in Valkenier's words, "that the Third World can well take care of its own interests and does not need Soviet support." [4]

B. Soviet Writings on the Third World, 1980–82: A Sampling

1. GENERAL CHARACTERISTICS: SKEPTICISM AND DIVERSITY

a. Affirmation of Valkenier's Judgment

A review of some 25 articles on the Third World by Soviet foreign policy specialists during 1980–82 supports Valkenier's general thesis on the diversity of Soviet approaches to Third World problems. Other Western scholars share this view.

While considerable overlapping and the sheer complexity of the subject make it difficult to establish clear-cut categories on the various schools of thought, still some distinctions are discernible, and in a general way could, perhaps, be identified as "Skeptical Realists" and "Skeptical Traditionalists." On the basis of this sampling alone it would seem that no serious Soviet student of foreign policy, perhaps even some conservative ideologues, approaches the problem of the Third World in the crude, propagandistic style of the late 1950's and 1960's.

b. Premise and framework for analysis: Marxism-Leninism

All analyses in the articles reviewed are based on Marxism-Leninism. Upon these principles rest the premises of argument and the structural framework for discussion, from which there can be no permissible deviation. Basic Leninist laws of development and the ideological presumption of the historical destiny of the Third World as a component of the world community of socialist nations to take shape sometime in the future are never doubted.

Within this accepted ideological structure, however, great intellectual freedom is exercised as scholars attempt to apply Marxist-Leninist theory to practice—much like to scholasticism of the Middle Ages that permitted a variable and finely tuned intellectualism but within the narrow bounds of Christian principles. Their ultimate purpose is to seek solutions to the concrete problems of development using the ideological tools of Marxism-Leninism. Variation within this narrow ideologically defined structure is, therefore, the norm for analysis.

Andropov reaffirmed this methodological approach in his article in Kommunist in February 1983, commemorating the 100th anniversary of Karl Marx's death. In this article in which he made a strong case for ideological flexibility, Andropov notes that Marx himself never adhered strictly to some "abstract ideal of neat, sleek socialism." On the contrary, he asserts that Marx's ideas are

---

[4] Ibid.

not a "dogma", but a guide to action that must be "imaginatively" applied. Times have changed since Marx and other founders of socialism wrote and experience has shown, he says, that socialism has not developed exactly as they had expected. For this reason theory must be continually and "creatively" developed, Andropov counsels, adding that in seeking solutions to problems the works of Marx, Engels, and Lenin should first be consulted, but that one need "no longer limit himself to doing only this." In affirming Marxism-Leninism, its values, prescriptions for development, goals and purposes, Andropov calls particular attention to the "multiform experience of the fraternal socialist countries"; though not identical in everything, this experience provides, nonetheless, "vast material for theoretical interpretation."[5]

Soviet scholars are thus given considerable latitude in their analysis of the Third World. Accordingly, differences occur among them on such disputed points as the pace of development, variations on the social structures of Third World countries, and prospects for success. Presistent themes running through these analyses are, however, the complexity of Third World problems, the difficulty (and time needed) to cope with these problems—no easy solutions, for example—and the uncertainty of establishing reasonable expectations about the future. Such appraisals, while certain about the ultimate long-term outcome on the victory of socialism, are, nonetheless, tempered by realism and uncertainty about the near-term. Skepticism seems to be the operating word.

c. General views of Soviet scholars

(1) I. Zorina, "The Developing Countries in the Political Structure of Today's World [6]

To get the flavor of Soviet writings on the Third World, two articles among those reviewed are summarized below, with added commentary on what they suggest in the context of this analysis. The first is by I. Zorina; the second by E. Khrishtich.

Abstract: Discusses developing world as a component of the international political community, stresses the element of diversity and structural differences among LDC's, and notes that their main problems as a whole is to win the right to participate in world politics, overcome dependency and underdevelopment. States that the Non-Aligned movement is an important rallying point and center for effective action in world politics, that nationalism is a collective weapon in foreign policy and an important part of the "anti-imperialist" struggle, and that diversity is a characteristics of nationalism within the developing world whose components are in search of alternative models, e.g., Islam as an alternative.

Argues that the growing independence of the LDC's in foreign policy is an "indisputable fact" (e.g., the Group of 77), underscores the diversity and complexity of political systems in

---

[5] Andropov, Yuri. The Teaching of Karl Marx and Some Questions of Building Socialism in the U.S.S.R. Moscow Tass in English. 0925, Feb. 23, 1983, in FBIS Daily Report: Soviet Union, v. 3, Feb. 24, 1983, p. R1–R14.
[6] Mirovaya Ekonomika I Nezhdunarodnyyi Otnosheniya (MEMO), no. 8, Aug. 1982, JPRS, p. 33–46.

the Third World and the irreversibility of active involvement of the Third World in the world economy and world politics. Contends that the "tremendous" economic, social and political problems facing the LDC's cannot be solved without "purposeful and coordinated action" by the entire international community and in an atmosphere of detente and peace, and concludes that specific problems of the LDC's along with the necessity of overcoming underdevelopment and including them in the world community has become "one of the most urgent global issues of the present day."

Commentary: This article, marked by great candor, reveals the Soviet awareness of the diversity and complexity of the LDC's and their role in the international order. It is no simple ideological statement, but a careful analysis that invites credibility on what lies ahead in Soviet attempts to influence the destiny of the LDC's. It is a realistic statement of the LDC's today, the role they now play and may play as they develop further. The article conveys the feeling that development is a long time acoming, but that it is an urgent global problem. A spirit of caution and restraint in dealing with the very difficult problem of development seems to permeate this article. The writer recognizes the difficulties and cautions that there are no easy solutions. The reader comes away with the feeling that if the future belongs to socialism, it will be a long way off and that the road to that end will be hard-going and the obstacles many and formidable. In this critical article the writer appears to take the globalist view.

(2) E. Khrishtich, "The Program of 'Collective Self-Reliance': (Critical Analysis)" [7]

Abstract: Discusses "collective self-reliance" as an emerging concept in the LDC's, e.g., Group of 77 and the Non-Aligned Movement. Acknowledges the technical, economic and social achievements of the liberated countries but contrasts this success with the growing gap in development levels between newly liberated and the industrially developed countries. Catalogues the tendency towards united action among LDC's in a program of "collective self-reliance," noting the emergence of regional economic associations in the developing world, the role of UNCTAD and other mechanisms for international economic cooperation. Indicates the appeals from the LDC's to the socialist countries for technical assistance. Stresses the "indisputable" importance of external factors in determining the fate of the "collective self-reliance" program, but notes that "the main condition for its success lies primarily within the developing world and consists in the degree to which the liberated countries are ready and willing to act on the program."

Records the diverging views of supporters of "collective self-reliance" in the LDC's, namely, the isolationists and integrationists: the former seek economic separation from the devel-

---

[7] Mirovaya Ikonomika I Mezhdunarodnyye Otnosheniya, in Russian, No. 6, June 1982, p. 120–28, in U.S.S.R. Report, World Economy and International Relations, No. 6, 1982, JPRS 82191, Nov. 8, 1982, p. 90–102.

oped countries with no distinction between the "imperialist" states and socialist countries; the latter "take a more realistic stance," reject economic isolation and advocate engagement and diversification. Calls attention to the diversity among LDC's "in terms of natural and geographic features," notably in resources, the erosion of the base of "collective self-reliance" by uneven development in the liberated countries, now "more pronounced than the overall gap between the developed and developing worlds." Observes that "collective self-reliance" is impeded by "external obstacles" stemming from their involvement in the world capitalist economy, the influence of social factors on the emergence of "collective self-reliance," and the negative results on development under the influence of capitalism—"an increase in poverty, unemployment and inequality in income distribution." Suggests alternative socialist "positive plan of action" linked with the "general movement of economic decolonization" that was proposed at the Havana conference of the Non-Aligned Movement.

Argues that economic cooperation and integration "have more chance of success in countries with similar socio-economic and political aims" and that supporters of this theory and practice of "collective self-reliance" realize that "it can only be accomplished in an atmosphere of lasting peace, international security and the observance of democratic principles in relations between any states." Contends that this program is backed by "the objectively anti-imperalist potential" of the "collective self-reliance" movement and that the struggle to implement it "could promote the reorganization of international economic relations and progressive democratic reforms in the developing world." Concludes that the socialist states regard this movement for "collective self-reliance" as a "reality of contemporary international life," that they support the "progressive undertakings and demands" of the LDC's directed at "economic decolonization," and regard the proposal for this program as a "sovereign affair of the liberated states and another sign of their independent role in world affairs."

Commentary: In many respects this is a remarkable article, highly sophisticated, analytically subtle, rationally argued within the Communist context, giving evidence of considerable depth of understanding of the Third World. This is no simplistic view of the LDC's. It is a realistic appraisal of forces at work and a prescription for success through socialism. As in the case of other Soviet scholars, the writer lays out comprehensively and clearly, though within the Marxist-Leninist context, the complexities of the Third World and the difficulties of underdevelopment brought on by the impact of geographical location, the unevenness of development, and the negative influence of unequal distribution of resources. He acknowledges the achievements of the LDC's, notably in their efforts to seek solutions to their problems of under-development through organizational mechanisms of self-help. By taking into account the diversity within this movement, as within the Third World as a whole, he implies the limits of Soviet influence and ultimately of control. No hardline approach, this analysis describes the forces at work in the Third World, especially those tending toward unity, rejects the capitalist solution to development, and holds out the Havana proposals (and thus the socialist model) as the best road to modernity. This article suggests an outlook of socialist traditionalism mixed with reasonable skepticism.[8]

2. "SKEPTICAL REALISTS"

a. Emphasis on Restraint, Realism and Limitations

Unlike the utopians in the Khrushchev days of the late 1950's and early 60's, the "skeptical realists" are far less confident of Soviet success in the Third World, at least in the near term. Serious failures have tempered Soviet enthusiasm and self-confidence in the Third World. More conscious of the enormity of its problems and of their ability to cope with them, they have tended to emphasize the limitations on Soviet policy and the wisdom of patience, restraint and realism.

As products of the foreign policy and regional institutes set up by Khrushchev to study the Third World (and thus be able to deal with it more effectively for Soviet policy purposes), the "skeptical realists" have in the course of time become better equipped intellectually to analyze Third World realities, having mastered the analytical tools of the social sciences.[9] With this new enlightenment Soviet scholars have become better able to see the Third World for what it really is, not for what it seems to be through the distorted prism of Communist ideology.

A sense of realism, pragmatism and skepticism has, accordingly, entered Soviet scholarship on the Third World, moderating the exaggerated expectations of primitive ideology.

b. Counsel of caution and realism from Novopashin

(1) Impact of economic decline on Socialist model

Counsel of caution and realism came from Yuriy Novopashin, sector Chief of the U.S.S.R. Academy of Sciences' Institute of the Economies of the World Socialist System, in an article published in Problems of Philosophy, no. 8 of August 1982. In brief, Novopashin argues that declining Soviet domestic economic performance is undermining the credibility of the socialist model abroad and that increasing economic stringencies at home requires rethinking of current Soviet policies on aid to the Third World.

Progress in advancing the socialist revolution, Novopashin contends, depends not only on direct assistance to "leftist regimes" and revolutionary movements, but also on the "demonstrative

[8] Among other Soviet writings examined were, Gavrilov, Y.N. Problems of the Formation of Vanguard Parties in Countries of Socialist Orientation. Narody Azii I Afriki in Russian, no. 6, 1980, in U.S.S.R. Report, Political and Sociological Affairs, no. 111, JPRS 77660, Mar. 24, 1981, p. 1–9; and in the same source, Yashkin, V.A. Liberated Countries in the System of World Social Relations, JPRS, p. 9–21. Also, Third World Nationalism, Marxism-Leninism Linked in Common Struggle. Asia and Africa Today in English, no. 2, Mar.-Apr. 1982, p. 2–5, in U.S.S.R. Report. Political and Sociological Affairs, no. 1239, JPRS 80593, April 16, 1982, p. 1–7. and, Polonskaya, L. Analysis of Ideological Trends in Developing Countries. Aziya I Afrika Segodnya, Oct. 1981, in U.S.S.R. Report, Political and Sociological Affairs, no. 1247, JPRS 80755, May 7, 1982, p. 1–10.
[9] HFAC, Soviet Diplomacy and Negotiating Behavior, 1979, p. 267–79.

effect" of successes in the socialist world. He points out that a socialist country has to provide an attractive model of "effective socioeconomic growth" and "just social relations." He criticizes those who attempt to gloss over the imperfections of the socialist system in an effort to impress world public opinion. The best way to influence world opinion, he notes, is through self-criticism of socialism "in all its complexity and contradictoriness."

In his assessment of Soviet Third World policy Novopashin calls attention to the decline in growth rates of economic production and national income in CEMA states during the latter half of the 1970's, buttressing his criticism with statistical evidence. He acknowledges that this downward trend has continued into the 1980's; he attributes the cause largely to defects in the economic system. Accordingly, the level of economic development in the socialist countries "cannot yet preclude shortages of certain food products and consumer goods and, frequently, low-quality of such goods." Such shortcomings, he argues, impedes their ability to point to the Communist system as an attractice alternative model to capitalism.

(2) On restructuring strategy of assistance to the Third World

On the matter of economic competition with the West in the Third World, Novopashin notes that the Soviet Union is at a disadvantage. He acknowledges that the Soviet Union and its socialist allies have found it difficult to help Third World client states "in all the many salients where such assistance would be desirable." But he criticizes "leftist" Third World leaders for expecting the socialist states to finance dubious efforts to "force" socioeconomic change through rapid industrialization. Overemphasis on developing basic industry, the traditional goal of Soviet economic aid, has been too costly, he says, for both the Soviet Union and its clients, usually resulting in a decline in the living standard and an alienation of the population.

Novopashin, therefore, calls for a restructured strategy of Soviet assistance to the Third World, one that he claims would serve more effectively both Soviet domestic and foreign policy needs.

(3) Recommendations for change in Soviet Third World policy

Among the changes Novopashin recommends in Soviet Third World policy are the following:
- —Shifting the emphasis on economic aid from developing basic industry to increasing agricultural production. The interests of both sides would be served, particularly because of the existing food problem in the socialist countries.
- —Exercising greater care in selecting client states. A more discriminating approach, he implies, would not only save money but also enhance Soviet international prestige by avoiding "compromising ties with repressive, antipopular regimes." Some self-proclaimed "socialist oriented" Third World leaders, he contends, actually "discredit the idea of socialism" with their harsh "mobilization" policies.
- —Instituting greater coordination among the socialist states in their policies of aid to the LDC's. CMEA countries, he notes, should pool their resources in order to compete with Western

efforts to accelerate their "economic expansion" in the Third World. And finally,

—Giving "special attention" to improving the training of "national cadres" within the socialist states for the LDC's. Such an undertaking would further enhance the effectiveness of socialist trade, economic, scientific and technical ties with the LDC's "which is one way of positively influencing them."

(4) On the importance of Novopashin's article

Novopashin's critique of Soviet economic performance and Third World policy and his appeal for caution and realism in dealing with the LDC's is remarkable for four reasons: it stands as counterargument against the traditionalists who have effusively praised Soviet economic aid to the Third World and specifically defended Soviet emphasis on developing basic industry; it represents an effort by those seeking economic reform in the U.S.S.R. to emphasize the global implications of Soviet economic performance; it exemplifies an attempt to generate pressures within the Soviet elite for changes in their approach to economic performance at home and to policy in the Third World; and finally, in the word of one observer, it is an acknowledgement that Soviet Third World relations ought to be based on what amounts to "a traditional colonial industrial-agrarian pattern."[10]

c. Principles governing relations between the Soviet Union and Third World clients

(1) A call to realism

In article published in The Working Class and the Contemporary World of July-August 1982, L.N. Lebedinskaya, candidate of historical sciences and senior scientific staff member in the Central Committee's Institute of Marxism-Leninism, reinforces several of the points made by Novopashin.[11]

Clearly a "skeptical realist," Lebedinskaya sets forth the following 11 principles (among others) governing relations between the Soviet Union and its Third World clients:

1. A realistic, scientifically well-grounded, and multifaceted evaluation of the specifically historical needs of the revolutionary development of the parties entering into interaction within a careful posing of the current and prospective problems of this development.

2. The coincidence of the general evaluations of the international situation, the disposition of forces in the international arena, and the over-all anti-imperialist position.

3. The coincidence in the basic and main views of the leading forces of the liberation movement in the young states with the views of the party and state leaders of the fraternal socialist countries on the imminent program of action of the revolution-

---

[10] Soviet World Outlook, Advanced International Studies Institute, v. 7, Oct. 15, 1982, p. 6. Novopashin's article is summarized on pages 5 and 6.

[11] Lebedinskaya, L.N. People of the Former Colonial World and Real Socialism. Rabochiy Klass I Sovremennyy Mir in Ruissian, no. 4, July-Aug. 1982, p. 16–26, in U.S.S.R. Report, Political and Sociological Affairs, no. 1331, JPRS 82234, Nov. 15, 1982, p. 6–15.

ary forces and the need for foreign support brought about by it.

4. Mutual trust, respect of the parties involved, and good will.

5. Non-interference in domestic affairs and foreign policy, the lack of any kind of compulsion or dictates in relations.

6. Taking into account the real limits of economic possibilities or other resources of the socialist countries in rendering aid to the developing states.

7. The impermissability [sic] of misusing aid, utilizing it for purposes which are contradictory to the interests of the struggle for socialism and national liberation, to the interests of the toiling masses.

8. The impermissability [sic] of parasitical attitudes in connection with obtaining aid from the socialist countries, as well as positions under which the socialist countries are put on the same level with capitalist ones (the rich "North") in regard to the historical debt to the former colonial countries.

9. The maximum possible consideration of the historical experience of all the revolutionary forces which have solved analogous problems under similar conditions. Persistent analysis of the mistakes which have been permitted in order to avoid their repetition.

10. Recognition by both sides of the fact that the international interests of revolutionary development and the development of the world revolutionary process as a whole take precedence over narrowly national interests.

11. Active propaganda among the masses of actions directed at strengthening and expanding the alliance of world socialism and the consistently democratic forces of national liberation, propaganda for the principles of international solidarity among all the revolutionary forces of the present day.[12]

(2) Other sobering thoughts

Lebedinskaya's principles are placed securely within the larger framework of accepted Soviet doctrine on the Third World. A distinction is made between "real socialism" (as in the Soviet Union) from the local varieties proliferating throughout the Third World. Complexity of forces within the "democratic strata" of the LDC's is realistically recognized. Class differences and profound social antagonisms that disrupt unity are objectively observed.

Understandably, the writer eulogizes positive Soviet contributions to economic development in the Third World, such as the building of more than 1,000 industrial enterprises and facilities, including the As-Saur Hydroelectric Power Complex in Syria. Reiterating many of the ideas set forth at the 26th Party Congress, Lebedinskaya appears to move safely along the line of accepted policy and ideology. She dutifully holds up to leaders in the National Liberation Movement the Soviet experience as a model, an inspiration, and a "reliable guarantee" of a "bright future."

---

[12] Ibid., p. 7–8.

Lebedinskaya also describes the dynamics of Soviet policy and activities in the Third World well within the confines of Marxism-Leninism:

The influence of victorious socialism on the forces of national liberation is carried out along the following three lines: in the first place, the fraternal socialist countries weaken imperialism, thereby creating favorable external conditions for the anti-imperialist struggle of the national, democratic forces within the former colonial countries; in the second place, victorious socialism influences the peoples who are struggling for their full national liberation and social progress, by the force of example it demonstrates the visible advantages of the new structure over the system of capitalist exploitation; in the third place, it renders direct international aid in support of its own allies in the anti-imperialist struggle within the former colonial world.[13]

(3) From a realist's perspective

But Lebedinskaya's analysis, though firmly based on Marist-Leninist premises and principles, still bears the mark of pragmatism and realism; implied or explicitly stated in the 11 principles are the requirements for a nononsense, cost-effective, realistic approach to client-patron relationships in the Third World. As Lebedinskaya notes, "practical experience" has demonstrated that "the greatest effectiveness of inter-action between liberation struggle in the former colonial world and real socialism" is achieved for both sides "within the unconditional observance of a number of general principles"—principles which she insists, with a modernist's appeal, should be observed, *"with their creative, flexible application, using newer and newer forms."*[14]

d. On broadening ties with Third World capitalist states

(1) Response to "imperialism's aggressiveness"

In another critical appraisal of Soviet Third World policy appearing in Pravda on February 2, 1982, Karen Brutents, a deputy chief of the Central Committee's International Department, candidly assesses the consequences of increased Western opposition to Soviet involvement in the Third World.[15] A Doctor of Historical Sciences and leading Soviet advisor, Brutents tempers the customary optimism about Soviet successes in the Third World with statements of concern about the death of East-West detente and the consequent impact of U.S. efforts to check Soviet influence. Brutents urges a pragmatic strategy to meet that challenge, emphasizing the expansion of Soviet ties to the capitalist and traditionally pro-Western Third World states as well as "leftist" regimes.

The unifying theme in Brutents' article is the hightened threat from the West to the LDC's brought on by the deterioration in East-West relations during the past several years. The LDC's, he writes, are "among the first to suffer" from "an exacerbation of the international situation." "The most aggressive representatives of imperialist policy," he continues, "immediately shift the emphasis to strong-arm methods, to crude pressure and diktat. And this is

[13] Ibid., p. 9.
[14] Ibid., p. 7 Underlining added.
[15] Brutents, Karen. Questions of Theory: The Soviet Union and the Liberated Countries. Pravda in Russian, Feb. 2, 1982, p. 4–5, in FBIS Daily Report: Soviet Union, v. 3, Feb. 10, 1982, p. CC5–CC10.

precisely what is happening now." Brutents cautions against Western efforts to disrupt the ties established with many LDC's during the 1970's and to reclaim their lost influence. Under U.S. leadership the Western powers have made Soviet cooperation with the Third World their chief target because the Soviet Union presents "a serious obstacle to imperialist expansion." Soviet propagandists have expressed optimism about the futility of such "imperialist" machinations, he notes, but warns that the impact of these "imperialist" efforts on the Soviet position in the Third World "must not be underestimated."

(2) Links to Third World capitalist states

To counteract "imperialism's increasing aggressiveness" toward the liberated LDC's Brutents suggests a strategy for expanding Soviet ties in the Third World that implicitly recognizes the increasing diversity and predominance of non-Marxist regimes. Prominent among Soviet advisers who have criticized dogmatic views on the LDC's and have stressed the independent behavior of many capitalist-oriented states, Brutents gave the customary official sanction to the "socialist-oriented" states that have been the traditional focus of Soviet diplomacy and resources. But he concentrates on the projects for improving ties with two other types of states; namely, those following the "capitalist road" to development, but preserving a large measure of independence in economic and foreign policy matters; and those historically susceptible to Western dominance in both domestic and foreign policy.

The Soviet Union, Brutents insists, has a "solid base" for cooperation with countries of the first group, countries like India, Mexico and Brazil whom he praises for pursuing a "policy of defending and enhancing national sovereignty in politics and economics." And he is optimistic about expanding Soviet ties with countries in the second group, those "which are still in many ways dependent on the West's imperialist powers in the economic and political respects and which follow a pro-imperialist course on a number of important issues."

Three factors operating in most Western countries, Brutents contends, provide the Soviet Union an opening for greater influence:
—"Influential" forces within the "ruling circles" which "look to the national interest and would like to lessen" dependency on Western countries;
—The inability of governments to ignore strong "patriotic feelings" among the mass population; and
—The tendency of "the politicians of imperialism" to act "crudely" and "brazenly" in seeking to win over local leaders, producing a negative reaction among them that gives a "special attractiveness" to cooperation with the Soviet Union.

(3) Realism in analysis

As in the cases of Novopashin and Lebedinskaya, Brutents places his analysis solidy within the restricted context of Marxism-Leninism and makes an obligatory nod in the direction of standard political and ideological formulations. But what is significant in this analysis is the realistic recognition of diversity of systems within the Third World, the attempt to differentiate among them, and to suggest a Third World strategy based not upon some simplistic ideological notion of the past but rather on realism and rationality.[16]

3. "SKEPTICAL TRADITIONALISTS"

a. Georgy Kim on the Third World

Inclined more towards traditionalist values and perceptions but still somewhat cautious and realistic in their appraisals of the Third World are the "skeptical traditionalists." Indeed, a sampling of recent Soviet literature on the Third World suggests that perhaps only the outright political propagandists—"political hacks," in American parlance—in contrast to serious Soviet scholars adhere to the gross simplifications of the past.

Prominent among the "skeptical traditionalists," and, therefore, representative of this line of thought, is Georgy Kim, a Corresponding Member of the Soviet Academy of Sciences and a leading Soviet authority on the Third World.[17]

In recent articles Kim focuses specifically on the relationship between the National Liberation Movement and world socialism. With the critical eye of a skeptic and realist, Kim acknowledges changing realities in the Third World, records the many problems and obstacles facing the LDC's in reaching socialism, and firmly points to the Soviet experience and model as the only successful way to development.

---

[16] Articles by Academician Ye. Primakov, a leading Soviet authority on the Middle East, convey the same spirit of realism, rationality and pragmatism. In one article published in Dec. 1980, Primakov describes the transition from the simplistic view in the early years to a more differentiated approach to the Third World. Not until the 1970's and the collapse of colonialism was the complexity of the Third World fully realized. As he wrote in 1980, "Reality . . . turned out to be far more complex, as expressed in the processes of differentiation among the liberated countries, in which the changes in the socioeconomic area are of the greatest significance." And with this differentiation came an awareness that achieving socialism, having once established a revolutionary government, takes a very long time, particularly in LDC's that begin with a limited material base for society. This article is an example of the high degree of analysis that Soviet specialists put into their study of the Third World. The problem is highly intellectualized, but within the confines of Marxism-Leninism, for beneath it all is a conviction that socialism is the wave of the future in the Third World. (Primakov, Ye. The Law of Uneven Development and the Historical Fate of Liberated Countries. Mirovaya Ekonomika I Mezhdunarodnyye Otnosheniya in Russian No. 12, Dec. 1980, p. 28–47, in U.S.S.R. Report, Political and Sociological Affairs, No. 1129, JPRS 77924, April 24, 1981, p. 10–26.)

[17] Prof. R. Ulyanovskiy is another prominent Soviet scholar on Third World matters who could be grouped among the traditionalists. See, National Liberation and Nationalism. Aziya I Afrika Segordnya in Russian, no. 10, Oct. 1980, p. 2–6, in U.S.S.R. Report, Political and Sociological Affairs, no. 1109, JPRS 77569, March 12, 1981, p. 1–9. This article presents a very sophisticated argument for the use of nationalism for Communist purposes in the Third World. Highly rationalized within the context of Marxism-Leninism, it is an attempt to show the positive nature of nationalism in the National Liberation Movement and how it can be used or understood in the Third World. Especially skillful is the analysis of Islam as a positive force in Iran. For another example of Ulyanovskiy's work, see Robbery Under the Guise of "Interdependence," Kommunist in Russian, no. 16, Nov. 1981, p. 76–87, in U.S.S.R. Report, Translations from Kommunist, no. 16, Nov. 1981, JPRS 79862, Jan. 15, 1982, p. 79–90. For examples of other traditionalists, see Medovoy, Alexander. High Economic Growth Cannot End Third World Poverty. Asia and Africa Today in English no. 2, Mar.–Apr. 1982, p. 7–9, in U.S.S.R. Report, Political and Sociological Affairs, no. 1239, JPRS 80593, April 16, 1982, p. 7–19; and, Agafonov, V.P. and R.I. Khasbulatov. Problems of Neocolonialism at the Present Stage. Rabochiy Klass I Sovremennyy Mir in Russian no 5, Sept.–Oct. 1980, in U.S.S.R. Report, Political and Sociological Affairs no. 1096, JPRS 77252, Jan. 27, 1981, p. 1–10.

b. Some characteristics of Kim's writings

(1) Perceived historical trends

Characteristics common to Soviet scholars on the Third World are readily discernible in Kim's writings. Most evident is recognition of the organic connection between the National Liberation Movement, the Soviet Union and world socialism as a central component of the present historical epoch.

By the second half of the 1970's, colonialism had reached a state of "practically complete and irreversible collapse," Kim contends, accelerating the crisis of capitalism and magnifying the success of world socialism.[18] For Kim this epochal tendency represents a "qualitative leap" in the liberation process marked by "radical changes" in the political map of Indochina and by the "formation of socialist oriented revolutionary regimes in a number of Asian, African and Latin American countries."[19]

It is, therefore, a Soviet "truth" that the historical trends of the 1980's have thus been clearly defined and that their direction in the long term considered irreversible.

(2) Diversity and complexities of the Third World

"Skeptical traditionalists" readily perceive the diversity and complexity of the Third World. They do not conceal these realities; nor do they deny the ultimate favorable outcome for socialism.

Today, Kim insists, social evolution within the LDC's is accelerating, and the tasks facing these developing countries are "particularly complex and varied."[20] Thus, the problem of choosing a path for future development is becoming "very crucial." Some African and Asian countries have not yet made a "final choice." Admittedly, the socio-economic evolution "can still vacillate and is fraught with the danger of reversals." But Kim insists that the "over-riding factor" is that the people of the LDC's, only recently "free from colonial or semi-colonial dependence," are now "rejecting all the neo-colonialist forms of dependence more and more resolutely" and "are deciding ever consciously in favour of genuine social progress"; that is, socialism. The "progressive course" of the National Liberation Movement during the 1970's has borne this out.[21]

But Kim cautions that the future road to development coincides with "increasingly intensive social differentiation which is a fairly complicated process." Differences exist in the LDC's both at the rate and level of socio-economic development and in the basic principles of their economic organization. Kim acknowledges that the LDC's are "a conglomeration of countries of different types, a complex of nations which are qualitatively heterogeneous and diverse." But he insists that they have something in common: a socio-economic background inherited from colonial days, exacerbated by the

---

[18] Kim, G. The National Liberation Movement Today. International Affairs (Moscow), no. 4, April 1981:27.

[19] Kim, G. The Soviet Union and the National Liberation Movement. Mirovaya Ekonomika I Mezhdunarodniye Otnoshenia, no. 9, spet., 1982, p. 19-33, in Current Digest of the Soviet Press, v. 34, No. 10, 1982, p. 9. Also translated in, FBIS Daily Report: Soviet Union, v. 3, Sept. 30, 1982, Annex no. 060, p. 1-7.

[20] Kim, National Liberation Movement Today, p. 28.

[21] Ibid.

"neo-colonialist policies of exploitation," as well as "the massive poverty plaguing their societies, poorly developed class structures, and the preponderance of traditional social institutions." [22]

Accordingly, the LDC's are beset by problems that cannot be ignored. And Kim wisely cautions that "the logic of social delimination and social progress" in the LCD's is such that "some reversals and set-backs do emerge as by-products of progressive development." As he notes in this epigram: "Social delimitation is not always a one-way process; it has a dialectic of achievements and losses." [23]

Though acknowledging the reality of uneven development, Kim nevertheless accents the positive, insisting that the National Liberation Movement as a whole is "historically on the offensive and has scored major victories." And more important, this continuing offensive has produced a "qualitative turning point from which socialist orientation has begun to deepen and expand." [24]

Kim thus acknowledges diversity and complexity on the one hand, but on the other, as a Marxist-Leninist traditionalist, he insists that their course is true and the outcome of a socialist victory assured. As he observes, "We are witnessing the *irreversible* process of revolutionary movement growing in depth." [25]

(3) Differentiation within the Third World

(a) Capitalist development "from above" and "from below"

Diversity and complexities in development suggest the importance of differentiation within the LDC's. As Kim explains, "Revolution is created by millions of people, and no one can invest universal patterns." [26] Nonetheless, Kim is fairly precise in categorizing the various stages of development and differentiating the countries within them.

In what he calls a "jig-saw puzzle of social delimitation" cutting through the developing world, Kim differentiates between countries with capitalist development and those with "socialist orientation."

Within the capitalist category, which admittedly engulfs "large areas of the Afro-Asian world," he makes further distinctions between those whose capitalism was instilled "from above" through "authoritarian means" (as in Iran, Taiwan and South Korea), or emerged spontaneously "from below" that is, "democratic" capitalism (as in India, Sri Lanki, the Philippines, and Nigeria). Kim gives a highly complex analysis of the shades of difference within the development process in this general category. [27]

(b) "Soviet type of development"

Various types exists within the LDC's having a "socialist orientation" or "non-capitalist development." Historically, the first is

---

[22] Ibid.
[23] Ibid., p.30.
[24] Ibid.
[25] Ibid. Underlining added. Many of the ideas in this section appear in Kim's, Alliance of World Socialism, National Liberation Movement, p. 1–3.
[26] Kim, National Liberation Movement Today, p. 29.
[27] Ibid., p. 30–33, and Kim, Alliance of World Socialism, National Liberation Movement, p. 4–5.

what Kim calls the "Soviet type of development" which was followed by the peoples of Soviet Central Asia and Kazakhstan after the Bolshevik Revolution.

The distinctive features of this type reflect the Soviet experience: a backward people (in this case Asian), under the leadership of the Bolshevik Party, within a centralized "proletarian state" that transformed society on the principles of "socialist construction," advancing towards socialism while bypassing the capitalist stage in their social evolution.[28]

By linking the historic Soviet experience in Central Asia with that of the Third World today, Soviet writers infer that theirs is the proven way towards development. (In the material examined nothing seems to have been said about China as a model for the Third World, a deficiency Beijing would strongly protest.) [29]

(c) "People's revolutionary type"

The "people's" or "popular revolutionary type" is the second category of nations seeking non-capitalist development. Representative of this type are Mongolia, Vietnam, Laos, among others.

The specific features of the "people's revolutionary" way of building socialism is the "class alliance" of the national peasantry and the other "working masses" with the peoples of the world socialist system—in the case of Mongolia with the Soviet Union, the world's first socialist state. The "subjective factor" plays the primary role, particularly "by the revolutionary political leadership whose efforts gradually convert the revolutionary democratic party of all the people into a Marxist-Leninist vanguard." Lacking conditions characteristic of the Soviet type of non-capitalist development, this interim process requires "strict adherence" to a stage-by-stage development, the "gradual introduction of reforms," (socialist reforms, that is), and the preservation of the "broader social base" for the "people's revolutionary power."

In brief, the "people's revolutionary type" assumes an organic connection with the U.S.S.R. and provides for the gradual transformation to the "Soviet type" through socialist reform and the conversion of the "national revolutionary democratic party" into the "guiding Marxist-Leninist vanguard," that is, the Communist Party.[30]

(d) "National revolutionary type"

The "national revolutionary type" of non-capitalist development, as manifested in Algeria, Syria and Tanzania, has distinctive features. "Major anti-imperialist, anti-feudal, and even some anti-capitalist measures" are being carried out under the leadership of national parties, according to Kim's definition. These parties repre-

---

[28] Ibid., p. 5, and Kim, National Liberation Movement Today, p. 34.

[29] For a Soviet view of Chinese activities in the Third World, see the review of the book, The Hegemonic Policy of China—A Threat to the Peoples of Asia, Africa and Latin America, by Yu. Plekhanov, in Ploitcheskoye Samobrazovaniye (Moscow) in Russian, no. 12, 1981, p. 132–135, translated in U.S.S.R. Report, Political and Sociological Affairs, No. 1245, JPRS 80705, April 30, 1982, p. 1–6.

[30] Kim, National Liberation Movement Today, p. 34, and Kim, Alliance of World Socialism, National Liberation Movement, p. 5.

sent chiefly the interests of the middle class urban strata, and partly those of the "working people" in the towns and countryside.

"The revolutionary transforming potential of this type of development," Kim observes, "may be different and depend largely on the correlation between nationalism and socialism in the ideology and practices of the ruling circles in those countries." The "leading forces" in this "national revolutionary type" declare adherence "most resolutely" to socialist principles. As the National Charter adopted in 1976 by the Algerian People's Democratic Republic states,

Socialism is a product of modern development. . . . Socialism has the advantage over all preceding social systems in that it combines the principles of the most rational, just and humane organization of society with the outstanding achievements of modern science and technology.[31]

Thus, the "national revolutionary type" embraces an indeterminate mixture of nationalism and socialism, but in sufficiently favorable proportions to qualify for the Soviet imprimatur.

(e) "Revolutionary democratic type"

The "revolutionary democratic type" of noncapitalist development is unique among Afro-Asian countries having a "socialist orientation." Among this group are South Yemen, Angola, Mozambique, the People's Republic of the Congo, and Socialist Ethiopia.

Essentially, the "revolutionary democratic type" forms the "left wing of the socialist orientation." Kim notes that this type is a "qualitatively new phenomenon," observable only since the mid-1970's, but nonetheless "objectively law-governed." As the "vanguard of socialist orientation," countries of the "revolutionary democratic type," Kim points out,

are developing along progressive lines under the leadership of the parties of a new type—the vanguard parties of the working people, whose ideology is scientific socialism and who rely on political alliance of the originating working class, peasantry and other working people with the international proletariat.

What seems most distinctive about the "revolutionary democratic type" is that it manifests "more clearly," in Kim's view, "signs of a new, social stage" in the National Liberation Movement. That stage constitutes a full and open embrace of "scientific socialism," that is presumably, Marxism-Leninism of the purer Soviet variety. As Samora Machel, leader of the FRELIMO party and President of Mozambique, recently said,

We reject the idea that there can be "African socialism" or "Mozambiquan socialism." We firmly and persistently declare: there is only one kind of socialism, precisely scientific socialism.

South Yemen shares similar sentiments. The Program of the Yemen Socialist Party, adopted in 1978, clearly states that the Party, in Kim's words, "is the vanguard of the Yemeni working class in alliance with the peasantry and other working sections of the people, and sets itself the aim of,"

revolutionary transformation of the society for the completion of the tasks of the democratic revolution and transition to building socialism, guided in the attainment

---

[31] Ibid., and Kim, National Liberation Movement Today, p. 34.

of this noble aim by the theory of scientific socialism with due regard for the local peculiarities.[32]

As the form approaching closest to the Soviet criteria for Marxism-Leninism, the "revolutionary democratic type" would seem to be the most desirable road to non-capitalist development in the Third World. That Kim places this type at a "new, social stage" in the National Liberation Movement and regards it as a "qualitatively new phenomenon" is significant in itself.

(4) "Contradictions" facing LDC's with a "Socialist orientation"

(a) Affect "social transformations" with "extremely weak" productive forces

Theoretical formulations that give some rational structure to the Third World may be intellectually satisfying to Soviet specialists, but it must be somewhat disconcerting when they address the concrete problems of development. Still, writers like Kim do not shy away from the hard realities: they seem to be generally forthright in singling out existing problems or "contradictions." As Kim cautions,

The very scope of measures planned and carried out in the socialist oriented countries indicates that the non-capitalist road to development is fraught with contradictions and specific difficulties which should not be ignored.[33]

The reality of uneven development is seen as a common problem in the LDC's. According to Kim, those countries seeking the route of capitalist development, with their "limited domestic markets," "large armies of paupers," and uncertainty of their relationship with the capitalists world, run the risk of widening the gap between themselves and the developed capitalist countries.[34]

Countries with a "socialist orientation" face the particular "contradiction," he says, of seeking to carry out "social transformations" that are "historically extensive in scale" while their productive forces are "extremely weak." Thus, it is "very difficult," he notes, to link these transformations not only with the proceses inherent in the scientific-technological revolution but also with the state sector itself. What is needed, Kim says,

is a long period of the gradual and purposeful formation of qualitatively new productive forces, a period of introduction and stimulation on new (transitional) forms of social relations necessary to overcome this objective contradiction.[35]

(b) "Progressive" ruling elite at variance with undeveloped class structure

Another "contradiction" is the difference in class structure among the countries of "socialist orientation"; namely, "the progressive, advanced character of the leading class . . . being at variance with extremely undeveloped class structure of society." Par-

---

[32] Ibid., p. 5–6, and Kim, National Liberation Movement Today, p. 34–35.
[33] Ibid., p. 35.
[34] Ibid., p. 31 and 33.
[35] Ibid., p. 35. Kim quotes Boris Ponomarov, a high ranking Soviet official, as saying that "economic policy is a most important sphere of activities for vanguard parties. Its complexity lies in the necessity to combine the creation of a new material and technological base with the improvement of living standards for the working people. In this situation, the leaders of socialist oriented countries see the way out in making measured progress, trying to avoid an artificial acceleration of social reforms."

ticularly "vexing" is the "weakness of the national proletariat" which prevents it from assuming a leadership role in the "national democratic revolution." Kim explains that the function of "class leadership" in countries with vanguard parties are fulfilled by a "coalition of non-proletarian revolutionary democratic forces." He foresees the easing and disappearance of this "contradiction" with the emergence of a "national proletariat" and with the growth of its "class self-awareness and political organization."[36]

(5) Solutions through linkage with world socialism

(a) Urgency of linkage

Solutions to Third World problems and the resolution of "contradictions," particularly those with countries of "socialist orientation," can best take place in close association with the world socialist system. At this point Kim's conservatism, despite suggestions of a reassuring realism and even skepticism in other aspects of Third World matters, shines through.

In Kim's view the unity of world socialism with the forces of national liberation becomes "particularly urgent" as national liberation revolutions develop into "national democratic revolutions." At this penultimate stage economic cooperation between the socialist countries and the LDC's, faced as they are with the task of social and economic transformation, becomes "especially great." In such arrangements "the principles of mutual benefit, equality and respect for the partners' political and economic interests" constitute the basis of economic relations. "Principal attention," he notes, is directed toward "establishing and strengthening" the state sector with priority given to industry and engineering projects. For Kim is convinced, like other conservatives, that industrialization "lays the foundation for speeding up the transformation of the developing states' backward economies and social structures."[37] And for a development model, Kim points to the successful Soviet experience in Central Asia.[38]

(b) Record of Soviet assistance

In Russia's leading journal on international affairs, World Economy and International Relations, of September 1982, Kim records the extent of Soviet cooperation with the LDC's of Asia, Africa and Latin America, suggesting the magnitude of Soviet involvement, the intensity of commitment and energy expanded, and the irreversibility of their Third World policy. In 1981, the Soviet Union had in force economic cooperation agreements with 65 Afro-Asian and Latin American countries, as well as trade agreements with almost all of the newly independent states. Economic assistance from the socialist states takes the form of "design, geological-prospecting and research work, deliveries of complete sets of equipment, construction-and-installation work, agricultural assistance, the training of personnel, etc." Priority is given to the development of in-

[36] Ibid.

[37] Kim, The Soviet Union and the National Liberation Movement, p. 10.

[38] To Kim, the Soviet Union is "a real beacon" for emulation among the LDC's "striving for progress and social justice." Kim, G. The U.S.S.R. and National-State Construction in Developing Countries. International Affairs (Moscow), no. 1, Jan. 1983: 35, 37, 41–44.

dustry and "power engineering," which account for over 70 percent of CMEA economic and technical aid and over 50 percent of the Soviet Union's contribution. In the LDC's of Asia and Africa, which had a combined electric power capacity of about 17 million kilowatts in 1960, over 40 power stations, with a total capacity of 7.4 million kw, have been built with Soviet aid, and 18 more, with a total capacity of 8.4 million kw, are under construction. Dozens of machinery and metalworking plants are being built.

As a result of socialist assistance, according to Kim, the LDC's will have the "option of using or exporting" more than 30 billion cubic meters of natural gas. Some 69 irrigation and land reclamation projects, making it possible to put about 740,000 hectares of land into cultivation, are also being created with Soviet help.

"The steadily growing credits provided by the socialist states," Kim continues, "are playing an important role in expanding economic cooperation with the developing countries." Total credits from the socialist states incrseased from approximately 5 billion rubles in the mid-1960's to 16 billion rubles in early 1979. Kim observes that the LDC's get credit on favorable terms, usually extended for a period of 10 to 15 years at 2 percent to 3 percent annual interest and a grace period of one to three years.

Kim emphasizes also the extent of Soviet technical training. Students from the Afro-Asian and Latin American countries are trained at Lumumba University, 11 state universities and more than 40 other schools of higher learning. As of 1981, over 40,000 people from almost 100 LDC's had received an education in Soviet higher schools, and about 39,000 more students, graduate students and trainees received instruction. In addition CMEA built and equipped, or is building, 250 higher and secondary schools, training centers and vocational-technical schools—231 with Soviet help.

In the matter of trade, Kim states that trade turnover between the Soviet Union and the LDC's of Asia, Africa and Latin America is "increasing steadily." It rose from 3 billion rubles in 1970 to 12 billion in 1980—a 300 percent increase, and reached a record level in 1981 of 16.5 billion rubles. The share of these states in the Soviet Union's trade turnover with nonsocialist states rose from 27.5 percent in 1980 to 31.8 percent in 1981.

Moving into the foreign policy realm in this particular article, Kim becomes highly contentious in his defense of Soviet policy in the Third World and attacks on that of the United States and the West. He charges that the "imperialists" were trying to "strangle the young independent states—first of all the ones with progressive regimes." And then he defends efforts by the "socialist commonwealth" as an "international duty," to "prevent the export of counterrevolution," "to foil the imperialist's plans," and to help the LDC's "defend their independence." [39]

(c) Certainty of the Third World's future destiny

Kim has no doubt about the future direction of Third World development. Analysis of the National Liberation Movement in its various stages provides "substantial grounds" for his belief that "in

[39] Kim, The Soviet Union and the National Liberation Movement, pp. 10–11.

the future there will be greater unevenness, leaps and bounds in the revolutionary process" in the Third World. He is convinced that "a still greater social gap will separate the two political poles in the developing world": one tending towards capitalist development, the other towards "socialist orientation." Using Brezhnev's speech at the 25th Party Congress for his textual justification, Kim predicts that "the role of the countries on the left wing of the socialist orientation will be on the upswing." And he continues,

As the positions of the vanguard parties of the working people become consolidated, and they themselves turn into genuinely Marxist-Leninist parties, these states may well become ready to be integrated with the world socialist system, which in turn, will become another factor deepening the overall crisis of modern capitalism.

Kim concludes with a statement affirming the Soviet ideological belief in the preordained connection between world socialism and the National Liberation Movement in the Third World. Strengthening this linkage, he notes, "will open up new broad prospects for the revolutionary renovation of the huge multifaceted world of the developing countries." The development of this unity, he declares, will largely determine the "outcome of the struggle between the two sociopolitical systems throughout the world today."[40]

4. COMPLEXITY BUT CERTAINTY IN PURPOSES AND GOALS

It seems clear from this review of Soviet writings on the Third World that Soviet thought on approaches to the Third World is by no means linear. The complexity of Third World problems produces distinctive variations in the writings of Soviet scholars, and though hardly models of simplicity, clarity and comprehensiveness, they suggest, nonetheless, creativity and intellectualism. Theirs is creativity and skillful analysis, but within a dogmatically accepted context and according to officially established rules and assumptions. It is not really intellectualism as understood in the Modern Age, but rather an intellectualism carefully constricted within the narrow bounds of a Communist constructed neo-scholasticism—an intellectualism that rejects the inductive scientific method in open and unfettered inquiry for the selective use of deductive acceptance of unproven propositions and assumptions.

Nonetheless, these analyses represent the exercise of thought, and among their virtues convey a clear conviction of belief in the role of Marxism-Leninism in the Third World. Doubts never arise on basic ideological propositions and assumptions, but only on how best to achieve officially and ideologically established goals. Hence, there is a permanency in purposes and ends, with marked variety here and there on means.

Finally, these commentaries focus mainly on economic development in the Third World. Little or nothing is said about military assistance. And yet military aid, along with generously given political support, as will be shown in subsequent parts of this study, is a major component of Soviet involvement in the Third World, used particularly in exploiting targets of opportunity. Unlike economic aid, it is a means for spreading Soviet influence and power "on the cheap." And while questions may arise among Soviet leaders and

---

[40] Kim, The National Liberation Movement Today, pp. 36–37.

scholars about the extent of commitment on the economic level, few such reservations appear on the policy of military assistance.

PART II—THE SOVIETS IN ASIA, AN EXPANDING PRESENCE [1]

First of all, turning to this issue of perspective, what we see in Asia . . . is part of a worldwide buildup. It is not that the Soviet Union has decided to zero in on Asia. Rather, this is part of a systematic Soviet military build-up and growth of political aggressiveness that we have seen globally over a number of years.
> —Thomas Perry Thornton of SAIS on the growth of Soviet power, in testimony before the House Foreign Affairs Committee, 1983.

From Afghanistan to North Korea, the Soviet Union's relations with almost every country in Asia have been worsened by its invasion of Afghanistan and by its support of Vietnam's military takeover of Cambodia. The only exceptions are the invaded countries themselves, where pro-Soviet regimes were established by armed force, and Vietnam and Laos, where regimes earlier came to power or consolidated their power with Soviet military assistance.
> —Bruce Porter, The Soviet Union in Asia, 1983.

II. SOVIET INVOLVEMENT IN ASIA

A. OVERVIEW

1. THE SOVIET UNION, AN ASIAN POWER [2]

The Soviet Union claims to be a "natural ally" of the Third World. This claim is based largely on the ideological notion of a shared anti-imperial outlook. But paradoxically the relationship is also "unnatural" in that it is based on the historical and geographic fact that the Soviet Union shares the imperial legacy of the Czars whose expanding empire had absorbed vast contiguous territories in Asia. For Russia is a Eurasian state with roots in both continents, the Asian as well as the European.[3] Three quarters of Soviet territory today lies in Asia, and thus its people, as in the case of the over 40 million Soviet Muslims, share common cultures, languages and religions with their neighbors along the Soviet-Asian border. Constituting one-sixth of the 260 million Soviet population making the Soviet Union the fifth Muslim power in the world, and expecting to constitute one-third of the estimated 310–320 million Soviet population at the end of the century, the Soviet Muslims by the numbers alone not only justify Russia's claim of

---

[1] Prepared by Joseph G. Whelan, Senior Specialist in International Affairs, Congressional Research Service. First published on March 27, 1984 as CRS Report No. 84 56S.

[2] For a comprehensive examination of the Soviets in Asia, see, U.S. Congress. House. Committee on Foreign Affairs. The Soviet Role in Asia. Hearings before the Subcommittee on Europe and the Middle East and on Asia and Pacific Affairs. 98th Congress, 1st session. Washington, U.S. Govt. Print. Off., 1983. 576 p.

[3] Gerald Segal, a Lecturer at University of Leicester, makes this fine distinction: "The Soviet Union is not an east Asian power, but it is a power in east Asia." (Segal, Gerald, ed. The Soviet Union in East Asia: Predicaments of Power. London, Heinemann, and Boulder, Colorado, Westview, 1983, p. 1.)

being an Asian power but represent that formidable Soviet Asian connection to the outer world of Islam.[4]

Expansion has been and continues to be one of the most dynamic forces in Russian history. Beginning from its small Kievan base in the 9th to the 13th Century, Russia was to expand beyond its European territories from the borderlands of Iran, Afghanistan and India in southwestern and southern Asia to the frontiers of China and Mongolia in East Asia and on to Siberia and the maritime provinces in the northeast. By the end of the 19th Century Russia could claim a vast colonial empire with colonies in Asia that covered three times the size of European Russia. Further ambitions eastward were checked, however, by the competing ambitions and interests of Britain, China and Japan. Remarkably, Russian territory in Asia exceeded many times the Asian possessions of the European colonial powers active in Asia. Half of the Asian continent was under European control, of which approximately four-fifths was Russian and one-fifth British.[5]

European colonialism was to recede completely in Asia during the post World War II period, except for Russia. (See Map 1) Rejecting charges of colonialism and casuistically distinguishing between the "classical" or "maritime", that is, overseas, colonialism of the other European powers from their "continental" contiguous colonialism, and building on the Czarist territorial legacy, Soviet Russia was to carry on the Czarist tradition and expand further into Asia, reaffirming the historic quasi-protectorate over Mongolia and now establishing a protectorate over Afghanistan, absorbing Tanna Tuva, acquiring southern Sakhalin as a wartime concession, and claiming by right of conquest the disputed southern Kurile Islands. By virtue of this continuous expansion, the Asian territories of Russia were to account for more than one-third of Asia.[6]

---

[4] Heinzig, Dieter. Russia and the Soviet Union in Asia: Aspects of Colonialism and Expansionism. Berichte des Bundesinstituts fur Ostwissenschaftliche und Internationale Studien, v. 48, 1982:59–60. For a discussion of Soviet Muslims, see, Bennigsen, Alexandre. Islam in the Soviet Union. Soviet Jewish Affairs, v. 9, no. 2, 1979:3, and Hetmanek, Allen. Afghanistan· The Soviet Muslim Factor. Washington. The Library of Congress, Congressional Research Serv.ce, Feb. 12, 1980, 8 p. (Issue Briefs: IB80019).

[5] Heinzig, Russia and the Soviet Union in Asia, p. 60.

[6] Ibid., p. 59.

Map 1
U.S.S.R. and Asia

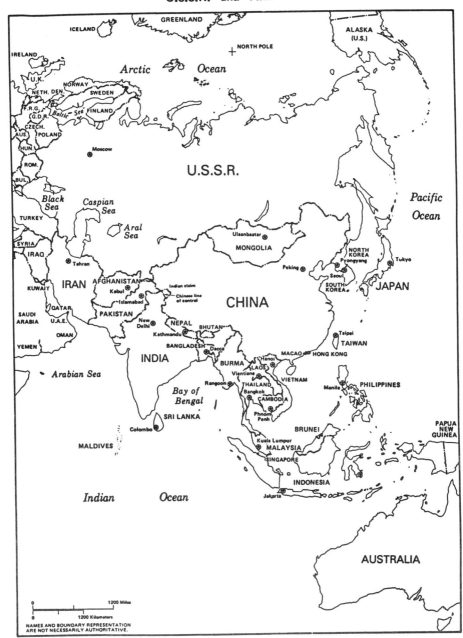

Hence the Soviets, as their Czarist antecedents, claim to be an Asian power with sovereign rights, extensive economic resources, especially in Siberia, and security interests to protect.[7] For in their perception of areas affecting their national interests, as Dr. Robert A. Scalapino, a specialist on Asian affairs at the University of California, notes, "Asia has a priority next to that of Europe and growing rather than diminishing in importance."[8] But in contrast most Asians perceive the Russians as "outsiders" and as a "great external power," not really "belonging" to their continent.[9] Be that as it may, the fact remains that the Soviet Union, though feared by many Asians as a global superpower, is in reality an Asian power; indeed, it is more than that, it is a Pacific power as well.[10] Thus when Brezhnev visited Tashkent in March 1982 to inaugurate a major new phase of his peace offensive in Asia, replete with overtures to China and Japan, he was reminding the world that the U.S.S.R. is an Asian as well as a European power whose history has been intertwined with the international politics of Asia as a principal actor.[11]

2. GEOSTRATEGIC NEEDS, AMBITIONS, AND POLICY GOALS

a. Soviet purposes and expectations

As an Asian power the Soviet Union has geostrategic needs, ambitions, and goals in that part of the world. It has the power, the instrumentalities and the tactics to pursue its ends. And it has pursued a policy that has taken on defensive and offensive characteristics.

Soviet purposes and expectations in the Third World countries of Asia sharpen when viewed in the larger context of Soviet Asian policy. A cosmic view of the Asian continent suggests the following general and specific Soviet interests to be secured:

—To develop Siberia's vast natural resources for use internally and internationally and to establish in its Far Eastern territories a strong regional power base from which to project Soviet power and influence into Northeast Asia and into the North and Western Pacific.[12]

---

[7] Palmer, Norman D. Soviet Perspectives on Peace and Security in Asia. Asian Affairs, v. 9, Sept.-Oct. 1981:4.

[8] Scalapino, Robert A. The Political Influence of the U.S.S.R. in Asia. In, Zagoria, Donald S., ed. Soviet Policy in East Asia. New Haven, Yale University Press, 1983, chapt. 3, p. 57–58.

[9] D'Encausse, Helen Carrere. Moscow's Aims and Capabilities in Asia. Defense Nationale (Paris), Nov. 1979:17–27, translated in, U.S.S.R. Report, Political and Sociological Affairs, No. 1013, JPRS 75152, Feb. 15, 1980, p. 1–9.

[10] Dr. Norman D. Palmer, Asian specialist at the University of Pennsylvania, wrote in his report on the Pushtchino Symposium during May 10–14, 1981 (in which Soviet specialists on Asia at the Academy of Sciences participated) "Emphasizing the fact that the Soviet Union was an Asian and a Pacific as well as a European power, Dr. Sladovsky stated that 'the Soviet Union has always sought to preserve peace in Asia,' and that 'naturally, developments in Asia and the Pacific are immediately related not only to the Soviet Union's economic interests but to its security as well." Dr. M. I. Sladkovsky is the Director of the Institute of Far Eastern Studies and a Corresponding Member of the U.S.S.R. Academy of Sciences. (Palmer, Soviet Perspectives on Peace and Security in Asia, p. 4.)

[11] Porter, Bruce. The Soviet Union in Asia: A Strategic Survey. RFE–RL. Radio Liberty Research, RL 148/82, April 1, 1983, p. 1. For a commentary on Asian concern for the Soviet status as superpower, see, Dibb, Paul. Soviet Capabilities, Interests and Strategies in East Asia in the 1980's. Survival, v. 24, July-Aug. 1982:155.

[12] Dibb, Soviet Capabilities, Interests and Strategies in East Asia, p. 155–56.

—To establish a strong military presence, especially a naval presence, in East Asia and to gain easy egress from bases on the continent through the strategically vital straits near Japan and Korea into the North and Western Pacific. Soviet objectives here are to counter U.S. power in the Pacific, isolate Japan, prevent regional domination by China and support national liberation movements and social revolutions by expanding Soviet power and influence in the area.[13]

—To neutralize Japan politically. By taking advantage of Japan's dependency on imports by sea through a strong naval presence, the Soviets seek to intimidate Japan to accommodate to their policy requirements and to drive a wedge into the American regional security system.[14]

—To isolate, encircle and contain China, while building influence in a disinterested, opportunistic North Korea. Soviet aims here are to keep China weak, preventing it from becoming in the long run a dangerous adversary as it moves along the course of modernization.[15]

—To build a strong regional power base in Southeast Asia by supporting Vietnam and helping it to consolidate the Indochinese states of Vietnam, Laos and Cambodia into a group of pro-Soviet Communist states, ultimately drawing them into the Soviet orbit; by reducing Chinese influence and preventing the ASEAN states (Malaysia, Singapore, Philippines, Indonesia, and Thailand) from developing into a pro-Western bloc with security ties with the West and/or China; by influencing ASEAN governments towards a neutralist posture; and by gaining increased and regular access to air and sea facilities in Vietnam and elsewhere for projecting Soviet seapower.[16] A strong Soviet naval presence in Southeast Asia could enable the Soviets to project their power and potentially gain influence, if not control, over the vital Strait of Malacca and other strategic features in the area that lead into the South Pacific, Indian Ocean and on to the Middle East.[17] (See Map 5)

—In South Asia, to strengthen its relations with India, the centerpiece of its Third World policy, and counteract the negative impact of the Soviet occupation of Afghanistan; to pacify Afghanistan, thus securing what the Soviets perceive to be a vital interest along their southern border; and to pressure Pakistan into reducing its support for the Afghan rebels.

—And, finally, in general, to compete with the United States for influence in Asia and the Western Pacific, to weaken key American alliances in the area, and to project a dual image of the Soviet Union; namely, that of a revolutionary society and development model in the Marxist-Leninist tradition with an appeal to the Third World, at the same time that of a formida-

---

[13] Thomas, Gerry S. Lieut. Comdr., USN. Their Pacific Fleet. U.S. Naval Institute Proceedings, v. 108, Oct. 1982: 82–83.

[14] Ibid., p. 86.

[15] Zagoria, Donald S. The Strategic Environment in East Asia. In, Zagoria, Soviet Policy in East Asia, chapt. 1, p. 2–3.

[16] Zagoria, Donald S. and Sheldon W. Simon. Soviet Policy in Southeast Asia. In, Zagoria, Soviet Policy in East Asia, chapt. 6, p. 154.

[17] Ibid., p. 153–54, and Thomas, Their Pacific Fleet, p. 86.

ble superpower dedicated to peace and the orderly advancement of state relations.[18]

b. Defensive and offensive aspects of Soviet policy

To achieve these presumed and asserted goals in Asia, the Soviets have pursued a policy that has in general been both defensive and offensive. Consider first the defensive aspects.

The notion of "encirclement," a Soviet bugaboo harking back to the Stalin era and magnified by the negative impact of war in Afghanistan, has contributed to the defensive character of Soviet policy. Everywhere the Soviets looked in 1979–1980, by their own admission, they saw real or potential enemies. With some truth, they reasoned that the Soviet Union was "encircled," by an inhospitable China, North Korea and Japan in the Far East; unreliable allies in Eastern Europe, demonstrated anew by the renewal crisis in Poland; a volatile southern flank comprising Iran, Turkey and Pakistan; and a hostile NATO alliance in Western Europe in the throes of an arms modernization program and supported by their most powerful capitalist adversary, the United States. The invasion of and continuing war in Afghanistan, purely defensive from their perspective, aggravated still further Soviet relations with the West, outraged much of the Muslim Third World, and deepened the feeling of "encirclement."[19]

Accordingly, the stage was set for Brezhnev's peace offensive which he launched at the 26th Party Congress in February 1981. The Soviets attempted to break out of their self-induced isolation. They did this by opening a dialogue with China and Japan. It was directed towards easing tensions and reconstituting relations on the basis of the proposed "confidence building" measures. This diplomatic demarche suggests the defensive character of Brezhnev's policy in Asia, a policy appealing to those who sought to decompress what was appearing to be the renewal of the cold war.[20]

Yet Soviet policy had an offensive side as well, and this was highlighted by the continuing war in Afghanistan; military, economic and political suppport for Vietnam in its war in Kampuchea; and the acceleration of the massive buildup of Soviet military power in the Far East. The combination of all three offensive elements of Soviet policy negated whatever positive effects were expected from the peace offensive in Asia; proved to be counterproductive in relations with Japan by accelerating its move towards rearmament; further alienated the ASEAN countries, making any possible Soviet inroads in this Third World federation unlikely; and produced not only a cooling in Soviet-Indian relations but encouraged India to diversify its arms procurement and in other ways distance itself from its heretofore favorite patron. The Soviet connec-

---

[18] Scalapino, Political Influence of the U.S.S.R. in Asia, p. 64, and Palmer, Soviet Perspectives on Peace and Security in Asia, p. 5.

[19] This subject is discussed in, Whelan, Joseph G. Brezhnev's Peace Offensive, 1981: Propaganda Ploy or U.S. Negotiating Opportunity? Washington, Library of Congress, Congressional Research Service, May 17, 1982, p. 13–14. (Report No. 82–96S) For a commentary on the peace offensive in the context of the Third World, see, Asian Security, 1982. Tokyo, Japan, Research Institute for Peace and Security, 1982, p. 54.

[20] Dibb, Paul. The Soviet Union as a Pacific Power. International Journal, v. 38, Spring 1983:243–44.

tion to this most preferred client in the Third World seemed to be loosening.[21]

3. THE SOVIET MILITARY BUILDUP IN ASIA

a. *Estimates of the buildup*

The Soviet military buildup in Asia, along with the Soviet invasion of Afghanistan and military involvement in Kampuchea as Vietnam's patron and mentor, have largely determined the relationships between the Soviet Union and the countries of Asia—Communist and non-Communist, both economically advanced and developing. The effects of this buildup, particularly in naval and strategic forces, and the aggressive use of military power, have reveberated throughout the entire continent and have fundamentally and adversely impacted upon Soviet-American relations in Asia and the Western Pacific.[22]

Sources abound that catalog what Admiral Robert Long, USN, Commander-in-Chief Pacific, terms, the "unparalleled growth of Soviet military power in the Far East."[23] (See Map 2 and Figure 1) This "impressive array of forces," as Donald S. Zagoria, an American specialist on Asian affairs, describes it, includes central strategic nuclear forces capable of reaching any point in Asia; a specifically Asian directed nuclear theater force that includes over 140 SS–20's and 70 Backfire bombers having a strategic range; a modernized ground force of about 51 divisions also directed against China; expanding forces near Japan, including new and permanent bases on some of the disputed Kurile Islands near Japan's northernmost island of Hokkaido; some 2,000 combat planes, including advanced fighter bombers and attack fighters; and, finally, a rapidly growing Pacific fleet with some 128 submarines including 31 nuclear ballistic missiles SSBN's, the most advanced of which can strike targets in the United States from near the Asian mainland. This force, based at an enlarged naval complex in Vladivostok and Petropavlovsk, is supplemented by Soviet naval and air facilities in Vietnam. Bases as far away as the Middle East, notably South Yemen and Ethiopia, significantly expand the scope of Soviet power projection in a vast region from the Pacific to the Indian Oceans.

---

[21] For discussions on Soviet overemphasis on the military side of its policy in Asia, see, Dibb, Soviet Capabilities, Interests and Strategies in East Asia, p. 159, and Menon, Rajan. The Soviet Union in East Asia. Current History, v. 82, Oct. 1983:313–314. For a recent appraisal of Soviet failures in East Asia, see, Dibb, The Soviet Union as a Pacific Power. p. 241.

[22] With respect to the Soviet buildup in Asia, Dr. Thomas Perry Thornton, an Asian specialist at The Johns Hopkins University, states: ". . . what we see in Asia . . . is part of a worldwide buildup. It is not that the Soviet Union has decided to zero in on Asia. Rather, this is part of a systematic Soviet military buildup and growth of political aggressiveness that we have seen globally over a number of years." (HFAC, Soviet Role in Asia, 1983, p. 3.) For other evaluations of the quality and quantity of the Soviet buildup, see, Langer, Paul F. Soviet Military Power in Asia, in Zagoria, Soviet Policy in East Asia, chapter 10.

[23] Oka, Takashi. Pacific Commander Sees Fresh, Strategic Focus on the Region. The Christian Science Monitor, June 15, 1983, p. 3. For estimates on the Soviet military buildup in Asia, see, U.S. Department of Defense. Soviet Military Power. 2nd. ed. Washington, U.S. Govt. Print. Off., 1983, 107 p.; Langer, Paul F. Soviet Military Power in Asia. In, Zagoria, Soviet Policy in East Asia, chapt. 10; and Asian Security, 1982, p. 1–8 and 54–60.

Map 2.
Military Buildup in the Soviet Far East

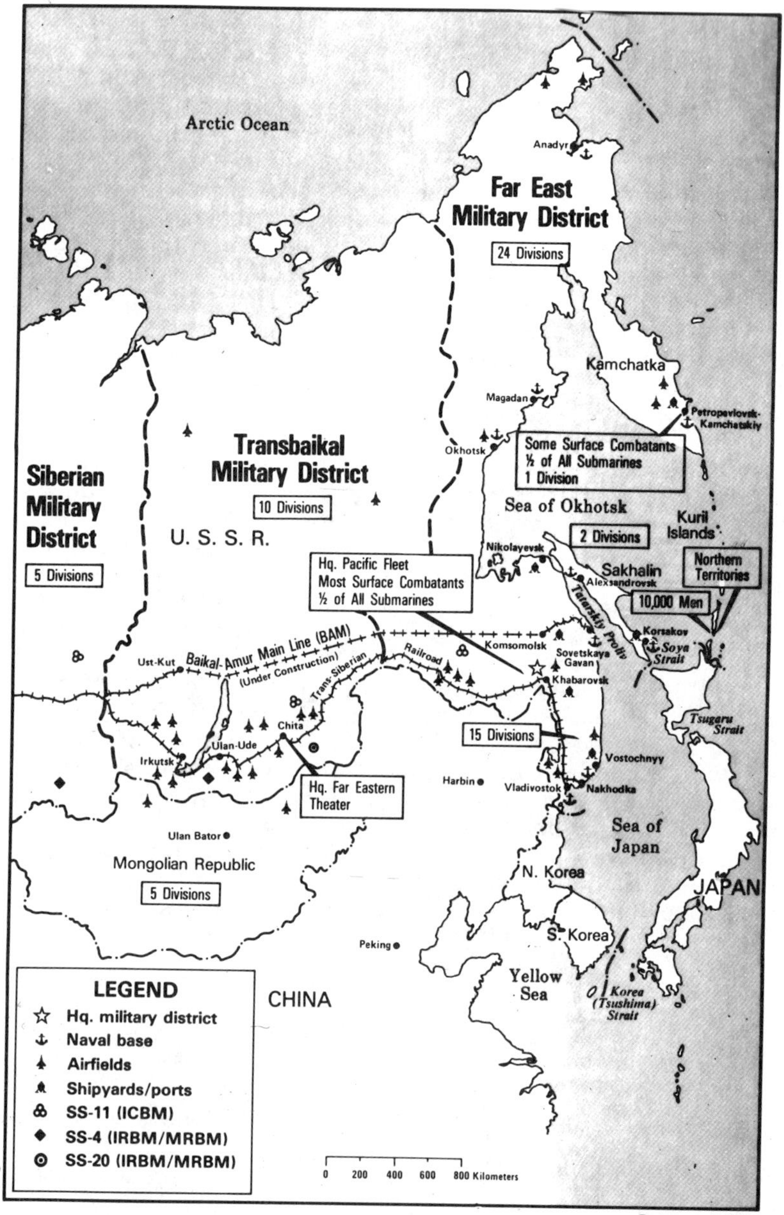

Arctic Ocean

Anadyr

Far East Military District

24 Divisions

Kamchatka

Magadan

Petropavlovsk-Kamchatskiy

Okhotsk

Siberian Military District

5 Divisions

Transbaikal Military District

10 Divisions

U. S. S. R.

Some Surface Combatants ½ of All Submarines 1 Division

Sea of Okhotsk

Kuril Islands

2 Divisions

Nikolayevsk

Sakhalin
Alexsandrovsk

Northern Territories

Hq. Pacific Fleet Most Surface Combatants ½ of All Submarines

10,000 Men

Ust-Kut Baikal-Amur Main Line (BAM)
(Under Construction)

Komsomolsk

Korsakov

Soya Strait

Railroad

Sovetskaya Gavan

Ust-Kut

Trans Siberian

Khabarovsk

Tsugaru Strait

Chita

15 Divisions

Ulan-Ude

Irkutsk

Vostochnyy

Hq. Far Eastern Theater

Harbin

Vladivostok Nakhodka

Ulan Bator

Mongolian Republic

5 Divisions

N. Korea

Sea of Japan

JAPAN

Peking

S. Korea

Yellow Sea

Korea (Tsushima) Strait

LEGEND
☆ Hq. military district
⚓ Naval base
✦ Airfields
✣ Shipyards/ports
♋ SS-11 (ICBM)
◆ SS-4 (IRBM/MRBM)
◎ SS-20 (IRBM/MRBM)

CHINA

0   200   400   600   800 Kilometers

Data as of 1982

Sources: Collins, John M. *U.S.-Soviet Military Balance: Concepts and Capabilities, 1960-1980.* Washington, McGraw-Hill, 1980, p. 134 and 356; *Asian Security 1982.* Research Institute for Peace and Security, Tokyo, Japan, 1982, p. 56.

FIGURE 1

Military buildup in the Soviet Far East [1]

Ground forces:
Army divisions 39
Naval infantry regiments 4
Tanks (medium) 13,020
Air and anti-air forces
Bombers... 435
Interceptors.. 750
Fighter/attack aircraft 815
ASW.. 50
SAMS.. [2] 7,500
Naval forces:
Aircraft carriers (Helicopter) 1
Cruisers.. 13
Destroyers 20
Frigates.. 50
Amphibious... 12
Submarines 122
Strategic... 31
Attack.. 91
Strategic rocket forces:
SS-20 .... [3] 140

[1] Except where indicated the source for these figures is, Collins, John M. and Thomas Peter Glakas. U.S.-Soviet Military Balance. Statistical Trends, 1970-1982 (As of January 1, 1983). Washington, Congressional Research Service, The Library of Congress, Aug. 1, 1983, p. 127-128.

[2] Goldman, Stuart D. Soviet Policy Toward Japan and the Strategic Balance in Northeast Asia. Washington, Congressional Research Service, The Library of Congress, Feb. 27, 1984, p. 8. (Report No. 84-64 F) On April 27, 1984, the Japanese Defense Agency reported that the Soviet Union had doubled to 40 the number of MIG-23 fighters deployed on Etorofu, the disputed island in the southern-most Kuriles chain. The Soviets first deployed the fighters last September as part of its military buildup in the Far East. They had b sed about 20 MIG-17 fighters for 15 years on four northern islands claimed by Japan but last year replaced them with MIG-23's. (Tokyo, Kyodo in English, 0303 GMT, April 27, 1984, in FBIS Daily Report, Soviet Union, v. 3, April 27, 1984, p. VI.)

[3] The Washington Post, November 30, 1983, p. A15.

Additional information from research institute for peace and security, Tokyo, 1982 [1]

Total Soviet ground forces (in 184 divisions)... 1,850,000
Divisions assigned to Sino-Soviet border .... Some 51
Divisions deployed:
East of Transbaikal Military District (39 of 51 divisions).. (360,000)
Vladivostok and surrounding area.................................... 15
Sakhalin Island 2
Kamchatka Peninsula 1
Northern Territories (rather less than a division).......... About 10,000
Headquarters, Far Eastern Theater, Established in Chita, 1979:
Commands three Soviet military districts: Siberian, Transbaikal, Far Eastern, Plus forces in Mongolia (5 divisions), Has operational control of navy and air force units in Far East. Army Corps Headquarters on Sakhalin Island: Recently raised to status of Army Headquarters.
Total ICBM launchers, July 1981 1,398

About 30 percent of strategic missiles deployed along Trans-Siberian Railway and SLBM in Pacific Fleet.[2]

Improved quality: SS-9 replaced by SS-18, part of SS-11 force replaced by SS-17 and SS-19.

84 SSBN's with 989 SLBM's:

> Being upgraded with Delta II and III classes each with 16 SS-N-8 or SS-N-18 with MIRV.
>
> SS-NX-20 to be replaced on Typhoon Class SSBN (25,000 tons) in latter half of 1980's, with greater rante and accuracy.

[1] Asian Security, 1982, p. 54-59.

[2] Dibb writes of the Soviet buildup in the Far East: "The Soviet Union has formidable military forces stationed in Siberia, including about 35 to 40 percent of her ICBM force and ballistic missile firing submarines, 25 percent of her ground forces and fighter aircraft, and over 30 percent of her strategic bombers and general purpose naval forces. Moreover, Soviet forces in the region have been provided, in recent years, with some of the most modern weapons in the Soviet military inventory. Since 1979, the U.S.S.R. has established a wartime theatre-level command in the Soviet Far East, which gives her Asian regions a degree of operational autonomy that would facilitate Soviet command and control in the event of a two-front war." (Dibb, Soviet Capabilities, Interests and Strategies in East Asia, p. 155.)

In the past 15 years the Soviet Pacific Fleet has more than doubled its tonnage to 1.5 million tons, adding some 270,000 tons of new ships between 1977 and 1980 alone. This fleet now ranks largest of the four Soviet fleets.[24] As Mike Mansfield, U.S. Ambassador to Japan, recently put it, in the last three years the Soviet Pacific Fleet has become "the biggest, the best, and the fastest-growing of the four Soviet fleets." The Soviets, he says, are "concentrating quite heavily on the Far East." [25]

The Soviet Unon has thus invested considerable military resources in Asia. According to a Defense Department estimate in 1983, "Soviet military forces in the Far East are second only to those forces opposite NATO in size, modernization and capability." "The quality and quantity" of these forces, the appraisal continues, "have been substantially improved", and predicts that "these trends will continue in the future." [26]

b. Effects of the military buildup

The effects of this Soviet military buildup in Asia have been far-reaching. In brief, it has enabled the Soviets to establish an unprecedented military presence in Asia and the Western Pacific for the projection of its power and influence. The Defense Department asserts that the Soviet leadership perceives this increased power "as a key means of accomplishing political and economic as well as military objectives." [27] However, the major problem confronting the Soviet Union is how to translate this military power into political influence, which up to now it has failed to do. Mansfield chides the Russians for being "so heavyhanded" in dealing with the Japanese; another diplomat remarks, "The biggest advantage we have in this part of the world is the incompetence of the Russians"; both agree, as Mansfield notes, "they make us look good by comparison." [28]

[24] Zagoria, Strategic Environment in East Asia, in Soviet Policy in East Asia, p. 17-18.

[25] Southerland, Daniel. Asia: Economic, Political Bright Spot for West: Strong U.S. Presence in Region Despite Soviets. The Christian Science Monitor, Feb. 17, 1983, p. 9.

[26] Soviet Military Power, 1983, p. 51 and 55.

[27] Ibid., p. 51.

[28] The Christian Science Monitor, Feb. 17, 1983, p. 9.

On the other hand, while the buildup may have yielded certain benefits to the Soviets, it has also proved to be counterproductive in the larger political and strategic sense. According to Paul Dibb, an Asian scholar at the Austrialian National University, the Soviet buildup has created "an atmosphere of apprehension in East Asia, particularly in China and Japan." Dibb foresees an emerging anti-Soviet coalition formed by China, the United States and Japan, and speculates that for the Soviet leadership, "this new strategic alignment, together with the NATO alliance in the west, raises the spectre of strategic encirclement in the 1980's." [29]

And finally military analysts underscore the constraints that exist on any successful projection of Soviet naval power in the Pacific. Faced with formidable logistical problems of supply, the absence of suitable operational bases and naval allies, along with the presence of the Seventh Fleet, the Soviets operate under serious limitations, at least for the present. John M. Collins, a leading American authority on the Soviet-American military balance, notes that all of Russia's Far Eastern forces "are at the extreme end of a tenuous logistic system." The combination of logistic and operational constraints, he concludes, "will limit the practical application of Soviet combat power anywhere in the Western Pacific for long time to come." [30]

But many of these limitations are being corrected in a long term military buildup. With this in mind Paul F. Langer, a specialist at RAND Corp., warns, ". . . whatever the various elements in the Soviet military posture in Asia in whatever numbers, there appears to be an unmistakable trend toward building Soviet military power throughout the spectrum of military preparedness." "The gap between the two Pacific navies," he stresses, "is likely to diminish considerably during the coming decade as the Soviet naval construction program steadily removes existing inadequacies." [31]

4. MAJOR TRENDS IN SOVIET ASIAN POLICY

a. U.S. withdrawal, Soviet resurgence, U.S. recommitment

Russia's persistent and massive military buildup has provided the kinetic energy for Soviet policy in Asia. This policy has contributed to shaping three major trends that were to affect fundamentally Soviet political relations in this Third World area: (1) U.S. withdrawal, Soviet resurgence, and a U.S. recommitment in Asia; (2) the continuing negative impact of the Soviet Union's invasion of Afghanistan and its support for Vietnam's aggression in Kampuchea; and (3) an evolving stalemate and enduring paradox in a Soviet policy that proclaims peaceful intent but pursues an aggressive military course.

U.S. withdrawal, Soviet resurgence and a U.S. recommitment has been a major trend in the larger context of international politics in Asia since the mid-1970's. The "precipitious" U.S. withdrawal from Vietnam and the decline of its power in the Pacific region, as Commander Gerry S. Thomas, U.S.N., a specialist in naval affairs,

---

[29] Dibb, Soviet Capabilities, Interests and Strategies in East Asia, p. 155–156.
[30] Collins, U.S.-Soviet Military Balance, p. 359.
[31] Langer, Soviet Military Power in Asia, p. 274–275, and 269–270.

terms it, created a power vacuum in Southeast Asia and the Western Pacific that was to have repercussions throughout the continent.[32] U.S. naval power was sharply reduced; its political commitment diminished; and its will to be involved in Asia deadened by the "Vietnam syndrome." China was left as the key bulwark against Soviet expansion.[33]

The Soviets, emerging in the mid-1970's as a successful protagonist in the Third World, moved rapidly into this power vacuum. By supporting the successful Vietnamese invasion of Kampuchea, it was able to dramatize the resurgence of Soviet power and influence in East Asia. Alert to a growing alignment between China and Japan in response to Soviet pressures, the Russians accelerated their military buildup in Northeast Asia. In the Pacific they instituted what Thomas refers to as a "dramatic rise" in their general purpose naval forces to fill the vacuum left by the U.S. withdrawal. As a result, according to Thomas, the Soviet Union had the opportunity to establish "a new, dominant Soviet naval presence in the Western Pacific."[34]

Thus a new balance of power was taking shape that seemed to tilt towards the Soviet advantage. For the first time the Third World ASEAN states, alarmed by Russia's involvement with Vietnam in Kampuchea, began to perceive the Soviets as a threat to their security, perhaps, equal to that of the Chinese.[35]

The United States, concerned also about the growth of Soviet power in East Asia and the Western Pacific, moved to strengthen its ties with China. But it was the Soviet invasion of Afghanistan that led eventually to a strong recommitment of the United States to Asia.[36] Under the Reagan Administration particularly, this recommitment has been deepened and expanded, leading to a substantial buildup of American military power in the Pacific, along with efforts to strengthen Japan's defense and bring China into a closer relationship. The tone of official statements by the Administration on national security matters projected what could be described as a "forward strategy" across a global front.[37] Zagoria portrayed the emergence of an anti-Soviet coalition comprising the United States, Japan and China as representing a "massive barrier" to further Soviet and Vietnamese expansion in East Asia.[38]

---

[32] Thomas, Their Pacific Fleet, p. 84.

[33] Porter, Soviet Union in Asia, p. 1.

[34] Thomas, Their Pacific Fleet, p. 84.

[35] Porter, Soviet Union in Asia, p. 2.

[36] Zagoria, Strategic Environment in East Asia, p. 5-7. For a discussion of the Soviet invasion's impact on the United States during 1979–1980, see, HFAC, Soviet Policy and United States Response in the Third World, 1981, p. 97–101.

[37] For the Administration's perception of the Soviet threat, see, Soviet Military Power, 1983, 107 p. See also, U.S. Department of Defense. Report of the Secretary of Defense Caspar W. Weinberger to the Congress, Feb. 1, 1983. Washington, U.S. Govt. Print. Off., 1983, p. 19–29; and U.S. Department of Defense. Joint Chiefs of Staff. United States Military Posture for FY 1984. Washington, U.S. Govt. Print. Off., 1983, p. 1–34. With respect to the Far East, the Joint Chiefs note: "Soviet forces constitute the most significant military threat to regional security and deployed U.S. military forces." (p. 25.)

[38] Zagoria, Strategic Environment in East Asia, p. 7. See also, Heinzig, Russia and Soviet Union in Asia, p. 66–67.

b. Lingering impact of Afghanistan and Kampuchea

The lingering effects of Soviet military action in Afghanistan and their support for the Vietnamese conquest of Kampuchea is the second major trend in Soviet Asian policy. Bruce Porter, Soviet specialist with Radio Liberty, states categorically:

> From Afghanistan to North Korea, the Soviet Union's relations with almost every country in Asia have been worsened by its invasion of Afghanistan and by its support of Vietnam's military takeover of Cambodia. The only exceptions are the invaded countries themselves, where pro-Soviet regimes were established by armed force, and Vietnam and Laos, where regimes earlier came to power or consolidated their power with Soviet military assistance.[39]

Thus Soviet armed forces invaded and occupied Afghanistan, and Vietnam, supported by the Soviet Union, established its hegemony over Indochina, but in both cases a high price had to be paid: For this aggression increased what is perceived to be the Soviet threat, as Porter notes, "in virtually every other country in Asia."[40] Military success may thus have given the Soviets some benefits and rewards, but in diplomacy they proved to be serious setbacks.[41] China and Japan, Pakistan and India were clearly shaken by these events, and cooled their relations with the Soviet accordingly.[42] ASEAN came to see the Soviet Union equal to the long-standing threat posed by China.[43]

That the Soviet military occupation of Afghanistan had lost none of its bitter meaning in the United Nations was demonstrated for the fourth consecutive year on Nov. 23, 1983 when, by an overwhelming vote of 116 to 20 with 17 abstentions, the General Assembly approved a resolution calling for the withdrawal of Soviet forces from Afghanistan. The vote was seen as an affirmation of Third World opposition to the Soviet Union.[44]

c. Stalemate and enduring paradox

(1) Stalemate in Soviet Asian policy

Stalemate and an enduring paradox constitute elements in the third major trend in Soviet Asian policy during 1980–82. Stagnation and stalemate set in as the negative impact of Afghanistan and Kampuchea began to be felt in the Asian Third World. Military intervention in these two countries put a brake on the forward progress of Soviet policy and exacted a heavy economic and political cost for the Soviets, raising questions as to whether Third World clients were really a political asset or imperial burden.[45] For, whatever influence the Soviets had in Asia it was based almost entirely on military power and that component in the calculus of power is not easily translated into political influence.[46] It

[39] Porter, Soviet Union in Asia, p. 4.
[40] Ibid.
[41] Ibid.
[42] Ibid., p. 3.
[43] Ibid., p. 2.
[44] Bernstein, Richard. U.N., for 5th Year, Bids Soviet Withdraw from Afghanistan. The New York Times, Nov. 24, 1983, p. A18.
[45] Asian Security 1982, p. 7 and 31, and Thornton, Thomas Perry. The U.S.S.R. and Asia in 1982: The End of the Brezhnev Era. Asia Survey, v. 23, Jan. 1983:11.
[46] Asian Security 1982, p. 7.

was an influence created out of fear, seldom the basis for building a lasting relationship.

For many influential non-Communist Asians the appeal of ideology had vanished in the 1950's, and the appeal of the Soviet Union as a development model for the 1980's had declined sharply in the preceding two decades.[47] Moreover, relative stability in the area, notably the growing economic strength of the Third World countries (especially the ASEAN states), offered few opporunities for Soviet influence and adventurism and contributed much to an evolving equilibrium of power.[48]

Finally, Russia's preoccupation with the unsettling East-West global problems, particularly those arising from the Polish crisis and NATO/Warsaw Pact modernization, diverted much of its energy away from Asia towards Europe.[49] Troubling developments in Europe compelled the Russians, at least temporarily, to place Asia on a back burner.

In brief, many factors worked more for stalemate than for success of Soviet policy in Asia.

(2) An enduring paradox

An enduring paradox in the conduct of foreign relations was demonstrated again by Soviet Asian policy; namely, the Soviet inclination to make real enemies out of, perhaps, only potential ones. The Soviet emphasis on military solutions to protect themselves against perceived potential enemies often results in creating an opponent that may not have even existed initially. This happened in Asia. Heavily accented military solutions and an obsessive concern for frontier security caused the Soviets to miss major opportunities in East Asia; it contributed to bringing about the alienation of ASEAN; and ultimately it encouraged the building of an anti-Soviet coalition with the United States as a driving force.[50]

In brief, excessive Soviet fears for its security and the tendency to overmilitarize foreign policy, as in the case of Asia, tend to produce something of a self-fulfilling prophecy. As Thomas W. Robinson, a specialist on Asia, wrote in a survey of Soviet policy in Asia during 1981:

> The Soviet Union also professed to see a grand design in American Asian policy. The U.S. was attempting to "knock together" an unholy alliance of Chinese expansionists, Japanese militarists, and Western imperialists to encircle Russia in Asia and upset the continuing process of national liberation. Such concepts as "Pacific community" and balance of power were denounced as figleaves for mere anti-Sovietism. And when leaders of these countries met to discuss what should be done to counter the Soviet military buildup, Moscow's support of Vietnamese conquest of Indochina, and Soviet intervention in Afghanistan, Moscow saw further proof that its several opponents were ganging up against it.[51]

Hence Zagoria rightly concludes in 1983 that the Soviets are indeed "faced in the Asian-Pacific region with countervailing military

---

[47] Ibid.

[48] Ibid., p. 15-16. See also, Dibb, Soviet Capabilities, Interests and Strategies in East Asia, p. 157.

[49] Asian Security 1982, p. 31.

[50] Dibb, Soviet Capabilities, Interests and Strategies in East Asia, p. 157, and Menon, Soviet Union in East Asia, p. 314-15.

[51] Robinson, Thomas W. The Soviet Union and Asia in 1981. Asian Survey, v. 22, Jan. 1982, p. 14.

power, regional cohesion, and socioeconomic resilence of a kind that thwarts their ambitions."[52] Thus what once may have been an illusion in the minds of Soviet policymakers has become a reality. Or as Dibb observes:

> In no other region of the world is the disproportion between Soviet military power and political influence greater. Save in Mongolia and Indochina, the U.S.S.R. seems to lack the necessary political, economic and ideological levers of influence. . . . [Soviet] diplomacy in the region has been marked by a rigidity that has served the U.S.S.R.'s interests poorly and has earned the hostility and enmity of most of its Asian neighbors, except for Indochina. To a large extent this is because of the growing Soviet military buildup.[53]

A final point is the paradox of proclaiming peaceful intent, while building military power; denying aggressive purposes, while attributing them to an adversary. This is a contradiction that makes the pursuit of such a policy not only counter-productive but self-defeating in relationships with a politically aware international public. It is difficult to pursue convincingly a peace offensive, as Brezhnev had attempted to do in Asia during 1981–1982 and Andropov continued in 1982–83, while simultaneously threatening with a military buildup, occupying another nation with armed forces, supporting the military suppression of another, and conducting an aggresive and provocative propaganda campaign against opponents of the Soviet Union. The Third World nations of Asia were not taken in by this illusion of peace but rather saw in Soviet conduct a clear distinction betwen the truth of reality from the fiction of illusion.

B. AFGHANISTAN: CATALYST AND STALEMATE

1. A QUALIFIED SOVIET MILITARY SUCCESS

a. General military situation: Stalemate

Like Lady Macbeth after the killing of Duncan, the Soviets have thus far failed to cleanse their hands of guilt for invading Afghanistan. For Afghanistan, now in its fifth year of prolonged distress, has proved to be a troubling reminder to Asians that the Soviet Union will use its awesome military power for expansionist purposes. Afghanistan is a classic case of Soviet military aggression against a Third World country, and thus acts as a continuing catalyst for arousing Asian's suspicions of Soviet purposes.[54] (See Map 3 and Figure 2.)

---

[52] Zagoria, Strategic Environment in East Asia, p. 12.
[53] Dibb, Soviet Union as a Pacific Power, p. 238.
[54] For a comprehensive examination of Soviet involvement in Afghanistan, see, Bradsher, Henry S. Afghanistan and the Soviet Union. Durham, N.C., Duke University Press, 1983, 324 p.; Hammond, Thomas T. Red Flag Over Afghanistan: The Communist Coup, the Soviet Invasion, and the Consequences. Boulder, Col., Westview Press, 1983. 300 p,; and Newell, Nancy Peabody and Richard S. Newell. The Struggle for Afghanistan. Ithaca, Cornell University Press, 1981. 236 p. For a view from the Soviet side by one of their leading specialists on the Third World, see, Ulyanovskiy, R. Development of the Revolutionary Process in Afghanistan. Mirovaya Ekonomika I Mezhdunarodnyye Otnosheniya (Moscow) in Russian, no. 8, Aug. 1983: 16–31, translated in, U.S.S.R. Report, World Economy and International Relations, no. 8, Aug. 1982, Nov. 25, 1982:3–20 (JPRS 84825). In preparing this section the writer consulted in typescript the survey and analysis of Richard P. Cronin, Specialist in Asian Affairs, CRS, on developments in Afghanistan during 1983, to be published in the Hoover Institution's 1984 Yearbook on International Communist Affairs. For a recent report giving a Congressional perspective, see the staff report by John B. Ritch III of the Senate Foreign Relations Committee, U.S. Congress. Senate. Committee on Foreign Relations. Hidden War: The Struggle for Afghanistan. 98th Congress. 2d session. Washington, U.S. Government Printing Office, April 1984, 55 p. (Committee print, S. Prt. 98–181.)

Map 3.
Soviet Presence in Afghanistan

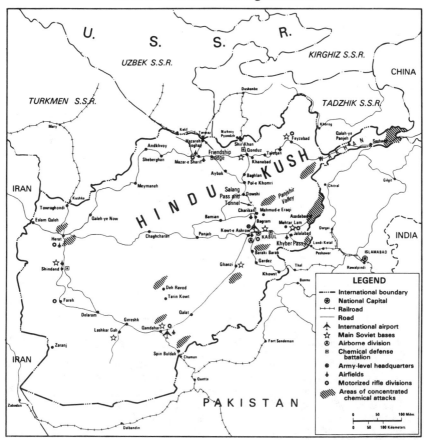

Data as of 1982

Sources: Hansen, James H. "Afghanistan: The Soviet Experience." *National Defense,* v. 66, Jan. 1982: 20-24,82; Isby, David C. "Afghanistan, 1982: The War Continues." *International Defense Review,* v. 15, no. 11, 1982: 1523-1528; *The Christian Science Monitor,* June 22, 1982, p. 6 and July 2, 1982, p. 12; U.S. Dept. of State. *Chemical Warfare in Southeast Asia and Afghanistan.* Special Report No. 98. Washington, March 22,1982, p. 14-18.

FIGURE 2

DATA ON SOVIET MILITARY FORCES IN AFGHANISTAN, 1982 [1]

Soviet Army Order of Battle, Afghanistan 1982 [2]

Army-level Headquarters, Balahisar Fort, Kabul.

105th Guards Airborne Division, Bagram Airfield, Kabul—3 to 6 Airborne Rifle Regiments, one Artillery Regiment.

54th Motorized Rifle Division, Herat—81, 118, 337 Motorized Regiments, (54) Tank Regiment, 86 Artillery Regiment.

66th Motorized Rifle Division, Farah—33, 108, 341 Motorized Rifle Regiments, (68) Tank Regiment, 161 Artillery Regiment.

201st Motorized Rifle Division, Jalabad—92, 122, 191 Motorized Rifle, (201) Tank Regiment, 220 Artillery Regiment.

360th Motorized Rifle Division, Kabul—"Nevel–Polozk Division".

1193, 1195, 1197 Motorized Rifle Regiment, (360) Tank Regiment, 920 Artillery Regiment.

346th Motorized Rifle Division, Kandahar.

"Debolzevo Division": 1164, 1166, 1168 Motorized Rifle Regiments, (346) Tank Regiment, 915 Artillery Regiment.

5th Motorized Rifle Division, Fezyabad—"Orel.Volkovsk-Bialystock Division": 142, 190, 336 Motorized Rifle Regiments, (5) Tank Regiment, 27 Artillery Regiment.

16th Motorized Rifle Division, Mazar-e-Sharif—156, 167, 249 Motorized Rifle Regiments, (16) Tank Regiment, 224 Artillery Regiment.

Up to 5 Air Assault Brigades, various locations.

Soviet Troop Strength [3]

Divisions and separate brigades (90 percent war establishment). 90,000.

Non-divisional troops, (support and combat). 50,000.

Air Force.. 10,000.

Advisors to Kabul Regime forces................. 2,000.

[1] Isby, David C. Afghanistan, 1982: The War Continues. International Defense Review, v. 15, no. 11, 1982:1524. Isby, is an authority on military affairs, author of "Weapons and Tactics of the Soviet Army" published by Jane's, and a long-time analyst, writer and editor on military subjects.

[2] Isby gives the following explanation of the order of Battle:

"Determining Soviet divisional deployments and compostions is always difficult, even in peacetime. The monitoring of the Soviet order of battle in Afghanistan is made more difficult by the Soviet practice of seldom committing full divisions to single operations. Even when a division-sized force is used, it is normally a composite force formed from more than one division.

"The reports of Soviet divisional designations in Western open-source literature have been somewhat contradictory, and it is possible that the 346th Motorized Rifle Division is actually the 357th [1188, 1190, 1192 Motorized Rifle Regiments, (357) Tank Regiment, 932 Artillery Regiment]; the 201st Motorized Rifle Division may be actually the 275th [980, 982, 984 Motorized Rifle Regiments, (201) Tank Regiment? Artillery Regiment]; the 66th Motorized Rifle Division may be actually the 68th [313, 480,? Motorized Rifle Regiments, (68) Tank Regiment, 139 Artillery Regiment]; and that the 5th Motorized Rifle Division is in fact the 201st Motorized Rifle Division. Regimental designations in the Soviet Army have, in most cases, remained the same since 1945, maintaining the traditions of that war. However, there have been some changes, including the provision of a tank regiment in motorized rifle divisions which normally has the same designation as the division itself. Thus, all regimental designations must be considered as less than certain."

[3] Isby notes that—

"In addition to these forces, there are substantial MVD and KGB forces reportedly present in Afghanistan; 'several hundred' advisors from the German Democratic Republic are reportedly reorganizing the Afghan police; and several thousand Soviet civilian advisors are employed at all levels of the Afghan civil sector.

Most Soviet Army units are deployed in company to regimental sized positions throughout the divisional area of operations."

It is also significant to note that in March 1980, the Soviets concluded a protocol with Afghanistan to install two ground communication stations using the Soviet Intersputnik System. (FBIS 08. Afghan-Soviet Satellite Station Protocol Signed. Kabul in English to Europe, 1900 GMT, Mar. 19, 1980.)

According to Karen McKay, executive director of the Committee for a Free Afghanistan, the Soviets have deployed SS-20's outside of Kabul. Afghan resistance sources also report, in the words of McKay, that "there is some kind of massive underground base in the middle of a mountain up in the Wakkhan corridor." "Every day a long convoy of armored personnel carriers bearing covered materials," she continues, "enters that mountain and comes out empty." In other parts of the country Afghans report "seeing gigantic missiles being transported on lowboys and other smaller missiles stacked like cordwood on the backs of long trucks entering these bases." McKay adds that the Soviets are "stepping up their entrenchment in Afghanistan" and lists the following evidence: 34 bases; 6 or 8 are strategic long-range offensive bases along the borders of Iran, Pakistan and China; Shinand is "one of the most sophisticated combined arms bases in the word"; hardened underground hangers; long runways capable of handling their biggest aircraft; fighter-bombers, long-range bombers, MI-24 Hind helicopters, transfer helicopters, tanks; and long-range surface-to-air missiles in Shinand as well as in other bases. (The Washington Times, March 21, 1984, p. 3C.)

The Soviets have achieved only a qualified military success in Afghanistan. The war is being waged in most parts of Afghanistan. Heavy fighting has been repeatedly reported in the Panjshir Valley and in the vicinity of Paghman, Herat and Kandahar. In late May and early June 1983, for example, reports were made of especially intense bombing attacks in and around Herat and in the vicinity of Kabul. The Soviets are employing helicopter gunships, massive artillery bombardments, flame-throwing tanks, and waves of air strikes against the ill-equipped, resisting rebels.[55]

Despite the commitment of some 105,000 troops (now placed at 180,000 by guerrilla sources, with fresh reinforcements expected) and some 30,000 held in reserve along the border, armed with the most up-to-date equipment to fight a poorly equipped, disorganized and untrained force of Afghan tribesmen, they have succeeded in controlling only the major cities, towns and communication networks, leaving the countryside (roughly 85 percent of it) to the mujahidin resistance fighters variously estimated from 20,000 to 100,000. Military analysts speak of a stalemate with a Soviet strategy geared to the long term erosion of resistance and gradual strengthening of their hold on the country through assimilation of the opposition, rather than one that calls for a massive investment of manpower and resources to bring the issue to a quick decision.[56] The Afghan army, largely ineffective, has been rapidly eroding from an initial force of some 100,000 to an estimated 20,000 in 1983, though recent U.S. estimates show a partial rebuilding to 40,000–50,000.[57] A Pentagon report published in 1983 concluded, "After more than three years, the Soviets find themselves embroiled in a counter-insurgency campaign that cannot be won with current force levels."[58]

As the war has dragged on into a stalemate, the guerrilla forces have grown in strength and resources, though weakened organiza-

---

[55] Rubenstein, Soviet Union and Afghanistan, p. 320.

[56] Branigin, William. Afghanistan, Oct. 21, 1983, p. A14. In this six-part award-winning series, Branigin provides a great deal of information on the war in Afghanistan, particularly from the mujahidin perspective. [Branigin, The Washington Post's Southeast Asian correspondent, was named the winner of this year's award for Distinguished Service in Foreign Correspondence of the Society of Professional Journalists, Sigma Delta Chi. Branigin was cited for this series based on a six-week trek in the Soviet war zone in Afghanistan, which judges declared had "greatly illuminated our knowledge of that long-running conflict." (The Washington Post, May 4, 1984, p. A30.)]

[57] Moritz, Frederick A. Soviets Prepared for a Long Fight in Afghanistan. The Christian Science Monitor, Mar. 30, 1983, p. 5 and Middleton, Drew. Afghan War Isn't Over But Soviets Seem to be Winning. The New York Times, May 1, 1983, p. E3. Richard P. Cronin, Specialist in Asian Affairs, CRS.

[58] Gelb, Leslie H. U.S. Said to Increase Arms aid for Afghan Rebels. The New York Times, May 4, 1983, p. A1. For other commentaries on the war, see, Isby, David C. Afghanistan 1982: The War Continues. International Defense Review, v. 15, no. 11, 1982: 1523–28, and Cole, Stephen V. The War in Afghanistan. Review of the News, v. 19, Jan. 26, 1983: 51–53, 55, 55–58.

tionally by a lack of internal unity. According to military analysts, they are insufficiently strong to change the military balance that continues decidedly in favor of the Soviets. The United States, China, Iran, Saudi Arabia, Egypt and other Muslim countries have successfully dispatched supplies covertly to the guerrillas through Pakistan, increasing what military resources they have been able to accumulate from the defecting Afghan army and those abandoned by the Soviets.[59] Nonetheless, they do not have the strength to make a decisive challenge and ultimately expel the Russians. The war in Afghanistan has thus been reduced to a guerrilla insurgency in which the main Soviet tactic, according to one close observer, is to institute "a reign of terror" until Afghanistan is conquered.[60] Or as Alvin Z. Rubinstein, a Soviet specialist at the University of Pennsylvania, puts it, "Militarily, Moscow is bent on the systematic destruction of as much Afghan tribal society as is necessary to break the will of the freedom-fighters." [61]

On April 23, 1984, U.S. officials reported that the Soviets launched a major new offensive in Afghanistan with the Panjshir Valley as the "prime target"—see Map. 3. Panjshir, a guerrilla stronghold that has successfully held off six Soviet attempts to control this strategically important valley, is one of the other critical valleys in northern Afghanistan through which supplies from the Soviet Union to Kabul must pass. A column of 20,000 Soviet and Afghan army troops with 600 to 800 vehicles and supported by substantial air cover were reported moving north from Kabul towards Panjshir. On April 17, American sources had reported new Soviet deployments along the Afghan border including 36 TU–16 Badger bombers and about 100 lighter bombers and ground attack planes along with large amounts of munitions, arousing speculation that the Soviets might be planning large-scale aerial bombing as part of their expected spring offensive. Nayyar Zaidi, a leading Pakistani journalist, corroborated reports of an "elaborate" offensive in the making. Zaidi had recently returned from visiting Afghan refugee camps and meeting with many resistance leaders in Peshawar, Pakistan. In the last two or three months the Soviets were said to be rapidly building up their military forces and, according to resistance sources, 50,000 additional troops poured into Afghanistan, raising the total to 185,000, with another 30,000 deployed along the Soviet side of the Afghan border in reserve. The presence of increased air power and the character of the opening attack using heavy bombers suggest the possibility that the Soviets may have been entering a new phase of their war against the mujahidin, one intended to break the stalemate. [62]

---

[59] Ibid. Zbigniew Brzezinski stated on Dec. 12 that the United States should increase its support for Afghan resistance fighters by supplying them with more sophisticated Western weapons rather than the Soviet-style guns they now receive. The "gradual addition to the weapon capability" of the guerrillas, he said, should be coupled with an enlarged diplomatic effort to get the Soviets to end their occupation of Afghanistan. (The Washington Post, Dec. 13, 1983, p. A9.)

[60] Malhuret, Claude. Report from Afghanistan. Foreign Affairs, v. 62, Winter 1983/84: 426–435.

[61] Rubinstein, Alvin Z. The Soviet Union and Afghanistan. Current History, v. 82, October 1983: 319.

[62] Hiatt, Fred. Bombers Near Border: Soviets Bolster Afghan Force. The Washington Post, April 17, 1984, p. A1; Zaidi, Nayyar. Afghan Resistance Fighters Expect Massive Soviet Push. The Washington Times, April 17, 1984, p. 7A; Hiatt, Fred. Soviets Uses Bombers in Afghanistan. The Washington Post, April 24, 1984, p. A1; and, Middleton, Drew. Big Soviet Attack Reported on Routes to Afghan Capital. The New York Times, April 24, 1984, p. A8.

b. Soviet objectives and acceptable solution

The Soviets have inflexibly held to their initial objectives in Afghanistan; namely, "to defend the socialist gains" of the Afghan revolution of April 1978 and "to protect the country" against the "interference and provocations" of its external enemies. When the conditions that promoted Soviet military intervention in the first place have been satisfied and satisfied with guarantees, then they will withdraw their military forces.[63] In brief, the Soviets will settle for nothing less than a socialist Afghanistan as now exists and in character with those established in Eastern Europe. Mongolia is presumed by many to be the Soviet model.

Hints of possible indirect negotiations through United Nations auspices stimulated interest in the West but failed to achieve any progress.[64] And this is where matters now stand. To a delegation of visiting United States Senators in August 1983, probing Soviet intentions in Afghanistan, Andropov gave this firm and authoritative response: The Soviet position is unchanged; "we will leave" when a stable political solution has been achieved, meaning the satisfaction of their initial condition.[65]

Movement on the international level, like that on the military, thus seems to be stagnated. Military observers generally agree that the Soviets have settled in for a long, dragged out war in Afghanistan, presuming to rely upon the forces of sovietization for ultimate conquest, forces that have long been operating internally in Afghanistan. In brief, a similar scenario as had been initiated many decades ago against the non-Russian nationalities of the U.S.S.R.[66]

c. Adverse impact on Soviet-Pakistani relations

On the international level Russia's war in Afghanistan has had an adverse effect on relations with Pakistan, though the Soviets had already largely written Pakistan off by their close relationship with India. The adverse impact was much greater and more costly on the Islamic countries.[67] Soon after the invasion of Afghanistan, Pakistan became a new home for the fleeing refugees, a sanctuary and military staging area for the mujahidin, and a pipeline for the covert inflow of military supplies to the anti-Soviet forces. Pakistanis, among the staunchest critics of the Soviet Union in the Third World, were placed in a variable dilemma: They could not antagonize the Soviets by going too far in supporting the Afghan guerrillas lest they provoke Soviet retaliatory military action along their borders, yet they were obliged to assist their oppressed

---

[63] HFAC, Soviet Policy and United States Response in the Third World, 1981, p. 86–88.

[64] The Christian Science Monitor, March 30, 1983, p. 5, and Sego, Steve. Soviet Policy in Afghanistan Under Andropov. RFE-RL. Radio Liberty Research, RL418/83, Nov. 8, 1983, p. 2.

[65] U.S. Congress. Senate. Dangerous Stalemate: Superpower Relations in Autumn 1983. A Report of a Delegation of Eight senators to the Soviet Union. 98th Congress, 1st Session. Washington, U.S. Govt. Print. Off., 1983, p. 7. (S. Doc. 98–16)

[66] For appraisals at the end of 1983, see, Giradet, Edward. Soviet's Dismal Four Years in Afghanistan: Despite High Losses in War, Kremlin Seems Determined. The Christian Science Monitor, Dec. 29, 1983, p. 1., and Middleton, Drew. 4 Years of Afghan Battle: No Vietnam for Moscow. The New York Times, Dec. 26, 1983, p. A8. Moscow appears to be projecting a prolonged stay for its forces in Afghanistan. Soviet media reports convey the impression that the insurgency remains powerful and widespread, and there is no hint that Moscow is actively seeking a way out through a political solution.

[67] Richard P. Cronin, Specialist in Asian Affairs, CRS.

Muslim Afghan brothers; they hesitated to close off their borders to the refugees (even if it were possible), yet they risked internal political but especially economic instability by admitting too many Afghans. In this dilemma lay the makings of a possible arrangement with the Soviets.

Like other LDC's in Asia, Pakistan's relations with the Soviet Union were, as Thomas Perry Thornton, a specialist on Soviet Asian affairs, notes, "distinctly chilly."[68] Yet, the Soviets saw Pakistan as the key to underecutting the insurgency in Afghanistan. Their tactic was to wear down the mujahidin not only militarily but politically; Pakistan, vulnerable to Soviet pressure, was the insurgents' strongest supporter, and thus Moscow's primary target.

Pakistan, burdened by 2.8 million refugees, according to their count (1 to 1.5 million found refuge in Iran), understandably sought relief especially because of the drain on their economic resources.[69]

Thus, despite deep mutual animosities—open Soviet criticism of Parkistan for supporting the mujahidin and maintaining close ties with China and the United States, and Pakistani criticism of the Soviets for occupying Afghanistan—both sides kept the door open for an accommodation.[70] For the Soviets could bargain on the basis of withdrawal of forces from the Pakistani border and deployment into the interior of Afghanistan in exchange for Pakistan's cutting back on support for the mujahidin.[71] However, the fact that Soviet forces by and large are not directly *on* the Pakistan border tends to minimize this bargaining point.[72] The issue became one of the subjects discussed in the U.N. sponsored negotiations in Geneva between representatives of Pakistan and the Soviet-backed Karmal regime. Pakistan was anxious to resolve the refugee issue, though not without withdrawal of Soviet troops—assurances that it willingly gave to the Afghan insurgents.[73]

Success of the talks was jeopardized by the refusal of the two major warring parties in Afghanistan to attend, the mujahidin and the Soviets. Negotiations seemed to stall, despite the optimism of U.N. officials who perceived here the first step in resolving the Afghan issue. By the fall of 1983, one close-in observer of the Afghan scene, William Branigin, correctly described the situation when he wrote, having in mind action on both the military and diplomatic fronts, "Thus, neither a political nor a military solution is yet in sight."[74]

[68] Thornton, U.S.S.R. and Asia in 1982, p. 22.
[69] Branigin, William. Afghanistan: Feuding Guerrilla Groups Rely on Uneasy Pakistan. (Last in Six-Part Series.) The Washington Post, Oct. 22, 1983, p. A10.
[70] Thornton, U.S.S.R. and Asia in 1982, p. 22.
[71] Weaver, Mary Anne. Pakistan Questions U.S. Desire for Afghan Settlement. The Christan Science Monitor, May 10, 1983, p. 3.
[72] Richard P. Cronin, Specialist in Asian Affairs, CRS.
[73] The Washington Post, Oct. 22, 1983, p. A10.
[74] The Washington Post, Oct. 22, 1983, p. A10. See also, Wiznitzer, Louis, Moscow Inches Closer to Troop Pullout from Afghanistan. The Christian Science Monitor, June 14, 1983, p. 3 and Stevens, William K. Pakistani Adie Doubts Afghan Solution is in Sight. The New York Times, June 16, 1983, p. A6. For a summary of the Geneva talks, see, Thornton, U.S.S.R. and Asia, 1982, p. 21–22. See also, Harrison, Selig S. A Breakthrough in Afghanistan? Foreign Policy, no. 51, Summer 1983:3–26 and his article in The Washington Post, Dec. 29, 1983, p. A17, "Are We Fighting to the Last Afghan?"; and Hammond, Thomas T. Will the Soviets Pull Out of Afghanistan? Survey, v. 27, Autumn—Winter 1983: 232–246. Harrison seems to take a more opti-

Continued

In pursuit of its consistent "carrot and stick" approach to Pakistan, seeming to alternate between blunt warnings on interference in Afghanistan and offers of economic assistance, the Soviets concluded a substantial economic and technical assistance agreement in December 1983 with particular stress on the development of energy resources. The purpose of this "carrot", according to Western diplomatic source, was "to try to persuade the government to change its policy in Afghanistan and acquiesce to the Soviet occupation and give legitimacy to the . . . Karmal regime." "I think we will see more of it," he predicted.

A senior Pakistan Foreign Ministry official insisted, however, that no quid pro quo arose in the talks, but he acknowledged Soviet purposes in the transaction, observing, nonetheless, that "we are clear in our own mind about what we want for a settlement in Afghanistan." Pakistan demands an early Soviet Troop withdrawal (4 to 6 months is said to be a practical timetable); consultation with Afghan refugees in Pakistan to ascertain conditions for their return; and guarantees on non-interference in Afghanistan.[75]

a. Process of cultural and political Sovietization underway

Though stalemated on the military and diplomatic fronts, the Soviets have, nonetheless, managed to carry forward their program of sovietization, meaning the reconstruction of a country along Soviet lines. In so doing they have followed a scenario remarkably similar to that pursued in their own country against such non-Russian nationalities as the Baltic nations, those in the Caucasus and in Soviet Central Asia.

Many academic and U.S. intelligence specialists concur in the belief that Russia's long-term solution is the absorption of Afghanistan into the Soviet Union as a Soviet Socialist Republic.[76] In fact, Soviet policy under Brezhnev and Andropev has been a direct continuation of Russia's strategy in Central Asia devised over a century ago called, "Russification," but in the Soviet era termed, "sovietization." This strategy passes through various stages, beginning first with directly extending Russian influence, followed by the undisguised use of military force, and ultimately bringing about political assimilation by political-cultural manipulation and if necessary by force. The Soviets refer to the process as, "the merger of nations"; that is, the unity of the Soviet state on the criterion laid down by the Soviet Russian leadership. Primarily, the northern part of Afghanistan, now the focus of Soviet attention, is geographically, historically, culturally and ethnically part of what is now Soviet Central Asia. (See Map 4) Speaking of Afghanistan as a

---

mistic view about a favorable outcome, while Hammond insists, "The U.N. can negotiate till doomsday, but Andropov is not going to abandon the sacred Soviet principle that once a country becomes communist is must remain communist, especially if it borders on the U.S.S.R." (p. 246).

[75] Claiborne, William. Soviets Increase Aid to Pakistan; New Tactic Seen. The Washington Post Jan. 27. 1984, p. Al and A20. By the terms of the agreement the Soviets agreed to provide Pakistan a credit of $277 million on fairly soft terms for the thermal power plant at Multan, to be repaid in the form of Pakistani goods. The Soviets also agreed to supply two deep drilling rigs, costing $6 million, for oil exploration. (Karachi Domestic Service in English, Dec. 20, 1983.)

[76] Sego, Soviet Policy in Afghanistan Under Andropov, p. 1-4, Robinson, Soviet Union and Asia in 1981, p. 15, The New York Times, May 1, 1983, p. E3.

whole, Steve Sego, a Soviet specialist at Radio Liberty, writes that the process has "passed beyond indirect pressure to military brutalization." [77]

Presently, the Soviets seem to have entered, almost lock-step with the military phase, the stage of cultural and political assimilation. Analysts state categorically that the weak Karmal regime, described as "hopelessly unpopular," is not a regime at all, but rather a fictitious administrative apparatus virtually totally controlled by the Soviet Union.[78] Nonetheless, the Soviets have a small but important leftist constituency that is by no means negligible, including the officer corps of the military.[79] From 10,000 to 20,000 young Afghans have been sent to the Soviet Union for Training and indoctrination for future leadership roles—"the satraps of the 1990's," as Rubinstein terms them.[80] The educational system, an early Soviet target even before the invasion, has been restructured for easy cultural assimilation. The Ministry of Education is patterned after that of Tajikistan, a Muslim republic of the U.S.S.R. Faculty members of Kabul schools of higher education come largely from the Soviet Union, and large numbers of Soviet teachers work in Afghan classrooms. "Such links," writes Sego, "are especially close among the large Tajik, Uzbek, and Turkmen populations of Afghanistan, who share similar languages with Soviet Central Asia." Radio broadcasts and school instruction in local languages conform to the patterns already existing in the Soviet national republics.[81]

In brief, Soviet policy amounts to a present day extension of the Leninist nationalities policy into Afghanistan. It focuses on the cultivation of national identities of the Tajiks, Uzbeks and Turkmen in Afghanistan with their ethnic kinsmen in the Soviet Central Asian republics. (See Map 4.) Some analysts contend that the utlimate goal is unity and assimilation. Mongolia is often cited as an interim model.[82]

Politically, the Soviets seem to have progressed rapidly towards their goal, at least to the point of establishing much of the infrastructure for control and manipulation. Operations of the Ministry of Justice in Afghanistan are controlled by Soviet advisers. New laws, for example, are first drafted in Russian.[83] Afghanistan's secret police organization, the KhAd, is directly controlled by the Soviet KGB. One recent defector said that the KhAd was essentially a new section of the Soviet KGB.[84] Two hundred Soviet KGB officers were said to work in the Ministry of Interior.[85] In January 1983, some 800 new Afghan agents returned to Afghanistan from the U.S.S.R. to take on their police duties.[86] Nearly 1,000 Soviet of-

---

[77] Sego, Soviet Policy in Afghanistan Under Andropov, p. 3.
[78] Ibid, Thornton, U.S.S.R. and Asia in 1982, p. 21, and Porter, Soviet Union in Asia, p. 5.
[79] Richard P. Cronin, Specialist in Asian Affairs, CRS.
[80] Rubinstein. Soviet Union and Afghanistan, p. 321.
[81] Sego, Soviet Policy in Afghanistan Under Andropov, p. 4.
[82] For a discussion of "the Mongolian Model" as an element in Soviet Asian policy, see Segal, Soviet Union in East Asia, p. 133-136.
[83] Ibid.
[84] The Washington Post, Oct. 21, 1983, p. A14.
[85] The New York Times, May 1, 983, p. E3.
[86] Sego, Soviet Policy in Afghanistan Under Andropov, p. 4.

ficers are said to work in the Defense Ministry.[87] Though strife among the Khalq and Parcham factions, "irreconcilable" as one Afghan source said, creates problems of control and organization in occupied Afghanistan, still there seems little doubt that the Soviets with their 3,000 to 5,000 "advisers" on hand in the Afghan Government, as sources generally indicate, have matters well under their control.[88]

Significantly, the Soviets have confined their sovietization measures to those areas nearest the Soviet border and in the cities and towns primarily under their control, though "control" is a condition not easily determined given the geographic conditions and the absence of reliable information.[89] This area of concentration corresponds roughly to the non-Pushtan areas of Afghanistan.[90] (See Map 5.)

---

[87] The New York Times, May 1, 1983, p. E3.
[88] The Washington Post, Oct. 21, 1983, p. A14.
[89] Richard P. Cronin, Specialist in Asian Affairs.
[90] Sego, Soviet Policy in Afghanistan Under Andropov, p. A14. Traditional tribal areas of the "fiercely independent Pushtuns," Sego notes, remain largely outside the control of the Soviet-Afghan forces. Some, not engaged in actively resisting the Russians, have been "bought into unreliable support for Kabul." Many others, however, have sought refuge across the Durand Line into Pakistani Pushtunistan.

Map 4.
Ethnic Groups in Afghanistan

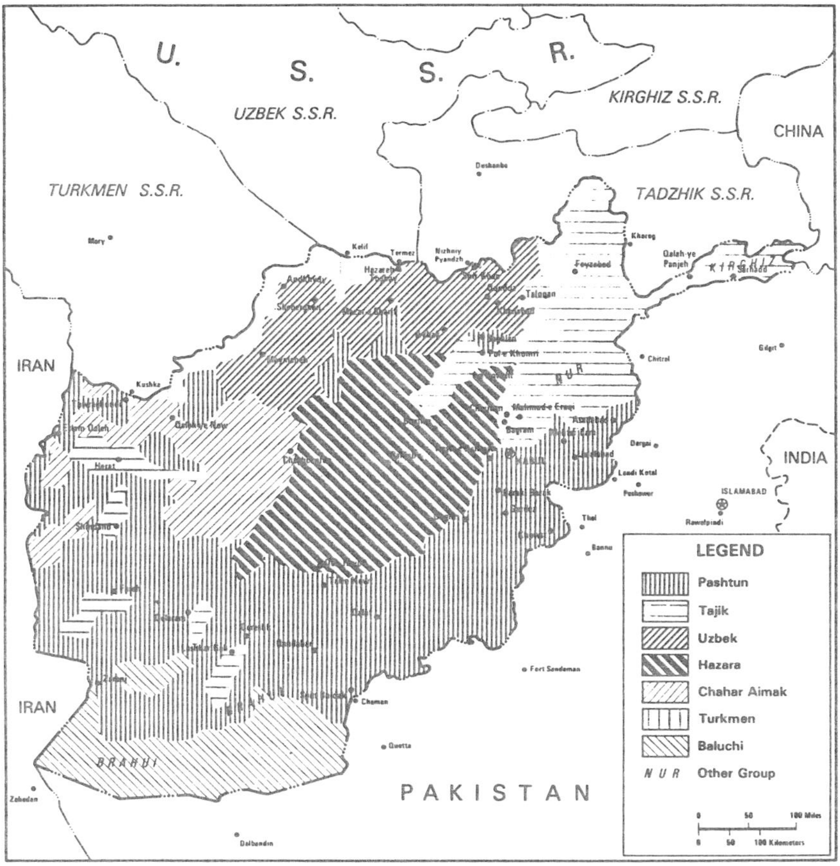

LEGEND

▦	Pashtun
	Tajik
▨	Uzbek
▩	Hazara
▨	Chahar Aimak
▥	Turkmen
▨	Baluchi
N U R	Other Group

0   50   100 Miles

0   50   100 Kilometers

b. Economic integration

(1) Soviet economic assistance

Economic integration has also gone apace, particularly in the geographic area between the Hindu Kush range along northern and northeastern Afghanistan and the Soviet border adjoining the Central Asian republics.[91] The area contains transnational roads and a rail crossing along with port facilities for traffic along the Amu Darya River that divides Afghanistan and the Soviet Union at the strategically important Friendship Bridge joining Termez in Russia with Hairatan in Afghanistan.[92] (See Map 3.) Certain northern areas are to be included in the electric power grids in nearby Tajikistan.[93] Such widespread economic connections can encourage not only economic but political gravitation northward toward Soviet Central Asis until absorption by the stronger economy could become a real possibility.

In 1982, the Soviets increased their efforts to build the infrastructure of Afghanistan. These efforts included the expansion of the airfield at Shindand in the west with a capability of operating strategic bombers. Improvements were also made in the airfield at Kandahar.[94] In general, the Soviets are upgrading some of Afghanistan's 36 airfields and constructing some new ones as well. A new military airfield is being constructed at Dasht-e-Atishan, some 40 kilometers east of the Iranian border in Herat Province.[95]

The Soviets have also embarked on an extensive road building program in the Wakhan Corridor, the only part of Afghanistan to border China; according to David Isby, it was annexed in 1981. (See Map 3.) Indicative of what may come is the Soviet practice (as elsewhere in the non-Russian areas of the Soviet Union) of displacing the native population (Afghan Tadjiks in this case) with Soviet settlers from the Tadzhik U.S.S.R. (See Map 4.) There are also unconfirmed reports that the Soviets have begun work on a railroad linking Kabul with the Soviet Union, a monumental task since it would involve much tunneling, but as David C. Isby, an American specialist on military affairs, notes, if true, "would indicate that the Soviets have little doubt that their presence will be a permanent one."[96]

A central feature of the Soviet effort is a wide-ranging program to expand the lines of communication between Soviet Central Asia and Afghanistan, an effort that could greatly assist the overall Soviet logistics and resupply plan and set the stage for greater economic and political integration.

The extent of Russia's long term commitment in Afghanistan and its expectations of perhaps a Mongolian solution can be meas-

---

[91] Sego, Soviet Policy in Afghanistan Under Andropov, p. 4. For a discussion of long-term Soviet activities in the area, see, Rubinstein, Soviet Union and Afghanistan, p. 318–19.

[92] Approximately 86 percent of Afghanistan's foreign trade now goes through the river port of Hairatan on the Amu Darya, whose facilities, along with those at Shir Khan, are being rapidly expanded. Reportedly, three or four convoys of craft leave the Soviet port of Termez daily with cargoes for Afghanistan. The Friendship Bridge, crossing the Amu Darya near Hairatan and opened in May 1983, carries both road and rail traffic, thus making it possible for the Soviets to establish a railhead for the Soviet railway system on the Afghan side of the border.

[93] Sego, Soviet Policy in Afghanistan Under Andropov, p. 4.

[94] Isby, Afghanistan, 1982, p. 1528.

[95] Hansen, Afghanistan: The Soviet Experience, p. 23.

[96] Isby, Afghanistan, 1982, p. 1528.

ured somewhat by its economic assistance. According to a 1983 report published by the State Department entitled, "Soviet and East European Aid to the Third World, 1981," the Soviet Union extended $2,120 million (East Europe, $210 million), to Afghanistan during the aggregate period 1954–1981. In 1980, the Soviets extended $395 million (East Europe, $135), and in 1981, $25 million, an estimate judged by one source to be low.[97] In addition, the Soviet Union and Eastern Europe sent 3,750 technicians to Afghanistan in 1981;[98] and as of Dec. 1981, 8,700 Afghan academic students were being trained in the Soviet bloc.[99]

Soviet economic assistance has served many purposes in Afghanistan. In Dec. 1982, Soltan Ali Keshtmand, Chairman of the DRA's Council of Ministers, elaborated on the forms of economic assistance that the Soviets were providing the Afghans. Approximately 170 different national economic projects are planned for construction under agreements on economic cooperation, of which 80, he states, "have already been commissioned and are working successfully." Keshtmand explains,

The U.S.S.R. is currently giving the DRA assistance in constructing and operating 85 projects in transportation, industry, power generation, communications, agriculture, irrigation, and public health, in prospecting for and exploiting mineral deposits, and in training national cadres. Over the past 2 years alone a transshipment base and a railroad station have been constructed at (Khayraton) through the joint efforts of the two countries' construction workers and specialists, as has a road bridge over the Amadarya. In addition, a (Lotos) space communication station, a compressor station on the Khodzha Gugurdak gas field, a motor transport enterprise to service Kamaz trucks, and other projects have been commissioned.

Today more than 5,000 highly skilled specialists, trained both in Soviet VUX's and technical colleges and in DRA educational institutions set up with Soviet assistance, are working in DRA industrial enterprises and state establishments. Approximately 70,000 skilled Afghan workers have been trained at Afghan-Soviet economic cooperation projects.[100]

(2) Soviet-Afghan trade

Trade also plays a prominent and integrative role in Soviet relations with Afghanistan. As Premier Keshtmand notes in his interview with Sovetskaya Rossiya,

Trade between the two countries is also developing successfully. Trade turnover has increased more than 200 percent over the past 5 years. The U.S.S.R. is rightly considered Afghanistan's major trading partner. Approximately half the Soviet exports to our country are machinery and industrial-transport equipment. In addition, the Soviet Union supplies the DRA with important commodities for the national economy, such as petroleum products, rolled ferrous metals, chemicals, and also consumer goods.

The DRA in turn supplies the U.S.S.R. with natural gas and carbamide. Cotton, wool, rawhide, citrus fruits, olives, dried fruits, and nuts occupy a significant place in exports to the Soviet Union. Trade between our countries is conducted on the basis of 5-year agreements—which imparts to it a regular, stable nature. The current agreement for the period 1981–1985 provides for an approximate trebling of trade turnover compared with the previous 5-year period.[101]

---

[97] U.S. Department of State. Soviet and East European Aid to the Third World, 1981. Washington, Feb. 1983, p. 19. Richard P. Cronin, Specialist in Asian Affairs, CRS.

[98] Ibid., p. 21.

[99] Ibid., p. 23.

[100] DRA Premier Interviewed on U.S.S.R.-DRA Relations. Sovetskaya Rossiya (Moscow), Dec. 4, 1983, 1st ed., p. 3, in FBIS Daily Report, Soviet Union, v. 3, Dec. 6, 1983, p. D1–D3.

[101] Ibid., p. D3.

Afghanistan, as Keshtmand indicates, is a heavy provider of natural gas and other minerals to the Soviet Union. But this Third World Soviet client has not been treated fairly. According to a NATO report on Soviet aid to its clients published in 1983, the Soviet Union, despite its aid, "is draining resources from Afghanistan." [102] The Soviets buy most of Afghanistan's largest export, natural gas, at a 40 percent discount from the world price, according to diplomatic and Afghan sources. Moreover, the meters are located on the Soviet side of the border so that the Karmal Government cannot tell how much Afghan gas is flowing into the U.S.S.R. "The Soviets are just helping themselves," a European diplomat notes. [103]

Furthermore, the Afghans pay for most of the military weapons purchased from the Soviets. Thus Soviet military and economic aid may reach some $2 billion a year, as some diplomatic sources estimate, but the Soviets get a return by exploiting Afghan resources. [104]

To sum up, Soviet economic aid and trade clearly play an integrative role in Soviet-Afghan relations. Combined with the political and cultural instrumentalities and judged in the context of long term success on the battlefield, the Soviet Union appears to have the means for ultimately converting their Third World Afghan client into another Mongolian People's Republic.

3. ASSESSMENT, COSTS, AND PROSPECTS

a. Military and diplomatic stalemate

Stalemate on both the military and diplomatic fronts seems best to characterize the Afghanistan problem at the end of 1983. Military specialists who have closely observed the military scene see the conflict as a classic example of a limited war in which the Soviets have carefully measured their commitment of men and resources. Their strategy, both military and political, seems designed, as Branigin notes, "for a long haul," a view commonly held by analysts, rather than for a quick solution. [105] Against a foe that is

---

[102] Fouquet, David. Moscow's Helping Hand: How Dependable? The Christian Science Monitor, Jan. 4, 1983, p. 8.

[103] Gigot, Paul A. Bitter Struggle: Afghans Are Determined, But So Are the Soviets, and They Appear Ready to Stay a Long While. The Wall Street Journal, April 26, 1983, p. 60. Gigot continues: "Soviet geologists have mapped out mineral deposits, too, and Soviet miners have already begun exploiting lodes such as the 1.7 billion-ton iron-ore deposits near Hajigak, northwest of Kabul."

[104] Ibid. For explanations from the Soviet side on what they are doing economically in Afghanistan, see, Vekshin, G. U.S.S.R.-Afghanistan: Economic Links. New Times (Moscow), no. 16, 1983: 26–27, and Mironov, Leonid. In Afghanistan's Industrial Belt. New Times (Moscow) no. 49, 1983: 20–21. To demonstrate the growth in Soviet-Afghan trade, Vekshin published the following table (p. 26) of statistics in millions of rubles:

	1977	1978	1979	1980	1981	1982
Exports from the Soviet Union	114	139	184	248	339	112
Imports into the Soviet Union	76	76	140	257	317	279
Total	190	215	324	505	656	691

[105] The Washington Post, Oct. 17, 1983, p. A1, Asian Security, 1982, p. 9, and The New York Times, May 1, 1983, p. E3.

weakened organizationally and limited in its military resources, the Soviets appear to have determined to fight a limited war of attrition, allowing political, economic and cultural forces to gradually work in their favor. Military analysts foresee little chance for the mujahidin expelling the Soviets so long as the Soviets are determined to hold Afghanistan.[106]

Nonetheless, the guerrilla forces, growing in strength and operational boldness, can no doubt pose a continuing problem for the Soviet occupiers particularly when a determined insurgent leadership has no apparent intention of breaking off the engagement; indeed, it does not even foresee a resolution until some three or four years more of fighting.[107] As Ahmed Shah Massoud, the Panjshir Valley commander, said, "If everything goes right . . ., the Russians will understand that this jihad cannot be defeated." He argues that a "certain stage in military warfare" will have been reached by then allowing for a settlement, that stage presumably meaning establishing a balance of military forces.[108]

On the diplomatic front stalemate also continues. There seems to be little possibility for a negotiated settlement, an appraisal strengthened by the demonstrated failure at Geneva in 1983. Both sides hold rigidly to their opposing positions, allowing little room for agreement.[109] Simply stated, the Soviets insist upon recognition of the Karmal regime as the legitimate government of Afghanistan; the mujahidin refuse to do so.

b. Gains and costs to the Soviets

(1) Some political, military, and economic gains

Thus far the Soviets have achieved some apparent gains in their occupation of and continuing war in Afghanistan, despite the price exacted by the mujahidin. Analysts speak of the potential use of air bases in the country for any future strikes in the strategically important Persian Gulf area, but the possibilities are low given the strategic, tactical, and logistical limitations. A final solution with Afghanistan under Soviet control, states Rubinstein,

> gives Moscow enormous political and military leverage in the region, and Soviet leaders, whose geostrategic outlook places a high value on prime real estate, may decide that the costs of countering the insurgency are not high enough to warrant relinquishment of the country.[110]

Moreover, Soviet involvement in Afghanistan has given the Soviets certain advantages in pressuring Pakistan politically. Fear of Soviet retaliation has compelled the Pakistans to measure carefully their support of the mujahidin and soften their long held antagonism towards the Soviet Union.[111]

---

[106] Ibid., and Porter, Soviet Union is Asia, p. 5.

[107] For observations by European diplomats on the willingness of the Soviets to tolerate the guerrilla resistance "for decades," see, The Washington Post, Oct. 20, 1983, p. A14.

[108] Branigin, William. Afghanistan: Inside a Soviet War Zone. Guerrillas Use Cease-Fire to Arm. Third in a Six-part Series. The Washington Post, Oct. 18, 1983, p. A13.

[109] For a discussion of various options for a settlement, see, Rubinstein, Soviet Union and Afghanistan, p. 338. For an insight into the durability of the Soviet commitment in Afghanistan, see, Gabriel. Afghanistan: The Nature of the Problem. Rahva Haal (Tallinn, Estonia), Aug. 27, 1983, p. 3, in, U.S.S.R. Report. Political and Sociological Affairs, No. 1475, JPRS 84740, Nov. 14, 1983, p. 1–3.

[110] Rubinstein, Soviet Union and Afghanistan, p. 338. Richard P. Cronin, Specialist in Asian Affairs, CRS.

[111] The Washington Post, Oct. 22, 1983, p. A10.

Trade and economic assistance has also enabled the Soviets to tighten their hold on Afghanistan, particularly its northern territories, thus contributing to eventual absorption through sovietization, if indeed that is the final Soviet goal. And finally, in justification for their main purposes for invading Afghanistan, the Soviets can claim to have secured their southern borders against what they perceived to be threats from their enemies.

Thus the Soviets have made some apparent gains, but at a cost.

(2) Some political, military, and economic costs

Afghanistan has exacted a heavy cost for the Soviets on the international scene. In October 1981, nearly two years after the invasion, Rajan Menon, an Asian specialist at Vanderbilt University, declared that within the Muslim world and within the Non-Alignment Movement (NAM)—in brief probably in nearly the entire Third World—"the Soviet Union has been isolated and left with but few defenders" on the issue of Afghanistan.[112] Recent voting in the U.N. General Assembly calling for Soviet withdrawal from Afghanistan registered again the seemingly lasting dissent and distrust of the Soviet Union among the LDC's and Muslim nations. Yet this apparent isolation of the Soviet Union may be misleading. Clearly many Third World states continue to support the U.S.S.R. on many other issues, while maintaining diplomatic opposition to the invasion of Afghanistan.[113]

Soviet relations with the United States have yet to recover from the serious blow dealt by the invasion. Setbacks in arms control have had a prolonged adverse effect on relations as the arms race, stimulated by the failure of the INF and START talks in 1983, appears to be taking off on a new cycle of escalation. Instead of a United States somewhat quiescent militarily and still caught up in the "Vietnam syndrome," the Soviets now face a United States determined to strengthen its military power, to play a much larger role in the Third World, and to pursue a more aggressive forward strategy globally. The Soviet response, generated by their own deep fears of U.S. aims and power, not only appears to have increased the world's anxiety for peace but thrusts a heavier economic burden on the Soviet Union as it seeks to match the U.S. buildup.

The military cost of Afghanistan has also been high for the Soviets. Though guerrilla estimates of Soviet casualities often appear to be "grossly exaggerated," according to Drew Middleton, military analyst for The New York Times, still in 1983 U.S. intelligence specialists estimated Soviet costs for the entire operation probably at 5,000 killed and 10,000 wounded.[114] That the Soviet leadership is sensitive to these losses is indicated by their recent efforts to publicize the heroism and sacrifices of the Soviet soldiers fighting in Afghanistan in order to build support on the home front, rather than

---

[112] Menon, Rajan. China and the Soviet Union in Asia. Current History, v. 80, Oct. 1981:332.
[113] Stuart D. Goldman, Analyst in Soviet Affairs, CRS.
[114] The New York Times, May 1, 1983, p. E3. Branigin notes that estimates on Soviet casualties vary considerably. Western diplomats place it between 8,000 and 15,000 total Soviet casualties since the Dec. 1979 invasion. An Afghan brigadier general who defected in April 1983 placed the figure at 19,000. The mujahidin usually give the high-side estimate of 25,000 to 30,000. U.S. sources, Branigin notes, put Soviet dead at 5,000 to 6,000 with an additional 12,000 to 15,000 wounded. But some analysts believe that as many as 12,000 Soviets may have been killed in this war. (The Washington Post, Oct. 21, 1983, p. A14.)

conceal their involvement as earlier was the case. Troop rotations every six months that show signs of the reentry of more Central Asian units suggest that the losses of Uzbeks and Kazakhs create fewer ripples of concern in their isolated communities than in the large Slavic cities like Moscow and Kiev.[115] Defections still occur among Soviet forces, and reports of low morale, stimulated by doubtful purposes of the mission, drug abuse and alcoholism, suggest a rising level of discontent among the troops. Trained to fight a European war, the Soviet soldier finds himself fighting a wholly unsuitable guerrilla war in the mountains of Afghanistan with entirely different requirements and risks. The prestige of the Soviet Army has no doubt suffered by this prolonged and often agonizing conflict. Gaining confidence and no longer overimpressed by Soviet military might, the guerrillas now tend to see the struggle as a David vs. Goliath mismatch in which they are not necessarily doomed by fate as the losers.[116]

Then there is the loss of military equipment destroyed in the fighting or through defections. According to Massoud, 80 percent of the military supplies for his guerrilla forces were captured from the Soviets.[117]

Finally, the economic costs of operations in Afghanistan are considerable. The adjective "severe" is often used to describe the financial costs of the war to the Soviets—"more than $4 mn a day being said to be expended in Afghanistan in one way or another," according to Tokyo's authoritative Research Institute for Peace and Security.[118] A more recent estimate placed the cost at "more than 3 billion dollars a year" being spent to support 105,000 Soviet troops in Afghanistan.[119] If the number of troops has been expanded to the estimated 180,000 with fresh reinforcements likely to be soon dispatched, as recently reported in a Yugoslav source, then the costs could rise appreciably. Though some of the expense may be borne by Afghan exports to the Soviet Union, as in natural gas, the exploitation of minerals, and other offsetting expenses, still the costs will no doubt remain very high, especially for an economy that already suffers from serious shortcomings. Stretched out over a long period of time, which responsible analysts assert will be the case given the persistence of the Soviet commitment and their corresponding lack of total success, it seems clear that burden of empire for the Soviet Union in Afghanistan could be heavy indeed.[120]

---

[115] Ibid.
[116] The Branigin articles, based largely on field research and interviews, exude this growing spirit of defiance. See the first installment, Afghanistan: Inside a Soviet War Zone. Rebel's Resolve Pitted Against Kremlin's Might, The Washington Post, Oct. 16, 1983, p. A1 and A18. He writes: "While the *mujaheddin* fear and respect Soviet air power, their increased familiarity with their enemy has bred a measure of contempt for the fighting abilities of Soviet soldiers. Reports of low morale, drug and alcohol abuse and poor motivation among Soviet troops appear to be borne out by examples of ineffectiveness in combat."
[117] The Washington Post, Oct. 18, 1983, p. A1.
[118] Asian Security 1982, p. 34–35.
[119] U.S. News & World Report, Nov. 14, 1983:40.
[120] For a recent appraisal of the war, see, Update: Russia's 'Hidden War' in Afghanistan. U.S. News & World Report, Aug. 1, 1983:22–25. See also, Brumas, Michael. The Soviet Forces in Afghanistan. RFE-RL, Radio Liberty Research, RL 459/83, Dec. 6, 1983, 3 p.

c. Prospects for the future

Prospects for at least the immediate future appear not to be particularly bright for either the Soviets or the mujahidin. For the essence of military stalemate is that it renders final or long term judgments inconclusive. After a searching inquiry into the conflict, notably the effective building of a guerrilla infrastructure, Branigin made this projection, "if, as the conventional wisdom has it, Soviet forces are in Afghanistan for the long haul, then so too is the Afghan resistance."[121] A State Department official, while putting it another way, said essentially the same thing: "The Soviets aren't winning. But the mujeheddin—the holy warriors—cannot force them out."[122]

Yet the Soviets appear determined to continue this conflict. To that extent they seem clearly prepared to pay the price, whatever that may be. Still, it is instructive to determine what this could mean through an historical analogy. Historical analogies can give guidance and insight, though they have their limitations. Foreign policy observers have drawn the analogy of Soviet involvement in Afghanistan with difficulties, and final defeat, of the United States in Vietnam. In many respects the analogy is an accurate one, but in other more essential respects it is not.

However, the historical analogy of the Boer War between the British and the white Africaner farmers of South Africa is accurate, at least in one way, and it is in the comparisons of the forces involved and the investment made by the British Government to "win." It took the largest empire in the world nearly three years, 1899–1902, to defeat a rag-tag, guerrilla-commando force of Boer farmers, but many of whom fought as mounted infantry, were by and large well equipped with modern rifles, and guided by skillful innovative military tactics. Only by massive, in the parlance of the Vietnam War, "search-and-destroy" operations reminiscent of the Vietnam War and the setting up of concentration camps across much of South Africa was it possible for the British to defeat the Boer insurgents. Victory was finally achieved at the cost of 200 million pounds; over 100,000 casualties of all kinds among the 365,693 Imperial and 82,742 Colonial soldiers, 22,000 deaths. Among the Boers, over 7,000 perished from a fighting force of only 87,365 men. Official estimates of those men, women, and children dying in concentration camps varied between 18,000 and 28,000. Apparently an estimated 12,000 black Africans perished. Over 400,000 horses, mules and donkeys were expended. Thomas Pakenham wrote with much truth in his recent history of the Boer War that, "The fruits of victory tasted sweet and sour to the British army." And as he further observed, the Boer War "proved to be the longest . . . the costliest . . . the bloodiest . . . and the most humiliating war for Britain between 1815 and 1914."[123] Yet, as one Asian specialist asserts, no doubt the Soviets will not so willingly give away the fruits of their victory as did the British.[124]

---

[121] The Washington Post, Oct. 17, 1983, p. A20.
[122] U.S. News & World Report, Aug. 1, 1983:22.
[123] Pakenham, Thomas. The Boer War. New York, Random House, 1979, pp. 607–8 and xixx.
[124] Richard P. Cronin, Specialist in Asian Affairs, CRS.

Even if this analogy does not completely fit the Soviet case in Afghanistan, still it does suggest the magnitude of ultimate costs for complete military "victory." It is possible that the Soviets, rejecting any diplomatic solution, might take this course, throwing more military resources and men into the conflict until a decisive military solution is achieved. Whatever the political wisdom of this course, they have, nonetheless, the military power to do this. And aided by the forces of sovietization already underway (as their forebears were aided by Russification), they might well eventually conquer Afghanistan as they had so many other non-Russian nations in the past either under the Czars or the Commissars. The Russian conquest of Central Asia clearly demonstrates that this possibility could become a reality.

Yet, powerful forces exist in the world today, like those effectively organized and often skillfully used by nations in the Third World and by the Islamic peoples. These forces could make such a course too costly, at least politically. And this is where the judgment of Norman D. Palmer, Asian specialist at the University of Pennsylvania, on Afghanistan's future may have both the merit of vision and prophecy, however inconclusive, when he wrote, "There will certainly be a non-Soviet tomorrow for Afghanistan; but that tomorrow . . . [is] clearly a long way into the murky future."[125]

C. CHINA: BARRIER TO EXPANDING SOVIET POWER

1. INTERSECTING POINTS OF CONFLICT

The after-shock of Russia's invasion of Afghanistan continues to reverberate throughout Northeast Asia. China, for a long time at odds with the Soviet Union, was visibly alarmed by this act of military aggression against a weak and defenseless Third World country. These fears were further heightened by Soviet support for Vietnam's military conquest of Kampuchea and by the general, and continuous, Soviet military buildup in the Far East. The militarization of the Sino-Soviet border has added to growing tensions over the years. But China's rivalry with the Russians extends beyond the Asian continent, to the Third World where for over two decades they have competed fiercely for influence.[126] Thus, Sino-Soviet interests conflict at four intersecting points, all of which directly or indirectly impinge upon Soviet policy in the Third World.[127]

---

[125] Palmer, Soviet Perspectives on Peace and Security in Asia, p. 17. Rubinstein concludes, "The Afghan crisis is likely to be with us for a long time to come." (Rubinstein, Soviet Union and Afghanistan, p. 338.) Allan and Stahel note that the guerrilla war in Afghanistan "pits tribes against a colonial power." Drawing on a series of scenarios of previous struggles of this type, they conclude that "the guerrillas are relatively successful during the period retained for analysis (1980–1985) and inflict relatively heavy losses on Soviet forces. Only a very large Soviet escalation (over 300,000 troops) could make a difference, and even then, the resistance would be hard to eradicate because of the support of the population and the primitive state of the country." Hence they predict that "the Afghan war will be with us for quite some time." (Allan, Pierre and Albert A. Stahel. Tribal Guerrilla Warfare Against a Colonial Power: Analyzing the War in Afghanistan. Journal of Conflict Resolution, v. 27, Dec. 1983:590–617.)

[126] See, Rubinstein, Alvin Z., ed. Soviet and Chinese Influence in the Third World. New York, Praeger, 1975. 231 p.

[127] For an extensive commentary on Sino-Soviet relations, see, HFAC, Soviet Role in Asia, 1983, pp. 235–513. Among Asian specialists giving testimony are Harry Gelman, Senior Staff Member, Rand Corp. and Professor Kenneth G. Lieberthal, University of Michigan. Dr. Seweryn Bialer, Soviet specialist at Columbia University, addresses the Soviet side of the relationship.

2. ON CONCILIATING CHINA

a. Rationale for rapprochement

The Soviets have had ample reason to moderate tensions in their relations with China. Though lacking in comparable military and economic power (China is often considered by western analysts as a developing country and a regional power), China still represents perhaps more in potential than in reality the most formidable barrier to Soviet expansion in Asia.[128] Alarmed by Russia's action in Afghanistan and Indochina taken against a background of a disturbing military buildup and apprehensive about Moscow's efforts to fill the power vacuum caused by the U.S. withdrawal from Asia in the 1970's, China responded with a multiple diplomatic effort to bring the United States, Japan and the Third World countries of ASEAN into a loosely constructed anti-Soviet coalition.[129] Virtually isolated from the Muslim world and the Non-Alignment Movement within the Third World, plagued by deep anxieties for its security aroused by the Polish crisis and the uncertain loyalties of its allies manifested in the crisis, and fearful of the new defense measures undertaken by the United States to strengthen NATO and the U.S. world position, the Soviets faced what they perceived to be an evolving "encirclement" of potential adversaries. China's counteraction—an "'obsession" with the Soviets, Palmer notes, in describing Russian attitudes towards the Chinese—only quickened already existing Soviet anxieties and encouraged a reassessment of its policy toward Beijing.[130]

Success in reconciling differences with China could bring about a shift in the balance of forces in Asia. This shift could have far-reaching and favorable effects for Moscow. It could: Secure the Soviet position in Indochina; pressure India away from China and into a closer alliance with the Soviet Union; have a salutary effect on relations with Japan and North Korea; and, finally, open up the ASEAN countries to Soviet influence.[131]

In brief, success could diminish the effectiveness of any anti-Soviet coalition the Chinese might construct in Asia, while at the same time relieving pressure in the East and allowing greater concentration of energy on even greater problems in the West.

b. An opening to the East

The 26th Soviet Party Congress in February 1981 provided the opportunity for Brezhnev to initiate an opening to the East.[132] Recognizing the inter-related power interests of China, the United States, Japan and the Soviet Union in the Far East, Brezhnev announced that the Soviet Union was prepared to "conduct concrete talks on confidence building measures in the Far East with all interested nations."[133] Other overtures followed, notably a personal

---

[128] Porter, Soviet Union in Asia: A Strategic Survey, pp. 1–3 & 5–6.
[129] Ibid., pp. 2–4, and Menon, China and the Soviet Union in Asia, p. 332, 341–42.
[130] Palmer, Soviet Perspectives on Peace and Security in Asia, p. 5.
[131] Porter, Soviet Union in Asia: A Strategic Survey, p. 5.
[132] For an analysis of recent trends in Sino-Soviet relations, see, Zagoria, Donald S. The Moscow-Beijing Detente. Foreign Affairs, v. 61, Spring 1983:853–873.
[133] Dibb, Soviet Union as a Pacific Power, p. 242–243.

letter to the Chinese leadership on March 12, 1981, a Brezhnev speech in Tashkent on March 24, 1982, another in Baku, and an authoritative Pravda article on May 20, 1982.[134] The Soviets sought normalization of relations based on open dialogue, mutually beneficial agreements, and confidence building measures along the Sino-Soviet border.

Beijing responded cautiously to these overtures, emphasizing the importance of concrete acts of Soviet intent and, according to the Soviets, setting unacceptable conditions. In the months ahead some cultural exchanges took place as the polemics of the dispute were somewhat moderated. The movement towards conciliation culminated with the meeting in October 1982 between Soviet Vice Foreign Minister Leonid Ilyichev, a top-ranking Soviet trouble-shooter on Chinese matters, and senior Chinese officials. The attendance of Foreign Minister Huang Hua at Brezhnev's funeral in November 1982, the highest ranking Chinese official to visit the Soviet Union in nearly two decades, and the lengthy talks between him and Andropov seemed to signal another important but uncertain step in the direction of of rapprochement. The conciliatory mood could not be fully sustained in 1983, however, as sharp underlying differences surfaced and polemical attacks resumed, though at a less vitriolic level. The Ilyichev meeting in Beijing with Chinese leaders in October proved to be inconclusive beyond a willingness to keep the dialogue going.[135]

c. Results: An ongoing dialog at best

Russia's three year effort to normalize relations with the Chinese has largely, but not entirely, failed. China has, for example, moved away from earlier efforts to build an anti-Soviet alliance with the United States and claims a position of equidistance between the superpowers. At best, an on-going dialogue has been established and continues; the atmospherics of the relationship have somewhat cleared.

China's preconditions for normalization have proved to be a formidable stumbling block to rapprochement with Moscow. The Chinese insist that the Soviets: Withdraw their troops from Afghanistan;[136] stop supporting the Vietnamese in their occupation of Kampuchea; reduce Soviet military strength along the lengthy Sino-Soviet and Sino-Mongolian border; and recently, reduce the number of SS-20's targeted at China.[137]

In brief, the Chinese demand virtually a total reversal of Soviet policy in Asia. Besides PRC conditions, other Chinese actions precluding rapprochement include strengthened economic ties with the United States and Japan, support for the Japanese defense buildup and dialogue with the United States and Japan on Korea.[138]

---

[134] Ibid., p. 244, and Thornton, U.S.S.R. and Asia in 1982, p. 13.
[135] Oka, Takashi. Moscow Tries to Keep Chinese Talking, But Are They Listening? The Christian Science Monitor, Nov. 2, 1983, p. 12.
[136] The depth of Chinese feelings on the Afghan issue is evident in their criticism of the Soviets for waging a "war of extermination." Routine Chinese references to Afghanistan speak of the Soviet "scorched earth policy" and allegations of Soviet "slaughter" of Afghan women, children and other noncombatants.
[137] Ibid.
[138] Larry A. Niksch, Specialist in Asian Affairs, CRS.

3. A DURABLE CONTRADICTION IN SOVIET POLICY

a. Formula for failure

Chances of Sino-Soviet rapprochement at some future time cannot be ruled out, but in the near term such chances seem to be very slim.[139] For a durable contradiction underlies Soviet policy towards China that preordains failure. Russia's policy and activities reflect the intention of establishing military predominance and political hegemony in Asia.[140] Events in the past near decade bear this out, and so it is viewed by Russia's adversaries in the region. This being the case, it is not likely that the Chinese, who would be the losers in any substantial accretion of Soviet power in Asia, would seriously enter a relationship of rapprochement. They already suffer from the negative effects of a serious imbalance of power.[141] Moreover, the Chinese have to compete strenuously, and not always successfully, with the Russians for influence over the strategically important Korean Peninsula.[142] This rivalry, rooted in geopolitics, is not likely to be diminished by political rapprochment.

Conflicts of interests, reflected in their negotiating positions on key issues, are, furthermore, far too profound to expect a return to the pre-1950 era of Sino-Soviet relations. Experience in recent years has demonstrated that Chinese interests, as they themselves profess, are best served in pursuing a policy of parallelism with the

---

[139] Estimates on the likelihood of a rapprochement vary. Dibb sees little possibilities for a fundamental rapprochement in the foreseeable future. Even if some improvement takes place, "it will be limited and fragile, and unlikely to lead to major changes in the strategic situation in East Asia." Dibb believes that for the remainder of the 1980's China will continue to be "a major policy preoccupation" of the Soviets, ranking second only to relations with the United States and NATO Europe. (Dibb, Soviet Union as a Pacific Power, p. 244–45.) Menon predicts progress on secondary issues that could result in creating a "less polemical and more hopeful relationship." But, he adds, "the primary issues" (agreement on Vietnam, Mongolia, Afghanistan and military deployments along the Sino-Soviet border) "will not disappear, and so mistrust and rivalry . . . will remain, with each continuing to view the other as a major danger to its security." (Menon, Soviet Union in Asia, p. 317.)

Soviet commentators seem to be more hopeful. Georgiy Arbatov, Director of the U.S.A. and Canada Institute and leading Soviet Americanist, acknowledged that the solution to problems in Sino-Soviet relations "is not simple." But observing that the Sino-American rapprochement began with "ping pong diplomacy," he noted that "we still can pin our hopes on whatever is started in a small way." Arbatov believes that normalization of relations "is in the interests of both nations." Other Soviet political commentators and scholars have expressed similar hopeful expectations. Aleksandr Bovin, a leading Soviet political commentator and advisor on foreign policy, emphasized the improvements in Sino-Soviet relations in an interview in December 1983, particularly in the economic sector. Politically, he said, both countries face the Afghan, Kampuchean and other difficult problems, but he noted that the Soviet Union was ready to patiently overcome the hostile relations between both countries. (Mainichi Shimbun [Tokyo], Dec. 30, 1983, p. 5.)

[140] For judgments on this matter, see, Dibb, Soviet Union as a Pacific Power, p. 239; Menon, China and the Soviet Union in Asia, p. 331; and Thomas, Their Pacific Fleet, p. 84–85. Thomas comments on the "alarm" with which both China and Japan viewed the Soviet naval buildup in the Pacific (p. 85).

[114] Menon elaborates on the "fundamental inequality of power" that characterizes the Sino-Soviet competition, China being a developing nation and regional power with global ambitions, and the Soviet Union, a superpower with great economic and military assets that give it a global reach. (Menon, China and the Soviet Union in Asia, p. 329–30.)

[142] For discussions of the role of Korea in Sino-Soviet relations, see, Asian Security 1982, p. 39; Robinson, Soviet Union and Asia in 1981, p. 20–21; and Scalapino, Political Influence of the U.S.S.R. in Asia, p. 68–69. Scalapino explains the strategic importance of North Korea, noting that it has a very short border with the Soviet Union but one that is extremely close to Russia's principal military base at Vladivostok. A North Korean alignment with Moscow would make China "highly vulnerable" since important Chinese industrial centers are located near its extensive border with North Korea. "In any policy dedicated to the containment of China or in the event of a Sino-Soviet conflict," Scalapino concludes, "the orientation of North Korea is crucial." (p. 67)

non-Communist countries in the Asian-Pacific region who share with them many interests in common. In Chinese eyes the Russians are clearly the adversary and a threat to these interests.[143]

b. Effects on Soviet policy in the Third World: resurgence of China as competitor

This "hegemonic" Soviet policy in Asia, as Beijing terms it, also works at cross purposes with Soviet goals and expectations in the Third World.[144] It has closed off potential avenues of influence with the LDC's of Southeast Asia. Alarmed by Soviet support for Vietman in Kampuchea, the ASEAN cuntries (especially Thailand) have gravitated towards China in search of a protective counterbalance to the Soviet-Vietnamese threat.[145] And China welcomes them, encouraging the gravitation even to downgrading to the level of "moral and political" ties its connection with Communist guerrillas active in the area.[146] Thus China gains in a vital strategic area, while the Soviet Union loses in their prolonged contest to claim the role of spokeman and leader of the Third World.[147]

Yaacov Vertzberger, an Israeli specialist on Asian affairs at Jerusalem's Hebrew University, believes that the Soviet invasion of Afghanistan may prove to be a watershed in China's relations with the entire Third World. China and the Soviet Union have been competitors in the Third World since the 1960's. For material rather than ideological reasons the Soviet have always had a "clear lead." Yet Vertzberger contends that since Afghanistan, China has been in a much stronger position, having three assets with which to embarrass the Soviets and win more influence for itself in the

---

[143] For a commentary on the creation of this new equilibrium in East Asia, see, Zagoria, Strategic Environment in Asia, p. 5-13.

[144] Premier Zhao Ziyang made a distinction between Soviet and American hegemonism, a term the Chinese press has routinely applied to both powers. "Any big power, if it pursues a hegemonistic policy, is hegemonists and China cannot but oppose it," he said. Referring to the Soviety military buildup along the northern borders of China, he continued: "I believe that we know better than the Americans where our threat comes from. In this regard, we do not equate the United States and Soviet Union either." (The New York Times, Jan. 4, 1984, p. A6.)

[145] The extent of Beijing's support for Thailand is evident by its guarantees of military support if Vietnam attacks, the military pressure the PRC has been applying on Vietnam's northern border, and its arming of the Khymer resistance forces in Kampuchea. China is determined to bring Vietnam down. It sees Southeast Asia as its sphere and in fundamental conflict with a Soviet presence there. (Larry A. Niksch, Specialist in Asian Affairs, CRS.)

[146] Menon, Soviet Union in East Asia, p. 316.

[147] For a comprehensive analysis of Chinese policy in the Third World, see, Harris, Lillian Craig. China's Third World Courtship. Washington Quarterly, v. 5, Summer 1982:128–136. Among the points Harris makes are the following: The PRC is demonstrating an increased interest in the Third World as part of its "broader international strategy to counter Soviet influence"; this activity reflects "the growing pains of a future great power"; Beijing believes that strengthened ties with the Third World are necessary "to allow it the political independence and the authority it seeks," particularly to enhance its drive for Third World leadership; the Soviet invasion of Afghanistan had energized the Chinese drive to build an anti-Soviet coalition that included the Third World as an integral part; the Chinese have moderated their revolutionary approach to the Third World, placing greater stress on state-to-state relations, particularly in Southeast Asia; the Chinese have undertaken a vigorous effort to expand their influence first in East Asia and Southeast Asia, the Middle East and Southwest Asia, Africa and to a certain extent Latin America; rhetoric remains China's major foreign policy tool in the Third World, since, as a developing country itself, it has few economic incentives to offer the Third World; and finally, in the next few years China is likely to assume a much more active role in Third World international organizations as confidence in its own ability increases and as a manifestian of the Chinese effort to maintain independence from both East and West, while delicately maintaining its good relations with the United States upon whom it depends (along with other industrialized countries) for progress in modernization.

larger global dimension of the crisis: Afghanistan is Muslim; Afghanistan is Asian; and Afghanistan *was* nonaligned.[148]

Chinese interest and activity in the Third World has taken a decided upward surge in recent years, stimulated no doubt by the militarization of Soviet foreign policy in Asia. Premier Zhao Ziyang visited Africa from late 1982 through early 1983, the first time in nearly two decades for a Chinese premier to do so. This ten-nation tour provided the occasion for the Chinese to demonstrate not only their commitment to Africa but also to the Third World. By this trip they reaffirmed their credentials to leadership of the Third World, and so it was interpreted. Particularly notable in this persistent promotion of Chinese interests in the Third World was the meeting on "South-South cooperation" held in Beijing in April 1983 under the joint auspices of the Academy of Social Sciences of China and the Third World foundation.

China identifies itself as a Third World country; it supports the idea of a New International Economic Order in its own right; and it has begun to show increased interest in the developing programs of the LDC's. A growing feeling has occurred in China that its foreign policies can be more effective when approached from a Third World point of view, using the "strong assets of the weak." As Professor Tatsumi Okabe of Tokyo Metropolitan University speculates on the future of China in the Third World:

The more diversified the international situation becomes, the more China's efforts to side with the Third World become meaningful as a countervailing force against more powerful countries.[149]

And one powerful country whose interests and goals conflict with those of the Chinese in the Third World is their socialist rival, the Soviet Union. The rivalry of the past may be only a prologue to the future. For as China moves more forthrightly along its course of economic modernization and thus becomes more dependent upon the economies of the United States, Japan and Western Europe, the Third World can be expected to take on even greater importance in the Beijing's foreign policy priorities. Accordingly, its rivalry with the Soviet Union could quicken. For such Third World areas as the oil-rich Persian Gulf region and the sea lanes around Southeast Asia then become matters of vital concern: This means free of Soviet domination.[150]

---

[148] Vertzberger, Yaacov. Afghanistan in China's Policy. Problems of Communism, v. 31, May–June 1982:17.

[149] Okabe, Tatsumi, Prof. Chiness Diplomacy as Reflected at the Recent National People's Congress. China Newsletter, no. 47, 1983:5.

[150] The Chinese have been active competitors with the Russians in the Third World. One source perhaps described their commitment correctly when it spoke of concern for any damage to China's reputation in the Third World "which it is cultivating so hard and with considerable success." (Wallace, James. U.S. and China Go From Enemies to "Suspicious Partners." U.S. News & World Report, Feb. 21, 1983:38.)

Chinese criticism of Soviet involvement in Kampuchea has been put in the Third World context. In November 1983, Li Shenzhi, Director of the Institute of American Studies, Academy of Social Sciences of China, noted that there was only one solution to his type of conflict: "The Third World should be left alone to solve its own problems. Hegemonism practiced by the Big Powers is the foremost problems of the contemporary world."

Sino-Soviet rivalry in Third World has taken on a special seriousness in the Persian Gulf region. China's policy of courting both sides in the Iran-Iraq war was described by diplomatic sources as being part of a larger strategy to compete for economic and political influence in the oil rich Persian Gulf area. According to these sources, this policy, involving a program of aggressive trading and possibly military sales to both combatants, was aimed at challenging the Soviet

Continued

D. Reawakening of Japan

1. FROM ISOLATIONISM TO INVOLVEMENT

Soviet policy of expansion and military buildup in Asia has also had a profound impact on Japan.[151] Arousing long suppressed Japanese anxieties and fears for its security, this aggressive Soviet policy has accelerated the changing direction of Japanese policy, in general highly flavored with pacifism up to this time, from isolationism and virtually a total dependence on U.S. protection, to playing a far more active role in international affairs and beginning to assume a much greater share of the defense burden for the Asian-Pacific region. It has also deepened Japanese political and particularly economic involvement in Southeast Asia, to the detriment of Soviet interests in that Third World area. As in the case of China, Russia's Asian policy and its aggressive behavior in the Far East have conjured up the authentic reality of a Soviet threat, spurred the building of an anti-Soviet coalition, created a new, more outgoing role for Japan in the international politics of Asia, and adversely affected Russia's larger designs on the Third World countries of Southeast Asia.[152]

2. THE GEOSTRATEGIC SETTING

a. Conflict preordained

The geostrategic setting for Soviet-Japanese relations enhances the potential for conflict. It is no historical accident that both countries have been adversaries since the opening of Japan by Commodore Matthew C. Perry in the mid-19th Century; indeed a potential Russian presence had spurred Japanese leaders at that time to incline towards the United States. A major war in 1905, Japanese military intervention in the Far Eastern Theater of the Russian Civil War during the early 1920's, an undeclared border war in the late 1930's, and a brief engagement as World War II came to a close in August 1945, attest to the record of discord in their relations.

---

strategic pretentions in the region, strengthening China's claim to Third World leadership, and positioning Beijing for a lucrative share of the postwar reconstruction business. As in the case of nations in both East and West, China realizes that its access to the political capitals and markets of the Middle East depends on keeping the area free of Soviet domination. Equally important to China is the necessity of keeping the oil flowing freely to Western Europe, Japan and the United States from whom the Chinese expect to get much of the technology and knowhow for carrying forth their own modernization. (Weisskopf, Michael. China Plays Both Sides in Persian Gulf War. The Washinton Post, Jan. 13, 1983, p. A21 and 25.)

[151] For commentary on the Soviet role in Northeast Asia and Soviet relations with Japan, see, HFAC, Soviet Role in Asia, 1983, p. 91–109, testimony of Dr. Allen S. Whiting, Asian specialist at the University of Arizona, and p. 110–128, testimony of Dr. Herbert J. Ellison, Secretary, Kennan Institute for Advanced Russian Studies.

[152] For a comprehensive analysis of Soviet-Japanese relations, see the following articles and monograph by Dr. Hiroshi Kimura, Professor of Political Science at the Slavic Research Center, Hokkaido University and one of Japan's leading Soviet specialists: Soviet Policy Toward Japan. Working Paper #6. Providence, Rhode Island, The Center for Foreign Policy Development, Brown University, August 1983, 51 p.; Recent Japan-Soviet Relations: From Clouded to "Somewhat Crystal." Journal of Northeast Asian Studies, v. 1, Mar. 1982:3–22; The Love-Hate Relationship with the Polar Bear: Japanese Feeling Toward the Soviet Union. Japan Quarterly, v. 28, Jan.–Mar. 1981:39–44; and, Soviet and Japanese Negotiating Behavior: The Spring 1977 Fisheries Talks. Orbis, v. 24, Spring 1980:43–68.

b. Three straits vital to Japanese security

As an island nation, Japan is wholly dependent upon free access to the seas. It must import 88 percent of its energy, 90 percent of essential raw materials, and 70 percent of its food. Nearly 60 percent of Japan's export trade is within the Pacific region.[153] Moreover, Japanese security hinges on three straits or "chokepoints" that control Soviet access to the Pacific: Soya between Soviet-controlled Sakhalin and Japan's northern island, Hokkaido; Tsugaru between Hokkaido and the main island of Honshu; and Tsushima between South Korea and southern Honshu and the island of Kyushu.[154] (See Map 2.) Japan is, therefore, vulnerable to Soviet pressure at these three points, particularly threats of using their superior military and naval power for political purposes, if not for outright military conquest.

c. Straits and islands essential for projection of Soviet power

Unhindered access through the Soya, Tsugaru and Tsushima Straits and possession of the Kuril Islands, now under Soviet jurisdiction, are considered essential by the Soviets for the projection of their seapower from the Soviet Asian mainland into the Asian-Pacific region and beyond, to the China Sea, through the Formosan Strait, the vital straits in Southeast Asia and on to the Indian Ocean and the Middle East.[155] For the Soviets, the chain of Kuril Islands, extending from the Kamchatka Peninsula to Japan proper, act as an essential defensive shield of protection across the maritime approaches to the Sea of Okhotsk. From this area they can securely deploy their fleet of ballistic missile submarines (SSBN's) targeted against the United States.[156] Continued Soviet possession of the Kurils is governed largely by the strategic geography of the area that denies Soviet land access to its key military base at Petropavlosk at the southern tip of the Kamchatka Peninsula.[157] Accordingly, the strategic importance of Vladivostok as Russia's principal naval base in the Far East and eastern terminus of the Trans-Siberian Railroad is enhanced still further and the necessity of unhindered access through the three straits magnified.

The economic development of Siberia and the Soviet Far East in general as a prime target in long term Soviet planning increases the strategic value of the three straits. Completion of the Baikal-Amur Main Line (BAM) to Sovetskaya Gavan north of Vladivostok and in the near proximity of Sakhalin and the Soya Strait is expected to quicken the economic development of the region.[158] Accordingly, further pressure can be expected to be added to insure Soviet egress to the open seas. One Soviet authority on the Far East states that 60 percent of the goods going to Vladivostok is shipped by sea. It is not surprising, therefore, that the Russians

[153] Thomas, Their Pacific Fleet, p. 86.
[154] Train, The Growing Soviet Naval Menace, p. 59.
[155] Ibid., p. 56–57.
[156] Dibb, The Soviet Union as a Pacific Power, p. 243–244.
[157] Okazaki, Hishahiko. Japanese Security Policy: A Time for Strategy. International Security, v. 7, Fall 1982: 190–191, and Asian Security 1982, p. 8.
[158] Vertzberger, The Malacca/Singapore Straits, p. 614–615.

have accelerated plans to build the largest and most advanced container terminal in the Soviet Union near Vladivostok.[159]

d. Conflicting strategic interests

Conflicting strategic interests of the Japanese and the Russians are fundamental. The intersecting points of these interests are the three straits and the Kurils. In establishing a credible sea denial capability by its military and naval buildup in the Far East, the Soviets have created an effective political weapon against the sea-dependent Japanese.[160] As Admiral Harry D. Train, NATO's Supreme Allied Commander Atlantic, explains in an analysis of the "vital" connection between "control of the chokepoints" and the gaining of maintaining control of the sea lanes of communications,

> The international political, economic, and military maneuvering to gain control of these geographically restrictive sea lanes, either by intimidation, subversion, or outright control, is clear evidence that the strategic importance of these waterways is fully recognized by the Soviet Union, and demonstrates their determination to exercise control of these passages as part of their global expansion strategy.[161]

As for the importance of the Kurils to Soviet strategic planning, possession of this island chain makes it all the more unlikely that the Russians will make any concessions to the Japanese on returning the disputed Northern Territories (which comprise the southernmost group of the Kurils). (See Map 2.)

The upshot of these strategic realities has been to solidify Japanese security ties with the United States, propel Japan into a closer relationship with China, quicken the tempo of defense preparedness, and encourage the Japanese to establish closer political and especially economic ties with the countries of Southeast Asia. The effect of this Japanese counter-strategy is to reduce the chances of Soviet penetration of this important Third World region.

3. SOVIET PROVOCATIONS AND PERCETPTIONS

a. Soviet objectives and strategy toward Japan

Within this geostrategic setting, the Soviets have pursued their policy of expansion, military buildup, and intimidation of the Japanese; and within it also their perceptions of Japan and its people have been cast.

Soviet foreign policy objectives toward Japan can be briefly summed up as follows:

—Weaken the Japanese-American alliance and Japanese willingness to cooperate with the United States against the Soviet Union;

—Limit Japan's cooperation with China, especially any military cooperation;

—Gain Japan's acceptance of Soviet jurisdiction over the Northern Territories;

---

[159] Journal of Commerce, Jan. 14, 1983, p. 1.
[160] Thomas, The Growing Soviet Naval Menace, p. 86.
[161] Train, The Growing Soviet Naval Menace, p. 59. Among the chokepoints Train cites are Soya, Tsushima, Hormuz, Malacca, Gibralter, the Bosporus, the Skaggerak, and the Panama Canal.

—Prevent a Japanese military buildup, particularly one designed to threaten Soviet naval and air access to the open seas; and
—Induce Japan to cooperate economically with the Soviet Union in the development of its Siberian resources and in order to gain access to Japanese technology.[162]

Soviet strategy has developed in three general directions, summed up in the term, "the carrot and stick approach" to foreign policy:

—The proffer of agreements intended to lessen Japanese-American cooperation and to draw Japan closer to the Soviet Union; for example, a treaty of friendship and an agreement on the non-use of nuclear weapons and long term cooperation;
—The intimidation of Japan, effected by the Soviet military buildup, military maneuvers and provocations near Japanese land and air space, and verbal threats; and finally,
—The targeting of key Japanese groups, such as the fisherman of Hokkaido, that might oppose the Government's anti-Soviet policies.[163]

b. Military power as means of intimidation

The Soviet Union has tried to intimidate Japan by its impressive military buildup and by the use of that military power to threaten and badger the Japanese into political accommodation if not complete submission. (See Map 2 and Figure 1.) Sources record the details of this buildup, highlighting such features as,

—The establishment of theater headquarters in the Far Eastern region, subdivided into three military districts, thus strengthening Soviet capacity for integrated operations;
—The deployment of some 51 divisions along the Sino-Soviet border and 39 of them with a strength of 360,000 east of the Trans-Baikal Military District, closer to Japan;
—The deployment of 15 divisions in Vladivostok and the surrounding area, two on Sakhalin, one on Kamchatka, and less than a division (10,000) on the Northern Territories;
—The steady buildup (and renewal) of its Pacific Fleet to some 720 naval vessels and 420 aircraft, including 128 submarines;
—The deployment of long-range Backfire bombers, SU-24 fighter bombers, and modern tactical fighters, and the replacement of older undersea craft with 31 long-range SSBN's;
—The deployment of some 140 SS-20's in the Soviet Far East, well within range of Japan.[164]

Recent Soviet military activities in Northeast Asia seem designed for a mission of intimidation. Among significant activities are:

—The staging of large-scale integrated military and naval maneuvers, as in the combined exercise Zapad 81 involving the Soviet Pacific Fleet;
—The frequent passage of Soviet warships through the three straits, often carrying out firing exercises without warning; and

---

[162] Niksch, Larry A. Briefing Book: Japan. Washington, Congressional Research Service, Library of Congress, Aug. 1983, p. 11-12.
[163] Ibid.
[164] Asian Security 182, p. 54-58, and The Washington Post, Nov. 30, 1983, p. A15.

—The flight of Soviet aircraft over the Sea of Japan and the straits, coming dangerously close to Japanese airspace. In March 1981, the Japanese Air Defense Force scrambled 783 time to monitor Soviet aircraft approaching Japanese airspace, a figure 23 percent higher than in 1980.[165] In November 1983, the Japanese scrambled 30 jet fighters on one occasion, the largest number in recent years, when 9 Soviet bombers flew close to southwest Japan before dispersing. A Japanese Defense Agency spokesman said that a new Soviet missile cruiser was identified sailing south through the Tsushima Strait as bombers flew overhead.[166]

c. *Propaganda and verbal pressure*

The Russians have also carried on a vigorous propaganda campaign designed to intimidate the Japanese as they have gravitated closer to the United States. A review of media materials for the past year suggest the growing intensity and hostility of this campaign, seeming to culminate in the KAL–007 incident of September 1983.[167]

One of the main themes in the Soviet propaganda attack is the charge that Japan is exhibiting a "dangerous militaristic tendency" and that militarism is on the rise. Soviet Foreign Minister Andrei Gromyko's diatribes against the alleged revival of Japanese militarism has placed the official stamp of approval on this particular propaganda line.[168]

Japanese Prime Minister Yasuhior Nakasone's statement that Japan should be "like an unsinkable aircraft carrier" against Soviet forces elicited perhaps the ultimate Soviet threat; namely, that such a policy "could spell a national disaster more serious than the one that befell [Japan] thirty-seven years ago."[169]

Aleksandr Bovin, a leading Soviet commentator for Izvestia and foreign policy adviser to the leadership, referring to the Nakasone remark in an interview in Japan, observed that "there are no unsinkable aircraft carriers." In a clear warning to the Japanese, he added: "to keep afloat, it is essential for Japan not to build up its military strength. . . ."[170]

Georgiy Arbatov, Director of the U.S.A.-Canada Institute and leading Soviet Americanist, made the same point a month before, also speaking to a Japanese audience. Responding to the Chinese panelist who charged that the SS-20's were a grave threat to

---

[165] Asian Security 1982, p. 58–59 and 6–8.

[166] The Washington Post, Nov. 30, 1983, p. A15.

[167] For a recent example, see, Modenov, S. Tokyo's Militaristic Syndrome. International Affairs, v. 12, Dec. 1983:83–87, 117.

[168] Dobson, Christopher. The Carrot and the Stick: Moscow Launches a Good Guy-Bad Guy Campaign Aimed at Discouraging Japan from Beefing Up its Defense Forces. Far Eastern Economic Review, June 2, 1983: 28–29.

[169] Wise, Allie. Missiles in Soviet Far East Likely to Dominate Soviet-Japanese Talks. RFE-RL, Radio Liberty Research, RL 264/83, July 14, 1983, p. 1–2. See also, Dobson, The Carrot and the Stick, p. 28–29. Actually what Nakasone said in Japanese in an interview with Washington Post editors on January 18, 1983, was that Japan should be "a big aircraft carrier" (Okina koku bokan) to block Russian planes. Nakasone's translator rendered this statement as "unsinkable aircraft carrier." (Goldman, Soviet Policy Toward Japan and the Strategic Balance in Northeast Asia, p. 13, footnote 15.)

[170] Mainichi Shimbun (Toyko), Dec. 30, 1983, p. 5, and Menon, Soviet Union in East Asia, p. 340.

Japan, China and other Asian nations, he said that the deployment may become necessary because of the "existing factors of instability as seen in the rapid militarization of Japan and the buildup of the U.S. 7th Fleet." Arbatov acknowledged that the Far East has become "an extremely dangerous region" and that the Soviet Union "cannot but be concerned about."[171]

d. Ambiguous aspects of Soviet perceptions of Japan

Virtually any action that the Japanese have taken in defense against what they perceive as a Soviet threat to their security has been judged by the Soviets to be a manifestation of militarism. Conclusion of the Sino-Japanese peace treaty in 1978 with its statement of warning against hegemonism in Asia was seen by Moscow as offensively anti-Soviet and fraught with serious long term strategic consequences.[172] Japan's acceptance of responsibility for patrolling the sea lanes 1,000 miles from the Home Islands and participation with the United States and other Pacific powers in joint sea lane safety exercises were met with Soviet charges that Japan and the United States were engaged in a "qualitative reorientaion" of their Security Treaty and that Japan had become the "Pentagon's hostage."[173]

With respect to the Northern Territories, the Soviets state categorically that there is simply nothing to discuss. In response to Japan's designation of February 7 to be "Northern Territorial Day," the Soviet Embassy made a representation to the Japanese Foreign Ministry, declaring that the decision was "an unfriendly act." to the Soviets, "There is no territorial issue of any kind existing in relations between the Soviet Union and Japan."[174]

Yet, so long as this matter is unsettled, relations between Japan and the Soviet Union will no doubt remain cool, and under these unfriendly conditions Japan is not likely to conclude a peace treaty with the Soviet Union. Thus the Soviet Union seems to be on an inflexible course regarding Japan. In fact an element of condescension colors the Russian attitude towards the Japanese—"a perfidious" people, one Soviet specialist on Asia described the Japanese. The Russians look upon Japan, Dibb notes, as a "fairly weak country militarily." They see no Japanese threat at present, but do foresee a danger in the future.[175]

Nonetheless, the Soviets value Japan as a trading partner and foresee a Japanese role in the development of Siberia, though under current conditions prospects have dimmed considerably.[176] Trade has grown from under $1 million in 1955 to $3.4 billion in 1979. Also Japan's use of the "trans-Siberian land-bridge" for trade from Japan to Western Europe overland across the Soviet Union has increased from 2,309 containers in 1971 to one million in 1982. Since 1970, $3 billion in Japanese credits, along with equipment

[171] Yomiuri Shimbun, (Toyko), Nov. 14, 1983, p. 12–13.
[172] Dibb, Soviet Capabilities, Interest and Strategies in East Asia, p. 157.
[173]Thornton, U.S.S.R. and Asia in 1982, p. 15.
[174] Asian Security 1982, p. 40.
[175] Dibb, Soviet Union as a Pacific Power, p. 243.
[176] For a commentrary on the failure of the economic connection, see, Thornton, U.S.S.R. and Asia in 1982, p. 14–16.

and advisers, have been given to the the Soviet Union for an assortment of projects in Siberia.[177]

Thus the Soviets perceive the Japanese ambiguously. They see them as a potential military adversary in their political and strategic orientation towards the United States, China and South Korea, an "awesome military power," one Soviet source said, by the end of the 1980's should their defense expenditures continue to increase by more than 7 percent.[178] To the Russians the thought of this vast configuration of power raises the specter of the historic "two-front threat," one in Europe, the other in Asia. Yet, on the other side of the equation is the positive reality that Japan, its economic power and technological know-how, has much to offer for strengthening the Soviet economy and particularly for developing the resources of Siberia. Japanese economic assistance could relieve the Soviets of a great and pressing economic burden.[179]

4. JAPAN'S RESPONSE: TOWARD A STRONGER DEFENSE

a. Popular awareness of the Soviet threat

The Japanese have perceived Soviet policy and activities in Asia as a threat to their security, and accordingly they have undertaken defense measures within the allowable limits of public opinion. Consequently, they have drawn closer to the United States and other politically like-minded countries of East Asia. And they have increasingly directed much of their constructive energies, notably economic assistance, to the area of historic Japanese influence, Southeast Asia.[180]

Awareness of the Soviet threat in Japan has been amply recorded in public opinion surveys. Despite the deep strains of pacifism in Japan as a result of defeat and destruction in World War II, and despite the inclination of the economic sector to stress the value of economic relations with Russia over military preparedness, the Japanese public in general clearly identifies the Soviet Union as its principal adversary. In a survey released on September 20, 1981 by the Prime Minister's office, 84 percent polled said that they "could not entertain friendly sentiments" toward the Soviet Union (the

---

[177] Menon, Soviet Union in East Asia, p. 340-341. See also Hewett, Ed. A and Herbert S. Levine. the Soviet Union's Economic Relations in Asia. In, Zagoria, Soviet Policy in East Asia, Chapt. 8. According to more recent statisitcs, Soviet-Japanese trade increased to $5.7 billion in 1982, but declined 25 percent in 1983 to $4.2 billion. (Stuart D. Goldman, Analyst in Soviet Affairs, CRS.)

[178] Menon, Soviet Union East Asia, p. 340-341, and Asian Security 1982, p. 40.

[179] For an analtyical commentary on the view of Soviet specialists on the Far East, see, Palmer, Soviet Perspectives in Asia, p. 9-13. One principal adviser to the CPSU placed the blame on the United States for "pressing Japan in an increasingly militaristic direction." Others denied Soviet responsibility, ridiculing the bogey of a "nonexistent Soviet military threat." To one scholar, the Japanese were simply a "perfidous people." For other commentaries, see U.S.A., Japan, South Korea: Sinister Triangle. New times (Moscow), November 1983:12-13; and Latyshev, I. Soviet-Japanese Relations at the Present Stage. Mirovaya Ekonomika I Mezhdunarodnyye Otnosheniya (Moscow), in Russian, No. 2, Feb. 1983:27-36, Translated in, U.S.S.R. Report, World Economy and International Relations, No 2, Feb. 1983, JPRS 83543, May 25, 1983.

[180] For a commentary on aspects of Japanese-American cooperation in response to the Soviet threat, see, Mike Mansfield. U.S. Ambassador to Japan. Danger Signals Across the Pacific: The Challenge of U.S.-Japan Cooperation. Speaking of Japan, v. 4, April 1983: 27-32. See also, Ambassador Mansfield's interview, Ways U.S. Can Cope with the Japanese Challenge. U.S. News & World Report, Nov. 28, 1983: 33-34. For a current assessment, see, Niksch, Larry A. Defense Issues in Japan-U.S. Relations: A Status Report. Washington, Congressional Research Service, Library of Congress, Feb. 14, 1984, 21 p.

same as in 1980). Other categories in the poll registered in descending percentages (and in importance) the same common theme; namely, distrust of Russia. Leading foreign policy specialists at the Tokyo's Research Institute for Peace and Security conclude: "These figures almost certainly give a fair picture of the view of the average Japanese toward the Soviet Union."[181]

Still, specialists like Scalapino have warned that the Japanese would move slowly and cautiously toward a limited defense program.[182]

But the KAL–007 crisis in September 1983 seems to have increased the Japanese public's antipathy toward the Soviet Union. A public opinion survey taken in the fall of 1984 reported that more than 90 percent of the Japanese now consider Soviet military power a threat to Japan, as compared with slightly more than half in polls taken in the spring of 1984.[183]

b. Elements in the Japanese response

Seemingly within the allowable limits of public opinion, the Japanese Government, particularly under Nakasone who assumed the Premiership in November 1982, has continued the pace of defense preparedness. In the heat of increased internal debate on defense Japan has taken other measures tightening its alignment with the anti-Soviet coalition taking shape in Asia.[184] Among the measures are:

—Conclusion of the Treaty of Friendship and Cooperation with China and the expansion of economic cooperation, solidifying the relationship in a new era of good feeling and linking Japan, via the "anti-hegemony clause," to China's efforts to counter Moscow's expansion in Asia;

---

[181] Asian Security 1982, p. 39.

[182] According to Scalapino, writing in the Spring of 1981, ". . . barring a major crisis in its relations with the U.S.S.R., Japan is likely to move in a cautious, incremental fashion during the next few years with respect to security policies. There is no evidence, for example, that Tokyo will go beyond extended sea-air lane patrols, military consultation with neighboring Asian states, joint military planning and exercises with the United States, assumption of U.S. base expenditures, and a commitment to a small, highly modern, defense-oriented military force taking little more than one percent of gross national product." (Scalapino, Robert A. Pacific Prospects. Washington Quarterly, v. 4, Spring 1981:7).

[183] DeYoung, Karen. Japanese See Soviet Saber Rattling as Aiding Nakasone's Policies. The Washington Post, Nov. 30, 1983, p. A15.

This writer was in Japan when the Korean 747 was shot down, addressing what could be termed "foreign policy elite groups" for USIA on Soviet-American relations in Tokyo, Sapporo, Osaka and Fukuoka. Even this limited exposure was sufficient to sense the widespread anger of the Japanese at the Soviet shoot-down. Many in the audiences felt that President Reagan's response was much too moderate.

For a brief but comprehensive report on the KAL incident, see, Soviet Downing of a South Korean Airliner. Washington, D.C., Foreign Affairs and National Defense Division, Library of Congress, Nov. 9, 1983, 20 p., Issue Brief: IB83146. See also, Westwood, James T. Japan and Soviet Power in the Pacific. Strategic Review, v. 11, Fall 1983: 27–35. Westwood writes: "The downing of the South Korean airliner over the Sea of Japan manifested both the extent of the Soviet Union's power base in the Pacific and Moscow's sensitivity regarding its military stakes in the region. . . . The airliner incident is thus a harbinger of troubled waters in the western Pacific, portending also increased demands on the military dimension of the U.S.-Japanese alliance."

[184] For a recent appraisal of Nakasone's diplomacy, see, Takubo, Tadae. First Round of Nakasone's Diplomacy. Asia Pacific Community, No. 21, Summer 1983: 1–10. Takubo writes: "Prime Minister Yasuhiro Nakasone's diplomacy . . . shows a fairly distinct direction. At least, his diplomacy is clearer and more easily understood than the diplomacy of his predecessor, former premier Zenko Suzuki . . . It would seem that Nakasone has chosen the role of a 'world statesman.' Perhaps, the circumstances of the present world situation left Nakasone little choice but to come forth with clear cut diplomacy." See also, Sherwin, Lawrence, Soviet-Japanese Relations Since Yasuhiro Nakasone Took Office. RFE–RL, Radio Liberty, RL 74/83, Feb. 9, 1983, p. 4.

—The steady tightening of the security bond between the United States and Japan (the Soviets described Japan as the newest member of NATO). Japan has taken such defense steps as: allowing the basing after 1985 of fighter bombers at Misawa in northern Honshu, placing them within range of strategic targets in the Soviet Far East; participation in "allied" naval exercises (for example, RIMPAC in 1980 and 1982); assuming responsibility for defending the sea lanes 1,000 miles southeast of Japan in response to the buildup of the Soviet Pacific fleet and to compensate for the diversion of vessels from the U.S. 7th Fleet to the Persian Gulf; and pledging to increase defense spending in 1982 and 1983.[185] The 1984 defense budget is 6.5 percent larger than that of 1983, totalling $12.5 billion, an increase over the 1983 budget of about $1 billion, amounting to just under 1 percent of Japan's GNP;[186]

—The decision to loan South Korea $4 billion after a Nakasone goodwill visit.[187]

—Meeting head-on such serious differences with the Russians as the fisheries issue and the Northern Territories. With respect to the latter question the Japanese have raised the Northern Territories issue to national prominence, making it a seriously and deeply felt irredentist matter;[188]

—In concert with the United States, instituting economic sanctions against the Soviet Union after the invasion of Afghanistan and initially supporting sanctions during the Polish crisis;[189] and finally,

—The adoption of a "comprehensive security" strategy, implying the use of Japan's vast economic power for security purposes, in combination with but subordinate to the military component,[190] though mindful of the constraints on Japan's military growth.

c. Focus on the LDC's of Southeast Asia

Japan's "comprehensive security" strategy, notably the economic component, has been directed partly at Southeast Asia, an historic region of Japanese interests. The irony of Soviet policy in Asia is that it is creating conditions in Southeast Asia and elsewhere in

---

[185] Dibb, Soviet Union as a Pacific Power, p. 243–244, and Menon, Soviet Union in East Asia, p. 340.

[186] The Washington Post, Jan. 25, 1984, p. A15, and The Christian Science Monitor, Jan. 26, 1984, p. 32. Still, Japan's defense spending remains under the one percent of GNP ceiling, and Nakasone's election defeat in December 1983 was interpreted by many as a set-back to his rearmament plans. (Stuart D. Goldman, Analyst in Soviet Affairs, CRS.)

[187] Menon, Soviet Union in East Asia, p. 340.

[188] On November 18, 1983, staff of CRS including the writer met with Mr. Kensaku Nomura, a member of the Hokkaido Prefectural Assembly and Chairman of the Special Committee on the Northern Territories. At the meeting Nomura emphasized that the reversion of the Northern Territories to Japan has received nationwide support: 40 of 47 prefectures have committees on reversion; 30 million people signed petitions for reversion.; and it is expected all 47 of the prefectures will have committees and accordingly raise the figures from 30 to 50 million. According to Nomura, this national aspiration for reversion cannot be suppressed; it is felt nationwide. "The Soviets took them," he said, "as a thief would steal. Thus there can be no conditional return; no quid pro quo." (Notes on the meeting.) For a presentation of the Japanese case, see, Japan's Northern Territories. Japan, Hokkaido Government, Sept. 1982, 21 p. (Compiled by the Japanese Ministry of Foreign Affairs.)

[189] Thornton, U.S.S.R. and Asia in 1982, p. 15.

[190] Asian Security 1982, p. 78. See also, Kraft, Joseph. Anchoring a Newly Assertive Japan. The Washinton Post, June 28, 1983, p. A15.

the Pacific region by resorting to military threats and pressures that have opened up renewed economic possibilities for Japan with political overtones.[191] A compelling force behind this renewed Japanese attention to Southeast Asia has been the natural search for markets; but, more importantly for the purposes of this study, it has also been the Soviet threat to Japan and its neighbors in the Asian-Pacific region that has created parallel if not common interests.

Perhaps one of Japan's most important contributions to reconstituting the balance of power in Asia against the Soviets and thus its most crucial contributions to international stability lies in maintaining the steady growth of the LDC's in the Pacific Economic Basin community. According to Jospeh Kraft, an American foreign policy observer, a Pacific Economic Basin community, akin to the European Economic Community, is "only a gleam in the eye so far." Disparate political systems, rival economic interests plus bitter memories of past grievance now stand in the way of progress. No organizing principle has yet come into view, (though the Soviet threat is now providing a good deal of kinetic energy in that direction). In the long run, Kraft avers, the Pacific Basin "provides the natural context for Japan's outward thrust, and eventually for that of China."[192]

Other foreign policy specialists have called attention to Japan's economic role in Southeast Asia. Seweryn Bialer, Soviet specialist at Columbia University, recently predicted in a discussion in Japan that Japan's role in international relations "will become increasingly important." He explained:

We are entering a new era of technological revolution; Japan and the United States will be the superpowers for that era. I think that Japan will be playing a greater role in world politics. It would then be impossible to separate a political role from an economic, technological role.[193]

Li Shenzhi, Director of the Institute of American Studies, Academy of Social Sciences of China, agreed with this prognosis, attributing the importance of Japan's future role to its economic strength and foreign policy. Li Shenzhi forsees the friendship between China and Japan as becoming "one of the pillars of peace in Asia." [194]

Speaking for the Japanese, Seizaburo Sato, a professor at Tokyo University, contrasted Soviet reliance on military power ("more than any other country") with Japan's economic success. He recalled that South Korea and the ASEAN nations had achieved "remarkable developments" in the early 1970's. While crediting those countries and their peoples with these achievements, Sato added quite rightly but with restraint, "I believe that Japan's role particularly its economic cooperation and investments, should also be appreciated."[195]

Japan is also playing a prominent economic role in India. With its basic industrial plant in place, India is looking toward more advanced technology from Japan and the West to fill its future needs.

---

[191] Asian Security 1982, p. 7–8, and Dibb, Soviet Union as a Pacific Power, p. 239, ff. 5.
[192] The Washington Post, June 28, 1983, p. A15.
[193] Yomiuri Shimbun (Tokyo), Nov. 14, 1983, p. 12–13.
[194] Ibid.
[195] Ibid.

For example, India is collaborating with the Japanese on automobile design and production and is searching for collaborative arrangements for the transfer of high technology from the West. Japan is clearly destined to play a most important role in this foremost of Third World countries.[196]

Japan's desire to strengthen its roots as an Asian power, play a larger role in Asian affairs, and forge closer political and economic ties with the Third World and Nonalignment Movement was graphically demonstrated in mid-May 1984 when Prime Minister Nakasone toured India and Pakistan, the first Japanese leader to visit these countries in 23 years. Since taking office in November 1982, Nakasone has visited virtually every Asian country for the purpose of getting personally acquainted with their leaders, learning firsthand their views on regional and world issues, and gaining knowledge of their problems. In Pakistan, Nakasone pledged more economic assistance. In India, he gave assurances that Japan would work hard to breathe new life into the "North-South" dialogue for liberalized trade and soft loans for poor countries, stressing particularly that Japan should make more effective use of its economic strength to promote friendly relations with the LDC's. Japanese Government sources hailed the diplomatic tour as a "magnificent success." [197]

5. RUSSIA'S POLICY TOWARD JAPAN: CONTRADICTORY AND COUNTERPRODUCTIVE

a. Forsaking economic gains to project military power

Running through Soviet policy towards Japan is the persisting contradiction that the Russian's obsessive concern for projecting military power is creating a formidable, and heretofore quiescent, adversary out of the only Asian nation that could be the most useful in easing the burden of their failing economy and particularly in developing their most valuable but vulnerable region, Siberia and the Soviet Far East. Caught up in an action-reaction syndrome, tensions have spiralled in Soviet-Japanese relations. It is hard to escape the conclusion that the Soviet Union was in this case as often times in East-West relations the prime move of discord.

Japan and the Soviet Union are, as American economists Ed. A. Hewett and Herbert S. Levine note, "the most natural trading partners," where the economic power of the one and the economic needs of the other are complementary.[198] But their economic-political relations continue to deteriorate with no prospect that the trend will be reversed in the near future. Thus Hewett and Levine echo the criticism of Ambassador Mansfield and others when they say, "it is striking how inflexible and clumsy the Soviets have been in their dealings with the Japanese." [199]

---

[196] The New York Times, March 15, 1984. p. A16.

[197] Murray, Geofrey. Nakasone Tries to have East Meet East by Touring Asian Nations. The Christian Science Monitor, May 10, 1984, p. 10.

[198] Hewett and Levine, Soviet Union's Economic Relations, p. 213.

[199] Ibid., p. 222. The quotation continues: "Soviet leaders seem unwilling to make political concessions of any sort, and negotiations on some economic cooperative projects frequently stall over Soviet insistence on very favorable terms."

But this clumsiness goes far beyond negotiations to the formulation and execution of foreign policy in Asia.

b. A self-fulfilling prophecy

Curiously, Soviet policy towards Japan is another case of a self-fulfilling prophecy. Soviet propaganda is rich with accusations of the revival of Japanese militarism. A reluctant pacifistically-inclined Japan is indeed rearming, but in a legitimate response to the projection of a threatening Soviet military power in Asia that places Japanese national interests, perhaps even survival, in jeopardy.

Soviet propaganda accuses the Japanese of reviving the age old dream of the Greater East Asia Co-Prosperity Sphere. Supplementing the accusation that Japan aspires to a leading role in Asia, if necessary by force, one high official in the Soviet Foreign Ministry said at a scholarly conference on Asia: "Most Japanese want Japan to be a great political power. In particular, they regard Southeast Asia as a sphere of influence." [200]

Yet, Russia's provocative and militarily-oriented foreign policy in Northeast Asia combined with the expansion of its military and political influence in Indochina has compelled the Japanese to look for like-minded allies in Southeast Asia. Their purpose: To reconstitute this future sphere of influence, but this time in an arrangement based on mutual self-interest. In fact, Scalapino predicts, speaking of Southeast Asia, "Japan is destined to play a growing economic role in the region, one of vital significance to all of the developing societies." [201]

Donald S. Zagoria and Sheldon W. Simon, American specialists on Asia, even urge the United States to encourage Japan to increase its economic role in the region, where the willing, but still suspicious, LDC's are reaching out for more economic assistance than the Japanese are yet prepared to offer. [202]

The Japanese have already greatly expanded their economic and political ties with ASEAN. According to Zagoria, Japan is now the first or second largest investor and trade partner of each noncommunist country in the area. In addition to establishing regular ministerial contacts with the ASEAN governments, Japan has also expanded considerably its cultural relations in the area. [203] The effect of this expanding Japanese influence is to deny the Soviets access to a strategically and politically important Third World area in Southeast Asia.

Thus what the Russians have done by their highly militaristic foreign policy and their heavy handed treatment of the Japanese is to close off access to a valuable and saving economic resource, and to push Japan into becoming a formidable part of what Zagoria calls that "massive barrier" of nations in the Asian-Pacific region blocking the expansion of Soviet power and influence in East Asia. [204]

---

[200] Palmer, Soviet Perspectives on Peace and Security in Asia, p. 10.
[201] Scalapino, Pacific Prospects, p. 12.
[202] Zagoria and Simon, Soviet Policy in Southeast Asia, p. 173.
[203] Zagoria, Strategic Environment in East Asia, p. 8.
[204] Ibid., p. 7.

E. Stiffening ASEAN Resistance to Soviet Expansion

1. Soviet Policy Objectives in Southeast Asia

a. Satisfy strategic needs for expansion

Soviet policy objectives in Southeast Asia seem designed to satisfy the larger strategic needs for expanding Soviet power in Asia, the Pacific and the Middle East. Acting initially in a power vacuum created by the withdrawal of the United States from Vietnam, the Soviets appear to have set their sights on expanding their influence throughout the Indochinese Peninsula, using Vietnam as their base and promoting a trend toward neutralism within the ASEAN nations. They seem bent on drawing the Communist states of Vietnam, Laos and Kampuchea into the Soviet orbit. Their ultimate purpose seems to be the removal of U.S. influence from Southeast Asia, having once again been committed in the region, the containment of China, and the creation of a new balance of power favorable to Moscow.[205]

Linked to these political objectives are the strategic, and they can be summed up in the word, "chokepoints." For critical chokepoints athwart the sea lanes connecting Northeast Asia with the oil-rich Middle East lie in the region of Southeast Asia. The most significant is the Strait of Malacca bounded by Malaysia and Singapore on the north and Sumatra on the south. By having secure naval and air bases in Vietnam, the Soviets accrue two strategic benefits. First is the potential for influencing, and, in extremis, interdicting the flow of traffic along the sea lanes from the Sea of Japan and the East China Sea in Northeast Asia, through the Formosan Strait, the South China Sea, and on to the Indian Ocean and the Middle East. The second benefit is access to the South Pacific, opening up still further the Asian-Pacific Basin to the projection of Soviet power.[206] (See map 5.)

---

[205] Asian Security 1982, p. 35, and Zagoria and Simon, Soviet Policy in Southeast Asia, p. 153–155. For a detailed examination of Vietnam's activities in Indochina and its implications for U.S. policy, see, U.S. Congress. Senate. Committee on Foreign Relations. Vietnam's Future Policies and Role in Southeast Asia. Prepared by the Foreign Affairs and National Defense Division, Congressional Research Service, Library of Congress. 97th Congress, 2d Session. Washington, U.S., Govt. Print. Off., 1982, 72 p. (Committee Print). See also, U.S. Congress. House. Committee on Foreign Affairs. Subcommittee on Asian and Pacific Affairs. Asian Security Environment: 1980. Report of the Special Study Mission to Asia , January 5–23, 1980. 96th Congress, 2d Session Washington, U.S. Govt. Print. Off., 1980, 96 p. (Committee Print).

See also, HFAC, Soviet Role in Asia, 183, p. 205–235 (Testimony of Dr. Douglas Pike, Southeast Asian specialist at the University of California, Berkeley.)

[206] For articles discussing this important problem, see, Vertzberger, Yaacov. The Malacca/Singapore Straits. Asian Survey, v. 22, July 1982: 609–629, and his, The Malacca/Singapore Straits: The Suez of South-East Asia. London, Institute for the Study of Conflict, 1982. 28 p.; Leifer, Michael. The Security of Sea-lanes in South-East Asia. Survival, v. 25, Jan.-Feb. 1983: 16–24; Train, The Growing Soviet Naval Menace, p. 56–61; Menon, China and the Soviet Union in Asia, p. 331, (Menon speaks of Chinese concern for the "premeditated Soviet effort to control the 'dumbbell' area formed by the Straits of Malacca and the two great bodies of water to its east and west"); and Leighton, Marian K. Soviets Still Play Dominoes in Asia. The Wall Street Journal, Oct. 14, 1983, p. 30.

106

Map 5
Southeast Asia

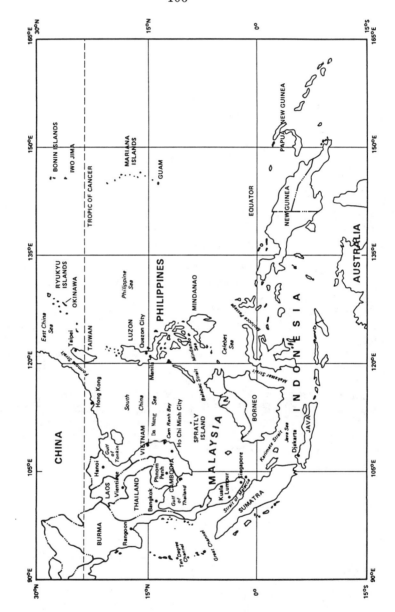

b. Military power: Factors determining relations

Soviet relations with the Third World states of Southeast Asia have been determined, as elsewhere in Asia, by three critical developments: the Soviet invasion of Afghanistan; Soviet support for the Vietnamese invasion of Kampuchea; and the Soviet military build-up in Asia.

The Soviet Union's material and political support of Vietnam's invasion of Kampuchea early in 1979, more than Afghanistan, seems to have decisively shaped the international politics of Southeast Asia. Soviet power was introduced directly into Southeast Asia via its alliance with Vietnam, the strongest regional military power. For the first time, ASEAN nations began to look at the Soviets as a threat to their security, perhaps equal to the long-standing threat posed by China.[207]

In brief, Kampuchea became the central element determining ASEAN relations with Moscow, particularly in circumscribing the range of Soviet influence in this area of the Third World.

The Soviet military buildup in Asia reinforced ASEAN concerns about Soviet ambitions in the region. Their anxieties were particularly heightened by the growing presence of Soviet naval and air power in neighboring Vietnam. A Soviet threat to the vital sea lanes and chokepoints of Southeast Asia could no longer be viewed as an abstract geopolitical problem but rather as a real possibility.[208]

2. EFFECTS OF SOVIET POLICY IN SOUTHEAST ASIA

a. Increased cohesion of ASEAN

Russia's expansionist policy in Asia, particularly its support of Vietnam's invasion of Kampuchea, accelerated the unity of ASEAN. For these Third World countries, Kampuchea was to become, as Japan's Research Institute for Peace and Security termed it, "a rallying call" for greater cohesion within ASEAN against the Russians and the Vietnamese. A high mark in this cohesion was perhaps reached in July 1981 when the ASEAN Foreign Ministers conference urged the withdrawal of foreign troops from Kampuchea and the dispatch of a United Nations Peacekeeping Force, a proposal later endorsed by the United Nations.[209]

Prior to the Kampuchea invasion, ASEAN had looked upon the Soviet Union with "guarded reserve," as Dr. Dieter Heinzig, a specialist at the Federal Institute for Eastern and International Studies in Cologne, West Germany, put it. They hoped for an eventual neutral and pacified Southeast Asia. But the invasion, along with other acts of Soviet-Vietnamese solidarity, transformed ASEAN's perception of the Soviet Union. Since then, the member states have seen the Soviets, in Heinzig's words, "as a power commanding a

---

[207] Porter, Soviet Union in Asia: A Strategic Survey, p. 3.

[208] For commentary on the Soviet-Vietnamese alliance in the context of the growing importance of Southeast Asia's waterways, see, Zagoria and Simon, Soviet Policy in Southeast Asia, p. 153–154.

[209] Asian Security 1982, p. 10.

concrete threat potential." [210] For as Menon writes, the reality is that Kampuchea is "garrisoned with Vietnamese troops and ruled by a government beholden to Hanoi and Moscow." [211]

ASEAN has reacted in a variety of ways to the Soviet threat in Southeast Asia. They have taken such united measures as significantly increasing defense spending, staging joint exercises and supporting standardization of weapons. [212] They rejected Moscow's request for berthing rights for warships; they took stronger action than ever before against the spread of Soviet espionage; they have looked upon Soviet proffers of good intentions with considerable official skepticism; and they have turned aside Soviet threats and other displays of official displeasure. According to Heinzig, "the ASEAN countries appear to have accustomed themselves to Moscow's policy of mixing threats with enticements in much the same way as the Western European countries have done." [213]

Singapore seems to have been the most outspoken of ASEAN member states in condemning the Soviets and Vietnamese for their aggressive policies. Among the actions taken is their expressed willingness to invoke a form of economic sanctions against the Soviets by cutting back repair of Soviet merchant ships, a major economic undertaking by the two countries. [214]

Differences exist in ASEAN on approaches to the Kampuchean question; they revolve around qualitative perceptions of the Sino-Soviet threat. ASEAN strategy, both regional and global, is based on the assumption that the most effective way of countering Soviet influence in Southeast Asia is to checkmate Vietnam's expansion into Kampuchea. An alternative policy has been advanced in Indonesia which shares with Malaysia a deep distrust of Beijing and together have a somewhat different perception of the threat from that of the other ASEAN states. This policy suggests that agreement with Hanoi on a Vietnamized Kampuchea would significantly reduce Vietnam's dependence on Moscow, bring about the Soviet withdrawal from Southeast Asia, and convert Indochina into a welcomed buffer against China. (Yet it is important to note that Malaysia never fully endorsed the Indonesian view and has strongly backed a Vietnamese withdrawal from Kampuchea.) [215] This idea has failed to gain acceptance in ASEAN, notably among Thailand, Singapore and the Philippine Islands. Seeing the threat from a different perspective, Thailand, supported by Singapore and the Philipines in their inclination toward Beijing, refute any compromise that does not include Vietnam's withdrawal from Kampuchea. [216]

Nonetheless, despite differences all ASEAN countries share to a greater or lesser extent the belief that they are potentially threatened in the long term, particularly by China. For the short and medium term, however, they see Vietnam by itself and as a proxy linked in alliance with the Soviet Union as the principal

[210] Heinzig, Dieter. The South-East Asian Countries' Perception of the Soviet Union. Cologne, West Germany, Federal Institute for Eastern and International Studies, Report No. 24/1983, p. 35.
[211] Menon, Soviet Union in East Asia, p. 341.
[212] Menon, China and the Soviet Union in Asia, p. 340.
[213] Heinzig, South-East Asian Countries' Perception of the Soviet Union, p. 36.
[214] Zagoria and Simon, Soviet Policy in Southeast Asia, p. 171.
[215] Larry A. Niksch, Specialist in Asian Affairs, CRS.
[216] Zagoria and Simon, Soviet Policy in Southeast Asia, p. 157–158, 161–162.

menace.[217] This shared concern has brought them together as a vital part of the much larger "massive barrier" taking shape against Soviet expansion in Asia, and though divided in some respects, Scalapino predicts an optimistic outcome; namely, "the gradual strengthening of regional ties through ASEAN and reasonably rapid economic gains."[218]

b. Restructuring the international politics of Southeast Asia

(1) The Soviet Union: "The agent of major change"

Soviet policy in Southeast Asia has also brought about the restructuring of the international politics of the region. In Indochina, as Menon, notes, Soviet military power has been "the agent of major change" in recent years.[219] Once on the fringe of Southeast Asian politics, the Soviet Union has now become a principal actor in the area as Vietnam's mentor, major supporter and ally. The Soviets seek to achieve their purposes in a contradictory policy that supports Vietnam's military aggression and yet attempts to conciliate the ASEAN countries with proffers of trade and aid [220] and a willingness to oppose further Vietnamese military expansion. Soviet policy in Southeast Asia, based on regional, global and strategic expectations, envisions the projection of its power into the Asian-Pacific region. In brief, to transform the status quo into a balance of forces more favorable to Moscow.[221]

(2) China and ASEAN on the Defensive

China, now encircled by adversaries and on the defensive, hopes to counter the Soviet thrust to the south by creating a power balance that includes ASEAN, Japan and the United States.[222]

The ASEAN countries look to a future Southeast Asia pacified and neutral. Meanwhile, they must reconcile their own differences and unite with China and other nations in the Asian-Pacific region in a protective anti-Soviet coalition.[223]

(3) Japan's "comprehensive strategy": "Bridge" to Vietnam

In pursuit of its "comprehensive strategy,"Japan has carved out a special place for itself in the politics of Southeast Asia.[224] It supports ASEAN countries politically and particularly economically with outlays of foreign aid, trade and investment; but at the same time Japan maintains a limited dialogue with Hanoi.[225] In their search for stability in Southeast Asia and curtailment of the Soviet presence in a more independent Vietnam, the Japanese see their

---

[217] Heinzig, South-East Asian Countries' Perception of the Soviet Union, p. 36.
[218] Scalapino continues: "Here, the rich resources, trained manpower, and leadership commitments combine to offer more hope than in many parts of the late-developing world. For the Singaporeans, the Malaysians, the Thai—and even the Filipinos and Indonesians—the era ahead promises a better life, punctuated, however, in some instances with periodic ethnic troubles and political upheavals." (Pacific Prospects, p. 12.)
[219] Menon, Soviet Union in East Asia, p. 341.
[220] Robinson, Soviet Union and Asia in 1981, p. 23–24.
[221] Zagoria and Simon, Soviet Policy in Southeast Asia, p. 162–163.
[222] Ibid., p. 160; Menon, Soviet Union in East Asia, p. 343; and Harris, China's Third World Courtship, p. 132–133.
[223] Zagoria, Strategic Environment in East Asia, p. 3–13.
[224] Zagoria and Simon, Soviet Policy In Southeast Asia, p. 173.
[225] Zagoria, Strategic Environment in East Asia, p. 7–9, and the Washington Post, June 6, 1983, p. A15.

role in this complex international structure as a "bridge" connecting Vietnam with ASEAN and the other nations opposed to Soviet-Vietnamese aspirations.[226]

(4) United States: A recommitment

The United States, having once again been committed to Southeast Asia (as recently demonstrated by the tour of Secretary of State George Shultz of the Far East in January-February 1983 and of South and Southeast Asia in June and July), now seems to be moving in the direction of greater involvement, though not sufficiently rapid to please some ASEAN leaders.[227] Like the Soviet Union, U.S. interests seem to be regional, strategic and global. Accordingly, it plays a major role in thwarting Soviet expanionist ambitions in the region.[228]

(5) Taiwan: Reevaluating an "Outcast"?

And finally Taiwan, a virtual "outcast" in the politics of East Asia, has potentially an important place in the evolving anti-Soviet alignment. Along with South Korea, Taiwan has come to be looked upon, particularly in the international business community, as an important part of the evolving East Asian economic order.[229] Strategically located along the Formosa Strait, Taiwan also holds what some may term a commanding position along the interior sea lanes stretching from Northeast to Southeast Asia.[230]

This strategic reality has not escaped Soviet attention. From March 1979 to July 1982, Soviet combat vessels and merchant ships have transited the waters off the east and west coasts of Taiwan some 2,392 times, according to the Taipei report. On June 27, 1982, a Soviet task force composed of one missile launching destroyer, one frigate and one corvette, moved through the Formosa Strait southward.[231] One authoritative high ranking military source stressed the frequency of Soviet transiting the Strait both with bombers and warships. As recently as February 6, 1984, a TU-95 Soviet bomber violated Taiwan's airspace. Taiwan's fighter aircraft scrambled and kept close watch of the plane before it flew away.[232]

Should Soviet activity become more threatening in East Asia, it is possible that Taiwan's part in an anti-Soviet arrangement could be more seriously considered, despite the enduring controversy with Beijing.[233]

---

[226] Murray, Geoffrey. Japan Seeks Diplomatic "Bridge" to Vietnam, But No Results So Far. The Christian Science Monitor, Jan. 19, 1984, p. 14.

[227] Quinn-Judge, Paul. Vietnam Legacy Curbs U.S. Role in Southeast Asia. The Christian Science Monitor , June 30, 1983, p. 1.

[228] Asian Security 1982, p. 10; Moritz, Frederic A. Southeast Asia: ASEAN and Its Communist Neighbors. the Christian Science Monitor, Mar. 4, 1983, p. 1213; the Washington Times, June 28, 1983, p. 5A; the Christian Science Monitor, June 15, 1983, p. 3; and Scalapino, Pacific Prospects, p. 12.

[229] Ibid., p. 11. Scalapino speaks of Taiwan doing "extraordinarily well" economically.

[230] Prittie, Terence. Strategic Balance in the Pacific. Soviet Analyst. v. 11, Jan. 27, 1982:4-5.

[231] Military Requirements for Advanced Aircraft. Part 2: Current Threat Assessment. Taipei, Taiwan, Institute of International Relations, National Chengchi University, June 1982, p. 22.

[232] FBIS 049, Taipei CNA in English, 1450 GMT, Feb. 6, 1984.

[233] For a discussion of Taiwan's role in defense of the Asian-Pacific region, see, Cross, Charles T. Taipei's Identity Crisis. Foreign policy, no. 51, Summer 1983:60-63. Cross explains the growing U.S. interest in the Western Pacific, notably the increase of Soviet naval power, adding, "Moreover, the concern of East Asian countries over oil increases the importance of protecting

Reaction within East Asia to Soviet policy has thus had the effect of restructuring the international politics of Southeast Asia. Forces are at work that suggest a growing alignment of countries opposed to Soviet expansion in Asia.[234]

c. Denying Soviets a Third World target

(1) Political alienation

Moscow's policy in Southeast Asia has also had the effect of denying the Soviet Union a choice Third World target. As in the case of Japan and China, Russia's pursuit of an expansionist foreign policy using military means has converted ASEAN into an inveterate adversary.

The alignment of international forces in Southeast Asia has placed the Soviet Union clearly on the outside. As an outsider, its range of influence has been drastically reduced. Soviet sources convincingly reveal the extent of their political estrangement in the region.[235] And this estrangement is reinforced by the dim prospects for peace in Kampuchea upon which partly hinges justification for the Soviet presence in the region.

In recent years the Soviets have witnessed a worsening of their relations with ASEAN. For example, attempts to coerce or seduce Thailand into a collective security arrangement by exploiting its fears of Vietnam led to rejection and a closer alignment with China.[236]

Specific anti-Soviet actions taken by ASEAN countries suggest the depth of their distrust of and disaffection with Moscow—Zagoria and Simon speak of a "massive suspicion."[237] Singapore and Indonesia, for example, expelled Soviet diplomats in early 1982 for

---

the sea lanes; Taiwan's location puts it in a key position for the naval defense of the lifelines of Japan, South Korea, and a large portion of the Chinese mainland as well." (p. 61–62)

For a comprehensive commentary on the problem of security of sea lanes (SLOC's) in the Pacific Basin with some emphasis on the Formosan Strait as one of other critical chokepoints, see, Tun-hwa Ko and Yu-ming Shaw, eds. Sea Lane Security in the Pacific Basin. Taipei, Taiwan, ROC, The Asia and World Institute, 1983, 136 p. (The Asia and World Monograph Series, No. 29, September 1983). This monograph contains the proceedings of The Conference on Sea Lane Security in the Pacific Basin held in San Francisco on Sept. 23–25. Papers were delivered and commented upon by specialists from the United States, Japan, South Korea and Taiwan. In the Executive Summary of general conclusions agreed to by the Conference is the statement that the "recent growth of the Soviet military in the Far East provides the greatest potential threat to the SLOC's, particularly in case of war." (p. 132)

See also, Lasater, Martin L. Taiwan: Facing Mounting Threats. Washington Heritage Foundation, 1984. 78 p., and Scalapino, Robert A. Uncertainties in Future Sino-U.S. Relations. Orbis, v. 26, Fall 1982:681–696.

[234]Zagoria, Strategic Environment in East Asia, p. 7. See also, Pike, Douglas. Southeast Asia and the Superpowers: The Dust Settles. Current History, v. 82, Apr. 1983:145–148, 179–180. Pike examines Southeast Asia's relations with the United States, the Soviet Union and China, and suggests that regionalism provides the best hope for peace, stability and economic development in Southeast Asia.

For a recent appraisal of Taiwan in the East Asian political setting, see, Johnson, Chalmers. East Asia: Another Year of Living Dangerously. In, America and the World, 1983. Foreign Affairs, v. 62, 1984:737–738. Johnson concludes: "The political skill shown in recent years by the Taiwanese in running their high-growth capitalist developmental state is, or should be, a model for the rest of the East Asia and much of the Third World." (p. 738)

[235] See, for example, Bulai, I. The Shady Aims of the "Pacific Community." International Affairs (Moscow), Jan. 1983:128–132.

[236] Porter. Soviet Union in Asia: A Strategic Survey, p. 3.

[237] Zagoria and Simon, Soviet Policy in Southeast Asia, p. 170.

espionage in what was described as a concerted display of their animosity against the Soviet Union.[238]

(2) Economic deterrent

Economic growth within ASEAN has acted as a strong deterrent to Soviet economic penetration. ASEAN has experienced a remarkable sustained economic growth rate of 6–10 percent per year.[239] According to Kishore Mahbubani, Deputy Chief of Mission of the Singapore Embassy in Washington, "The ASEAN countries have the fastest growing economies of the Third World and, combined together, form the fifth largest trading partner of the United States." A "testimony to the growing significance of ASEAN," Mahbubani continues, is the fact that the foreign ministers of the United States, Japan, the European Community, Canada, Australia and New Zealand participate annually in the meetings of ASEAN's foreign ministers.[240]

Moreover, Soviet trade with the ASEAN countries has been small, and with all East Asia, "meager," according to Menon. No other East Asian states, except for Indochina, Mongolia and North Korea, send more than 4 percent of their exports to the Soviet Union or imports more than 4 percent from it. ASEAN buys less than 0.5 percent of its imports from the Soviet Union.[241] Even for military assistance, the non-Communist states of East Asia have looked to the United States and Western Europe; between 1970 and 1980 none purchased arms from the Soviet Union.[242]

Soviet economic aid has been minimal, and technical assistance negligible.[243] Examination of standard U.S. Government sources on Soviet aid to the non-Communist Third World suggests little or no recent activity in ASEAN. Indeed, ASEAN looks to the United States and especially Japan, the latter now playing a major role in the economic diplomacy of Southeast Asia.[244] However, the Soviets

---

[238] Porter, Soviet Union in Asia: A Strategic Survey, p. 3, and Thornton, U.S.S.R. and Asia in 1982, p. 18. For examples of Thailand's displeasure with Soviet practices, see, Zagoria and Simon, Soviet Policy in Southeast Asia, p. 170–171. Thailand has served as a regional center for Soviet diplomatic and intelligence activities for some years with an embassy staff much larger than required for normal business.

[239] Thomas, Their Pacific Fleet, p. 86. See also, Asian Security 1982, p. 15–16, and The Washington Post, June 30, 1983, p. A27.

[240] Mahbubani, Kishore. The Kampuchean Problem: A Southeast Asian Perception. Foreign Affairs, Winter 1983/84: 421. Mahbubani quotes approvingly Lawrence B. Krause, an Asian specialist, who wrote that ASEAN countries "have been experiencing what can be described as a peaceful and orderly revolution. Dramatic changes have occurred in their political, social and cultural life." And then Mahbubani cites these supporting facts: Thailand now enjoys a per capita income of $800, compared with Vietnam's $189; Thailand's gross national product is larger than that of Vietnam, Laos and Kampuchea combined. ASEAN's combined population is 275 million, five times that of Vietnam. ASEAN's combined GNP amounts to over $200 billion, more than 20 times that of Vietnam. (p. 411)

[241] Menon, Soviet Union in East Asia, p. 314.

[242] Ibid.

[243] Ibid.

[244] Zagoria, Strategic Environment in East Asia, p. 8. The Japanese Cabinet adopted a 1984 budget on January 25, 1984, allowing for an increase in foreign aid of 9.7 percent or a total of $2.3 billion. On a percentage basis foreign aid was the only area to get a larger increase than the defense budget. (The New York Times, Jan. 26, 1984, p. A3.) Most of the aid funds will go to large development projects—an electronics factory in India, a power plant in Malaysia, rather than small-scale food or health programs. The largest share of foreign aid, 70 percent, has been allocated to Asia. (The New York Times, Jan. 29, 1984, p. E5.) For an analysis of Japan's role in Southeast Asia, see, Matsuzaka, Hideo. Future of Japan-ASEAN Relations. Asia Pacific Community, No. 21, Summer 1983:11–22.

have enjoyed some success in shipping services, notably in ship repairs and in cross trades linking foreign ports.[245]

Perhaps Zagoria and Simon best summed up Soviet economic activity in ASEAN when they described it as being "miniscule" and a "weak reed" upon which to build influence.[246] According to Hewett and Levine, the Soviet Union is a "minor economic factor" in Southeast Asia, but they add the qualifier, *"now"*, explaining that Russia's superpower status and its constant interest in the region suggest "the possibility of a much more significant economic role in the future." [247]

In brief, an economically strong ASEAN with prospects for a bright economic future acts as a formidable deterrent to Soviet penetration, and along with the factors noted above has thus far effectively denied the Soviet Union a choice area of the Third World.[248] Mahbubani concludes, "There is virtually no other part of the Third World that the United States can point to as a similar 'success story' of U.S. foreign policy." [249]

(3) Unrelenting Soviet drive for advantage: the Philippine case

Yet the Soviets do not acquiesce passively in the multiple counterpressures from the ASEAN states. They do seek out cracks in its unity to exploit. In the case of the Philippines, the Soviets have given special attention to the Philippines in recent years.[250] For example, the Soviets voiced steady criticism of the agreement on U.S. bases in the Philippines when it was being reconsidered in 1983. They underscored the power of the opposition movement within the country against "the American military presence," citing the relationship as a classic case of "neo-colonialism." As one Pravda commentator said, the "Filipinos to do not want to remain hostages to the Pentagon.[251]

Moreover, the Soviets have also been politically active. For example, they have undertaken extensive international exchanges, such as exchanges of visiting political leaders. They have clearly sought to exploit these exchanges to their advantage.[252] And the Filipinos on their part have welcomed visiting Soviet officials, creating thereby an opening for Soviet political messages. In April 1983, I.P. Kalin, deputy chairman of the U.S.S.R. Supreme Soviet Presidium, headed a Soviet delegation to the Philippines. On this occasion

---

In 1982, the Soviet Union concluded a scientific and technical cooperation agreement with the Philippines to build a cement plant. If completed, this project will represent the first Soviet-built industrial plant in the region. (Thornton, U.S.S.R. and Asia in 1982, p. 19.) For a commentary on increased cultural, scientific and economic cooperation, see, Metro Manila Times in English, Dec. 4, 1983, p. 4, in FBIS, Daily Report, Soviet Union, v. 3, Dec. 7, 1983, p. E1-E2.

[245] Hewett and Levine, Soviet Union's Economic Relations, p. 210-211, and Zagoria and Simon, Soviet Policy in Southeast Asia, p. 169-170.

[246] Zagoria and Simon, Soviet Policy in Southeast Asia, p. 169-170.

[247] Hewett and Levine, Soviet Union's Economic Relations, p. 202.

[248] Scalapino not only foresees "the gradual strengthening of regional ties through ASEAN" but also "reasonably rapid economic gains." Economic resources, trained manpower and leadership commitments combine with ASEAN "to offer more hope than in many parts of the late-developing world." (Scalapino, Pacific Prospects, p. 12.)

[249] Mahbubani, Kampuchean Problem, p. 421.

[250] See, HFAC, Soviet Union and the Third World, 1977, p. 92-94.

[251] Pravda (Moscow) in Russian, June 5, 1983, 1st ed., p. 5, in FBIS Daily Report, Soviet Union, v. 3, June 7, 1983, p. E1.

[252] See, for example, the coverage of the visit to Moscow by a group of Philippine parliamentarians in December 1982. (Izvestiya [Moscow] in Russian, Dec. 8, 1982, Morning ed., p. 4, in FBIS Daily Report, Soviet Union, v. 3, Dec. 17, 1982, p. E1-E2.

Kalin acclaimed the expansion of trade and cultural ties between both countries, and, reiterating the standard peace theme, noted that this visit gave him the opportunity to explain "the immutable course of the peace-loving foreign policy of the Soviet State, which advocates the development of equitable and mutually advantageous cooperation with all countries." Speaking of cultural relations, Kalin said, "Cultural ties between our countries are developing exceptionally fruitfully."[253]

And the Filipinos themselves have responded agreeably to this exceptional Soviet attention. A report in a Manila newspaper in December 1983 headlined, "U.S.S.R.-Philippines: Successful Rapprochment," provides a measure of this reaction. The occasion was the conclusion of the Philippine exhibition of industrial and consumer goods in Moscow. The account elaborated effusively on the State of relations, concluding that "the experience of the past seven years provides concrete evidence of the fact that Soviet-Philippine relations are developing in the right direction."[254]

Thus the Soviets have achieved some success in the area of political and cultural exchanges and in getting some economic access to the Philippines. In addition, there are vulnerabilities that could potentially be exploited that if successful could open the way for greater Soviet influence. One such vulnerability is the existence of a deep nationalistic, anti-American element in the Government and an opposition that might favor closer ties with Moscow. The other is the potentiality for internal political and economic turmoil that could endanger U.S.-Philippine ties and give the Soviets greater opportunities for expanding their influence.[255]

Thus, the Soivets do not take their political alienation from ASEAN as a fait accompli. Nor are they deterred by ASEAN's economic success. As in other parts of the Third World, they aggressively seek our targets of opportunity whether it be for modest political, economic and foreign policy gains or larger stakes as in outright support for "wars of national liberation" as in Central America.

d. Soviet presence in Vietnam: Benefits and costs of empire

(1) Benefits accrued

(a) Access to Vietnam's naval and air bases

The central focus of Soviet policy in Southeast Asia has been Vietnam; the effects of this involvement have been to accrue certain benefits but also to impose certain costs on the Soviet Union. Perhaps the greatest gain for the Soviets was to achieve access to the American-built naval and air bases at Cam Ranh Bay and Da Nang in Vietnam.[256] (See map 5.) The Soviets have access, but not

---

[253] Izvestiya (Moscow) in Russian, Apr. 22, 1983, Morning ed., p. 5. in, FBIS Daily Report, Soviet Union, v. 3, April 26, 1983: E1–E2.

[254] Metro Manila Times (Manila) in English, Dec. 4, 1984, p. 4, in FBIS Daily Report, Soviet Union, v. 3, Dec. 7, 1983, p. E1–E2.

[255] Larry A. Niksch, Specialist in Asian Affairs, CRS.

[256] Douglas Pike describes the Soviet Union and Vietnam as being "bound together in an extraordinarily close and even intimate association. It is a relationship built on and the product of

base rights, though their presence seems "permanent"—a fact demonstrated by the continuing, perhaps even alarming, increase of their forces and growing Vietnamese dependence on Soviet support. In brief, access to these facilities has given the Soviets the only operating military base between Vladivostok and the East Coast of Africa. The implications of this strategic coup are far-reaching.

Soviet forces at these bases are impressive. An estimated 10-15 naval warships are regularly in port at Cam Ranh Bay for refueling, repairs, and rest and rehabilitation for the crews.[257] Included in this revolving task force are 2 submarines, 3 cruisers or destroyers, a landing craft and 6 auxiliary ships.[258] A number of TU-16 (Badger) and TU-95 (Bear) bombers are based at Da Nang.[259] Advanced TU-22M (Backfire) bombers are also reportedly based there.[260] Six Badgers were spotted at Da Nang in late 1983.[261] Soviet electronic intelligence and communications facilities located in Vietnam are said to be the largest in the world outside the Soviet Union, with the exception of those in Cuba and Aden.[262]

From these bases, the Soviets have been able to project their naval and air power regularly and extensively into the nearby areas, the Pacific and Indian Oceans, and along continental Asia; the pace of their activity has quickened in the last six months of 1983.[263] The strait of Malacca falls within easy range, and proximity to U.S. naval and air operations in Subic Bay and Clark Field bases in the Philippines provides important monitoring capability.[264]

On February 15, 1984, an official at the Japanese Foreign Ministry revealed that the 43,000 ton Soviet aircraft carrier *Novorossiysk,* which had been deployed in the Indian Ocean, was presummed heading for Vietnam. Earlier unconfirmed reports indicated that the vessel had passed through the Strait of Malacca. According to the Japanese official, the re-deployment of the aircraft carrier was likely meant to be a display of Soviet military power in

---

opportunism and dependency, opportunism on the part of the Soviet Union and dependency on the part of the Vietnamese." (HFAC, Soviet Role in Asia, 1983, p. 205-206.)

In explaining the importance of the Cam Rahn Bay facility to the Soviets, Harry Gelman notes: "The Soviet Navy, I think is quite jealous of the fact that the United States has a great many more bases overseas. There is a far larger presence. They are striving to catch up. They would like to have more bases. They regard the acquisition of whatever they have in Cam Ranh Bay as an important step forward, inadequate though it is. It offers important conveniences for the operations in the Indian Ocean, which they feel they badly need. It also offers important intelligence collection convenience, both against the United States and against China, and these in their view are not to be sneezed at." Gelman adds, "they would like also, I think, in the back of their mind, to expand on this and get more from the Vietnamese than they have been able to so far." (Ibid, p. 392.)

[257] McWilliams, Edmund. Vietnam in 1982: Onward into the Quagmire. Asian Survey, v. 23, Jan. 1983:70.

[258] Dibb, Soviet Union as a Pacific Power, p. 246, ff. 14.

[259] The Christian Science Monitor, Jan. 19, 1984, p. 14.

[260] Asian Security 1982, p. 36.

[261] Middleton, Drew. Soviet Buildup in Far East Causing U.S. Concern. The New York Times, Jan. 30, 1984, p. A2.

[262] Dibb, Soviet Union as a Pacific Power, p. 246, ff. 14.

[263] The New York Times, Jan. 30, 1984, p. A2.

[264] McWilliam in 1982, p. 70. For a recent report on the Soviet buildup in Vietnam, see, DeYoung, Karen. New Arms, Troops Expand Soviet Military role in Southeast Asia. The Washington Post, Dec. 21, 1983, p. Al. See also, Jacobs, G. Soviet Forces and the Pacific Basin. Jane's Defense Review, v. 4, No. 2, 1983: 131-137, 141. Jacobs observes: "In terms of strict military force there appears evidence that the Soviets may be attempting to change the delicate equilibrium of military forces (between the U.S.A. and U.S.S.R.) that has existed for the last decade."

the region. It was also speculated that the carrier planned to use the naval facilities at Cam Ranh Bay as a base of operation.[265]

Acquisition of these facilities has "far-reaching implications" for South and Southeast Asia, according to Commander Thomas. In one move the Soviets by-passed mobile logistics weaknesses and acquired the capability to maintain 20 warships in the Indian Ocean and more than 10 others in the South China Sea. Thomas notes that China sees the acquisition of these bases as an extension south of the Soviet naval presence by more than 2,000 miles, a further Soviet move to encircle China, and a renewed Soviet attempt to penetrate the Third World.[266]

By having these military facilities the Soviets have demonstrated that they are now a major military force in the region. New opportunities are thus given them for intervening in times of a Southeast Asian crisis. A case in point is the Chinese incursion into Vietnam in February 1979 to "punish" the Vietnamese for their invasion of Kampuchea. The Soviets responded by deploying a flotilla of 10 ships to the South and East China Seas as a warning no doubt to Beijing not to go too far.[267]

Such displays of force for political purposes have apparently become commonplace.

In May 1980, the Soviets were reported to have stationed for the first time nuclear-powered attack submarines in the South China Sea. According to an International Herald Tribune report, this deployment was carried out "in apparent demonstration of its power to disrupt some of the world's busiest shipping lanes."[268]

In 1980, the Soviet aircraft carrier *Minsk* led a four-ship naval flotilla on what was called "an unprecedented cruise" through the Gulf of Thailand. In February 1983, the *Minsk*, carrying vertical-takeoff YAK–36 fighter planes, sailed virtually within view of the water front business district of Singapore. According to U.S. Ambassador to Philippines Michael Armacost, Soviet aircraft have carried out "hundreds of violations of Philippine air space."[269]

On April 16, 1984, Pentagon officials reported that the Soviet Navy staged amphibious landings on the Vietnamese coast, the first time Soviet marines have operated outside their coastal waters and in this part of the world. One official said that the amphibious landing exercises are another indication, following the deployment of a helicopter carrier to the Caribbean, of Russia's willingness and ability to project force beyond its borders. The most recent exercise on April 12, about 90 miles south of Haiphong, in-

[265] Tokyo Kyodo in English, 1106 GMT, Feb. 15, 1984.

[266] Thomas, Their Pacific Fleet, p. 86. The most authoritative weekly magazine in Asia recorded what Leifer calls the following "expression of apprehension" about the Soviet naval buildup and its use for political purposes in Southeast Asia: "If the Soviet Union succeeds in securing naval and air bases in Vietnam and in having Soviet forces permanently stationed there, the problem that the Soviet Pacific Fleet now has of having to pass through narrow straits in order to gain access to the Pacific will be partly solved. The resulting change in the U.S.-Soviet naval balance in the South China and the Indian Ocean could seriously affect vital Western sealanes in those waters." (The Power Game. Soviet Forces in the Far East. Asia 1981 Yearbook. Hong Kong, Far Eastern Economic Review, 1981, p. 23, quoted in, Leifer, Security of Sea-lanes in Southeast Asia, p. 20.)

[267] Zagoria and Simon, Soviet Policy in Southeast Asia, p. 155.

[268] International Herald Tribune, May 2, 1980, quoted in Leifer, Security of sea-lanes in Southeast Asia, p. 20.

[269] Leighton, Marian K. Soviets Still Play Dominoes in Asia. The Wall Street Journal, Oct. 14, 1983, p. 30.

volved a 14,000-ton *Ivan Rogov* class amphibious assault ship, the 38,000-ton helicopter carrier *Kiev,* several support ships and 400 to 500 Soviet marines. The exercise of April 9 took place at Cam Ranh Bay and involved four amphibious landing ships. Militarily the exercises were described as "routine," but one Pentagon official said they were of "major significance politically" in that they appeared to be "sending a message" to ASEAN states that they could be "a target of Soviet aggression." [270]

Presumably it was such displays of power along with the continuing Soviet military buildup in the Far East that led President Reagan to warn in a speech on the state of U.S. national security in March 1983,

They have taken over the port we built at Cam Ranh Bay in Vietnam, and now, for the first time in history, the Soviet Navy is a force to be reckoned with in the South Pacific.[271]

(b) Political benefits

Alliance with Vietnam, one of the few diplomatic victories in the region for the Soviets in recent years, has given Soviet Union for the first time a major strategic foothold in Southeast Asia.[272] Politically and militarily, the Russians have become a principal player, a "major agent," in a region that once was a Western preserve, and one that is bound to grow in strategic and political importance.[273] For it is axiomatic that power often begets power by pulling into its gravitational orbit the lesser, the weak, the indefensible.

The potential threat, with political implications, of Soviet naval and air force operations out of Vietnam to sealane communications vital to Japan and the United States has been persistently emphasized by U.S. Navy authorities.[274]

Russia's military and strategic presence has given its leaders the potentiality for manipulating the political forces in the region, perhaps to their advantage. As their naval forces increase with the steady buildup of military power in East Asia, the Soviets can be expected to use it for political profit, for example, in pressuring ASEAN governments to allow port calls for their warships.[275]

Fear of China among Southeast Asians and of the unassimilated overseas Chinese, particularly in Malaysia and Indonesia where considerable numbers are looked upon with resentment and suspicion, can be exploited politically.[276]

The Soviets can offer themselves to ASEAN nations as an alternative to China, an "insurance policy," so to speak, to a China that might one day become too powerful, or to a U.S. whose leadership has in the past been seen as unreliable and erratic.[277]

---

[270] The Washington Post, April 17, 1984, p. Al, and Andrews, Walter. Soviets May Intensify Fight in Afghanistan. The Washington Times, April 18, 1984, p. 3A.
[271] Congressional Record, March 24, 1983, p. S3911 (Daily Edition).
[272] Dibb, Soviet Union as a Pacific Power, p. 240.
[273] Zagoria and Simon, Soviet Policy in Southeast Asia, p. 164.
[274] Stuart D. Goldman, Analyst in Soviet Affairs, CRS.
[275] Zagoria and Simon, Soviet Policy in Southeast Asia, p. 155.
[276] Ibid.
[277] Ibid., p. 156.

The Soviets can also selectively support radical and opposition groups in politically unstable Southeast Asian LDC's to their advantage, should these groups come to power.[278]

Even Japan is potentially vulnerable in Southeast Asia, despite its economic largesse. Past wartime memories can be exploited by a resourceful Soviet Union.

In brief, as Zagoria and Simon conclude,

the Soviets have a variety of levers they can use in an effort to insert themselves increasingly into the region as one of the great-power "security managers" whose views and interests must be taken into account.[279]

(2) Costs imposed

(a) The economic burden

There is, however, an imperial cost to be exacted, and for the Soviets it comes in the form of bearing a heavy economic burden and sacrificing some potential political gains elsewhere.

Vietnam is an expensive ally. Its economy, suffering from prolonged dislocations from earlier wars and now from military stalemate in Kampuchea after 5 years, continues to stagnate and deteriorate. In foreign trade it is practically bankrupt.[280] Deprived of international assistance (except from the Soviet bloc, Sweden, France and India), the Vietnamese economy, in Mahbubani's words, "has no realistic prospects of improving."[281] Vietnam's GNP decreased from $257 per capita in 1978 to $189 in 1982. Malnutrition levels remain extremely high after 40 years of war. In 1981, Vietnam could not even guarantee the daily minimum of 1,500 calories for its population. Political and social costs are considerable as the slow process of societal deterioration continues. For Vietnam must bear the formidable cost of maintaining 180,000 troops in Kampuchea, 40,000 in Laos and another 600,000 at or near the Chinese-Vietnamese border.[282]

The pacification of Kampuchea has settled into a long-term stalemate, and for this, Mahbubani notes, "Vietnam is still bleeding."[283] He concludes, as do other analysts, that "the prospects for Vietnam succeeding are bleak." Careful analysis of the political, economic and military realities, he maintains, "shows that Vietnam may be headed for disaster."[284] Facing important challenges within Kampuchea, Vietnam is said to be "losing the political battles" to opposition forces, leaving the Vietnamese-installed regime "shaky."[285]

Vietnam's policy appears to be three-fold: to outlast ASEAN until the international coalition formed by ASEAN collapses; to build up a puppet government, party and army to take over some of the burdens; and to exploit cracks in ASEAN's unity and among

---

[278] Ibid.
[279] Ibid.
[280] Heinzig, South-East Asian Countries' Perception of the Soviet Union, p. 34.
[281] Mahbubani, Kampuchean Problem, p. 407.
[282] Ibid., and Heinzig, South-East Asian Countries' Perception of the Soviet Union, p. 34, and Zagoria and Simon, Soviet Policy in Southeast Asia, p. 165.
[283] Mahbubani, Kampuchean Problem, p. 407.
[284] Ibid., p. 424.
[285] Ibid., p. 408.

other ASEAN supporters. In short, a long term struggle can be foreseen in which Soviet backing is essential to Vietnam.[286]

Vietnam, increasingly isolated diplomatically, has become almost totally dependent on the Soviet Union.[287] "Without Soviet economic and military support," notes Mahbubani, "the Vietnamese economy would crumble," with unacceptable consequences for its relations with China and its position in Kampuchea.[288]

For this dependency the Soviets pay a heavy price. Most analysts put that price at $3 million a day, a total of $1 billion a year.[289] But Thomas W. Robinson, a specialist on Asian affairs, records a figure of $5–6 million a day in 1981.[290] At present Vietnam takes about one-fourth of worldwide Soviet aid; only Cuba gets more (one half).[291] External indebtedness for Vietnam, most to the Soviet block, doubled during 1980–1982 and now stands at approximately $3.5 billion. During 1981–1982, Vietnam dispatched over 30,000 "trainees" to work in the Soviet bloc in partial payment for their indebtedness.[292]

The Soviets have also sent hundreds of technicians to assist in the Vietnamese economy. Many technicians hold key positions, and in some instances down to the production unit level. The Soviets have undertaken long-term, large-scale projects with final completion dates late in the 1980's. Accordingly, Edmund McWilliams, an Asian specialist, taking the long-term view, concludes, "The Soviets appear to have designed their assistance program to anchor the Soviet presence in Vietnam."[293] A long-term agreement on development of economic, scientific and technical cooperation was concluded with Vietnam in 1983. It covers the period up to the year 2000. This alone suggests the intended longevity of Moscow's commitment to Vietnam.[294]

Costs to the Soviets are also evident by the fact that Moscow is funding more than half of Vietnam's current five-year plan at a cost of about $3.2 billion and including about 40 major projects. The Soviets also supply nearly all of Vietnam's arms (at a cost of about $1 billion since 1980), including the expansion of its naval forces, the modernization of its air force, improvement in its air defense with anti-aircraft missiles and radar stations, and logistical support for the Vietnamese military campaign in Kampuchea.[295]

The Soviets have also extended large-scale economic aid to Kampuchea, further increasing its costs for involvement in Vietnam. Moscow claims to have provided $134 million in 1980 and $95 million in 1981. Some 200 Soviet technicians also work in Kampuchea. In addition, the Soviets provide military assistance, especially in training pilots, artillery officers and senior staff officers.[296] Soviet

---

[286] Larry A. Niksch, Specialist in Asian Affairs, CRS.

[287] McWilliams, Vietnam in 1982, p. 62–63.

[288] Mahbubani, Kampuchean Problem, p. 419–420.

[289] Ibid, p. 419.

[290] Robinson, Soviet Union and Asia in 1981, p. 22.

[291] Heinzig, South-East Asian Countries' Perception of the Soviet Union, p. 34.

[292] McWilliams, Vietnam in 1982, p. 65–66.

[293] Ibid., p. 69.

[294] Izvestia, Nov. 16, 1983, p. 5, in, Current Digest of the Soviet Press, v. 35, no. 46, Dec. 14, 1983:12 and 24. This article summarizes the extent of Soviet aid planned under this agreement.

[295] Zagoria and Simon, Soviet Policy in Southeast Asia, p. 159–160, and Thornton, U.S.S.R. and Asia in 1982, p. 17.

[296] Carney, Kampuchea in 1982, p. 81.

advisers are active within the PRK Armed Forces General Staff, and presumably others are engaged elsewhere in the PRK military apparatus. East Germany concluded an agreement to rebuild the PRK armed forces and develop air defense installations.[297]

Close-in Soviet involvement has caused friction with the Vietnamese. A persistent Soviet complaint is the inefficient use of their aid by the Vietnamese and the need for greater Soviet control over it.[298] Vietnam has bristled at the doubling of oil prices since mid-1981, seriously aggravating the balance of payments problem.[299] Certain Vietnamese misgivings about Soviet political purposes in Indochina, especially in Kampuchea, and the risk of a "sell out" as in earlier times has also put a strain on the alliance.[300] Not always have regional and global interests coincided. Vietnam is believed to resent particularly the Soviet role and the size of its presence in Kampuchea.[301] Also, Hanoi has watched the oscillations of the Sino-Soviet dialogue with anxiety, fearing a rapprochement at its expense despite Moscow's assurances to the contrary.

To some extent, therefore, the Soviets not only must pay a heavy economic cost to sustain Vietnam and its own position there; but it must also suffer the ingratitude of what Mahbubani calls a country "too proud and too tough" to accept "a totally subservient role."[302]

(b) Political Costs

The Soviets pay a high political price for their involvement in Vietnam. At the international level they have generally been unstinting in their political support of Vietnam, particularly in the United Nations and within the Non-Alignment Movement (NAM) where they have been Hanoi's leading backer in efforts to legitimize its client government in Kampuchea led by Heng Samrin.[303] Yet, Soviet support of Vietnam has effectively polarized the politics of Southeast Asia; the effect has been to worsen Soviet relations with China and the United States, two prime international competitors whose security interests are closely intertwined with those of Moscow.[304]

Moreover, by arousing suspicions within ASEAN, the Soviets have alienated a potential source for political influence, driving its member states into the arms of China, the United States and Japan.[305] The Soviets have strong latent interests in Indonesia which it sees as the most powerful country within ASEAN.[306]

---

[297] Ibid.
[298] Asian Security 1982, p. 81, and McWilliams, Vietnam in 1982, p. 66.
[299] Ibid.
[300] Mahbubani, Kampuchea Problem, p. 420.
[301] McWilliams, Vietnam in 1982, p. 70.
[302] Mahbubani, Kampuchean Problem, p. 419. For a commentary on Vietnamese attitudes towards the Russians, see, Kendal, Harry H. Vietnamese Perceptions of the Soviet Presence. Asian Survey, v. 23, Sept. 1983:1052-1061. The writer attempts to portray relationships between the Vietnamese citizens and the Soviet advisers; to relate individual Vietnamese experiences and attitudes; and to draw some tentative conclusions about the future of the relationships. An indirect economic cost to the Soviets is their being shut out of ASEAN trade. (Stuart D. Goldman, Analyst in Soviet Affairs, CRS.)
[303] Zagoria and Simon, Soviet Policy in Southeast Asia, p. 160.
[304] Ibid., p. 157.
[305] Ibid., p. 157-158, and Dibb, Soviet Capabilities, Interests and Strategies in East Asia, p. 157.
[306] Dibb, Soviet Union as a Pacific Power, p. 247-248.

Gains are also possible in the other ASEAN states through astute political manipulation of the competing internal forces. But the Soviets have chosen the military option, and China, the United States and Japan appear to have been the clear beneficiaries.

(3) On balance: The military problem

On balance, the Soviets appear to have judged that the costs for a deep involvement in Vietnam are acceptable in light of the available benefits, real and potential.[307]

The transcending reality in Moscow's view would seem to be the long-term strategic gain of establishing a strong military and naval position in Southeast Asia. As noted above, this position gives the Soviet Union the potentiality for: containing China and projecting its power into the Pacific and Indian Oceans; countering and ultimately removing American influence in Southeast Asia and beyond; bringing about the neutrality of ASEAN; imposing its power and influence around the vital Southeast Asian straits; securing the communication lanes from Northeast Asia along the Asian continent to the Indian Ocean; altering the prevailing balance of power in its favor and enhancing the possibility of being a major actor, perhaps even a decisive actor, in the entire Asian-Pacific region.

In brief, the military option seems to have served Soviet purposes very well and the recent visits to Vietnam by leading Soviet bloc military authorities, including Marshal Nikolai V. Ogarkov, chief of the Soviet General Staff, is much more than a symbolic affirmation of policy choice: It would seem to be a clear signal of Soviet intentions for the present and future.[308]

---

[307] Zagoria and Simon, Soviet Policy in Southeast Asia, p. 158.

[308] In February 1982, Marshal Ogarkov visited all three Indochinese states, the most senior officer to visit the region since 1974. According to Thornton, "the trip highlighted the increasing military value of Vietnam to Moscow as the regional roles of China and the United States grow." (Thornton, U.S.S.R. and Asia in 1982, p. 17.) In January, the East German Defense Minister visited the area, and in April the Czechoslovak Defense Minister. (Carney, Kampuchea in 1982, p. 81.)

II. INDIA, CENTERPIECE OF SOVIET THIRD WORLD POLICY

A. Afghanistan and Kampuchea: Soviet Setbacks in the NAM

1. SOVIET VIEW OF THE NAM AND INDIA

a. A "natural ally"

The Soviet approach to India has differed remarkably from that of its approach to other Asian countries.[1] India is a special case; it is an exception.

Since the beginning of the Non-Alignment Movement (NAM) in the Third World during the mid-1950's, India, one of the founders and leaders of the movement, has been the centerpiece of Soviet policy in the Third World. In Khrushchev's tripartite view of world politics, reaffirmed by succeeding Soviet leaders in justification of peaceful coexistence, the LDC's of the Third World were designated socialism's "natural allies" in the Soviet struggle against the imperialism and colonialism of the West.[2] As the driving force and potentially strongest country in the NAM, India has held a special place in this ideological construct.[3] Accordingly, the Soviets view India as a valuable, and vulnerable, political target, an influential partner sharing many mutual foreign policy interests. With Russia's split with China in the 1960's these interests have broadened and deepened.

In general, the Indian connection has enhanced Soviet opportunities to influence the NAM, suiting quite well its larger Asian policy

---

[1] For an extensive examination of the Soviet role in South Asia, including Afghanistan, see, HFAC, Soviet Role in Asia, 1983, p. 235–324. The subcommittee heard testimony from, Roger E. Kanet, a specialist on Third World affairs, University of Illinois, Selig S. Harrison, an Asian specialist at the Carnegie Endowment for International Peace, and Stephen P. Cohen from the University of Illinois.

[2] Vselvolod Ovchinnikov, a Moscow political observer, explains Soviet alignment with the NAM in his article in Pravda on Nov. 18, 1982, particularly in countering U.S. attempts "to impose American hegemony on the world." The writer stresses identical Soviet interests with the LDC's of Asia, Africa and Latin America in frustrating the "neocolonialist policy" of imperialism, that is, the West. "Soviet-Indian relations," he writes, "serve as a convincing example" of carrying out the five basic principles that will assure independence. As the people in India "well know," he continues, "these ties have not been and are not, for the Soviet Union, either a means of extracting maximum profit or an instrument of political pressure and diktat." Nor are the ties of friendship and cooperation "detrimental to the interests or security of any third countries," but have "a beneficial effect on the situation in Asia and the international climate in general." (Moscow, Pravda, in Russian, Nov. 18, 1982, 2nd ed., p. 4, in FBIS Daily Report, Soviet Union, v. 3, Nov. 23, 1982, p. CC4–CC7.)

[3] See, Zorina, I. Developing Countries in the Political Structure of Today's World. Mirovaya Ekonomika I Mezhdunarodnyee (Moscow), in Russian, No. 8, Aug. 1982:80–91, translated in JPRS, 1982, p. 33–46. According to Zorina, "India warrants special discussion as a great Asian state. After waging a long and persistent struggle for independence, India presided at the cradle of the non-aligned movement and has pursued a balanced and even foreign policy line with the aim of stable relations on the subcontinent." Praising its opposition to "Beijing hegemonism" and "U.S. political pressure," Zorina emphasizes that "India has a stable and friendly relationship with the U.S.S.R." (p. 43.)

and the global purposes of contesting American power and expanding its own.[4]

b. Solidifying and nurturing the relationship

Since the mid-1950's, the Soviet Union has persistently attempted to solidify its relationship with India by a timely dispensing of political support and equally large-scale outlays of economic and military assistance.[5] Having interests of its own to be achieved, such as satisfying its sense of insecurity and achieving its goals of regional predominance, India has generally been an eager recipient of Soviet largesse.[6]

Brezhnev's report at the 26th Soviet Party Congress in February 1981 clearly conveys the degree of Russia's special regard for India. In his sober commentary on Soviet relations with the Third World, lowering somewhat the degree of Soviet economic involvement, Brezhnev singled out India, in contrast, for high praise. He spoke of India as occupying "a major place" in Soviet relations with the Third World; welcomed its "increased role" in international affairs; and described Soviet-Indian friendship as "a deep-rooted popular tradition." [7]

Less formal but still meaningful are the comments of one Soviet specialist on Asian affairs who told a recent Moscow conference of East-West scholars on Asia:

We consider India a growing power in the non-aligned movement. We trust India. We devote much attention to India. We consider it to be a big factor in international policy. We care about it.[8]

Nor did this favorable Soviet view of India change with the appointment of Konstantin Chernenko to succeed Andropov as General Secretary of the CPSU. Chernenko's 25-minute meeting with India's Prime Minister Indira Gandhi on the occasion of Andropov's funeral in mid-February 1984 provided the opportunity for reaffirming Soviet-Indian friendship. Chernenko, who in the past has had little to say about the Third World beyond pro forma statements, assured Gandhi that Soviet policy toward India would not change and even expressed a determination to strengthen the relationship.[9]

---

[4] For a recent Soviet commentary on Moscow's relations with "this friendly Asian country," see, Zhegalov, L. January 26 is India's Republic Day: At the Head of the Non-Aligned. New Times (Moscow) No. 4, Jan. 1984:12–13.

[5] The Soviet Union has consistently supported India in its conflicts with neighboring Pakistan. With respect to economic and military assistance, during the period 1954–1978, the Soviet Union extended a total of $2,282 million in economic credits and grants to India. For the same period the countries of Eastern Europe extended $445 million. Soviet interest in South Asia as a whole is apparent by the fact that Soviet military agreements and deliveries to South Asia during 1956–1978 were valued at $4,290 million and $3.375 million respectively. During 1973–1977, the value of Soviet arms transfers to India alone was placed at $1,100 million; arms transfers from Czechoslovakia were valued at $10 million, and from Poland, $40 million. During 1955–1978, 2,200 Indian military personnel were trained in the Soviet Union. In May 1980, the Soviet Union agreed to sell India $1.6 billion in weapons, the largest arms agreement ever concluded between the two countries. (HFAC, Soviet Policy and United States Response in the Third World, 1981, p. 82.)

[6] Robinson, Soviet Union and Asia in 1981, p. 25. Richard P. Cronin, Specialist in Asian Affairs, CRS.

[7] Brezhnev, Leonid I. Report of the CPSU Central Committee. Moscow Domestic Service in Russian, 0720 GMT, Feb. 23, 1981, in Foreign Broadcast Information Service (FBIS), Daily Report, Soviet Union. Proceedings of the 26th CPSU Congress, v. 1, Supplement 1, Feb. 24, 1981, p. 11.

[8] Palmer, Soviet Perspectives in Asia, p. 17.

[9] FBIS 024. Hong Kong, AFP, in English, 0456 GMT, Feb. 15, 1984.

Indicative also of the Soviet leadership's favorable attitude towards India and the desire to keep the relationship intact was the 6-day visit by Soviet Defense Minister Marshal Dmitri Ustinov to India during March 1984. Ustinov was accompanied by Admiral Sergei G. Gorshkov, chief of the Soviet Navy. Originally scheduled in February, the Ustinov visit had been cancelled three days before Andropov's death. During his stay in India Ustinov was accorded "the full honors of a visiting chief of state," according to one New Delhi observer.[10] Upon arriving in New Delhi, Ustinov expressed the hope that "talks with Mrs. Gandhi would yield fruitful results as before." Referring to the Soviet-Indian Friendship Treaty of 1971, Ustinov noted that since then relations between the two countries had "advanced towards the correct direction." [11]

In a later address to workers at the Nasik aircraft factory where India is manufacturing Soviet-designed MIG aircraft, Ustinov remarked that "the example of your factory . . . show[s] well the fruitful character of all-round cooperation between our countries." Repeating a time-honored Soviet phrase in singling out India for special praise, Ustinov described the relationship as having become "a deep-rooted tradition", one that meets the "interests of the Soviet Union and India." Ustinov expressed confidence that Soviet-Indian cooperation "will continue to expand and strengthen for the benefit of the peoples of the two countries, in the name of peace and progress on earth." [12]

Indians expressed a special pleasure for the attention being paid to them. Defense Minister Ramaswamy Venkataraman noted that the Ustinov visit, so soon after Andropov's death and election of Chernenko to leadership, demonstrated to Indians "the importance which the Soviet Union attached to India." For Indians the visit was regarded as "a landmark in Indo-Soviet relations." [13]

Later Ustinov had a meeting with the Indian chief of naval staff, suggesting to some observers that India may make extensive purchases of Soviet naval equipment. Ustinov was scheduled to visit Vishakhapatnam, India's largest naval headquarters on the eastern coast; the Nasik aeronautics factory; the Avadi tank factory in Madras where the T-72 tank is being built under Soviet license; and the Indian military Academy.[14]

In brief, the Chernenko leadership sent a signal to New Delhi, that the Soviet commitment to India was firm and that Moscow looks forward to an expanding, fruitful relationship.

---

[10] Weaver, Mary Anne. Soviets Woo India to Buy Arms. The Christian Science Monitor, March 9, 1984, p. 9.

[11] The Washington Post, March 6, 1984, p. A9.

[12] Moscow Tass in English, 1428 GMT, Mar. 6, 1984, FBIS 061.

[13] The Washington Post, March 6, 1984, p. A9.

[14] Ibid. For a report on Ustinov's visit to India, see, Sen Gupta, Bhabani. Indo-Soviet Relations: For Better or for Worse. India Today, Mar. 31, 1984: 79–81. In this incisive commentary, Sen Gupta makes the following appraisal: "The Ustinov visit, . . . was one of the important landmarks in the 34-year-old Indo-Soviet friendship. In political and strategic importance it is comparable to the India visits of Khrushchev and Brezhnev." As a result of the visit, "India will now receive frontier military technology from the Soviet Union at par with the Warsaw Pact countries. More than 60 percent of the new weapons and technologies for the IAF and Indian Navy will be coming from the Soviet Union."

c. The ultimate purpose?

The Soviet-Indian relationship has thus been carefully nurtured by Moscow over the past near three decades. India has been bound to the Soviet Union by a network of political, economic, scientific and military agreements, including one of Moscow's now ubiquitous "friendship" treaties. Perhaps the ultimate purpose of Soviet policy is best described by Robinson in his survey and analysis of Soviet policy in Asia during 1981, "In Moscow's view a socialist India today could well become a communist India tomorrow, through evolution if not revolution." [15] Yet, on the other hand, there are those who contend that it is questionable whether the Soviets hold out any real hope for a Communist India, or even whether such an outcome would serve their purposes. The Soviet experience with China suggests the limitation on relations with a Communist state sufficiently large to go its own way whatever the polity that governs it. [16]

2. INDIA'S VIEW OF THE SOVIET CONNECTION

a. "Coincidence of interests"

India has its own interests to be achieved through the Soviet connection. These interests flow from the need for foreign assistance in internal economic development. But more importantly, they flow from a perceived need for Soviet support in defense and foreign policy. It would be incorrect, therefore, to assume that India is being innocently ensnared in a Soviet trap. What is called a "coincidence of interests" is a persistent theme running through analyses by specialists on Indian foreign policy. It is not surprising, therefore, as Professor Robert C. Horn, an Asian specialist at the California State University at Northridge, concludes, that by the end of the 1970's (and before Afghanistan) relations between Moscow and New Delhi developed "to a point of closeness and cooperation few other major power-Third World relationships had achieved." [17]

b. Regional interests

From the regional perspective India has looked upon the Soviet Union as a crucial counterweight to a potential threat from China. (See Map 1) Border differences, long a source of contention between India and China, together with China's close ties with neighboring Pakistan, India's foremost adversary, have made the Soviet connection most desirable. Similarly, U.S. policy of using China and Pakistan as strategic counterweights to Soviet expansion in Asia has tended to encourage India to look to Moscow for protection of its regional interests.

Thus, the Soviets play a key role in India's objectives of maintaining military preponderance over Pakistan and deterring China. Arms, aid, and coproduction arrangements with Moscow are ac-

---

[15] Robinson, Soviet Union and Asia in 1981, p. 25.
[16] Richard P. Cronin, Specialist in Asian Affairs, CRS.
[17] Horn, Robert C. Afghanistan and the Soviet-Indian Influence Relationship. Asian Survey, v. 23, March 1983:244.

cordingly very important. For the main concern of India is the disruption of the regional military and political balance, revival of U.S.-Pakistani ties, and a new U.S. military role in the region, all of which counters India's own political ambitions.[18]

c. Geopolitical interests

A close alignment with Moscow has also served India's larger geopolitical and international purposes. India has found a shared interest with the Soviets in the effort to turn the Indian Ocean into a "zone of peace," as the Soviets term it, not necessarily as a genuine ally of Moscow, but rather in response to its own national interests; namely, to reduce the role of external powers and increase its own influence in the region, and especially to prevent outside military support of rivals or domination of smaller neighbors by outside powers. Converting the Indian Ocean into a "zone of peace" is an Indian proposal mooted through Sri Lanka in 1970. The Soviets simply give lip service to the idea, and the Indians know it; but it serves their objectives.[19]

On the other hand, the Soviets may be really sincere about this proposal. From their perspective U.S. SSBN's in the Indian Ocean are a threat to the Soviet homeland, just as the U.S. military presence in the Indian Ocean is a threat to their vital sea lane communications.[20]

Constraints on the non-littoral powers contiguous with the Indian Ocean would also reduce the level of tension in the area brought on by escalating naval deployments of the superpowers. The Indians are not blind to Soviet purposes in the area. But they worry less about the problem than the United States since American policy has tended to support their enemies in contrast to the Soviets.[21]

Finally, the Soviet connection can be perceived as an asset advancing India's role in the NAM, though since the invasion of Afghanistan it has been something of an albatross for India. Nonalignment, based on often genuine grievances of past colonial experiences, represents a substantial component of power in world politics. However unfounded Soviet claims on the organization may seem to the West, nonetheless, many radical members, if not most, see truth in the Soviet argument and equate the West and the United States with colonial and imperial policies and aspirations. Hence close ties with Moscow can give India wider access for building the influence and power it already has within the movement.

d. Gains for India

Thus India has had something to gain from the Soviet connection, both from the regional and geopolitical perspective—not to speak of the domestic where Soviet pressure on the Communist

---

[18] Richard P. Cronin, Specialist in Asian Affairs, CRS.
[19] Richard P. Cronin, Specialist in Asian Affairs, CRS.
[20] Stuart D. Goldman, Analyst in Soviet Affairs, CRS.
[21] Richard P. Cronin, Specialist in Asian Affairs, CRS. For a commentary on Indian policy, see Sagar, Imroze. Indo-Soviet Strategic Interests and Collaboration. Naval War College Review, v. 34, Jan.-Feb. 1981:13–33.

Party of India (CPI) for support has often been sought.[22] And while Horn can rightly say that "Moscow could hardly have a better Third World ally to work with" in pursuing its Asian and global policy, it could also be rightly said that India too has a useful Soviet ally in pursuing its own regional and geostrategic interests.[23] This relative "equality" or "partnership" that characterizes Soviet-Indian relations appears to be unusual, if not unique, in Soviet Third World relations.[24]

3. AFGHANISTAN AND KAMPUCHEA: TEST OF THE RELATIONSHIP

a. The Indian response

The Soviet invasion of and the continuing war of attrition in Afghanistan and Vietnam's invasion and military occupation of Kampuchea have tested the Soviet-Indian relationship as nothing before. Afghanistan, particularly, has had the potential for disrupting the relationship. Most of the non-aligned Third World have voiced sharp and unrelenting opposition to the Soviet move into Afghanistan.[25] For India, the invasion by actual Soviet army units into a country nonaligned and not part of the Soviet bloc (as in the case of Czechoslovakia in 1968 which similarly India did not condemn but expressed disapproval and "anguish") was, as Horn notes, "a situation repugnant to its historic foreign policy principles."[26]

And yet India, as noted above, needed Soviet support. By this time, for example, the Soviet Union had become even more important economically for India; in 1981 it m..y have passed the United States as India's largest trading partner. Total trade in 1981 reached almost 2.4 billion rubles and was steadily rising.[27]

Clearly, India had a problem. Its response had to be carefully crafted: on the one hand to avoid sanctioning the invasion and thus preserving intact its principles and support within the NAM; but yet not alienate the Soviet Union, its principal supporter. Politically, India was more important to the Soviet Union than the Soviet Union was to India.[28] Its bargaining position was strengthened substantially.

In responding to Afghanistan, the Indian leadership was spared an enraged public opinion, and accordingly could orchestrate its response within a wide range of acceptability. According to the Indian Institute of Public Opinion, the Soviets have consistently retained "high popularity" in India, and the armed intervention brought about "only a very marginal decline—from 168 to 157 points." With the passage of time, the Soviet image improved, swinging "steadily upward on the popularity chart," according to

---

[22] See, Ghosh, Partha S. and Rajaram Panda. Domestic Support for Mrs. Gandhi's Afghan Policy: The Soviet Factor in Indian Politics. Asian Survey, v. 23, March 1983:261–279.
[23] Horn, Afghanistan and the Soviet-Indian Influence Relationship, p. 224.
[24] Stuart D. Goldman, Analyst in Soviet Affairs, CRS.
[25] Rand, Moscow Shows Concern Over Change in Non-aligned Leadership, Mar. 4, 1983, p. 2.
[26] Horn, Afghanistan and the Soviet-Indian Influence Relationship, p. 244.
[27] Thornton, The U.S.S.R. and Asia in 1982, p. 19.
[28] Ibid., p. 20.

Indian scholarly sources. Sympathetic respondents perceived the Soviet Union as "a friend in need."[29]

In general, the Indian response was set by Prime Minister Charan Singh late in December 1979 and modified according to the needs of the moment by Gandhi who became Prime Minister in January 1980. Two themes predominate:

—India has "always opposed outside interference in the internal affairs of one country by another"; it urges that the Soviets withdraw their troops from Afghanistan and return the country to "normal" conditions.

—India perceives a major danger in the Afghanistan crisis; namely, the reintroduction of the United States into the region and resumption of arms aid and security assistance to its regional rival, Pakistan.[30] Accordingly it has insisted that no country or external power should aggravate conditions. Under Gandhi this initial position was extended and softened to express confidence in Soviet assurances that their forces would remain in Afghanistan no longer than necessary. Failure of India to take a harder stand, as in the U.N. debate on the nonaligned resolution condemning the intervention, caused, according to Horn, "a good deal of shock and surprise."[31] In contrast to confrontation, India has preferred to work behind the scenes to quietly bring about the withdrawal of Soviet troops and to express its displeasure privately with the Soviet armed intervention.

The initial Indian response was thus moderated by realism in the direction of seeking an accommodation with Moscow, or as some observers term it, a "realistic approach."[32] In general, this broad approach continues to guide Indian policy on Afghanistan.

b. Equivocation on Kampuchea

India's approach to Kampuchea was similarly accommodating, and equivocal—characterized, it might be said, by the false hope that it would be the vanguard of recognition.[33] India maintained close relations with Vietnam, and in July 1980, as promised in the election campaign, Gandhi recognized the Heng Samrin regime in Kampuchea. On the other hand, India has unfailingly expressed its opposition publicly to the presence of foreign troops in the country, though carefully not mentioning Kampuchea by name.[34]

---

[29] Ghosh and Panda, Domestic Support for Mrs. Gandhi's Afghan Policy p. 267. The writers note: "By and large, the respondents were inclined to see the Afghan crisis in the framework of a regional crisis to which the U.S. had contributed not insignificantly by promising arms aid to Pakistan." A survey in March 1980 indicated that 28 percent of the respondents found the basic interests of India and the Soviet Union "very much in agreement," and 44 percent thought that during the two to three months that followed the Soviet intervention their interests had drawn closer. A study of international images over the period 1971-1981, conducted by the Indian Institute of Public Opinion, revealed that the Soviet Union "has almost always led the United States in popularity."

[30] Richard P. Cronin, Specialist in Asian Affairs, CRS.

[31] Horn. Afghanistan and the Soviet-Indian Influence Relationship, p. 245–246.

[32] Thorton, The Soviet Union and Asia in 1981, p. 20.

[33] Richard P. Cronin, Specialist in Asian Affairs, CRS.

[34] Horn, Robert C. Soviet-Indian Relations: Issues and Influences. New York, Praeger, 1982, p. 206.

Thus in both cases India has maintained a very delicate balancing act, attempting to preserve simultaneously both its principles and its "friendly" ties with Moscow.

c. Effects of Afghanistan on Indian policy

Within this carefully designed cautious and equivocating policy, India, nonetheless, was to take steps in the aftermath of Afghanistan that caused concern in Moscow. Robinson spoke of a "near-revolution" in Indian foreign policy, noting that Gandhi was "perhaps more shocked than anyone at the Soviet use of force in Southwest Asia." [35] For the Soviets, Indian policy was proceeding in a direction that could weaken, even disrupt, their relationship. Briefly, New Delhi's policy was to strengthen relations with China (Foreign Minister Huang Hua visited New Delhi in June 1981), the United States (including a Gandhi visit) and even institute talks with Pakistan; and to diversify arms acquisitions by negotiating deals with France, Britain and the United States. The purpose: to lessen India's dependency on Moscow. [36]

B. SALVAGING A DAMAGED RELATIONSHIP

1. ACTIVITY AT THE DIPLOMATIC LEVEL

a. Official Soviet visits, 1980

After Afghanistan, the Soviets faced a major task with India; namely, to salvage a damaged relationship. They sought to accomplish this task by exerting countervailing pressures on the diplomatic level and by an increased outpouring of aid on the economic and military level.

Moscow's principal diplomatic device for this damage limiting operation was high-level official visits. A veritable parade of Soviet officials to New Delhi took place in the aftermath of Afghanistan from 1980 to the end of 1982. Brezhnev, Gromyko and leading Soviet political and military officers visited India; Andropov was to visit in 1983, but his failing health and passing prevented it. Such visits provide the Soviets with the opportunity for stressing such appealing political themes as the "identical interests" existing between India and the Soviet Union, for example, concurrence on certain Third World issues and ostensible opposition to militarizing the Indian Ocean and the Persian Gulf; and also emphasizing the threat inherent in the evolving Sino-American relationship particularly military aid to Pakistan which has been presented as a concerted attempt to "encircle" India. [37]

The Soviets moved into action quickly. In mid-February 1980, less than 2 months after the invasion, Foreign Minister Andrei A. Gromyko visited New Delhi. His mission was to explain the Soviet position, the causes and necessity of the intervention; to justify the intervention; and to seek India's support. [38] Two months later,

---

[35] Robinson, The Soviet Union and Asia in 1981, p. 25.
[36] Thornton, The U.S.S.R. and Asia in 1981, p. 19–22. It is significant to note that Mrs. Gandhi declined Soviet overtures to go to Moscow to commemorate the 10th anniversary of the 1971 friendship pact.
[37] Horn, Afghanistan and the Soviet-Indian Influence Relationship, p. 248–249.
[38] Ibid.

Soviet Deputy Foreign Minister Nikolai P. Firyubin continued applying Soviet pressure during his short visit to New Delhi. And in December 1980, Brezhnev himself led an entourage of nearly 300 to New Delhi, again to plead the Soviet case, hoping to win Indian support. Loss of such support, according to Horn, would have been "devastating" for Soviet prestige and its position within the Third World.[39]

b. An emphasis on the military, 1981-82

Throughout 1981 and 1982 Soviet officials, both political and military leaders, descended upon New Delhi, lobbying vigorously for their cause and India's support—even to directly intervening in India's internal politics through the CPI.[40] On one occasion Chief of Staff Marshal Nikolai V. Ogarkov and on another Soviet Defense Minister Dmitri F. Ustinov, along with Admiral Sergei G. Gorshkov, Russia's leading naval authority, and a military delegation of 80 including over 30 top-ranking army generals, paid their respects to the Indian leadership in so-called goodwill visits, seizing the opportunity to continue applying seemingly unrelenting Soviet pressure. In many instances economic and military agreements were concluded as an apparent earnest of Russian interest in maintaining India's friendship. India's leaders, both political and military, made return visits to Moscow in concerted efforts to advance India's own policy of conciliation yet disapproval of the Soviet presence in Afghanistan. These exchanges of visits are recorded and analyzed in detail by Horn in his published works on Soviet-Indian relations.[41]

Reduced to the simpliest terms, the sum and substance of efforts on both sides has been to influence the other on fundamental policy: On the specific issue of Afghanistan, the Russians to get India's support, often obliquely but other times forcefully, for their continuing military involvement; and the Indians to pressure the Soviets behind the scene to moderate their policy and withdraw their military forces.

2. ECONOMIC AID, MILITARY ASSISTANCE, AND TRADE

a. Agreements in 1980

(1) India's Defense Ministry negotiates arms agreement

In attempting to shore up the relationship, the Soviets were forthcoming in extending economic and military assistance to India and expanding their trade on favorable terms. On two occasions in 1980, the Russians demonstrated their largesse, for clearly political reasons.

In what Horn calls a clear example of "Moscow's anxiety to solidify the relationship" occurred on the occasion of a visit to Moscow by an India Defense Ministry team in May. The delega-

---

[39] Horn, Soviet-Indian Relations: Issues and Influence, p. 197.

[40] Soviet Candidate Member of the Politburo E.A. Shevardnadze made a special plea for support of Gandhi's "peaceful foreign policy" at the CPI's 12th Congress. (Horn, Afghanistan and the Soviet-Indian Influence Relationship, 256-257.)

[41] Horn, Soviet-Indian Relations: Issues and Influence, chapter 7, and Afghanistan and the Soviet-Indian Influence Relationship, p. 244-260.

tion, made up of top officials, armament specialists and financial advisers, went to Moscow to resume negotiations last held in September 1979. The results of the mission were, as Horn put it, "substantial to say the least."

The Soviets agreed to a $1.63 billion credit for India to purchase weapons and equipment over a period of 10–15 years. On terms beneficial to India, the agreement called for credit repayable over 15 years after a two-year grace period at 2.5 percent interest. Important for India were the weapons made available, including 5 highly sophisticated MIG–25 Foxbat aircraft, an undisclosed number of fast attack boats equipped with missiles, 100 T–72 tanks with another 600 to be produced in India under license.[42]

India had good reason to conclude this agreement—the first one of its kind outside the Warsaw Pact—particularly in light of the expected delivery of new U.S. arms to Pakistan. But it was an eager Moscow that pressed the attractive offer.[43]

(2) Brezhnev's appealing economic offer

When Brezhnev visited New Delhi in December 1980, he brought along appealing inducements for the Indians. The Soviets agreed to provide economic assistance for a broad range of projects totalling over Rs. 40 billion in India's next five-year plan. Steel and aluminum expansion and oil exploration were especially emphasized.

Another Soviet incentive was to lay before the Indians an attractive trade offer. Soviet-Indian trade had been growing substantially. The Soviets were by this time India's third largest trading partner and second best customer for Indian exports. Under a signed protocol both sides pledged to double the total value of trade by 1985 to the equivalent of $13.33 billion. Brezhnev was also reported to have spurred the negotiations for supplying India the MIG–25 and indicated that the Indian air force would soon be getting the first supply.[44]

Brezhnev's most appealing, and significant, offer was, however, an agreement to raise the Soviet Union's crude oil supplies to India by one million tons per year. For India, then scrambling for new oil resources since the outbreak of the Iran-Iraq war (from whom India received some 70 percent of its oil imports), this agreement was in Horn's words "of tremendous importance."

Soviet priorities were clearly demonstrated in this transaction. In order to increase oil supplies to India and other Third World countries, the Soviets would have to reduce exports to Western Europe and thus lose precious hard currency. India would pay by more exports to the Soviet Union, not in hard currency, leading Gandhi to express her appreciation in Parliament for "this friendly

[42] Horn, Afghanistan and the Soviet-Indian Influence Relationship, p. 249, and Stuart D. Goldman, Analyst in Soviet Affairs, CRS.

[43] Horn, Soviet-Indian Relations: Issues and Influence, p. 189, and Menon, China and the Soviet Union in Asia, p. 333.

[44] Horn, Afghanistan and the Soviet-Indian Influence Relationship, p. 252, and Horn, Soviet-Indian Relations: Issues and Influence, p. 189. Soviet appeal as a trading partner for India was said to be declining as India was running up large export surpluses and the Soviets were unable to supply the quality of technology and trade that India needed. (Thornton, the U.S.S.R. and Asia in 1982, p. 20. See also, Ali, Salamat. Oil, Weapons and Friendship, Far Eastern Economic Review, Jan. 2, 1981:19.)

gesture." Indian MP's greeted the announcement with "rousing cheers." [45]

b. Other Soviet proffers of aid and trade, 1982-83

(1) Ustinov's military mission, March 1982

Against a background of flux in India's complex relations with the United States, Pakistan, China, Britain and France, on the one hand and the Soviet Union on the other, generated by a desire to distance itself from Moscow and diversify its weapons acquisitions, Soviet Defense Minister Ustinov made a 6-day official visit to New Delhi in March 1982. Backed by a formidable delegation of Soviet military officers whose size was described as unprecedented, an "eager" Ustinov attempted to nullify the impending arms deal with France by offering India the latest generation of military hardware at what was generally described as cutrate prices and soft terms. Among the weapons Moscow was prepared to supply India were the T-82 tank and advanced MIG-27 tactical fighter-bomber. The latter was said to be equivalent to or better than the French Mirage 2000 then under consideration.[46]

(2) Gandhi's visit to Moscow, September 1982

In an apparent effort to strengthen India's non-alignment credentials after visiting the United States in March 1982, Prime Minister Gandhi went to Moscow the following September and there conferred with Brezhnev and other Soviet leaders.[47]

The visit provided Gandhi the occasion to stress India's traditional non-alignment policy and to express her displeasure with the Soviet presence in Afghanistan. For the Soviets, it provided the opportunity to conclude an agreement increasing their mutual trade from $2.6 billion to $3.9 billion annually over the next four years.[48] Soviet Prime Minister Nikolai A. Tikhonov conveyed the Soviet offer to build a 1,000 megawatt nuclear power plant in India that would double the size of the Tarapur atomic plant. The visiting Indians agreed to study the offer. In addition, Tikhonov offered to build a thermal plant with a capacity ranging between 800 to 1,000 megawatts. The Russians also agreed to assist India in the second stage of the Vishakhapatham steel plant, proposing commercial credits on the same terms as the first stage.[49]

Pravda gave the following instructive appraisal of the Gandhi visit:

[45] Horn, Soviet-Indian Relations: Issues and Influence, p. 199, and Horn, Afghanistan and the Soviet-Indian Influence Relationship, p. 252. See also, Rangan, Kasturi. India is Showered with Soviet Largess. The New York Times, Dec. 14, 1980, p. 11.

[46] Auerbach, Stuart. Soviets Pledge to Aid India Against Pakistan. The Washington Post, Mar. 21, 1982, p. A18, and Kaufman, Michael T. Soviet Says It is Eager to Help India Produce Arms. The New York Times, Mar. 20, 1982, p. 11. See also, Porter, Bruce. Soviet Defense Minister to Visit India. RFE-RL. Radio Liberty Research, RL 117/82, 4 p. On April 17, 1982, the French Defense Ministry announced that India had chosen the Mirage 2000, agreeing to buy 40 with an option to purchase 110 others. (The New York Times, April 18, 1982, p. 6.)

[47] Southerland, Daniel. Mrs. Gandhi Seeks to Change Pro-Soviet Image. The Christian Science Monitor, July 30, 1982, p. 3.

[48] Facts-on-File, Oct. 1, 1982, p. 729B2-C3. See also, Andersen, Walter. India in 1982: Domestic challenges and Foreign Policy Successes. Asian Survey, v. 23, Feb. 1983:111-122.

[49] Delhi Domestic Service in English, 0249 GMT, Sept. 22, 1982, in FBIS Daily Report, Soviet Union, v. 3, Sept. 22, 1982:D2.

The Soviet-Indian talks in Moscow took place in an atmosphere of mutual under-standing, warmth and cordiality. The sides noted the high level and large scale of bilateral cooperation in the economic, trade, scientific and technical spheres, which is being implemented on a planned basis and is of a mutually advantageous and long-term nature. They agreed to examine the possibility of further widening coop-eration in such spheres as ferrous and nonferrous metallurgy, the coal and petrole-um industries, machine building and power industry and confirmed their determi-nation to increase trade 50–100 percent in 1986 and also to maintain the high rate of trade growth until 1990.[50]

Thus the Gandhi visit enabled the Soviet leaders to reassert their commitment to India, particularly in matters of economic aid, and inferentially to reinforce their claim to India's friendship and sup-port internationally. In a larger sense the visit provided the oppor-tunity for the Soviets to restate their credentials as a reliable patron of the Third World.

(3) Activities in economic relations, 1983

The year 1983 was marked by continuing exchanges of visits by leading officials and the conclusion of scientific, technical and eco-nomic agreements that provided suitable occasions for the Soviets to call attention to their largesse in relations with India.

In December 1983, Ivan V. Arkhipov, First Deputy Chairman of the U.S.S.R. Council of Ministers, conferred with his Indian coun-terpart in New Delhi as cochairman of the Soviet-Indian Intergov-ernmental Commission for Economic and Scientific-Technical Coop-eration. In reporting on the Commission's meeting, Soviet corre-spondent Dimitri Biryukov underscored the importance of Soviet-Indian cooperation in developing India's economy by stressing a common theme in Soviet media; namely, that over 70 industrial projects had been built in India with Soviet assistance. Economic ties were "constantly expanding," he said, citing particularly the Soviet role in building the Visakhapatnam Combine ("proceeding successfully") and the "giant" Vindayachal thermal power sta-tion.[51]

On December 9, the Soviet Union and India concluded a trade agreement for 1984, providing for "further growth" in their trade. The Tass report reflected Soviet satisfaction and pride in their rela-tions with New Delhi when it stressed that the Soviet Union is India's "biggest trading partner" and that India is the "biggest trading partner of the U.S.S.R. among the developing states." In 1983, trade turnover exceeded 30 billion rupees.[52]

Thus the Soviet connection has continued to be reinforced by sig-nificant activity in the economic sphere, though problems were sur-facing, notably the serious imbalance in trade to India's favor that imposes an economic cost on India since the issue is not settled in hard currency.[53] And despite displays of Indian independence in its

---

[50] Strengthening Friendship. Editorial. Moscow Pravda in Russian, Sept. 28, 1982, p. 1, in FBIS Daily Report, Soviet Union, v. 3, Sept. 29, 1982, p. D1.
[51] Moscow Domestic Service in Russian, 1900 GMT, Dec. 7, 1983, in FBIS Daily Report, Soviet Union, v. 3, Dec. 8, 1983, p. D2. An earlier report indicated that the number of industrial and other projects totaled some 60 with another 30 or so facilities under construction or on the draw-ing boards. (Moscow Tass in English, 1955 GMT, Sept. 14, 1983, in FBIS Daily Report, Soviet Union, Sept. 14, 1983, p. D1.)
[52] Moscow Tass in English, 1321 GMT, Dec. 9, 1983, in FBIS Daily Report, Soviet Union, v. 3, Dec. 12, 1983, p. D2. For an analysis of this agreement, see, Gidadhubli, R.G. Indo-Soviet Trade Protocol for 1984. Economic and Political Weekly (India), Jan. 14, 1984:60.
[53] Richard P. Cronin, Specialist in Asian Affairs, CRS.

relations between the superpowers, the Soviet leadership could view the state of their relations with New Delhi with some measure of satisfaction, as Pravda noted in a hortatory editorial effusive with praise in the fall of 1983:

India is an active champion of reorganizing international economic relations on a just and democratic basis, of establishing the new economic order, and of putting an end to the exploitation of liberated countries by the developed capitalist states.

It is natural that India's independent and dynamic foreign policy would generate dissatisfaction and opposition by imperialism, and primarily U.S. imperialism. This was particularly sharply manifested during U.S. President Reagan speech at the 38th U.N. General Assembly session, in which, according to the Indian newspaper TIMES OF INDIA, he "launched unjustified attacks against the Nonaligned Movement," whose chairman is India. Replying to similar statements in the past about the "tilt" toward the U.S.S.R. tolerated by India, I. Gandhi said: "The point is not that we are with the Soviet Union but that the Soviet Union is with the countries of Asia and Africa and is supporting the independence movement and the struggle against colonialism."

India's relations with the Soviet Union and the other socialist countries are a component of its foreign policy. Soviet-Indian relations have become an important factor of peace and stability in Asia and all over the world. The friendship and all-round cooperation between our countries have withstood the test of time. India and the U.S.S.R. share common positions on such major international problems of our time as ensuring peace, liquidating the threat of the outbreak of war, curbing the arms race—and primarily the nuclear arms race—adhering to the principles of peaceful coexistence, and taking practical steps to liquidate existing and prevent the emergence of new armed conflicts.[54]

C. THE MATTER OF INFLUENCE

1. EXTENT OF SOVIET INVOLVEMENT

The central issue in Soviet-Indian relations, viewed as a problem in Moscow's Third World policy, is the matter of influence. After nearly three decades the Soviet Union has become deeply involved in India. One simple measure of this involvement are the Tass estimates of 1980 that enterprises in India built by Soviet technological assistance accounted for over 30 percent of the petrochemical products, 20 percent of its electricity, 80 percent of the heavy metallurgical equipment it manufactures, and 60 percent of its turbo and hydrogenerators. The Soviet Union is also a key source for India's crude oil.[55] And as noted above Soviet-Indian trade has grown to an impressive degree, requiring extensive interaction on both sides.

---

[54] India: Important Role in the System of International Relations. Editorial. Moscow Pravda in Russian, Oct. 22, 1983, 1st ed., p. 4–5, in FBIS Daily Report, Soviet Union, v. 3, Oct. 31, 1983, p. D6.

In October 1983, the Soviet Union and India held high level talks on a major new arms deal under the terms of which the Soviet Union agreed to supply India with the latest version of MIG aircraft, tanks, missiles and other weapons. Included in the transaction was the MIG-31, the Soviet's latest fighter planned for manufacture in the next few years. Though still on the drawing boards, the Russians indicated that they will supply it to India when it has been successfully flight tested. Meanwhile the MIG-29, known as the Fulcrum, is to be supplied to India with licensing rights to manufacture this highly sophisticated fighter plane. The Soviets also agreed to supply the T-80 tank, the latest to have undergone successful field trials. Many of India's existing armored regiments were said to be using the T-72 which are expected to be gradually replaced by the T-80. (Financial Times [London], Oct. 19, 1983, p. 6.)

A manuscript by S. Nihal Singh, an Indian journalist, entitled, "Why India Goes To Moscow For Arms," (1983, 26 p.) was made available for use in this study. This problem is also discussed in a series by Russell Warren Howe entitled, "India: New Military Giant?" published in The Washington Times beginning, March 20, 1983, p. 1A.

[55] Rand, Robert. Brezhnev to Visit India Next Week. RFE-RL. Radio Liberty Research, RL 467/80, Dec. 5, 1980, p. 2.

There are other indicators. Since the mid-1960's the Soviet Union has been India's primary arms supplier.[56] Space cooperation has also been extensive and has acted as a binding element in the relationship, the most symbolic aspect being the training of an Indian cosmonaut for an expected Soviet space flight sometime in 1984.[57]

On April 3, Rakesh Sharma, an Indian Air Force pilot, joined two Soviet cosmonauts for an eight-day visit to Salyut 7 space station. All three returned safely to earth on April 11 after a successful spaceflight, to the acclaim of the Soviet leadership and Mrs. Gandhi.[58]

Other aspects of the Soviet presence in India that suggest the depth of involvement are:
—The presence of about 500 Soviet officials functioning in various capabilities;
—The sizeable Communist Party of India (CPI—585,000 claimed members). However, it is split and, according to Singh, its influence is limited, as in Parliament (percentage of vote in 1980, 6.2 percent; 12 MPs of total 544); [59]
—The large network of trading and friendship societies, operating at an estimated annual cost of $50 million and being financed surreptitiously;
—Four Soviet cultural centers with the Soviets promoting at least 48 publications in 12 languages;
—Extensive broadcasting from Radio Moscow and Radio Tashkent in up to 8 languages;
—Over 200 branches of the Indo-Soviet Cultural Society; and
—The availability of what is termed "pro-Soviet" newspapers.

A press account from New Delhi on the occasion of the Ustinov official visit in March 1984 notes that, despite evidence of Indian independence from Moscow, the signs of a close relationship "remain abundant." The Indian newspapers were "effusive in their posthumous praise" of Andropov as a "friend of India." Moscow radio broadcasts to New Delhi on a number of channels "overshadowing all other stations." Russian tanks are a "spectacular feature" of every Republic Day parade. Soviet bookstores and Russian cultural societies "abound," and the exchange of official visitors on both sides are "a constant stream." Finally, the ranks of Indian academia, notably in the social sciences, are "often markedly pro-Soviet and anti-American." One influential newspaper editor said, "The Soviets have penetrated the Indian intelligentsia to a remarkable degree." [60]

---

[56] Singh, Why India Goes to Moscow for Arms, p. 1.

[57] For a survey of Soviet-Indian space cooperation, see, U.S. Congress. Senate. Committee on Commerce, Science, and Transportation. Soviet Space Programs: 1976–80. 97th Congress, 2d session. Washington, U.S. Govt. Print. Off., Dec. 1982, p. 290–295. The Indian cosmonauts, Rakesh Sharma and Ravish Malhotra, both test pilots, completed another stage of their training at the Yuri Gagarin Cosmonauts Training Center near Moscow in December 1983. Their flight with the Russian cosmonauts is scheduled for 1984. (Moscow Tass in English, 1141 GMT, Dec. 21, 1983, in FBIS Daily Report, Soviet Union, v. 3, Dec. 22, 1983, p. D1–D2.)

[58] Schmemann, Serge. Indian Joins Soviet Pair in 8-Day Space Mission. The New York Times, April 4, 1984, p. A16, and the Washington Post, April 12, 1984, p. A33.

[59] Interview in CRS, April 7, 1983, and Wesson, Robert, Checklist of Communist Parties, 1982. Problems of Communism, Mar.-Apr. 1983:97.

[60] Stevens, William K. India Still Looks to Soviet but Elsewhere too. The New York Times, March 15, 1984, p. A16.

The Soviet presence in India is indeed far-reaching and formidable. But have the Soviets been able to influence Indian policy proportionate to their presence?

2. EXTENT OF SOVIET INFLUENCE

a. On the Afghan issue

It is extraordinarily difficult to measure accurately the extent of Soviet influence over Indian policy. Horn attempts to do this by tracking the course of India's relations with the Soviet Union under the impact of the Afghan issue. That Moscow influenced India's views on Afghanistan, there can be little doubt; but that influence, if not marginal, may have emerged from Soviet insistence, perhaps indirectly, on political payment for past favors from an India that knew what was expected and the costs of resisting Moscow's pressures.[61] Horn concludes,

What these twists and turns in Soviet-Indian relations over the Afghanistan issue point to is the effort each has made to influence the other and the difficulty both have had in being successful. India has not been able to obtain a Soviet withdrawal and the U.S.S.R. has not been able to obtain an Indian endorsement of the Soviet occupation. Moscow's invasion has not been fully supported by New Delhi, but neither has it brought about a rupture in relations, the two alternative scenarios many in the West foresaw. That reality has "wandered" between these two extremes gives testimony to the fabric of Soviet-Indian relations and to their mutual need for one another.[62]

On the broader issue of an Asian Collective Security System first proposed by Brezhnev in 1969—obviously very "pro-Soviet," as Horn notes, India still refuses to sign on.[63] Clearly, its interests are not served; Soviet efforts to pressure New Delhi in this important diplomatic undertaking have failed.

b. On arms transfers

Nor has extensive military assistance to India given the Soviet Union sufficient leverage for altering its policy. In a penetrating study on Soviet arms trade in the Third World and its capacity to influence policy, Menon concludes, though not all would agree, with respect to India that "India has been willing to take Soviet foreign policy interests into account in instances where the cost is low."[64] Generalizing on the broader Soviet experience in the Third World, Menon further concludes:

The Soviet Union has thus been able to employ arms transfers to create a stable presence in a number of countries by supporting their security goals, and to evoke responsiveness towards Soviet interests when the recipient views the costs as tolerable. The Soviet leaders have not, however, been able to induce their major arms customers to make costly adjustments in policy to propitiate the U.S.S.R.[65]

---

[61] Richard P. Cronin, Specialist in Asian Affairs, CRS.

[62] Horn, Afghanistan and the Soviet-Indian Influence Relationship, p. 257.

[63] Ibid., p. 259.

[64] Menon, Rajan. The Soviet Union, The Arms Trade and the Third World. Soviet Studies, no. 3, July 1982:390, and Richard P. Cronin, Specialist in Asian Affairs, CRS.

[65] Ibid. Roger F. Pajak, National Security Adviser to the U.S. Secretary of the Treasury, concludes that 25 years of military assistance has "served Soviet interests reasonably well." The Soviets have acquired no "ideological converts" as a direct result of arms transfers, but they have "acquired a substantial, though unquantifiable, degree of influence in the Third World." He notes also the Soviet military sales to India "have enhanced Moscow's stature in New Delhi

c. In the nonalignment movement

Finally, the Soviet Union has not been successful in exerting any decisive influence on India within the Nonaligned Movement (NAM). A case study is the most recent meeting of the NAM in New Delhi during March 7-12, 1983.

At the NAM's previous meeting in Havana during September 1979, India, along with Yugoslavia and other member states, successfully resisted pressure from Cuba, Ethiopia and Vietnam (supported aggressively by the Soviet Union) to accept the "radical thesis" espoused by Castro identifying the Soviet Union as a "natural ally" of the NAM against imperialism.[66] At new Delhi the proceedings of the NAM took a decided shift away from the radical left towards the moderate center, a shift sharply contested in the Soviet media.[67] Prior to this meeting Moscow had lobbied extensively, particularly India, giving a clear indication that it was, so to speak, "calling in the chits" for past favors. A principal Soviet concern was the damaging impact of Afghanistan on its efforts to win over the NAM. As one Soviet source put it, the Soviet Union needed "a voice of support and assistance," "words of sympathy," and "a helping hand." New Delhi owed this much to the Soviet Union, it was said, given their repeated "sacrifices" for India.[68]

But the Soviets only partially succeeded in their attempts to influence Indian behavior at the conference. As the host country, India prepared the draft declaration. Critics described this "blandly worded" document as a "draft with no teeth." Many of the nonaligned member states perceived it to be "blatantly anti-United States and pro-Soviet." This slant towards Moscow was evident on three central issues in Soviet-Indian relations: Afghanistan, Kampuchea and the Indian Ocean.

India's initial positions in the draft did not constitute dramatic reversals of previous policy, but, as Horn notes, "the shifts in emphasis and nuance were definitely there and definitely in Moscow's favor." If it were true that the Soviets had influenced India, then the Indians were forced to backtrack when the conference got underway. For the final declaration called for the withdrawal of foreign troops from Afghanistan and strict observance of non-intervention. The declaration expressed concern over continuing conflicts in Southeast Asia, reaffirmed the principles of "non-interference and the inadmissibility of the use of force," and expressed the hope that the problem of Kampuchea would be resolved through negotiations, mutual understanding and self-determination free of outside interference. And finally it called for the resumption of Soviet-American negotiations on reducing their military presence in the Indian Ocean.[69]

---

and circumscribed that of the West. . . . " Despite an uneven experience with respect to creating a durable influence, the Soviet Union, he contends, "will continue to use arms transfers as a primary foreign policy instrument for maintaining and expanding Soviet influence in the Third World." (Pajak, Roger F. Soviet Arms Transfer as an Instrument of Influence. Survival, v. 23, July/Aug. 1981:170-172.) A standard work on arms transfers is, Pierre, Andrew J. The Global Politics of Arms Sales. Princeton, N.J., Princeton University press, 1982, 253 p.

[66] Horn, Soviet-Indian Relations; Issues and Influence, p. 173-175.
[67] Rand, Moscow Shows Concern Over Change in Nonaligned Leadership, p. 1.
[68] Horn, Afhganistan and the Soviet-Indian Influence Relationship, p. 253-255.
[69] Kessing's Contemporary Archives, August 1983, p. 32349-32355.

The results of the conference were disappointing to the Soviets. They were cool towards India. They believed, apparently, that India had conceded too easily on the pro-Soviet draft declaration. (It is conceivable, however, that India slanted the initial declaration toward Moscow was a negotiating ploy, knowing full well that it would be revised at the conference by the more moderate forces, thus playing both sides of the street at once.)

Thus, while the Soviets may have had some influence over India initially, the conference as a whole left the general impression in India and the West that the "pro-Soviet tilt" that had dominated the NAM in recent years had now ended. Indeed, India emerged from the conference as one of the chief spokesmen for unity within the NAM, meaning a decided shift toward the center and an orientation more in keeping with its initial purpose; namely, nonalignment.[70]

Another interpretation is that the pro-Soviet stance left India isolated and accordingly would have reduced its influence.[71]

3. ON THE DURABILITY OF SOVIET INFLUENCE

a. Horn: An unchanging relationship

The durability of Soviet influence in India is an open question, and must remain so given the vagaries of international politics and the volatility of political influence. Yet students of Soviet-Indian relations have made some general and plausible conjectures.

Horn acknowledges the "strains and coolness" that the continuing Soviet presence in Afghanistan has caused, yet the failure of a close Pakistan-U.S. security arrangement, he contends, has enabled India to distance itself from Moscow and accordingly retain its own independent stance between the superpowers. Hence, Horn concludes, "A break in Soviet-Indian relations over Afghanistan is as unlikely as an Indian policy transition from 'realistic' to 'pro-Soviet.'"

Nor are changes to be expected in the Brezhnev succession regime. Horn underscores an important characteristic in Soviet-Indian relations when he concludes that, "Dramatic changes in relations have not been the rule in relations between Moscow and New Delhi, particularly since the end of the 1960's and such changes are just as unlikely in the future."[72] Horn elaborates in the conclusion of his larger work:

For the future, India and the Soviet-Indian relationship are faced with the same dynamics as in 1969 and ever since: for India, how can its independence from big powers be further developed, and its ties with China and the United States expanded, while still maintaining its strong relationship with the Soviet Union? For the Soviet Union, how can it limit such diversification while expanding its own role in the South Asian region and maintaining its strong relationship with India? While the future will not duplicate the past, the themes, patterns, dynamics, and trade-offs are likely to be the same for New Delhi and for Moscow as they have been. Each will successfully influence the other on occasion, but, generally, such influence will likely remain limited. The Soviet-Indian relationship, nevertheless, will continue to

---

[70] Ibid., and Horn, Soviet-Indian Relations: Issues and Influence, p. 254-255. For a comprehensive survey of nonalignment, see, Non-alignment. International Studies, v. 20, Jan.-June 1981; whole issue.
[71] Richard P. Cronin, Specialist in Asian Affairs, CRS.
[72] Horn, Afghanistan and the Soviet-Indian Influence Relationship, p. 258-259.

be highly significant for the two countries involved in the region, China and the United States, and for the overall world political scene.[73]

b. Scalapino: An unweakened alignment

In his prospective glance at South Asia in the context of the Pacific region, Scalapino acknowledges the "substantial" chance that India may gravitate towards an authoritarian or quasi-authoritarian political system. But the current Indian alignment with the Soviet Union "does not necessarily indicate that such an authoritarian trend would take a communist form." Odds are currently against such a development, he contends. Nonetheless, Scalapino cautions, "there is no reason to believe that the Soviet-Indian alignment will weaken in the near future."[74]

c. Menon: Continuing reliance on arms transfers for a "visible presence"

In his analysis of Soviet arms tranfers and their impact on the Third World, Menon asserts this principle that, "India has been willing to take Soviet foreign policy interests into account in instances where the cost is low." [75] Heavy dependency on Soviet arms transfers, he contends, has not deterred states from turning away from the Soviet Union, citing the case of Egypt, when they felt that "close ties with the Soviet Union were no longer in their interests." [76]

But Menon states (and Roger F. Pajak, National Security Adviser to the U.S. Secretary of the Treasury and specialist on arms transfers agrees) that the "driving force" behind Soviet arms transfers "will continue to be political." He continues,

Though the export of weapons has provided the Soviet leaders with only limited influence in the developing world, it has provided them with a visible presence. This, together with the realization that some influence is better than none, will ensure Moscow's continued heavy reliance on this instrument of diplomacy.[77]

d. For India, a matter of interests

From these judgments it can, therefore, be inferred that the Soviet presence in India will probably remain formidable and that Soviet economic and military assistance will remain a principal instrument of its policy. Yet India has succeeded in keeping its principles and interests in its relations with Moscow firmly intact. Mrs. Gandhi reiterated these principles simply and directly at the New Delhi meeting of the NAM, "we have neither natural allies nor natural adversaries," and on other occasions, "We are neither pro-Western nor pro-Soviet, but pro-Indian." [78] Thus Soviet influence in the future as in the past will no doubt have to be measured by what New Delhi perceives to be its own interests.

---

[73] Horn, Soviet-Indian Relations: Issues and Influence, p. 221-222.

[74] Scalapino, Pacific Prospects, p. 12-13.

[75] Menon, The Soviet Union, the Arms Trade and the Third World, p. 390.

[76] Ibid., p. 391.

[77] Ibid., p. 393. Pajak writes: "The Soviet leadership undoubtedly will continue to use arms transfers as a primary foreign policy instrument for maintaining and expanding Soviet influence in the Third World." (Pajak, Soviet Arms Transfer as an Instrument of Influence, p. 172.)

[78] Kessing's Contemporary Archives, v. 19, Aug. 1983:32355, and The Christian Science Monitor, Mar. 9, 1984, p. 9.

III. SOVIET INVOLVEMENT IN ASIA: ITS MEANING

A. TAKING THE MILITARY OPTION

This brief survey of Soviet involvement in Asia from the perspective of its Third World policy suggests certain broad generalizations that give meaning to the unfolding events described here and to the general direction of Soviet policy in the 1980's. The first point to be made is the Soviet inclination to base its policy on military power and its willingness to use the military option, notwithstanding the sacrifice of potential political and economic benefits.

One aspect of the military option in action is the Soviet military buildup over the years that has been perceived by Moscow's potential adversaries in Asia as a genuine threat. And this buildup gives no indication of receding, but rather of increasing. The continuing buildup and deployment of the Soviet Navy, based in the Soviet maritime provinces in Northeast Asia and in Vietnam in the southeast, both within easy range of vital chokepoints in the world's sea communications, pose a new challenge to the nations of the Pacific and Asian region. The continuing buildup of Soviet military forces, particularly of strategic weapons systems, in Northeast Asia seems to have made both a qualitative and quantitative difference in the balance of forces in that area. Though the Soviet Union as a continental power still suffers many constraints in projecting its power, nonetheless, the trend seems in the direction of building a strong and threatening military presence in Asia and the Pacific.[1]

Another aspect of the Soviet military option in Asia is the attempted pacification of Afghanistan and Kampuchea, the latter through its proxy Vietnam. Both endeavors suggest the Soviet inclination to look primarily for military solutions when their perceived interests are threatened, as in Afghanistan, and when opportunities arise for expanding Soviet power and influence, as in both regions.

In an era when Soviet ideology has lost the appeal it once had, when the Soviet model of development in the Third World has been tarnished by failures, when many Third World countries in Asia have been making striking economic advances, and when the possibility of a national liberation movement rising against established indigenous postcolonial governments has been minimized, the military option seems to have taken on a new meaning, one that more correctly fits into the traditional mold of classical imperialism and colonialism.

---

[1] With respect to Southeast Asia, Douglas Pike writes, "The Soviet Union is clearly determined to increase its military presence in Southeast Asia and to translate this if possible into political power. What is not clear is the extent of its ambition." (Pike, Douglas. Southeast Asia and the Superpowers: The Dust Settles. Current History, v. 82, April 1983:148.)

B. POLARIZING THE INTERNATIONAL POLITICS OF ASIA

The militarization of Soviet policy has polarized the international politics of Asia.[2] This is the second point to be made.

China, the United States, Japan, ASEAN, South Korea and Pakistan to a degree have rallied in a loosely concerted effort to counteract what they commonly perceive to be a Soviet threat to their interests. Even the strategic relevance of the "outcast" Taiwan is apparently being reconsidered in this new alignment of forces, particularly the importance of the Formosan Strait in the defensive strategy of East Asia.

Thus, a balance of power, reflecting a new and changing structure of relations, seems to have been taking shape since 1979. Zagoria calls this loosely configured power bloc a "massive barrier" opposing Soviet expansionism. Curiously, the Soviet peace offensive, launched by Brezhnev in 1981, has revealed the depth of this new alignment of forces, as the militarization of Soviet policy and the declaration of peaceful intent have worked at cross purposes revealing a fundamental contradiction.

"Stalemate" thus seems best to describe the state of Soviet policy in Asia at this point. As a result of political polarization the Soviets have made gains in Indochina through their fraternal alliance with Vietnam, though at a high price. But they have been effectively closed down in their efforts to build influence within the Third World states of ASEAN. These countries have looked to their own inner resources for development and to the Pacific community of nations, particularly Japan and the United States. The Soviets have lost ground in India. And paradoxically Soviet expansionism in Asia has regenerated Beijing in its efforts to compete more effectively with Moscow for influence in the Third World.

Finally, Soviet policy in Asia constitutes a self-fulfilling prophecy, a behavior characteristic of the Soviets amply demonstrated in the postwar period: The militarization of its policy, in apparent response to a declared threat to Soviet security, has created real adversaries when in many instances none may have existed in the first place. This curious circular behavioral pattern of action-reaction and reaction-to-the-reaction adds a preservative to tensions in Soviet relationships. The overall effect is to downgrade the value of diplomacy already overburdened by problems, to perpetuate tensions, and to reduce the possibility of achieving a genuine peace.

C. INDIA, THE NATION IN BETWEEN

India, as the nation in between the major contending forces in Asia, is an exception to Russia's Asian policy. Nonetheless, the militarization of Soviet policy—apparently only as it relates to Afghanistan and Kampuchea—has imposed serious limitations on Moscow's effectiveness in India. This is the third point.

India, as noted above, is the centerpiece of Soviet policy in the non-Communist Third World. Through the Indian connection

---

[2] For the polarization of Southeast Asia, see Pike, Southeast Asia and the Superpowers, p. 145–148, 179–180. Pike examines Southeast Asia's relations with the United States, the Soviet Union and China and suggests that regionalism provides the best hope for peace, stability and economic development in Southeast Asia.

linked closely with the Non-Alignment Movement, the Soviets have sought to widen their influence in the Third World and thus advance their cause globally. From the perspective of global strategy the Soviets also seek Indian support in making the Indian Ocean a "zone of peace," meaning for Moscow at least the exclusion of U.S. naval forces.

But, after Afghanistan and Kampuchea, the Soviets have had difficulty claiming the unqualified loyalty of New Delhi. Shocked by the violation of much revered international principles, India has attempted to distance itself from Moscow, playing off one adversary against the other in Asia. Accordingly, the Soviets have doubled their efforts to strengthen the relationship with New Delhi, using economic and military assistance along with direct political pressure and extensive propaganda. The measure of Soviet influence in India, however, has been determined strictly by Indian self-interest.

By and large India's perception of its interests in the Soviet relationship seems to be more regional than strategic. Support for the Soviet peace policy in the Indian Ocean seems to be based on the expectation that it will reduce the military, and thus political, pressure from its adversaries, Pakistan and China. Russia's larger strategic role in Asia does not appear to be given equal weight of importance. Thus, it can be argued, a certain narrowly conceived regional myopia seems to govern India's policy towards the Soviet Union, a policy open to the charge that it fails to take into account those larger strategic threats that the Soviets pose elsewhere in Asia and that are apparent to other Asian nations, including those belonging to the NAM.

D. A New Stage of Russian Expansionism?

Soviet involvement in Asia in recent years suggests the final point; namely, that Russia may be entering a new stage of expansion in Asia.

The Soviet imperial system is unique in the Modern Age. Much evidence suggests that Russia, both Czarist and Soviet, has been an organically expansionist power, driven by a deep-rooted historical dynamism that is fueled by an abiding sense of territorial insecurity.[3] As a contiguous empire, in contrast to the "maritime" empires of other European states, the Russian has maintained a territorial cohesiveness that did not undergo the dissolution characteristic of other European imperial systems in the 20th Century. This unique Russian imperial entity has thus become an organic part of the whole Russian historical experience, Czarist and Soviet. Moreover, the historic Russian imperative for expansion, strengthened by the sense of territorial insecurity, has never diminished over the years. The dynamic impulse for empire, fortified by the messianism of Communism, has never really been arrested, nor has the sense of territorial insecurity, which on the contrary has magnified with each accretion of territory.[4] In the current era another powerful

---

[3] Aspects of this problem are elaborated on in, Brzezinski, Zbigniew. Tragic Dilemmas of Soviet World Power: The Limits of a New-Type Empire. Encounter, v. 61, Dec. 1983:10–17. See also, HFAC, Soviet Diplomacy and Negotiating Behavior, 517–520.

[4] See, Sonnenfeldt, Helmut, and William G. Hyland. Soviet Perspectives on Security. Adelphi Papers: 150. London, International Institute for Strategic Studies, 1979, 24 p.

and potentially dangerous ingredient has been added; namely, the fact that the Soviet Union is a one-dimensional military world power.[5]

All of this suggests that the elements for continuing Soviet expansionism remain in place, at least in the near future. From the Soviet perspective, the fusion of history, ideology and military power seems to be complete. Hence the growing Soviet presence and deepening involvement in Asia, to a degree never before attained, tends to support the view that the Soviet Union may indeed be entering a new stage of expansionism in Asia. Accordingly, this expanding presence provides ample evidence to show that the Soviet commitment to the Asian part of the Third World continues to be essential, even vital, to its worldview, and that this commitment is firm and, indeed, expanding.[6]

While there are strong indications that the Soviet Union will continue to try to expand its influence in Asia in the foreseeable future, still the factors that can deter, perhaps even undermine, that effort are significant. There are potentially debilitating internal factors that Soviet leaders must take into account as they calculate the costs and gains of empire: the distortions, strains and overall shortcomings in the performance of the Soviet economy; the continuing excessive demands on the resources of the nation for military purposes; serious problems now plaguing Soviet society (vital matters such as poor public health care and the declining rate of population growth in the Great Russian and other Slavic areas) that have affected the vigor of national growth; the potentially troubling nationality problem that could threaten the unity of the Soviet state in the future; and the logistical problems that some defense specialists judge to be virtually insolvable in their efforts to maintain a strong and independent defense structure in the Soviet Far East far away from their main source of strength in European Russia.

Externally, the Soviet leaders will have to take into account the growing resistance of Asian nations to their expansion. But more importantly they will be faced at some point with the problem of cost-effectiveness in maintaining an empire and in determining the extent of their commitment to the Third World—a matter that will be expanded upon in the final part of this study. As in the case of

---

[5] Brzezinski, Tragic Dilemmas of Soviet World Power, p. 10.

[6] Malcolm Mackintosh, a British specialist on Soviet affairs, concludes that the nature of the Soviet attitude towards Asia is "not likely to change . . . It will almost certainly continue to be that of a superpower with a 'European' or 'imperial-European' kind of nationalism, combined with the Soviet Union's contemporary form of communist ideology, which is often rather remote from classical Marxism. It is bound to be dependent on the Soviet concept of the role and size of Soviet military power in the area, and the Soviet Union will for strategic and traditional Russian reasons, interpret the situation in Asia as a series of groupings, spheres of influence leading to a balance of power in Asia in political and military terms. If this turns out to be the case, the possibility that the Soviet Union's role in Asian affairs will change and acquire genuinely Asian characteristics with a real understanding of Asian thinking, Asian standards and Asian associations will, as far as we can see, be rather remote." (Mackintosh, Malcolm. Soviet Attitudes Towards East Asia, in, Segal, ed. The Soviet Union in East Asia, chapter 2, p. 15.) Paul Langer foresees military power as the primary instrument in achieving Soviet policy goals in Asia. He concludes: "In the absence of a better outlook for the Soviet economy than exists today and in view of the unlikelihood of a reversal of the decline in the Soviet Union's political-ideological appeal, military power and its political uses seem destined to remain the preferred and virtually the sole instrument of Soviet policy abroad. Soviet military might in Asia must then be expected to continue its steady growth in the years ahead." (Langer, Soviet Military Power in Asia, p. 270–271.)

imperial systems of the past, expansion tends to reach a point of diminishing returns where the cost of empire, rather than being a political asset, becomes a burden too heavy to bear. And the Soviets, despite the assurances inherent in their ideology and their confidence in the continuing growth of their military power, are not immuned to these historical forces. Thus, despite their expanding presence in Asia at the present time, they will face serious problems in the future imposed by the limits of imperial power.

PART III—THE SOVIET UNION AND THE MIDDLE EAST [1]

> We regard the countries of Asia, Africa and Latin America that make up the majority of the non-aligned movement—an influential force of today—as our fellow-fighters in the struggle between those who work for peace and those who work against it. It is the intention of the Soviet Union to continue to do all in its power to deepen and develop friendly ties with these countries.
>
> —Andrei A. Gromyko's speech at the U.N., Sept. 27, 1984.

I. SOVIET POLICY TOWARD THE PERSIAN GULF, THE ARABIAN PENINSULA, IRAN, AND IRAQ

A. SOVIET STRATEGY IN THE GULF

The Arabian Peninsula and the Persian Gulf became a focus of superpower competition in the 1970s. Providing the West with a large proportion of its energy needs, the region came under increasing Soviet military pressure, peaking after the fall of the Shah and the invasion of Afghanistan in 1979. By the early 1980s, Western military capabilities and political presence were seen as diminishing, while Soviet interests and capabilities were perceived as growing.

The trend began in 1977 when the massive airlift of arms and supplies to Ethiopia and the stationing of Cuban proxy forces there demonstrated that the Soviets were prepared to come to the aid of a client state and to maintain a presence on the periphery of the Arabian Peninsula. This was followed by the Soviet naval build-up in the Indian Ocean, and then Soviet jockeying for position in the North-South Yemeni confrontations from 1979 to 1981. The Iranian revolution and the Soviet takeover of Afghanistan immediately raised fears in the West and among the Persian Gulf sheikdoms of a Soviet military challenge in the area. Western security remains threatened by the possibility of Soviet military advances in the region.

The advantages gained by the Soviet Union's vigorous military adventures in areas close to the Arabian Peninsula were mitigated by the reaction of the Gulf states to the Soviet military threat. The Gulf states came together in May 1981 to form the Gulf Cooperation Council, a grouping of six conservative monarchies, whose goal was to create a unified voice against Soviet encroachments that was not simply an invitation to dependence on a Western military presence. At the same time, the United States acquired local support (from Saudi Arabia, Oman, and Somalia in particular) for a stepped up military profile in the Persian Gulf and Indian Ocean.

Growing Soviet military opportunities in the area have not been translated into local influence in the Persian Gulf. Although a

---

[1] Prepared by Michael J. Dixon, Research Analyst in Soviet and East European Affairs, Congressional Research Service. First published on December 12, 1983, as CRS Report No. 83-229 S.

Soviet military operation cannot be discounted in a crisis, the Soviets currently appear to pursue a moderate policy of trying to achieve normal relations with as many Arabian Peninsula governments as possible, with the aim of reducing Western influence and checking the expansion of U.S. military presence. Moscow has attempted to moderate its image in the Gulf by pushing for an agreement with the West, China, and Japan prohibiting foreign military bases and the use of force in the Persian Gulf as well as declaring the Indian Ocean a demilitarized "zone of peace." The Soviets have implied that they will not intervene in the Gulf as long as the United States is excluded from the region and they have warned the Gulf states that the U.S. Rapid Deployment Force is intended for use against their oil installations. However, the obstacles to improved Soviet relations with the Gulf states are its continued occupation of Afghanistan, close ties to "national liberation" movements, and the relationship with the PDRY, the most radical state on the peninsula. These countries also hold a profound religious aversion to Communism that is strengthened by Islamic nationalism. As a consequence of Soviet activities in the region, Saudi Arabia has mounted a diplomatic offensive, using its economic leverage, to undermine Soviet policies.

The success of Soviet policy in the Persian Gulf will depend on a number of developments. The course of the Soviet war in Afghanistan could determine how the sheikdoms will view the Soviet Union in the future. Soviet consolidation of power in Afghanistan and the subjugation of the guerrilla movement could spell increasing apprehension over Soviet capabilities and intentions towards the Gulf. So far, however, the stalemate in Afghanistan has not provided the USSR with a measurable strategic advantage in the region; indeed, the war in Afghanistan has demonstrated the obstacles the Soviets might have to face should a military option be undertaken. Nonetheless, Gulf fears of the Soviet military presence nearby grow out of the demonstrated willingness of the USSR to take advantage of instability should the opportunity arise.

The Iran-Iraq war is of great importance to Soviet policy in the region. The instability in the region created by the two belligerents has aroused fears of an increasing Soviet presence in Iran and Iraq and temptations to interfere in the domestic affairs of the smaller Gulf states. However, the Soviets have to date been unable to maintain balanced relations with both Iran and Iraq. External issues, such as the Arab-Israeli conflict, also influence Soviet ties to the Gulf states. Continued U.S. identification with Israel over Palestinian rights and a settlement in Lebanon could weaken the willingness of Gulf states to maintain security ties to the United States and encourage them to accept affiliations with the USSR. On a number of occasions, Arab leaders have stated that Israel, not the Soviet Union, is the principal threat to peace in the region.

Future Soviet energy needs could affect Soviet policies toward the Persian Gulf states. Although it is not clear whether the Soviet Union or its East European allies will require oil imports in the decades ahead—estimates of future Soviet oil production and consumption vary—growing demand for Persian Gulf oil could intensify Soviet pressures on Gulf states to provide oil to the USSR and its allies and to normalize relations.[2] Saudi officials have estimated that the USSR will be a net oil importer in the late 1980s.

The Soviets maintain a strong and secure foothold in the People's Democratic Republic of Yemen (PDRY), strategically located at the southern tip of the Arabian peninsula on the Bab al-Mandab Strait. With its airfields and port facilities, the PDRY provides Moscow with the capability to project power in the region, help defend its interests in Ethiopia, and pressure Saudi Arabia and the Gulf states. In North Yemen, or the Yemen Arab Republic, Moscow has maintained a significant presence after supplying the Sana'a government with arms during its 1979–1981 wars with rebel insurgents and PDRY forces also armed by the USSR. Recent developments indicate that the PDRY, with Soviet encouragement, may be moderating its policies towards its neighbors in order to acquire sorely needed economic aid from its richer Gulf neighbors, an adjustment that could aid Soviet efforts to normalize relations with those countries but also reduce PDRY dependence on Moscow.

Saudi Arabia continues to treat the Soviet Union as anathema to its interests. While Saudi leaders have tempted Moscow with the possibility of resuming severed diplomatic relations, there is no immediate likelihood that the two countries will improve relations. On the other hand, Kuwait, with whom the Soviets have diplomatic relations, appears to be a model that the Soviets hope will be emulated by other Gulf states. Kuwait has concluded an arms deal with the Soviet Union and supported Soviet efforts to demilitarize the Gulf and the Indian Ocean. Kuwait has also been the most vocal of the GCC nations against a U.S. military presence.

The region, because it lies proximate to the Soviet southern border, is one in which the Soviets maintain strong interests in political and military developments. They have acknowledged that the United States has vital interests in the Gulf, but they have opposed any U.S. presence to defend these interests. The Soviets have concentrated primarily on anti-Western elements in the Gulf states and on undermining Western influence there, while encouraging cooperation with the USSR in certain specific objectives. The Gulf and Arabian Peninsula will remain an object of Soviet diplomatic pressure backed by strong military capabilities in the region.

B. The U.S.S.R. and Iran

1. SUMMARY

The Soviet Union welcomed the fall of the Shah and the victory of Ayatollah Khomeini in 1979. The Iranian revolution suddenly ended decades of U.S. and Western predominance and the reign of a strong, pro-Western government. The Shah and Moscow had, however, achieved stable and cooperative relations in the areas of economic and military affairs before the Iranian revolution upended all regional equilibrium. With the denial of U.S. access to Iran, the Soviets reaped immediate gains from the collapse of the Shah's government, and its replacement appeared to offer rich opportuni-

---

[2] See, U.S. Congress. Joint Economic Committee. Soviet Economy in the 1980's: Problems and Prospects. Part I. December 31, 1982. (Section IV, p. 351–507.)

ties for the expansion of Soviet influence beyond the cooperative relationship achieved with the Shah. But, Moscow's early political gains in Iran have been mitigated by Iran's displeasure with the Soviet invasion of Afghanistan, Moscow's support for Iraq, and allegations of Soviet interference in Iranian domestic affairs through the communist Tudeh party.

Soon after the consolidation of power by the Khomeini government, it became clear that new problems had been created for the Soviet Union in its relations with Iran. Iran apparently adopted the principle of "negative equilibrium" in its relations with the two superpowers. The concept maintained that Iran's foreign policy must prevent either the USSR or the United States from acquiring influence in the military, political, economic, and cultural life of Iran.[3] This principle limited the normalization of relations between the two countries. By mid-1983, Soviet-Iranian relations were at their lowest point since the revolution.

Soviet strategic gains were substantial nonetheless, and they reflected Khomeini's national security concepts, which were much more favorable to Soviet interests because they removed U.S. influence from the country. Iran's foreign policy is no longer pro-Western but neutralist and anti-Western. Khomeini has virtually eliminated U.S. influence in the country and sought to damage U.S. prestige, most dramatically by the taking of the hostages at the U.S. Embassy. The already moribund Central Treaty Organization (CENTO) collapsed as a consequence of the revolution's policy of nonalignment, thus calling into question the U.S. policy of containment and undermining Western security systems in general. Iran also closed down the two U.S.-run electronic surveillance stations, which had kept watch on Soviet ICBM tests and constituted an important means of verifying strategic arms limitation treaties. The government decided to drastically curtail arms purchases, cancelling all those with the United States, and it reconsidered its role as policeman of the Persian Gulf. Khomeini sided with the anti-imperilist, anti-American coalition of radical Arab states, a development that complicated the U.S. Camp David approach to achieving a peaceful settlement of the Arab-Israeli conflict. Iran under Khomeini dropped its support for the policies of Egyptian President Anwar Sadat, broke ties with Israel, and embraced the Palestine Liberation Organization (PLO).[4]

In this "zero-sum" evaluation of successes in the USSR-Iran-U.S. triangle, Soviet gains vis-a-vis the United States have been great. Nonetheless, Soviet ability to affect the foreign policy of the Khomeini government in the past two years has been minimal. A number of problems continue to generate friction in the Soviet-Iranian relationship. These issues are: the Iran-Iraq war; the Soviet invasion of Afghanistan; trade, particularly in natural gas deliv-

[3] Chubin, Shahram. the Soviet Union and Iran. Foreign Affairs. Spring 1983. p. 930.
[4] For background on Soviet-Iranian relations before 1981, see: Hirschfield, Yair P. Moscow and Khomeini: Soviet-Iranian Relations in Historical Perspective. Orbis, Summer 1980. Also, Cooper, William P. The Impact of the Iranian Revolution on the Soviet Union. In, The Economic Consequences of the Revolution in Iran. Joint Economic Committee. U.S. Congress. 96th Congress. 1st Session. November 19, 1969. And, Rubinstein, Alvin Z. Soviet Policy Toward Turkey, Iran and Afghanistan. New York, Praeger. 1982.

eries to the USSR; and Soviet involvement in Iranian domestic politics.

2. NARRATIVE OF SOVIET RELATIONS WITH IRAN

Since 1980, Moscow has observed political developments in Iran unfold in an environment of confusion and near-anarchy. Despite this turmoil, Soviet policy toward Iran has been consistent. Its major goals have been to acquire some measure of influence in the country by improving relations with the regime of Ayatollah Ruhollah Khomeini. To promote this objective, Moscow's second aim has been to encourage anti-Western (particularly anti-American) sentiments in Iran by stressing the dangers to the revolution posed by the West, and it has supported leftist influence in the Islamic government. The Soviet Union has presented itself as the defender of the Iranian resolution, and it has attacked criticism of the Soviet Union by various Iranian factions as counter-revolutionary. The Soviets have also attempted to deter any normalization of ties between Iran and the West.

Soviet warnings to Iran of the dangers facing its revolution from the West aim to increase Iran's sense of isolation and weakness and to promote reliance on the Soviet Union for assistance and protection. Leftist terrorist attacks, principally by the Marxist and Islam-inspired Mujahedin-e Khalq, against Khomeini's Islamic Republic have led to Soviet offers of "security assistance," presumably counterintelligence training and expertise to "protect the revolution." [5]

The Soviet attitude toward the Iranian revolution and Islamic fundamentalism in general was considered at the 26th Congress of the Communist Party of the USSR in February 1981, two years after Khomeini had returned to Iran from exile. In his report to the delegates, General Secretary Leonid Brezhnev spoke of the Iranian revolution in favorable, but cautionary terms. Despite "its complications and contradictions," Brezhnev noted, "it is fundamentally an anti-imperialist revolution even though internal and foreign reaction is striving to change its nature." Brezhnev also offered Iran Soviet cooperation, on the basis of "equality" and "reciprocity." About the Islamic revival, Brezhnev said, "the liberation struggle can unfold under the banner of Islam," but added that "reaction also operates with Islamic slogans while raising counter-revolutionary mutinies." [6] Thus Brezhnev reiterated the Soviet view of the progressivism of the Islamic revolution in Iran, and somewhat downplayed the contradictions apparent between Islam and Marxism.

While the Soviet attempted to dismiss the problem of religious fundamentalism, two other major developments threatened normalization with Iran: the Iran-Iraq war and the end of the hostage crisis. The resolution of the hostage crisis in January 1981 was par-

---

[5] Chubin, Shahram. Gains for Soviet Policy in the Middle East. International Security. Spring 1982. p. 140–142. There are also reports of a Soviet-run "listening post" in southeastern Iran that monitors Pakistani assistance to Afghan guerrillas. In exchange for Iran's permission to establish the station, Moscow tips off the Khomeini government about Iranian refugees attempting to flee to Pakistan. (See *Time* magazine, March 8. 1982. p. 32 and 41.)

[6] Foreign Broadcast Information Service (FBIS). Soviet Union Daily Report. Proceedings of the 26th CPSU Congress. Vol. I. February 24, 1981. Vol. III. No. 36, Supp 001. p. 10–11.

ticularly worrisome for the Soviets because it might have opened the way for a possible U.S. rapprochement with Tehran just months after the start of the Iran-Iraq war in September 1980.[7]

Soviet leaders considered their ties with Iran endangered by the continued influence in the government of President Abol Hassan Bani-Sadr and Foreign Minister Sadegh Ghotbzadeh. Both figures urged that Iran seek some measure of normalization with the West, primarily for the purpose of economic reconstruction. Success for the policy of the centrists would mean the possible end of Iran's isolation and potential reliance on the Soviet Union. The ouster of Bani-Sadr in June 1981 was considered a positive development for Soviet policy. And in June and August 1981, two bombings, which eliminated a number of top Iranian officials, aided Soviet interests. The assassinations were used by Moscow to try to fuel Iran's suspicions of U.S. and CIA involvement in its domestic affairs.[8]

Although the Soviets did not expect a great deal of improvement in relations with the post-Shah regime, they have been disappointed by the slow pace of normalization. On March 9, 1982, an authoritative evaluation of relations with Iran appeared in *Pravda,* the official Communist Party newspaper, written by Pavel Demchenko, its primary commentator on Middle East affairs. The article was the first high-level assessment of the Kremlin's ties with Tehran since Brezhnev's appraisal at the 26th Party Congress. Demchenko's theme was that although the Iranian revolution had produced positive changes in Moscow's ties with Tehran, Iran's antagonistic behavior has prevented relations from improving even further. The author complained about the reduction in the number of Soviet diplomats and journalists permitted to work in Iran; the closing of Russian cultural centers; the termination of Iranian-Soviet banking activities; the government-supported anti-Soviet propaganda in Iran; and the clerical regime's inclination to equate Soviet and U.S. motives in Iran.[9] Demchenko blamed right-wing influences around Ayatollah Khomeini for the obstructionism in the development of Soviet-Iranian relations. He did, however, assert that the USSR continues to support the revolution, but not its anti-Soviet elements.

A pessimistic evaluation of the Iranian revolution also appeared in the July 1982 issue of *Kommunist,* the Communist Party's official theoretical journal, written by Rostislav Ulyanovsky, the deputy head of the International Department of the CPSU Central Committee and a leading writer on Third World affairs. The author accused the Islamic clergy of undermining the revolution with the establishment of "absolute rule." This, the "third stage" of the Iranian revolution, is marked by clashes between the clergy and the "left-radical and revolutionary-democractic organizations" and pop-

---

[7] Freedman, Robert O. Soviet Policy towards the Middle East Since 1970. New York, Praeger, 1982, p. 413. Freedman also notes that the Soviets attempted to sabotage the hostage release by warning of an impending U.S. attack.

[8] Ibid.

[9] Rand, Robert. Pravda Assesses Soviet-Iranian Relations. Radio Liberty Research. RL 127/82. March 11, 1982. See also, Dawisha, Karen. The USSR in the Middle East: Superpower in Eclipse? Foreign Affairs, Winter 1982/83. p. 446–448. Dawisha concludes that "while the objective of influencing events in Iran remains a feature of Soviet policy, their capability of doing so, given the increased hostility of the current regime and the widespread persecution of pro-Soviet elements, is increasingly limited." (p. 448)

ular "disillusionment" with the leadership that has forsaken the revolution. Ulyanovsky claimed that leftist opposition groups (presumably elements best represented by the Communist Tudeh party and the Mujahedin-e Khalq) "express the aspirations of the Iranian working people most fully," and take "sharply anti-American and truly anti-imperialist positions." [10]

This frank talk by Soviet commentators, which continued throughout 1982, suggests a change in Soviet attitudes towards Iran with intensified criticism of the Islamicization underway in the country.[11] In the January 7, 1983 (#2) issue of New Times, editor Dmitry Volsky suggested that the Iranian revolution has not lived up to its original promise, that it has "stopped halfway." Volsky carefully avoided criticizing Khomeini, but attacked the government for postponing land reform, prolonging the war with Iraq, and persecuting leftists, including members of the communist Tudeh Party.

After a further deterioration in relations between the Soviet Union and Iran and the crackdown on the Tudeh party in the spring of 1983, Ulyanovsky again attacked the Islamic Republic in another authoritative article. Tudeh Secretary General Khianuri had been arrested in February along with thirty other party officials, and the party was dissolved by government proclamation in May. Anti-Soviet religious elements of the clergy were increasing power and sought to eliminate the capability of the Soviets to influence Iranian domestic politics in the future. Ulyanovsky, writing in the June 22 issue of *Literary Gazette,* said that Iran's revolution had become "Islamic despotism," and that the current regime was undemocratic and intent solely on self-perpetuation. The present campaign of anti-Sovietism was the consequence of a political struggle led, according to Ulyanovsky, by the "right-wing, conservative and traditionalist wing of the Shi'ite clergy, gravitating more and more toward rapprochement with the pro-Western bourgeois merchants and entrepreneurs and the feudal and landowning circles." [12] The article avoids any criticism of Khomeini himself and offers no judgments on the future course of events in Iran. But it reflects Moscow's frustration over how to deal with the fundamentalist Tehran regime. Moscow has seemed prepared to avoid provoking Tehran in order to improve the atmosphere for the normalization of ties, although in 1983 Soviet commentary stepped up criticism of the Iranian clerical leadership. The Soviets view Iran's policy of nonalignment with either superpower as having given way to bitter anti-Sovietism.

---

[10] Ulyanovsky, Rostislav. The Iranian Revolution and Its Special Features. See the abstract in the Current Digest of the Soviet Press, Vol. XXXIV, No. 52, p. 11–12. The first stage of the revolution, according to Ulyanovsky, ended with the fall of the Bazargan government in November 1979. The second, which represented the "commercial and entrepreneurial bourgeoisie," ended when President Bani Sadr was removed from power in June 1981.

[11] From August to October 1982, for example, Moscow Radio held a series of weekly talks by Vladimir Volinskiy on Soviet-Iranian relations. In them, Volinskiy combined praise for Soviet assistance and cooperation with criticism of Tehran.

[12] Soviet World Outlook, July 15, 1983. See also, FBIS, Soviet Union Daily Report, June 30, 1983, p. H1–8 for a complete text of the article.

3. THE IRAN-IRAQ WAR

a. Soviet policies

The Soviet Union has officially remained neutral in the war which began in September 1980 when Iraq invaded Iranian territory. Because of the existence of a treaty of friendship between the USSR and Iraq and the fact that the Iraqi military is armed by the USSR, Moscow's neutrality was interpreted as, in effect, a swing in favor of Tehran. The USSR's policies suggested it was more interested in wooing Iranian trust than reinforcing Iraq. Prospects of strategic gains for Moscow appeared greater in Iran, and the Soviets were distrustful of Iraq, which has sought better relations with the conservative monarchies of the Arabian Peninsula, signed major industrial and military contracts with the West, and suppressed the Iraqi Communist Party. However, the Soviet Union appeared to be engaged in a balancing act for it did not wish to seem to be sacrificing its longstanding partnership with Iraq. But the Soviet Union undermined its image of neutrality when Ambassador Vladimir Vinogradov reportedly hinted at supplying Iran with arms and spare parts.[13]

Since then Iran has sharply criticized Moscow for aiding Iraq with arms deliveries and military advisers. Moscow's apparent objective is to maintain close ties with both Baghdad and Tehran to prevent a shift by either towards the United States and the West[14] and to force both nations to remain beholden to the USSR for arms. A *pax sovietica* to end the Gulf war seemed a likely aim of its foreign policy, although it is not probable now. So far, the war has frustrated Soviet efforts to develop close ties with each of the hostile parties and increase its influence in the Persian Gulf.

In late 1982, the Soviet Union registered a slight but definite shift in its support from Iran to Iraq because of an Iranian battlefield success and Soviet decision to view a decisive victroy by one side or the other as harmful to its interests. Until late 1982, Moscow had refused to deliver military equipment to Baghdad which led to poor relations with Iraq. By early 1983, the Soviet Union had resumed military shipments to Iraq, thus jeopardizing relations with Iran and making an improvement in ties more difficult to achieve.[15] The Soviets apparently gave up hoping for Iranian reasonableness in ending the Gulf war and saw no prospects for better ties with Tehran even should Moscow maintain its course of official neutralism.

The Soviets campaigned for a negotiated settlement of the conflict, a war which does not entirely serve Soviet interests in the region. The war has increased the influence of the moderate,

---

[13] Porter, Bruce. Soviet Arms and the Iraqi-Iranian Conflict. Radio Liberty Research. RL 382/80. October 16, 1980.

[14] Rubinstein, Alvin Z. The Soviet Union and Iran Under Khomeini. International Affairs. Autumn 1981. p. 610–611. The French weekly magazine, *L'Express,* reported in December 3, 1982 that Iran and the Soviet Union had signed a secret military pact in May 1981. The purported agreement provides for Soviet technicians to be sent to Iran and Iranian officers to be trained in the USSR. It reports that the agreement has been fully implemented although Iranian authorities deny its existence. The article suggests the agreement may be the continuation of one signed by the Shah for the supply of arms.

[15] Rand, Robert. Iran-Iraq War continues to Frustrate Soviet Policy Goals. Radi Liberty Research. RL 297–83. August 4, 1983.

wealthy Arab states of the peninsula, eased Egypt's return to the Arab mainstream as a result of its military support of Iraq, isolated Syria, which has sided with Iran, and raised fears on the Arabian peninsula of an Iranian-led Shiite revolution against Sunni Arab monarchies.[16] The Soviets also view the war as contributing to the power of the more conservative, anti-Soviet wing of the Islamic Republican Party. The Kremlin sees the conflagration as aiding U.S. interests by softening Arab opposition to a U.S. military presence in the region.[17]

b. Soviet military aid to Iran

The Soviet Union has attempted to make Iran militarily dependent on it for its national security, but it has been unwilling or unsuccessful in turning Iran into its direct arms client. Because the Soviet Union wishes to keep close ties with both nations, it has been sending modest amounts of arms to Iraq through East European intermediaries and in turn permitting Syria, Libya, and North Korea to transfer stocks of weapons to Iran. The Soviet Union and its Eastern bloc allies are reported to have some 2,000 military advisers in Iran, including several hundred East Germans working with Revolutionary Guards[18] and SAVAMA, the secret police. But Iran's capacity to absorb Soviet weaponry is limited because most of its inventory is of U.S. origin. Reliable reports state that Israel has been an important supplier of U.S. spare parts and ammunition throughout the war.

During the first year and a half of the war, the Soviets virtually boycotted arms deliveries to Iraq. In late 1982 however, Moscow resumed limited supplies of sophisticated arms, including MIG-23 and -25 aircraft and T-72 tanks. The turn towards Iraq may be the result of Iran's drive against Iraqi territory in late 1982 and early 1983 and the Soviet Union's inability to use the war to acquire measurable influence in Iran. This has been due to Iraq's failure to seriously threaten Iran (which is therefore not desperate for foreign military assistance), Iranian stockpiles of U.S.-made weapons purchased by the Shah and Iran's success in finding spare parts for them from Western sources, and the combat skill of the Revolutionary Guards (the Pasdaran).

Iran has received large supplies of arms from other sources. North Korea and Iran have had an arms-for-oil agreement since the early stages of the war. The North Koreans delivered 40 percent of Iran's $2 billion in military arms imports in 1982. This includes 150 T-62 tanks, 1,000 mortars and other smaller weapons. Military analysts feel North Korea is working with the Soviet Union to exert leverage on Tehran. It has sent about 300 military instructors to Iran.[19] China is also involved in the Iran-Iraq war

[16] Middleton, Drew. Gulf War Said to Strengthen More Moderate Arab Nations. New York Times. November 24, 1982. p. A6.
[17] Vladimir Gudev, a Soviet commentator writing in the weekly *New Times* (November 1982, #47), says a settlement "would inevitably strengthen the positions of the Middle East countries opposed to U.S. interference in regional affairs and endanger Washington's interests in the vast Persian Gulf area and its plans to establish military and political domination there."
[18] Gelb, Leslie. Iran Said to Get Large/Scale Arms from Israel, Soviets and Europeans. New York Times. March 8, 1982. p. A10.
[19] New York Times, December 19, 1982, p. 1 and 14.

and the pursuit of influence there. Peking desires to restrict Soviet influence in both Iran and Iraq, and so it has reportedly shipped military equipment to both sides, although Chinese officials deny it. Both Iran and Iraq are said to be paying for Chinese arms with exports of oil. In January 1983, Iran and China agreed to a 150 percent increase in annual trade, with a total turnover planned to reach $500 million in 1983. A significant portion of the trade is suspected to be in Chinese arms flowing to Iran.[20] If reports of an increasing arms trade with China—as well as with Israel, North Korea, and Libya—are accurate, Tehran may be displaying a reluctance to depend further on Moscow for diplomatic and military support that could represent a further setback for Soviet policy in Iran.

The Gulf war has not aided Soviet policy in the region, although it has distracted attention from the war in Afghanistan and reduced oil supplies to the West, probably keeping oil prices higher than would be the case without the war. Moscow has insisted on a neutral pose, provoking the enmity of Tehran and Baghdad, while limited arms deliveries to both sides have seemingly further damaged the Soviet position. Soviet actions have aroused Iraqi hostility and suspicion without earning real gains in Iran. Without a peaceful resolution of the war, the Soviets appear to be in a no-win situation. An Iraqi victory would strengthen Baghdad's independence from the USSR and perhaps lead to a reconciliation between a defeated Iran and the United States. On the other hand, an Iranian victory might solidify and spread the Islamic regime to Baghdad and deepen anti-Soviet animosities in Tehran.

4. THE SOVIET OCCUPATION OF AFGHANISTAN

The Soviet invasion of Afghanistan remains an impediment to better relations between Moscow and Tehran. In December 1982, Iran marked the third anniversary of the invasion by denouncing the Soviet Union's continued presence in Afghanistan. The Iranian Foreign Ministry on December 26 condemned Moscow's "hegemonistic move against the oppressed and Muslim people of Afghanistan," and demanded the withdrawal of Soviet troops. The statement called the Soviet Union "the world oppressor" and condemned the "savage behavior" of its troops in Afghanistan. Thousands of Iranian protesters staged a demonstration at the Soviet Embassy in Tehran, which led to an official protest by the Soviet government and a response from TASS charging that the protest was organized with "the obvious connivance of the Iranian authorities." The Afghanistan issue has been the principal cause of a number of other anti-Soviet demonstrations in Iran in recent years.[21]

---

[20] Weisskopf, Michael. China Plays Both Sides in Persian Gulf War. Washington Post. January 13, 1983. p. A21 and A25. See also, The Economist (May 14, 1983, p. 55-56) which says Peking has supplied Iran with its version of Soviet MIG-19 and -21 aircraft (called the F-6 and F-7 by the Chinese) by way of North Korea. Also: Hiro, Dilip. Iran Plays China Card. Wall Street Journal. September 22, 1983. p. 30.

[21] See, Rubinstein, Alvin Z. The Soviet Union and Iran under Khomeini. International Affairs. Autumn 1981. p. 604-609. For Soviet charges of Iran's interference in Afghanistan, see The Current Digest of the Soviet Press, Vol. XXXV, No. 31. August 31, 1983. p. 6.

Ayatollah Khomeini has described the conflict in Aghanistan as "a sacred holy war" for the Muslim guerrillas. In 1980, Foreign Minister Sadegh Ghotbzadeh led charges that the Soviet invasion called into question Soviet amibitions in the region. Even though Ghotbzadeh was removed from office in late 1980, his views probably represent the opinion of most Iranian leaders, who are deeply suspicious of Soviet intentions. The continued occupation of Afghanistan by Soviet troops will place limits on Soviet-Iranian relations.

In the summer of 1983 Moscow sharply escalated its criticism of Iranian support of the Afghan resistance. Iran is host to some one million Afghan refugees and permits its border regions to be used by Afghan guerrillas. Tehran has also refused to take part in the United Nations-sponsored talks in Geneva on a settlement of the Afghanistan problem. Iran has instead opted to keep itself informed by U.N. mediators on the status of the talks between the Pakistani and Afghanistan governments.

5. SOVIET TRADE WITH IRAN

Trade with Iran has provided the Soviet Union with the opportunity to maintain official government-to-government ties and encourage Iran's economic reliance on Moscow during conditions of political strain between the two countries. The Soviets have tried to cultivate a new relationship with Iran by avoiding political differences and focusing on economies ties. Early efforts to establish relations with the Islamic Republic by offering economic and military aid were rejected. Later, however, Western economic sanctions and the war with Iraq compelled Iran to seek limited economic ties with the USSR. Although trade has expanded since the political turmoil of 1978 and 1979, the Soviet Union has been dissatisfied with the disinclination of the Khomeini government to allow trade to lead to closer political relations.

Under the Shah, Soviet economic relations with Iran were developed extensively. A reduction in trade followed the political crisis that led to the overthrow of the Shah, although this was caused more by the inability of the Iranian economy to absorb imports and to provide exports of natural gas, rather than by conscious Iranian policy. Trade with the Soviet Union and Eastern Europe grew quickly after 1979, however, as a result of Western economic sanctions during the hostage crisis and the Gulf war, which closed down a number of Iran's southern ports. *Izvestia* claims that 1981 Soviet-Iranian trade had reached a record 800 million rubles ($1.1 billion), double the level of 1980, and higher than the 671 million rubles in 1978, the last full year of the Shah's rule. The 1981 trade figure was particularly notable because it was achieved without the resumption of Iranian natural gas sales to the USSR, Iran's largest export item to the Soviet Union under the Shah. However, trade declined in 1982 to below 800 million rubles.[22] The most surprising factor in the trade was the Soviet purchase of 2.2 million tons of Iranian oil, the first oil deal between the two countries. (The crude

---

[22] Klochek, V. USSR's Foreign Trade in 1982. Ekonomicheskaya Gazeta. March 1983 (#13). FBIS, Soviet Union Daily Report, March 31, 1983, p. S8.

oil was reportedly bought for direct shipment to Vietnam.) A similar expansion in trade occurred between Iran and Eastern Europe, primarily the result of purchases of Iranian crude oil.

The most sensitive trade issue remains the suspended gas deliveries through the Iran Gas Trunkline (IGAT I), which were halted in early 1979 but resumed in mid-1979 without reaching former levels, and then ceased entirely in March 1980 when the Soviets refused to pay the Iranian price of five times the previous rate. By late 1982, deliveries had not resumed. Another casualty in Soviet-Iranian trade was the IGAT II pipeline, to have been completed in 1981. The Iranians further angered the Soviet Union when the government announced in September 1982 that it had decided to route the IGAT II pipeline through Turkey, using materials already supplied by the USSR.[23] This project, with European participation, involved Iranian gas deliveries to Soviet Trans-Caucasia to offset Soviet exports of Siberian gas to Eastern and Western Europe in exchange for hard currency earnings.

Soviet-Iranian trade relations seemingly improved—at least temporarily—in early 1982. In February, the Soviet Union and Iran signed an accord for cooperation in the construction of two power plants during the visit to Moscow of Energy Minister Hasan Ghafurifard, the first Iranian Cabinet official to visit the USSR since early 1979. The visit was notable more for the restraint demonstrated by both sides, who emphasized the value of bilateral cooperation, rather than the benefits to be derived by an economic agreement. Ghafurifard refrained from calling for a Soviet withdrawal from Afghanistan and for a halt to Soviet arms shipments to Iraq. He dispelled western reports that Iran was considering a Soviet offer of a Treaty of Friendship similar to those signed with Cuba, Vietnam and Ethiopia, but described the USSR as a "friendly country." The minister added that ideological differences should not hinder good relations as long as both nations did not intervene in the other's affairs.

The Soviet media have regularly pointed out (and exaggerated) the benefits to Iran of economic ties with the Soviet Union. In January 1983, the Soviets completed the electrification of the railway line between the Soviet border and the northern Iranian city of Tabriz, easing overland commerce between the two countries. *Izvestia* noted that of 153 joint ventures, 104 have been completed. According to Soviet sources, Iran shipped 3.4 million tons of goods through the USSR in 1981. The Soviets also laud the construction of the Isfahan steel mill which was built with Soviet assistance before the revolution, the construction of hydroelectric and irrigation dams along the border river of Arras, and the presence of 1,000–2,000 Soviet technicians in Iran.[24]

---

[23] For a detailed discussion of the natural gas agreements, see, Hanningan, J. B. and McMillan, C. H. The Soviet-Iranian Gas Agreements: Nexus of Energy Politics, East-West Relations, and Middle East Politics. Soviet Union/Union Sovietique. Vol. 9, Pt.2 (1982). p. 131–153. The authors note that the barter agreements allowed the Soviet Union to penetrate Iran with material, technical, and financial assistance in the development of Iranian industry. This contributed to a growing Soviet economic "presence" and increased its political influence. The agreements also eased Soviet domestic natural gas transportation problems.

[24] The U.S. Government estimates Soviet and East European economic technicians in Iran during 1981 at 2,450. U.S. Department of State. Soviet and East European Aid to the Third World, 1981. February 1983. p. 21.

An important development in Soviet-Iranian relations has been Iran's growing trade with Soviet allies, such as East Germany, Czechoslovakia, Bulgaria, South Yemen, and North Korea. In 1982 Iran concluded agreements with East Germany (for petrochemical projects), Czechoslovakia (for geological surveys), South Yemen (for continued refining of oil at Aden), Libya and Algeria (for oil and gas cooperation), Syria (for arms and food), and India (for atomic energy). Trade with North Korea, which is providing arms and assistance to Iranian industry, was projected to rise to $500 million in 1983, from $14 million in 1980.[25]

Although the Soviet Union has attempted to encourage trade with Iran, the level of economic activity is comparatively low. Further, Moscow has been unable to translate its bilateral economic relations real agreements in the political sphere. The heavily publicized visit by Minister Ghafurifard produced virtually no lasting political gains. The natural gas issue, the most important source of contention, remains unresolved. The economic agreements that have been signed with the Soviet bloc are the result of pragmatic decisions by both sides. Iran has been isolated by western sanctions and the Gulf war, while the USSR has found a limited number of trade accords useful in maintaining ties to Iran.

6. THE TUDEH AND SOVIET INTERFERENCE IN IRANIAN AFFAIRS

One objective of Soviet policy in Iran has been to support the pro-Moscow communist Tudeh (Masses) Party as a political force within Iran as the revolution unfolds. Soviet leaders presumably hope that should the present regime collapse, the left will gain power, placing the Tudeh in the position to shape the course of events in Iran to Soviet advantage, perhaps in a national front-style coalition. The Tudeh ensures that the Soviet Union has a voice to influence internal Iranian politics. Although small in numbers (probably no more than 5,000 members before 1983), the Tudeh's limited popular base is made up for by its organizational discipline and Soviet assistance. Most observers believe the Tudeh has little chance of assuming sole power in Iran. However, the Soviet Union has hoped that the Tudeh could assume a pivotal role in a post-Khomeini government, and it has been careful not to be seen as supporting any opposition to Khomeini.[26]

Under the Shah, the Tudeh party was banned. And under Khomeini, until February 1983, the party was tolerated and did not suffer the persecution inflicted on other leftist groups because of its unstinting support of the Islamic Republic. The party's secretary general and leader Nurredin Khianuri said it would aid the government as long as the "progressive" nature of the revolution is maintained and it follows the course of "anti-imperialism." Unlike other leftists groups in Iran, the Tudeh has rejected overt armed

---

[25] Kelly, S.B. The Soviet Penetration of Iran. A Contemporary Paper, Vol. XII, No. 1, 1983. Center for International Security.

[26] See, Chubin. Gains for Soviet Policy in the Middle East. p. 143. "The obvious Soviet asset—the Tudeh party—can be used either as a pressure group or as a power base for an alternative government. It would be a mistake to see the Soviet's choices as confined solely to the Tudeh party members and its sympathizers." Rubinstein (Soviet Policy Towards Turkey, Iran, and Afghanistan. p. 114) writes that the Tudeh's current aim is more to sustain anti-American and prevent an opening to the West than to seize power.

violence as a political tool, and this approach helped ensure its survival.

In February 1983, however, the government turned against the Tudeh, detaining the leadership of the party, including Khianuri, on charges of espionage and plotting to overthrow the Islamic republic. The move seemed to reflect both the worsening relations with the USSR and the ascendance of anti-Soviet elements in the Iranian clergy. In May, the government cracked down further by dissolving the party and two other small pro-Soviet groups. Eighteen Soviet diplomats were also ordered expelled. Tehran's actions reportedly were taken mainly as a consequence of the USSR's decision in late 1982 to resume arms sales to Iraq and for reasons of internal factional politics in Iran. The party has also endorsed the Soviet invasion of Afghanistan. Moscow quickly launched a campaign against the arrests and disbanding of the Tudeh.[27]

Ultimately, the Tudeh strategy failed because of the contradictions of its policies. One observer described the Tudeh's relationship towards the revolution as essentially "parasitic." [28] The legal dissolution of the Tudeh necessarily reduced the party's organizational strength and most of its political influence. However, a revival of the communist party's activities with Soviet assistance cannot be ruled out in the future.

Another area of Soviet interference in Iran's internal affairs has traditionally concerned ethnic divisions in Iran. Recently, the Soviet Union has not encouraged separatism or decentralization, as it did in 1945-46 when it established the puppet Kurdish and Azerbaijan republics. Other nationalities in stages of rebellion include the Turkomans, the Baluch, the Arabs of Khuzistan province on the Gulf, and the Qashqai in the south, all of whom could represent a threat to the territorial integrity of Iran. However, the Soviet Union has not actively sought to encourage their nationalism, and instead has identified them with American interests and monarchist counter-revolutionary unrest. Generally, the Soviets have supported ethnic rights in Iran, but have also suggested that the "progressive" nature of the Khomeini revolution aids nationalist rights. Moscow does not want to be seen as supporting ethnic and nationalist hostilities that may sabotage the revolution.[29]

The most serious involvement of the Soviet Union in ethnic unrest is in Azerbaijan and Kurdistan. In Azerbaijan, the large Muslim People's Republic Party of Ayatollah Mohammad Kazem Shariatmadari, the religious head of the Turkish-speaking minority, is seeking greater, autonomy from Tehran. The Soviet Union emphasizes Iranian Azerbaijanis' ties with the Azerbaijani republic of the USSR, and Soviet propaganda has lauded Azeri cultural contributions in Iran. The pro-Moscow, communist Azerbaijan Democratic Party (ADP) also resumed operations under the Khomeini government, but does not claim a following as large as Ayatollah Shariat-Maradi's party. The aim of Soviet policy here, however, is

[27] Soviet World Outlook. March 15, 1983. And, Soviet World Outlook. July 15, 1983.
[28] Devlin, Kevin. The Rise and Fall of the Tudeh Party. Radio Free Europe. RAD Background Report/112. May 17, 1983. p. 3. See also, Rand, Robert. Iran's Crackdown on Pro-Soviet Communists Continues. Radio Liberty Research. RL 201/83. May 19, 1983.
[29] Atkin, Muriel. Soviet Relations with the Islamic Republic. SAIS Review. Winter-Spring 1983. p. 191-192.

not to encourage separatism, as it was after World War II but, it appears, to exert leverage over the central government. Soviet leaders may be wary of launching a separatist movement in Iranian Azerbaijan that could spill over into the Soviet Azerbaijan republic.[30]

The issue of Kurdish independence receives more attention—if not consistent support—from the Kremlin. The Kurdish independence movement has suffered under superpower maneuverings and political developments between Iran and Iraq. The Soviets have also had trouble working out an alliance with the dominant Kurdish Democratic party (KDP), with whom it has had close ties in the past. Moscow has on occasion given the appearance of pushing the KDP into supporting the central Tehran government, in the hopes of currying favor with the Khomeini government. But, Moscow has apparently chosen to maintain a strategy of keeping its options open in Kurdistan by aiding from time to time both anti-Iranian and anti-Iraqi Kurdish factions. Most observers believe that Soviet arms supplies to Kurdish separatists are a means of pressuring Tehran, and are not a concerted effort to overthrow the government.[31]

C. Soviet Foreign Policy and Iraq: Outmoded Alliance?

1. INTRODUCTION

Following a period of expanding ties in the 1960s and early 1970s, Iraq has more recently loosened its bonds to the Soviet Unon. This was the consequence of changes in Arab and regional politics, Iraq's growing oil wealth, its des re for expanded economic relations with the West, and the pragmatic, less ideological attitude towards foreign affairs that characterizes the government of President Saddam Hussein.

Iraq has seen its national interests conflict sharply with those of the USSR, while its independence from Moscow and maneuverability have increased. President Saddam Hussein has followed a policy of pan-Arabism and nonalignment at the expense of Soviet interests in the region. Rising revenues from oil exports have led to expanded commercial, political, and military ties with the West and the relative decline of economic relations with the Eastern Bloc. Moscow's decision to resume arms shipments to Iraq in 1982 does not necessarily signal a qualitative turn in Soviet-Iraqi ties, though there have been some improvements. Relations will continue to be affected by the changing Middle East political environment and national interests.

The view from Moscow has been frustrating. In the past three years, Iraq has condemned the Soviet invasion of Afghanistan, initiated a war with Iran, thus undermining the Soviet goal of shaping an anti-imperialist coalition of Mideast states, and adopted a more amenable posture towards the West, including greater economic and military ties. Saddam has ended the ruling Baathist Party's cooperation with the Iraqi Communist Party, which was

---

[30] Ibid., p. 192–193.
[31] See, Rubinstein. Soviet Policy Toward Turkey, Iran, and Afghanistan. p. 115–116. See also, Atkin. Soviet Relations with the Islamic Republic p. 191–192.

seen as an instrument of Soviet policy in the country. The Soviet calculation to remain neutral in the Gulf war (a policy that, under the circumstances, constituted a gain for Iran) was intended to curry favor with Tehran without losing all influence in Iraq. Although the 1972 Treaty of Friendship and Cooperation remains in force, in practice there is now clearly less than an alliance relationship.

2. MILITARY AND ECONOMIC RELATIONS

To increase its influence in Baghdad, the Soviet Union had extended economic and technical aid and military assistance while developing informal exchanges between government and party organizations. Soviet economic aid has been substantial over the years, totaling some $705 million from 1954 to 1981; during the same period, Eastern Europe provided $495 million. The commitment to Iraq's military capabilities has been even more impressive. Baghdad has been the USSR's largest arms buyer, with purchases of about $4.9 billion from 1975 to 1979.[32] Commercial considerations have spurred Soviet arms sales to oil-rich Iraq since the early 1970s.

Until the mid-1970s, the Eastern bloc had supplied nearly all of Iraq's weaponry and military training. This dependence on Soviet training continues. Western estimates of Soviet and East European military advisers currently in Iraq range from 1,000 to 2,200, at least double the number in the early 1970s. The Iraqi armed forces (together with Syrian forces) have received the most advanced military equipment that the Soviets have offered to a Third World country, with deliveries of MiG–21s and MiG–23s, Scud missiles, T–62 and T–72 tanks, and other advanced weapons. In January 1983, the Soviets agreed to deliver another $2 billion in arms. With Soviet supplies, Iraq maintained one of the best trained and well-equipped armies in the Middle East until the Iran-Iraq war broke out in 1980.

Moscow and its East European allies have also undertaken large commercial projects and significant investment in technical assistance that have led to a growing trade. East European countries have been active in Iraqi development. Romania has contracts for power and oil development; Bulgaria is involved in construction projects; Poland has 8,000 technicians in Iraq; and Cuba had 3,5000 construction and road workers in the country in 1981.[33]

The Soviet Union won bids to construct major irrigation and power projects worth some $1 billion in the late 1970s. The Soviets earned valuable hard currency from sales of arms and heavy machinery, and Iraqi deliveries of oil to the USSR (from a high of 220,000 barrels a day in 1973, to a low of 70,000 b/d in 1979 and

---

[32] U.S. Department of State. Soviet and East European Aid to the Third World, 1981. p. 19.
The U.S. Government estimates that Iraq has received $5.0 billion in arms from the Soviet Union from 1976 to 1980. U.S. Arms Control and Disarmament Agency. World Military Expenditures and Arms Transfers, 1971–1980. March 1983, p. 119.
The Christian Science Monitor reports (January 31, 1983, p. 13) that Iraq paid $10 billion to the Eastern bloc for Soviet arms in the first two years of the Gulf war. Although no reliable and comprehensive statistics are available, if the foregoing estimates are reasonable, Iraq has purchased over $20 billion in arms from the USSR and Eastern Europe since 1955.
[33] U.S. Dept. of State. Soviet and East European Aid, 1981. p. 8 & 21.

almost zero in 1981) enable Moscow to sell more of its own oil to the West. In 1981, the Soviets concluded a number of large commercial contracts with Iraq, and Soviet exports reached $1.2 billion.[34] As trade grew, however, the Soviet share of Iraqi foreign trade dropped. During this period, Iraqi trade with the West and Japan multiplied as a consequence of Iraq's oil wealth.[35]

In the mid-1970s, Iraq decided to diversify its source of arms supplies. One development that contributed to this decision was the Soviet Union's reluctance in 1975 to provide additional artillery and infantry weapons to the Iraqi forces attempting to subdue Kurdish separatists in the north. Iraqi's largest arms deal was with France, but minor purchases of weapons were made with Britain, West Germany, Italy, and more recently with Brazil. The Iraqi-French agreement provided for sales of Mirage F–1 aircraft, tanks, missiles, and naval vessels valued at $1.5 billion, in exchange for guaranteed oil supplies. Iraq also negotiated the sale of a nuclear reactor with France, which caused widespread concern that Iraq was moving to produce its own atomic bomb. In January 1983, during the visit to Paris of Deputy Prime Minister Tariq Aziz, France agreed to permit Iraq to continue buying French arms on credit while France triples its purchases of Iraqi crude oil The French government's decision in 1983 to provide Iraq with Super Etendard bomber aircraft armed with Exocet air-to-surface missiles is seen as further evidence of Baghdad's reliance on the French connection. France has sold Iraq about $4 billion in arms since the Gulf war began, excluding the Etendards.[36]

Increasingly, Iraqi and Soviet evaluations of their security interests have come into conflict, leading to a relative downgrading of economic and military relations. Although Iraq continues to purchase large numbers of weapons systems from the Eastern bloc, as a consequence of Moscow's ambivalent policies in the Gulf war it has come to rely less and less on the Soviet Union for its national security. The Soviet invasion of Afghanistan provoked Iraqi condemnations at the United Nations and Islamic conferences. The Iranian revolution has also compromised the Soviet allegiance to Iraq. After the start of the Iran-Iraq war, Moscow adopted a neutral stand (it officially favors neither side) and refused to step up direct arms shipments to Baghdad. After Iranian forces advanced into Iraqi territory in 1982, the Kremlin resumed arms shipments to Iraq. The apparent improvement in relations has not led to a corresponding expansion of Soviet influence among the Baathists. In fact, Iraqi leaders may be generally skeptical of Soviet dependability in a crisis.[37] Furthermore, Iraq's dependence on Saudi and other conservative Arab political and financial support may carry the price of maintaining distance from the USSR.

---

[34] Ibid., p. 8.

[35] Soviet government sources claim that total trade with Iraq grew from 600 million rubles in 1975, to 909 million in 1981 and 994 million in 1982. Klochek. USSR's Foreign Trade in 1982. (In, F.B.I.S., Soviet Union Daily Report, March 31, 983, p. S8.)
    In 1982, Iraq's total trade with the industrial West was $19.4 billion, with Soviet bloc just $1.95 billion, of which $1.3 billion was with Romania alone. (See, International Monetary Fund. Direction of Trade Statistics, 1983 Yearbook. p. 219–220.)

[36] New York Times. January 8, 1983. p. 4.

[37] Smolansky, Oles M. The Kremlin and the Iraqi Ba'th, 1968–1982: An Influence Relationship. Middle East Review. Spring/Summer 1983. p. 67.

President Saddam Hussein has repeatedly declared that the two superpowers have a vested interest in seeing the Gulf war continue, and he cites as evidence the flow of arms into Iran from both the Eastern bloc and the West. Saddam has said that Iraq's treaty with Soviet Union "has not worked" during its war with Iran, and he has indicated his government is seriously considering steps to improve relations with the United States under the proper circumstances.[38] Contributing to Iraq's resentment of the USSR's neutrality is the fact that most of Moscow's friends (Libya, Syria, South Yemen and the PLO) support Iran in the Gulf war, while Iraq depends on the more conservative, pro-Western states for aid. Iraq views the Soviet policy of improving ties with the Shiite Islamic Republic in Iran as detrimental to its interests. Ayatollah Khomeini has consistently called for the overthrow of Saddam Hussein and the creation of a Shiite, clergy-ruled government in Baghdad.

Of particular worry to the Soviets have been the first steps towards a possible rapprochement between Iraq and the United States. U.S. Deputy Secretary of State Morris Draper travelled to Baghdad in April 1981 soon after the Reagan Administration had approved the sale to Iraq of five Boeing airliners. Mideast specialist Robert Freeman points out that one of the side effects of the Israeli bombing of the Osirak nuclear reactor in June 1981 was limited U.S.-Iraqi cooperation at the United Nations in formulating a Security Council resolution condemning the Israeli action.[39] And in December 1982, the Reagan Administration provided Iraq with a $460 million loan at low interest for grain purchases. Moscow is concerned that Iraq may abandom its support for the anti-Israeli Steadfastness Front and join the centrist states of Jordan and Saudi Arabia, with whom it has developed closer relations.

3. NON-ALIGNMENT AND PAN-ARABISM

Baghdad's campaign against the Iraqi Communist Party is another cause of strain in Soviet-Iraqi ties and has resulted in the spectacular decline in the party's fortunes. In 1978 and 1979, a total of forty-eight members of the ICP were executed by the government for allegedly infiltrating the armed forces. Further arrests and persecution of Communists followed that resulted in driving the ICP underground.[40] The Soviets have interpreted Iraqi anti-communist domestic policies as indications of an anti-Soviet foreign policy, while Baghdad sees the hand of the Kremlin behind the Communist Party. At the 26th Congress of the CPSU in February 1981, the head of the ICP Mohammad Aziz, apparently under Soviet direction, denounced the Iraqi government's treatment of the ICP and the Kurds, condemned the Iran-Iraq war, and called for Iraq to withdraw from Iranian territory. The Communist Party declared in early 1982 that it was actively promoting revolution against the central Baghdad government together with Kurdish se-

---

[38] Middleton, Drew. Iraq Says its Treaty with Soviet Union Hasn't Worked. New York Times, November 17, 1982, p. A3.
[39] Freedman. Soviet Policy Toward the Middle East. p. 408–410. Freedman acknowledges that the Osirak raid gave new life to the Steadfastness Front and indeed led to limited shipments of Soviet arms to Iraq.
[40] Smolansky. The Kremlin and the Iraqi Ba'th. p. 63.

cessionists. For the Baathists, the 1978 Communist takeover in Afghanistan, followed by the Soviet invasion in 1979, demonstrated the danger of permitting a Communist party to operate freely organizing workers and students and infiltrating the armed forces.[41]

Underlying Iraqi hostility towards the Soviet Union and the Communist Party is Baghdad's attempt to project itself as the head of the pan-Arab and non-aligned movements, a policy that has conflicted with Soviet interests in Iraq.[42] Baghdad has increasingly seen its interests served by following the principles of nonalignment: equidistance between the superpowers and avoidance of dependence on either. Iraqi Baathist ideology has also recently supported pan-Arab nationalism, with emphasis on Arab unity, not socialist internationalism based on the Soviet model. Iraq has become concerned by Moscow's growing assertiveness in regions surrounding the Gulf—in the Horn of Africa, the Yemens, and Afghanistan. After the Soviet invasion of Afghanistan, Iraq denounced Moscow for spreading Marxist ideology in the region. In February 1980, Saddam Hussein proposed the "Pan-Arab Charter," which called for all Arab states to reject the presence of any non-Arab military forces on their territory.

Increasingly, the Kremlin and the Baathists are political competitors in the Arab world. Iraq has had a running fued with South Yemen; Baghdad announced in 1980 the creation of a front to oppose the Marxist government in Aden, with the explicit intention of ridding the country of Soviet influence. Iraq has supported the Eritrean independence movement in Ethiopia, another Soviet client state, citing concern over the Cuban and Soviet presence in the Horn of Africa. Iraq has been consistent in its opposition to superpower presence in the Persian Gulf and its relations with Syria have deteriorated. The Iraqis have denied Soviet requests for naval facilities at Um-Qasr, on the Persian Gulf. Iraq's recent pragmatism is also explained by the change in leadership in 1979 from President Ahmad Hassan al-Bakr to Saddam. Saddam is considered to be far less pro-Soviet than his predecessor and more eager to develop the country's economy with Western technology.[43]

4. CONCLUSION: SOVIET SUCCESS AND FAILURES IN IRAQ

Soviet influence on the ruling Baathist government has been sharply limited in recent years. Moscow has been unable to modify Baghdad's position on a number of issues of importance to Iraq: the Soviet invasion of Afghanistan, ending the war with Iran (although Saddam has been more forthcoming than the Iranians), and concessions to the Iraqi Communist Party. The ICP remains a principal obstacle to improve relations. The Soviet Union has endeavored to include the Iraqis in the Steadfastness Front of Arab antiimperialist states along with Syria, Libya, Algeria, the PLO, and South Yemen, but the dynamics of international politics have mitigated against Iraqi participation. Baghdad has seen relations with Syria

---

[41] See, Kashkett, Steven B. Iraq and the Pursuit of Nonalignment. Orbis, Summer 1982. p. 478–480

[42] See Hottinger, Arnold. Arab Communism at Low Ebb. Problems of Communism, July/August 1981. p. 22–24.

[43] Kashkett. Iraq and the Pursuit of Nonalignment. p. 480.

worsen as a result of rivalries between the two Ba'th parties and Syria's support for Iran, while Libya remains isolated in Arab politics. Instead of weakening Western influence in the region, Iraqi foreign policy has contributed to drawing Western involvement into the area at Soviet expense.

During the 1970's, the Soviet Union's economic aid and military sales and training were useful in promoting Iraqi dependence on Moscow, but as Iraq cultivated its relationship with France and Western Europe, the value of these ties diminished. The arms supply relationship remains, to a large degree, an important means of influencing Iraqi behavior because of Iraq's reliance on Soviet-built weapons in its war with Iran. Nonetheless, Iraq is unlikely to permit this dependence to alter its fundamental security policies developed in the past decade at the expense of Soviet interests.

D. SOVIET POLICY TOWARD SAUDI ARABIA

Saudi Arabia is crucial to Soviet policy in the Arabian Peninsula and would present a diplomatic prize for Moscow should there be a renewal of relations between the two countries. So far, Saudi leaders have held out the lure of diplomatic recognition to moderate Soviet policies on issues of importance to them. In addition, it seems fairly clear that the Saudis have flirted with the Soviets in order to exert leverage over the United States and keep Washington committed to the region. Because the two nations have no political or economic relations and the region is dominated by conservative monarchies, Soviet influence among the conservative states of the Arabian peninsula is negligible. The possibility of improved formal relations hinges on the prospects of re-establishing diplomatic ties with Riyadh, severed in the late 1930's. The resumption of relations and the expansion of Soviet influence will depend to a large degree on Saudi confidence in U.S. foreign policy and the possible need of Saudi Arabia accommodating Soviet power in the region.[44] In the past, Saudi Arabia has been receptive to Soviet overtures to improve ties as a means of exerting leverage over U.S. policy, particularly towards Israel, and to balance the country's dependence on the United States for military security. In recent year Saudi-Soviet ties have fluctuated between apparent moves to normalize and careful distancig by the Saudis.

The Soviet Union has had ambivalent reactions towards the Saudi monarchy. Saudi Arabia is a leading Arab state which has resolutely opposed the U.S.-sponsored Camp David peace accords while providing financial and diplomatic support for the Palestine Liberation Organization, a close ally of the USSR. On the other hand, the Saudis are anti-communist and maintain close military ties to the United States, while opposing Soviet policy throughout the Middle East.

1. SOVIET OVERTURES TO SAUDI ARABIA

The Soviet Union has been intent on demonstrating to the Saudis that Moscow is a reliable ally on issues of importance to the Arab world, and that ideological and religious differences need not

---

[44] Quandt, William, Riyadh Between the Superpowers. Foreign Policy, Fall, 1981. p. 38.

obstruct proper if limited political relations.[45] Moscow notes with optimism any signs of Saudi disappointment with the direction of U.S. foreign policy in the Middle East and interprets this weakness as a signal to pressure the monarchy into some form of dialogue.[46]

The latest occasion for Moscow's statements on the possibility of improving ties with the Saudis came on the fiftieth anniversary of the founding of the Saudi Kingdom in September 1982. Radio Moscow lauded Riyadh's leadership of the Arab world, its stance on Palestinian independence, and its financial aid to the underdeveloped nations, while reminding its listeners that the USSR was one of the first states to establish diplomatic ties with Saudi Arabia in 1932.[47]

More recent and substantial speculation over the possibility of a Soviet breakthrough with Saudi Arabia arose during the visit to Moscow in December 1982 of Saudi Foreign Minister Prince Saud al-Faisal as a member of the Arab League's peace delegation. This was the first known visit by a senior Saudi official since diplomatic ties with Moscow were severed in the late 1930s. Although Prince Saud was in the Soviet Union not as an official representative of Saudi Arabia but as an Arab League spokesman, Saud and Foreign Minister Andrei Gromyko held talks that presumably touched on bilateral ties as well. The Soviet media gave little publicity to the meeting, apparently in recognition of Saudi sensitivities. Prince Saud's participation in the delegation suggests that Saudi Arabia sees some benefit in maintaining contacts with the USSR. In particular, Saud's visit may have been an attempt to induce the United States to pressure Israel to compromise on peace negotiations.

It is not yet clear whether the Saud-Gromyko talks will lead to an improvement in Saudi-Soviet relations. However, a number of Saudi officials have implied on repeated occasions that Riyadh is keeping the door open, perhaps as leverage on the United States. The Saudi deputy prime minister, Prince Adbullah ibn Abdulaziz, was quoted in December 1982 as saying that the monarchy "sees no objection to a dialogue with any party within the context of Arab interests."[48]

---

[45] Igor Belyayev, an expert on the Middle East, has written a number of authoritative articles in the Soviet press on the need for a Saudi-Soviet rapprochement. In July 1980, he wrote in *Literaturnaya Gazeta* that the time was ripe for the two nations to open diplomatic relations. He noted the poor state of U.S.-Saudi relations: "Not a trace remains of the former confidence that special relations with the United States were a panacea for all ills." (FBIS, Soviet Union Daily Report, July 11, 1980, p. H5) In January 1979, in the same journal, Belyayev said that communism, Islam, and the Saudi monarchy were not incompatible with productive diplomatic relations, an argument repeated in more general terms by Secretary General Brezhnev at the CPSU Congress in February 1981.

[46] William Quandt, a specialist on Saudi foreign policy, says that the Saudi attitude is that the United States is "not particularly adept at translating its armed strength into diplomatic influence," and that a series of U.S. decisions revealing a lack of will have tempered Saudi enthusiasm for close ties to the United States. (See, Quandt. Riyadh Between the Superpowers. p. 39–41.)

[47] FBIS, Soviet Union Daily Report, September 23, 1982. p. H11.

[48] Quoted in, Rand, Robert. U.S. Officials See No Early Breakthrough in Saudi-Soviet Ties. Radio Liberty Research, RL 498/82, December 10, 1982. p. 3. In early 1980, then-Crown Prince Fahd acknowledged the Soviet peace offensive towards Riyadh: "We have recently observed a postive development in the Soviet Union's policy. It began through its information media with the expression of some views indicating that it behaves as though it understands us. * * * On our part, we began dealing with it even indirectly in a reasonable way." (Quoted in Quandt. Riyadh Between the Superpowers. p. 51.) Quandt also notes (p. 52) that Saudi officials have acknowledged that Saudi and Soviet diplomats meet regularly throughout the world to discuss bilateral issues.

Although the Soviet Union is virtually excluded from directly influencing Saudi policy, it is satisfied with a number of Saudi actions. Riyadh has refused to grant the United States permanent facilities for its Rapid Deployment Force (RDF) and it has identified Israel, not the U.S.S.R., as the principal threat to its national security. The Saudis have also been unwilling to support the Camp David peace process and sought Soviet support for the Fahd peace plan in 1981.[49] Shahram Chubin, a specialist on Soviet policy in the Middle East, notes that because of the invasion of Afghanistan, the Saudis have come to recognize the proximity of Soviet power as a potential threat. Saudi leaders reportedly believe that the Soviet Union seeks to establish a guaranteed supply of oil from the Gulf states, including Saudi Arabia. The Soviet presence in South Yemen, combined with pressure on North Yemen and Soviet influence in Libya, Ethiopia, and Afghanistan, provides Moscow with some measure of influencing Saudi policy. In Chubin's words, "Soviet power, proximity, and ability to pose indirect threats to the Saudi regime will constitute a continuing incentive to the Saudis to avoid offending the Soviet Union and to acknowledge its interests." [50] For the time being, this may be the most effective, if sole, means of exerting influence on Saudi Arabia.

2. SAUDI ARABIA BETWEEN EAST AND WEST

Soviet policy in the Arabian Peninsula may also be aided by Saudi perceptions of superpower capabilities in the region. William Quandt, a Middle East specialist with the Brookings Institution, has written that Saudi Arabia increasingly sees its interests in maneuvering between Moscow and Washington.[51] Although the Saudis fear Soviet encroachments on the Gulf, according to Quandt, this is not sufficient—or they are not confident enough of U.S. protection—to induce Riyadh to ally itself completely with the United States. Saudi leaders have doubts over the capability and will of the United States to insure its security and are tempted by Soviet peace overtures. And they know that Moscow has influence over radical, destabilizing Arab regimes hostile to Saudi Arabia. As the superpower rivalry increasingly focuses on the Persian Gulf and as Gulf states face greater pressure from the Soviets, for the Kremlin a positive development would be for Riyadh to induce the United States to moderate its military presence in the region.

In 1981, the Soviet Union suffered a defeat when the United States approved the sale to Saudi Arabia of AWACS aircraft (Airborne Warning and Communications System). According to Robert Freedman, a specialist in Soviet relations with the Middle East, Moscow feared that congressional approval of the AWACS sale would lead to Saudi Arabia's support for the Camp David process and to facilities for the U.S. Rapid Deployment Force. After the U.S. Senate failed to vote down the AWACS sale (thus supporting the Administration's decision to sell), Pravda wrote on October 30

---

[49] Chubin, Shahram. Gains for Soviet Policy in the Middle East. International Security, Spring 1982, p. 134–136.
[50] Ibid., p. 135–136.
[51] Quandt. Riyadh Between the Superpowers.

that Saudi Arabia would now assume "the role of bridgehead" for U.S. policy in the Gulf.[52]

Although the Saudis do not wish to see their security ties to the United States broken, their reluctance to expand these relations is viewed as a positive trend by the Soviets. A Saudi-Soviet rapprochement, should it materialize during the reign of the current Saudi leadership, will be constrained by historical Saudi worries of Soviet hostility to the conservative monarchy and Moscow's aid to radical, "progressive" Arab governments.

E. SOVIET POLICY IN THE YEMENS

1. INTRODUCTION

The People's Democratic Republic of (South) Yemen (PDRY) is Moscow's most valuable and reliable strategic asset in the Arabian Peninsula and Persian Gulf area and the closest approximation to a satellite the Soviets have in the region. The PDRY has maintained close ties with the Soviet Union since it became independent in 1967; Moscow in turn has provided military and economic assistance and diplomatic support. South Yemen's ruling political party, the "vanguard" Yemeni Socialist Party (YSP), espouses Marxist ideology and "proletarian internationalism" and maintains close links to the Soviet Communist Party. While Aden will continue to align itself with Moscow, it seems recently to have adopted more moderate, pragmatic policies in order to acquire economic assistance and develop commercial trade from conservative Arab states and the West. South Yemen will probably continue to depend on the Soviet bloc for political and military support and serve as a bridgehead for Soviet involvement in northwest Africa and the Arabian Peninsula.[53]

The Soviet presence in Southern Yemen has been longstanding; but since the 1960s the USSR also has achieved some success in North Yemen, known officially as the Yemen Arab Republic (YAR). Soviet influence in the YAR has in large measure been aided by the Northern Yemenis' suspicions of Saudi desires for hegemony in the peninsula. As a consequence, government leaders in the capital of Sana'a have attempted a balancing act by promoting a military relationship with Moscow to offset Saudi influence. The Soviets have taken full advantage of Sana'a's vulnerability. Since the February 1979 border clashes between Sana'a and Aden, which flared up again in early 1981 and early 1982, the Soviets have opportunistically drawn North Yemen into a military aid relationship, even while North Yemen continues to purchase weapons from the United States largely with Saudi financing. As a result, Soviet influence in North Yemen has increased markedly, while the U.S. presence has diminished.

---

[52] Quoted in Freedman. Soviet Policy Towards the Middle East Since 1970. p. 419.

[53] For general information on the PDRY and its relations with the USSR, see the following recent works: Viotti, Paul R. "Politics in the Yemens and the Horn of Africa: Constraints on a Superpower." In, Mark V. Kauppi and R. Craig Nation, eds. The Soviet Union and the Middle East in the 1980s. Lexington, Mass. D.C. Heath, 1983. And, Freedman. Soviet Policy Toward the Middle East; Efrat, Moshe. "Scientific Socialism on Trial in an Arab Country." In, Peter Wiles, ed. The New Communist Third World. New York, St. Martin's Press, 1982; Novik, Nimrod. "Between Two Yemens: The Soviet Challenge and U.S. Response." In, Nimrod Novik and Joyce Starr, eds. Challenges in the Middle East. New York, Praeger, 1981.

The Soviet Union plays a careful double game in North Yemen. The USSR supplies arms and military training to Sana'a, while indirectly supporting the rebel National Democratic Front (NDF), a Marxist political organization tied to the PDRY.[54] Although talks concerning a union of North and South Yemen have been conducted by officials from both governments in recent years, there is little likelihood that a single Yemeni state will be formed in the near term. Unification, with a combined population base of nine million, and under PDRY political and military domination with the aid of the NDF, is a possible objective of Soviet policy, but short-term gains on the Arabian Peninsula will not be sacrificed for this longer-term goal. Moscow must weigh the competing advantages of such a provocative development with the costs of a possible increase in U.S. military presence in the region, closer Saudi-U.S. relations, and worsening Soviet relations with the Gulf states and Saudi Arabia. Thus Moscow desires to maintain close ties to North Yemen with an eye on improving relations with the states of the Persian Gulf and Arabian Peninsula.

2. SOVIET MILITARY AND STRATEGIC POLICY IN THE YEMENS: THE DOUBLE GAME

a. The PDRY

PDRY-Soviet relations were consolidated in October 1979 when President and General Secretary of the Yemeni Socialist Party Abd al-Fattah Ismail visited Moscow. Ismail was installed as PDRY leader in June 1978 after the coup overthrew the more moderate Ali Salim Rubayi. As the most pro-Soviet of Aden's leaders, Ismail signed a 20-year treaty of friendship and cooperation similar to those Moscow has concluded with Ethiopia, Iraq, and Syria. The two countries also signed a "plan of contracts" between the CPSU and the Yemeni Socialist Party to cover the years 1980-83. The PDRY was given observer status in the Soviet bloc Council for Mutual Economic Assistance (CMEA), and in July 1980 Soviet economic planning experts were in Aden to aid in the drafting of a 5-year economic development plan. South Yemen became more important to Soviet strategy in the mid-1970s with the re-opening of the Suez Canal. Until then, Soviet bloc military and economic aid was negligible. After the loss of the port of Berbera in Somalia, Aden assumed the role of principal staging area for Soviet military penetration in the Horn of Africa and northwest quadrant of the Indian Ocean.

Soviet interests are served in the PDRY by a Marxist-Leninist ruling party with a solid ideological and organizational foundation that cannot easily be overturned by new leaders. The YSP, guided by the "principles of scientific socialism," has earned Aden the Soviet confidence as a "country of socialist orientation." The Kremlin, by all accounts, considers the PDRY ruling party a reliable ally and sufficiently strong to remain loyal to the Soviet bloc and to resist challenges to the government.

---

[54] See, for example, Van Hollen, Christopher. North Yemen: A Dangerous Pentagonal Game. The Washington Quarterly, Summer 1982. p. 137-142.

The Soviet Union secured its ties to Aden in April 1980 when Ismail was abruptly replaced by Prime Minister Ali Nasir Muhammad for unexplained reasons. Speculation suggests that Ismail was ousted in an inter-party struggle for being too closely tied to the Kremlin and, as a result, straining relations with Arab states. Nasir Muhammad was initially given credit for supporting some measure of rapprochement with Yemen and Saudi Arabia. Another view gives a somewhat different explanation and might serve to illuminate Soviet policy in the Yemens: Ismail was edged out of power with the aid of Moscow because he jeopardized the USSR's new and growing relationship with Sana'a. Ismail was too belligerent towards Sana'a and thus contributed to Saudi and U.S. influence in North Yemen. The Soviet reaction was to sacrifice Ismail and ideology for the more pragmatic geo-strategic gains North Yemen offered. The change from Ismail to the Kremlin-picked Nasir Muhammad thus achieved two objectives: the PDRY was made more respectable in the Arab world and Yemeni co-existence was assured, although, to be sure, ideological and historical obstacles remain between the North and South.[55] Thus, Aden's relations with the YAR could be a future source of tension in its relations with the Soviet Union as Aden does not always appear to be in close step with the USSR's desire to improve relations with the North.

Whatever the circumstances, the new leader moved rapidly to reassure the Soviets that Aden's close ties with Moscow would not be altered. In May 1980, while on a visit to Moscow, Nasir Muhammad publicly supported the Soviet invasion of Afghanistan. Relations with the Soviet bloc have been buttressed by the signing of friendship and cooperation treaties with Hungary and Bulgaria in November 1981.

In the PDRY, Soviet rewards have been significant. The USSR has had the use of port facilities at Aden, a base at Khormaksar (used as staging areas for Soviet and Cuban troops to Ethiopia), anchorages at Socotra in the Gulf of Aden and at the island of Perim in the Bab al-Mandab straits, as well as numerous airfields for reconnaissance missions over the Indian Ocean and the Horn of Africa.[56] The facilities and privileges provided by the PDRY enabled the Soviets to provide support on Ethiopia's side in the 1977–78 Ethiopian-Somali war.

Soviet military and economic aid to Aden has been extensive; the USSR supplied all of the PDRY's foreign arms purchases of $775 million in the half decade from 1976 to 1980.[57] The Soviet bloc provided some $330 million in economic aid from 1954 to 1981. In 1981, 1,100 Soviet and East European military technicians were stationed in the PDRY, together with 500 Cuban advisers. Also in 1981, the Soviet bloc (including Cubans) maintained approximately 2,850 economic advisers in Aden.[58] East Germany is reported to be aiding

[55] Perlmutter, Amos. The Yemen Strategy. The New Republic, July 5 and 12, 1980. p. 17.
[56] Foreign Report. August 25, 1983. p. 4.
[57] U.S. Arms Control and Disarmament Agency (ACDA). World Military Expenditures and Arms Transfers, 1971–1980. March 1983. p. 119.
[58] U.S. Department of State. Soviet and East European Aid to the Third World, 1981. p. 14, 19, and 21.

the PDRY internal security forces. In late 1980, there were indications that the Soviet Union had reached a secret agreement with South Yemen whereby Aden would permit the Soviets liberal access to its military facilities in exchange for a Soviet guarantee to protect South Yemen. The PDRY in turn would be granted full membership in the CMEA and eventual observer status in the Warsaw Pact. Since the purported signing of the agreement, there have been reports of Soviet military construction on the islands of Socotra and Perim and at Jabl Alhal, near Aden. The latter facility, according to some reports, is to be a regional command center for Soviet armed forces.[59]

b. North Yemen

Over the years, Soviet policy has been to enhance its control over the strategic, 17-mile-wide Bab al-Mandab straits at the mouth of the Red Sea, expand its influence in North Yemen, and prevent a PDRY-Saudi rapprochement that potentially could lead to a lessening of Soviet influence. While much attention has been focused on the strategic significance of the Red Sea straits and the Suez Canal, the Soviet presence in the Yemens serves equally to exert pressure on the Persian Gulf states.[60]

Soviet interests in Sana'a have opposed the creation of a government strong enough to threaten its position in Aden. With extensive military and economic aid, Moscow intends to cultivate a government more responsive to Soviet desires and opposed to U.S. and Saudi influence. A neutralist government in Sana'a would induce the Saudi monarchy to be more cautious on issues affecting Soviet interests in the Persian Gulf. The Soviets also may intend to prevent hostilities with the PDRY, which could draw the United States and Saudi Arabia into closer agreement on the need for a greater military response to the Soviet presence in the region.[61]

The Saudis are mindful of North Yemen's strategic importance, but equally suspicious of its latent irridentism. Indeed, Saudi officials are reported to have interpreted the February 1979 border clash between North and South Yemen as a PDRY–USSR–Cuban test of Saudi and Western resolve in the wake of the fall of the Shah in Iran.[62] The combined population of South and North Yemen (2.1 and 5.7 million, respectively) could also prove threatening to the Saudis who number just over 10 million. In October 1981, President Ali Abdullah Salih travelled to Moscow, thus underscoring his country's policy of maneuvering between Moscow and Washington. He supported Moscow's call for an international conference on the Middle East and a "zone of peace" in the Persian

[59] There are also intelligence reports that the Soviets have built two missile bases, one covering Aden, the other protecting the northwest from Yemeni attacks. South Yemeni troops at the sites are supported by Cuban soldiers and Soviet technicians. The USSR has also developed a number of airfields around Aden, one for its 12th Air Force Squadron, comprised of fighters, transports, and reconnaissance aircraft, used to support Ethiopian forces. Ali, Salamat. Moscow Widens the Gulf. Far Eastern Economic Review. November 6, 1981. p. 28–30.

[60] See, for example, Chubin, Shahram. Security in the Persian Gulf: The Role of the Superpowers. London, International Institute for Strategic Studies, 1982. p. 126–127.

[61] Page, Stephen. "Soviet Policy Toward the Arabian Peninsula." p. 90–91. In, Stoddard, Philip H., ed. The Middle East in the 1980s: Problems and Prospects. (Proceedings of a conference sponsored by the Defense Intelligence College and the Middle East Institute, at Washington, D.C. June 8–9, 1983.)

[62] Chubin. Security in the Persian Gulf. p. 60.

Gulf and Indian Ocean, and he condemned the establishment of foreign military bases in the Persian Gulf. Following the visit, Salih travelled immediately to Saudi Arabia to cover his position with that country.

The USSR maintains large military and economic missions in North Yemen. In 1981, there were some 700 Soviet and Eastern European military advisers training 11 of the army's 12 brigades and 175 economic technicians in North Yemen. Sana'a has also sent hundreds of academic students to the Soviet Union and Eastern Europe for higher education. About 1,500 North Yemenis, most of them officers and military personnel, are now in the Soviet Union for training. In contrast, to date, only 60 YAR officers have been trained in the United States, while scholarships number only 25 per year. From 1954 to 1981, the Soviet Union and its East European allies extended some $180 million in aid to Sana'a and trained over 2,000 North Yemeni military personnel in the USSR during the same period.[63]

The Soviet Union has also been the YAR's principal arms supplier over the past two decades.[64] More recently, to wage the war against the NDF guerrillas, the Sana'as government has been dependent on the weapons provided by the Soviets, which include 650 tanks, 450 armored personnel carriers, three squadrons of MiGs, one Sukhoi squadron, as well as about half of Yemen's helicopters.[65] In 1979, the Carter Administration agreed to deliver $390 million in arms, paid for by Saudi Arabia, to North Yemen to demonstrate its determination to contain Soviet expansionism in the region. Despite the YAR-Soviet arms connection, the United States continues to provide economic and military support to Sana'a in an attempt to prevent Salih's government from shifting too close to the USSR. (Riyadh also provides the YAR central government with about $400 million in aid annually.) However, delays in arms shipments, said to be caused by Saudi ambivalence towards supplying Sana'a with sophisticated arms, led President Salih to seek arms from the USSR. Estimates of Soviet arms shipments to North Yemen after 1979 run as high as $1 billion to $2 billion.[66] Consequently, North Yemen owes the USSR approximately $700 million, its largest outstanding debt to any foreign country. This relationship has fueled fears of a growing North Yemeni dependence on the Soviet Union.[67]

In the meantime, the Soviets continue to arm the PDRY and, indirectly, the National Democracy Front. The Front, which claims the government in Sana'a is a group of Saudi puppets, is comprised

[63] U.S. Department of State. Soviet and East European Aid to the Third World, 1981. p. 14, 15, 19, and 21.
    Ottaway, David B. North Yemen's War: Sana'a Turns to Soviets for Military Aid. Washington Post, April 21, 1982. p. A1 and A19.
[64] The U.S. Arms Control and Disarmament Agency (ACDA) estimates Soviet arms transfers to Yemen at $625 million in the half decade from 1976 to 1980, out of total YAR arms imports of $1,100 million. (The United States supplied about $170 million, according to the same estimates. These figures do not include the massive infusions of arms by the United States and the USSR after the North-South war.) See, U.S. ACDA. World Military Expenditures and Arms Transfers, 1971–1980. p. 119.
[65] Ottaway. North Yemen's War. And, The Military Balance, 1983–84. London, International Institute for Strategic Studies, p. 64–65.
[66] Ottaway. North Yemen's War.
[67] Richey, Warren. Christian Science Monitor, January 12, 1983. p. 13.

of Marxists, Ba'athists, Nasserists, and Yemeni army defectors. An estimated 5,000 guerrillas have waged a war against the central government for six years with Soviet-made weapons supplied by Libya, Syria, and the PDRY.

3. THE ADEN TRIPARTITE PACT OF AUGUST 1981

The Aden Tripartite Alliance of August 1981 links the PDRY, Libya and Ethiopia militarily and politically. Although the three nations derived different benefits from a alliance, the treaty, signed during a summit meeting of the three heads of state and formed presumably under the auspices of the Soviet Union, served to enhance the Soviet presence in the Horn of Africa. This agreement was anomalous in many regards. The three states do not share a common border; two are Arab and one is predominantly Christian; and their ideologies diverge on a number of important issues, such as commitment to Marxism-Leninism and subservience to Moscow. Tangible results of the agreement, according to various reports, include Aden's decision to station a brigade in Ethiopia and the delivery by Libya of 300 Soviet-made tanks to the PDRY. However, its principal purpose seems to be propagandistic and rhetorical with few concrete long-term consequences that would not have developed without the pact.

The pact was alarming to a number of Arab states because it appeared to encourage a trend towards regional alliances and polarization.[68] Triggered by the U.S.-Libyan confrontation over the Gulf of Sidra on August 19 in which two Libyan combat aircraft were downed, the pact was a reaction against the U.S. base facilities granted to Oman, Somalia, and Kenya and the formation of the Gulf Cooperation Council in May 1981, which groups six conservative Arabian Peninsula monarchies. The agreement was also seen as an instrument to pressure North Yemen into accomodating pro-Soviet positions. However, for Aden, the treaty ended its extreme isolation in the region at a time when only the USSR could be counted as a reliable alley. Aden has reportedly received hundreds of millions of dollars in Libyan financial aid, which it desperately needs. More importantly, the treaty is clearly aimed at consolidating the Soviet position around the Horn of Africa. In this way, the PDRY has helped promote Soviet interests in the regime.

4. SOUTH YEMEN BETWEEN EAST AND WEST: A REASSESSMENT?

There have been signs of a political struggle under way in Aden, often over the form of the country's ties to its neighbors and the Soviet Union. A number of developments in the country concerning economic and political relations with its conservative neighbors and the West may give some indication of the direction of PDRY-USSR future relations, although the implications of these signals still remain ambivalent. Close relations between the PDRY and the USSR have contributed to isolating Aden. South Yemen was one of

---

[68] The PLO, represented by chief-of-staff Abu Jihad, was also a signatory to the agreement. Present were the National Democratic Front, the Popular Fron for the Liberation of Oman, the Popular Fron for the Liberation of Bahrain, indenpent Palestinina movements, and Sudanese and Saudi communists. Also see, Dunn, Michael Collins. Defense and Foreign Affairs Daily, January 13 and 14, 1982.

just two Arab states (the other was Syria) that supported the Soviet invasion of Afghanistan. Recent purges in Aden have been interpreted as a demonstration of Nasir Muhammad's pragmatism and his desire to loosen ties with the Kremlin and improve the PDRY's relations with conservative, oil-rich Arab states in order to obtain money for South Yemen's economy.[69] In 1981, Nasir Muhammad succeeded in demoting Defense Minister Ali Antar to a minor ministerial post. Antar was considered to be pro-Soviet, along with a number of other leading officials who were removed from office in 1981.

While South Yemen undergoes almost inscrutable domestic political turmoil, there are additional signs that in foreign economic trade Aden has been successful in attracting Western investment. Aden's four largest trading partners are Japan, Britain, Australia, and France with China and the Soviet Union sixth and seventh. Observers note that government officials are increasingly dissatisfied with technology and technicians from the Socialist bloc.[70] Economic aid from the Soviet bloc has been minimal. According to U.S. Government sources, in 1981, the USSR and its East European allies gave no financial aid to the PDRY; in 1980, it was a mere $15 million.[71] Aden's dissatisfaction with the performance of Eastern economic assistance may not alone lead to worsening relations. One benefit to Soviet policy of improved PDRY economic ties to other Arab states is increased hard currency for the purchase of Soviet arms.[72] PDRY officials may also have grown envious of North Yemen's lucrative balancing policy between East and West, and may be tempted by the possibility of similar rewards with other Arab states.

Aden has also normalized diplomatic relations with almost all Arab nations, of particular importance the Gulf monarchies. It accepted Kuwaiti mediation of its long-standing dispute with Oman, and in November 1982 South Yemen and pro-Western Oman signed an accord establishing more friendly relations. Moscow is apparently hoping that the move will temper the Gulf Cooperation Council's (GCC) inclinations to evolve into a military pact that would accept U.S. military presence in the region. Another benefit for the Soviets of closer PDRY-Gulf monarchy relations would be economic aid to South Yemen from some Gulf states—especially Kuwait, the United Arab Emirates, and Saudi Arabia—and so lessen Aden's de-

---

[69] Rand, Robert, Prime Minister of South Yemen to Visit Moscow. Radio Liberty Research, RL 365/82. September 10, 1982.

[70] South Yemen: A Slow Move Towards the West. The Middle East, August 1982. p. 20–21.

[71] U.S. Department of State. Soviet and East European Aid to the Third World, 1981.

[72] Yukimasa, Chudo. "The Commercial Policies of the Communist Third World: The PDRY," in, E.J. Feuchtwanger and Peter Nailor, eds. The Soviet Union and the Third World. New York, St. Martin's Press, 1981. p. 108-112. Chudo says: "Although the PDRY stands firm in its verbal commitment to proletarian internationalism, the new regime has shown that it would like to withdraw, to some extent, from the neighboring conflicts in the Horn and Oman. It seems that the present regime intends to concentrate on its own internal development into a Marxist-Leninist state but to soft pedal, to attract aid from wealthy conservative Arab states, in spite of its deepening political and military commitments in its Soviet-type internal development." (p. 109) For additional views on PDRY commercial and development policy, see: Efrat, Moshe. "Scientific Socialism on Trial in an Arab County." Efrat agrees with Chudo that rapprochement with other Arab states "cannot prevent the PDRY—firmly committed to 'scientific socialism' as well as to Moscow—from pursuing the basic elements of its domestic and international policies." (p. 199)

pendence on the U.S.S.R.[73] The motives behind the rapprochement with Oman are not entirely clear, and it is still too early to say how successful the agreement will be. But the agreement suggests that South Yemen intends to expand its range of contacts with moderate Arab states, though it remains to be seen whether at the expense of Soviet interests.

5. SUMMARY AND CONCLUSIONS: SOVIET SUCCESS IN THE YEMENS

Soviet policy in the Yemens appears to have been a success thus far. The Soviets have maneuvered themselves into an influential position in North Yemen. The instrument of military assistance and arms sales has proved valuable in luring the Sana's government into serving Soviet interests at the expense of the West. The government of President Salih has moved leftward, in part to accommodate the pressures represented by the NDF, as its dependence on Moscow has grown. There is concern among a number of observers that the Salih government could collapse.[74] Yemeni unification, which should not be altogether discounted, may come about under South Yemen's terms. However, unification may compromise Soviet relations with moderate Arab states, except under all but ideal conditions. Moscow will continue to woo Sana'a with military aid to forestall Western influence and protect it against PDRY-and Soviet-supported guerrillas.[75] The Soviet Union benefits by its overwhelming presence in both countries and its proximity to the sources of political power. In North Yemen, Soviet influence is mitigated by Salih's deliberate policy of playing to East and West. However, it would appear that Salih will in the foreseeable future continue to remain in political debt to Moscow.

In the south, the Soviet Union stands at present uncontested for influence. The combination of economic and military aid has tied the PDRY into a close relationship with the USSR. Ideological compatibility between the two countries has been promoted by the institutionalization of the Yemen Socialist Party as the sole ruling party in the PDRY. The formation of a vanguard socialist party has contributed to the consolidation of Soviet influence in Aden.

South Yemen has proved its usefulness to Soviet foreign policy in a number of ways. It serves as a staging area for Soviet forces in the region, and together with North Yemen, as a means of exerting pressure on Saudi Arabia and other Gulf states. Aden has also been a training ground for revolutionary groups scattered throughout the world; for example, the Sandinista forces of Marxist Nicaragua have been reported to be trained in the PDRY. The moderation of Aden's isolation in the Arab world may aid the Soviet attempt to broaden relations with conservative Arab states. In recent years, Soviet policy towards Southern Yemen has increasingly

---

[73] Katz, Mark N. Oman Security Gets a Boost in Soviet-urged Moderation. Christian Science Monitor, January 18, 1983. At least one Middle East observer suggests that the PDRY-Oman agreement indicates a drift in Aden's policies away from the Soviet Union, rather than a USSR-sponsored move to lessen Aden's isolation. See, Andelman, David. Andropov's Middle East. The Washington Quarterly, Spring 1983. p. 112.

[74] Van Hollen. North Yemen. p. 141. Also, Van Dusen, Michael. Cloer U.S. Attention to Yemen. New York Times, February 12, 1982. p. A35.

[75] Page. Soviet Policy Toward the Arabian Peninsula. p. 95.

become a function of its goals in the strategic and unstable Persian Gulf region.

In short, the Soviet Union has successfully drawn North Yemen into what is for the West a dangerously close relationship without sacrificing its position in South Yemen. A similar policy of patronizing both sides in a conflict was unworkable in the Horn of Africa in 1976–78 when Moscow attempted to shift its support from Somalia to Ethiopia, all the while trying to maintain a dependency relationship with Somalia, and has so far proved unsuccessful in Iraq and Iran. Soviet policy in the Yemens for now remains on course: encouraging North Yemeni isolation from the Saudis and the West and dependence on the USSR, while exerting maximum pressure on the PDRY.

II. THE ARAB-ISRAELI ZONE

A. SOVIET-SYRIAN RELATIONS AFTER CAMP DAVID AND THE LEBANON CRISIS

Although the Soviet Union has drawn Syria into a closer relationship in recent years, Syria continues to follow a foreign policy that often clashes with Soviet goals in the region. Syria has viewed the Soviet Union primarily as a supplier of military equipment and diplomatic aid in conflicts with its neighbors, even though a friendship treaty signed in 1980 would suggest stronger ideological affinities. The reasons for agreeing to cement ties to the USSR with a treaty were not ideological, but pragmatic, stemming from Syria's political isolation in the Arab world, domestic troubles, and the need to ensure a steady flow of arms.[1] Bilateral relations have been constrained by each nation's overriding national interests; for example, Syria has been unwilling to ignore its security interests in Lebanon even if they collide with Soviet interests. And Moscow has hesitated to risk a superpower confrontation in the volatile Middle East for the sake of a regional ally. Unlike most other patron/client relationships, the Soviet-Syrian ties seem often a case of the client dictating policy to the patron.

Following the diplomatic and military defeat suffered by Syria and, in the eyes of many people, by the Soviet Union in 1982 during the Israeli invasion of Lebanon, the recent upgrading of Soviet arms transfers to Syria has been interpreted as a demonstration of Moscow's desire to increase its influence in the region through stronger support for Syria.

Indeed, the Soviet-Syrian relationship has relied increasingly in the last several years on military arms deliveries. Given the political issues that Syria must address in the context of the Arab-Israeli confrontation and conflicting Syrian regional interests vis-a-vis Soviet strategic objectives, it is unlikely that the two countries can develop an alliance without serious differences. Despite their differences, the Soviet Union and Syria have found common ground on which to base their relations since the Israeli invasion of Lebanon and deepening U.S. involvement there.

1. HISTORY: SYRIA AS MOSCOW'S MISCHIEVOUS ALLY

Throughout most of the 1970s, Syria was able to effectively play off one superpower against the other, while assuring for itself a leading role in Arab politics.[2] By 1980, a number of constraints on

---

[1] See, for example, Freedman, Robert O. Soviet Policy Toward Syria Since Camp David. Middle East Review, Fall 1981. p. 31–32.

[2] For an overview of Syrian foreign policy, see, Rabinovich, Itamar. The Foreign Policy of Syria: Goals, Capabilities, Constraints, and Options. Survival, July/August 1982. p. 175–176. Ra-

Syrian foreign policy had dictated closer relations with the USSR. In particular, burgeoning domestic unrest and the deterioration of relations with neighboring states drove Syria to cultivate its relationship with Moscow. Political protests fomented by fundamentalist Muslin groups followed the Syrian military intervention in Lebanon in 1976. Syrian diplomatic isolation was a result of President Hafez Assad's failure to forge a successful anti-Sadat front against the Camp David accords, which at the time were progressing without serious obstacles. Increasingly, Syria faced a hostile Iraqi-Jordanian alliance on its southern and eastern borders.

Syria also found the political and economic costs of sustaining a military presence in Lebanon increasingly high, even though it provided the Assad government with a sphere of influence and a means of controlling the PLO and undermining the Camp David peace process. By 1979, Palestinian-Israeli confrontations in Lebanon had threatened to draw Syria into the conflict, and Syrian aircraft were more frequently engaging Israeli aircraft.[3] The intensification of the confrontation with Israel resulted in a growing dependence on the Soviet Union, demonstrated in early 1980 with Syria showed its support of Moscow by refusing to criticize the Soviet invasion of Afghanistan. In October of that year, the two countries signed a Treaty of Friendship and Cooperation, a development that has been considered a victory for Soviet foreign policy given Syria's longstanding unwillingness to commit itself to formalizing its ties to the U.S.S.R.

The agreement, a standard Soviet Friendship Treaty, calls for increased military cooperation between Moscow and Damacus but does not specifically commit the Soviet military to assist Syria in case of war. In a vaguely worded clause, it provides only that the two parties "coordinate positions" and "cooperate" to defend Syria's sovereignty.[4] It also provides for cooperation in economic, scientific, technological, and cultural areas.

The treaty has not led to Syrian subordination of its interest to the Soviet Union. According to a number of observers, Syria has invoked the treaty for its own advantage in instances when Soviet support was actually nonexistent. The first instance occurred soon after the signing of the treaty, in November 1980, when, much to Soviet displeasure, President Hafez Assad mobilized the Syrian army on the border with Jordan during the visit to Damascus of Vasily Kuznetsov, at the time a candidate member of the Politburo. The timing of the mobilization with Kuznetsov's visit was designed to suggest Soviet agreement with the move. Syria invoked the treaty again in the spring of 1981 during the crisis over the stationing of Soviet-made missiles in the Bekaa Valley in Lebanon, and a third time in the winter of 1981–82 when Israeli formally annexed the Golan Heights.[5]

---

binovich writes that President Hafez Assad's foreign policy had reached its zenith by 1977: "By then Syria had won endorsement from the Arab world of her hegemony in Lebanon; together with Saudi Arabia and Egypt she had formulated a unified Arab strategy for a comprehensive settlement of the Arab-Israeli conflict; and she was able to set the conditions under which Assad met with both Presidents Carter and Brezhnev that year." (p. 175–176)

[3] Ibid., p. 177–178.

[4] The text of the treaty appears in the Middle East Review, Fall/Winter 1981–82, p. 74–75.

[5] Rand, Robert. Moscow, Damascus and the Crisis in Lebanon. Radio Liberty Research, RL 239/82. p. 1–2.

2. THE ISRAELI INVASION OF LEBANON

In 1982, during the Israeli invasion of Lebanon, Moscow was under pressure from Syria and other Arab states to act. Prolonged Soviet inaction damaged Moscow's prestige and brought into question its reliability as an ally of the Arab world. The Soviet response to the Lebanese crisis was viewed around the world as a test of Moscow's commitment to Syria and the Arab world even though the Soviet commitment to Syria has never extended to its activities in Lebanon. Early in 1983, the Soviet delivery of sophisticated, high altitude SA-5 missiles to Syria accompanied by some 1,000 Soviet troops appeared to signal Moscow's willingness to play a larger military role in the Middle East reminiscent of the Soviet relationship with Egypt in the early 1970s.

Even before the Israeli invasion of Lebanon the Syrians pressed for greater Soviet involvement, including an accord on a "strategic balance," in other words, more Soviet arms shipments to create military parity between Syria and Israel. Moscow's reaction was to give material and diplomatic support sufficient to ensure Syrian territorial sovereignty, without damaging long-term cooperation with Damascus. Moscow agreed, however, to consider the modernization of Syrian Air Forces and air defense systems. In March 1982, during a visit to Damascus, Soviet Air Force commander Marshal Kutakhov agreed to new arms transfers to Syria and to a speed-up in their delivery. But, the Soviet Union was also concerned that an all-out war between Israel and Syria could threaten the weak regime of President Assad and lead to a request by Assad for direct Soviet involvement. Moscow viewed the Israeli invasion as a limited war of attrition, which required less Soviet assistance than a fullblown engagement. Both Syria and the USSR saw eye-to-eye on the need to avoid full scale war with Israel. Notwithstanding, Syria sought definite political reassurances and more effective military equipment from Moscow, particularly after Israel attacked Syrian-held areas in Lebanon, threatened the strategic Beirut-Damascus highway, and struck Syrian missiles sites that had been deployed in the Bekaa Valley since April 1981. Similarly, once the Israelis invaded Lebanon, the Soviets became concerned that Israel's successful strikes against the missile sites could weaken Syria's defenses and cast doubt on the USSR's own air defense technology.[6] The Soviets did not hurry to aid Syria or the retreating PLO forces, but seemed content to watch from the sidelines. Some observers have suggested that Soviet inaction was caused by Soviet leader Brezhnev's deteriorating health and the consequent jockeying for power in the succession struggle.

In June, Brezhnev appealed to President Reagan to exert control over Israel and underlined Moscow's concern over a war so close to its southern borders. However, Brezhnev did not communicate an ultimatum or suggest stronger Soviet action should Israel not with-

---

[6] Roberts, Cynthia. Soviet Arms Transfer Policy and the Decision to Upgrade Syrian Air Defences. Survival, July-August 1983. p. 155. The author notes that the Israelis staged spectacular successes against Syrian missile sites, wiping out 17 SAM batteries and SA-2s. This led to the visit to Syria in June of the First Deputy Commander-in-Chief of the Soviet Air Defense Forces, Gen. Yevgeny Yurasov. By September, Israel had knocked out 29 Syrian SAM batteries and destroyed 90 aircraft and 400 tanks.

draw from Lebanon. Soviet demonstration of its military commitment was expressed by a willingness to replace, in time, Syrian equipment losses. According to one Middle East observer, the Soviet Union fulfilled its responsibilities to Syria with "little or no risk to itself." [7] Soviet restraint during the comparatively limited war was illustrated by the absence of massive airlifts similar to those undertaken during the Yom Kippur war of 1973 and high-level official exchange of visits, although Assad was rumored to have made a secret trip to Moscow. Considering the nature of the Israeli action, which was confined to Lebanese territory, and the lack of a united Arab response, Moscow's actions were standard.

Soviet caution has been further explained by Moscow's estimation that the Arab states did not have the military capability or will to win the war if they were called upon to wage one. Soviet leaders did not want the war to expand and lead to a superpower confrontation. Moscow hoped that, by limiting the scope of hostilities, the United States and Israel would pay a price for being branded the instigators of the crisis by the Arab world.[8] Furthermore, Arab leaders could not come to an agreement on a common Arab strategy. Soviet leaders were said to have been surprised by the Arab states' lack of material support to Palestinian fighters.

By the fall of 1982, after the evacuation of PLO forces from Beirut, Soviet influence in the Middle East was damaged considerably. It was the United States at the time that reaped the benefits of acting as mediator, supplying peacekeeping forces, and working towards a framework for an Israeli and Syrian force withdrawal, while the Soviet Union stood by.

The USSR declined to upgrade its relations with Syria during the conflict in a manner that would indicate an escalation of the war or an extension of the mutual security agreements in the Friendship Treaty. In June 1982, Syria again asked the Soviet Union to sign an agreement on a "strategic alliance" with Damascus, to offset the one signed between the United States and Israel in December 1981. A strategic understanding with Moscow is seen in Damascus as a means to end Syria's reliance on arms less advanced than those possessed by Israel. Syria's desire for a strategic bond with the Soviet Union was not new, however. In January 1982, one month after the Israeli government annexed the occupied Golan Heights, Syrian Foreign Minister Abdel Halim Khaddam travelled to Moscow to obtain a strategic agreement with the USSR, but was rebuffed by the Soviets.

Soviet-Syrian relations were further strained by Syrian accusations that Soviet military equipment was unreliable and inferior to American technology used by Israel. Moscow dispatched a number of high-ranking military advisers to inspect damaged weaponry and reassure Syrian military leaders. Chief of Staff of the Soviet Armed Forces, Marshal Nikolai Ogarkov, is reported to have visited Syria during the war. Soviet military planners were clearly sensitive to charges of having failed to support Syria with proper military

[7] Golan, Galia. The Soviet Union and the Israeli Action in Lebanon. International Affairs, Winter 1982/83. p. 8.
[8] See, Dawisha, Karen. The U.S.S.R. in the Middle East. p. 442–443. Doder, Dusko. Soviets See Invasion of Lebanon Rebounding Against U.S., Israel. Washington Post, June 25, 1982.

equipment and that their military technology was inferior to U.S. weaponry. Karen Brutents, a senior Middle East specialist and Deputy Chief of the International Department of the Central Committee, was sent to Syria in February 1983 to help smooth relations.[9] In March, the Soviet Union agreed to deliver additional T-72 tanks, BM-21 rocket launchers, SA-6 and -9 missiles, and Mig-23 aircraft.

The losses of the Syrian armed forces, equipped with Soviet weapons, and political considerations may persuade the Soviets to consider the strategic agreement more seriously.[10] The delivery of Soviet surface-to-air SAM-5 missiles was a response to the USSR's equipment's poor showing in the Lebanon crisis as well as a demonstration of diplomatic and military support of an important ally. But, an obstacle to greater military cooperation is the danger posed by the powerful Israeli armed forces which have dominated all past hostile exchanges with Syria. Nonetheless, the SAM-5s have been viewed as a deepening of the Soviet commitment to Syria and a response, perhaps, to the dispatching of U.S. Marines to participate in the multinational peacekeeping force in Beirut.

3. SOVIET MILITARY AID AND ARMS TRANSFER POLICY TOWARD SYRIA

Since the Lebanese crisis in the summer of 1982, the Soviet Union has upgraded its military presence in Syria and replenished Syrian battle equipment losses. In the spring of 1983, the U.S. State Department estimated Soviet military personnel in Syria at 6,000 to 7,000, 2,000 of which are advisers and 4,000–5,000 man and control the three new SAM-5 missile sites. In addition, there are an undisclosed number of Soviet troops providing security around the sites.[11] The Soviet Union has also trained over 5,500 Syrian military personnel from 1955 to 1981, second only to Egypt in the Middle East.

The Soviet share of the Syrian arms trade has been overwhelming, accounting for about 82 percent of Syrian arms imports from 1976 to 1980. It is clear that the rationale for the deliveries is political as well as commercial. (Saudi Arabia and Kuwait are reported to have financed large amounts of Syrian weapons purchases with hard currency.) From 1976 to 1980, Syria was the second largest importer of Soviet arms in the world with deliveries valued at $5.4 billion during the five-year period. (Libya was first with $5.6 billion, and Iraq fell in third, behind Syria, with $5.0 billion.)[12]

The closeness of Soviet-Syrain military ties was demonstrated in July 1981, during the Bekaa Valley missile crisis, when the two countries engaged in joint naval exercises off the Syrian coast. The USSR sent 53 ships into the Mediterranean to provide support for

---

[9] Oliphant, Craig. The Performance of Soviet Weapons in Lebanon. Radio Liberty Research, RL 68/83, February 7, 1983. And, F.B.I.S., Soviet Union Daily Report, February 8, 1983. p. H2.

[10] Rand, Robert. Syria Presses for Strategic Alliance with Moscow. Radio Liberty Research, RL 257/82, 1982. p. 2.

[11] See, U.S. House of Representatives. Committee on Foreign Affairs. Subcommittee on Europe and the Middle East. Hearings. (June 2, 1983) Developments in the Middle East, June 1983. p. 9–10.

[12] U.S. Arms Control and Disarmament Agency. World Military Expenditures and Arms Transfers. March 1983. p. 118–119. Czechoslovakia delivered an additional $440 million in arms to Syria during those five years. Thus, Soviet bloc arms supplies accounted for nearly 90 percent of Syrian weapons stockpile.

amphibious landing exercises with Syrian troops. The maneuvers were apparently intended, among other things, to warn Israel not to strike Syrian missile batteries.

The delivery of SAM-5 missiles to Syria, begun in late 1982 and made public by Israeli military authorities in January 1983, has received considerable attention.[13] Although the missiles are more advanced than any previously possessed by Syria, their delivery must be evaluated in the context of Soviet-Syrian relations. In this regard, it is instructive that the Soviets maintain almost complete control over the installations and, presumably, when to fire the missiles.[14] This recalls the manner in which the Soviets manned Egyptian air defenses until they were expelled in 1972, taking their missiles with them. Thus, the delivery of the advanced air defense technology assumes less risk for Soviet leaders.[15]

The Soviet-Syrian relationship rests to a large degree on Syria's dependence on Soviet military supplies. Unlike Iraq, Algeria, and even Libya which have diversified their sources of arms, Syria has chosen to rely essentially on Moscow for its weaponry. Other states which have close relations with Moscow have begun to purchase weapons from France, Great Britain, the United States, and Italy. Syria has not. While Syria is arguably the USSR's most important political and military ally in the region, Moscow has seen fit not to provide the most advanced technology it possesses.[16]

4. ECONOMIC ASSISTANCE

Although the Syrian economy is closely tied to the West, the Soviet Union and Eastern Europe are heavily involved in assisting Syrian development. Syria's total trade with the West is much greater than with the Soviet bloc—$3.7 billion compared with approximately $600 million (according to Soviet statistics) with Moscow alone in 1981.[17] Syrian arms purchases, often paid for by

---

[13] The SAM-5, code named Gammon by Western military authorities, has a range of 150 miles against high-flying targets up to 95,000 feet in altitude. The missiles are deployed in three sites in western Syria, with at least one battery of six missiles per site. They can cover all of Lebanon, most of Israel, northern Jordan, and into the Mediterranean. Because the missile poses little, perhaps no, threat to low-flying, high speed aircraft, its most likely targets are reconnaissance aircraft and E-2C Hawkeye airborne early warning aircraft. The Gammon has never before been deployed outside the Soviet bloc and Israel will have to develop electronic countermeasures or other means to neutralize the missiles. (See, Flight International, January 29, 1983. p. 246.) Although the SAM-5s represent a new threat to Israeli air superiority, it has been reported that Israeli authorities expect to be successful in dealing with the 1960's-vintage missiles. Nonetheless, the Israeli government interprets the deployment as a signal of Moscow's invigorated defense commitment to Syria. (See, Christian Science Monitor, February 24, 1983, p. 6.)

[14] U.S. House of Representatives. Committee on Foreign Affairs. Subcommittee on Europe and the Middle East. Hearings. (June 2, 1983) Developments in the Middle East, June 1983. p. 10.

[15] New York Times, May 16, 1983. p. A1 and A6. Also, Roberts. Soviet Arms Transfer Policy. p. 158.

[16] On these points, see Cynthia Roberts, op. cit. The author also notes that the Soviets have refrained from exporting the T-64 main battle tank, which is, according to some, more capable than the T-72. She suggests that the self-imposed restrictions on arms shipments to Syria are due to the risks of superpower confrontation in the Middle East. In other nations, such as Cuba and Ethiopia, Moscow is more willing to escalate arms transfers to aid a client where U.S.-Soviet relations are less likely to be affected. One aspect of Soviet arms transfer policy relating to Syria is that the Soviets have come to value the hard currency earnings of sales, a development that may indicate Moscow would like to sell more, but not necessarily better, gear.

[17] The International Monetary Fund places trade turnover between Syria and the USSR for 1982 at about $172.6 million, a tiny portion of its total foreign trade of $5.09 billion. See, Direction of Trade Statistics. 1983 Yearbook. p. 372-373.

wealthier Arab states, also provide the Soviet Union with valuable hard currency reserves. The USSR and Eastern Europe, however, maintain 4,100 economic advisers in Syria managing projects financed by $740 million in credits. In 1981, Eastern European countries signed trade agreements valued at over $3 billion for the next five years, and approximately $500 million in development contracts, repayable in Syrian goods. From 1954 to 1981, the Soviet Union and its allies extended nearly $2 billion in economic aid to Syria, but since 1979, new grants and loans have been virtually nonexistent.[18]

The lack of general aid is compensated by the concentration of communist countries on specific projects in Syria, such as oil refiners, phosphate plants, land reclamation, power, and transportation. The Soviets have built the railroad linking the port of Latakia with the industrial areas of the interior. East European countries and the USSR have coordinated their economic development activities in Syria. Like Iraq, Turkey, and the PDRY in the Middle East, Syria is a principal recipient of financial aid and bilateral projects from the Soviet bloc. Nonetheless, the Soviet Union must compete with the West for economic and commercial influence in the country.

B. SOVIET-EGYPTIAN RELATIONS AFTER SADAT

1. INTRODUCTION

The assassination of Egypt's President Anwar Sadat in October 1981 was seen by the Soviet Union as a potential watershed event in its policy towards the Middle East. Suddenly, the pillar of U.S. Mideast policy and an outspoken leader of the anti-Soviet bloc was removed. The Kremlin sought to take advantage of the opportunities presented by his death. Although Egyptian foreign and domestic policy did not undergo a radical change, the Soviet Union has maintained expectations that the new president, Hosni Mubarak, might soften some aspects of the strongly pro-American and anti-Soviet policies of his predecessor and seek to restore ties with Moscow. Despite signs of a normalization in relations and more numerous official contacts in the two years since Sadat's death, the Soviets have displayed frustration over the lack of real progress in improving ties. Soviet leaders may have come to reassess their initially sanguine hopes for better relations after Sadat's death. Close U.S.-Egyptian relations remain an impediment to Soviet progress in Egypt.

Nonetheless, Moscow sees a number of factors working in its favor in the post-Sadat era and, indeed, an atmospheric warming has occurred. Soviet leaders feel that alleged Israeli intransigence on the issue of Palestinian autonomy and Egyptian domestic political pressures will require Cairo to balance its association with the United States and Israel with at least normal relations with Moscow. The USSR considered Sadat's personal leadership largely responsible for Egyptian anti-Sovietism and Egypt's isolation in the Arab world. Without Sadat, Egypt is more likely to abandon the

---

[18] U.S. Department of State. Soviet and East European Aid, 1981. p. 8, 19, and 21.

"contradictions" of its foreign policy according to the Soviets, and return to its more natural position on the Arab political spectrum.

Egypt was the USSR's most important ally in the Middle East before 1973. The 1973 "October war" led Sadat to seek a U.S.-sponsored resolution of the chronic Egyptian-Israeli hostilities and to attract Western economic aid and trade to stimulate the nation's economy. Clearly in Sadat's mind, the Soviet Union could offer Egypt little in the way of satisfying these objectives. As Egypt and the United States developed a consensus on strategic, political and economic goals, relations with the Soviet Union deteriorated. As an indication of the decline of the Soviet presence, in the decade from 1967 to 1976, the USSR supplied Egypt with arms valued at nearly $2.4 billion; from 1976 to 1980, arms transfers were estimated at $20 million.[19]

By 1972, Sadat had begun to dismantle Egypt's relations with the USSR by ordering the withdrawal of the Soviet air defense forces and the contingent of Soviet advisers. In 1975, Egypt sharply restricted Soviet access to naval facilities at Mersa Matruh and Sollom. By March 1976, Sadat had abrogated the Soviet-Egyptian Friendship and Cooperation Treaty and ordered the USSR to shut down submarine operations in Alexandria, the last accessible port for Soviet operations. The Soviet Navy's Mediterranean Squadron thus lost its most valuable facilities, to which it had virtual free access for nearly a decade.[20] Thus the Soviet Union lost a stratetic military presence in the eastern Mediterranean and the Middle East which it will not regain in Egypt barring a radical change in government in Cairo.

2. THE ROAD TO NORMALIZATION

Soviet relation with Egypt had been deteriorating since the explusion of the Soviets in 1972, but they achieved a new low before Sadat's death. President Sadat declared that Egypt would lead an anti-Soviet bloc in the Middle East and announced that his country would send aid to the anti-government and anti-Soviet guerrillas in Afghanistan. Egypt gave the United States rights to use the military facilities at Ras Banas on the Red Sea for the Rapid Deployment Force, without granting permanent base rights. Egypt under Sadat was becoming the focus of the Reagan Administration's concept of a strategic alliance of anti-Soviet Middle Eastern states that was to include Israel, the Sudan, and Saudi Arabia.

One of Sadat's last decisions was to expel the Soviet ambassador and 1,000 economic and technical advisers in September 1981 as part of a crackdown on anti-government dissidents. Sadat also announced the cancellation of all outstanding contracts between the

---

[19] U.S. Arms Control and Disarmament Agency (ACDA). World Military Expenditures and Arms Transfers, 1967–1976. July 1978. p. 158. And, U.S. ACDA. World Military Expenditures and Arms Transfers, 1971–1980. March 1983. p. 119.

[20] For a discussion of the importance of Egypt to the Soviet naval presence in the Mediterranean, see Weinland, Robert G. Land Support for Naval Forces: Egypt and the Soviet Escadra, 1962–1976. Survival, March–April 1978. p. 73–79. Weinland writes that Alexandria "emerged quite early . . . as the 'center of gravity' of the Soviet naval presence in the Mediterranean, and it retained this position as long as the Soviet Union remained in Egypt. Alexandria appears to have served three major functions: it was the Squadron's 'headquarters,' it provided sheltered location from which replenishment and other ships of the service could operate, and it had those repair and maintenance facilities." (p. 76)

two countries. Since then, however, President Mubarak has refrained from antagonizing the Soviet Union. A number of Egyptian and Soviet decisions have given the appearance of placing relations on a course of normalization. In fact, Mubarak and leading Egyptian government officials have endorsed the idea of normalization, first by resuming full diplomatic ties, as long as it is not at the expense of U.S.-Egyptian relations.

The Soviet Union quickly signalled its desire for better relations after Sadat's death. In a message to Mubarak shortly after Sadat's death, Soviet leader Leonid Brezhnev said: "You may rest assured that your readiness for an improvement in relations between Egypt and the Soviet Union . . . will always meet with understanding and support from the Soviet side."[21] Moscow's initial broadcast on Sadat's death linked the assassination to dissatisfaction of the Egyptian people with Sadat's foreign and domestic policies, in particular the peace treaty with Israel and the military alignment with the United States. The Soviet Union attempted to counter U.S. moves to strengthen its ties with Sadat's successors with allegations that Washington was imposing a "gross diktat" and ordering the Egyptians in how to act. Moscow asserted that events in Egypt affected Soviet security. The USSR was clearly trying to reclaim a role in Egypt.[22]

One of Mubarak's first moves was to lift the ban on sales of cotton to the USSR placed by Sadat in 1977 and to request the return of Soviet technicians for the operation of Soviet-built projects, such as the Aswan dam, the Asyut cement plant, and a major aluminum plant. Egypt is reported to be considering the purchase of additional Soviet military equipment to balance its reliance on western supplies and to acquire sorely-needed spare parts for its inventory of Soviet-built weapons.[23] Egypt agreed in 1982 to purchase 200 Romanian tanks modeled on the Soviet T–55. The Egyptian decision in January 1982 to purchase French-built Mirage 2000 aircraft was further evidence to the Soviets that Egypt wished to diversify its military ties, reducing its dependence on the United States.

Soviet commentators view the course of Mubarak's foreign policy in a positive light. They note that Mubarak has freed a number of politicians imprisoned in Sadat's crackdown againt the opposition, including the heads of the Egyptian-Soviet Friendship Society and Egypt's leftist Socialist Labor party. Moscow has favorably commented on Mubarak's differences with Washington over the resolution of the Palestinian autonomy question. After Israel turned over to Egypt the last territory it held in the Sinai in April 1982, Mubarak refused to travel to Jerusalem, as the Israelis had planned, in order to avoid recognizing Israeli control of the disputed city. Egypt recalled its ambassador from Tel Aviv to protest alleged Israeli complicity in the Sabra and Shatila massacres in Lebanon in September 1982. Soviet observers have also tended to look at the criminal prosecution of Ismat Sadat, the former president's brother, on

---

[21] Soviet World Outlook, October 15, 1981. Vol. 6, No. 10. p. 2.
[22] Ibid.
[23] The Kuwaiti News agency, KUNA, carried one such report on October 29, 1982. See, FBIS, Soviet Union Daily Report, November 1, 1982. p. H3.

charges of fraud as a further sign of Egypt's break with the policies of the past, as well as evidence of the corruption of the Sadat government.[24] Mubarak sent a high-level delegation to the funeral of Leonid Brezhnev in November 1982, even though the Soviet government refused to send any representation to Sadat's funeral over a year earlier. The new Soviet leadership of Yuri Andropov chose the head of Egypt's delegation to be one of the few foreign representatives to meet privately with First Vice President Vasily Kuznetsov. Moscow television noted on December 19, 1982 that the Egyptian media have "made positive remarks in relations to the countries of the socialist camp," but added that it "would be wrong to think that Egypt has radically changed its foreign policy."[25]

In sum, Moscow has welcomed Mubarak's unwillingness to continue the anti-Soviet policies of Sadat and pursue a more "realistic" diplomacy. The Kremlin also cites Egypt's growing rapprochement with the Arab world and more frequent criticisms of Israel.

In December 1982, Deputy Prime Minister and Foreign Minister Kamal Hasan Ali said Egypt did not "oppose the establishment of normal friendly relations between Egypt and the Soviets." Ali noted that commercial and economic relations are good and that technical and cultural cooperation is getting better. In mid-February 1983, Ali said an exchange of ambassadors was "inevitable." In a December 1982 interview, President Mubarak compared Egypt's policy towards Moscow and Washington to India's: "India has special relations with the Soviet Union and normal relations with the United States. . . . We have a special relationship with the United States and, in contrast, normal relations with the Soviet Union."[26] An aide to President Mubarak, Osama al-Baz, recieved two Soviet experts on the Middle East in early 1983. Anatoly Gromyko, director of the African Institute of the USSR Academy of Sciences and son of the foreign minister, and prominent journalist Igor Belyayev travelled to Egypt in January.[27] In March 1983, Soviet Deputy Prime Minister Nikolay Baybakov was in Cairo to discuss the normalization of relations.[27]

Egypt remains an important trading partner of the Soviet Union in the Middle East although relations have worsened since 1973 and total trade turnover has dropped considerably. In 1975, Egypt ranked first among Soviet trading partners in the Middle East with total trade turnover at 710 million rubles; by 1982 this figure fell to

---

[24] The Soviet Union directs a great deal of its media propaganda towards Egypt. Commentary on international events frequently covers developments in Egypt and the prospects of Soviet-Egyptian rapprochement, although reports chide Cairo for failure to recognize the value of good relations with Moscow. See, FBIS, Soviet Union Daily Report, December 19, 1982 p. H3; January 27, 1983, p. H2; February 1, 1983, p. H8; February 2, 1983, p. H2. Also, Robert Rand. Moscow Remains Ready to Improve Ties with Egypt. Radio Liberty Research, RL 115/82. March 8, 1982. And, Egyptian Official Says Cairo Favors Improving Ties with Moscow. Radio Liberty Research, RL 15/83. January 6, 1983.

[25] The commentary was by Izvestiya political observer Stanislav Kondrashov. FBIS, Soviet Union Daily Report, December 27, 1982. p. H3–4. See also, Temko, Ned. Two U.S. allies in the Mideast Smile toward Soviets. Christian Science Monitor, January 20, 1983. On Mubarak's foreign policy, see, Egypt Back in the Picture. The Middle East, September 1982. p. 11–14.

[26] Quoted in, Robert Rand. Egyptian Official Favors Improving Ties with Moscow, op. cit.

[27] Mubarak Seeks Neutral Ground for Egypt. Journal of Commerce. January 26, 1983. p. 5A. Belyayev is the author of numerous articles on Soviet-Egyptian relations stressing the illegitimate nature of Sadat's rule. See his, Different Times? Egypt 1983. Asia and Africa Today, No. 7, 1983. p. 20–23. And: Egypt, Land of Wonders. Literaturnaya Gazeta, January 12, 1983.

521 million rubles, fourth bhind Libya, Iraq, and Iran.[28] Unlike the Soviet Union's other major trading partners in the Middle East which export large quantities of petroleum and minerals, Egypt relies on selling cotton, textiles, foodstuffs, and industrial consumer goods to the USSR. Thus, commercial relations between the two countries appear to be a possible inducement toward better ties. Furthermore, Egypt still has to reschedule approximately $10 billion in military aid debt to the Soviet Union. It is also interested in acquiring spare parts for its older Soviet weaponry.[29] However, the United States is Egypt's largest trading partner, providing 20 percent of Egypt's imports in 1981.

3. LIMITS TO NORMALIZATION

The extent to which the two countries are likely to improve relations in the near future has limits. Cairo has opposed the Soviet Union's presence in Afghanistan and is generally suspicious of Soviet motives in the region, particularly in its close relations with Libya and its history of undermining Sudanese stability. While the USSR and Egypt are ready to work towards better relations, political conditions may hamper the course. Egypt has declared that Moscow must agree not to interfere in its internal affairs. Clearly, Egyptian authorities are concerned over alleged Soviet support of muslim fundamentalists and opposition groups, such as the "Patriotic Front," led by former Egyptian General Shazli, exiled in Libya.

The Soviet government through its media has expressed disappointment with Egyptian foreign policy on a number of occasions. Soviet authorities apparently expected relations with Egypt to improve dramatically after the last bit of Sinai territory was handed over by the Israelis. Egypt, the Soviets reasoned, would have less stake in remaining tied to the Camp David accords and the peace process with Israel and so could begin to move towards positions compatible with Soviet objectives. However, in spite of Egypt's disapproval of Israeli policies in Lebanon and the West Bank, Mubarak has generally followed the spirit of the Camp David accords.

An editorial by Radio Moscow in January 1983 was indicative of the Soviet frustration towards Cairo. Commentator Nikolai Andreyev noted that the "double stance" of the Egyptian government towards expanding relations with Moscow is "raising concern."

On the one hand, the leaders of the regime declare their endeavors to abandon much of the former policy [of Sadat]; on the other hand, they are seeking to maintain . . . the course of developing the so-called special relationship with the United States and, subsequently, with Israel—a fact that harms other countries—and to follow the course of the so-called separate peace process within the spirit and framework of Camp David—the course established by As-Sadat.[30]

Andreyev said that Egypt's support for U.S. policies and Camp David is "incompatible with Cairo's declared course toward settle-

---

[28] Klochek. The USSR's Foreign Trade in 1982. (Appears in FBIS, Soviet Union Daily Report, March 31, 1983. p. S8.)

Soviet sources report that Egypt's exports to the USSR provide jobs for 150,000 Egyptians. One theme stressed by Soviet propagandists is the value to Egypt of economic ties with the Soviet Union and the assistance offered by Soviet technicians. See, Victor Kalikhin commentary, FBIS, Soviet Union Daily Report, February 1, 1983. p. H8–9.

[29] Price, D.L. Policy Shifts in the Middle East. Soviet Analyst. June 22, 1983. p. 2.

[30] FBIS, Soviet Union Daily Report, January 27, 1983. p. H2–4.

ment of relations with the Arab world and toward nonalignment." About the normalization of diplomatic relations between Moscow and Cairo, he said that Egypt must support its words by "tangible deeds." [31]

4. CONCLUSIONS

At the time of the death of President Sadat, Soviet-Egyptian relations were at an all time low and Soviet influence in the country was virtually non-existent. Since then President Mubarak has opened avenues of communication which could lead in time to a normalization of ties, beginning perhaps with the resumption of diplomatic relations. [32] For the Soviet Union, normalization would indicate that Egypt's preparedness to reassess policies of the Sadat era, moderate its anti-communism, and move toward the Arab mainstream. It seems reasonable to anticipate that Sadat's rigid opposition to the Soviet Union and close indentification with the West will continue to be moderated.

Soviet success in Egypt will be measured less by its presence there than by the accommodation of the Egyptian government to conditions in the Middle East compatible with Soviet interests. A de-emphasis of military ties to the United States, growing popular anti-Americanism, and a lessening of the commitment to the Camp David peace process would be positive developments for Soviet policy. However, aside from limited inroads, such as resuming economic assistance to major Soviet-Egyptian joint projects and expansion of trade, few targets of opportunity are currently available to the Soviet Union in Egypt.

---

[31] Ibid.
[32] Egypt Expect to Restore Ties to Soviet Soon. New York Times. May 5, 1983. p. A8.

III. THE U.S.S.R. AND LIBYA

A. INTRODUCTION

While the Soviet Union and Libya have maintained close relations for a number of years, the issues of Soviet influence in Libya has attracted much attention recently. Libyan adventurism in North Africa is seen by many as indirect Soviet expansionism, while a number of Col. Qadhafi's policies seem compatible with Soviet interests in the region. The Libyan leader is hostile to a U.S. military presence in the Middle East and the Mediterranean Sea, rejects the right of Israel to exist, undermines pro-western governments in the region, such as Egypt's, and maintains close military and internal security ties with the Soviet bloc. Although the degree of Soviet-Libyan cooperation and agreement in international affairs is open to question, it is apparent that the USSR sees opportunities in cultivating a relationship with Col. Qadhafi and in using his anti-Western policies to its own advantage.

Relations between the Soviet Union and Libya since 1969, when Col. Muammar Qadhafi led a military coup against the government of King Idris, have been ambivalent. Commercial and military contacts from the beginning of Qadhafi's leadership have flourished, while political and ideological objectives have often been in conflict. However, in recent years, military and political ties have expanded considerably without the benefit of a formal alliance agreement. Nonetheless, although the two nations' policies coincide on a number of issues critical to U.S. and Western interests, there exists a sharp divergence on other goals and a general Soviet reluctance to become too closely and irrevocably identified with the unpredictable Col. Qadhafi.

For the Soviet Union, Libya presents strategic and military opportunities to support its policy in the Middle East and the Mediterranean. In the early post-World War II years, Moscow endeavored to acquire from the allied powers authority to establish trusteeship control over Tripolitania in Western Libya. A foothold on the North Africa coast would facilitate a Soviet naval presence in the Mediterranean and challenge Western predominance in the area. Although the Soviets were not successful in getting rights in Libya at the time, recent history has presented Moscow with new opportunities in the country.

In Libya, Moscow finds a nation that promotes instability in the region, is strongly anti-Western, and hostile to U.S. influence, but at the same time unpredictable and uncontrollable. Col. Qadhafi has threatened his neighbors in Egypt, Tunisia, the Sudan, and Chad, which has forced these countries to take Libya into consideration in their defense planning. Libya has attempted to undermine the governments of such pro-Western African countries as Liberia, Ghana, Nigeria, and Senegal. Libya's anti-imperialist credentials in the Third World and its frequent confrontations with the United States have been embarrassing to Washington in some Middle East capitals and Africa. With its large arms inventory and belligerent foreign policy, Libya also poses a modest danger to NATO's southern flank.

Libya's wealth enables it to purchase arms, which for political reasons it can get in large quantities only from the Soviet bloc, while Qadhafi's desire for complete control of domestic affairs leads him to seek internal security assistance from Soviet and East European security organizations.

A number of Libyan policies have worked to limit closer Soviet ties to Qadhafi's government. Libya maintains important economic links to the West, centered around its oil exports, and it has refused to grant the Soviets a base on its territory.[1] Qadhafi's maverick image and aggressive foreign adventures have forced Moscow to periodically disassociate itself from Libya. Nonetheless, the Kremlin has in Libya a trading partner that provides it with vast amounts of hard currency in arms sales and a possible contributory source of energy in the future.[2] Although neither country is completely satisfied with the state of relations, Soviet influence in Libya is a legitimate source of concern in U.S. and Western foreign policy. The danger of Soviet military penetration in Libya and the North African littoral continues, although numerous observers have minimized the threats posed by Col. Qadhafi or the Soviet Union in Libya.

B. SOVIET POLICIES AND OBJECTIVES

Libya presents strategic opportunities for the Soviet Union. Its location on the Mediterranean coast provides the Soviet navy with convenient ports of call and possible basing privileges. Libya represents a counterweight to the strong U.S. influence in Egypt, and replaces, to some extent, the large Soviet military presence in Egypt. (The USSR maintained nearly 20,000 troops and advisers in Egypt until Sadat expelled them in 1972.) As a possible staging area for Soviet forces, Libya may also be figured into NATO military planning for southern Europe. In addition, the Soviet Union is eager to check the growing military relationships between the United States and the neighboring countries of Egypt, the Sudan, Morocco, and Tunisia, fueled in part by Moscow's own military patron-client ties with Tripoli.

Arms sales have been a useful instrument of Soviet policy in Libya; Moscow monopolizes Libyan arms purchases by providing about two thirds of its weaponry. The Soviets have signed arms agreements with Libya totaling approximately $15 billion from 1973 to 1981, half of which have been delivered.[3] Libya is said to

---

[1] NATO military planners are said to fear that Libya may grant the Soviets access to facilities on its territory in the event of a crisis. See, Middleton, Drew. A Soviet Peril: Bases in Libya. New York Times, March 1, 1981. Sec. 1, part 1, p. 11. In July 1981, two Soviet frigates visited the naval base at Tripoli, the first visit by the Soviet navy to Libya.

[2] For an overview of attitudes toward Libya in the Soviet press, see: Usov, V. Anti-Libyan Storm in Washington. International Affairs (Moscow). March 1982. p. 125–128.

[3] Soviet and East European Aid to the Third World, 1981. U.S. Department of State, February 1983. p. 9. One source places *total* Libyan arms imports from all sources from 1978 to 1982, a period of five years, at $4.48 billion. See, SIPRI, Yearbook of World Armaments and Disarmament, 1983. p. 270.

have the highest ratio of weaponry to troops in the world, with an arsenal of weapons valued at $12 billion. Although Libya's population is one percent of Africa's total, its purchases of arms amounts to about 40 percent of the continents total although most of its inventory lies in storage. These deliveries include 2,800 T–54/–55/–62/–72 main battle tanks, armored personnel carriers, artillery, and Frog, Scud, and Scaleboard (SS–12) surface-to-surface missiles for the army.

Libya's 55,000-man army has some 2,900 tanks compared with Egypt's 2,100 tanks, which has an army six times the size of Libya's. The Libyan air force, which now has MiG–23 and –25 fighters, is similarly heavily equipped, with 555 combat aircraft for 5,000 personnel, while Egypt's 27,000-man air force maintains 429 aircraft. The disparity in inventory is even greater between Libya's army and air force and the forces of its other neighbors, such as Algeria and the Sudan. The Libyan navy possesses five Soviet Foxtrot-class submarines and a dozen Soviet-built missile boats, in addition to Western-produced surface craft. However, the navy is much less over-armed than the other services.[4]

Soviet military advisers are estimated to number 1,000–2,000, operating down to the regimental and battalion level and maintaining tanks, rocket launchers, artillery, and aircraft. Between 600 and 1,000 Cubans assist in these roles, including road building and construction. Some 1,500 to 2,000 East Germans advise Libya's intelligence and internal security forces.[5] Libya is also reported to have sent soldiers to Poland for military training.[6]

Because its arms build-up so greatly exceeds Libya's capacity for absorption, many observers have suggested that it serves as a Soviet storage depot for activities in Africa and the Middle East. On the other hand, large quantities of arms are reported to be damaged and in disrepair as a result of Libya's limited ability to maintain the equipment. One inducement to purchase arms is Qadhafi's desire to re-export weapons to nationalists and separatists throughout the world for personal and political reasons.[7] Although, there may be no formal agreement for Soviet use of the equipment, it seems conceivable that the two nations could cooperate under the proper circumstances.

C. LIBYAN FOREIGN AND DOMESTIC POLITICS AND MOSCOW

Early Soviet-Libyan relations under Qadhafi offered little hope of ideological affinity. Qadhafi's revolutionary ideology is populist, Is-

---

[4] Zartman, I. William. "Arms Imports: The Libyan Experience." In, U.S. Arms Control and Disarmament Agency. World Military Expenditures and Arms Transfers, 1971–1980. March 1983. p. 16–18.

[5] Cooley, John K. Soviets in Libya: A New Mediterranean Power. Washington Post, March 10, 1981. Cooley also writes of East German assistance in putting down an anti-Qadhafi coup attempt. See, Libyan Sandstorm. New York, Holt, Rinehart and Winston, 1982. p. 282.

[6] New York Times. January 31, 1982. Section 1, p. 14. Over 200 Libyan cadets were sent to Poland, according to the news story. The deal was arranged by the USSR and is said to represent Qadhafi's support for the military takeover in Poland in December 1981 as well as Poland's intentions to secure oil supplies.

[7] Andrew Pierre, an arms transfer specialist, suggests that for Qadhafi arms purchases are primarily a means to spread revolution abroad, and are not intended for Soviet purposes. He notes also that Libya has been reluctant to expand the Soviet military training program and prefers Cuban advisers to Soviets. See, The Global Politics of Arms Sales. Princeton, Princeton University Press, 1982. p. 198–199.

lamic, and pan-Arab nationalist, with few similarities in Soviet ideology. In his Green Book of 1976, Qadhafi developed the concept of "third universal theory" based on a course of pure direct democracy that is neither communist nor capitalist, where complete sovereignty resides in hundreds of people's committees, not in western-style parliaments.[8] Although a number of observers have seen similarities between Qadhafi's brand of socialism and Marxism,[9] Moscow remains suspicious of the indigenous quality of Qadhafi's ideas and their nationalist and Islamic content. Suspicions are not lessened by Qadhafi's advice to the Third World to follow a course of "positive neutralism," or the rejection of both superpower camps.[10]

The Kremlin is perhaps concerned that Qadhafi's ideas may spread to the Muslim population of the Soviet Union. Qadhafi's ideological affinity with Iranian leader Ayatollah Khomeini cannot be reassuring to Soviet leaders. Libya's foreign policy is characterized by nonalignment and at least rhetorical support for avoiding encumbering ties with either bloc. Moscow's problems in cultivating a strong relationship with Libya were apparent in Qadhafi's official visit to Beijing in October 1982. The meeting with Chinese leaders reportedly was at Qadhafi's initiative with the goal of further diversifying Libya's contacts.[11]

Not all of Libya's specific foreign policy goals are shared by the Kremlin. However, Qadhafi's militance often serves Soviet interests. Libya desires war on Israel and the unification of the Arab world in a revolutionary, anti-imperialist alliance. Libya's military expansion is driven by Qadhafi's political objectives. These include a war with Israel, support for national liberation movements throughout the world,[12] and the creation of a greater Libya stretching across the Sahara Desert.[13]

Although the Soviet Union has little control over Libyan foreign policy, their objectives frequently coincide. Moscow often lauds Libyan policy and the goals of combatting colonialism, racism, and Zionism. Libya's interpretation of these objectives—such as support for the Polisario liberation movement in the Western Sahara and destabilizing efforts in other African countries, notably Chad—have not been officially endorsed by Moscow. But, the Soviet Union's continued sale of arms to Tripoli as an intrument of Soviet policy

---

[8] For interpretations of Libyan domestic and foreign policies, see: First, Ruth. Libya: The Elusive Revolution. New York, Africana Publishing Co., 1975. John K. Cooley. Libyan Sandstorm, op. cit. And, Libya-Sudan-Chad Triangle: Dilemma for U.S. Policy. Hearings before the Foreign Affairs Committee, Subcommittee on Africa. U.S. House of Representatives, 97th Congress. October 29 and November 4, 1981.

[9] Hajjar, Sami G. The Marxist Origins of Qadhafi's Economic Thought. Journal of Modern African Studies. September 1982. p. 361–375.

[10] See, Laipson, Ellen. "Libya and the Soviet Union." In, Laqueur, Walter, ed. The Pattern of Soviet Conduct in the Third World. New York, Praeger, 1983. p. 139–140.

[11] China's reception of Qadhafi was reported to be proper but restrained, reflecting the political differences between the two countries, particularly over approaches to a Middle East peace settlement and Libya's denunciations of "U.S. imperialism" without equal mention of Soviet threats to the region. Qadhafi continued on to North Korea where he signed a treaty of friendship and cooperation, which also provides for mutual defense arrangements and arms sales.

[12] Washington Times. May 29, 1983. p. 1A, 12A. The report said that Libya was involved in twenty Latin American countries by sending cash and arms to revolutionary groups. It has also extended an offer of $100 million to Sandinista regime in Nicaragua.

[13] Ogunbadejo, Oye. Qadhafi's North African Design. International Security, Summer 1983. p. 154–178.

suggests that it supports the general destabilizing activities of the Libyan government.[14]

A policy of nonalignment has led Libya to pursue economic relations with Western Europe. But, Libya has voiced its determination to avoid political or economic dependence on foreign countries, particularly non-Arab ones. Through the mid-1970s, Libya continued to receive substantial arms and aid from France, Great Britain, and the United States. Recent years have seen Libya acquire an increasing proportion of its principal weapons systems from the Soviet bloc and less from the West.

In the years immediately after the 1969 revolution, Libya limited its commercial relations with the Soviet Union to the purchase of arms. The first purchase was made in July 1970, followed by another deal in 1974 for $1 billion in military equipment. Large numbers of Soviet military advisers and technicians accompanied the arms, but to reduce Moscow's control the Libyan government also relied on advisers from Cuba, Pakistan, North Korea, Yugoslavia, and Taiwan. In the late 1970s, Western nations reconsidered their arms sales policies towards Libya with an eye to keeping a military balance in the region and withholding aid to a country with a record of militant anti-colonialism and strong links to terrorist organizations in the West. Libya's desire for modern military equipment had led to isolation from the West and increasing reliance on the Soviet Union. For Moscow, the Libyan requests for arms represented a new opening to the Middle East and North Africa after diplomatic setbacks in Egypt and the Sudan.[15]

Libya's isolation from the West has deepened since the election of the Reagan Administration. Two confrontations with the United States, in August 1981 and February 1983, may have reinforced Libya's dependence on the USSR for arms and led Qadhafi to fundamentally reevaluate his concept of avoiding alliance with superpowers. A challenge from the United States could lead Libya towards greater collaboration and perhaps a client relationship with the USSR. On August 20, 1981, during the confrontation with the United States in the Gulf of Sidra, Libya entered into an alliance with Ethiopia and the Peoples Democratic Republic of (South) Yeman (PDRY), two client states of the Soviet Union. The Tripartite Agreement should enhance Soviet efforts to increase pressure on the pro-western countries of Egypt, the Sudan, and Saudi Arabia. Libya presumably will be more likely to transfer its large inventory of armaments to its allies in the agreement and to provide financial assistance to them. The agreement gives Moscow a means to influence Libya indirectly without formal treaty bonds with the unpredictable Qadhafi.[16]

In March 1983, Libya and the Soviet Union agreed "in principle" to conclude a treaty of friendship and cooperation during a visit to Moscow of Abd as-Salam Jallud, Libya's second in command. The understanding came one month after the U.S.-Libyan confrontation arising from Washington's charges that Libya was attempting to undermine the pro-Western Sudanese government. The limited

[14] Zartman. Arms Imports: The Libyan Experience. p. 19.
[15] Ibid., p. 18.
[16] Hottinger. Arab Communism at Low Ebb. p. 29–30.

agreement suggested that the Soviet Union was avoiding an increase in its support for Qadhafi's government.[17] Moscow also declined to mention any increase in Soviet-Libyan military relations. While Qadhafi has sought a strengthened military agreement with the USSR, the Soviets have doubted his commitment to ties with Moscow.[18]

D. SOVIET ECONOMIC RELATIONS WITH LIBYA

The Soviet bloc also maintains profitable economic links with Libya, in addition to lucrative arms sales. But with large oil reserves, Libya does not need Soviet economic assistance and, instead, looks to the West for economic trade and development. According to Soviet sources, total Soviet trade turnover with Libya has soared from 19 million rubies in 1974 to 1,347 million rubies in 1982.[19] Eastern European nations have construction and services contracts valued at several billion dollars. The Soviet bloc is reported to be earning vast amounts of hard currency from service contracts and economic technicians estimated at over 30,000 in Libya. Cuba is reported to have 5,000 economic advisers stationed in Libya.[20]

With the exception of the nuclear development program, the USSR has been unable to provide the technological know-how to contribute to Libyan development. Moscow agreed in 1978 to construct a 300-megawatt nuclear power plant, and recently the two countries have discussed the possibility of cooperating on two more nuclear power plants of 400-megawatts each. Col. Qadhafi has been interested in developing nuclear power facilities but has denied intentions to build a nuclear weapon. The Soviet Union has also continued its involvement in the huge Misurata steel complex, built with Soviet assistance.

Future economic relations may center on Libyan oil exports, although in the past Libya has not been an important supplier of energy to the USSR and its Eastern European allies. Falling oil prices and Libya's declining hard currency reserves may improve the chances of barter arrangements with the Soviet bloc. However, Libya has traditionally been a price hawk within OPEC and may see little return in exporting to the Soviet bloc, which is poor in hard currency and technologically less developed than the West.[21] But, for the time being, the Soviet Union remains Libya's largest and most reliable supplier of weapons. Falling oil prices and the consequences of declining revenues may in the long run hinder Libya's efforts to export revolution abroad and reduce Libya's dependence on the Soviet Union for arms. However, if the Soviet

---

[17] See: Rand, Robert. A Look at Soviet-Libyan Relations. Radio Liberty Research, RL 307/83. August 11, 1983.

[18] During a September 1, 1981 speech, Qadhafi expressed Libya's "desperate" need for a "military alliance" with "any ally," but reiterated Libya's desire to remain "neutral and nonaligned forever." FBIS, Middle East and North Africa Daily Report. September 2, 1981 (MEA-81.-170). p. Q1-Q21.

[19] Klochek. The USSR's Foreign Trade in 1982. (Reprinted in FBIS,, Soviet Union Daily Report, March 31, 1983. p. S8.)

[20] U.S. Department of State. Soviet and East European Aid. p. 9 and 20.

[21] Stern, Jonathan P. "CMEA Oil Acquisition Policy in the Middle East and the Gulf: The Search for Economic and Political Strategies." In U.S. Congress. Joint Economic Committee. Soviet Economy in the 1980s: Problems and Prospects. December 31, 1982.

Union becomes a net oil importer, as some analysts predict, an arms-for-oil barter arrangement may result, particularly as a consequence of Libya's declining hard currency reserves. Moscow may be interested as well in initiating a barter deal for its East European client states.

E. CONCLUSION: SOVIET SUCCESSES AND LIMITATIONS IN LIBYA

Increasing isolation from the West and opposition at home may lead Col. Qadhafi towards more military cooperation with the Soviets, even if this means violating the Libyan revolution's principle of nonalignment. The balance in the relationship appears to be shifting towards greater Libyan dependence on Moscow and Soviet distancing from Qadhafi's policies. Although the two countries have deep ideological differences, closer political and military ties have been achieved. In recent years, Libya's isolation from the West and its "anti-imperialist" policies have more often coincided with Soviet interests. Nevertheless, there is little indication that Libya's policies are directly guided or influenced by the Soviet Union.[22]

Soviet policies in Libya are constrained by a number of factors—ideological, political, and economic—while the relationship has expanded on the strength of military dependence. Qadhafi's Islamic fundamentalism has been incorporated into the structure of Libyan society and is not merely a rhetorical set of principles. The international dynamics of Libya's politics continue to frustrate Soviet relations with other regional actors in the Middle East and Africa, and thus there seems to be little chance for a genuine political partnership.[23] Economic relations will necessarily be limited by the diverging structures of each country's economy. Soviet attempts to expand relations with Libya to coordinated political action may prove risky. Observers tend to view the Soviet-Libya relationship as resting on weak foundations, and pressure to alter the relationship of arms transfers, internal security cooperation, and economic development assistance could weaken the Soviet presence in Libya.[24] The Soviets appear to be prepared to offer Libya broader military association without legitimizing political identification with Qadhafi.

TABLE 1.—USSR AND EASTERN EUROPE: MILITARY AGREEMENTS WITH NON-COMMUNIST LESS DEVELOPED COUNTRIES (LDC'S), 1981

[In million of U.S. dollars]

	U.S.S.R.	Eastern Europe
Total [1]	6,060	2,030
North Africa		650

---

[22] St. John Ronald Bruce. The Soviet Penetration of Libya. The World Today. April 1982. p. 137.

[23] Libyan assistance to Chadian rebel forces in the summer of 1983 is perhaps a case of Soviet reluctance to support Qadhafi's policies in the region. The Soviet Union has refrained from publicly sanctioning Qadhafi's involvement in Chad. See, Rand, Robert. Chad Becomes Object of U.S. and Soviet Concern. Radio Liberty Research, RL 280/83. July 22, 1983. p. 2-3. However, another interpretation sees the Soviets backing Libya against Western interests as long as the Chadian conflict does not escalate. See, Yodfat, Aryeh. Soviet Analyst. October 12, 1983. p. 6.

[24] St. John. The Soviet Penetration of Libya. p. 138.

TABLE 1.—USSR AND EASTERN EUROPE: MILITARY AGREEMENTS WITH NON-COMMUNIST LESS DEVELOPED COUNTRIES (LDC'S), 1981—Continued

[In million of U.S. dollars]

	U.S.S.R.	Eastern Europe
Sub-Saharan Africa	1,910	5
Latin America	105	10
Middle East	3,505	1,365
South Asia	535	5

[1] Because of rounding, components may not add to totals shown.

Source: U.S. Department of State. Soviet and East European Aid to the Third World, 1981. February 1983. p. 2.

TABLE 2.—MILITARY TECHNICIANS IN NON-COMMUNIST LDC'S, 1981

[Number of persons] [1]

	U.S.S.R.	Eastern Europe	Cuba
Total [1]	16,280	1,925	[2] 39,175
North Africa	4,000	600	50
Sub-Saharan Africa	4,535	765	36,910
Latin America	165	60	1,715
Middle East	5,425	500	500
South Asia	2,155	NA	

[1] Numbers are rounded to the nearest 5.
[2] Includes combat units in Angola and Ethiopia.

Source: Soviet and East European Aid, 1981. p. 2.

TABLE 3.—U.S.S.R. AND EASTERN EUROPE: ECONOMIC AID EXTENDED TO NORTH AFRICA AND THE MIDDLE EAST, BY COUNTRY

[In millions of U.S. dollars]

	1954–81		1980		1981	
	U.S.S.R.	East Europe	U.S.S.R.	East Europe	U.S.S.R.	East Europe
Total	11,175	5,475	315	675	55	
North Africa (subtotal)	3,250	980	315			
Algeria	1,045	525	315			
Mauritania	10	10				
Morocco	2,100	215				
Tunisia	95	230				
Middle East (subtotal)	7,925	4,495		675	55	
Cyprus	15	10		5		
Egypt	1,440	1,225		300		
Greece	5	NA				
Iran	1,165	685				
Iraq	705	495				
Jordan	30	NA				
Lebanon		10				
North Yemen	140	40				
South Yemen	205	125		15		
Syria	770	1,155				
Turkey	3,400	755		355		
Other	55				55	

Source: Soviet and East European Aid, 1981. p. 17–19.

TABLE 4.—U.S.S.R. AND EASTERN EUROPE: ECONOMIC TECHNICIANS IN NORTH AFRICA AND THE MIDDLE EAST, 1981 [1]

[Number of persons]

	U.S.S.R. and Eastern Europe	Cuba
Total	73,020	8,900
North Africa (subtotal)	45,870	5,250
Algeria	11,150	250
Libya	31,700	5,000
Mauritania	50	
Morocco	2,350	
Tunisia	600	
Other	20	
Middle East (subtotal)	27,150	3,650
Iran	2,450	
Iraq	13,000	3,500
North Yemen	175	
South Yemen	2,700	150
Syria	4,100	
Other	4,725	

[1] Minimum estimates of number present for a period of one month or more. Numbers are rounded to nearest 5.
Source: Soviet and East European Aid, 1981. p. 20–21.

TABLE 5.—ACADEMIC STUDENTS FROM NORTH AFRICA AND THE MIDDLE EAST BEING TRAINED IN THE U.S.S.R. AND EASTERN EUROPE, AS OF DECEMBER 1981 [1]

[Number of persons]

North Africa	4,485
Algeria	2,225
Libya	275
Mauritania	280
Morocco	650
Tunisia	1,055
Middle East	18,650
Egypt	775
Iraq	2,275
Lebanon	545
North Yemen	775
South Yemen	1,335
Syria	3,665
Other	9,280

[1] Numbers are rounded to nearest 5. Most of the estimates are based on scholarship awards.
Source: Soviet and East European Aid, 1981. p. 22–23.

TABLE 6.—VALUE OF ARMS TRANSFERS, CUMULATIVE 1976–80, BY MAJOR SUPPLIER AND RECIPIENT COUNTRY

[In millions of current U.S. dollars]

Recipient	Supplier						
	Total	U.S.S.R.	United States	France	United Kingdom	West Germany	Others
North Africa	13,210	7,305	440	1,560	85	900	2,870

TABLE 6.—VALUE OF ARMS TRANSFERS, CUMULATIVE 1976–80, BY MAJOR SUPPLIER AND RECIPIENT COUNTRY—Continued

[In millions of current U.S. dollars]

Recipient	Supplier						
	Total	U.S.S.R.	United States	France	United Kingdom	West Germany	Others
Algeria..................................	2,300	1,800	....	....	20	370	100
Libya	8,600	5,500	....	410	50	460	2,155
Mauritania............................	90	....	....	40	....	....	50
Morocco................................	2,000	5	380	1,100	5	50	440
Tunisia	220	....	60	10	10	20	125
Middle East	38,600	12,500	14,200	3,500	2,700	1,400	4,265
Bahrain	40	....	5	20	....	....	20
Cyprus..................................	10	....	....	....	....	....	10
Egypt....................................	1,900	20	430	600	180	370	300
Iran	8,300	625	6,200	200	250	380	650
Iraq	7,800	5,000	....	950	90	160	1,560
Israel....................................	4,300	....	4,300	....	60	....	30
Jordan	1,000	....	725	....	280	5	50
Kuwait...................................	800	50	390	130	220	....	10
Lebanon................................	80	....	40	10	20	5	10
Oman	430	....	10	....	400	....	10
Qatar....................................	170	....	5	70	90	....	10
Saudi Arabia..........................	4,700	....	2,000	700	975	350	660
Syria	6,600	5,400	....	290	100	100	730
United Arab Emirates....................	575	....	20	450	60	40	20
North Yemen.............................	1,100	625	170	80	....	10	205
South Yemen...........................	775	775	....	....	....	....	10

Note: To avoid the appearance of excessive accuracy, all numbers in this table are independently rounded, with greater severity for larger numbers. Therefore, components may not add to totals.

Source: U.S. Arms Control and Disarmament Agency. World Military Expenditures and Arms Transfers, 1971–1980. Publication 115. March 1983. p. 117–220.

TABLE 7.—SOVIET TRADE WITH NORTH AFRICA AND THE MIDDLE EAST, 1972–82

[Million rubles]

	1972	1978	1980	1981	1982
North Africa:					
Algeria:					
Turnover...............................	115	140	155	198	179
Exports...............................	56	88	93	113	132
Imports	59	51	62	84	46
Libya:					
Turnover...............................	39	159	451	551	1,347
Exports...............................	9	52	163	190	221
Imports	30	107	288	361	1,126
Morocco:					
Turnover...............................	55	104	198	261	194
Exports...............................	32	57	93	127	136
Imports	24	47	105	134	59
Tunisia:					
Turnover...............................	10	13	25	15	11
Exports...............................	3	10	20	13	6
Imports	7	4	6	2	5
Middle East:					
Egypt:					
Turnover...............................	514	346	384	511	521
Exports...............................	266	148	173	244	219
Imports	247	198	211	267	302

TABLE 7.—SOVIET TRADE WITH NORTH AFRICA AND THE MIDDLE EAST, 1972-82—Continued

[Million rubles]

	1972	1978	1980	1981	1982
Iran:					
Turnover	230	671	335	879	766
Exports	96	433	259	409	577
Imports	134	238	75	470	189
Iraq:					
Turnover	152	1,084	732	909	994
Exports	90	674	473	906	976
Imports	62	410	259	4	18
Jordan:					
Turnover	(.6)	5	14	21	91
Exports	(.6)	5	14	20	90
Imports		0	(.2)	(.4)	(.2)
Kuwait:					
Turnover	15	37	17	18	6
Exports	15	37	15	13	6
Imports			2	6	0
Saudi Arabia:					
Turnover	5	8	31	26	14
Exports	5	8	31	26	14
Imports					
Syria:					
Turnover	112	205	321	530	512
Exports	59	131	168	279	211
Imports	54	74	153	252	301
North Yemen:					
Turnover	2.7	33	48	23	34
Exports	2.3	33	48	23	34
Imports	(.4)		(.2)	(.4)	(.3)
South Yemen:					
Turnover	6.5	27	61	99	73
Exports	6.5	26.5	56	93	67
Imports	0	(.5)	5	6	6

Note: Figures rounded to nearest million rubles. Therefore, components may not add up to totals.

Source: "Vneshniaia Torgovlia za SSSR," various years.

TABLE 8.—EXPORTS AND IMPORTS OF THE SOVIET UNION AND EASTERN EUROPE TO AND FROM NORTH AFRICA AND THE MIDDLE EAST, 1976-82 [1]

[In millions of U.S. dollars]

	Exports				Imports			
	1976	1979	1981	1982	1976	1979	1981	1982
North Africa:								
Algeria	190	209	265	252	162	93	84	71
Libya	104	237	215	204	87	189	408	346
Morocco	187	162	247	261	151	180	264	159
Tunisia	34	68	88	69	27	19	30	32
Middle East:								
Egypt	359	218	491	472	671	296	235	232
Iran	285	906	1,227	1,166	103	125	133	113
Iraq	263	246	281	267	20	30	33	28
Jordan	22	61	100	85	16	3	20	17
Kuwait [2]	54	73	75	71	129	5	253	215
Lebanon	117	168	185	158	49	72	79	67
Qatar	1	1	5	5				
Saudi Arabia	63	423	340	186	31	1	1	
Syria	166	257	300	255	150	147	202	171
United Arab Emirates	25	30	28	27	112	24	1	1

TABLE 8.—EXPORTS AND IMPORTS OF THE SOVIET UNION AND EASTERN EUROPE TO AND FROM NORTH AFRICA AND THE MIDDLE EAST, 1976–82 [1]—Continued

[In millions of U.S. dollars]

	Exports				Imports			
	1976	1979	1981	1982	1976	1979	1981	1982
North Yemen	9	24	14	12		1		
South Yemen	8	11	12	11				

[1] In the IMF statistics, Eastern Europe includes Albania, Bulgaria, Cuba, Czechoslovakia, East Germany, Mongolia, North Korea and Poland, but excludes Hungary, Romania and Yugoslavia.

[2] Soviet imports from Kuwait are f.o.b.

Note: Exports are f.o.b., import figures are given c.i.f.

Source: International Monetary Fund. Direction of Trade Statistics, Yearbook 1983. p. 56–59.

TABLE 9.—SOVIET TRADE WITH NORTH AFRICA AND THE MIDDLE EAST, 1976, 1979, AND 1982, IMPORTS AND EXPORTS

[In millions of U.S. dollars]

	U.S.S.R imports from—			Soviet exports to—		
	1976	1979	1982	1976	1979	1982
North Africa:						
Algeria	85	57	27	113	40	6
Libya				20	130	31
Morocco	54	71	62	67	101	183
Tunisia	7	4	3	16	20	18
Middle East:						
Egypt	372	145	135	191	76	176
Iran	58	68	60	126	565	744
Iraq				83	142	141
Jordan				5	11	31
Kuwait	129	5	215			
Saudi Arabia				15	39	29
Syria	92	82	116	44	79	57
North Yemen				7	14	7
South Yemen				6	8	8
United Arab Emirates					14	

Note: Soviet imports from countries are reported f.o.b., exports c.i.f. for the majority of countries. Some figures are estimates or extrapolations of part-year totals.

Source: Direction of Trade Statistics, 1983 Yearbook. International Monetary Fund. Washington, D.C. (Figures have been rounded to nearest million.)

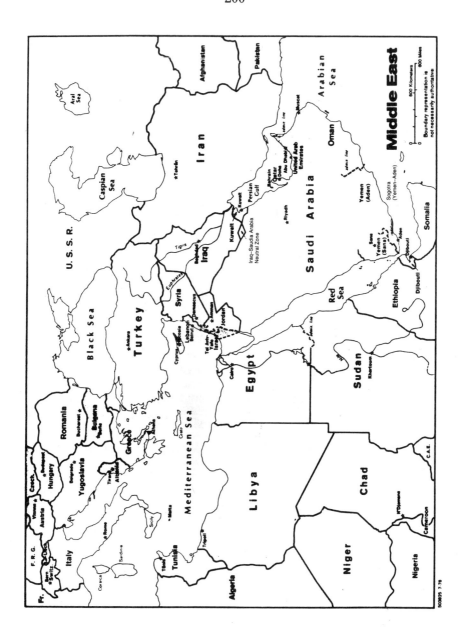

PART IV—THE SOVIET UNION IN AFRICA: CONSOLIDATION OF GAINS [1]

What kind of objectivity can be at issue . . . if the United States looks upon Africa not only as a "confrontation zone" with the Soviet Union, but also primarily as a raw materials and energy sources zone and a market for the United States! And if the USSR has dealings with the Africans, we are accused of "expansionism." In essence, the socialist countries are almost being denied the right to develop friendship and cooperation with Africa. At the same time, while it provides assistance to peoples which are struggling for their freedom, the Soviet Union does not seek any advantages for itself, is not hunting for concessions, is not trying to achieve political domination, and is not importuning military bases.
—Anatoliy Gromyko, Dec. 1982.

Ethiopian revolutionaries and working people, proceeding along the path of Lenin and the Great October Revolution, side by side with the Communist Party of the Soviet Union, consider themselves to be a component of the world system of socialism. They have taken into account the fact that the more than 50 years of the USSR's experience in the cause of building socialism is for them a model and a reliable guarantee of their bright future.
—Mengistu Haile Mariam, Ethiopia's leader, speaking at the 26th CPSU Party Congress, 1981.

I. THE SOVIET POSITION IN AFRICA IN THE 1970'S

In the 1970's, a new wave of decolonization precipitated by the withdrawal of Portugal from its territories in Southern and Western Africa provided Moscow with a number of opportunities to advance its influence in the region. For the first time, the Soviets were able and willing through arms aid, advisors, and Cuban troops to join Africa's military conflicts. The Soviet Union dramatically displayed its new ability to project its powers overseas, its will to use them (in the Horn and in Angola), and its intentions to make the most of opportunities that should arise (in Ethiopia, the Sudan, and throughout Southern Africa where "liberation" struggles were underway). Soviet leaders were clearly playing a larger role in Africa and wanted their interests protected. As Soviet-American relations began to worsen, Soviet activities in Africa were increasingly viewed in Washington through the prism of superpower competition. Soviet military involvement in Africa was one of the chief U.S. grievances against the USSR that led to the decline of detente.

A. INTERVENTION IN SOUTHERN AFRICA AND THE HORN

Moscow's efforts were concentrated on southern Africa and the Horn. The Soviet Union and Cuba cooperated in mounting massive military operations in 1975–77 to support the Popular Movement

---

[1] Prepared by Michael J. Dixon, Research Analyst in Soviet and East European Affairs, Congressional Research Service. First published on December 10, 1984 as CRS Report No. 85–675.

for the Liberation of Angola (MPLA), one of three factions claiming power in the former Portuguese colony. The combination of Soviet arms and Cuban troops (36,000 at their peak in 1976) was decisive in the victory of the MPLA. By October 1976, the USSR and the People's Republic of Angola had signed a treaty of friendship and cooperation. Moscow and Havana again combined their resources in Ethiopia to defend the revolutionary government of Lt. Col. Mengistu Haile Mariam, whose survival was threatened by internal rebellions and Somali attempts to seize control of the Ogaden region. By 1978, Moscow had delivered some $1 billion in weapons and supplies while Cuba had an estimated 20,000 troops stationed in Ethiopia. In November 1978, the USSR and Ethiopia signed a treaty of friendship and cooperation.

By the end of the decade, the Soviet Union had solidly entrenched itself in the Horn and in southern Africa, two important regions of Africa. Ethiopia, located on the Red Sea across from Saudi Arabia, guards the approaches to the Suez Canal and the Indian Ocean. With its vast mineral resources, Angola is considered to have significant economic potential. Elsewhere in southern Africa, the Soviets developed close security ties with Mozambique, formalized in a treaty of friendship and cooperation in April 1977. The Soviet Union also positioned itself to benefit possibly in Namibia (also rich in minerals) where a pro-Soviet, anti-Western government could emerge after eventual independence from South Africa.

B. Intensified African Radicalism

In the 1970's, the Soviet Union benefited from increased radicalization in Africa. The trend was set by the Peoples Republic of the Congo (Brazzaville) which declared its adherence to Marxism-Leninism in 1969. In the following decade, other countries did the same: Somalia, Angola, Guinea-Bissau, Sao Tome and Principe, Madagascar, and Benin. This development appeared to some observers to spell the end of "African" socialism in favor of "Marxist" socialism.

David Albright, a specialist on Soviet relations with Africa, suggests that during the decade Africa became much less wary of Soviet ambitions and impressed by its "anti-imperialist" rhetoric. This transformation of attitudes toward the USSR led Africans to re-examine their policy of non-alignment. In the 1960s, non-alignment dictated maintaining limited ties to the USSR; by the 1970s, economic aid from the Soviet Union and trade with it were viewed as advantageous. Furthermore, African leaders and opposition groups came to regard the Soviets as useful allies to promote their interests. The MPLA in Angola called on Moscow for aid against other factions; in Rhodesia, Joshua Nkomo received substantial Soviet assistance. This led some other African states to seek out relations with Moscow and welcome Soviet involvement in African affairs.[2]

---

[2] Albright, David. The USSR and Sub-Saharan Africa in the 1980s. The Washington Papers, No. 101. Georgetown Center for Strategic and International Studies, 1983, p. 22–24.

C. A Balance Sheet

Contrasted with this record of successes were a number of political setbacks suffered by Moscow in Africa. Soviet influence was lost completely in Somalia by 1977 after the USSR switched its allegiance to Ethiopia. In Egypt, the USSR was seen as an ineffectual partner, unable or unwilling to promote Egyptian interests in the Arab-Israeli conflict. Also disturbing to the Soviets was the lack of success that Soviet allies in Africa faced in consolidating secure, Marxist governments. Although the USSR strengthened its presence in southern Africa and the Horn, an extended military commitment has not yet led to unchallenged political or military victories on the pro-Soviet regimes in Angola, Mozambique, and Ethiopia.[3] Although the ruling parties of Angola and Mozambique proclaim themselves to be Marxist-Leninist, the Soviet Communist Party rejects these claims and classifies them as "revolutionary vanguard" parties.

The USSR's achievements outside the Horn and southern Africa are also noteworthy and should not be neglected. Moscow has been successful in developing relations with less radical governments in the region. In the mid-1970s, relations with Nigeria, Africa's most populous state and one of its leading voices, were carefully cultivated. In 1976, the USSR and Nigeria signed an agreement for the joint construction of a huge iron and steel plant. In 1978, Morocco signed an agreement with the Soviet Union for $2 billion in Soviet credits for the development of the Moroccan phosphate industry.

The 1970s also saw the Soviet Union markedly increase its military aid to the nations of sub-Saharan Africa. Arms transfers from 1965 to 1974 totaled $241 million. From 1975 to 1979, these sales increased more than tenfold, to $3.38 billion. Although approximately $2 billion went to new clients in Ethiopia and Angola, Moscow also forged new military bonds with other African states. The Soviet Union replaced China as Tanzania's principal arms supplier; Soviet deliveries soared to $300 million in the last half of the decade from almost nil during the previous ten years. Uganda, Zambia, Guinea, Mali, Mozambique, and Nigeria also became large purchasers of Soviet arms in this period.[4]

D. The China Factor

One consequence of Soviet policies was the loss of considerable Chinese influence in Africa. Indeed, an objective of the Soviet Union was to undermine Chinese charges of Soviet "hegemonism" or global expansionism. Moscow demonstrated itself to be the "natural ally" of liberation forces; its faction in the Angolan civil war was able to defeat those supported by the West and China. The West was branded the imperialist power in the region for its ties to South Africa, while China was caught in Angola siding with forces receiving aid from South Africa. Chinese military support for liberation in southern Africa was revealed as largely inconsequen-

---

[3] Katz, Mark. The Third World in Soviet Military Thought. Baltimore, MD. The John Hopkins University Press, 1982.

[4] Figures derived from: U.S. Arms Control and Disarmament Agency. World Military Expenditures and Arms Transfers, 1965–1974, p. 75. And, U.S. ACDA. World Military Expenditures and Arms Transfers, 1970–1979, p. 127.

tial.[5] In the last half of the decade, Chinese arms sales to sub-Saharan Africa were just $140 million.

By the end of the 1970s, the Sino-Soviet competition in Africa was nearly over. Beijing could not match Soviet arms shipments to the region, and China's economic aid programs declined sharply after a $400 million credit was extended for the construction of the Tanzania/Zambia Railroad. Chinese economic aid of $2.445 billion to sub-Saharan Africa in the two decades from 1959 to 1979 was double that of the Soviet Union. But by 1979, Chinese aid to sub-Saharan Africa was a mere $40 million a year, while the USSR and Eastern Europe extended $185 million.[6] USSR, too, had reduced its economic aid and began to rely increasingly on military and security ties to African states for influence. In turn, Africa turned to the West for large-scale aid and occasionally to China for lower cost projects in light industry and agriculture. The Chinese were probably satisfied with developments in Zimbabwe, however, where Robert Mugabe's liberation movement took control of the government after independence in 1980 at the expense of the Soviet-supported faction led by Joshua Nkomo.

E. CUBA AND EAST GERMANY: VALUABLE SOVIET ALLIES IN AFRICA

The decade of the 1970s was notable for the "quasi-alliance" or "quasi-coalition" formed between the Soviet Union, Cuba, and the (East) German Democratic Republic (GDR), chiefly in southern Africa and Ethiopia.[7] Moscow served as the principal supplier of arms; Cuba supplied the majority of military and civilian personnel; while the GDR specialized in providing security and intelligence services to radical governments. In 1979, Cuban military personnel in Africa numbered 33,000 and civilian economic advisers over 8,000.[8] In the early 1970s, GDR efforts were focused on the West African nations of Mali, Guinea, and Ghana, but shifted to the more promising targets of the national liberation movements in the Portuguese colonies of Guinea-Bissau, Cape Verde, Angola, and Mozambique. The GDR continues to nurture close ties with those states as well as Ethiopia, Benin, and Congo-Brazzaville, with whom it has had a long-standing relationship.[9]

On balance, despite some setbacks, the Soviet Union was able to expand its influence in Africa in gaining treaty-bound allies in Angola, Mozambique, and Ethiopia while making some advances elsewhere as in the Congo. These gains helped strengthen Soviet claims to be a global power with rights and responsibilities beyond

---

[5] Singleton, Seth. "Natural Ally: Soviet Policy in Southern Africa," In, Clough, Michael, ed. Changing Realities in Southern Africa. University of California, Berkeley. Institute of International Studies, 1982, p. 194–195. Singleton writes: "The Soviet Union could easily provide the one thing that the liberation movements need—guns. By the mid-1970's, with the burdens of Cuba and Indochina and an increasingly shaky economy at home . . . Soviet abilities to prop up friendly governments were almost nil. Expansion of Soviet presence and influence therefore depended on a local need for weapons or military protection."

[6] Central Intelligence Agency. Communist Aid Activities in Non-Communist Less Developed Countries, 1979 and 1954–79. October 1980, p. 18 and 39.

[7] Albright, David E. "The Communist States and Southern Africa." In, Gwendolen M. Carter and Patrick O'Meara, eds. International Politics in Southern Africa. Bloomington, IN. Indiana University Press, 1982, p. 4–15.

[8] Commuinists Aid Activities in Non-Communist Less Developed Countries, 1979 and 1954–79, p. 15 and 21.

[9] Croan, Melvin. A New Afrika Corps? Washington Quarterly. Winter 1980, p. 27–28.

regions adjacent to Soviet territory. Soviet military engagements in the Horn and Angola were regarded as legitimate and met with approval among African nations, while its Cuban and East German proxy forces became a new element in African politics. The USSR continued providing economic aid to Africa, but at levels below the ambitious programs of the early 1960's when Premier Nikita Khrushchev pioneered Soviet advances in Africa. The Soviet Union was successful in drawing considerable prestige away from China by the end of the decade, particularly after Soviet-supported forces came to power in Angola.

II. SOVIET STRATEGIC INTERESTS IN AMERICA

Developments outside Africa attracted most of the Soviet Union's attention from 1980 to 1983. In Poland, simmering domestic discontent, economic stringencies and Western scrutiny of conditions intensified Moscow's concern about the weakness of the Polish Communist Party and the danger of domestic opposition spreading to other East European nations. One hundred thousand Soviet troops in Afghanistan were unable to subdue anti-government rebels and restore order under the Soviet-installed government of Babrak Karmal. In the Middle East, the Arab-Israeli conflict continued to threaten a superpower confrontation. The Iran-Iraq war presented new challenges and opportunities for Soviet influence in the Persian Gulf region.

Both the Soviet Union and China appeared ready to take new steps to improve relations after twenty years of hostility. Talks aimed at normalization began in 1982, but little real progress was made toward a rapprochement. Moscow also displayed concern over increasing U.S.-Japanese security ties. In this period, the Soviet Union devoted greater resources and attention to its military strength in East Asia as well as Southeast Asia. The lack of progress on arms control, deepening U.S.-Soviet confrontation, and the proposed NATO deployment of intermediate-range missiles in response to Soviet deployments of its SS-20s posed new threats in Europe.

Although sub-Saharan Africa clearly ranks well below Europe, the Middle East, and Asia in geopolitical importance to the USSR, Moscow is determined to demonstrate its power and expand its influence on the continent. The expansion of the Soviet presence in Africa is intended to demonstrate the USSR's widening role as a global power with superpower responsibilities. Two regions of Africa—the Horn and Southern Africa—are of political and strategic importance to Soviet ambitions of projecting military force and political influence abroad.

A. THE SOVIET MILITARY PRESENCE IN AFRICA

The Soviet naval detachments along the West African coast and in the Indian Ocean should be viewed as part of the Soviet drive to overcome the geographical disadvantages of severely limited access to the open seas. The Soviet naval presence in waters around the African continent has increased dramatically since the 1960's. What was once an area of uncontested Western control has since seen the Soviet Union establish a peacetime presence in West Africa at Conakry, Guinea and Luanda, Angola and on the east coast in Mozambique and Ethiopia. Crises in the Middle East—for example, the Ethiopian-Somali war in 1976-77, the Iranian revolution (which precipitated increased U.S. naval deployments), and the

Iran-Iraq war—led the Soviets to augment their Indian Ocean naval forces.

The Soviet navy has several military missions with indirect security objectives for the USSR. It helps secure the southern sea route through the Indian Ocean connecting the European and Asian segments of the USSR. In the event of a major war in East Asia, it is widely thought that the Soviets would not be able to sustain their forces without this sea lane of communication. The Soviet navy's mission is to neutralize the presence of U.S. and Western naval forces in the Indian Ocean and it presents a latent menace to Western shipping through the critical "choke points" at the Straits of Hormuz and the Red Sea and the commercial sea lanes around the South African Cape. The navy also "shows the flag" in Africa and promotes Moscow's ambitions of becoming a principal actor in African affairs and regional conflicts.

Sub-Saharan Africa has geographic importance to the West and the USSR, although this should not be overstated. The Soviet Union could menace vital sea lanes of communications between North America and Western Europe to and from the Persian Gulf and its oil resources. Its naval presence in Ethiopia, South Yemen, and the Indian Ocean has grown steadily, to the point where it could muster sufficient military capabilities to block access to the Suez Canal from the Bab el Mandab and to the Persian Gulf at the Straits of Hormuz, at least for a short period. With its naval assets in the South Atlantic, the USSR could pose threats to the Cape route, an important commercial link and a sea route tying the West to allies in the Persian Gulf and the Far East.

The Soviet Indian Ocean Squadron, averaging 20 to 25 ships at any one time, uses facilities on Ethiopia's Dahlak Archipelago in the Red Sea for peacetime logistics and maintenance assistance. The Soviet navy has averaged about 70 visits per year at Dahlak from 1979 to 1983. The major asset there is an 8,500-ton floating drydock. Since 1983, ships from the Soviet Mediterranean fleet have also called at Dahlak.[1] This facility replaces the loss in 1977 of Soviet rights to the Somali port of Berbera. The Soviets also have access to South Yemeni ports on the Arabian Peninsula and the islands of Socotra and Perim.

The Soviet Union's West Africa Patrol, which usually numbers between five and eight ships and is much smaller than its Indian Ocean contingent, is based in Luanda. The patrol's apparent mission is to maintain a Soviet presence and provide a contingency show of force.[2] Other Soviet naval units have also called on the port of Maputo, Mozambique and Port Louis, Mauritius.[3]

Easy access to African ports and airfields facilitates the deployment of the Soviet naval and air forces. The Soviet Union now has rights to port visits, maintenance, and use of shipyards for overhaul, as well as the construction of storage depots in various countries. These facilities and privileges prolong the time Soviet vessels can remain on station and reduce costly transit time. Longer peri-

---

[1] Soviet Military Power. U.S. Government Printing Office. 3rd ed. April 1984, p. 125–126.
[2] There have been unconfirmed reports that Moscow has air and naval facilities on the West African island nation of Sao Tome and Principe. Christian Science Monitor. March 21, 1984, p. 2, Washington Times, September 13, 1984, p. 5A. Both reports relied on Portuguese sources.
[3] In May 1984, a detachment of three ships visited Mauritius.

ods of deployment permit the Soviet Union to meet force requirements with a smaller number of ships, freeing others for deployment elsewhere.[4]

The Soviet Union also uses African military facilities for air surveillance. Soviet forces staged surveillance flights from airfields in Guinea (until 1977), Somalia (until 1977), Angola (since 1977), and Ethiopia (since 1979). The Soviets have used Il–38 May anti-submarine warfare planes to support their naval forces and keep an eye on U.S. naval forces. Long-range Tu-95 Bear maritime reconnaissance aircraft have been stationed in Angola.[5] These aircraft provide coverage of U.S. naval forces in the Atlantic Ocean. During the Falkland Islands conflict in 1982, Soviet Tu-95s based in Luanda carried out surveillance of British naval maneuvers and reportedly relayed intelligence to Argentine forces.

Some military analysts speculate that the African continent could be used as a staging area for Soviet combat aircraft deployed against U.S. or NATO forces. In the event of hostilities in the Mediterranean, Soviet access to airfields in North Africa—Libya or Algeria—could initially complicate the defense problems of NATO forces in the region. Similarly, aircraft based in the Soviet Union could rely on North African or Ethiopian bases (unless those nations sought a neutral status) to rearm and refuel bombers for missions in the Mediterranean as well as the Indian Ocean.[6] Soviet aircraft stationed in Egypt until the early 1970's may have been intended for such use, although as far as is known, they were in fact used only for Egyptian purposes.

Soviet facilities in southern Africa could play a role in Soviet strategy in the event of a conflict in the Middle East. If hostilities in Southwest Asia were to lead to a U.S. decision to deploy forces in the region, the USSR could conceivably launch Backfire bombers from home territory to intercept U.S. warships rounding the Cape. Airfields in Mozambique and Angola, or elsewhere in the region, would, if the host nation permitted, enable Soviet aircraft to refuel and return home.[7]

The Soviet Union makes valuable use of rights to African airfields for the purpose of projecting power in intra-African disputes. During the 1975–77 Angolan civil war, the Soviets used Ethiopian bases to ferry weapons to its ally. Soviet and Cuban aircraft carrying Cuban troops to Angola used airbases in Guinea and Pointe Noire, Congo to refuel and resupply before reaching their final destination. There is evidence that Libya could assume a similar staging role for Soviet forces in conflicts in sub-Saharan Africa. Moscow can be expected to attempt to increase its network of reliable basing facilities if the costs are not high.

B. THE INDIAN OCEAN AND THE SOUTHERN SEA ROUTE

The Indian Ocean has become an arena of naval rivalry between the United States and the Soviet Union. In 1977, Somalia forced the evacuation of the Soviet navy from Berbera, but by 1978 the

---

[4] Remnek, Richard. Soviet Military Interests in Africa. Orbis, spring 1984, p. 125–126.
[5] Ibid, p. 126–127.
[6] Ibid., p. 127–130.
[7] Ibid.

Soviets had acquired rights to the former British base of Aden in Marxist South Yemen. With growing ties to Ethiopia, then at war with Somalia, the Soviets soon earned rights to call in Ethiopian ports. The fall of the Shah and the revolution in Iran followed by the Soviet invasion of Afghanistan in 1979 led to a Soviet (and American) buildup of naval forces in the Indian Ocean and Arabian Sea. The U.S. decision to develop an air and naval base on the remote island of Diego Garcia further impressed the Soviets with the importance of maintaining a naval presence in the region. New alliances with recently independent Mozambique and Angola aided the Soviet Indian Ocean naval effort. The Soviet Union saw that its geostrategic position required a greater naval presence. As Soviet power grew so did the West's perceptions that the USSR intended to challenge Western military supremacy and pose a potential threat to the commercial shipping routes through the Red Sea and around the Southern African Cape.

A primary objective of Soviet policy is to contain China and neutralize Japan and isolate these two countries with naval forces and states closely associated with the USSR. Soviet naval capabilities in the Indian Ocean region, sustained by a Soviet naval presence in the South Atlantic and Southern Africa, are a logical element of this strategy, particularly because of Japan's heavy dependence on Persian Gulf oil.

The Soviet interest in the Horn of Africa is in part due to its location at the southern approaches to the Suez Canal. Ethiopia and South Yemen, both closely aligned with the USSR, lie astride the 17-mile wide Bab el Mandab Strait, a choke point between the Indian Ocean and the Mediterranean Sea. With an ally in Marxist Ethiopia, the USSR has additional motives to station naval forces nearby.

Many scholars explain the Soviet Indian Ocean Squadron as a defensive concern to guard shipping routes from Soviet Europe to Soviet Asia and as protection for Soviet fishing and merchant fleets. At any one time, there are between 100 and 200 Soviet merchant and fishing vessels in the Indian Ocean. Between one-third and one-half of the Soviet merchant fleet is dedicated to the Southern Sea Route.[8] This route through the Black Sea, the Suez Canal, and the Indian Ocean to the Pacific Ocean is the most important link between western and eastern USSR, other than the Trans-Siberian Railroad. It is vulnerable to western naval interdiction.

The vulnerability of the railroad to Chinese disruption in the event of war increases the importance of the Indian Ocean as a sea lane of communication between the two halves of the USSR. Soviet military authorities view a U.S. naval and military capability in the Indian Ocean as a threat to its interests. In 1980, Izvestiya, the government newspaper wrote:

> The escalation of U.S. military might in this region cannot fail to be regarded . . . as a threat to the security of the Soviet Union . . . which uses the Indian Ocean as the only non-freezing sea route uniting two of its parts—the European and Far Eastern regions.[9]

---

[8] Westwood, Lt. Cmdr. James T. The Soviet Union and the Southern Sea Route. Naval War College Review. January/February 1982, p. 63.
[9] Quoted in ibid., p. 65.

The Suez Canal is thus critical to Soviet naval forces deployed in the Indian Ocean in the event of war. The distance from the Black Sea to the Gulf of Aden is only 4,000 miles when the canal is open, but is 12,000 miles if the Canal is shut and the South Atlantic route is used.

Since the late 1970s, the Soviet presence in the Indian Ocean has jumped sharply. In May 1979, the carrier *Minsk,* the amphibious warfare ship *Ivan Rogov,* and a Kara-class cruiser visited South Yemen. These were followed by visits by Echo-class submarines and their tenders. In December 1982, the *Minsk* called at Bombay, India after exercises in the Indian Ocean. Other ships have anchored off the South Yemeni island of Socotra, not far from the African coast. The Soviet navy deploys destroyers and frigates of the Kashin, Krivak, Kotlin, and Riga classes to patrol the Arabian Sea and the strategic Straits of Hormuz and Bab el Mandab and shadow U.S. combat vessels. In 1980, the Soviets strengthened their submarine operations in the Indian Ocean.[10] During the period that Iran held U.S. diplomats hostage, the USSR maintained 30 ships in the Indian Ocean and reduced their numbers only after the United States drew down its ships. The Soviet navy has demonstrated its capability to deploy forces in large numbers in peacetime and with new friends in Africa can be expected to project them in a crisis.

C. THE CAPE ROUTE AND STRATEGIC MINERALS

The Soviet Union, according to some analysts, intends to improve its capabilities to menace Western shipping routes around the Cape of Good Hope, the world's most heavily trafficked sea lanes.

The Cape route is used by supertankers plying between the Persian Gulf and ports in Europe and the United States. It is also an important alternate route tying Western Europe to Japan and is a vital artery for the deployment of U.S. forces to the Indian Ocean and the Persian Gulf. In 1980, 6,450 ships, 6,325 of them from Western countries, used the Cape route.[11] West European dependence on Persian Gulf oil (which must travel the Suez or the Cape route) stood at 36 percent of total oil consumption in 1982 (down from 63 percent in 1977). Japan's dependency was 68 percent, down from 78 percent in 1977.[12]

The U.S. Navy believes that the Soviets have the ability to operate against Western sea lanes and may threaten a cutoff for political leverage during a crisis.[13] The Suez Canal, closed from 1967 to 1974, is still regarded as vulnerable to a blockade, which stresses the importance of the Cape route.

Although the Soviet Union recognizes the importance of the Cape sea routes, a blockade of the route may be impractical for a

---

[10] Kelly, Capt. James F., Jr. Naval Deployments in the Indian Ocean. U.S. Naval Institute Proceedings. May 1983, p. 175–177.

[11] South Africa 1983: Official Yearbook. Johannesburg, Rensberg Publications, p. 314.

[12] Blechman, Barry M. and Luttwak, Edward N. International Security Yearbook, 1983/84. New York, St. Martin's Press, 1984, p. 224.

[13] Statement of Rear Adm. John Butts, Director of Naval Intelligence. In, U.S. Congress. House of Representatives. Committee on Armed Services. Seapower and Strategic and Critical Minerals Subcommittee. Defense Department Authorization and Oversight. Hearings on H.R. 2287. 98th Cong., 1st Session. February 24, 1983. Washington, U.S. Govt. Print. Off., 1983, p. 46.

number of reasons. If the Soviet Union were determined to halt the flow of oil to the West from the Persian Gulf, it might be more effective to do so at the Straits of Hormuz, the mouth of the Persian Gulf. The interdiction of shipping either from or around southern Africa would probably be in the context of much broader hostilities. Interrupting the flow of oil or minerals would be interpreted as an act of war and would presumably occur only after conflict has begun. In such circumstances, the Soviet Union's African friends might seek neutral status and close their facilities to belligerents. The Soviet navy may not have the capability of sustaining a blockade for more than a few months. At the time of a blockade, the Soviet merchant and fishing fleets would also become vulnerable to retaliatory actions by the West.[14]

Another argument for Southern Africa's strategic importance is the presence in the region of large reserves of minerals essential for industrial and defense production. The United States imports over 90 percent of its cobalt, manganese, chromium and platinum. European nations are entirely dependent on imports for these minerals. In addition, unlike the United States, they rely heavily on third countries for tin, tungsten, titanium, and copper. Southern Africa, particularly the Republic of South Africa, is an important producer of many of these minerals. South Africa and Zimbabwe have over 97 percent of the world's chromium reserves and South Africa alone holds 87 percent of available platinum, while Zaire and Zambia are important suppliers of copper and cobalt.[15]

Four minerals are particularly critical for defense purposes and are in short supply: chromium, manganese, vanadium, and platinum group metals. With the exception of Zimbabwe and chrome, only the Soviet Union produces or has reserves of these minerals in quantities rivaling or surpassing South Africa. U.S. allies in Western Europe and Japan are even more dependent on these materials.[16]

A 1982 study by the U.S. Senate Foreign Relations Committee concluded that the possibility of a Soviet interdiction of mineral shipments from Southern Africa was "unlikely except under such wartime conditions where shipping from the Persian Gulf would also come under attack."[17] It added that the loss of petroleum supplies would be far more critical to Western economies and warfighting capabilities that the long-term loss of mineral supplies. The report rated Soviet interference as the least likely cause of a disruption in mineral supplies from South Africa. The most likely was internal instability leading to labor unrest or a breakdown in society.

[14] Legvold, Robert. "The Soviet Union's Strategic Stake in Africa." In, Jennifer Seymour Whitaker. Africa and the United States: Vital Interests. New York, New York University Press. 1978 p. 169.
[15] See: U.S. Department of the Interior. Bureau of Mines. Mineral Commodity Summaries. 1983. And, Orme, John. Ore Wars: The Problem of U.S. Dependence on Foreign Minerals. Fletcher Forum. Summer 1982 p. 408–409.
[16] South Africa: Time Running Out. Study Commission on U.S. Policy Toward Southern Africa. Foreign Policy Study Foundation, Inc., Berkeley, CA. 1981 p. 311–314.
[17] U.S. Senate. Committee on Foreign Relations. Committee Print. U.S. Minerals Dependence on South Africa. October 1982, p. iii.

III. SOVIET ECONOMIC RELATIONS WITH AFRICA: PROGRESS WITH PROBLEMS

A. Forms of Soviet Aid

Although Soviet aid to—and trade with—Africa have increased tremendously since the 1950s, when the continent opened to Soviet influence, limited resources and poor economic performance are Moscow's principal handicap in dealing with Africa. As a consequence, Soviet aid programs are rarely directed at the neediest countries, but toward nations that can best contribute to the Soviet economy and Soviet political/military goals. Aid is rarely offered in the form of grants, but in concessional credits linked to a recipient's purchase of Soviet equipment and services. These arrangements generated most of the trade between the USSR and Africa. Aid is apparently designed strictly with Soviet political and economic consideration in mind, to complement the Soviet economy, bolster nations friendly to the USSR, and promote forces ideologically aligned with Moscow.

Soviet economic aid takes various forms. Soviet and East European personnel are dispatched to Africa; Africans are sent to the Soviet Union for civilian and military training at Soviet expense; and joint economic enterprises are established, often in fishing, mineral extraction, or transportation. These instruments of influence promote a Soviet presence in Africa, penetrate African markets, provide military and strategic assets, and, in the case of arms sales, earn valuable hard currency for the Soviet economy.

B. The Soviet Experience with Economic Assistance

Soviet attitudes towards economic relations with Africa have undergone several changes since the 1950's. During the period of Khrushchev's rule, after a time when the USSR had virtually no ties to Africa, economic assistance was designed to undermine the Western presence. Underdevelopment was seen as a positive factor aiding Soviet penetration and removing Western influence. Political, not economic, gains were significant goals in Soviet strategy as Khrushchev pumped expensive aid programs into newly independent, radical, non-capitalist states. In the decade after Khrushchev, roughly from 1965, Moscow evaluated aid programs on the economic advantage they would provide the Soviet Union. In so doing, the Soviets came to support raw materials exports from Africa to the USSR in place of the more popular import-substitution industrialization. The changes in Soviet economic relations called for a new international division of labor whereby the Soviet bloc supplied Africa with machinery, technology, and expertise in exchange for raw materials and other goods unavailable in the USSR. Although trade expanded considerably by 1975, the Soviet Union was unable to dislodge the West or penetrate the more stable, pro-Western African countries' markets.[1]

Although the last decade coincided with a second wave of decolonization, which brought independence to the Portuguese colonies and a black government to power in Zimbabwe, the Soviets have resisted demands from radical African states for more aid and admission to the Soviet block trading groups, the Council for Mutual Economic Assistance (CMEA). Moscow evidently now recognizes that Africa remains fundamentally tied to the Western market economies, and it often encourages African states to seek economic assistance from the West. While the radical pro-Soviet states are strategic Soviet assets, the USSR also stresses expanding economic relations with the wealthier and more stable African states, such as Morocco, Sierra Leone, and Senegal, whose trade complements the Soviet economy.[2]

C. Current Soviet Economic Assistance to Africa

Soviet economic aid to sub-Saharan Africa is small, and providing such aid clearly ranks low on the Soviet list of priorities. In 1981, according to U.S. Government figures, the Soviet Union signed economic assistance agreements valued at $125 million with the states of sub-Saharan Africa—down from $310 million in 1980. Eastern Europe committed $115 million in aid, less than half the 1980 figure of $280 million.[3]

Aid to Africa occupies a small portion of the Soviet worldwide aid effort, and it is dwarfed by Western aid programs. Given its commitments in other regions of the world such as in the Middle East, to its Communist client states in the Third World such as Cuba and Vietnam, and to its defense priorities at home, Moscow is in no position to provide large amounts of aid to Africa. Of the $22.4 billion in Soviet economic aid extended to the non-Communist Third World from 1954 to 1981, sub-Saharan Africa received less than $2.9 billion, or about 13 percent of the total. By comparison, North Africa and the Middle East, strategically more important to Soviet security, got four times as much Soviet aid; India alone received more aid than all of sub-Saharan Africa in the same period.[4]

[1] See: Valkenier, Elizabeth. Great Power Competition in Africa. Journal of International Affairs. Fall/Winter 1980/81, p. 259–268.

[2] Ibid., p. 266–268.

[3] U.S. Department of State. Soviet and East European Aid to the Third World, 1981. February 1983. Publication 9345, p. 16–17. The United States extended $743 million, $826 million and $874 million in loans and grants to sub-Saharan Africa in 1980, 1981 and 1982 respectively. Central Intelligence Agency. Directorate of Intelligence. Handbook of Economic Statistics, 1983. CPAS 83–10006 p. 106.

It is important to distinguish between aid committed and aid actually drawn or delivered. Although figures are not broken down for Africa, according to U.S. Government estimates, between 1954 and 1981, the Soviet Union delivered just 44 percent of the aid extended to all Third World countries. In contrast, the Development Assistance Committee of the OECD estimates that its members actually supplied over 80 percent of the aid they extended between 1977 and 1980. Organization for Economic Co-operation and Development (OECD). Development Co-operation. (Prepared by the Development Assistance Committee.) November 1982, p. 161–2 and 183.

[4] The Soviet Union provided just 4.9 percent of total world development aid in 1982, as defined by the Development Assistance Committee of the OECD, compared with 32.5 percent by the EEC and 21.9 percent by the United States. In absolute terms Soviet bloc aid to the Third World is minuscule. Total Western and Japanese aid in 1982 came to over $28 billion; CMEA aid was just $2.5 billion, $1.9 billion of which was Soviet. Development Co-operation, 1983 Review.

Continued

Nonetheless, economic assistance is an effective, if limited, instrument of Soviet policy in Africa. The Soviet Union claims that it has made intergovernmental agreements on economic and technical cooperation with 29 countries in sub-Saharan Africa, completed 127 projects with 175 more under construction or being drafted, and trained some 55,000 workers and specialists.[5]

The Soviets generally focus on programs and nations that promise the greatest return for their investment. In Africa, this means commercial ventures and long-range projects that contribute to Soviet economic plans. Of the approximately $3.5 billion in aid the Soviets offered to all of Africa from 1975 to 1981, $2 billion went to Morocco for the development of phosphate mining for shipment to the USSR for the production of fertilizer. Only $770 million went to sub-Saharan Africa in that time.[6] A 1984 NATO study concluded that "the non-communist developing countries are considered an area to be penetrated by political, trade, and military means, but they are not the target of a consistent and sustained economic aid policy."[7] The report also found that Soviet aid to the Third World declined steadily from 1975 to 1982, whicle military sales rose steeply. Africa, as one of the least important regions to Soviet security, receives less attention and resources from Soviet aid programs.

Although Soviet aid to Africa is low, a number of observers have suggested that its policy of concentrating its efforts on large publicized projects in a few countries has given Moscow political and propaganda rewards. Soviet aid is not meant to compete with Western aid programs, it is argued, but is designed to succeed in a few target areas. The Soviet Union has been largely successful in maximizing the political effect of its modest efforts in Africa. Its most ambitious industrial project is the Ajaokuta steel plant in oil-rich Nigeria. Some 3,000 Soviet advisers are at Ajaokuta, with the total expected to reach 6,000.

TABLE 1.—U.S.S.R. AND EASTERN EUROPE: ECONOMIC AID EXTENDED TO AFRICA, BY COUNTRY

[In million of U.S. dollars]

	1954–81		1980		1981	
	U.S.S.R.	Eastern Europe	U.S.S.R.	Eastern Europe	U.S.S.R.	Eastern Europe
Sub-Saharan Africa (total)	2,870	1,990	310	280	125	115
Angola	30	100				
Benin	10	NA			5	
Burundi		negl				

(Prepared by the Development Assistance Committee of the OECD.) November 1983 p. 185 and 186.

Using calculations different from those used by the DAC, NATO estimated that of $58 billion in Soviet aid to all developing countries, about $5.8 billion went to Communist developing countries, and more than $3 billion of this went to Cuba. See, Atlantic News. May 11, 1983 p. 4.

[5] TASS, November 5, 1982. In, F.B.I.S., Soviet Union Daily Report, November 9, 1982. p. Jl. See also, Anatoliy Gromyko. Africa Today. Kommunist. September 1982. Reprinted in, Joint Publications Research Service. No. 82435. October 12, 1982, p. 106–108.

[6] National Foreign Assessment Center. Communist Aid Activities in Non-Communist Less Developed Countries, 1978 and 1954–79. ER 80–10318U. October 1980, p. 7. And, Soviet and East European Aid, 1981 p. 17.

[7] Quoted in, Soviet Military Aid to Third World Soars as Other Aid Ebbs. Christian Science Monitor. April 5, 1984 p. 10.

TABLE 1.—U.S.S.R. AND EASTERN EUROPE: ECONOMIC AID EXTENDED TO AFRICA, BY COUNTRY—
Continued

[In million of U.S. dollars]

	1954–81		1980		1981	
	U.S.S.R.	Eastern Europe	U.S.S.R.	Eastern Europe	U.S.S.R.	Eastern Europe
Cameroon	10					
Cape Verde	5	5				NA
Central African Rep	5					
Chad	5					
Congo Brazzaville	45	60				
Equatorial Guinea	negl					
Ethiopia	400	355			10	5
Gabon		negl				
The Gambia	negl					
Ghana	95	145				
Guinea	215	110	5			
Guinea-Bissau	10	5				
Ivory Coast		NA				
Kenya	50					
Liberia	negl					
Madagascar	70	35	50	35		
Mali	100	25			5	
Mauritius	5					
Mozambique	175	100				
Niger	negl					
Nigeria	5	220				20
Rwanda	negl					
Sao Tome and Principe	NA	NA				
Senegal	10	35				
Sierra Leone	30					
Somalia	165	10				
Sudan	65	270		30		
Tanzania	40	75				
Uganda	25	25				
Upper Volta	5					
North Africa	3,250	980	315			
Algeria	1,045	525	315			
Mauritania	10	10				
Morocco	2,100	215				
Tunisia	95	230				

Source: U.S. Department of State. Soviet and East European Aid to the Third World, 1981. February 1983. Publication No. 9345, p. 17.

In January 1982, the Soviets signed a 10-year trade and economic cooperation agreement with Angola valued at $2 billion. In Mozambique, Soviet advisers are said to be developing coal mining and oil exploration. The Soviets have committed $42 million for road construction in Madagascar, a country increasingly allied with Moscow. Otherwise, the Kremlin has demonstrated little attempt to shift its aid and trade efforts from the economically advanced Middle East to the poorer regions of Africa. The Soviets have generally limited their aid projects to agriculture, technical training, and geological surveys, as well as the comparatively lucrative joint fishing companies, which provide export earnings and strategic political and military information.[8]

[8] Valkenier, Elizabeth. The Soviet Union and the Third World: An Economic Bind. New York, Praeger. 1983, p. 33.

Most African states seem increasingly to have realized that the USSR cannot provide sufficient economic resources to aid in economic development. Angola has turned to the West, particularly Portugal, it former colonizer, for experts to rebuild the nation's industrial infrastructure. Mozambique, facing drought conditions in 1983 and conflict with South African-backed rebels, has intensified its search for economic aid from Western sources—and for investment from South Africa—in exchange for a shift away from reliance on the Soviet bloc.[9] The Soviet bloc has reportedly not gained much influence in Mozambique's economic affairs because President Samora Machel's pragmatic policies have encouraged Western aid, trade, and investment. Machel is said to be dissatisfied with Soviet failures to fulfill aid promises and its rejection of Mozambique's bid for membership in the Council for Mutual Economic Assistance (CMEA). Furthermore, the Soviet economic experience may be irrelevant to Mozambique, as well as to much of the rest of Africa which must continue to rely on peasant farmers if there is hope of rapid advances in agricultural output. Mozambique has turned away from the state agriculture collectives pushed by Soviet advisers to encourage private farming.

D. Soviet Technicians in Africa and Scholarships Extended

The number of Soviet personnel in Africa has risen sharply since the early 1970s. In 1970, there were an estimated 7,200 Soviet and East European economic technicians in sub-Saharan Africa, rising to nearly 16,200 in 1975, and 14,730 in 1981, the last year for which reliable figures are available.[10] Cuban economic technicians numbered over 9,000 in 1981.

The Soviet Union has also focussed considerable efforts on the extension of scholarships to students and military personnel. The USSR was host to over 30,000 academic students from 39 African countries in 1981, up from 15,000 in 1975. The largest numbers were from Ethiopia (5,355), Nigeria (3,250), Mozambique (2,180), Congo-Brazzaville (1,845), the Sudan (1,560), Ghana (1,135), and many others came from pro-Western states such as Kenya, Zaire, Ivory Coast, Senegal, and Cameroon.[11] The granting of scholarships is a means of influencing Africa's future leaders. Although many students are said to return from the USSR disillusioned and embittered by their experiences, a significant number probably become supporters of the Soviet Union.

E. Fishing Rights and Maritime Transport: Expanding Soviet Presence in Africa

The fishing and merchant fleets of the USSR occupy a significant place in expanding Soviet influence in Africa. The fleets have been increasingly active in African waters as the Soviet Union has created a number of joint enterprises in shipping and fishing with African governments. The expansion of the merchant and fishing

---

[9] Mozambique: Preparing to Dump Moscow for Western Aid? Christian Science Mon'tor. October 7, 1983, p. 11.
[10] Soviet and East European Aid to the Third World, 1981, p. 14.
[11] Ibid., p. 22–23.

fleets has paralleled a similar growth in the capabilities of the Soviet navy in West Africa and the Indian Ocean. The merchant fleet has enlarged its share of shipping between African ports and other non-Soviet ports. The fishing fleets have successfully expanded operations in sub-Saharan Africa to the point where they have bilateral agreements with nearly every coastal West African country from Morocco to Nigeria, as well as Angola and Mozambique.

Under the fishing agreements, the Soviet fleet is usually provided rights to refuel and resupply, and in some cases it virtually controls the fishing industry of the countries. In others, the USSR has agreed to improve port facilities. Agreements with Equatorial Guinea, Guinea-Bissau, and Mozambique may also serve to create naval bases.[12] However, African governments have complained about Soviet fishing techniques that deplete coastal waters of fish. Although African nations receive between one-fourth and one-third of the Soviet catch in exchange for fishing rights, they derive little else in economic benefits as most of the fish is processed on board ships. Personnel from the fishing and merchant fleets are also suspected of engaging in intelligence activities when ashore.[13]

[12] Rothenburg, Morris. The USSR and Africa: New Dimensions of Soviet Global Power. (Washington, D.C.: Advanced International Studies Institute, 1980.) p. 81.

[13] Bissell, Richard E. "Union of Soviet Socialist Republics." Thomas H. Henrikson, ed. Communist Powers and Sub-Saharan Africa. Stanford, California. Stanford University Press, 1981, p. 14.

IV. SOVIET CULTURAL RELATIONS AND PROPAGANDA ACTIVITIES IN AFRICA

Soviet cultural diplomacy is intended to introduce other nations to Soviet culture, history, ideology, and economic achievements. Activities exposing African peoples to Soviet literature, language, arts, political doctrines, and even sports exhibits are carefully orchestrated to accomplish two objectives. The first is to overcome negative or indifferent impressions of the USSR; and the second is to marshal active support for Soviet policies. Cultural diplomacy (often described as propaganda) is also used to demonstrate that the Soviet revolutionary experience can be successful if applied in Africa and to discredit Western policies in the region.

The Soviet Union conducts a major cultural or propaganda effort attempting to present the Soviet Union as the natural ally of the African people and show that Western international corporations subject the continent to "hideous exploitation," and that the region's economic problems are the result of the colonial experience. The Soviets have presented statistics to support their claims. According to one TASS report, for example, the inflow of Western capital in 1970–1978 was $4.3 billion, while profits extracted from Africa were $16 billion.[1]

Soviet writers boast that the USSR has always sided with African nations "in their actions in the United Nations aimed against colonialism, racism, and neo-colonialism and in moves to curb aggression and strengthen peace."[2] The Soviet Union has stated its support for a proposal to declare Africa and the Indian Ocean nuclear-free zones. Moscow also claims that its economic aid has no strings attached, and "unlike capitalist countries, the USSR does not lay down terms that are incompatible with the national interests of African states."[3] Soviet assistance is said to truly benefit Africa, while capitalist aid allegedly suits only the interests of monopolies, is concentrated on developing private enterprise, and perpetuates the exploitation of Africa's wealth.

The Soviet Union frequently publicizes U.S. relations with South Africa and accuses the United States of wanting to "perpetuate the apartheid system . . ., [to] put an end to the international isolation of the racist regime . . ., and to install a puppet government in [Namibia]."[4]

The Soviets spread considerable disinformation about U.S. policies. The Soviet media has charged the United States with planning the overthrow of the new government of Jerry Rawlings of Ghana, President Kenneth Kaunda of Zambia, and President

---

[1] F.B.I.S. Soviet Union Daily Report. June 21, 1984, p. J1.
[2] Shvedov, A. and Litvin, V. The Soviet Union and African Nations. International Affairs (Moscow). June 1980, p. 59.
[3] Ibid., p. 61.
[4] Midtsev, V. 'Peacemaking' Masquerade. New Times. March 1984, #12, p. 12.

Robert Mugabe of Zimbabwe.[5] The United States is also said by Soviet commentators to have plans for a military alliance with South Africa and right-wing military governments in South America, to be known as the "South Atlantic Treaty Organization," or SATO. Soviet reports have also said that the United States and South Africa were cooperating in the production of chemical and biological weapons for use against South African blacks.[6]

A. Soviet Broadcasts to Sub-Saharan Africa

The Soviet Union directs considerable effort to broadcasting news and opinion to Africa. In 1982, this air time totaled 274 hours per week in English and African languges.[7] The USSR broadcasts in ten African languages, more than any other country; the United States, by comparison, broadcasts in three. More than a third of Soviet programming for broadcasts to Africa is tailored to African audiences, compared to a tenth for the Voice of America and the BBC. East European countries (mostly East Germany, Czechoslovakia, and Bulgaria) broadcast another 264 hours a week, Cuba 46 hours per week, and North Korea 107.

By comparison, China aired 101 hours of programming a week to sub-Saharan Africa, while the United States broadcast 136 hours, or about half the amount of Soviet programming.

B. Soviet Information Activities [8]

Soviet personnel in Africa actively promote the USSR with media placements, cultural exhibits, exchanges and trade fairs. Pro-Soviet African governments encourage propaganda activities favorable to the Soviet Union, while many others discourage Soviet efforts and welcome Western activities. The Soviet Union is able, nonetheless, to conduct information activities in virtually every African nation. The USSR has an estimated 100 personnel carrying out cultural and information work in sub-Saharan Africa. One-third are Tass, Novosti, or Moscow radio and television correspondents. The majority are embassy or cultural center officials. Moscow conducts its most intense Third World efforts in cultural and information activities in Africa, where media, educational, and cultural institutions are weak and their reliance on outside material is great.

Soviet information efforts assume various forms. Soviet officials are responsible for placing Tass and Novosti press reports and radio and television programs in the local media. Soviets are successful in obtaining frequent presentation of documentaries and feature films in a few countries sympathetic to the USSR.

[5] Copson, Raymond W. "The Soviet Union in Africa: An Assessment." In, Walter Laqueur, ed. The Pattern of Soviet Conduct in the Third World. Praeger, New York, 1983, p. 200.

[6] Ibid., p. 200. Quoted from F.B.I.S., Soviet Union Daily Reports, March 19, 1982, p. J2; March 25, 1982, p. J2. (Radio Moscow broadcast.)

[7] Information taken from: Communist International Radio Broadcasting to Sub-Saharan Africa Remains Virtually Unchanged in 1982. United States Information Agency. Office of Research. September 8, 1982.

[8] This section relies on information and analyses presented in: U.S. International Communication Agency. Office of Research. Soviet Cultural and Information Activities—1981. February 9, 1982, p. 17–23.

Soviet officials distribute periodicals in most African countries. *New Dawn,* for example, has a circulation of 3,000 to 5,000 in Nigeria and 3,000 in Botswana; in Tanzania, the Soviet weekly *Urusi Leo* (a Swahili title meaning "Russia Today") has a printing run of 25,000. Soviet books, translated into English and French, are available throughout Africa. The books typically deal with Marxist ideology, life in the USSR, and scientific topics. Soviet embassies frequently donate books to universities and secondary school libraries.

In 1981, the Soviet Union held 18 film festivals in Africa, ranging from documentaries to feature-length classics. Commercial theatres regularly show Soviet feature films in some African countries with close ties to the USSR. The USSR also conducts trade exhibits, but only four were held in all of 1981 in Africa. While the record is inconsistent in these areas, it seems that Africans' impressions of the Soviet Union are probably improved.

C. Cultural Exhibits and Exchanges [9]

The USSR also stages cultural exhibits and performances in Africa. Photo exhibits of Soviet life and technology are popular, and Soviet achievements in outer space are frequent subjects. Soviet sports teams travel in Africa for exhibition matches and exchanges, and Soviet athletic coaches help train African teams. Soviet performing arts groups visit African countries that include shows with folk singers, dancers, and acrobats.

While these visits generate a certain amount of interest, their impact seems marginal, particularly in view of the popularity of African cultural forms and the influence of Western culture, including Western music, dance, and fashions. Moscow has signed cultural and cooperation agreements with at least 16 countries in Africa. These provide for Soviet cultural activities in each country, including delegation exchanges, and performing arts, sports, and educational exchanges. The Soviet Union has large exchange programs in Africa that involve Soviet instructors teaching at universities, party schools, secondary schools, and technical institutes. Moscow is most active in conducting exchanges in Congo-Brazzaville, Guinea, Madagascar, Ethiopia, Ghana, Mali, and Tanzania. In most countries, however, these activities are on a smaller scale than comparable Western efforts.

The Soviet Union has cultural centers in at least 12 countries, often operated by local friendship societies. The cultural centers, like their more widespread American and European counterparts, sponsor lectures and exhibits and provide libraries and theatre facilities. Russian language instruction is offered, frequently to Africans intending to study in the USSR.

The USSR also sponsors bilateral friendship societies in nine countries, which in some cases count important officials as their members. The most important and active societies are in Ghana, Madagascar, Nigeria, and Mauritius. The societies usually perform activities similar to those of Soviet cultural centers and information offices.

---

[9] This section relies on information provided by: U.S. International Communication Agency. Office of Research. Soviet Cultural and Information Activities—1981. February 9, 1982.

D. SUMMARY

Soviet cultural activities may find a responsive constituency among those nations critical of the United States or former European colonialist nations and who are sympathetic to the Soviets. Patience and planning may help to develop Soviet ties with local elites over the long run. Exchanges and information activities are clearly more successful in pro-Soviet African countries and probably contribute to instilling positive attitudes toward the USSR, particularly among the younger generation of Africans. The success of the USSR's cultural diplomacy in Africa is difficult to measure because it usually complements Moscow's economic and military efforts in African countries. In any case, Africans are now far more aware of Soviet policies and objectives and indifference may have been replaced by some sympathy, through rarely outright support.

V. SOVIET MILITARY AID AND SECURITY ASSISTANCE TO SUB-SAHARAN AFRICA

The Soviet Union is now by far the largest supplier of weapons to sub-Saharan Africa. Until the early 1970s, deliveries to the continent were relatively small, with most arms coming from France and Great Britain, the former colonial powers. From 1976 to 1983, however, Soviet deliveries ($7.06 billion) to sub-Saharan Africa were more than ten times those of the United States (approximately $600 million). Total deliveries from all communist countries were approximately $4.44 billion from 1980 to 1983; from non-communist about $3.07 billion. The Soviet Union was the source of over half (51 percent) of the weapons delivered to Sub-Saharan Africa from 1980 to 1983. Former colonial powers, the United Kingdom and France, were large suppliers, together delivering about $1.2 billion in arms during the period, or about 16 percent of the total. West Germany and Italy were also important suppliers.[1]

A. MORE ARMS AND AN EXPANDING CIRCLE OF RECIPIENTS

Soviet arms deliveries are geographically concentrated in two countries in sub-Saharan Africa, Ethiopia and Angola, which together received about $3.15 billion in arms from 1978 to 1982. The USSR supplies weapons to 19 African nations and is the principal supplier to eleven of these, including Benin, Cape Verde, Congo-Brazzaville, Guinea, Madagascar, Tanzania, and Zambia.[2]

From 1976 to 1983, the Soviet Union delivered more arms in virtually every category of weaponry than did the United States and its West European allies. (See Table 2.) Presumably, Ethiopia and Angola absorbed most of these weapons, although a country breakdown of figures is not available. For example, the USSR delivered 1,590 tanks and self-propelled guns to Sub-Saharan Africa to about 203 by the West; 3,425 pieces of artillery to the West's 1,281; and 330 supersonic combat aircraft to the West's 70. In only three categories of weaponry, "major surface combatants," "minor surface combatants," and "other aircraft," did the entire West deliver more weapons. When compared with only U.S. supplies to Africa, the Soviet preponderance in weapons deliveries is overwhelming.

---

[1] Grimmett, Richard F. Trends in Conventional Arms Transfers to the Third World by Major Supplier, 1976–1983. Congressional Research Service. Report No. 84–82F. May 7, 1984, p. 25 and 27.

[2] ACDA. World Military Expenditures and Arms Transfers, 1978–1982. April 1984, p. 95.

TABLE 2.—NUMBERS OF WEAPONS DELIVERED BY MAJOR SUPPLIERS TO SUB-SAHARAN AFRICA

Weapons category	United States [1]	U.S.S.R.	Major Western European [2]
1976–1979			
Tanks and Self-Propelled Guns	23	1,250	10
Artillery	852	2,125	200
APCs and Armored Cars	11	1,750	450
Major Surface Combatants	0	4	7
Minor Surface Combatants	0	41	39
Submarines	0	0	0
Supersonic Combat Aircraft	21	160	40
Subsonic Combat Aircraft	0	120	5
Other Aircraft	5	60	125
Helicopters	4	80	140
Guided Missile Boats	0	1	1
Surface-to-Air Missiles (SAMs)	0	410	0
1980–1983			
Tanks and Self-Propelled Guns	20	340	150
Artillery	99	1,300	130
APCs and Armored Cars	89	625	975
Major Surface Combatants	0	3	10
Minor Surface Combatants	0	14	51
Submarines	0	0	0
Supersonic Combat Aircraft	4	170	5
Subsonic Combat Aircraft	0	5	50
Other Aircraft	35	40	95
Helicopters	0	100	35
Guided Missile Boats	0	9	0
Surface-to-Air Missiles (SAMs)	0	375	200
1976–1983			
Tanks and Self-Propelled Guns	43	1,590	160
Artillery	951	3,425	330
APCs and Armored Cars	100	2,375	1,425
Major Surface Combatants	0	7	17
Minor Surface Combatants	0	55	90
Submarines	0	0	0
Supersonic Combat Aircraft	25	330	45
Subsonic Combat Aircraft	0	125	55
Other Aircraft	40	100	225
Helicopters	4	180	175
Guided Missile Boats	0	10	1
Surface-to-Air Missiles (SAMs)	0	785	200

[1] U.S. data are for fiscal years given (and cover the period from July 1, 1975 through September 30, 1983). Foreign data are for calendar years given.
[2] Major Western European Includes France, United Kingdom, West Germany, and Italy totals as an agregate figure.

Source: U.S. Government. From figures compiled by Richard F. Grimmett. Trends in Conventional Arms Transfers to the Third World by Major Supplier, 1976–1983. Congressional Research Service. Report No. 84–82F. May 7, 1984. p. 32.

In the most recent period (1980–1983), the Soviet Union led in the delivery of tanks and self-propelled guns, artillery, supersonic combat aircraft, helicopters, guided missile boats, and surface-to-air missiles. The major Western European nations delivered more APCs and armored cars, major and minor surface combatants, subsonic combat aircraft, and other aircraft. The United States led in no weapons category.

In eight of the twelve delivery categories, Soviet arms shipments declined from the first period (1976–1979) to the second (1980–1983).

This probably reflects the let-up in hostilities between Ethiopia and Angola and their respective neighbors, and the consolidation of central authority after years of civil war. (Nonetheless, the value of Soviet arms transfers increased from one period to the next, from $3.19 billion to $3.87 billion.)[3] In only three categories did deliveries increase: supersonic combat aircraft, helicopters, and guided missile boats. (The USSR has made no deliveries of submarines.)

B. SOVIET POLITICAL OBJECTIVES

Arms aid has recently served as the most reliable and dramatic Soviet instrument for achieving a presence in Africa. In the case of Angola, Ethiopia and Mozambique, the military relationship grew with a strong political alliance that tied African governments to Soviet interests. Soviet military assistance to Angola, Ethiopia, and Mozambique was the instrument helping to build lasting relations with ruling governments or factions already sympathetic to the Soviets.

Military aid can be more quickly and efficiently applied than economic or technical assistance. Military equipment is often easily available from existing inventories and deliveries usually begin soon after agreement is reached. In the case of Ethiopia and Angola, massive airlifts succeeded in quickly supplying weapons which were crucial in achieving tactical military victories. Deliveries to these three African states were critical in the establishment of independent, pro-Soviet governments. Weapons deliveries to other African states have not been so clearly instrumental in securing Soviet influence.

The Soviet Union has used arms sales to develop relations with states in Africa regardless of the country's ideology or its propensity for Soviet-style socialist revolution. Moscow is unable to compete with the West for influence in Africa on the basis of economic aid or investment capital, and so turns to military assistance.[4] The dollar value of Soviet arms transfers to Africa is far greater than the economic aid it provides. The Soviets may have concluded, furthermore, that the military authorities in Africa, as in many areas of the Third World, are the most important elite in political development. As Robbin Laird, a Soviet specialist, has written, Soviet "military assistance is designed to exercise influence over the political orientations of Third World development by shaping the commitments of Third World military elites."[5]

C. AFRICA AS A SHARE OF MOSCOW'S ARMS EXPORTS

Arms sales also represent a large share of Soviet export earnings, or about 13.4 percent of total exports to all countries. Between 70 and 80 percent of Soviet arms delivered worldwide are sold for hard currency; about 60 percent are sold on comparatively favor-

---

[3] Grimmet. Trends in Conventional Arms Transfers, p. 25.

[4] For example, in the five years from 1978 to 1982, the Soviet Union transferred approximately $4.8 billion in arms to Sub-Saharan Africa. In the 28 years from 1954 to 1981, it extended (without necessarily delivering) just $2.87 billion in economic aid. See: ACDA. World Military Expenditures and Arms Transfers, 1978–1982. p. 95. And, U.S. Department of State. Soviet And East European Aid to the Third World, 1981, p. 17.

[5] Laird, Robbin F. Soviet Arms Trade with the Noncommunist Third World. Proceedings of the Academy of Political Science. Vol. 35. No. 3. 1984, p. 199.

able credit terms. (Presumably, sales to African countries are typical in this regard, although larger shares are possibly puchased on credit.) In the case of developing countries, arms were estimated to be 55 percent of total Soviet exports in 1983 (with comparable percentage figures in the years immediately preceding).[6]

Arms exports to Africa, however, are a comparatively small percentage of total Soviet arms transfers. In 1980–1983, arms deliveries to Sub-Saharan Africa accounted for about 10.7 percent of total Soviet arms deliveries to the Third World, according to U.S. Government estimates. The Middle East and South Asia received the lion's share of Soviet arms exports, about 68 percent, East Asia 12 percent, and Latin America 9 percent.[7] While Soviet shipments of arms to Africa are small compared to deliveries to other parts of the world, they represent a sharp growth since the early 1970s and are significant in a continent that is lightly armed.

Although Africa is the least heavily armed region of the world, with the smallest amount and least sophisticated weaponry, the trend is toward rapidly rising expenditures and imports of arms. In constant dollars, arms imports in Africa were almost ten times higher in 1980 than a decade earlier. The reason for the increased arms expenditures and imports is the greater potential for armed conflict in some parts of Africa, notably southern Africa and the Horn, and the demand for prestige weapons by a few governments.[8] Political instability is likely to create conditons for civil war and general unrest in countries such as Mozambique, Angola, Ethiopia, and Uganda. Military coups are a common form of transferring power and have occurred recently in Upper Volta, Liberia, and Ghana. Regional and ideological conflicts, as between Uganda and Tanzania or Zaire and Congo-Brazzaville, are common. Finally, racial conflict over the future of Namibia-Southwest Africa and South Africa could also contribute further to Soviet military assistance to national liberation groups.

D. Soviet Bloc Troops and Advisers in Africa

The number of Soviet bloc military personnel in Africa has grown. In 1981, Soviet and East European military advisers numbered 5,300 (up from 2,600 in 1975), concentrated in Angola, Ethiopia, Mozambique, Mali, Guinea, and Guinea-Bissau. From 1955 to 1981, some 13,800 Africans received military training in Soviet bloc countries. Most of these personnel were from one-time Soviet allies, as well as from Nigeria, Tanzania, and Zambia.[9] The value of such military training cannot be accurately measured, but it would be in the hundreds of millions of dollars.

Cuban troops and advisers—almost non-existent in Africa in the mid-1970s—totalled nearly 37,000 in 1981. Most were in Angola (23,000), Ethiopia (12,000), and Mozabmique (1,000).[10] In 1984, how-

[6] Developments in Soviet Arms Exports and Imports, 1980–83. Current Analysis. Wharton Econometric Forecasting Associates. No. 62. August 15, 1984, p. 1 and 3–4.

[7] Grimmett. Trends in Coventional Arms Transfers, p. 26.

[8] Pierre, Andrew J. The Global Politics of Arms Sales. Princeton, N.J. Princeton University Press, 1982, p. 255.

[9] Soviet and East European Aid, 1981. p. 14. And, Communist Aid to Less Developed Countries of the Free World, 1975, p. 4.

[10] Soviet and East European Aid, 1981, p.15.

ever, Cuba and Ethiopia reportedly agreed to cut the number of Cuban troops to 3,000 by mid-year. Ethiopia's cost of maintaining troops—estimated at $6 million a year—and the lessening threat from Somalia both influenced the decision to cut back.[11] To date, however, there has been little evidence of actual Cuban withdrawals from Ethiopia. Political developments in southern Africa, particularly South Africa's signing of peace accords with Angola and Mozabmique, also led to increased talk of the possibility of Cuban troops leaving Angola. Nonetheless, Cuban troops represent a force which, to many African observers, seems sympathethic to African interests. They reportedly do not arouse the suspicions among Africans that the presence of Soviet troops would.

TABLE 3.—U.S.S.R., EASTERN EUROPE AND CUBA: MILITARY TECHNICIANS IN AFRICA, 1981 (NUMBER OF PERSONS) [1]

	U.S.S.R. and Eastern Europe	Cuba [2]
Africa (total)	9,900	36,960
North Africa (subtotal)	4,600	50
Algeria	2,000	NA
Other	2,600	50
Sub-Saharan Africa (subtotal)	5,300	36,910
Angola	1,600	23,000
Ethiopia	1,900	12,000
Guinea	50	10
Guinea-Bissau	50	50
Mali	205	
Mozambique	550	1,000
Other	945	850

[1] Minimum estimates of the number of persons present for a period of 1 month or more. Numbers are rounded to the nearest 5.
[2] Including combat units in Angola and Ethiopia.

Source: U.S. Department of State. Soviet and East European Aid to the Third World, 1981. February 1983. Publication 9345. p. 14.

While the Cubans were particularly welcome in Africa in the mid- to late-1970s, there are increasing signs of African discontent with the Cuban military presence since some of the purposes of the Cuban troops—defending Ethiopia against Somalia and aiding the installation of the MPLA in Angola—have been achieved. Public opinion at home may also influence a reduced Cuban presence in Africa.[12]

In Angola, Cuba has suffered casualties in clashes with UNITA rebels, but Cuba has carefully avoided direct engagement with South African forces. In Ethiopia, they are not involved in fighting Eritrean secessionists whom they once supported during the reign of Emperor Haile Selassie. Instead, Cuban forces are deployed to defend Ethiopian territory against Somali incursions. Cuba's refusal to fight the Marxist Eritreans may have been one reason for the agreement to withdraw its troops.

---

[11] New York Times. January 25, 1984, p. A2.
[12] Duncan, W. Raymond. "Cuban Military Assistance to the Third World." In, Cooper, John F. and Papp, Daniel S. Communist Nations' Military Assistance. Boulder, Colo. Westview Press. 1983, p. 150.

E. Conclusions

With the scramble to build up military capabilities among African states, African governments are less inhibited by military dealings with Moscow. Economic constraints could limit the pace of militarization in Africa, but conflict and instability are not likely to lessen in the near future. Such conditions could afford the USSR new opportunities to build military and security relationships with African nations.[13] However, the Soviet Union has been criticized for its security relationship with Uganda's Idi Amin. The Soviets continued their close ties to the repressive Ugandan government despite its brutal behavior at home and its aggressive foreign policies. Moscow also suffered by its aid to Equatorial Guinea's brutal Macias Nguema, deposed in 1979.

The provision of military assistance has advanced Soviet interests in Africa by increasing its influence over regional political developments (as in the Horn and southern Africa), reducing Western influence, and expanding Moscow's power projection capabilities with access to military facilities and new security relationships. Moscow is aided by its ability to export large quantities of arms on short notice. However, the USSR's arms clients cannot always be considered its political clients as well. Moscow's close friends such as Ethiopia, Angola and Mozambique display independent policies at variance with Soviet interests. As Joachim Krause, a specialist on Soviet arms transfers, writes, "The decisive dilemma in the long run for Soviet arms transfer policy in Sub-Saharan Africa is that the Kremlin is hardly in a position to meet all the related military, political, and economic expectations of its client states."[14] The most obvious example of this situation is in southern Africa where dominant Soviet security ties with Mozambique and Angola are largely ineffective in thwarting the South African military threat and in securing Soviet participation in the negotiating process toward peace and a settlement of the Namibian independence issue.

Krause notes that elsewhere in Africa, where conflict is less fundamental, "an arms transfer relationship with the Soviet Union can often make good sense politically."[15] Moscow has demonstrated its reliability as a supporter of socialist governments threatened by internal instability. Also an arms relationship with Moscow serves to diversify a nation's political orientation. It ensures that African states' ties to the West are not complete.

In sum, the massive increase in Soviet arms deliveries to Africa in the 1970's and early 1980's has made Moscow an important actor in African affairs. It has also intensified U.S.-Soviet competition on the continent. Although arms transfers are not a guarantee of enhanced influence, they do make the USSR a more attractive partner in advancing a country's political objectives though often with doubtful or marginal benefits to the USSR.

---

[13] Albright, David E. The USSR and Sub-Saharan Africa in the 1980s. Washington Papers/ 101. Georgetown Center for Strategic and International Studies, Washington, D.C., 1983, p. 59–61.

[14] Krause, Joachim. "Soviet Arms Transfers to Sub-Saharan Africa." R. Craig Nation and Mark V. Kauppi (eds.). The Soviet Impact in Africa. Lexington, Mass. Lexington Books, 1984, p. 141.

[15] Ibid., p. 142.

VI. THE SOVIET PRESENCE IN THE HORN: CONSOLIDATION IN ETHIOPIA

A. HISTORY

Soviet policy makers certainly considered the geostrategic significance of the Horn of Africa when they sought closer relations with Ethiopia in the mid-1970s. The Horn may well be the most important region of sub-Saharan Africa as far as the Soviet Union is concerned. It lies at one end of the transit route between the Mediterranean Sea and the Indian Ocean, important in military and commercial terms. The Horn is on the southern periphery of the Middle East, a position which could allow the Soviets to pressure pro-Western Saudi Arabia, the Sudan, Egypt, and even Kenya.

The Soviet Union has long tried to gain a presence in the Horn of Africa. In the 1960s, the USSR tried with limited success to improve relations with pro-Western Emperor Haile Selassie's government in Ethiopia. In the early 1970s, the USSR courted Sudanese President Jaafar Nimeiri until an attempted Communist-led coup in 1971 induced Nimeiri to turn against the Soviets. It found its client in Mohamed Siad Barre who in 1969 seized power in Somalia, Ethiopia's natural adversary. The USSR acquired access to various Somali military facilities including the port of Berbera, and in 1974, the Soviets signed a treaty of friendship with Somalia, its first with an African nation. But Soviet relations with Somalia deteriorated after Moscow turned to Ethiopia to court the new revolutionary military regime which had overthrown the the conservative government of Emperor Haile Selassie in 1974. This led Siad Barre to expel Soviet advisers and revoke military access rights. Moscow chose to strengthen its ties to Ethiopia when in mid-1977 Somali forces invaded Ethiopia to seize control of the Ogaden region. It carried out a massive airlift of weapons, advisors, and Cuban combat troops which in early 1978 enabled Ethiopia to repel the Somalis.[1] The Soviet-Ethiopian relationship culminated in the signing of a Friendship and Cooperation Treaty in November 1978.

With Soviet and Cuban assistance, the Ethiopian government was able to repel regular Somali armed forces in a massive counterattack and achieve at least a stalemate in controlling rebel secessionists in Eritrea, Tigre, and Oromo provinces despite determined resistance. Soviet and allied security assistance (primarily from East Germany) has allowed Col. Mengistu Haile-Mariam to eliminate most of his domestic political opposition and prevent a coup.

---

[1] For more on the Soviet role in Ethiopia before 1980, see: Henze, Paul. "Getting a Grip on the Horn." Walter Laqueur, ed. The Pattern of Soviet Conduct in the Third World. New York, Praeger, 1983, p. 150–186. Ottaway, Marina. Soviet and American Influence in the Horn of Africa. New York, Praeger, 1982. Rothenberg, Morris. The USSR and Africa: New Dimensions of Soviet Global Power. Washington, D.C. Advanced International Studies Institute, 1980.

Since 1977, the Soviet role has expanded rapidly. The USSR probably sees in Ethiopia a strongly anti-Western government that supports Soviet policies in the region and provides Moscow with access to military bases. Ethiopia has generally proved to be a reliable partner although strains in the relationship occasionally surface. Ethiopia may present a Third World model of socialist development for the Soviets. It is avowedly Marxist-Leninist and has recently established a Soviet-style vanguard party that Moscow hopes will replace the military's dominant role in society and government. The Soviets have relied heavily on military and security assistance to maintain predominant influence. Although Col. Mengistu seeks greater military assistance to ward off external and internal threats to his rule, he appears unwilling to permit the Soviets a greater say in domestic policies.

Ethiopia is a poor and underdeveloped nation. Mengistu has reportedly been dissatisfied with the small amounts of development aid the Soviet bloc has extended to Ethiopia. The strong tradition of Ethiopian nationalism has created friction, while the Soviet Union has placed clear limits on the economic resources it will commit to Ethiopia's development. During the 1984 famine in Ethiopia, Moscow was unwilling or unprepared to assist the country to any great degree. To date, however, the USSR has invested heavily in Ethiopia's future, perhaps as much as $3.0 billion including arms and economic aid, without significant repayment from Ethiopia.

Soviet penetration of Ethiopia has been extensive and the recent formation of a Communist party should signal greater Soviet involvement in the country. The militarization of the conflict in the Horn in the past ten years and Ethiopia's relations with the Soviet Union are critical to Western interests in Africa and the Middle East.

B. SOVIET OBJECTIVES

The Soviet Union has sought considerable involvement and participation in managing Ethiopian affairs. The Soviets were decisive in their swing away from Somalia to Ethiopia and in repelling Somali forces. Soviet and Cuban military assistance has been critical to the survival of the Mengistu government. The Soviet and Cuban presence in Ethiopia contributes to Moscow's perceptions of its role as a global power and its ability to challenge Western forces in the region. Ethiopia's position on the Red Sea and its proximity to the Middle East give it strategic importance to the Soviets and the West. Ethiopia is also important in maintaining the USSR's north-south communication lines to black Africa.

Moscow has prodded the ruling Provisional Military Administrative Council (PMAC) to establish a vanguard proletarian party consistent with its conception of Marxist-Leninist principles to institutionalize the revolution and consolidate Soviet influence in the country. The Soviet Union seeks to reduce Ethiopia's ties to the West and simultaneously increase its reliance on the socialist East. Moscow was cautious about the possibility of genuine Soviet-style socialism developing in Africa during the Brezhnev period and under his successors. At the same time, the Soviet Union wishes to deepen economic ties between the socialist world and "socialist-oriented" Ethiopia, and thus has granted it associate membership in the Council of Mutual Economic Assistance. The Soviet bloc, however, has been unable to contribute significantly to economic development.

1. STRATEGIC OBJECTIVES

Ethiopia's location in the Horn of Africa is of increasing strategic importance to the Soviet Union, since the United States has negotiated military arrangements with neighboring Somalia, the Sudan, and Kenya. The superpower naval build-up in the Indian Ocean, the rising importance of Persian Gulf oil in Western considerations, and the significance of the Red Sea waterway have contributed to Soviet interest in the Horn. The USSR's loss of influence in the Sudan and Egypt, with the simultaneous improvement of U.S. relations with these countries and Saudi Arabia in the wake of the Iranian revolution, probably increases the importance of Ethiopia in Soviet calculations. Ethiopia is also close to the Persian Gulf and could serve as a base to interdict oil shipments in the event of hostilities. The Soviets used Ethiopia as a base to ferry weapons to Angola during its civil war and its conflicts with South Africa.

The presence of some 13,000 Cuban troops in Ethiopia in 1981 attests to the Soviet Union's strategic interests in the region. There have been reports that Cuban troops have been reduced to fewer than 10,000 in 1984, but these have not yet been confirmed.[2] The Soviet Union has delivered weapons valued at over $2.2 billion, which include 700 T-54 tanks, at least 10 coastal patrol vessels, 65 MiG-21 and 20 MiG-23 combat aircraft, about 20 transport aircraft, and 24 Mi-24 helicopters.[3] The Ethiopian armed forces have increased in size to 250,000 from approximately 50,000 before the revolution.

Soviet policy in Ethiopia appears to imply a recognition that advancement of Soviet global interests require heavier direct involvement. The Soviet Union sees that the "correlation of forces," deemed favorable for the advance of socialism worldwide, demand Soviet military assistance for success. Mark Katz, a specialist in Soviet policy in the Third World at the Brookings Institution, says in regard to the general rise in Soviet military adventures abroad that

No longer would it suffice for the USSR to play an indirect role while local forces undertook most of the fighting. Without a greater degree of direct Soviet involvement, the local forces whose victory the Soviets desire might instead be defeated. This is the result of the trend for indigenous Third World forces to have interests that not only differ from, but also conflict with Soviet interests. Thus the protection of Soviet interests in the Third World must increasingly be borne by the USSR itself.[4]

---

[2] Wise, Sallie. Ethiopian Leader Mengistu Pays Working Visit to USSR. Radio Liberty Research. RL 133/84. March 29, 1984, p. 1.
[3] Military Balance. p. 68–69. ACDA. World Military Expenditures, 1978–1982, p. 95. The $2.2 billion figure is for the years 1978–1982 only.
[4] Katz, Mark N. The Third World in Soviet Military Thought. Baltimore, The Johns Hopkins University Press, 1982, p. 115.

2. POLITICAL OBJECTIVES

Ideally, the Soviet Union would like Ethiopia to develop from a "socialist-oriented" nation into a full-fledged socialist state. The requirements of socialist orientation include a progressive limitation of the private sector and the nationalization of industry, an alliance of workers and peasants in a proletarian party, and a deepening of political and economic ties with the socialist bloc.[5] In this regard, Ethiopia is a model of Soviet development in Africa.

Although Col. Mengistu owes his political survival in large measure to the Soviet and Cuban presence, the 1980s have seen signs of considerable disagreement between Ethiopia and the USSR. So far, however, these strains have not threatened to undo their relationship. The principal source of irritation has been Moscow's demand that Mengistu transfer power to a vanguard Marxist-Leninist party from the military dictatorship of the PMAC, or "Derg" as it is known in Ethiopia. In the Soviet view, Ethiopia needs an organized revolutionary party to control political activity and maintain a pro-Soviet orientation.[6] Moscow regards Ethiopia as "national revolutionary" or "socialist-oriented," but not a full-fledged Marxist-Leninist state. A Marxist-Leninist party, according to Moscow, would promote a more permanent relationship between Moscow and Addis Ababa by replacing the personalized rule of the Derg with ruling structures similar to the Soviet system and bound by a common ideology. Military cooperation and common short-term regional strategies are insufficient, in the Soviet view, to sustain a long-lasting alliance.

Mengistu strongly resisted the idea of a revolutionary party to guide the Ethiopian revolution even though the Derg's rhetoric was increasingly Marxist and militant and ostensibly based on "scientific socialism." The PMAC leaders thought that such a party would give the Soviets more control of the government and erode the military's hold on policy.[7] In December 1979, however, Mengistu, under prodding from the Soviets, declared the formation of the Commission for Organizing the Party of the Working People of Ethiopia (COPWE). COPWE's stated objective, to establish a Soviet-style party, proceeded slowly. It had little identity other than as a propaganda outfit for the ruling PMAC. In its early years, there was no apparent intention to empower it with the authority to shape ideology or government policy, much less evolve into a genuine Marxist vanguard party.[8]

In January 1983, COPWE decided to devote its next meeting in September 1984, commemorating the tenth anniversary of the revolution, to the creation of a Workers Party of Ethiopia (WPE). The formation of the party, with Mengistu as its Secretary General,

---

[5] Gorman, Robert F. Soviet Perspectives on the Prospects for Socialist Development in Africa. African Affairs. April 1984, p. 175. Gorman adds: "These states should be distinguished from the romantic and populist versions of socialism, which, though clearly more progressive than capitalist-oriented states, had nevertheless embraced philosophies alien to the genuine Soviet top-down party inspired and constructed model of socialist development."

[6] Wise, Sallie. Ethiopia Forms Soviet-Style Party. Radio Liberty Research, RL 340/84. September 7, 1984.

[7] For more on the Ethiopian party, see Edmond J. Keller. The Ethiopian Revolution at the Crossroads. Current History. March 1984, p. 121 and 137.

[8] Soviet World Outlook. September 15, 1984, p. 5.

was welcomed by the Soviet Union. The party lends credence to Soviet theories about how "socialist-oriented" nations of the Third World are to progress toward genuine socialism and enhances the ligitimacy of the Soviet presence in Ethiopia. The Soviet Union was represented at the founding of the party by a high-level delegation led by Politburo and Secretariat member Grigoriy Romanov. He praised Ethiopia's action and compared the event to Soviet history.

The entire history of the Soviet state after the victory of the Great October Revolution and the living practice of revolutionary transformations in other socialist countries irrefutably prove that it is impossible to defend their gains from outside infringements and domestic counterrevolutions and to overcome economic and cultural backwardness without the leading and directing role of a party.[9]

Despite the formation of the WPE, many observers question the motives of Ethiopia's leaders. They note that Mengistu may wish to secure increased deliveries of Soviet weapons and delay repayment of debts to the USSR without the commitment to building a party. Perhaps as an inducement to form the party, the USSR agreed to step up aid. Romanov signed a comprehensive economic cooperation agreement for oil and gold exploration, an irrigation dam, textile factory, expansion of a cement plant, and hydro-electric feasibility studies. There is little evidence that the party will become more powerful than the army. For example, large numbers of WPE Central Committee members are active or former military officers.[10]

The Soviet presence is formidable. There are an estimated 4,000 Soviet advisers in the country, 1,000 East Germans involved in security and intelligence, 13,000 Cuban troops and another 1,000 Cuban technicians. They exert a strong influence in military affairs and in running the government ministries. The Soviets have also been influential in Ethiopian political development. Mengistu has set up "kebeles," Soviet-style neighborhood associations that serve the dual purpose of spying on citizens and disseminating propaganda.[11] The government has nationalized industries, expropriated property, and established state farms. The Soviet Union has also encouraged the formation of mass organizations of peasants, trade unions, and women to mobilize the population in support of the government.[12] The language of the revolution is Marxist-Leninist and "scientific socialism." Symbols of Ethiopia's socialism are everywhere, in huge public portraits of Marx and Lenin and slogans on billboards extolling the benefits of Marxism and the revolution.[13]

The extent to which Ethiopia is commited to Marxism-Leninism and ties to Moscow is not certain. David and Marina Ottaway, close observers of Ethiopian politics, wrote in 1981 that there was a symbiotic relationship between the two nations after Ethiopia's progressive official adoption of Soviet ideology.

The question thus arises whether the adherence to Marxism-Leninism can be considered genuine or is simply a facade adopted for convenience' sake, a lure used to attract the Soviet Unionn or indeed a requirement imposed by the Soviets as the

[9] Ibid. And, Christian Science Monitor. September 13, 1984, p. 10.
[10] On the make-up of the party see Africa Confidential. September 19, 1984.
[11] Mann, Matt. Assessing the Revolution. Africa Report. November-December 1983, p. 48–49.
[12] New York Times. October 8, 1984, p. A8.
[13] Keller. The Ethiopian Revolution at the Crossroads, p. 117–121.

quid pro quo for their support. The answer inevitably is somewhat mixed. As we perceive it, there is a genuine commitment on the Derg's part to certain policies which are in accordance with, and inspired by, the ideology. On the other hand, one may well question whether the present high pitch of Marxist-Leninist rhetoric would ever have been attained without the Soviet and Cuban presence. While there is no evidence that the Ethiopian government's policies were in any way modified after the Soviet Union became its major foreign ally, there can be little doubt of a much greater open commitment to the ideology.[14]

3. ECONOMY AND SOVIET ASSISTANCE

Although Moscow delivers generous amounts of military hardware to Ethiopia, it provides little economic assistance despite worsening drought conditions, extreme food shortages, and balance of payments difficulties. Ethiopia is approximately $3.0 billion in debt to the Soviets for the purchase of weapons and the garrisoning of Cuban troops and Soviet advisers. There are also reports of Ethiopian dissatisfaction with the performance of Soviet arms. Repairs on Soviet equipment reportedly must be performed in the USSR and transportation costs borne by the Ethiopian government.[15]

In 1980 and 1981, according to U.S. Government sources, the USSR and its allies extended $15 million in non-military aid to Ethiopia.[16] At the same time, Western sources have been providing Ethiopia with considerably more assistance and deliveries of food, estimated at about $190 million in the early 1980s.[17] As a poverty-stricken nation, Ethiopia holds little economic atraction for Moscow. The Soviet Union is careful to discourage Ethiopia from notions that it will become "adopted" in the form of an African Cuba. At the same time, there are few people who believe that Ethiopia actually will have to repay its massive debts to Moscow.

Trade with Ethiopia is hardly lucrative, but the Soviets have an overwhelming trade surplus. In 1982, the USSR exported goods valued at 182.3 million rubles and imported 13.2 million rubles from Ethiopia. In 1978, the trade imbalance was 64.2 million rubles in exports to 4.3 million in imports. By any measure, Soviet trade with Ethiopia is miniscule. Trade takes the form of barter arrangements, as with many other African nations.

Ethiopia's principal export to the USSR is coffee, which is used to help pay off its debts. Its principal import, besides arms, is petroleum. Some 70 percent of Ethiopia's export earnings in 1980 went to pay for oil imports.[18] The Ethiopian government has sought price advantages from the USSR in the past to little avail. The Soviets have agreed to explore for oil, but their record has not been as good as western prospecters.

In recent years, Ethiopia has suffered from severe famines, caused by drought, dislocation from continued warring between secessionists and the central government, and the application of "socialist principles" to the agriculture sector.[19] The agriculture

---

[14] David and Marina Ottaway. Afrocommunism. New York, Africana Publishing Co., 1981, p. 154.
[15] Albright. The USSR and Sub-Saharan Africa in the 1980s, p. 65.
[16] U.S. Department of State. Soviet and East European Aid, p. 17.
[17] Albright. The USSR and Sub-Saharan Africa in the 1980s, p. 65.
[18] Henze. Communism and Ethiopia, p. 70.
[19] Ibid. p. 71. Also, Ottaway, David B. Ethiopia Squeezed Between East and West. Washington Post. Sept. 23, 1984.

sector accounts for approximately 45 percent of gross domestic product and 85 percent of total exports, and it is the sector the Soviet are typically least effective in stimulating.

Ethiopia is the recipient of large sums of foreign assistance from the European Economic Community, the World Bank, and the International Development Association. The country runs a heavy trade deficit (up to $400 million in 1982 from $210 million in 1978) while financing the costs of its counter-insurgency campaigns.[20] There seems to be little possibility that Moscow will effectively contribute to an improved Ethiopian economy despite the strategic advantages influence might provide.

C. SOMALIA IN SOVIET STRATEGY TOWARD THE HORN

Somalia could present the Soviet Union with new opportunities in the 1980's. It is unlikely that Moscow could achieve a rapprochement with Siad Barre given its support for the anti-Barre Democratic Front for the Salvation of Somalia (DFSS) liberation movement based in Addis Ababa. Somali actions also have induced Moscow to criticize Siad Barre's government. Among these are the agreements with the United States permitting American use of Somali military installations and Somalia's closer alignment with conservative Arab powers such as Egypt and Saudi Arabia. The strengthening of opposition movements against Siad Barre has also demonstrated to the Soviets the weakness of his government.

Siad Barre's problems are complicated by the influx of ethnic Somali refugees from the Ogaden fearing Ethiopian military reprisals. (Ethiopia is reportedly giving direct military support to anti-Siad Barre rebels because of Somalia's aid to Ogaden insurgents fighting Ethiopian government forces.) Economic stringencies, ineffective military actions against Ethiopians-supported insurgents, and political unrest that has reached into the armed forces causing mutinies and defections all contribute to the weakness of the Siad Barre government. It is also reported that the Western Somali Liberation Front, the Somali-supported guerrilla movement seeking to free the Ogaden region from Ethiopian control, is divided over how closely it should identify itself with Siad Barrer.[21] David Albright argues that the Soviets may be pinning their hopes on a new government based on Ethiopian-supported DFSS elements to replace Siad Barre. Such a government would prove more accommodating to Soviet offers of better relations.[22]

An alternative argument is that the USSR is pursuing a policy of wooing Siad Barre away from Western and conservative Arab nations. It may have hopes of bringing about a peace agreement between Ethiopia and Somalia that could lead to a regional federation (to include South Yemen) similar to the one proposed by Fidel Castro in March 1977 in Aden. The Soviet Union perhaps anticipated that Somalia would be disappointed by the small amount of aid it received from the United States, Western Europe, and conserva-

---

[20] Selwyn, Michael. Politics Versus Trade: Ethiopia Seeks a Balance. Middle Economic Digest. June 14, 1984, p. 12-14.

[21] Albright. The USSR and Sub-Saharan Africa in the 1980s, p. 68-70.

[22] Ibid. p. 71. Also, Albright. "The USSR and Africa in 1982: The Quest for Global Power Status." In, Africa Contemporary Record, 1982-83. London, Africana, 1983, p. A160-161.

tive Arab states and therefore be receptive to improving relations with the USSR.[23] The Soviets may have the ability to "deliver" the Ethiopians and substantially end the security threats to Somalia's territory under the right circumstances.

D. Prospects for Soviet Influence in the Horn

The creation of the WPE should at least temporarily give Soviet-Ethiopian relations added momentum and perhaps deepen Soviet political penetration of the country. However, Ethiopian resistance to institutionalizing the Party and adopting further Soviet-style precepts of government may add to tension and to Soviet disillusionment with the course of the revolution. It is too early to tell. Other issues may intervene in Soviet-Ethiopian relations as well.

In addition to the severe economic stringencies that may encourage Ethiopia to seek closer ties with Western trade partners and aid donors, Ethiopia's deep Christian heritage may prove to be another major obstacle to the spread of Marxist influence. Thus far the revolutionary government has been fairly tolerant of the religious institutions of Ethiopian Orthodoxy. But the country's impoverished population appears to place great faith in religious worship which Marxist-Leninism may not be able to penetrate.[24]

The mounting costs of sustaining military campaigns and the apparent lack of success in ending rebel challenges to the central government could stretch Ethiopia's reliance on the Soviet bloc severely. The Cubans and Soviets (less so) are reportedly reluctant to participate directly in government offenses in Eritrea. This factor, combined with the high cost of stationing Cuban troops, may have been behind the announcement of Cuba's decision to withdraw a large portion of its troops by the summer of 1984.[25] The Soviet Union has apparently concluded that it must aid Mengistu's efforts against Eritrea. However, a 1982–1983 offensive carried out with the aid of Soviet and East German advisors ended unsuccessfully. There are reports that Mengistu replaced East German intelligence advisors with Israeli personnel.[26] Ethiopian troops have also supported the efforts of Somali liberation movements, particularly the Democratic Front for the Salvation of Somalia (DFSS), against the government of Siad Barre, through no evidence exists of direct Soviet and Cuban assistance on the warfront. Threats to Soviet consolidation of power in Ethiopia may lie in continuing ethnic divisions in the country and an economic crisis of catastrophic proportions exacerbated by resistance to the Marxist central government. So far, Moscow has successfully reinforced Ethiopia's inclinations to support the Soviet Union on issues important to its regional presence and the development of socialism in Ethiopia.

---

[23] Yodfat, Aryeh. Somalia: A Shift in Soviet Policy. Soviet Analyst. September 1, 1982.

[24] See Henze's brief treatment of the religion issue. Communism and Ethiopia, p. 68.

[25] New York Times. January 25, 1984. p. A2. See also, Ethiopia Feels Internal Strain as Rebels Gain Grounds in Eritrea. Christian Science Monitor. April 18, 1984, P. 10.

[26] Albright. The USSR and Sub-Saharan Africa in the 1980s, p. 66.

VII. SOUTHERN AFRICA IN SOVIET POLICY

Southern Africa is of special interest to the Soviet Union. The USSR achieved two major successes in the region in the 1970s when it signed Friendship and Cooperation Treaties with avowedly Marxist Angola (October 1976) and Mozambique (March 1977). During this period, the Soviets transported Cuban soldiers and weaponry to Angola; assisted Cuban and East German training of Southwest Africa People's Organization (SWAPO) guerrillas to fight in Namibia and of guerrillas of Umkhonto we Sizwe, the African National Congress's (ANC) military wing, to operate in South Africa. The USSR also trained and equipped about 10,000 men of Joshua Nkomo's Zimbabwe African People's Union (ZAPU) wing of the Patriotic Front for the war in Rhodesia. Thus far, the Soviets have failed to reap the benefits of their association with Nkomo, whom they evidently expected would head independent Zimbabwe's first government or at least share power with Robert Mugabe, the current prime minister of Zimbabwe. Instead, since independence in 1980, Mugabe has distanced himself from Moscow.

The impending independence of Namibia (Southwest Africa) from the Republic of South Africa presents the possibility of further Soviet gains, although the final details of a Namibian settlement have yet to be arranged. It may be that a Marxist regime likely to call on Moscow for support could come to power in Namibia. On the other hand, a Namibian settlement, if finally achieved, could contain guarantees and safeguards that could prevent this from happening. The Soviet Union probably also expects future revolutionary change in South Africa, but not in the near future. Moscow sees its identifications with black nationalism as enhancing its image throughout Africa and the Third World.

A specialist on Soviet policy toward Africa, Seth Singleton, suggests that Soviet interests in southern Africa dictate encouraging a polarization within the region and a Soviet-African alliance of "socialist orientation" against the United States and the West. One tactic is to induce the United States into closer ties with South Africa.[1] In southern Africa, the Soviet Union is in the position of aiding the cause against apartheid supported by all other Africans. Further, Soviet political interests in the area coincide with Western economic and geostrategic vulnerabilities.

The economic importance of southern Africa to the West is apparent to the USSR, while the region holds little strategic value to the Soviet Union. It is the major source, outside of the USSR, of four strategic minerals—platinum, chromium, vanadium and manganese. Southern Africa lies astride a major transit route between the Indian and Atlantic Oceans for commercial and military ships.

---

[1] Singleton, Seth. The Shared Tactical Goals of South Africa and the Soviet Union. CSIS Africa Notes. No. 12. April 26, 1983, p. 1.

Specifically, this sea route carries most of the crude oil destined for Western Europe. It is not certain that the Soviet Union has immediate strategic ambitions in southern Africa. Nor is it clear that the Soviets can threaten Western interests there in the near future. Nonetheless, Moscow appears ready to take advantage of opportunities in the region as they present themselves.

A. Soviet Relations With Angola and Mozambique

Since the late 1970s, Mozambique and Angola have faced increasing economic stringencies and, in the recent past, have come to a tentative *modus vivendi* with South Africa which may reduce their dependence on the Soviets and Cubans for security assistance. Long-term Soviet involvement in the region may have to rest on foundations other than military and security assistance to Angola and Mozambique. Until the agreements with South Africa in 1984, both countries were subject to direct South African military pressure and sought close ties to Moscow to ensure their security.

Southern Angolan territory was occupied by South African forces pursuing SWAPO guerrillas and attacking their bases.[2] In addition, the Luanda government has faced strong challenges from rebel guerrillas of the UNITA (National Union for the Total Independence of Angola) movement led by Jonas Savimbi. Savimbi claims his forces control up to a third of Angola. UNITA, according to numerous reports, also receives considerable assistance and military aid from South Africa.

Mozambique was raided for the first time in January 1981. South Africa asserted its right to "hot pursuit" against opposition forces operating from Mozambique. Before the Nkomati agreement of 1984, the African National Congress (ANC) had camps in Mozambique from which it carried out insurgent actions and sabotage in South Africa. The South African government was charged with providing covert support to the rebel Mozambique National Resistance Movement (RNM) trying to destabilize the FRELIMO (Front for the Liberation of Mozambique) government. The two countries signed the Nkomati accord in March 1984 by which each agreed to prevent the use of its territory for guerrilla activities against the other.

The Soviet Union has a major interest in the survival of the present MPLA (Popular Movement for the Liberation of Angola) government in Angola and a resolution of the Namibian independence problem that could promote its influence in the region. Moscow seeks to preserve the MPLA in power in Luanda, primarily by means of military assistance and the presence of some 25,000 Cuban troops in the country. Angola is one of two countries in southern Africa referred to by the Soviets as being "socialist-oriented." The MPLA faces continued challenges to its authority from UNITA rebels and from South African raids into Angolan territory. In Namibia, the USSR would like to see a Southwest African

---

[2] For information on domestic developments in Angola, see: Bender, Gerald J. The Continuing Crisis in Angola. Current History. March 1983. Ottaway, David and Marina. Afrocommunism. New York, Africana Publishing Co., 1981. Chapter V. And: Katsikas, Suzanne Jolicoeur. The Arc of Socialist Revolutions: Angola to Afghanistan. Cambridge, Mass., Schenkman Publishing Co., 1982. Chapter 2.

People's Organization (SWAPO) government installed with a strong pro-Soviet inclination.

1. ANGOLA

Angola is Moscow's principal political and military commitment in southern Africa, second only to Ethiopia among Soviet interests in Africa. Since 1975, the Soviet Union has supplied equipment and logistical support for Cuban troops to help the MPLA repel South African intervention and its assistance to rebel UNITA forces. The USSR has supplied large quantities of new, sophisticated military equipment, estimated at $950 million from 1978 to 1982.[3] It dispatched naval forces to Luanda to assert its interests in the region and to show the flag. In June 1982, a Soviet naval task group paid a visit to Angola. In that year, the Soviets stepped up their efforts to replace equipment Angolan forces lost to heavy South African attacks in 1981. A high-level Soviet military delegation travelled to Luanda in January 1982.

As a consequence of close military ties, Angola was reported to possess in 1983 a relatively sophisticated (for the African theater) air defense system, including the Soviet-built surface-to-air SA-8 and -9 missiles and perhaps SA-6 and -13s. The Angolan Air Force has two squadrons (26-30) of MiG-21 fighter aircraft and 14-16 MiG-23s as well as advanced helicopters, Mi-8s and Mi-24s.[4] The Soviet Union also stations some 1,000 military advisers in Angola, accompanied by approximately 1,000 East Germans, and 1,600 other East Europeans, mostly Bulgarians.

Angolan President Jose Eduardo dos Santos visited Moscow in May 1983 for talks with Soviet leader Yuri Andropov and Defense Minister Dmitri Ustinov. One result was an agreement for increased arms deliveries to Angola. Soviet-Angolan talks reaffirmed the position of both sides on the issue of Cuban troops in Angola. The joint communique justified the presence of Cuban troops and condemned U.S. and South African attempts to link Cuban troops withdrawals to a Namibian settlement.[5]

In January 1984, the Soviet Union and Cuba announced they would increase defense assistance to Angola. The decision was apparently made following defeats of Angolan forces in late 1983 at the hands of South African troops when South Africa launched "Operation Askari" to dislodge SWAPO camps in southern Angola. The Soviet decision also followed a diplomatic warning to South Africa not to destabilize the pro-Soviet Angolan government. According to TASS, the Soviet Union "strongly demanded that the racist regime stop its aggression against Angola and withdraw its troops." [6]

The Soviet Union has committed itself to long-range economic development assistance in Angola. In January 1982, Angola and the USSR signed an agreement for economic cooperation and trade through 1990 amounting to $2 billion, according to Soviet sources. A subsequent protocol agreement covered projects in energy, ship-

---

[3] ACDA. World Military Expenditures, 1978-82, p. 95.
[4] Where Lion Roam No More. Defense and Foreign Affairs. September 1984, p. 10-11.
[5] Moscow Radio. January 13, 1984. In: JPRS-UPS-84-013. February 9, 1984, p. 4.
[6] Current Digest of the Soviet Press. Vol. XXXV, No. 20, June 15, 1983, p. 14 and 23.

building, agriculture, and geological research. The Soviets agreed to develop projects in Malanje Province that would include a hydro-power station on the Cuanza River and a dam and reservoir for irrigation purposes. It remains to be seen how much of the promised assistance will actually be delivered or will result in completed projects. Angolan officials are known to be disenchanted with Soviet aid deliveries and accomplishments.

Despite Soviet and Western aid, Angola remains deeply in debt. Its foreign debt is estimated at $2.5 billion and 40 percent of its foreign currency earnings are spent on military equipment and defense.[7] The Cuban presence drains Angola's financial resources. One source reports that Angola pays the Soviet Union and Cuba between $1.8 and $2.4 billion a year for assistance.[8] Thus, the commitment to Angola may not cost the USSR much. Angola is a comparatively wealthy African nation with hard currency earnings from the export of oil and diamonds to the United States and Europe which it uses to compensate Moscow for arms deliveries and economic aid. The cost to the Soviets of training and equipping SWAPO guerrillas and a small number of ANC commandos is small. One estimate places the cost of Soviet activities in southern Africa at less than what it costs to maintain two Soviet army divisions.[9] One observer suggests that the USSR could sustain an increased level of support for Angola without strain.[10]

At the same time, the USSR appears unwilling to invest its own scarce resources in the country and may encourage it to look to the West for economic assistance and trade as long as these links do not weaken political and security ties to Moscow.

2. MOZAMBIQUE

Soviet relations with Mozambique picked up in 1982, when a guerrilla war led by anti-communist Movimento Nacional da Resistencia (MNR) forces in Mozambique intensified. The opposition movement reportedly has little political support in the country, but it has been successful in disrupting Mozambique's economy. Mozambique's security worries have been aroused by repeated South African incursions penetrating deep into Mozambique territory in search of anti-South African nationalists of the ANC.

In 1982, the USSR and Mozambique held a number of talks on military cooperation. In November, Defense Minister Dmitiri Ustinov and Marshal Nikolai Ogarkov, chief of staff of the Soviet armed forces, met with President Samora Machel. In December, a Soviet military delegation led by Col. Gen. A.N. Zotov, head of the Main Directorate of the USSR General Staff, toured parts of Mozambique. In October 1982, the head of the Mozambican air force held consultations with his Soviet counterpart in Moscow. The Soviet Union has frequently demonstrated its support for Mozambique. Following South Africa's raids in January 1981, units of the

---

[7] Time. January 23, 1984, p. 27.
[8] Foreign Report. April 7, 1983, p. 5.
[9] Singleton. The Shared Tactical Goals of South Africa and the Soviet Union, p. 1.
[10] Murphy, Bill. Probable Soviet Objectives in Angola and Namibia. Radio Liberty Research, RL 33/84. January 18, 1984, p. 2.

Soviet navy called at Maputo harbor.[11] In June and July 1982, three Soviet naval vessels again appeared in Maputo.

Soviet military assistance to Mozambique has been substantial, particularly since South African incursions beginning in 1981. Soviet weapons deliveries to Mozambique from 1978 to 1982 amounted to $250 million.[12] The Soviet Union currently maintains approximately 1,000 advisers matched by a similar number of Cuban advisers.

The Soviet Union's ties with Mozambique are deepened by more numerous exchanges at the government and party level. In recent years, the CPSU presumably advised FRELIMO on organization of the party and on ideological issues. Mozambique government officials travel to the USSR frequently, while Moscow often dispatches delegations to offer technical advice or simply to commemorate special anniversaries.

From 1975 to 1981, the Soviet Union extended to Mozambique about $175 million in economic assistance; East European allies added another $100 million.[13] The Soviet Union concluded an agreement with Mozambique in April 1982 valued at approximately $60 million to provide for Soviet exports, the establishment of large farming cooperatives, assistance in coal mining, and the search for energy resources. In October 1982, East Germany agreed to aid the repair of Mozambique's railroads.[14]

B. Limits of Influence in Angola and Mozambique

Soviet influence in Angola and Mozambique is limited by the mismatch between the two nations' needs for security assistance and economic development aid and Soviet provisions of it. The Soviet Union has been largely ineffective in contributing to their economic rebuilding efforts. Mozambique was turned down for a membership in CMEA, the Soviet bloc economic organization, in 1981, and the Soviets apparently placed clear limits on the amount of aid they would commit to the country. Angola's economy relies considerably on exports to the West, while Mozambique's principal source of revenues is trade with South Africa—laborers' wage remittances, railroad and port fees, and the sale of hydro-electric power to South Africa. Recent agreements with South Africa may usher in a period of peace that could allow Angola and Mozambique to concentrate on economic development—and perhaps further reduce the potential for Soviet influence.

There are signs that the two countries are increasingly interested in dealing with the West for trade and economic development. In October 1983, President Machel travelled to France and Great Britain where he won further aid pledges and the cancellation of certain debts. And in Belgium, Foreign Minister Joaquim Chissano appealed for "massive and immediate Western investment and aid."

[11] Albright, David E. "The USSR and Africa in 1982: Quest for Global Power Status." Colin Legum, ed. Africa Contemporary Record, Vol. XV, 1982-1983. New York, Africana Publishing Co., 1984, p. A157.
[12] ACDA. World Military Expenditures, 1978-1982, p. 95.
[13] U.S. Department of State. Soviet and East European Aid, p. 17.
[14] Albright, David E. "The USSR and Africa in 1982: Quest for Global Power Status." Africa Contemporary Record, 1982-1983, p. A158.

Mozambique officials are said to be increasingly irritated with the poor performance of Soviet bloc aid. The country was particularly hard hit by a drought in 1983 and a shortage of foodstuffs, causing 100,000 deaths from of starvation.[15] In 1982, the Mozambique government agreed to remove the diplomatic obstacles to full participation in the European Community's aid programs, which requires diplomatic recognition of the Federal Republic of Germany and its control of West Berlin. Mozambique also sought the benefits of adhering to the Lome Convention.[16]

Portugal is an important partner in the rapprochement with the West. Economic cooperation agreements were signed in 1981–82, following high level official exchanges. In April 1982, Mozambique and Portugal signed a protocol for military training while plans were reportedly made for the purchase of Portuguese arms.[17]

The benefits of trade with the West are increasingly apparent to Mozambique. U.S. companies are reported in larger numbers in Mozambique, while Mozambique officials extol the virtues of U.S. corporate efficiency.[18] There are also some reports of a major re-evaluation of its centralized socialist economy in favor of some degree of private enterprise, particularly in the agriculture sector.[19]

1. ANGOLA AND MOZAMBIQUE AGREEMENTS WITH SOUTH AFRICA

The Soviet Union has been the sole source of security assistance for both countries since independence. However, since 1981 South Africa has stepped up its attacks in Mozambique and Angola and increased its assistance to rebel forces of UNITA and the RNM. Both countries required greater military aid from the Soviet bloc which Moscow was not entirely willing to provide. As noted, the Soviet Union has been more forthcoming in providing arms and economic aid in recent years, but not in sufficient quantities to discourage South African challenges to those countries.

David Albright has suggested that the Soviet Union is not prepared to channel more resources to the region in the wake of South Africa's military and diplomatic advances. The USSR has rejected appeals for more economic assistance, and notes that it is providing as much as it can.[20] At the same time, military analysts doubt that the Soviet Union can bring military assets to bear in southern Africa to dissuade South Africa from carrying out its military actions against Mozambique and Angola.[21] Furthermore, Moscow knows that greater assistance may not in fact ensure a political

---

[15] Mozambique: Preparing to Dump Moscow for Western Aid? Christian Science Monitor. October 7, 1983. The Economist. October 22, 1983, p. 32. Time, January 30, 1984, p. 23.

[16] MacQueen. Mozambique's Widening Foreign Policy. The World Today, Jan. 1984, p. 25.

[17] Ibid. This agreement, according to MacQueen, precipitated Yepishev's visit to Maputo and Soviet efforts to keep Mozambique in line.
See also: Lisbon a Diplomatic Port of Call on African Issues, New York Times, January 25, 1984, p. A3.

[18] Mozambique Seeks Western Investment, New York Times, February 5, 1983, p. 34.

[19] Isaacman, Allen. Mozambique Rethinks Marxism, Christian Science Monitor, June 15, 1983. p. 18. Van Slambrouck, Paul. Mozambique Tones Down Marxist Rhetoric, Turns "Practical" on Economy. Christian, Science Monitor,. April 28, 1983, p. 5.

[20] Albright, David E. New Trends in Soviet Policy Toward Africa. CSIS Africa Notes. No. 27. April 29, 1984, p. 9.

[21] Ibid.

payoff. It has noted with disappointment Mozambique's turn to the West for economic aid since 1982.

In March 1984, Mozambique entered into a nonaggression pact with South Africa, the so-called Nkomati Accords, probably as a direct result of South African-supported destabilization, a severe drought, and economic decline. South Africa agreed to halt its support of the RNM, while Mozambique agreed to remove ANC strongholds from its territory. In April 1984, Angola and South Africa agreed to a cease-fire and disengagement to be monitored by a joint Angolan-South African commission. Angola must guarantee that SWAPO does not use Angolan territory evacuated by South Africa to launch attacks in Namibia. South Africia's diplomatic achievements may indicate a reduced role for the Soviet Union in the security policies of Angola and Mozambique.

2. SOVIET POLICY ON THE NAMIBIA SETTLEMENT

According to Singleton, the Soviet Union has several objectives in Namibia: discredit the U.S. role in the negotiations for independence; buttress the USSR's reputation as an indispensable ally of the liberation; expand Soviet influence within SWAPO; and, last, ensure the transfer of power in Namibia to a "socialist-oriented" government linked to the Soviet Union. Singleton also notes that the Soviet Union may not be able to capitalize on a SWAPO victory, particularly if its leaders follow the comparatively pragmatic economic and diplomatic course that Zimbabwe set for itself. Thus, the USSR may be shunted aside when its role as arms provider and military trainer is complete.[22] David Albright agrees that a successful Western-sponsored negotiated resolution of the Namibian problem under the auspices of the United Nations could eliminate Soviet opportunities in Namibia.[23] Furthermore, a Namibian solution could deprive the USSR of influence in neighboring Angola, no longer threatened by South African forces on its southern borders.

While the Soviet Union may not be opposed to a negotiated solution in Namibia, it may not support a specific settlement unless it is included in the negotiation process—something the United States and South Africa are not likely to permit. As long as it is excluded, its real interests may be to blame the United States and South Africa for the continuing violence, while SWAPO and Angolan depend on Moscow for military assistance.

Soviet strategy toward South Africa hinges on the ANC and the South African Communist Party (SACP), both banned in South Africa. Although the ANC is not a Marxist party, the USSR provides it with most of its arms and other assistance. Since the 1960s, the ANC and the SACP have cooperated through the armed wing of the alliance, Umkhonto we Sizwe ("Spear of the Nation"). Soviet policy probably rests on eventually establishing the SACP as the "vanguard" of the South African liberation struggle, operating within the ANC but dominating it. According to Singleton, Soviet policy in this instance is traditional:

---

[22] Singleton. The Shared Tactical Goals.
[23] Albright. The USSR and Sub-Saharan Africa in the 1980s, p. 80.

Its basic elements are the united front, the proletarian base and the worker-peasant alliance, the gradual escalation of armed struggle, the rejection of spontaneous revolutionary action, the rejection of national (ethnic) deviations, and reliance on the Soviet Union and the world communist movement. The main danger over the long run is not repression by the regime. That can be useful. The main danger is the emergence of a middle class which supports the regime.[24]

The Soviet Union does not expect revolution soon in South Africa, Singleton maintains, but escalating violence and repression are expected to encourage the creation of forces sympathetic to the liberation struggle. The Soviet Union may suffer by association with the ANC if divisions within the black political movements develop. A united black movement with a prominent ANC role would probably benefit future Soviet opportunities in South Africa. Present Soviet attitudes toward South Africa suggest a cautious approach with little political change there in the near future. Helen Kitchen, an African affairs specialist at the Georgetown Center for Strategic and International Studies, and Michael Clough, of the U.S. Naval Postgraduate School, believe that the USSR is not seeking a direct confrontation with South Africa.

It is enough for now that South Africa's domestic and regional policies provide a useful international issue that keeps the West, and particularly the United States, on the defensive in the United Nations and in its relations with other African states. Assuming that the Angolan situation does not escalate into an East-West confrontation, present Soviet policy with regard to South Africa costs little and is bringing good returns. But total onslaught it is not.[25]

---

[24] Singleton, Seth. "The Natural Ally: Soviet Policy in Southern Africa." Michael Clough, ed. Changing Realities in Southern Africa. Berkeley, Institute for International Studies, 1982, p. 225.
[25] Kitchen and Clough. The United States and South Africa: Realities and Red Herrings. Washington, D.C., 1984. Georgetown Center for Strategic and International Studies, p. 31.

VIII. OTHER COMMUNIST NATIONS' OBJECTIVES IN AFRICA

Assistance from Cuba and East Germany is particularly important for the success of Soviet policies in Africa. The Cubans supply troops, military advisers, and civilian technicians and the East Germans offer security and intelligence experts. These two countries are often described as "surrogates" of Soviet policy in Africa, but the relationships are more complex. As a consequence of their dependence on Soviet sponsorship, both states operate within limits that coincide with Soviet interests on the continent. Cuban and GDR involvement is an important dimension of Soviet influence in Africa, even if both nations pursue objectives that are sometimes different from those of Moscow.

Other East European nations have expanded their contacts with African states, but their activities are not as critical to Soviet successes. This section will concentrate on the policies and objectives of Cuba and East Germany and the degree to which they complement Soviet interests.

China's objectives in Africa, on the other hand, conflict sharply with Soviet/Cuban/GDR interests in the region. In the 1970s, the People's Republic of China was largely unsuccessful in competing for influence with the Soviets, especially in the former Portuguese colonies of southern Africa. Beijing stepped up its diplomatic activities in Africa in the early 1980s and turned its attention to achieving real political gains in the region.

A. The Case of Cuba: A Military Role

Cuban interest in Africa began soon after the Cuban revolution in 1960 and focuses on Cuba's view of its role in the world revolutionary movement. Cuba supported liberation movements in Guinea-Bissau, Cape Verde, Equatorial Guinea, and the MPLA in Portuguese Angola during the 1960's. Cuba maintained close ties to insurgents in the Portuguese colonies with whom it shares a similar culture and language. Castro gave assistance to Marxist Eritrean rebels during the reign of Ethiopian emperor Haile Selassie. Havana's activities in Africa before the heavy involvement in Angola suggest motives independent of Moscow's.[1] However, the two countries have similar policies toward Africa; both maintain close relations with other "progressive" states such as Mozambique, Guinea, Algeria, Benin, Congo-Brazzaville, Tanzania, Zambia, and Libya

---

[1] For historical treatments of Cuban policies in Africa, see LeoGrande, William M. Cuba's Policy in Africa, 1959–1980. (Berkeley, Institute of International Studies, 1980). And, LeoGrande. Cuban-Soviet Relations and Cuban Policy in Africa. Cuban Studies. January 1980, p. 1–37. Valenta, Jiri. The Soviet-Cuban Alliance in Africa and the Caribbean. The World Today. February 1981, p. 45–53. Dominguez, Jorge. Cuban Foreign Policy. Foreign Affairs. Fall 1978. Volsky, George. "Cuba." Thomas H. Henrikson, ed. Communist Powers and Sub-Saharan Africa. Stanford, Hoover Institution Press, 1981.

and distance themselves from conservative, pro-Western nations such as Kenya, the Ivory Coast, Morocco, and Zaire.

Cuba later took advantage of its new position in Africa by sending large numbers of troops and advisers. In 1981, Cuba had about 23,000 combat troops in Angola and 12,000 in Ethiopia, and 1,000 military advisers in Mozambique, with more in Guinea and Guinea-Bissau. Its economic technicians in Africa total over 9,400, according to U.S. government estimates—6,500 in Angola, 1,000 in Ethiopia, 1,000 in Mozambique, with smaller numbers in Madagascar, Guinea, and other nations.[2]

In Angola and Ethiopia, the strong Cuban presence bolsters governments with close Soviet ties. William LeoGrande, a specialist on Latin America, notes that Cuba was the initiator of Marxist involvement in Angola and less of a Soviet proxy than in Ethiopia. In Angola, Cuba aided a movement it cooperated with for many years. Cuba's military involvement following South African intervention preceded the USSR's commitment. Cuban forces in Angola increased quickly to 36,000 in late 1975, decreased to 12,000 in the late 1970's before rising again in 1982 to 23,000 in 1983. Although the USSR lent critical logistical assistance in transporting Cuban troops and providing essential weaponry, it was generally induced into further participation by Cuban success and leadership.[3] In this regard, the Cuban presence apparently induced the Soviets to commit themselves further in Angola.

In Ethiopia, by contrast, Cuba and the USSR coordinated their military assistance and Moscow played a dominant role. Cuba aided a new government with whom it had few historical contacts. In the past, Cuba supported Marxist rebels in Eritrea against the central government of Emperor Selassie and avowedly Marxist-Leninsist Somalia, a recipient of Cuban military aid at the time.[4] In Ethiopia, Soviet generals assumed operational command of Cuban forces in the war against Somalia. In the words of LeoGrande, "the ideological lines of the conflict [between Ethiopian and Somalia] were much less clearly drawn and the geopolitical dimension of the conflict loomed much larger. Cuba thus proved far more vulnerable to the charge of acting as a Soviet proxy."[5] The Soviets were willing to become more deeply involved in Ethiopia and perhaps requested the Cuban role in Ethiopia.

Nonetheless, policy differences appeared in both Angola and Ethiopia. Castro chose not to have his forces participate in Soviet and Ethiopian campaigns against Eritrean secessionists, although he also elected not to continue aid to Eritreans. In Angola, Cuba is reported to have intervened on behalf of President Agostino Neto in 1977 to put down an attempted coup led by a pro-Soviet faction.

[2] U.S. Department of State. Soviet and East European Aid, 1981, p. 20.

[3] LeoGrande. Cuban-Soviet Relations and Cuban Policy in Africa, p. 13. LeoGrande writes: "The evidence indicates that through the summer of 1975, Cuba and the USSR acted independently in expanding their assistance programs to the MPLA as the civil war became increasingly internationalized. As the compatibility of their policies became clear, the Cubans and Soviets began coordinating their actions. They did *not* hatch a premeditated plot to intervene in Angola as an opening move in a joint offensive against western influence in Africa. On the contrary, increases in Cuban and Soviet aid were essentially reactive."

[4] Ibid. p. 23. See also, Katz, Mark N. The Soviet-Cuban Connection. International Security. Summer 1983, p. 94–95.

[5] LeoGrande, p. 20–21.

It is not known how much assistance the group received from Moscow or whether Moscow knew of the coup attempt in advance. Even if there are policy differences between Havana and Moscow, they do not appear to substantially impair their cooperation in Africa.

Cuban motivations for its enterprises in Africa have various origins. Aside from its ideological commitment to Africa, Cuba desires to strengthen its ties to the "socialist-oriented" governments of Africa, and assume a greater role in world affairs. In particular, Havana would like to assume the leadership of the non-aligned and Third World movements. Another goal is radical reduction of both its real and apparent dependence on Moscow and a demonstration of its value as an ally to Soviet foreign policy goals. The Cuban presence in Africa probably reduces its monetary indebtedness to Moscow by increasing its bargaining leverage when its repayments on loans come due. Since the mid-1970's, relations with Moscow have strengthened and the Soviets have increased their economic assistance and arms transfers to Cuba. Cuba's role in Africa has enhanced Havana's position in the nonaligned movement. Cuba has pushed the movement to adopt positions more sympathetic toward the USSR and to portray Moscow as the Third World's staunch ally, a development of clear benefit to the Soviets.

Cuban and Soviet policies in Africa are generally mutually reinforcing and supportive, despite some different perspectives and objectives. In the early 1980s, however, Castro may have shifted his active emphasis from Africa to Central America where opportunities for revolutionary gains appear to be greater. There are signs of a reduced Cuban commitment in Angola where Cuban troops do not engage South African forces, and Ethiopia, which may wish to reduce the number of expensive Cuban troops as the war with Somalia winds down. However, Havana seems certain to maintain its military advisory capacities in the rest of Africa and to contribute modest economic and technical skills where they are wanted.

B. East Germany: Special Role

Without the Soviet connection, the GDR's activities in Africa would probably be much more circumscribed than Cuba's. Originally, GDR economic and military assistance was designed to marshal African support for its campaign against West Germany. The circle of GDR friends in Africa expanded quickly with the dissolution of the Portuguese empire in Africa and the intensification of the decolonization struggle in Rhodesia and South West Africa. The GDR's principal partners in Africa are Ethiopia, Mozambique, Angola, Libya, Cape Verde, Algeria, Tanzania, Guinea-Bissau, and the SWAPO and ANC liberation movements. In the late 1970's, the number of high-level East German visits to Africa demonstrated the GDR's interests in developing ties to radical governments. Minister of Defense General Heinz Hoffmann visited Angola, Congo, Guinea-Bissau in 1978. In 1979, he went to Zambia, Mozambique, and Ethiopia. The General Secretary of the Socialist Unity Party and chairman of the Council of State Erich Honecker has travelled to Zambia, Angola, Mozambique, and Ethiopia. Honecker signed long-term treaties of friendship in Ethiopia, Mozambique, and Angola.

East Germany has focused its efforts in Africa on building a Marxist-Leninist infrastructure in nations where it is welcome. In Ethiopia, for example, the GDR helps the Soviet Union develop cadres and mass organizations. The youth wing of the communist Socialist Unity Party of the GDR, the Free German Youth (FDJ), organizes "Friendship Brigades" in Africa and is active in establishing a "revolutionary consciousness." [6] One author described them as "ambassadors in blue shirts." [7] East Germany also establishes educational institutions in several African states, among them Ethiopia, Mozambique, Angola and Guinea-Bissau. GDR advisers have built, supplied and established Marxist-Leninist curricula for various schools at all levels in these countries.[8]

The GDR, through the National People's Army (Volksarmee, NVA) and the State Security Service (SSD), provides allies with security and military assistance. It is estimated that there are GDR troops and advisers in Algeria (250), Libya (400), Congo (750), Angola (450), Ethiopia (250), Guinea (120), Mozambique (100), and Madagascar (300).[9] It is suspected that SWAPO and ANC guerrillas are being trained by East Germans in Africa and the GDR. East German assistance to Angola has been significant in securing the Soviets' predominant position. An unknown number of East Germans were reported flying MiG-21 aircraft during the civil war, for example.[10] East Germany may also have had a hand in instigating the Shaba I and II operations against Zaire by the Angola-based Front for the Liberation of the Congo in 1977 and 1978.[11]

To date, the GDR is most active in nations undergoing some form of struggle, either internal or external, and it has offered valuable services as a supplier of military goods and training. Like the Soviets, East Germans have had little to offer in economic terms to Africa. The GDR extends economic assistance to Africa in modest quantities but concentrates on nations with a "socialist orientation." In Ethiopia, for example, it is reportedly responsible for port modernization at Asab and Massawa. In Angola, it offers similar services and provides technicians where there are critical shortages of skilled personnel. African states are not generally clients of the finished industrial machinery exported by the GDR.[12]

---

[6] Glass, George A. East Germany in Black Africa: A New Special Role? The World Today. August 1980, p. 307.

[7] Fischer, Hans-Joachim. ABC and Multiplication Tables—Weapons in the Class Struggle: On the GDR's Pedagogical Work in Developing Countries. Deutschland Archiv, June 1982. Translation in Joint Publications Research Service. East Europe Report. No. 2048. August 26, 1982, p. 16.

[8] Ibid., p. 13–16.

[9] Sivard, Ruth Leger. World Military and Social Expenditures, 1983. Washington, World Priorities, 1983, p. 9.

[10] For more on GDR military assistance to Africa, see Melvin Croan. A New Afrika Korps? The Washington Quarterly. Winter 1980. p. 27. Croan says East Germans may have flown in the Nigerian Air Force against Biafra. He adds that GDR's involvement adds up to a "role as a chief proxy for the Soviet Union in plying arms, probably now supplanting the role traditionally played by Czechoslovakia as a supplier of arms and military equipment." (p. 28) Another source describes GDR activities in Ghana under the government of Flight Lt. Jerry Rawlings. East German intelligence services are said to discredit West German and U.S. policies with disinformation. See, Foreign Report. June 9, 1983.

[11] Valenta, Jiri and Butler, Shannon. "East German Security Policies in Africa." Michael Radu, ed. Eastern Europe and the Third World, p. 153–154.

[12] Sodaro, Michael. "The GDR and the Third World: Supplicant and Surrogate." Michael Radu, ed. Eastern Europe and the Third World. New York, Praeger, 1981, p. 121–122.

East Germany appears to have established itself as an important partner of the Soviet Union in building socialism in Africa and allying friendly African states more closely with the Soviet bloc. The economic aspects of the East-West competition in Africa pose the question of how the GDR can best remain an actor in African affairs since it has few economic resources and little trade with Africa. The resolution of military conflict in nations where the GDR is committed may lead East Germany to expand its efforts to institutionalize Leninist forms of government in order to ensure lasting influence in Africa for itself and the Soviet Union. Peaceful resolution of conflicts may contribute to the reduction of GDR non-economic assistance to some African states.

C. CHINA: COMPETITOR FOR SOVIET INFLUENCE

The early 1980's witnessed a revival of Chinese interest in African affairs coinciding with its generally greater activism among Third World nations. In the last half of the 1970's, Beijing sought a "strategic alliance" with the United States and Western Europe against Soviet "hegemonism." China also pursued stronger commercial ties with the West to modernize its economy. Both developments de-emphasized relations with the Third World. In 1982, at the 12th party congress, China announced a policy of equidistance between the superpowers in which the United States was identified, like the USSR, as a state with "hegemonist" aspirations. China's leaders began encouraging contacts with the Third World, supported the non-aligned movement more than before, stressed North-South economic issues, and stepped up its modest foreign aid programs.[13] Africa became an important part of Beijing's Third World activism which included Southeast Asia and the Middle East. China's renewed interest in Africa was demonstrated by the eleven-nation tour of Africa by Premier Zhao Ziyang from December 1982 to January 1983—the first by a high level Chinese leader since Premier Zhou Enlai visited Africa in 1964. China's return to the Third World reflected its concerns that it had ignored the region for too long and had thus lost considerable influence.

Although China has stressed its ties to the Third World since its creation in 1949, its credentials as a leader of the underdeveloped world had tarnished. The modernization drive of the late 1970s slowed as China reassessed its international role and Beijing saw better ties to the Third World as enhancing its political independence and promoting its leadership of the non-aligned movement. China's new assertiveness in the Third World is also permitted by stable political development since the death of Mao Zedong in 1976 and the end of the tumultuous Cultural Revolution. Signs of political stability apparently persuaded African states that Beijing can be a reliable partner. Beijing is far less concerned with the need for revolution than it was in the 1960s and nearly 1970s, and is worried more by the threat of Soviet advances in the Third World.[14]

China has apparently returned to the conclusion that it has much in common with the Third World in terms of economic devel-

---

[13] Copper, John F. China and the Third World. Current History. September 1983, p. 245.
[14] Harris, Lilian Craig. China's Third World Courtship. Washington Quarterly. Summer 1982, p. 129–130.

opment and political influence, but with different policy results. According to one China specialist, China realized that it is "disadvantageous to try to play 'power games' on the same level with such superpowers as the United States and the Soviet Union," and that "Chinese foreign policies can be more effective when approached from a Third World standpoint, using the 'strong assets of the weak.'" [15] China's increased involvement in the Third World reflects its judgment of the rising influence of Third World nations in international affairs. A Chinese commentator observed that "Today, the broad masses of African people, in opposing the power politics of the big powers, in their bid to preserve national independence and develop national economy and establish a new international economic order, have grown into a vigorous force in international politics." [16]

China's stated political objectives in Africa are to increase political stability and to promote economic development. Most interstate conflict and instability, in its view, serve only to invite Soviet and U.S. interference in the form of military aid that undermines Chinese influence. Participation in economic development promotes China's image of noninterference in African affairs. China tries to stress positive themes of independence, unity, economic development, and equidistance between the superpowers and attempts to identify itself with African views on issues. China also denies any aspirations to leadership or "hegemony" and attempts to present its involvement in Africa as a neutral, non-partisan actor interested only in what Africa itself desires. [17]

In the 1970's, China's prestige in Africa may have suffered when it sided with the United States and South Africa against Soviet and Cuban-supported forces in Angola. In 1978, Beijing unsuccessfully pressured African states to expel Cuba from the nonaligned movement in retaliation for its military involvement in Africa and its close ties to the Soviet Union.

In late 1982, however, China and Angola agreed to establish diplomatic relations despite the continued presence of Cuban troops and the history of Chinese assistance to anti-government UNITA rebels. Angola's reliance on Cuban forces had been an obstacle to a normalization of Chinese-Angolan relations. Beijing publicly conceded on both issues when it declared that the Cuban troops were an internal Angolan matter and it dismissed allegations that it was supporting UNITA forces. [18]

Premier Zhao's 1982–83 trip to Africa took him to Egypt, Algeria, Morocco, Guinea, Gabon, Zaire, Congo, Zambia, Zimbabwe, Tanzania, and Kenya. He stressed opposition to hegemonism and cooperation with the Third World. During the trip, Zhao cancelled a $100-million debt owed by Zaire, extended a $33 million loan to

---

[15] Okabe, Tatsumi. Chinese Diplomacy as Reflected at the Recent National People's Congress. China Newsletter. No. 47.

[16] Unsigned commentary. China & the World. No. 4. Beijing Review Foreign Affairs Series. 1983, p. 6.

[17] Ibid., p. 7–8. "In no way does China wish to seek hegemony, nor is it interested in a so-called position of leadership. What it is after is that all countries in the world, be it large or small, strong or weak, may take part in international affairs on an equal footing and live together in a friendly, peaceful way."

[18] Larkin, Bruce D. "China's Year in Africa: Renewal and Continuity." In, African Contemporary Record, 1982–83, p. A96.

Zimbabwe, and agreed to raise imports from Kenya. He refused to cancel a huge debt owned by Tanzania and Zambia for the Tanzam Railroad (linking Zambia to the seaport of Dar es Salaam), though the debt is a financial burden on the two African nations. He also agreed to sell between 60 and 80 F–7 fighters to Egypt. Zhao gave effusive support to black African political aspirations and castigated South Africa for its system of apartheid.[19] Zhao met with leaders of SWAPO (the Southwest African People's Organization) and the president of South Africa's African National Congress (ANC), Oliver Tambo. SWAPO President Sam Nujoma has in recent years visited China frequently which suggests that China is trying to forge close ties to the group despite its links to Moscow and that Nujoma may wish to diversify SWAPO's external relations.

Zhao repeatedly told his African hosts that threats to their stability came from Washington and Moscow, not Beijing. The Chinese Communist Party newspaper, the People's Daily, editorialized that "the African continent still remains unstable due to the disturbances and destruction caused by * * * the rivalry for spheres of influence between the superpowers. This has seriously affected the stability and development of African countries."[20] In the words of the Far Eastern Economic Review, Zhao's pitch was: "While developing countries can side with the United States or the Soviet Union if they wish, they can count on China for political support in helping to mould an independent voice for the Third World."[21] Zhao's aim was to persuade African states to reduce their reliance on the two superpowers and to burnish China's image as a champion of the Third World.

China hopes to check the spread of Soviet influence in Africa by enhancing its own image in the region. China has few economic resources to offer and little ability to export arms to Africa.[22] It cannot compete on the same level as the Soviet Union or the United States for influence in Africa. Nonetheless, Beijing's renewed campaign for better relations with regional African states may give some African states options to diversify their ties that they otherwise would not have. As a nation with a Marxist-Leninist doctrine, it can be an attractive partner for some African states who wish to maintain distance from European nations and the United States, as well as the USSR.

---

[19] Copper. China and the Third World, p. 247–248.
[20] Quoted in, Tyrrell, Roland. Zhao's African Odyssey. Far Eastern Economic Review. February 3, 1983, p. 24.
[21] Ibid.
[22] According to U.S. Government figures, China exported $555 million in weapons to sub-Saharan Africa from 1978 to 1982 (and an additonal $310 to Libya).

IX. CONCLUSION

The record of Soviet involvement in Africa has been mixed. In the past decade, the Soviets suffered setbacks in a number of countries including Uganda, Somalia, Egypt, Equatorial Guinea, Guinea, and the Sudan. Moscow would identify as successes Angola, Ethiopia, Mozambique and perhaps nations of lesser significance such as Benin, Cape Verde, Congo-Brazzaville and Guinea-Bissau. The military achievements and expansionism of the 1970's in Angola and Ethiopia gave way in the early 1980's to an emphasis on consolidation in Africa. Seth Singleton, a specialist on Soviet policies in Africa and the Third World, writes, in the context of the Soviet Union's Third World policy:

> Since 1980 Soviet efforts have shifted from expansion to consolidation; from exploitation of local quarrels to widespread 'friendship' and promotion of fronts against the United States; from emphasis on guns and the reach of Soviet 'might' to improving the Soviet image and discrediting the United States. The present Soviet policy tries to hold on to as many 'gains of socialism' as it can while playing on the Reagan administration's preoccupation with military power and its seeming conviction that Third World upheavals are of Soviet origin.[1]

Singleton's thesis seems an apt description of Soviet policy in sub-Saharan Africa. Moscow invested heavily in Ethiopia, Angola, and Mozambique and it is unclear whether similar opportunities will present themselves soon.

The presence of Cuban troops in Africa and the record of Soviet military involvement set a precedent that could embolden the USSR to act militarily in the future. The Soviet presence has quantitatively and qualitatively altered the balance of forces in Africa in its favor, but for how long remains to be seen.

The Soviet's capacity to deliver economic assistance has been questioned repeatedly by African countries. Moscow itself seems unwilling to set aside more than the comparatively modest amounts of aid it has extended in the past. Soviet aid will probably continue to be concentrated in nations allied to it or where the Soviets can expect commercial benefits for their own economy, as in Morocco and Guinea. At the same time, the USSR will attempt to increase its trade with capitalist African nations if it is in its interests, and similarly it will not object if its African friends seek Western economic aid as long as they remain "socialist-oriented" and, especially, dependent on Soviet security ties and are loyal to Soviet regional interests.

The trend in Soviet military assistance is as yet unclear. The possible winding down of the wars in Ethiopia (and the Ethiopian famine, which the Soviets can do little to alleviate) and in southern Africa (where recent agreements between Angola and Mozambique

---

[1] Singleton, Seth. 'Defense of the Gains of Socialism:' Soviet Third World Policy in the mid-1980s. The Washington Quarterly. Winter 1984, p. 102.

and South Africa indicate a temporary reduction of conflict) may lessen the opportunities for the expansion of Soviet influence. In the late 1970's and early 1980's, the Soviet Union demonstrated its readiness to deliver arms to sub-Saharan Africa in large quantities. Soviet arms transfers—concentrated in Angola, Ethiopia, and Mozambique, however—were much greater than those from the West. However, the USSR has cultivated other, new arms clients since the mid-1970's which may turn to Moscow for future aid and training. In any case, military deliveries are no more than crisis aid and are not a sure means of acquiring durable political influence. The dynamics of Africa's regional politics appear to guarantee a certain number of arms clients and temporary allies. Africa's chronic instability and the willingness of its leaders to seek outside support suggest that Moscow will always have a number of opportunities to spread its influence by means of military and security assistance.

While there are strong indications that Moscow will continue to expand its influence where possible, the current stress appears to be on the consolidation of gains in Africa. There are a number of factors that make further Soviet achievements difficult and may contribute to a mood of restraint and retrenchment in Africa. The leadership crisis in the USSR, since at least 1980 when Leonid Brezhnev fell ill, probably has dominated the attention of Kremlin officials. The effects of the leadership transition on Soviet foreign policy is hard to assess, but many speculate that it has inhibited Soviet policies in Europe and toward the United States and China; it is not unreasonable to suspect a similar effect in sub-Saharan Africa where Soviet interests are less compelling. Soviet leadership continuity may lead to the Kremlin giving greater attention toward its African clients as well as other African states.

Moscow also faces foreign policy issues of considerably greater importance than Africa. The deployment of NATO's intermediate-range nuclear weapons, arms control negotiations with Washington, attempts at rapprochement with China, the continuing war in Afghanistan, political unrest in Eastern Europe (particularly Poland), and security commitments in the Middle East and northeast Asia are drains on Soviet political and military resources. It is unlikely that Kremlin leaders lose much sleep over the dilemmas of Soviet policymaking in Africa when confronted with intransigent security issues closer to home.

Soviet officials also appear to be less optimistic about the possibilities of socialist development in Africa, despite the recent formation of a Marxist party in Ethiopia. African states, the Soviets know, are inherently unstable and they are governed by weak institutions. The dynamics of Africa's regional quarrels, tribal and ethnic identity, African nationalism, and the quest for economic progress are factors that can undermine the spread of Soviet (as well as Western) influence.

The Soviet Union appears to have come to a turning point in assessing whether it is cost-effective to maintain a strong presence in Africa. Moscow is now facing daunting costs in simply sustaining its influence as African states—particularly the USSR's close allies—face grave economic and military difficulties requiring substantial external assistance. The costs of expanding its influence by assuming heavier burdens in these countries may, for the time being, be too high when measured against the likely security, political, or economic gains. Soviet expansion in Africa could well have reached a point of diminishing returns. The Soviets may now look toward consolidating their impressive advances of the past decade, while waiting for another favorable "correlation of forces" to emerge at some future time.

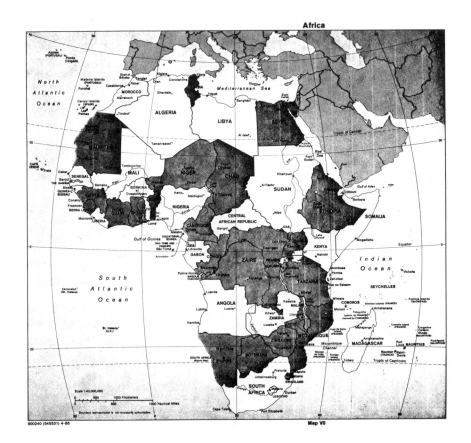

Africa

Map VII

PART V—LATIN AMERICA IN SOVIET THIRD WORLD POLICY, VARIATIONS ON REVOLUTION AND TRADITIONALISM [1]

> Warm greetings to the peoples of Latin America who are fighting against imperialism and reaction and for peace and democratic development of their countries! Peoples of the world! Demand an end to the aggressive actions of the United States against Nicaragua! Strive for the liberation of Grenada from American occupation!
>
> —Soviet slogans on the 67th anniversary of the Bolshevik Revolution, 1984.

> We Nicaraguans join today in the fraternal Soviet people's festivities since we are guided by the same desire to be free and independent and to struggle for peace, equality and solidarity among the world's peoples. That is why our two countries are united by ties of brotherhood and solidarity.
>
> —Daniel Ortega on the 67th anniversary of the Bolshevik Revolution, Nov. 10, 1984.

I. PERSPECTIVES AND TRENDS; OBJECTIVES AND INSTRUMENTALITIES

A. MULTIPLE PERSPECTIVES IN HARMONY AND CONTENTION

1. THE VIEW FROM LATIN AMERICA

a. *"Multipolarization" of power: Stimulus to independence*

At least potentially, Latin America is a major configuration of political and economic power in world affairs. Collectively comprising 20 of the independent republics of the New World, Latin America covers over 95 percent of the territory in the Western Hemisphere lying south of Mexico's northern border. (See Map 1) Rich in natural resources, with an estimated population of 370 million in 1981, including the Caribbean Islands, and having within its geographic reach some of the principal sea lanes of world communications, and being in close proximity to one world superpower, the United States, Latin America constitutes an impressive concentration of regional power and a geopolitical entity of the first order.

Yet only in recent years has Latin America attracted Soviet attention. Until Fidel Castro's successful revolution in Cuba in the late 1950's and early 1960's, it had a low priority in Soviet foreign policy calculations. "Geographic fatalism," as the Soviets say— meaning close proximity to the United States and thus geopolitically within its sphere—had placed limitations on their interests and accordingly on their activity.

---

[1] Prepared by Joseph G. Whelan, Senior Specialist in International Affairs, Congressional Research Service. First published on Dec. 17, 1984, as CRS Report No. 85–40 S; revised and updated.

Map 1

Two developments occurred in the post-World War II era that changed the context of the Soviet role in Latin America and fundamentally altered Latin American perceptions not only of the Soviet Union but perhaps equally important perceptions of their own role in international relations: One was the "mulitpolarization" or diffusion of power in world politics; [2] the other, the emergence of détente in East-West relations.

The global redistribution of power, recorded in Part I of this study, gave rise to the Third World as a new and prominent force in world politics. "Multipolarization" provided a stimulus to independence. Third World regions such as Latin America, heretofore relegated to a dependency status, were now able to play a much larger and more independent role in world affairs.

Detente in East-West relations further opened up possibilities for change: Detente made the Soviets more acceptable as a "traditional" participant in international relations; detente broadened Soviet access to Latin America and other Third World regions, increasing the possibilities for penetration and influence; but detente also gave Latin America a new opportunity to exercise its own power regionally, independently, bilaterally, and collectively.

Many Latin American leaders welcomed expanding ties with the Soviet Union. However much they despised the Soviet system, distrusted its leadership, and perceived Soviet foreign policy and local Communist Party leaders as antithetical to their countries' interests, still they saw rewards to be accrued in an expanding relationship with Moscow. No doubt they also gained some psychic satisfaction from exercising their right as sovereign independent states, as Cole Blasier, a Soviet and Latin American specialist at the University of Pittsburgh, suggests. Establishing closer relations with the Soviets, moreover, gave them room for maneuvering and potential bargaining leverage in any dealings with the United States. And finally, material benefits such as trade and technical assistance were to be gained, allowing sufficient economic diversity to reduce their dependency on the United States. [3]

In brief, Latin America has viewed international problems mainly from a regional North-South perspective, not from an East-West geostrategic perspective. Expanding relations with Moscow, therefore, caused no special problem for them. On the contrary it held out the promise of playing a larger and more independent role in world affairs and of improving their prospects for economic development.

b. Impact of anticolonialism and resentment of U.S. hegemony

A second major influence in shaping a distinct Latin American view of Soviet involvement in the Western Hemisphere is the anticolonial tradition in Latin American history and the subsequent

---

[2] Varas, Augusto. Ideology and Politics in Latin American-USSR Relations. Problems of Communism, v. 33, Jan.–Feb. 1984: 35. See also, Varas, Augusto. Soviet-Latin American Relations under United States Regional Hegemony. Washington, The Wilson Center, Smithsonian Institution, 1984. No. 140, p. 2. Prepared under the auspices of The Wilson Center's Latin American Program. Varas was a visiting fellow during 1983–1984.

[3] Blasier, Cole. The Giant's Rival: The USSR and Latin America. Pittsburgh, Pa., University of Pittsburgh Press, 1983, p. 132.

pervasive resentment among Latin Americans of U.S. hemispheric hegemony.

Not until the early 19th Century did the countries of Latin America, spurred on by the same historical forces of nationalism and a more distant vision of democratic idealism that had inspired the American Revolution, finally win their independence from Spain and Portugal. Much of the political disorder that followed these wars of national independence provoked U.S. military action for reasons of national security and in some cases to satisfy the popular demands of "Manifest Destiny." At mid-century, U.S. military forces conquered Mexico and annexed the so-called Mexican cession—much of what is now the American West and Southwest. In 1898, the United States went to war with Spain, liberating Cuba but also absorbing many of Spain's territorial possessions in the Caribbean and far Pacific. During the first three decades of the 20th Century U.S. military forces intervened intermittently in Central America, Mexico and the Caribbean. Military intervention was undertaken during this latter period largely for reasons of national security, and when the danger subsided, the United States withdrew its forces and encouraged adherence to the principle of collective security in the Western Hemisphere.

Nonetheless, however justified, these military conquests and interventions combined with a history of economic adventurers to create in the Latin American mind a deep-rooted, lasting tradition of hatred for "Yankee imperialism." Much of this attitude and resentment of U.S. presumptions of hemispheric hegemony exist today readily available for the Soviets to exploit.

Soviet efforts to cast their Third World policy in the context of anti-colonialism and anti-imperialism, specifically linking the United States to the reactionary colonial and imperial forces of today, have found fertile soil in Latin America. Speaking of Soviet attempts to "Satanize" the United States in Latin America, Robert S. Leiken, a Latin American specialist and senior fellow at the Carnegie Endowment for International Peace, rightly observes:

Many Latin Americans have come to regard world events as a contest between reactionary forces, led by "Yankee imperialism," of which they have had first-hand knowledge, and progressive forces, led, or at least assisted, by the Soviet Union, with which they have no direct experience.

Capitalizing on this deeply engrained prejudice, Soviet propagandists, aided by their Cuban allies have disseminated this worldview throughout Latin America in efforts to discredit the United States; but again as Leiken correctly notes, acceptance of this propaganda "has resulted primarily from U.S. economic, cultural, political, and military actions in Latin America." [4]

Thus, the Soviets are able to exploit to their political advantage an American vulnerability rooted largely in the past, while through distorted propaganda they minimize such culpabilities of their own as the conquest of Eastern Europe, military interventions in Hungary and Czechoslovakia, and the military occupation of Afghanistan.

---

[4] Leiken, Robert S. Eastern Winds in Latin America. Foreign Policy, no. 42, Spring 1981, p. 105.

c. Drawing on a revolutionary tradition

(1) The Iberic-Latin legacy

Linked to the second aspect of the Latin American view of Soviet involvement in the Western Hemisphere, that of anti-colonialism, is the vigorous revolutionary tradition that permeates the region. Three distinctive traditions seem to have shaped Latin American views on political philosophy, with each in different ways creating political tensions that often times led to revolution: The Iberic-Latin legacy; democratic idealism fostered by the Enlightenment; and Marxist Socialism. Elements of all three superimposed upon Latin American society have been in contention, often under adverse political and socio-economic environmental conditions that fueled a deeply engrained revolutionary spirit.

Integrated within the distinctive Iberic-Latin legacy, emanating from southern Europe, were such ideas, institutions and formative experiences as Roman Law and governance, the Thomistic tradition set within a hierarchically structured Roman Catholic Church, feudalism and the system of medieval guilds, and the prolonged struggle to expel the Moors. Assumptions about the governance of man were transformed concretely into absolutist centralization, the unification of social groups, and a militantly narrow religious outlook. "Running through this tradition," writes John D. Martz, III and David J. Myers of the Pennsylvania State University, "was the vision of an organic political community, the components of which were to harmonize the quest of man's self-fulfillment." [5]

This unique form of Iberian monism had branched off from the mainstream of Western intellectual thought before the Enlightenment and prior to the works of the major social contract theorists. Consequently, what took root in Latin America as a result of this legacy and the fortifying works of Spanish thinkers was a persisting belief that a well ordered political community was necessary. The impact of this intellectual stream that congealed in a theory of corporatism has remained, in the words of Martz and Myers, "strong and vibrant" in Latin America. [6]

(2) Influence of the enlightenment

In due course ideas associated with the enlightenment, that is, rationalism and humanism, were communicated to Latin America by Jesuit scholars. [7] Other strains of liberal-pluralist thought, such as those of Montesquieu, Voltaire, Locke, and Rousseau, also reached the New World. So important was their influence by the end of the 18th Century that scholars traditionally have acknowledged France and the United States as the ideological source of both the structure and substance of Latin American governments since 1810, while the influence of Spain has been minimized or ignored. [8] Nonetheless, such ideas of the enlightenment that fostered

---

[5] Martz, John D., III and David J. Myers. Understanding Latin American Politics: Analytic Models & Intellectual Traditions. Polity, v. 26, Winter 1983: 216–217.
[6] Ibid., p. 219.
[7] Ibid.
[8] Ibid., p. 221.

individual rights over collectivist ideas did not displace the earlier tradition, but rather were superimposed upon it.[9]

(3) Introduction of Marxism

The third tradition, Marxism with its emphasis on collectivism and social equality, was introduced into Latin America in the 20th Century. But the absence of advanced industrial capitalism, theoretically the nurturing ground for Marxism, among other factors, created obstacles to the spread of its influence. Nonetheless, efforts have been made to adapt Marxism to local conditions—witness the multiple variations in Latin America today—thereby contributing to the vitality of the Marxist tradition.[10] Thus Martz and Myers conclude:

> The Marxist current, then, further underlines the coexistence and admixture of intellecutal traditions in Latin America. Its intrinsic durability seems assured by the anguishing conditions under which so many still live.[11]

(4) Environmental conditions as spur to revolution

Specialists writing on expanding Soviet opportunities in Latin America uniformly emphasize the impact of the distressing social, economic and political milieu—the "anguishing conditions," noted above—that exist in much of the Latin American region. What Jiri Valenta, an American specialist in Soviet bloc and Latin American affairs, wrote about the "ongoing conflict" and "reasons for the revolutionary transformation occurring" in Central America in 1983 is applicable to many parts of Latin America:

> The present crises in Central America cannot be attributed solely to Cuban and Soviet interference. What is occurring in El Salvador and to varying degrees in other Central American counties, particularly the northernmost, is the rapid decay of *anciens regimes*. This process has been witnessed already in other Third World countries such as Ethiopia. The decay of outmoded political and economic structures and social orders is the result of the dynamic interaction of a number of factors internal to the countries themselves. The societies of Central America are polarized by antagonism between a small upper class and a very poor majority; in most of these countries the middle class remains weak and underdeveloped. Socioeconomic polarization and the past and existing oppressive regimes have contributed significantly to the rise of internal and interregional conflict in these countries.[12]

Societies in clear need of political and social reform, economic reform and development coexist with political traditions and institutions that span the spectrum from political-military authoritarianism on the right, through regimes and political forces professing democratic liberalism in the center, on to those like Castro's brand of Communism and other Socialist varieties (Maoism, for example) on the extreme left. Adverse environmental conditions activate revolutionary traditions that in turn create opportunities for Soviet intervention. Thus W. Raymond Duncan, a specialist on the Third World at the State University of New York (Brockport), could cor-

---

[9] Ibid., p. 222.
[10] Ibid., p. 225.
[11] Ibid. For an analysis of the difficulties in establishing an American-style pluralistic democracy in Latin America, see Dealy, Glen C. The Pluralistic Latins. Foreign Policy, No. 57, Winter 1984-85: 108-127. Valuable insights into this problem were provided by Rubens Medina, Chief, Hispanic Law Division, Law Library, Library of Congress.
[12] Valenta, Jiri. Soviet and Cuban Responses to New Opportunities in Central America. In, Feinberg, Richard E., ed. Central America: International Dimensions of the Crisis. New York, Holmes and Meier, 1982, Chap. 6, p. 128-129.

rectly say in writing on the Cuban Revolution, "In one sense at least Latin America fell into the Soviet lap." He gave this explanation:

The Soviet-Cuban affair matured against a background of change in the rest of Latin America that created conditions favorable to an increased Soviet presence there. Foremost among these forces was the drive for economic development, which evolved out of the region's rapid urbanization. population explosion and the food shortages accompanying it, an increased skewing of income, and worsening of the ever-present unemployment. By 1973 when OPEC . . . sharply increased the price of oil, all of the above problems were aggravated. The drive for economic development was accompanied by openness to political experimentation: to wit, Mexico's mixture of capitalism and socialism in the postwar period; Cuba's . . . revolution; military reformism in Brazil (1964) and Peru (1968); Chile's socialist experiment (1970–1973); a leftist socialism in Guyana (1970 onward) and Jamaica (1972–1980).[13]

d. Distinctive hemispheric self-interests

(1) Tendency toward independence and decline of U.S. hegemony

The redistribution of world power in the postwar era, the impact of anti-colonialism combined with widespread resentment against U.S. hemispheric hegemony, and the reality of a durable, vibrant and relevant revolutionary tradition appear to have had maturing effect on Latin America. For not only has Latin America come to have its own distinctive hemispheric interests, but also the desire and often the wherewithal to seek and achieve those interest independently, bilaterally, and collectively.

The Cuban Revolution in 1959 now appears to have been a watershed in the international politics of Latin America. Leiken asserts that it "marked the beginning of the end of the U.S. era in Latin American history."[14] He could also have asserted that it marked the beginning of a new Soviet era in Latin America. Thereafter, the United States could not prevent the Cuban Revolution from becoming a symbol of the resurgent popular nationalism of the 1960's and a powerful new revolutionary force in this hemisphere linked to the Soviet Union. Nor could it prevent the intrusion of the Soviet presence and the inclination of many Latin Americans to use Moscow as a leverage against the United States.[15] Valuing less dependency on the United States and more the pursuit of an independent course particularly in economic development, they tended to give greater importance to North-South regional issues than to East-West geostrategic problem

In brief, Latin Americans, like so many other Third World peoples, began to see new opportunities for themselves in a changing international political environment; and when possible, they took them.

---

[13] Ducan, W. Raymond. Soviet Interests in Latin Amercia: New Opportunities and Old Constraints. Journal of Inter-American Studies and World Affairs, v. 26, May 1984: 165–166.
[14] Leiken, Robert S. Soviet Strategy in Latin America. Published with The Center for Strategic and International Studies, Georgetown University. The Washington Papers/93, v. 10, New York, Praeger, 1982, p. 3.
[15] Varas, Ideology and Politics in Latin-American-USSR Relations, p. 35–36.

(2) Concrete forms of independent action

(a) Expanding diplomatic relations

Latin American perceptions of their own self-interest have taken on a variety of concrete forms.[16] Displaying a new self-confidence and global assertiveness in the 1970's, Latin American nations established full diplomatic relations with the Soviet Union. In 1960, the Soviets had diplomatic relations with only three Latin American countries—Cuba, Brazil, and Argentina. By the mid-1970's virtually every major South American and several Caribbean and Central American countries had established relations with Moscow.[17]

(b) Expanding economic relations

Expansion of diplomatic ties led to further expansion of trade. In 1964, the Soviet Union had trade relations with only four Latin American countries; by 1975, the number increased to 20.[18] Soviet commerce with Latin America, excluding Cuba, increased from $124 million in 1970 to $4.9 billion in 1981.[19] Latin America also looked to Moscow for technical assistance, particularly in the development of its vast hydroelectric resources.[20] Soviet military goods also found markets in Latin America. In 1981, for example, the Soviet bloc concluded agreements in Latin America valued at $115 million.[21]

Moreover, nationalization of foreign holdings in Latin America, another indicator of independence, gained momentum during the late 1960's. Legislation restricting foreign equity and profit repatriation was also widespread in the 1970's, as were protests against discriminatory U.S. commercial legislation. By the end of the 1970's, less than 33 percent of Latin American exports went to the United States, a decline from 50 percent two decades before.[22]

(c) Going it alone in foreign policy

In foreign policy Latin American independence has been forcefully registered, the most extreme cases being Cuba, Grenada and Nicaragua. In the 1970's, Latin American countries, uniting behind Panama, demanded reform in the Organization of American States (OAS), spurned the Inter-American Treaty of Reciprocal Assistance (the so-called Rio Treaty of 1947), lifted the embargo against Cuba (still maintained by the United States), voted for Communist China's admission to the United Nations, and supported Arab positions against Israel. Widespread spurning of the U.S. boycott of the 1980 Olympic Games in Moscow demonstrated how far Latin America had moved from the days of dependency on the United States.[23]

---

[16] See, Leiken, Soviet Strategy in Latin America, p. 2–6.
[17] Luers, William H. The Soviets and Latin America: A Three Decade U.S. Policy Tangle. The Washington Quarterly, Winter 1984: 8.
[18] Leiken, Soviet Strategy in Latin America, p. 6.
[19] Duncan, Soviet Interests in Latin America, p. 166.
[20] Blasier, The Giant's Rival, p. 134.
[21] U.S. Dept. of State. Bureau of Intelligence and Research. Soviet and East European Aid to the Third World, 1981. Washington, 1983, p. 2. (Publication 9345).
[22] Leiken, Soviet Strategy in Latin America, p. 3–4.
[23] Ibid., p. 4–5.

This tendency towards independence in foreign policy was evident also in the deepening of Latin American political contacts in the Third World and Western Europe.[24] It has been most recently manifested in efforts by the Contadora Group (Colombia, Mexico, Panama, and Venezuela), acting on their own, to bring about peace in Central America. Less significant but still making the point is Panama's insistence during negotiations with the United States that the 38-year-old School of the Americas located in Panama for training Latin American military officers be placed under Panamian and not U.S. leadership.[25]

Notably, the same spirit of independence has sometimes characterized the relationship between Cuba and the Soviet Union. During the mid-to-late 1960's Castro pursued an avowed revolutionary line in open defiance of Moscow which at the time was pursuing a more conciliatory tactic.

The same Latin American independent attitude was only recently manifested in another way; namely, opposition to the Vatican's doubts about the Christian validity of the so-called "Liberation Theology." This new theology, heretical some critics contend, is an attempt by some Latin American theologians to reconcile Christianity with Marxism as a means of revitalizing and reconstituting the Roman Catholic Church in Latin America. It has been described as being "above all else an indigenous theology of the oppressed and poor."[26] "To the skeptical eye" of one critic, however:

liberation theology for all its good intentions promises a mirror image of the Latin American authoritarian societies of the past, but this time of the left rather than the right. Once again, economic decisions will be state-controlled. Once again, many theologians will identify Christianity with the Latin American state.[27]

Though this doctrine of socio-economic reform has been criticized by the Vatican, it has, nonetheless, won acceptance among many of Latin America's 325 million Roman Catholics.[28]

(3) Projecting a different image: Confidence, maturity and independence

The view from Latin America has changed markedly in the three decades since the Soviets, redirecting their policy from continentalism to globalism, moved out into the Third World. No longer a dependency of the United States, Latin America seems to project a different image, one of confidence, maturity and independence. As realists, Latin Americans, except for Cubans, value the American connection for economic and political reasons, but they also want to do business with the Soviets, as an exercise of their own national sovereignty, when their interests dictate such a course. And these interests vary, from the Cubans who find the Soviet Union a pro-

---

[24] Ibid., p. 5.
[25] Halloran, Richard. U.S. Military School to Quit Panama. The New York Times, Aug. 18, 1984, p. 4.
[26] Pastor Jeffrey A. Galbraith, St. Paul's Lutheran Church, Greenfield, Mass., in, The Wall Street Journal, Sept. 14, 1984, p. 29.
[27] Novak, Michael. The Case Against Liberation Theology. The New York Times Magazine, Oct. 21, 1984: 94.
[28] For a discussion of this problem along with excerpts from the Vatican's essay entitled, "Instructions on Certain Aspects of the 'Theology of Liberation,'" see, The New York Times, Sept. 4, 1984, p. A1 and A10; and Goodman, Walter. Church's Activist Clerics: Rome Draws the Line. The New York Times, Sept. 6, 1984, p. A1 and A14.

tector and maintainer of their revolution and the Sandinistas who welcome Soviet political, economic, and military support in the winning of their revolution; to the Argentines who value the Soviet market for their grain no less than Soviet political support against Britain in the Falklands War; and to the other South American countries, except Chile, who look to the Soviet Union for economic assistance in developing their hydroelectic power, military purchases, and profitable markets for their agricultrual products.

Latin Americans have, apparently, accepted the decline of the hemispheric community idea and the expanding Soviet presence in the Western Hemisphere as something of historic inevitabilities— though recently concern for Soviet-Cuban intervention has been growing in neighboring Latin American governments.[29] In brief, Latin Americans seem to feel confident of their ability to manage their own destiny. Thus the essence of the view from Latin America, one that tends to emphasize regionalism over global geostrategic concerns, is hemispheric self-determination.[30] Perhaps William D. Rogers, former Assistant Secretary of State for Inter-American Affairs, best summed up this view when he wrote:

> Latin America—on this matter [that is, resistance to encroachments on their national sovereignty]—seeks independence and freedom from intervention beyond all else. Different countries experiment with different ways of arranging their domestic order and responding to the international economic crisis. But all are committed to the preservation of their own independence and integrity.[31]

2. THE VIEW FROM THE UNITED STATES

a. From hegemonism to hemispheric cooperation

The United States views Soviet encroachments into Latin America in pursuit of its Third World goals as a contending superpower. The United States is determined to protect American vital national security interests and ultimately to maintain a position of preeminence in the Western Hemisphere. This preeminence, bound so closely to preserving vital national interests, has been transformed in the present era from what had been called a coercive "hegemonic presumption"[32] to a spirit of hemispheric cooperation. The report of the Kissinger Commission on Central America captured the essence of this transformation when it defined U.S. purposes in the late 20th Century, internationally and in this hemisphere, as "cooperation, not hegemony or domination; partnership, not confrontation; a decent life for all, not exploitation."[33]

---

[29] Leiken, Soviet Strategy in Latin America, p. 102.

[30] Varas writes: "My main hypothesis is that the Soviet-Latin American linkages are conditioned by United States-Soviet Union relations; that these relations [that is, Soviet-Latin American] are politically and economically profitable for both parties; and that these developments pose no threat against the United States nor a reduction in its strategic security." (Varas, Soviet-Latin American Relations under United States Regional Hegemony, p. 1.)

[31] In the preface to Leiken's, Soviet Strategy in Latin America, p. ix.

[32] Leiken, Soviet Strategy in Latin America, p. 1.

[33] U.S. President. Report of the National Bipartisan Commission on Central America. Washington, Jan. 1984, p. 8.

b. The perspective of history

(1) Expansion at the expense of Hispanic America

Three elements seem to constitute the American perspective on Latin America: the historical, the geostrategic, and the regional.

Consider first the historical. The history of the United States has been inextricably bound to the history of Hispanic America.[34] At its beginning the United States was confined to the sparsely inhabited territory east of the Mississippi; Britain held Canada; and Spain possessed the Floridas and claimed the territory west of the Mississippi. Territorial expansion, the driving force of American history, was achieved at the expense of a reluctant but weakened Spain and a still weaker Mexico, sometimes by purchase as in the case of the Floridas and others by military conquest as in the territory acquired in the Mexican War.

U.S. success in national expansion at the expense of Hispanic America, carried forth against a background of international contention on the respective virtues and vices of Latin and Anglo-Saxon civilizations, deposited a residue of resentment mixed with envy among many Latin Americans. Americans, confident that their Manifest Destiny in the mid-to-late 19th Century was ordained by Providence, took on an air of supreme confidence and seemed not to doubt their superiority over their Latin neighbors, culturally, socially, politically, economically and even in matters of religion.[35]

(2) Monroe's Doctrine: Hemispheric privilege as a "natural right"

American hemispheric power evolved within the textual confines of the Monroe Doctrine.[36] This fundamental American shibboleth categorically, and unilaterally, ruled out further European colonization in the Westen Hemisphere; termed the extension of the European system to any portion of this hemisphere "as dangerous to our peace and safety"; and pledged U.S. abstention from European affairs. Until the United States itself became sufficiently powerful to enforce this doctrine, it had to rely on British power and diversionary intra-European conflicts to prevent any infringements.[37]

Applied selectively in the area comprising Mexico, Central America and the Caribbean Basin where American security interests

---

[34] For an earlier interpretive analysis of U.S. policy in Latin America by a leading American diplomatic historian, see, Bemis, Samuel Flagg. The Latin American Policy of the United States: An Historical Intrepretation. New York, Harcourt, Brace, 1943. 470 p.

[35] To sample the flavor of this intense spirit of American nationalism, see, Smith, J.H. The War With Mexico. New York, Macmillan, 1919. 2 vols.

[36] The standard work on the Monroe Doctrine is, Perkins, Dexter. A History of the Monroe Doctrine. Revised edition. Boston, Little, Brown, 1955. 467 p. This is a synthesis of the published monographs by Perkins on the Monroe Doctrine.

[37] A significant precursor of the no-transfer principle in the Monroe Doctrine was Jefferson's statement in 1808 strongly opposing the acquisition of Cuba by Britain or France. Suggestive of the American presumption that its national security was bound close to Cuba is the instruction by Secretary of State John Quincy Adams in April 1823, eight months before the declaration of the Monroe Doctrine, to the U.S. Legation in Madrid in which he states that "the annexation of Cuba to our federal republic will be indispensable to the continuance and integrity of the Union itself." Adams saw this outcome as a result of the "law of political gravitation" in which Cuba, "disjoined from its own unnatural connexion with Spain, and incapable of self-support, can gravitate only towards the North American Union, which, by the same law of nature, cannot cast her off from its bosom." Implied in the Adams statement was the reaffirmation of Jefferson's "no-transfer" principle. (Bailey, Thomas A. A Diplomatic History of the American People. Seventh edition. New York, Appleton-Century-Crofts, 1964, p. 286.)

were most vulnerably exposed, the Monroe Doctrine and its corollaries, stated and unstated, provided the textual basis for American hegemony in the Western Hemisphere and essentially established the conditions for relations between the United States and its Latin neighbors. In times of national danger, as in the onset of World War I, the United States responded to political disorders and revolutionary upheavals in the Caribbean, Mexico and Central America with military power in order to forestall any threats to its security. Prolonged military occupations, often times intended to protect and preserve private American economic interests, were customary.

Thus the United States became the policeman of this hemisphere, and the Monroe Doctrine was its "big stick." As Walter Lippmann wrote four decades ago, many Americans came to think that "our privileged position" in this hemisphere was "a natural right." [38] Only with the softening spirit of the Clark Memorandum in 1928 that repudiated the intrusive "corollaries" of the Monroe Doctrine, set into motion the eventual withdrawal of American occupation forces, and ended the protectorate over Cuba—in brief returning the doctrine to its initial purpose directed against Europe, not Latin America—and only with the "Good Neighbor Policy" of President Franklin D. Roosevelt in the 1930's, did the United States in effect multilateralize the meaning and application of the doctrine basing hemispheric relationships on the principle of collective security. [39]

Thus the United States was able to enter World War II with the assurance that its "strategic rear" would be protected. And so it remained, at least for about 15 years into the postwar period when an anti-Soviet hemispheric consensus took shape during the Cold War.

(3) Castro's revolution; enter the Soviets

Castro's successful revolution in Cuba during 1959–60 opened a new era in U.S.-hemispheric relations. It was, as the Kissinger Commissions report said, "a seminal event in the history of the Americas," adding, "a fact appreciated almost immediately by the Soviet Union." [40] For Cuba was to become an instrument and Castro a "point man" for Soviet Third World policy not only in Latin America but also in Africa. Though ridiculed by Soviet leader Nikita S. Khrushchev as having "outlived its times" and had died "a natural death," the Monroe Doctrine, as it matured since the 1930's into a hemispheric concept of collective security, provided the unstated premise for the U.S. response, supported by Latin America, to the Soviet threat of threats, the 1962 Cuban missile crisis.

Whether this concept will ever again be a premise for collective hemispheric action in response to an outside threat will no doubt depend upon the degree of a shared awareness of the threat, acknowledgment of a binding mutual interest, and a collective willingness to confront it. Recent upheavals in Central America and

[38] Quoted in, Kissinger Commission's Report, p. 91.
[39] Bailey, A Diplomatic History of the American People, p. 681.
[40] Kissinger Commission's Report, p. 88.

the Caribbean Basin, notably the U.S. invasion of Grenada carried out at the invitation of some Caribbean governments, reveal a clear conflict between the Reagan Administration, which perceives an imminent threat in that region from Soviet-Cuban sponsored Communist-left wing subversion, and some of the Latin American countries, which appear to be less certain of the danger and look to deeper economic and social problems as primary causes of concern. Expressing the texture and tone of the Administration's approach to the Central American crisis, the Kissinger Commission report reflects the deep anxiety felt by many Americans:

> The United States cannot accept Soviet military engagement in Central America and the Caribbean beyond what we reluctantly tolerate in Cuba.
> We will also need to define specific situations as precisely as possible and to make those definitions clear to Moscow. At the same time we must avoid the inference that Soviet actions we have not proscribed are thus acceptable to us. If we do challenge directly any particular Soviet military activity in the region, we must be prepared to prevail.[41]

In a strict construction of the Monroe Doctrine, Gaddis Smith, an American diplomatic historian at Yale University, concludes an historical commentary on the legacy of the doctrine with this somewhat ironic but relevant statement on possible unilateralism in the future:

> Despite an occasional call from the political right to "remember the Monroe Doctrine," it is unlikely that 10 million school children will ever again have to endure a reading of the old message or that a high official will again call the doctrine "the most fundamental of our foreign policies." But the Doctrine's concepts will remain alive, although unnamed, as long as the American Government and people believe it is right and necessary for the United States to act unilaterally in this hemisphere, to intervene in the affairs of other nations or to define alone what standards of international law the United States will or will not follow.[42]

A return to the original meaning of the Monroe Doctrine, at least in its reference to an outside threat to U.S. national security, has never been ruled out. Given the diffusion of power in this hemisphere, the decline of the community idea and the differing perceptions of regional interests within a global context, such a reversion to old patterns of national behavior, especially in times of an acute East-West crisis, could become an acceptable, necessary, even irresistible, option.

(4) Uncertainty on U.S. historic role

In brief, the American historical experience in Hispanic America inevitably colors its perspective on relations with Latin America and on Moscow's role in this hemisphere. Many Americans perceive the stakes to be high; the degree of potential threat to U.S. security, real; and the global character of the Soviet-American contest in which Latin America is now a vital part, a fact of international life. Such attitudes seem destined to rekindle the deep-rooted spirit of American nationalism in defense of U.S. hemispheric interests. But there are dissenters, many powerful and well placed, as in the Congress, who caution against a U.S. military interven-

---

[41] Kissinger Commission's Report, p. 122–123.
[42] Smith, Gaddis. The Legacy of Monroe's Doctrine. The New York Times Magazine, Sept. 9, 1984: 128.

tion in Central America that might create another Vietnam: They tend to downgrade the Soviet-Cuban danger.[43]

c. From the East-West geostrategic perspective

(1) Threats to SLOC

The second element of the American perspective on Latin America and Soviet involvement in the Western Hemisphere is the geostrategic; that is, the inclination to see the region, particularly Central America and the Caribbean Basin, strictly within the context of the Soviet-American global rivalry and specifically in terms of U.S. security requirements.

Russia's global reach into the Third World, backed by expanding Soviet nuclear and conventional forces, particularly the expansion of the Soviet Navy, has alarmed many Americans. Reflecting the geostrategic perspective, Leiken categorically states that the Soviet-Cuban intervention in Angola during the mid-1970's, the first major overseas projection of Soviet power, "marked the beginning of a Soviet global strategic offensive" [44] and that this forward policy of globalism threatens American security interests in Latin America. Observers from this perspective focus principally on the Soviet threat to the vital sea lines of communication (SLOC) in the Atlantic, Caribbean, and Central American region.[45] (See maps 2, 3, 4, 5, and fig. 1.)

The United States has always been a sea-faring nation and commerce its life's blood which explains why the first principle in its diplomatic history since the founding of the Republic has been "freedom of the seas." Maps 2, 3, 4 and 5 visually portray the importance of SLOCs in the Latin American region to U.S. security; Figure 1 provides the official explanations. The relevance of the Caribbean and Gulf of Mexico to U.S. security interests is highlighted by the historical fact that in every major Pacific-Asian war involving the United States—World War II, the Korean War and war in Vietnam—logistical support for military supplies came largely from the East Coast and Gulf Coast ports of the United States, not from the West Coast which seems more logical. The reason for this is the lack of what is called "through-put" facilities on the West Coast for logistically sustaining military operations in the Pacific-Asian region.[46] Official acknowledgment of the estimate that the center of gravity of the world economy may be shifting to

[43] For a discussion of Congress in the unfolding Central American crisis, see, Destler, I.M. The Elusive Consensus: Congress and Central America. In, Leiken, Robert S., ed. Central America: Anatomy of Conflict. Published in cooperation with Carnegie Endowment for International Peace. New York, Pergamon, 1984. Chapt. 15.

[44] Leiken, Soviet Strategy in Latin America, p. 102.

[45] For Leiken's perception of the geostrategic threat see, Eastern Winds in Latin America, pp. 94–96. Taking into account the Soviet's global strategy, Leiken suggests that the Soviets have undertaken "an extensive flanking movement directed at the maritime life lines of Europe and Japan." Cuba and the Central American-Caribbean Basin play a vital part in this movement; as he says: "Soviet military writers recognize publicly that U.S. strategic freedom in other parts of the globe depends on stability in the Caribbean." (p. 95) Leiken elaborates on the strategic significance of the Caribbean Basin projecting various scenarios to emphasize its importance in his, Soviet Strategy in Latin America, pp. 61–72.

[46] This matter is discussed in, Gannon, Edmund J. The Panama Canal and the Panama Canal Zone: Some of Their Contributions to Strategic Mobility and Logistic Support. Washington, The Library of Congress, Congressional Research Service, Dec. 19 1977, 68 p.

the Pacific-Asian region suggests still further the importance of un-impeded SLOCs to U.S. security.[47]

President Reagan shares this perspective, as evidenced in his radio address of April 14, 1984. Repeating his concern about Nicaragua's joining with the Soviet Union and Cuba in trying "to install Communism by force throughout this hemisphere," the President cited statistics as proof of the vast military investment the Soviets and their Cuban allies have been making in Nicaragua. "What I've said today is not pleasant to hear," he said, "but it is important that you know that Central America is vital to our interests and to our security." "We cannot turn our backs on this crisis at our doorstep," he said.[48]

The Kissinger Commission report spells out in geostrategic terms the potential threat emanating from a Soviet-Cuban presence in Central America, citing the adverse effects on the global balance, the threat to the Nation's sea lanes, and the impairment of U.S. credibility globally—"The triumph of hostile forces in what the Soviets call the 'strategic rear' of the United States would be read as a sign of U.S. impotence" it says.[49] The report sums up the "large stakes" the United States has in the present Central American conflict; they include preventing:

A series of developments which might require us to devote large resources to defend the southern approaches to the United States, thus reducing our capacity to defend our interests elsewhere.

A potentially serious threat to our shipping lanes through the Caribbean.

A proliferation of Marxist-Leninist states that would increase violence, dislocation, and political repression in the region.

The erosion of our power to influence events worldwide that would flow from the perception that we were unable to influence vital events close to home.[50]

(2) Seeing Central America through geostrategic glasses

Supporters of a more vigorous and intrusive policy in Central America thus tend to place great emphasis on the geostrategic aspects of the problem. For them the central question is one of geopolitics: They tend to be more concerned about the role of Moscow and its ally Cuba and less about the regional aspects of the prob-

---

[47] Pacific Rim: America's New Frontier. U.S. News & World Report, Aug. 20, 1984: 45–51. President Reagan said: "You cannot help but feel that the great Pacific basin—with all its nations and all its potential for growth and development—that is the future." Former Under Secretary of State Lawrence Eagleburger noted that the consequences for the United States is a "shift of the center of gravity of U.S. foreign policy from the transatlantic relationship toward the Pacific basin and particularly Japan."

[48] Gwertzman, Bernard. Reagan Says Crisis in Region Compels Aid to Salvador. The New York Times, April 15, 1984, p. 12.

[49] Kissinger Commission's Report, p. 92–93. In underscoring the importance of the sea lanes, the Commission notes: "Such a deterioration in Central America would also greaty increase both the difficulty and the cost of protecting these lines of communications themselves. Under present plans, some 50 percent of the shipping tonnage that would be needed to reinforce the European front, and about 40 percent of that required by a major East Asian conflict, would have to pass from the Gulf of Mexico through the Caribbean-Central American zone. These same sea routes also carry nearly half of all other foreign cargo, including crude oil, shipped to this country."

[50] Ibid., p. 93.

lem—matters such as economic poverty, political oppression, and social injustices that have fueled discord and revolution in the region.

d. The view of the regionalist

(1) Examining the problem at its roots

The regionalist, the third element in the American perspective, tends to go to the source of the problem. Though conscious of other perspectives and their importance, the regionalist, nonetheless, seems more inclined to view the problem from the Latin American side and accordingly examines the regional roots of the problem as a first priority. In brief, looking from the inside out rather than the outside in.

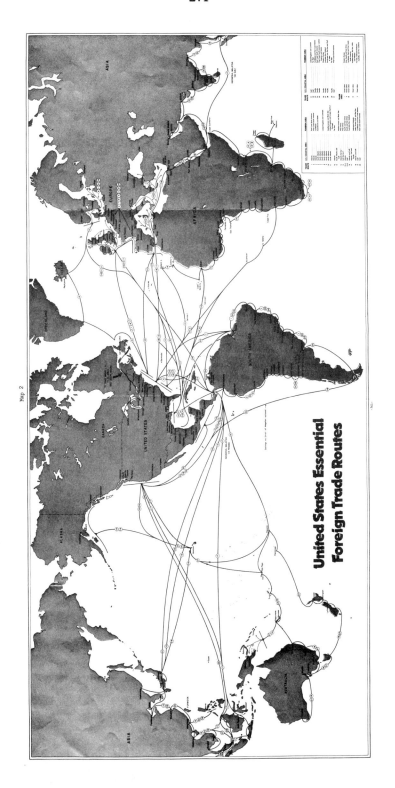

Map 2

United States Essential Foreign Trade Routes

See key (Legend) on page 272.

LEGEND

	U.S. coastal area	Foreign area
Trade route:		
1	Atlantic	East Coast South America
2	Atlantic	West Coast South America
4	Atlantic	Caribbean
6	North Atlantic	Scandinavia and Baltic
5	North Atlantic	United Kingdom and Continent
7	North Atlantic	United Kingdom and Continent
8	North Atlantic	United Kingdom and Continent
9	North Atlantic	United Kingdom and Continent
10	North Atlantic	Mediterranean and Black Sea
11	South Atlantic	United Kingdom and Europe North of Portugal
12	Atlantic	Far East
13	South Atlantic and Gulf	Mediterranean and Black Sea
14	Atlantic-Service 1	West Africa
14	Gulf-Service 2	West Africa
15–A	Atlantic	South and East Africa
15–B	Gulf	South and East Africa
16	Atlantic and Gulf	Australia-New Zealand
17	Atlantic, Gulf and Pacific	Indonesia-Malaysia
18	Atlantic and Gulf	India, Persian Gulf and Red Sea
19	Gulf	Caribbean and East Coast Mexico
20	Gulf	East Coast South America
21	Gulf	United Kingdom and Continent
22	Gulf	Far East
23	Pacific	Caribbean and East Coast Mexico
24	Pacific	East Coast South America
25	Pacific	West Coast South America, Central America and Mexico
26	Pacific	Western Europe
27	Pacific	Australia New Zealand
28	Pacific	Southwest Asia, Red Sea and Gulf of Aden
29	Pacific	Far East
31	Gulf	West Coast South America
Trade area:		
I	Great Lakes	Western Europe
II	Great Lakes	West, South and East Africa
III	Great Lakes	Caribbean, East and West Coasts South America
IV	Great Lakes	Mediterranean, Red Sea, India and Pakistan
V	Great Lakes	Far East, Indonesia, Malaysia, Australia, and New Zealand

Source: U.S. Maritime Administration, Dec. 7, 1983.

273

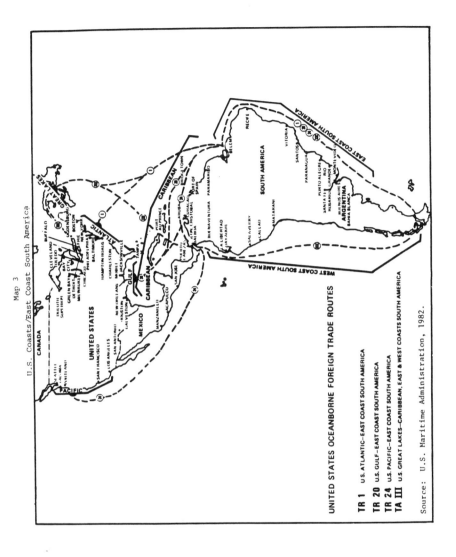

Map 3
U.S. Coasts/East Coast South America

UNITED STATES OCEANBORNE FOREIGN TRADE ROUTES

TR 1 U.S. ATLANTIC–EAST COAST SOUTH AMERICA

TR 20 U.S. GULF–EAST COAST SOUTH AMERICA

TR 24 U.S. PACIFIC–EAST COAST SOUTH AMERICA

TA III U.S. GREAT LAKES–CARIBBEAN, EAST & WEST COASTS SOUTH AMERICA

Source: U.S. Maritime Administration, 1982.

Map 4

U.S. Coasts/West Coast Central America, South America and Mexico

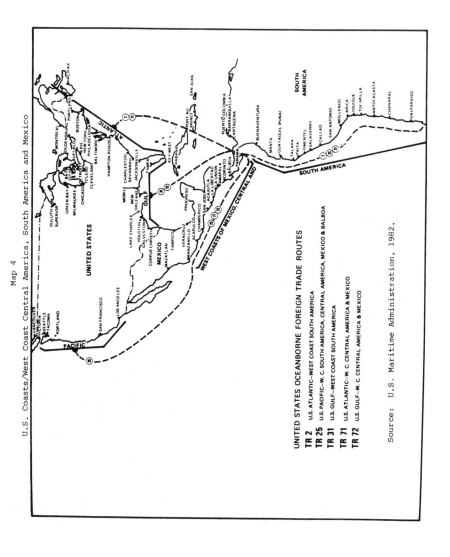

UNITED STATES OCEANBORNE FOREIGN TRADE ROUTES

TR 2 U.S. ATLANTIC—WEST COAST SOUTH AMERICA

TR 25 U.S. PACIFIC—W. C. SOUTH AMERICA, CENTRAL AMERICA, MEXICO & BALBOA

TR 31 U.S. GULF—WEST COAST SOUTH AMERICA

TR 71 U.S. ATLANTIC—W. C. CENTRAL AMERICA & MEXICO

TR 72 U.S. GULF—W. C. CENTRAL AMERICA & MEXICO

Source: U.S. Maritime Administration, 1982.

275

Map 5

U.S. Coasts/Caribbean

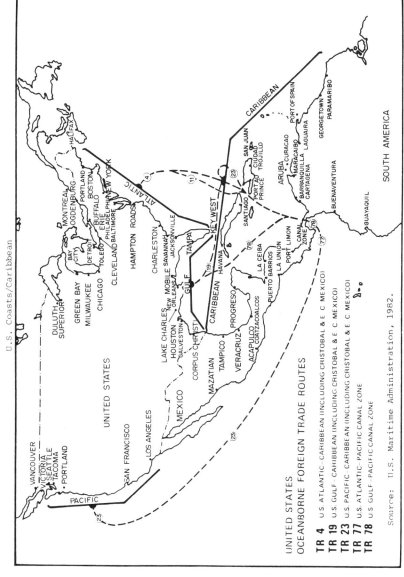

UNITED STATES
OCEANBORNE FOREIGN TRADE ROUTES

TR 4 US ATLANTIC–CARIBBEAN (INCLUDING CRISTOBAL & E C MEXICO)
TR 19 US GULF–CARIBBEAN (INCLUDING CRISTOBAL & E C MEXICO)
TR 23 US PACIFIC–CARIBBEAN (INCLUDING CRISTOBAL & E C MEXICO)
TR 77 US ATLANTIC–PACIFIC CANAL ZONE
TR 78 US GULF–PACIFIC CANAL ZONE

Source: U.S. Maritime Administration, 1982.

FIGURE 1—STRATEGIC IMPORTANCE OF SEA LINES OF COMMUNICATION IN CENTRAL
AMERICA AND THE CARIBBEAN BASIN

REPORT OF THE NATIONAL BIPARTISAN COMMISSION ON CENTRAL AMERICA, 1984

Strategic Implications for the United States

Through most of its history, the United States has been able to take for granted our security in our own hemisphere. We have come to think, as Walter Lippmann wrote four decades ago, "that our privileged position was a natural right." In fact, it was the rivalries in Europe and the supremacy of British seapower that allowed us to uphold the Monroe Doctrine with minimal effort for more than a century—until the intrusion of communism into Cuba.

The ability of the United States to sustain a tolerable balance of power on the global scene at a manageable cost depends on the inherent security of its land borders. This advantage is of crucial importance. It offsets an otherwise serious liability: our distance from Europe, the Middle East, and East Asia, which are also of strategic concern to the United States. Security commitments in those areas require the United States to supply its forces overseas at the far end of trans-oceanic lines of communication whose protection can be almost as costly as the forces themselves.

At the level of global strategy, therefore, the advance of Soviet and Cuban power on the American mainland affects the global balance. To the extent that a further Marxist-Leninist advance in Central America leading to progressive deterioration and a further projection of Soviet and Cuban power in the region required us to defend against security threats near our borders, we would face a difficult choice between unpalatable alternatives. We would either have to assume a permanently increased defense burden, or see our capacity to defend distant trouble-spots reduced, and as a result have to reduce important commitments elsewhere in the world. From the standpoint of the Soviet Union, it would be a major strategic coup to impose on the United States the burden of defending our southern approaches, thereby stripping us of the compensating advantage that offsets the burden of our transoceanic lines of communication.

Such a deterioration in Central America would also greatly increase both the difficulty and the cost of protecting these lines of communications themselves. Under present plans, some 50 percent of the shipping tonnage that would be needed to reinforce the European front, and about 40 percent of that required by a major East Asian conflict, would have to pass from the Gulf of Mexico through the Caribbean-Central American zone. These same sea routes also carry nearly half of all other foreign cargo, including crude oil, shipped to this country.

The Soviets have already achieved a greater capability to interdict shipping than the Nazis had during World War II, when 50 percent of U.S. supplies to Europe and Africa were shipped from Gulf ports. German U-boats then sank 260 merchant ships in just six months, despite the fact that Allied forces enjoyed many advantages, including a two-to-one edge in submarines and the use of Cuba for resupply and basing operations. Today this is reversed. The Soviets now have a two-to-one edge overall in submarines and can operate and receive aircover from Cuba, a point from which all 13 Caribbean sea lanes passing through four chokepoints are vulnerable to interdiction.

The Soviet ability to carry out a strategy of "strategic denial" is further enhanced by the presence near Havana of the largest Soviet-managed electronic monitoring complex outside the Soviet Union, as well as by the regular deployment of TU-95 Bear naval reconnaissance aircraft.

Now there is the added threat of an entire new set of problems posed by Nicaragua. It already serves as a base of subversion, through overland infiltration of people and supplies, that can affect the entire region, Panama included. Panama is gradually assuming full responsibility for the security of the Canal; this means that any threat to the political security of that country and to the maintenance of its friendly relations with the United States automatically constitutes a strategic threat.

As Nicaragua is already doing, additional Marxist-Leninist regimes in Central America could be expected to expand their armed forces, bring in large numbers of Cuban and other Soviet bloc advisers, develop sophisticated agencies of internal repression and external subversion, and sharpen polarizations, both within individual countries and regionally. This would almost surely produce refugees, perhaps millions of them, many of whom would seek entry into the United States. Even setting aside the broader strategic considerations, the United States cannot isolate itself from the regional turmoil. The crisis is on our doorstep.

Beyond the issue of U.S. security interests in the Central American-Caribbean region, our credibility worldwide is engaged. The triumph of hostile forces in what the Soviets call the "strategic rear" of the United States would be read as a sign of U.S. impotence.

Thus, even in terms of the direct national security interests of the United States, this country has large stakes in the present conflict in Central America. They include preventing:

—A series of developments which might require us to devote large resources to defend the sourthern approaches to the United States, thus reducing our capacity to defend our interests elsewhere.

—A potentially serious threat to our shipping lanes through the Caribbean.

—A proliferation of Marxist-Leninist states that would increase violence, dislocation, and political repression in the region.

—The erosion of our power to influence events worldwide that would flow from the perception that we were unable to influence vital events close to home.[1]

The regional approach tends to encourage a greater awareness of the complexity of the problems, the limitations on U.S. efforts to correct them particularly through military solutions, and the limitations on Soviet involvement that can induce restraint in Moscow. It does not ignore the globalist view, but holds that regional problems are important in themselves, perhaps even of primary importance, and are the basis of Soviet involvement. Eliminate the regional problems and the Soviets cease to be a threat. Regionalists tend to see their problems as impinging only indirectly on global superpower politics.

Perhaps the consummate regionalists among Americans are neither Government nor academic specialists but rather the missionaries who work in the grass roots of Latin America, dealing with the peoples and their problems on a day-to-day basis. Often times victims of left and right wing extremists, they lead what they believe to be a rewarding but others perceive as a precarious existence trying to improve the society in which they work.

(2) Perspectives in conflict: East-West vs. North-South

William H. Luers, a top-ranking U.S. career Foreign Service Officer of ambassadorial rank with training and experience in Eastern Europe and Latin America, explains the lack of consistency in U.S. relations with Latin America partially in terms of the "divided community of foreign policy specialists." This split among specialists, he contends, "severely inhibits" the formulation of policy on questions relating to Soviet Union and Latin America.[51]

Simply stated, Luers makes the distinction between foreign policy elites (government specialists, academics and journalists) who are preoccupied professionally with East-West and North-South issues. The East-West specialists, he notes, have tended to dominate in the State Department, the National Security Council, the Defense Department and other agencies dealing with national security issues. They have focused mainly on such issues as military weaponry, arms control, defense strategy, alliance matters and the general requirements of global politics—issues, in brief, that go to the heart of Soviet-American relations.

In contrast, the North-South specialists, relatively new to the Government, academia and journalism, have tended to be preoccu-

---

[1] U.S. President. Report of the National Bipartisan Commission on Central America, January 1984, p. 91–93.

[51] Luers, Soviets and Latin America, p. 5–6.

pied with Third World nations and their problems—such issues as regional development, human rights, and social questions.

According to Luers, the difference in mind-sets between the East-West Sovietologists and the North-South Latin Americanists is "most striking." Twenty years exposure to meetings of these specialists in their professional organizations (that is, the American Association for the Advancement of Slavic Studies and the Latin American Studies Association) led Luers to conclude that, "The participants' vision of foreign policy and U.S. society are at opposite poles of the American political spectrum." Luers makes this contrasting comparison:

The Latin Americanists are often influenced by the Latin left, severely critical of the U.S. government and the U.S. private sector, sympathetic to and supportive of Latin criticism of the United States, worried about people and development problems. They tend to be idealistic about the U.S. ability and desire to shape events and about Latin American motivation.

The Russian-East European specialists tend to be critical of the Soviet Union, communism, and revolution. They are not given to idealism, are hard nosed about the limits of U.S. policy, and convinced that there are virtually no issues so important as those involved in the U.S.-Soviet relationship. Soviet specialists and Europeanists in general give low priority to North-South issues and tend to be either patronizing toward those who do, or worse, instant experts when they engage the issues. . . .

. . . The Soviet specialists tend to think of Latin America as a minor side show in U.S. foreign policy. To the Latin Americanists the region is of major interest to the United States for humanitarian and political reasons which are only confused, in their view, by the introduction of "extraneous" East-West issues. Therefore the Soviet and Latin American specialists tend at times to reinforce each others low tolerance for discussing seriously the Soviet threat in the Caribbean Basin but for completely different reasons.[52]

Wayne S. Smith, a former State Department official posted in Cuba, Director of the Department's Office of Cuban Affairs, and now Senior Associate of the Carnegie Endowment for Peace, seems to reflect the perspective of the regionalists in one of his published works. (This illustration and the others below do not imply strict adherence to a single perspective.) In 1982, he chided the Administration for its over-emphasis on East-West matters at the expense of the regional in dealing with Central America. In a sharply critical article entitled, "Dateline Havana: Myopic Diplomacy," he wrote:

Although concern over Cuban involvement in any turmoil so near the southern border of the United States is justified, U.S. policy would have been more effective had it addressed the turmoil in its proper context [meaning, regional context]. Treating the situation as a major East-West test of wills, however gratifying to the administration's confrontational instincts, did not and still does not contribute to a sensible solution.[53]

In a similar critical review of the Administration's policy towards Cuba and Central America from the regionalist perspective, William M. LeoGrande, Latin American specialist at American University, charges that, "Washington ignores the real source of insurgency in Central America—decades of economic inequality and political oppression." LeoGrande offers what he terms a "per-

[52] Ibid.

[53] Smith, Wayne S. Dateline Havana: Myopic Diplomacy. Foreign Policy, no. 48, Fall 1982, p. 162.

fect example" of what has been wrong with the U.S. response to provocative Cuban initiatives abroad:

By treating Cuba [backed by the Soviet Union] as the source of Central America's problems, the United States loses sight of regional dynamics, focusing only on the East-West dimension of local conflicts. The United States would respond more effectively to Cuban initiatives by focusing on the regional conflicts themselves, seeking solutions that deprive Cuba of political advantage.[54]

Other scholarly observers of the Latin American scene, such as Valenta tend to combine both perspectives. A specialist in Soviet-East European affairs who had fled his native Czechoslovakia at the time of the 1968 crisis and who has in recent years shifted to Latin American studies, Valenta points to "the rapid decay of *anciens regimes*" as the cause of the Central American crisis and proceeds to catalog economic, political and social injustices in the area. The present crisis "cannot be attributed solely to Cuban and Soviet interference," he avers.[55] But Valenta insists that, "It is the Soviet presence in otherwise local or regional disturbances which creates the potential military threat and elicits a U.S. response."[56]

The Kissinger Commission's report reflects the same mixture of North-South and East-West perspectives. A common threat running through the report is the belief that, "the roots of the crisis are both indigenous and foreign." On the regional level, the report says that, "Discontents are real, and for much of the population conditions of life are miserable; just as Nicaragua was ripe for revolution, so the conditions that invite revolution are present elsewhere in the region as well." The Commission's recommendations address these developmental needs. But on the globalist, East-West side, the report clearly establishes the geopolitical, Soviet connection:

. . . these conditions have been exploited by hostile outside forces—specifically, by Cuba, backed by the Soviet Union and now operating through Nicaragua—which will turn any revolution they capture into a totalitarian state, threatening the region and robbing the people of their hopes for liberty.
. . . indigenous reform, even indigenous revolution, is not a security threat to the United States. But the intrusion of aggressive outside powers exploiting local grievances to expand their own political influence and military control is a serious threat to the United States, and to the entire hemisphere.[57]

e. Division and uncertainty; Soviet opportunity

Thus, Americans view Latin America and Soviet involvement in this Third World region from many perspectives. They share a common historical experience with policies, a doctrine and its corollaries exclusively designed to expand, maintain and protect American power in the Western Hemisphere. Adjustments have been made to suit changing times and changing requirements, at least until the entry of revolutionary-directed Soviet and Cuban power into the region. Since then, perceptions have mirrored the

---

[54] LeoGrande, William M. Cuba Policy Recycled. Foreign Policy, no. 46, Spring 1982, p. 115. Blasier, who also tends toward the regionalist perspective, though he was trained in both areas, sharply criticized Leiken's article "Eastern Winds in Latin America" (Foreign Policy, no. 42, Spring 1981) for exaggerating the Soviet threat. He likened "Leiken's alarming panorama of communist advances, penetrations, threats and perils" to what had once been called, "Sovietophobia." (Foreign Policy, no. 43, Summer 1981: 187.)
[55] Valenta, Soviet and Cuban Responses in Central America, p. 128.
[56] Valenta, Jiri. Soviet Policy in Central America. Survey, v. 27, Autumn-Winter 1983: 287.
[57] Kissinger Commission's Report, p. 4.

geopolitical needs of a superpower wanting to protect its global position and the regional needs of a hemisphere whose deprived and underdeveloped countries create fertile soil for revolution and Soviet-Cuban intervention. Though sharing a common history, Americans of the mid-1980's seem divided and thus uncertain on how best to address the current Soviet-Cuban challenge in Central America and the Caribbean Basin. It is this uncertainty and division that can create opportunities for the expansion of Soviet influence in this Third World area.

3. THE VIEW FROM THE SOVIET UNION

a. Latin America in the Soviet worldview

(1) Impact of "geographic fatalism"

Geographic, ideological and geopolitical elements have constituted much of the Soviet view of Latin America.

Not until the Cuban Revolution had the Soviet Union directed any serious attention to the region. Heretofore, the doctrine of "geographic fatalism," the notion that Latin America was in the U.S. sphere of influence and accordingly would not permit leftist governments or a strong Soviet influence so close to its borders, had been the guiding principle in Soviet attitudes. U.S. intervention in Guatemala in 1954, to forestall what it perceived to be a Communist-leftist Arbenz regime, confirmed the validity of this doctrine.[58] The invasion of Grenada no doubt has strengthened this belief.

Politically, the Soviets benefited from their self-imposed physical abstention from Latin America. Unlike the Americans they were able to approach the Latin American scene without the surfeit of historic prejudices that have plagued the United States. The Soviets have exploited this vulnerability much to their advantage, invariably linking the United States, as in one case, to the oppressive regimes of the "scoundrel generals."[59]

(2) Ideological influences

Marxist-Leninist ideology provides the larger philosophical construct within which the Soviets perceive Latin America. At least theoretically this ideology teaches that the completion of history will occur with the global triumph of Communism. Since the Bolshevik Revolution, world development, the Soviets contend, has tended towards that ultimate end. Socialism, combined with the National Liberation Movement and Russia's "natural allies" in the

---

[58] Rothenberg, Morris. The Soviets and Central America. In, Leiken, Central America: Anatomy of Conflict, chapt. 6, p. 131.

[59] V.V. Volskiy, director of the Latin American Institute, records the multiple offenses of the United States in a report on the U.S. role in Central America. "Latin America remembers well its history" of imperial exploitation, he states accusingly. "Washington's present actions do not allow anyone to forget this history, which is a direct continuation of the tradition of its aggressive policy." Volskiy concludes that "hypocrisy and demagoguery hide the true goals and actions of U.S. foreign policy in Central America, one thing is perfectly clear: The U.S., as it has in the past, reflects the greed of American monopolies and aspirations of the U.S. rulin circles for world supremacy." (Volskiy, V.V. U.S. Role in Central America. Latinskyaya Amerika [Moscow], no. 11, Nov. 1983, translated in, USSR Report. Political and Sociological Affairs, March 2, 1984 p. 22-25. JPRS-UPS-84-022.)

Third World, are looked upon by the Soviets as central, irreversible forces in the modern era.[60]

Latin America plays a key role in the fulfillment of this perception and in the unfolding of this unchanging historical process. As Georgiy Arbatov, Director of the USA and Canada Institute, said, "The Soviet Union is not bent upon threatening U.S. security in Central America. We cannot be blamed for the socialist revolutions in Cuba and Nicaragua"—meaning events in Central America and the Caribbean are part of the larger historical forces enveloping the world, not something necessarily engineered by Moscow but rather a natural unfolding of history.[61] Perhaps, Anatoliy P. Butenko, a Soviet scholar and specialist on Socialism and Third World matters, best summed up this idea when he recently wrote in his impressive book, "Socialism as a World System":

> Whereas at the start of the century socialism had taken only the first steps in post-October Russia, it now exists and is developing as a powerful world system of socialist states of Europe, Asia and Latin America, a system with which countries of a socialist orientation [Ethiopia, for example] are joining up and with which revolutionary detachments of the non-socialist world [Sandinista-supported guerrillas in El Salvador, for example] are interacting increasingly closely, multiplying the impact of socialism and gradually turning it into a force capable of exerting a decisive influence on all world politics.[62]

(3) Geopolitical ingredient

The geopolitical ingredient completes the triad of elements shaping the Soviet perception of Latin America within its worldview. Central to the Soviet worldview is the belief that the correlation of forces now favors the Socialist world and that world Capitalism is in decline. Soviet policy towards the Third World is inextricably tied to the assumption of an existing symbiotic relationship with the Third World and the reality of expanding Soviet global power within its vast regions.[63] Soviet power, particularly military power, constitutes the main ingredient in their assessment.[64] Accordingly,

---

[60] For a complete explanation of the linkage between the Nonalignment Movement (NAM) with the Soviet Union and the assumption of a "natural" alliance with the Third World, see, Artemyev, P. Nonalignment—Important Factor in World Politics. Mirovaya Ekonomika I Mezhdunarodynyye Otosheniya (Moscow), no. 3, Mar. 1981: 61–72, translated in USSR Report, Political and Sociological Affairs, no. 1157, Aug. 10, 1981, p. 35–47 (JPRS 78708.)

[61] Yomiuri Shimbun (Tokyo), Nov. 14, 1983, p., 12–13.

[62] Butenko, Anatoliy P. Socialism as a World System. Moscow, Politizdat, 1984, p. 238. That Latin American Communists are kindred spirits with the Soviets in sharing this Socialist perception of the future was revealed in the published statement of the Conference of South American Communist Parties held in Buenos Aires in July 1984. The statement concluded: "At the Conference of Communist Parties of Latin American and Caribbean countries held in Havana in 1975, we emphasized once again that our parties are an actively operating constituent of the world communist movement. They firmly adhere to the principles of Marxism-Leninism and proletarian internationalism. We are part of the powerful stream that is changing the course of history and creating a new society without exploiters or exploited. Here, in South America, through our actions, unity and our daily struggle, we are making a contribution to liquidating dependence, backwardness, social injustice, unemployment, and illiteracy for millions of people, and are helping to create a more just humane world, a new world, which must be a socialist world moving toward its highest stage of development, the creation of a communist society." (Pravda, Aug. 8, 1984, 1st edition, p. 4, in, FBIS Daily Report, Soviet Union, v. 3, Aug. 9, 1984, p. K3.)

[63] Valenta, Soviet Policy in Central America, p. 289–290.

[64] On the appeal of Soviet military power to the Third World, Dimitri K. Simes, a specialist on Soviet affairs at the Carnegie Endowment, writes: "The USSR is still active in the Third World and its involvement is often eagerly sought by local rulers. But these requests rarely result from any illusions about Soviet motives, and almost never reflect the belief that communist Russia is a model for Third World development. Moscow's military power and its willingness to provide arms and geopolitical protection, not the appeal of Soviet ideas and accomplish-

Continued

the Soviets nourish the idea that they must be recognized as a superpower and claim the "rights" of a superpower actor on the international scene.

From this view flows the further belief that U.S. influence, even in its "own backyard," Latin America, is on the wane. Revealed in their published discussions is an awareness of the crisis within the Organization of American States (OAS) and the inability of the United States to use the organization as it once did.[65]

The Soviets also appreciate, as Brezhnev noted at the 26th Party Congress, that "the role in world affairs of Latin American countries such as Mexico, Brazil, Argentina, Venezuela, and Peru has grown considerably"—further evidence that U.S. hemispheric influence is on the wane. They acknowledge setbacks, as in Jamaica, Peru and Bolivia, but, nonetheless, they perceive the overall trend toward Latin American independence from the United States to their advantage and as a mark of the changing international politics of Latin America.[66]

Still, Moscow is aware of the special importance of Latin America for the United States and the power it can bring to bear. It values the Cuban relationship as an important breakthrough against previous "geographic fatalism" about U.S. hegemony and perceives Nicaragua as offering a second possible breakthrough; other countries in Central America, a third and fourth. But, conscious of great power responses to serious threats by strong counteraction, the Soviets see the need for caution in their approach to Central America.[67]

Thus, the Soviets seem to perceive Latin America from both the regional and geopolitical perspective. They are cognizant of the changing social structures of the nations and the force of revolution and discord in such areas as Central America. Given the high degree of political oppression and the continuation of historic economic and social inequities, Latin America, at least the Caribbean and Central American area, is no doubt seen by the Soviets as a classic case of a region "ripe for revolution" and expansion of the Soviet brand of Socialism.

But the Soviets also fix their views in the concept of the changing correlation of world forces that has such significant geopolitical implications as increased opportunities for spreading Soviet influence in the region, the diminution of U.S. influence, and the growing independence of Latin America from U.S. hegemony—all of which have a fundamental effect on East-West relations since it has the potential for magnifying aggregate Soviet power and diminishing that of the United States globally.

---

ments, are what normally motivate Third World overtures to the Soviet Union." (The New Soviet Challenge. Foreign Policy no. 55, Summer 1984: 124.) Robert A. Ford, a long-time Canadian diplomat posted in Moscow for more than 20 years, observes with respect to Soviet reliance on military power, "If the Soviets are unable to solve their economic, ethnic and social problems, there will be a tendency to rely, as at present, on military strength to exert their claims to superpower status." (The Soviet Union: The Next Decade. Foreign Affairs, v. 62, Summer 1984: 1140.) For an analysis of the role of military power in Russian expansionism, see Brzezinski, Zbigniew. Tragic Dilemmas of Soviet World Power: The Limits of a New-Type Empire. Encounter, v. 61, Dec. 1983: 10–17.

[65] Rothenberg, Morris. Since Reagan: The Soviets and Latin America. The Washington Quarterly, v. 5, Spring 1982: 178.

[66] Ibid.

[67] Ibid., p. 178–179.

From the Soviet perspective, therefore, the problems of Latin America may in a narrow sense be regional ones, but Latin America itself is, nonetheless, firmly fixed and perceived as a geopolitical entity within the larger global context of Soviet-American and East-West relations. For the Soviets, regionalism and the geopolitics of the Latin America seem to be indivisible.[68]

b. Moscow's three-part approach to Latin America

(1) An ally of Socialist Cuba

The Soviets view Latin America and deal with it essentially in three distinct categories: (1) Socialist Cuba, a Marxist-Leninist state, the first in Latin America, with revolutionary ambitions in Latin America and elsewhere, and a reliable Socialist ally internationally; (2) the explosive Caribbean Basin and Central America where revolutionary ferment is intense and targets of opportunity are opening up; and finally, (3) the settled, established governments of Mexico and South America where the objective realities of stability dictate the pursuit of traditional diplomacy.

The Soviets were slow to recognize the revolutionary potential of a successful Cuban revolution and, subsequently, were annoyed at Castro's erratic tendency, until the late 1960's, to pursue a revolutionary tactic of support for guerrilla warfare in opposition to the preferred Soviet approach of détente internationally and the "united front" regionally. But the Soviets came to value Socialist Cuba as a model for revolution in Latin America and as a persistent goad to its rival, the United States. As opportunities unfolded in Central America, the Soviets gave its sanction to Castro's revolutionary approach, launching what one Soviet Latin American specialist saw as "the beginning of a new stage in the struggle of the entire continent."[69]

In brief, Castro became Moscow's "pointman" for revolution in Latin America, an instrument of Soviet Third World policy, particularly of intervention in Africa, and, as Morris Rothenberg, a Soviet specialist and director of the Advanced International Studies Institute in Bethesda, Maryland, notes "an important adjunct" of Soviet political, military, propaganda and intelligence activities in Latin American and the Third World areas.[70] Though paying a steep price by underwriting the Castro regime economically (an estimated $8 to $10 million per day)[71] the Soviets have been able to gain such benefits as, strengthening their claim of legitimacy as a special force in world history, establishing an important base in a strategically vital area in the Western Hemisphere, and magnifying the image of its power and prestige in the geopolitics of the

[68] Blasier, Giant's Rival, p. 130.

[69] Jacobsen, C.G. Soviet Attitudes Towards Aid to and Contacts with Central American Revolutionaries. Prepared for the State Department, April 10, 1984, p. 9–10. The setting for this remark was a roundtable discussion after the Sandinista victory explicity approved Che Guevara's previously rejected stress on the primacy of armed struggle which was published in Latinskaya Amerika, nos. 1, 2 and 3, 1980.

[70] Rothenberg, The Soviets and Central America, p. 131–132.

[71] Ramet, Pedro and Fernando Lopez-Alves. Moscow and the Revolutionary Left in Latin America. Orbis, v. 28, Summer 1984: 351.

East-West struggle.[72] Socialist Cuba was to become a symbol of Russia's breakout from the constricting influence of the doctrine of "geographic fatalism" and the introduction of its power directly into Latin America; and beyond that, the symbol of a unified strategy with Russia in the Third World.[73]

(2) Revolutionary opportunities in Central America and Caribbean Basin

Upheaval in Central America and the Caribbean Basin has called for a distinctive Soviet approach, that of revolutionary opportunism in search of new political conquests.[74] The Soviets, surprised by the Sandinista success in Nicaragua in July 1979, seem to have considered their victory a watershed in Soviet Third World policy in Latin America; in brief, a step beyond Cuba, a further opening of the breach in "geographic fatalism." The importance of developments in Central America to the Soviets was underscored by Sergio Mikoyan, editor-in-chief of the Soviet scholarly publication Latinskaya Amerika, when he declared in 1980 that the Sandinista revolution was of "colossal international importance—one of those events that demand reexamination of established concepts."[75]

The main thrust of Soviet policy in this area has been to give political and military support to Nicaragua and the rebel guerrillas fighting in El Salvador and to use Cuba and its East European allies, notably Bulgaria, Czechoslovakia and East Germany, as a channel for transmitting Soviet military assistance.[76] For Moscow perceives Nicaragua as a new opportunity for spreading its influence in the Western Hemisphere. Like Cuba, Nicaragua seems destined to become a staging area for further Soviet penetration of Latin America.

But the Soviets, aware that Central America and the Caribbean are vital parts of the "strategic rear" of the United States, have been cautious in pursuing its policy of opportunism, despite the intense propaganda support for the Sandinistas—at least until the fall of 1984. The invasion of Grenada clearly demonstrated to them the limits of U.S. tolerance in the region. This and the U.S. mili-

---

[72] Ibid. Soviet use of Cuban naval facilities reached a new level when in April 1984 a Cuban Koni-class frigate joined the Soviet 20,000 ton helicopter cruiser *Leningrad* and accompanied by the 8,000 ton guided missile destroyer *Idaloy* participated in joint naval exercises in the Gulf of Mexico 75 miles off the coast of Louisiana. A senior U.S. Defense Department official said that "this is just the beginning of combined operations with the Cuban navy" but the "bigger significance" was that "the Cuban navy is how reaching the stage where it's capable of combined exercise" and that "This is just one, initial step to make sure they [the Cubans] understand Soviet doctrine and tactics." (Andrews, Walter. Cuba Joins Soviets in Exercise Off U.S. Coast. The Washington Times, April 10, 1984, p. 2A.)

[73] Valenta writes: "In spite of past disagreements and existing differences, the Soviets and Cubans now have a unified Third World strategy which reflects the overall coordination of their foreign policies." (Soviet Policy in Central America, p. 288.)

[74] Luers writes with respect to Soviet opportunism in the Third World: "Soviet behavior in the Third World, in general, and Latin America, in particular, has generally been governed more by perceived opportunities and developments in the region than by the current state of U.S.-Soviet relations." (The Soviets and Latin America, p. 25.)

[75] Ibid., p. 13–14. The Soviets seemed enthusiastic in their support, at least in the beginning. In an address on Nov. 6, 1979 honoring the 62nd anniversary of the Bolshevik Revolution Andrei Kirilenko, a top-ranking Soviet leader, asserted that "the Soviet people rejoice that in recent years the people of Angola, Ethiopia, Afghanistan, Nicaragua and Grenada have broken the chains of imperialist domination and have embarked on a road of independent development." (Rothenberg, The Soviets and Central America, p. 133.)

[76] Ibid., p. 132–134.

tary support for the Government forces fighting Nicaraguan-supported guerrilla rebels in El Salvador and other demonstrated forceful efforts to counter the Sandinistas seem to have introduced into Soviet thinking an element of unpredictability regarding U.S. behavior. Grenada's radical leftists, aided by the Soviet Union and Cuba, had been rapidly moving towards establishing a Marxist-Leninist regime, but were forestalled by a timely U.S. military intervention.

Thus Central America and the Caribbean Basin appear to be a prime Soviet target within an otherwise diversified Soviet strategy in Latin America. Conditions seem ripe for Soviet exploitation, but the objective realities, carefully measured in risks and gains, dictate a policy of opportunism tinged with caution with respect to an unpredictable Reagan Administration.[77]

(3) Pursuit of traditional diplomacy: The case of Argentina

Finally, the Soviets have pursued a policy of traditional diplomacy towards Mexico and the nations of South America, the third of their multi-directional approach to Latin America. This does not mean that they abjure revolutionary tactics when appropriate—though they have pursued this line cautiously in the Southern Cone having been badly burned by the Allende setback in Chile; but rather that the main concentration of their effort is on traditional state-to-state relations.

A case in point is Argentina. As the second largest nation in South America, strategically positioned on the South Atlantic and traditionally the maverick of the Western Hemisphere consistently opposed to the United States, Argentina was a logical Soviet partner for establishing long-term state-to-state relations.[78]

Moreover, Argentina and the Soviet Union are bound by mutual economic interests. Argentina has been a main supplier of agricultural products much needed by the Soviets. This economic connection paid off in 1980 when Argentine grain exports helped the Soviets fend off the negative effects of the U.S. grain embargo.[79]

On their part the Argentines have had much to gain from this traditionally-flavored relationship. The Soviet Union has been a major dependable market for Argentine exports. In 1980, they made up 33.7 percent of Argentine exports for a total value of $2.9 billion; yet Argentina purchased only 3 percent of its imports from the Soviet Union, an imbalance the Soviets have accepted for apparently long-term political and economic reasons. Also, the only major Soviet cooperation program in Latin America, outside of Cuba and Nicaragua, for the past decade has been with Argentina. The Soviets have supplied Argentina with heavy water, enriched uranium and technological assistance under a bilateral nuclear energy agreement.[80]

---

[77] On the matter of Soviet caution, Rothenberg writes: "The strategic importance attached by the United States to the region makes the extension of Soviet influence an attractive target, but also convinces the USSR to exercise caution in pursuing such an objective." (The Soviets and Central America, p. 145.)

[78] Luers, The Soviets and Latin America, p. 13.

[79] Ibid.

[80] Ibid.

Politically, the Soviets defended the Argentine military governments who were busy liquidating by the thousands alleged revolutionaries, subversives (probably including Communists) and Marxists at home. The Soviets also gave Argentina full support in the
Falklands War with Britain and in the dispute with Chile over the
Beagle Channel.[81]

In brief, the Soviet-Argentine relationship has evolved out of the
workings of traditional diplomacy. A relationship based on "mutual
convenience," as Luers terms it, it has been characterized as being
"increasingly pragmatic, close, but not intimate"—somewhat akin
to Russia's relationship (except for military assistance) with another Third World nation, India. Still, Soviet opportunities for
changing this traditional approach could be a future possibility
given the endemic Argentine political-economic disorder, particularly for a Soviet Union attracted by the strategic importance of a
large Latin American country positioned in the South Atlantic.[82]

c. Ideology combined with pragmatism

A central theme running through the Soviet view of Latin America as a target area and Third World problem is the importance of
ideology in creating the framework for policy. Combined with ideology is a high degree of pragmatism in the execution of their policy.
Ideology provides the schematic strucuture and the philosophical
underpinnings for perceiving policy; it provides the analytical tools
for examining policy alternatives; and it provides the unifying principles, notably proletarian internationalism, for carrying it out.
Ideology thus has an important value of its own.

Ideology is, however, buttressed by a solid, feet-on-the-ground realism that deals with the sensible and the possible. Hence the
three-part Soviet perception of Latin America as a rationalization
for action in this Third World region. Accents on the pragmatic
tends to support Duncan's view that Soviet policies in Latin America are "essentially those of a great power in quest of traditional
great power concerns," and that Soviet national interests appear to

---

[81] Ibid. Volskiy, Moscow's leading Latin Americanist, said in an interview that "The Malvinas
crisis united the Argentine nation in the struggle against imperialism. England and the USA—
NATO allies—acted not against any particular class of Argentine society, but against the entire
people, against the entire Argentine nation, and against its legitimate aspiration to make the
Malvinas Islands once again Argentine." It was "natural," he continued, that the British-Ameri-
can effort "could not fail to strengthen the struggle of the Argentine people for the democratiza-
tion of the counry, and the struggle for an independent foreign policy." Enlarging the frame of
reference to include all of Latin America, Volskiy concluded: "And today these sentiments are
characteristic not only of Argentina but also of an every growing number of countries on the
continent, which are rejecting a policy which calls for following Washington's adventuristic
course in an unthinking manner. The mood of change is felt everywhere. Everything indicated
that the future of this part of the world lies not with dictators and tyrants but with democracy
[meaning Socialism and Communism] and progress instead. And in this regard there is particular meaning in the words of the late president of Chile, Salvador Allende, who said that the day
is not far off when once again there will open up a broad road along which many will walk in
order to build a better society." (Volskiy, V.V. Interview on Regional Developments. Komsomolskaya Pravda [Moscow], Mar. 30, 1983, p. 3, translated in USSR Report, Political and Sociological
Affairs, no. 1411, May 24, 1983, p. 4–5, JPRS 83532.)

[82] Luers, The Soviets and Latin America, p. 13. In describing the Soviet focus on the Southern
Cone, Leiken emphasizes it strategic importance: "That region has appreciated in strategic
value as aircraft carriers and supertankers have outgrown the Panama and Suez Canals, and
maritime traffic in the South Atlantic has multiplied. Mounting interest in offshore petroleum,
in the deep seabed, in fishing, and in Antarctica, together with the appearance of the Soviets'
blue water navy in the South Atlantic, have further enhanced the region's strategic prominence
for the superpowers." (Leiken, Eastern Winds in Latin America, p. 98.)

be "defined primarily in terms of economic and political power." The direct promotion of Communism in Latin America, as an ideological goal, is thus "over-shadowed by the interests of Moscow as an evolving great power with traditional world requirements." [83]

Soviet pragmatism dictates a course that avoids confrontation with the United States. This is a key element in the Soviet perception. Duncan puts it this way: "The Soviet Union . . . is clearly unwilling to risk open confrontation in a geographical region where sensitive US interests abound." [84] Robert A. Ford, a Canadian diplomat seasoned by more than two decades of service in Moscow, reinforces this view. Speaking of the Third World as a whole, he observes that the Soviet leaders, guided by a "high degree of realism," will do "nothing intentionally that would endanger Soviet security. Hence, support for pro-Soviet movements [in the Third World] will be carefully calculated to avoid a direct confrontation with the United States, particularly in areas [like Central America] of vital importance to the latter." [85]

Thus the conclusion that Moscow, despite its alluring Third World rhetoric, still gives Latin America a low priority in its calculation of foreign policy interests.

B. SUMMARY OF MAJOR TRENDS IN SOVIET-LATIN AMERICAN AFFAIRS

1. CUBA: GEOPOLITICAL FULCRUM FOR KHRUSHCHEV'S GLOBALISM

The broad, general trends in Soviet involvement in Latin America follow roughly, and interchangeably, the lines of Russia's three-part approach explained above. Until the Cuban Revolution in 1959–1960, Latin America had been politically terra incognito for the Soviets. Though Latin America was to play a minor role in Soviet global revolutionary strategy within the Comintern during the 1920's and 1930's, Moscow generally adhered to the concept of "geographic fatalism." [86]

The Cuban Revolution coincided with three developments in Khrushchev's foreign policy, each mutually reinforcing: The Soviet move from continentalism to globalism, that is, Khrushchev's bold thrust into the Third World; his claim on the loyalties of the National Liberation Movement (NLM) in what he called the Third World "zone of peace"; and the reckless use of power to demonstrate his case that the balance of world forces, because of this alignment of Third World forces, had shifted in favor of the Social-

---

[83] Duncan, W. Raymond, Soviet Power in Latin America. In, Donaldson, Robert H. ed. The Soviet Union in the Third World: Successes and Failures. Boulder, Col., Westview Press, 1981, chapt. 1, p. 10.

[84] Ibid., p. 11.

[85] Ford, Soviet Union: The Next Decade, p. 1141.

[86] For recent commentary on this early period, see, Varas, Ideology and Politics in Latin American-USSR Relations, p. 36–38, and his, Soviet-Latin American Relations Under United States Regional Hegemony, p. 3–8. See also, Blasier, The Giant's Rival, p. 76–79. For a critical review of Blasier's observations on early Latin American Communist Party relations with the Comintern, see, Smith, Wayne S. Russians and Latins. The New York Times Book Review, Dec. 25, 1983, p. 15. Smith notes that, "As a result of the disasters of 1928 to 1935, the Latin American Communist Parties remain exceedingly dubious about armed struggle as a tactic and are usually reluctant to be in the forefront of a revolutionary movement." (p. 15). In obedience to the Comintern's directives, the Latin American parties had pursued an active revolutionary course that led to these "disasters."

ist camp led by the Soviet Union and away from that of the Capitalist world under U.S. leadership.[87]

Cuba was to be the geopolitical fulcrum upon which Khrushchev would rest the lever of Soviet power to prove his case. Hence his claim that the Monroe Doctrine had died a "natural death," meaning an end to U.S. sway in the Western Hemisphere. Khrushchev's was a geopolitical ploy of the first magnitude: It was intended to force the United States to knuckle under and submit to the Soviet diktat in global politics, though ostensibly Soviet missiles and bombers in Cuba were to serve only defensive purposes. However, the U.S. response in the Cuban missile crisis of 1962—Khrushchev's consummate power play—frustrated that effort, but by no means entirely: The offensive missiles were removed, but the Soviets got a foothold in Cuba that has expanded incrementally and, some observers say, dangerously in the next two and a half decades.[88]

After the missile crisis, detente constituted the main trend in Soviet foreign policy until the mid-1970's. This policy was reflected in the Soviet approach to Latin America. But serious strains developed in Soviet-Cuban relations over tactics. Until the late 1960's, Castro went his way, opting for a course of armed struggle in open defiance of his mentors in Moscow. However, the Soviets, through economic sanctions and unfriendly persuasion, were finally able to bring him into line.[89] From this point on Cuba was to become a dependency of the Soviet Union.

2. PURSUIT OF A DUAL POLICY: DETENTE AND ARMED STRUGGLE

From the mid-1970's until the early 1980's Brezhnev pursued a dual policy, one of detente in East-West relations, particularly in Europe where the threat of nuclear war was most acute; while at the same time reactivating Khrushchev's policy of a bold global thrust into the Third World.[90]

Using Castro as his "point man," Brezhnev became deeply involved in the revolutionary struggles for Angola and Ethiopia. Yet in other regions of the Third World, particularly in Latin America, Brezhnev carefully differentiated his emphasis on armed struggle in pursuit of traditional diplomacy. But Allende's peaceful accession to power proved to be a bittersweet experience for the Soviets. From Moscow's perspective Allende had moved too rapidly toward Socialism in Chile, and accordingly provoked a counter-revolution that resulted in his overthrow and death—and consequently a serious setback for the Soviets in Latin America.[91]

---

[87] HFAC, Soviet Union and the Third World, 1977, p. 17–25.

[88] For recent commentary on the transition in Soviet policy from abstention to involvement in Latin America, see, Valenta, Soviet Policy in Central America, p. 287–288, 291–293; Rothenberg, Latin America in Soviet Eyes, p. 1–3; and Ramet and Lopez-Alves, Moscow and the Revolutionary Left in Latin America, p. 344–346.

[89] Blasier, The Giant's Rivals, p. 16–20; Varas, Ideology and Politics in Latin American-USSR Relations, p. 39–40; Jacobsen Report, p. 9; and Ramet and Lopez-Alves, Moscow and the Revolutionary Left in Latin America, p. 344–346.

[90] For a review of this strategy and its consequences, see, Ulam, Adam B. Dangerous Relations: The Soviet Union in World Politics, 1970–1982. London, Oxford University Press, 1983. 325 p.

[91] Ramet and Lopez-Alves, Moscow and the Revolutionary Left in Latin America, p. 347–350, and Blasier, The Giant's Rival, p. 85–87.

Taking full stock of this setback, Brezhnev adopted a policy of greater caution and pursued a traditional course in diplomacy. Gradualism became the accepted path to power. The Allende experience, indeed, strengthened the Soviet case against the volatile ultra-leftist forces pushing for revolution "now" in favor of detente and flexibility in its relations in the Latin American Third World.[92]

3. SANCTIONING ARMED STRUGGLE AFTER SANDINISTA VICTORY

The perennial argument over tactics shifted in favor of Castro and the ultra-leftists after the unexpected victory of the Sandinistas on July 19, 1979. (It is ironic and curiously instructive to recall that SALT II, the centerpiece of détente in East-West relations, was signed almost one month to the day before the Sandinista conquest, June 18, 1979.) Soviet Latin Americanists, such as Sergio Mikoyan, hailed the victory as one of "colossal international importance—one of those events that demand re-examination of established concepts."[93] And the Soviets, in general, portrayed the Sandinista success as an historic watershed, reversing the decline in Communist fortunes following the overthrow of Allende in 1973, and heralding a new revolutionary upsurge not only in Central America but throughout all Latin America.[94] A reformulation of policy was in the making as the Soviets began to refer to "armed struggle" as "most promising in the specific conditions of most of the Latin American countries."[95]

In the aftermath of the Sandinista revolution (along with leftist success in Grenada), the Soviet leadership thus began to sanction the tactic of armed struggle, at least in Central America and the Caribbean Basin. Simultaneously, they have continued the pursuit of traditional diplomacy in the context of detente with other countries of Latin America.[96]

---

[92] With the cutback in Cuban revolutionary activity in the Western Hemisphere in 1968, the emergence of detente in East-West relations, and the growing self-confidence and global assertiveness of Latin America in the 1970's, the Soviets pursued traditional diplomacy to its fullest. They began to expand state-to-state diplomatic and commercial relations in the Hemisphere and in general pursued its own version of a "good neighbor" policy. In 1960, the Soviets had diplomatic relations with only Cuba, Brazil and Argentina. By the mid-1970's, it had opened relations with virtually every major South American and several Caribbean and Central American countries. Thus the Soviets were to establish "substantial diplomatic presences" and expand commercial an cultural relations impressively. According to Luers, Soviet trade with Latin America grew tenfold between 1970 and 1977. (Luers, The Soviets and Latin America, p. 8.)

[93] Luers, The Soviets and Latin America, p. 13.

[94] Rothenberg, The Soviets and Central America, p. 133.

[95] Duncan, Soviet Interests in Latin America, p. 177.

[96] "United fronts" were still advocated among the parties in such countries as Argentina, Brazil, and Mexico where armed struggle had dim prospects of success. (Ibid., p. 177.) State-to-state relations also continued to flourish, as in the case of Moscow's relations with Argentina. A recent example of dualism in Soviet policy is their continued vigorous support for the Sandinista cause, politically and militarily, while carrying on apparently fruitful relations with Mexico, a country in the forefront of the Contadora group seeking peace in Central America. For example, on Sept. 18, 1984, President Miguel de la Madrid of Mexico received the USSR Supreme Soviet delegation led by I.V. Kapitonov, deputy of the Supreme Soviet and secretary of the CPSU Central Committee. On the occasion of Mexico's National Day, Mexican Ambassador to the Soviet Union Horacio Flores de la Pena addressed the Soviet people over Moscow television on Sept. 16, a common Soviet practice, but one clearly appealing to the Mexicans and other Latin Americans. (Moscow Television Service in Russian, 1030 GMT, Sept. 18, 1984, and Moscow Television Service in Russian, 1430 GMT, Sept. 16, 1984, in FBIS Daily Report, Soviet Union, v. 3, Sept. 19, 1984: K1.)

Even the Soviet commitment to the Sandinista cause, though forthright in many respects, has been marked by caution (at least until the fall of 1984) as in the use of third parties as instruments in their interventionist policy and restraints in their commitments to Nicaragua—points emphasized by many observers.[97] Things seemed to change qualitatively, however, in the fall of 1984. Reports of Soviet delivery of MIG fighters, later proved to be untrue, alarmed many Americans particularly leaders in the Administration. But the Soviet action was widely regarded as a test of U.S. will to determine the measure of its tolerance of a Soviet military buildup in Nicaragua rather than an invitation to direct confrontation. Though cautiously testing the United States, the Soviets still seemed to respect that "strategic rear" of the United States. Nonetheless, the risk of confrontation is always there; for seemingly cautious Soviet probing actions of this type, as in the initial stages of the Cuban missile crisis, can escalate and overstep the line of U.S. permissibility, producing as a result a first-class confrontation and crisis. This matter is examined below in greater detail.

4. GENERALIZATION ON GEOPOLITICS AND TACTICS

a. The primacy of geopolitics

Certain generalizations surface even from this brief sketch of the general trends in Soviet policy towards this Third World region. Perhaps the most visible is the Soviet tendency to construct their Latin American policy within the larger context of East-West relations and of their on-going commitment to the Third World. Thus it seems evident that however important the internal-regional developments in these Third World nations may be, their importance is judged by Moscow in large measure by their geopolitical significance; that is, their value in strengthening the Soviet Union and its world position, the relative "ripeness" of the area for revolution, its correlation with the larger world forces, and the risks of confrontation with the United States.

b. Variations on tactics

A second point to be made is the variations in the Soviet approach. Multiple instrumentalities are crafted to suit the desired purposes and achieve the desired ends, whether the tactic be armed struggle as in Central America, peaceful penetration and gradualism using traditional diplomacy as in Argentina, or a mixture of both.

For the Soviets, the option is always open, and in the Central American and Caribbean region they have opted for armed struggle. Leiken puts it this way:

> The geopolitical center of gravity of Soviet Latin American strategy has shifted from tactics of peaceful transition in the southern cone to those of armed struggle in the Caribbean Basin.[98]

Duncan supports this view with this added observation:

---

[97] For example, Luers, The Soviets and Latin America, p. 16.
[98] Leiken, Soviet Strategy in Latin America, p. 102.

The significant point to be made . . . is the specific linking of Cuban and Soviet support of armed struggle with a theoretical underpinning, both legitimizing, and implying a predisposition toward external support of guerrilla movements.[99]

In brief, variations on tactics in the service of a larger political purpose.

C. A SPECTRUM OF APPARENT SOVIET OBJECTIVES

1. ON SOVIET OBJECTIVES: "AN IMPERFECT LEARNING PROCESS"

Soviet objectives in Latin America appear to have spanned a broad spectrum generally reflecting in recent years the three-part categories of maintaining Socialist Cuba, seizing revolutionary opportunities in Central America and the Caribbean Basin, and carrying on traditional diplomacy in Mexico and South America.

Luers contends that it is "difficult to discern a unifying coherent strategy that has driven Soviet policies" in Latin America other than "the objective of increasing their influence and weakening that of the United States." [100] Beyond this proposition, Soviet objectives, deduced imperfectly from the dogmatic rhetoric of their propaganda and variable perceptions of their behavior, appear to be at once utopian, inconsistent, often vague and uncertain, and almost always dissembling.

Henry Kissinger cautions that both superpowers tend to make the mistake of ascribing to the other "a consistency, foresight and coherence that its own experience belies." [101] And so it has been in Latin America. Reality is often quite different from perception. For in Latin America, as Luers notes, the Soviets have "stumbled, stepped back, and probed further with limited understanding [and means, it could be added] of the region or vision about how to pursue their own interests." Americans often make the mistake of "believing that the Soviet steps are sure-footed and carefully planned years in advance." [102]

Such behavior elucidates the proposition stated by Alexander Dallin, a Soviet specialist at Stanford University, that Soviet behavior in foreign policy can be seen "as the product of an encounter between expectation and values of Soviet decision makers and the reality as they found and perceived it." But carrying out a foreign policy, however, "has required (and in turn reflected) a series of adaptations—an imperfect learning process." [103]

To sketch briefly Soviet objectives—their policy assumptions, strategy and tactics—in Latin America for the past quarter century is essentially to describe this "imperfect learning process." For the Soviet experience in that Third World region reveals a mixture of such characteristics as excessive ideological pretentions and expectations, crass revolutionary opportunism, military adventurism, bold imperial ambition, realpolitik in the extreme, a conscious dissembling in a propaganda of non-truths and half-truths; and yet a

---

[99] Soviet Interests in Latin America, p. 177.
[100] Luers, The Soviets and Latin America, p. 8–9.
[101] Ibid.
[102] Ibid.
[103] Ibid.

caution marked by restraint and the pursuit of traditional diplomacy customary in any modern nation-state.

2. LONG-TERM SOVIET OBJECTIVES

a. Unswerving pursuit of ideological goals

Ideology cannot be disregarded as a powerful contributing element to Soviet objectives in Latin America, however irrelevant and impractical it may seem to the outsider. Ideology establishes Soviet legitimacy, at least formally: It links the Soviet Union to the historical process, defining its mission in history and providing the historical context for the development of Soviet policy. Communist goals of global triumph were set by revolutionary principles emanating from the Bolshevik Revolution, reaffirmed and refined by succeeding Soviet leaders and theoreticians. They remain fixed in Soviet thinking and thus in their worldview.

Accordingly, ideology projects the broad design for the transformation of Latin America to Socialism—a Socialism, not of the West European Democratic Socialist variety, but that of the Communist-directed Soviet Union. This design is not precisely defined in any detailed way but rather projects a general but viable pattern for future development. In a practical sense ideology firmly links the Soviet Union to the revolutionary movements now shaking the foundations of Latin American society. Unlikely Soviet success in achieving their long-term goals in the present era or near future beyond their gains in Cuba and Nicaragua has dictated a strategy of political opportunism.[104] Nonetheless, the ultimate Soviet ideological goal is affirmed as an abiding principle of Soviet international life, and it does condition Soviet thinking and behavior in foreign policy.[105]

b. Presumed geopolitical objectives

Soviet ideological goals are ideals, great expectations to be achieved at some point in history; Soviet geopolitical goals are realities that reflect the hard facts of international life. Great power politics enter in to create an hegemonic contest for global turf. Latin America, as part of the Third World, is a principal region in this contest.[106]

---

[104] Blasier writes: "Given the realities, many of the time-encrusted goals of the international Communist movement, voiced generations ago by Lenin, are no longer reliable guides to contemporary Soviet behavior. It is not that Lenin's goals have been repudiated or that Soviet leaders do not pay them lip service from time to time. Rather, it is because Lenin's goals, such as the establishment of world communism, the spread of socialism everywhere, and the like are simply not viable in today's world and probably not in tomorrow's." For this reason, Blasier adds, "the Soviet leadership must seize its opportunities where it finds them." (The Giant's Rival, p. 131.) See also, Simes, The New Soviet Challenge, p. 125-126.

[105] Though Blasier may question the practicality of Soviet goals and their ability to achieve them in "today's world" or "tomorrow's," nonetheless, he recognizes the Soviet commitment to these goals when he wrote, "The Soviet leadership is irrevocably committed to national liberation movements and the ultimate achievement of socialism in Latin America." (The Giant's Rival, p. 68.)

[106] Duncan observes that Soviet policies in Latin America "strikes one as essentially those of a great power in quest of traditional great power concerns . . . the search for influence to guarantee territorial security . . ., access to markets and resources so necessary for economic prosperity. . . . Although Moscow's objectives turn in part upon ideological considerations . . ., Soviet national interests appear to be defined primarily in terms of economic and political

Khrushchev's updating and refinement of Soviet ideology placed Latin America in a new context. It linked Latin America to the Third World, not directly at first—his attention had been drawn initially to Asia and Africa—but soon after the emergence of Castro. The effects of the Khrushchev synthesis were to globalize Soviet foreign policy, bring Latin America more directly into the Soviet worldview, and create a specific set of Soviet geopolitical objectives in the Western Hemisphere.

Long-term Soviet objectives are briefly, to weaken the U.S. hemispheric position, encourage Latin American independence, and expand Soviet influence. The full effect, if successful, would be to enhance Russia's superpower status globally and reduce that of the United States; increase Soviet prestige and that of Socialism; and introduce Soviet power as an enduring factor into the international politics of the Western Hemisphere.

Moscow's presumed geopolitical objectives have distinctive characteristics. Notwithstanding exaggerated Soviet ideological rhetoric, Russia and the United States have been engaged in an old-fashioned struggle for power. Assuming an enduring adversarial relationship with the United States, the Soviets have long sought to transform the existing international status quo, tipping the balance of power in their favor. They seek to establish a new international Socialist system under their hegemony. In the judgment of some observers, they have seemed to pursue a singular grand geopolitical design, initiated in the mid-1970's, intended to reduce American power globally by executing a long range economic, political and military flanking movement, a projection of the Mackinder thesis, so to speak, that suggests a Soviet geopolitical envelopment of the United States and Latin America from its Eurasian base.[107] Superior military power has been essential for the success of this geopolitical strategy that seems rooted in Russian history and energized by new expectations promised in Marxism-Leninism.[108] Possessing extensive raw material resources and holding strategic positions along crucial sea lane communications in the Caribbean and South Atlantic, the denial of which to the United States could inflict serious injury, Latin America has become a principal part of this geopolitical design.[109]

Duncan sums up long-term Soviet objectives in Latin America in this sweeping but compressed statement:

---

power. This is not to say that Marxist-Leninist ideology does not condition Soviet conceptions of power; quite the contrary. But it does suggest that the direct promotion of communism in Latin America is overshadowed by the interests of Moscow as an evolving great power with traditional world requirements—particularly in terms of its ideologically and territorially perceived adversaries, the United States and mainland China." (Soviet Power in Latin America, p. 10.) For a commentary on the inter-relationship between Soviet great power interests, their buildup of military power, and its impact on the United States and the Third World, see Luers, The Soviets and Latin America, p. 3-4.

[107] Leiken elaborates on his views of this flanking movement in, Reconstructing Central American Policy, Washington Quarterly, v. 5, Winter 1982: 50; Eastern Winds in Latin America, p. 94-96; and Soviet Strategy in Latin America, p. 11-14.

[108] Simes, The New Soviet Challenge, p. 120-126.

[109] For a commentary on the importance of raw material resources, see, Duncan, Soviet Power in Latin America, p. 5-6. "Any redirection of raw materials trade of this type during the last quarter of the 20th century, in the context of shrinking global supplies of raw materials and increasing demands, helps the Soviets in the game of power politics and great power status," Duncan concludes. He goes on to explain the importance of other raw materials, for example, oil, coal, iron, and uranium, in Soviet Strategy in Latin America.

All of these transformations [that is, economic development and expanding trade, the impact of economic and political nationalism, and the decline of the Western Hemisphere Community idea] combined to present opportunities for the Soviet Union to insinuate its presence and gain influence wherever possible, hopefully at the expense of the United States. Adapting its foreign policy to the new realities, Moscow concentrated on five main types of activity: (1) to pursue any opportunity that promised to weaken the United States, short of provoking direct confrontation; (2) to establish bases for its ships, including its blue water navy as well as those engaged in intelligence-collecting, commercial fishing, and merchant marine activities as a projection of its power in the region; (3) to gain access to strategic raw materials and food; (4) to expand diplomatic, commercial, and trade relations wherever possible; and (5) to promote Marxist-Leninist models of economic and political change, hopefully communist-party-led, in as risk-free a manner as possible (i.e., with minimum financing and, again, short of provoking U.S. intervention).[110]

Soviet long-term objectives in Latin America, as perceived by serious-minded American students of Soviet and Latin American policy, seem ambitious—perhaps over-ambitious—imperial, and somewhat impractical, given the limited Soviet resources. Still, this is how they seem to see their tasks in this hemisphere and accordingly should be taken seriously.

3. SHORT-TERM SOVIET OBJECTIVES

a. Socialist Cuba, a base for projecting Soviet power

The starting point for a brief summary of short-term Soviet objectives in Latin America is Socialist Cuba. Central to Soviet policy in Latin America, and especially in the Caribbean and Central America, is to maintain and protect Socialist Cuba and to strengthen Moscow's hold on Cuba as a permanent base for projecting Soviet power.

The Soviets have accumulated, in Rothenberg's words, "an enormous strategic stake in Cuba and to that degree in Latin America."[111] Their physical presence, linked to Cuba's military potentiality, places Soviet power in a position to challenge the United States in its "strategic rear."[112] An "important adjunct" of Soviet political, military, propaganda and intelligence activities in Latin American and Third World areas, Cuba provides a base for projecting Soviet influence throughout the Caribbean and Latin America in a manner now taking place in Central America.[113]

Cuba also serves as a model for Latin American leftist regimes, the Sandinistas and the New Jewel Movement in Grenada, for example. It is an instrument of revolution in Latin America and a channel for enlarging Soviet influence in the Third World through such organizations as the Non-Alignment Movement (NAM). Unable to exercise influence in the Third World through interna-

---

[110] Duncan, Soviet Interests in Latin America, p. 167.

[111] Rothenberg, The Soviets and Central America, p. 132.

[112] For detailed elaborations on the strategic importance of Cuba to the Soviets, see Leiken, Soviet Strategy in Latin America, p. 61–72; and Valenta, Soviet and Cuban Responses in Central America, p. 137–139. Valenta notes that the Soviets have use of modern docking facilities, potential submarine facilities in Cienfuegos, air facilities for reconnaissance aircraft, satellite stations, and sophisticated intelligence facilities for monitoring U.S. satellite and microwave conversations and also NATO advanced weapons testing in the Atlantic. Since 1978 Soviet pilots have been flying MIG-27's on patrol missions in Cuba and Soviet TU-95's conduct regular reconnaissance missions monitoring U.S. naval activities in the Atlantic. Cuba is also a center for close Soviet-Cuban coordination in gathering intelligence information in the Caribbean Basin (p. 137).

[113] Rothenberg, The Soviets and Central America, p. 131–132.

tional economic bodies or regional organizations, the Soviets have sought to build military-political clients such as Cuba: Their purpose, to magnify Soviet prestige globally, to fortify its claim to legitimacy as a special representative of world history, and to seek parity with the United States as a superpower in the military and political field.[114]

Finally, Cuba is "a key maritime strategic piece on Moscow's global chessboard," as Duncan puts it, as well as a port of call for merchant marine fishing fleet operations, trade activities, and oceanographic work. Soviet investments in Cuba's marine activities have accounted for its "spectacular growth" and when linked to that of the Soviets, and compared with U.S. shortcomings, magnifies its importance as a Soviet power asset.[115]

In brief, Cuba is a principal power resource for the Soviets in seeking their goals in Latin America, and, accordingly, must be maintained even at considerable economic cost and protected as an extended, highly important but not necessarily a "vital" Soviet interest.

b. Exploiting opportunities in Central America and Caribbean Basin

In Central America and the Caribbean Basin, the Soviet short-term policy objective is to exploit whatever revolutionary opportunities that might arise, as in Nicaragua, El Salvador and Grenada, and to do so at a low risk to itself. They have sought to foment revolutionary upheaval and encourage so-called "anti-imperialist" forces and regimes in the region.[116]

At this juncture, the security issue seems to be the most important component of Soviet objectives. "One Soviet security objective," writes Valenta, "is gradually and cautiously to secure access to and maintain naval facilities in the Caribbean Basin so as to project Soviet power while undermining that of the United States and its allies."[117] According to Valenta, the Soviets lack facilities and logistical support needed for the permanent deployment of a fleet in the region. Cuba is their only significant military base; it is speculated that the Soviets want to upgrade and expand their naval presence in the Caribbean.[118]

Using Cuba as a model for military modernization, the Soviets also seek to develop close military ties with new client regimes through arms transfers and other forms of military cooperation. In so doing the Soviets want to become a major military supplier to the "anti-imperialist" forces in the Basin. A case in point, and future precedent, is Soviet-Cuban arms transfers to Nicaragua that have destabilized the region.[119]

Economic objectives play only a minor role in Soviet strategy in the region. Trade is minimal, and, as Valenta notes, "The Soviets do not view the Caribbean as economically attractive."[120] Howev-

---

[114] Luers, The Soviets and Latin America, p. 25.
[115] Duncan, Soviet Power in Latin America. p. 7.
[116] Valenta, Soviet Policy in Central America, p. 291.
[117] Ibid., p. 293.
[118] Ibid., p.294.
[119] Ibid.
[120] Ibid., p. 295.

er, the presence of important natural resources, especially in Mexico and Venezuela, has doubtless spurred Soviet interest.[121]

The Soviets also seek to divert U.S. attention from Europe and Asia where they are involved in unresolved conflicts in Poland and Afghanistan by preoccupying the United States with trouble in its own "strategic rear."[122] It is further speculated that the Soviets want to get the United States bogged down in Central America, as it had been in Vietnam, thus reducing its resources and energy from other troubled global areas in the East-West conflict.[123]

Thus, the Soviets pursue political-military objectives in this Third World region of Central America and the Caribbean Basin. Though concealing their involvement behind the Cuban and East European screen—thus complicating the task of creating an effective U.S. response, they, nonetheless, have established clearly defined revolutionary and expansionist objectives and have sought to achieve them through military means, but in a cautious, yet incremental manner.

c. On the path of traditionalism in Mexico and South America

The Soviets have selected the path of diplomatic traditionalism in pursuing their short term objectives in Mexico and South America. In a strategy of political gradualism, the Soviets have encouraged a "united front" with a common opposition in Communist Party matters, and by and large abjure the path of armed struggle; however, the Chilean party, in defiance of this line, advocates violent revolution.[124] On the state-to-state level they have sought over the past 25 years to establish long-term stable government realtions with traditional trade, economic, and political objectives.[125]

A "distinct pragmatism" underscores Soviet objectives in this region, Duncan observes, "an inclination to ride with Latin American nationalist aspirations rather than trying to force-feed doctrinaire Marxism-Leninism to unwilling subjects."[126] A striking example of this pragmatism was I.V. Kapitonov's visit to Mexico in September 1984. A top party leader and member of the Supreme Soviet, Kapitonov headed a delegation of Soviet parliamentarians to Mexico at the invitation of Mexico's National Congress. Kapitonov was received by President Miguel de la Madrid, and he addressed the National Congress. In the course of the visit, according to an Izvestiya account, Kapitonov emphasized that "the USSR advocates the further development of traditional ties with Mexico." As if to prove his point, he cited the great number of bilateral agreements that had been concluded in the last few years, paving the way for cooperation in economic matters, science and technolo-

[121] Ibid.
[122] Ibid., p. 289.
[123] Kissinger Commission's Report, p. 93.
[124] Luers, The Soviets and Latin America, p. 16–17.
[125] Ibid.
[126] Soviet Power in Latin America, p. 8. In describing this traditionalist approach, Duncan writes: "Despite the Soviet willingness to welcome delegates from the pro-Soviet Latin American Communist parties to the capital, the Kremlin continues to pursue active diplomatic, trade, and technical assistance programs in countries where Communist parties are proscribed (Bolivia, Brazil, Uruguay), where the government makes life difficult for Marxists associated with guerrilla movements (as in Argentina in the mid 1970's), and where transnational corporations strongly link the Latin American countries with western capitalism."

gy, shipping, air communications, radio, television and sport. "However, the potential here is far from exhausted," Kapitonov said, "there is much to be done by both sides in the common interest."[127]

4. ADAPTING OBJECTIVES TO REGIONAL REQUIREMENTS

The Soviet pursuit of objectives in Latin America, both long- and short-term, are thus adapted to the requirements of the time and the region. Policy is shaped according to hard political realities.

D. INSTRUMENTALITIES DIFFERENTIATED BY CIRCUMSTANCE

1. BUILDING ON A MILITARY-IMPERIAL BASE

In pursuit of their objectives in Latin America, the Soviets have many instrumentalities differentiated by circumstance. The starting point is the military character of the Soviet state from which all else flows; for military power and its use are the principal criteria guiding Soviet policy in the Third World. This characteristic is forcefully demonstrated in Part II of this study on the expanding Soviet presence in Asia.[128]

Formal adherence to Marxism-Leninism ideology serves a useful philosophical, institutional and conceptual purpose in organizing the government, in policy planning and in appealing especially to the downtrodden of the Third World who seek a saving organizational principle. But Marxism-Leninism, as an organizing principle and an alluring utopianism, has long lost its appeal not only in the Third World but within the Soviet Union itself. One seasoned American diplomat with decades of service in the Soviet bloc rightly termed Soviet ideology, "dry bread."[129]

What remains, therefore, is Soviet militarism, whose guiding criterion is building and using military power for imperial purposes. Allocation of political and economic resources are made with this in mind. A sustaining force is the lingering influence of the old imperial Russian tradition of expansionism and the vision of a promised future of global hegemony in Marxism-Leninism.[130]

---

[127] Izvestiya (Moscow), Sept. 19, 1984, Morning Edition, p. 4, in, FBIS Daily Report, Soviet Union, v. 3, Sept. 25, 1984, p. K1 and K3.

[128] For a discussion of the militarization of Soviet policy, see, Brezezinski, Zbigniew. Tragic Dilemmas of Soviet World Power: The Limits of a New-Type Empire. Encounter, v. 61, Dec. 1983: 10–17. See also, HFAC, Soviet Diplomacy and Negotiating Behavior, p. 510–520.

[129] Simes attributes the "pitiful state" of Soviet culture to the "deadly and oppressive political and intellectual climate." "No wonder the ability of the USSR to act as a leader of the international communist movement had declined, perhaps irrevocably," he continues, adding, "The days of the Communist International are over." According to Simes, "The nationalist, conservative Soviet police state has no genuine universal appeal beyond the reach of its tanks." On the Soviet influence in the Third World. Simes writes: "The USSR is still active in the Third World and its involvement is often eagerly sought by local rulers. but these requests rarely result from any illusions about Soviet motives, and almost never reflect the belief that communist Russia is a model for Third World development. Moscow's military power and its willingess to provide arms and geopolitical protection, not the appeal of Soviet ideas and accomplishments, are what normally motivate Third World overtures to the Soviet Union." (The New Soviet Challenge, p. 123–124.)

[130] Simes notes the nationalization of Soviet ideology and the melding of its with Russian historical tradition. "The czars' internal policies are routinely exposed," he notes. "But as far as foreign policy is concerned. Soviet Communists positively endorse the Russian imperial heritage." "Marxist-Leninist cliches," he writes, "are increasingly used to legitimate goals formerly associated with imperial Russia." (The New Soviet Challenge, p. 120–122.) For observations on

Continued

2. THE POLITICAL DIMENSION

Politics set the course of Soviet policy in such Third World areas as Latin America. Defined strictly in terms of Soviet interests, it carefully discriminates among the governments and regimes deserving Soviet support and accordingly determines the character of that support. Opportunity, legitimately gained or through clandestine means carried on by overstaffed embassies, provides the opening wedge; and incrementalism, the carefully measured means for dispensing Soviet political largesse, and for building and expanding its influence. Soviet prestige and power engaged in support of a client is the essence of the political dimension.

By the early 1960's the Soviets had determined to support Socialist Cuba. Except for a brief period of tactical misunderstanding, they have sustained that support for a quarter century. At the United Nations, through the NAM, and in the international arena generally, the Soviets have consistently supported Castro's positions, particularly in his jousts with the United States.[131] The Soviets have also used their military power for political purposes, both to their advantage and that of Cuba. Extensive naval visits and maneuvers with Cuba in the Caribbean and Gulf of Mexico have been intended to make a clear political point; namely, to demonstrate Soviet support of Cuba and to affirm the legitimacy of a Soviet naval presence in the area.

Much the same has been true of Nicaragua. With the Sandinista victory, the Soviets threw their political support behind the revolutionary regime, sealing the relationship with political agreements, both party and state, and manifesting their support by frequent visits to Moscow by Sandinista leaders and return visits by Soviet officials.[132] There are no doubts where the Soviets stand on this issue, though they cast a cautious eye towards Washington. Characteristic of Soviet political support has been a vigorous propaganda campaign designed to win over world opinion on behalf of the Sandinistas and discredit the United States.[133]

---

the militarization of Soviet foreign policy, see Luers, The Soviets and Latin America, p. 18-20. Luers writes of Brezhnev's efforts in bringing the Soviet Union "to a superpower status as a military, not an economic nor an ideological power. . . ." That military emphasis to Soviet development over the past eighteen years, he continues, "has affected the party, Soviet society, and Soviet foreign policy. This military emphasis in Soviet foregin policy has made the Kremlin such a formidable and disturbing competitor in the third world, and particularly in the Western Hemisphere." For another commentary on Soviet military power and foreign policy, see Ford, The Soviet Union: The Next Decade, p. 1140.

[131] Duncan, Soviet Power in Latin America, p. 16.

[132] Rothenberg discusses the wide range of interaction between the Soviets and Sandinistas in, Latin America in Soviet Eyes. Problems of Communism, v. 23, Sept.-Oct. 1983: 9-11; Since Reagan: The Soviets and Latin America, p. 175-178; and The Soviets and Central America, p. 132-134. A recent illustration of Soviet support for Communists and leftists in Cuba and Central America was Soviet Foreign Minister Andrei Gromyko's speech at the U.N. on El Salvador: "We are witnessing gross interference in the internal affairs of El Salvador. No effort is spared to prop up the regime of the stooges who are committing brutal crimes against the Salvadoran people." On Nicaragua: "A real siege—military, political and economic—has been mounted against Nicaragua whose people, defending their national freedom, independence and democratic achievements, are heroically resisting in the face of the undeclared war organized against it by Washington." On Socialist Cuba: "They still cannot reconcile themselves to the existence of Socialist Cuba. Threats are being made against Cuba to force that country off the course to which it has been committed both in words and deeds." Gromyko gave Soviet support to efforts to achieve peace in Central America. (FBIS 089, Take 10, Moscow Tass in English, 1545 GMT, Sept. 27, 1984.)

[133] In its attack on the Republican Party platform for 1984, Tass places particular stress on American "imperialism." "The United States insatiably devours one after another integral parts

Continued

Among the more settled traditional governments of the Southern Cone, the Soviets have seized available opportunities to introduce their political influence. Support for Argentina in the Falklands War stands as a classic case of Soviet political support given virtually unstintingly to a Third World country at a moment of crisis. All the ingredients are there: an opportunity to discredit Britain, the United States and their NATO allies; an enlarging wedge for further expanding Soviet influence in Argentina; an occasion for the Soviets to affirm their own credentials as a "natural ally" of the Third World; a chance to point out the weaknesses of the inter-American system; and a dramatic event that could arouse and magnify Latin American suspicions of the United States and accelerate the movement away from dependency.[134]

Pro-Soviet Latin American Communist Parties have also served as a useful political instrument for Russian policy. Though limited in membership, appeal and effectiveness, they can be counted on for support.[135]

3. ARMS TRANSFERS AND MILITARY ASSISTANCE, THE PRINCIPAL WEAPON

Arms transfers and military assistance (training personnel, providing equipment and constructing facilities) are the Soviet's principal weapons for building and spreading influence in Latin America. This is what the Soviets do best, a device proven many times in the Third World since the first arms transfer to Nasser's Egypt in 1955. Moscow cannot compete with the United States, Japan and the West in economic aid; they can, and do, in the military sphere. Their purpose is to further solidify relationships in the Third World. Military assistance serves basic needs for both the Soviets and their clients. For the Soviets it provides the lure, and for the Third World clients it promises: an alternative to the West who many still distrust; practical support for revolutionaries on the road to power; security against adversaries, internal and external; stability for unstable revolutionary regimes; and a means for expanding revolution beyond a client's borders. During the period 1976–1979 and 1980–1983, Soviet arms deliveries to Latin America were valued at $1.92 billion and $3.16 billion respectively.[136]

Soviet military assistance to Socialist Cuba has been the critical factor in Castro's ability to: solidify his regime at home; expand the revolution into Latin America; support Soviet policy in such Third World areas as Angola and Ethiopia, even supplying its own troops;

---

of the U.N. trust territory of the Pacific Islands (Micronesia)," Tass charges. "We do not mention Latin American countries which the United States views as Texas' backyard where Washington can do whatever it likes." According to the Soviets, the platform adopted at the Dallas convention "is permeated with imperial arrogance." (FBIS 043, Tass, Aug. 22, 1984.)

[134] Duncan, Soviet Interests in Latin America, p. 181–182.

[135] Rothenberg, Latin America in Soviet Eyes, p. 16. For commentaries by Blasier, see his, The Giant's Rival, p. 68, 143–145. For a discussion of the regional apparatus and the Russian staff within the CC CPSU, see p. 72–76.

[136] Grimmett, Richard E. Trends in Conventional Arms Transfers to the Third World by Major Supplier, 1976–1983. Washington, Congressional Research Service, The Library of Congress, May 7, 1984, p. 25. (Report No. 84–82 F). For a commentary on Soviet military assistance to the Third World, see, Krause, Joachim. Soviet Military Aid to the Third World. Aussenpolitik, v. 34, no. 4, 1983: 392–404. With respect to criteria for military aid, Krause writes: "The Kremlin tries to gain economic advantage from the sale of weapons, but political criteria alone decide who is given arms aid under what circumstances." (p. 397)

and play a credible role as a Soviet client state in the NAM and other international organizations where Third World countries are politically active. Total Soviet military assistance to Socialist Cuba has been estimated to be $3.8 billion during 1961–1979.[137]

Similarly, Soviet military aid, apparently transshipped through Cuba and their East European allies, has been a critical factor in sustaining the Sandinista regime at home and expanding its military operations into adjoining El Salvador. Estimated Soviet military assistance to the Sandinistas has been placed at some $125 million during 1979–1982. Subsequent deliveries in early 1983, according to the State Department, were "speeded up." [138] In the fall of 1984, deliveries seemed to have accelerated to an alarming degree.

Soviet military assistance had also been a factor in attempting to consolidate the leftist regime in Grenada. After the U.S. invasion and occupation of Grenada in October 1983, it was discovered from captured documents that five secret military cooperation agreements had been concluded by the former Bishop government with Cuba, North Korea and the Soviet Union. The agreements provided for $37 million in additional military equipment to Grenada and the dispatching of a permanent delegation of 27 Cuban military advisors. The Soviets had planned to send $27 million in military equipment; the North Koreans $12 million in supplies; and the Cubans were to train the armed forces.[139]

Military assistance has also been a useful instrument for expanding Soviet influence in the Southern Cone, though hardly on the scale as in Cuba and Nicaragua. The Soviets have given substantial assistance to Peru, but in recent years the Peruvians have sought to diversify their purchases. Troubled by a recent outburst of violence from the Shining Path Maoist Communist faction, Peru has found a ready source of arms supply in the Soviet Union. In July 1984, the Peruvian Government was considering the purchase of over $50 million in arms from the Soviet Union in what could be the largest sale by Moscow to Peru since it returned to democracy four years ago. American officials have long expressed uneasiness over the Soviet-Peruvian military relationship, the only South American country that has made major arms purchases in Moscow. About 160 Soviet military advisers are stationed in Peru, including about 90 with the Peruvian Army.[140]

Soviet military aid is thus a vital component of Soviet Third World policy. Joachim Krause, a West German scholar, concludes: "Arms supplies, training aid, technical assistance and if need be direct military support (or the provision and provisioning of such backing) are currently the main instrument of Soviet foreign policy in the Third World." There can be little doubt that this conclusion

---

[137] Blasier, The Giant's Rival, p. 100. Blasier notes that this is an estimate of cumulative military aid calculated on the basis of the amount granted in 1961–1968 ($1.5 billion). He indicates that "the total probably is much higher." According to a report prepared by a contractor for the State Department, Soviet military aid to Cuba averaged 15,000 tons from 1963 to 1980. Military aid rose to 63,000 tons in 1981 and 68,000 tons in 1982. (Jacobsen Report, p. 14.)

[138] Jacobsen Report, p. 15. For Cuban military aid to Nicaragua and Central American revolutionaries, see, p. 17–18.

[139] Duncan, Soviet Interests in Latin America, p. 170.

[140] Diehl, Jackson. Peru Considers Purchase of More Soviet Weapons. The Washington Post, July 27, 1984, p. A20.

has special relevance to Latin America. Perhaps equally important is Krause's further conclusion—in line with what was said above about the militarization of Soviet foreign policy—that, "Military aid, one might almost say, has emerged as the foreign policy instrument of the Soviet military machine." [141]

4. ECONOMIC AID AND TRADE: A CASE OF MULTIPLE PURPOSES

Soviet economic aid and trade in Latin America has served multiple purposes as an instrument of Soviet Third World policy, though not necessarily succesfully. Blasier, who has examined Soviet economic relations with Latin America in some detail, concludes that "on the whole" these relations have been "disappointing." [142]

The Cuban economy, based on the Soviet model since the early 1970's, has not yet become viable, and accordingly has had to be sustained by the Soviets with formidable subsidies. During the period 1961–1979, Soviet economic aid to Cuba amounted to an estimated $16.7 billion.[143] In 1981, Socialist Cuba received about $3.6 billion in aid from the Soviet bloc. In 1982, this subsidy was increased to $4.9 billion, largely through the mechanism of preferential pricing of Cuban sugar and the artificially low price Cuba pays for Soviet oil.[144] It is estimated that Soviet economic support of Cuba amounts to $8 million per day, a figure judged to be low. The annual total amounts to $3 billion, approximately 25 percent of Cuba's gross domestic product or approximately five times the total U.S. aid to Latin America.[145]

In the case of Nicaragua, Soviet economic largesse has been carefully measured. Initially, Moscow encouraged the Sandinistas to get aid anywhere they could, but in the past two years an increasing share of Managua's international transactions has gradually been redirected toward the Soviet sphere. During 1981 and 1982, an economic protocol provided for a $50 million Soviet credit, supplementing $100 million in credits from Libya, $64 million from Cuba, and over $50 million more from East Germany, Czechoslovakia and Bulgaria. In May 1982, the Soviets extended an additional $100 million credit to Nicaragua.[146]

Cautious about unnecessarily provoking the United States, the Soviets have moved slowly in taking on Nicaragua as a full-fledged client. But more important, particularly for the purposes of this study, the Soviets appear to have been unwilling thus far to underwrite the Sandinista economy to the extent that they have in Cuba. Socialist Cuba has proved to be a heavy economic burden for the Soviets, and observers of Soviet activities in Latin America believe that, given mounting economic and social difficulties at home as well as increasing liabilities on the foreign policy front, the Soviets are not anxious to add another burden to their accumulating prob-

[141] Krause, Soviet Military Aid to the Third World, p. 403.
[142] Blasier, The Giant's Rival, p. 129, 141-143.
[143] Ibid., p. 100.
[144] Duncan, Soviet Interests in Latin America, p. 176.
[145] Valenta, Soviet Policy in Central America, p. 298.
[146] Rothenberg, Latin America in Soviet Eyes, p. 9.

lems.[147] Hence the argument among Soviet scholars for greater diversity in dealing with the Third World, and particularly in Latin America.[148]

In trade relations with Latin America, the Soviets have had to pay a stiff price because of a serious and persistent trade imbalance. Large deficits characterize this economic relationship, sometimes constituting a substantial fraction of the total Soviet deficit. Latin America has become a major source of Soviet imports of traditional agricultural products such as grain, meat, hides, coffee and cocoa. In return, the Soviets have attempted to sell heavy industrial equipment for large projects such as irrigation, hydro and thermal power and transport. The trade balance has persisted in favor of Latin America, and the difference is paid in hard currency.[149] Nonetheless, Soviet-Latin American trade has grown "quite rapidly," Rothenberg writes, "though it remains an extremely small percentage of the foreign trade of both sides." According to Soviet trade figures, turnover (excluding Cuba) in 1969 amounted to 116.5 million rubles; by 1979, this had increased to 595 million rubles, and by 1981, it reached 3,124.4 million rubles (about $4.5 billion). Over the years the bulk of the trade has been with Argentina and Brazil. Increased Soviet interest in Latin America is clearly indicated by the fact that in 1960 the Soviets traded with only four Latin American countries; now they trade with more than 20.[150]

Trade relations as recorded here are normal among nations and reflect certain traditionalist aspects of Soviet policy in Latin America. But such tangible and viable connections strengthen the Soviet presence in Latin America, with all the known political implications. For multiple reasons, therefore, economic aid-and-trade, though a costly instrument, serves a useful Soviet political purpose in this Third World region.[151]

---

[147] Blasier, The Giant's Rival, p. 129. Valenta comments on aspects of this economic burden in, Soviet Policy in Central America, p. 297-298. According to Jacobsen, in the context of overall aid to Third World nations, "Moscow's commitment to Nicaragua is modest." (Jacobsen Report, p. 21.)

[148] See Part I of this study, the Soviet "Commitment in Perspective," p. 54-88. See also, Valkenier, Elizabeth Kridl. The Soviet Union and the Third World: An Economic Bind. New York, Praeger, 1983, 188 p.

[149] Blasier, The Giant's Rival. p. 129-130, 141-142.

[150] Rothenberg, Latin America in Soviet Eyes, p. 15.

[151] Leiken explains the strategic aspects of Soviet economic relations in Latin America: "In Latin America . . . the Russians have 'difficulties in selling their industrial products.' Hence, they suffer a trade deficit. However, the Soviets turn this shortcoming to their strategic advantage. Once the Russian market becomes critical to a foreign country, the Soviets exploit this dependence to extract industrial and military sales, together with political support. This has happened in Egypt, India, Indonesia, and Cuba. Currently the Soviets purchase one-fifth of Argentina's exports and more than half of its traditional exports of meat and grain. Seeking to establish footholds, Soviet trade with Latin America shot up from 3 per cent of their non-military Third World trade in 1970 to 11 per cent in 1977." Leiken continues: "In Latin America power projects, the 'fractional' Soviet role is the provision of turbines and generators. In Latin America's most advanced nuclear program, the Soviets provide the Argentines with the critical components of heavy water and enriched uranium. In all these projects, the Russians occupy a decisive place in the techno-productive process. This again follows a pattern previously seen in Afghanistan, Cuba, Egypt, India, and Somalia. Like other Third World countries, Latin American nations resist Soviet penetration: Peru has been revising its relationship with Moscow. Nevertheless, the Olmos project has not been abandoned and refinancing is being sought from the Russians, as well as from the Swedes." Leiken reply to Blesier's critique, Foreign Policy, no. 43, Summer 1981: 189-190.)

5. PUBLIC DIPLOMACY: A BENIGN BUT EFFECTIVE INSTRUMENT OF
INFLUENCE

Public dipomacy, a benign instrument of influence, has played an important and seemingly effective role in Soviet policy in Latin America. According to Rothenberg, the expansion of Soviet activity in the general area of culture and information has been "substantial." One "striking" statistic is in the growth of Soviet Spanish language publications. During the decade 1949–1959, the Soviets published about 53 such titles totaling half a million copies per year. In 1975, they issued 353 Spanish titles and published 13 million copies; and in 1980, 370 titles and 10.6 million copies. In 1958, the Soviets published only seven Spanish language serial titles; by 1980, the number increased nearly five-fold. In 1972, Communist countries broadcast 708.5 hours per week to Latin America; by 1979, the figure increased to 793 hours; Cuba accounted for 241.5 hours, or almost one-third of the total.[152]

Student education has also been an important component of the Soviet effort in Latin America. According to C.G. Jacobsen, a specialist on the Soviets in Latin America, the number of Soviet scholarships to Central American students rose "dramatically" during the early 1980's. Deputy Secretary of State Kenneth W. Dam reported that between 1972 and 1982 Soviet scholarships "for a handful of Central American and Caribbean countries rose over 500 percent, to nearly 4,000." By 1983, the Soviet Union and Cuba provided 7,500 scholarships to Central American students.[153] Jacobsen notes that Central America probably constitutes "the second largest Soviet scholarship program aimed at Latin America, though the total of South American students is difficult to compute." The largest program is directed at Cuba which during 1983–1984 had some 9,000 students attending Soviet institutions of higher learning.[154]

Increased Soviet interest in Latin America is also evident by the establishment of a major research institute and by the expanding scope of Soviet research on the region. Intellectually underpinning much of the Soviet effort in Latin America is the Latin American Institute. Founded in 1961 and staffed by leading Soviet Latin Americanists, the LAI serves as a Soviet "think tank" for the guidance of policymakers in the Party and Government. The LAI parallels the work of another institution in the Soviet Academy of Sciences that deals with Soviet-American relations; namely, the USA and Canada Institute.

In 1969, the LAI began publishing the journal Latinskaya Amerika with a circulation of about 3,000. Its main purpose was to serve as a clearinghouse for the published work of Soviet Latin Americanists. As Soviet interest increased, the journal's circulation rose

---

[152] Rothenberg, Latin America in Soviet Eyes, p. 15. For a listing of Soviet magazines and Communist broadcasts, see, Blasier, The Giant's Rival, p. 191–192.

[153] Jacobsen Report, p. 29.

[154] Ibid. For other sources on Soviet educational efforts in Latin America, see, U.S. General Accounting Office. Report to the Congress. U.S. and Soviet Bloc Training of Latin American and Caribbean students: Considerations in Developing Future U.S. Programs. Washington, August 16, 1984, 67 p. (GAO/NSIAD-84-109); The Economist Foreign Report, no. 1835, Aug. 9, 1984: 6–7; and The Christian Science Monitor, May 18, 1983, p. 1. According to the Monitor, "Latin Americans on Soviet bloc scholarships currently outnumber those on US government scholarships by about 18 to 1." "We're definitely out-scholarshiped," confirms David Larsen of the International Institute of Education, the largest U.S. education exchange agency.

steadily reaching a plateau of about 7,000 by the late 1970's. Within six months after the Sandinista victory, the journal, issued in Russian and Spanish, was changed from a bimonthly to a monthly and its circulation increased to 9,000. This number was reduced in 1982 and 1983 to 7,500.[155] The prominence and growing resources of the LAI and the wide circulation of its journal suggest the seriousness with which the Soviet Union looks upon its future in Latin America.[156]

Scholars differ on the impact of this interconnecting network between the Soviet Union, Cuba and Latin America. Blasier concludes:

> One finds in Latin America an incongruity. There is extensive Soviet influence over the thinking of many Latin Americans, particularly because aspects of the Soviet program, with adaptations, appeal to the needs and interests of some groups, but the Soviet model as a whole rarely dominates, and it is attractive only to a very few.[157]

Rothenberg is more skeptical in his concluding appraisal of the Soviet impact. He writes:

> These diplomatic, economic, cultural, and ideological connections do not yet make the Soviet Union a full-fledged "superpower" in the Western Hemisphere, but they do enable Moscow to exert some influence on selected target groups and to hold out the possibility of alternatives to the United States. Especially in situations such as the present one of strained US-Soviet relations, Latin American links with the USSR can be interpreted as demonstrations of independence from Washington. It is in this context that one should look at the growing complex of Soviet activity in the region—and at evolving Soviet assessments of the erosion of US dominance there.[158]

Whatever the proper balance of influence, the fact remains that the Soviets have an expanding presence in this Third World region; they are determined in their commitment; and they have differentiated instrumentalities for achieving their larger political goals.

---

[155] Rothenberg, Latin America in Soviet Eyes, p. 15.

[156] For a commentary on the debate carried on among Latin Americanists, see, Hough, Jerry F. The Evolving Soviet Debate on Latin America. Latin American Research Review, v. 16, no. 1, 1981: 124-143. For a descriptive commentary on the LAI and its scholars, see, Blasier, The Giant's Rival, Appendix 2.

[157] Ibid., p. 15.

[158] Rothenberg, Latin America in Soviet Eyes, p. 16. With respect to the press, Leiken states: "The satanization of the United States is widely disseminated in the Latin American press, over which the Soviets have considerable influence." Leiken elaborates on this charge. (Leiken, Eastern Winds in Latin America, p. 105.) Some observers dispute this charge.

II. CUBA, AN INSTRUMENT OF SOVIET POLICY

A. IDEOLOGICAL PURITY OF CASTRO'S REVOLUTION

1. THREE POINTS FOR CONSIDERATION

Socialist Cuba, the first in Moscow's three-tiered approach to Latin America, is an instrument of Soviet policy in Latin America and the Third World. Three points emerge in this relationship that bear directly on Soviet strategy: the ideological defects of Castro's revolution and its relevance to Soviet policy; the Soviet militarization of Cuba, transforming it into a disciplined and effective instrument of military power; and the use of this instrument in pursuing Soviet goals in Latin America and the Third World.

2. IN THE BEGINNING: IDEOLOGICAL IMPERFECTIONS

a. Castro, a "primitive"

It is said that John McCormack and Fedor Chaliapin, the great classical singers of the early 20th Century, were "primitives" whose art was nurtured in their native soils of Ireland and Russia, enabling them to achieve world renown. Fidel Castro was also a "primitive" whose revolutionary spirit was nurtured in the soil of his native Cuba, enabling him to achieve world recognition as a charismatic revolutionary leader.

b. Victory without communism

Castro was not a professed Communist, at least not initially, though later he claimed to have "deep Socialist and Communist convictions." [1] He had reacted to the stimuli of his environment; his revolutionary consciousness appears to have been formed by the social, economic and political injustices of the Batista regime and the violent Cuban political culture: He opted for revolution as a way of correcting the inequities and deformities about him. According to Blasier, the Cuban Communist Party had offered its support "late and grudgingly" to the armed struggle against Batista; they and Moscow had contributed "little or nothing" to the success of the July 26th Movement. [2]

In brief, Castro, who was regarded with hostility by Cuban Communists, made it on his own. [3] As Blas Roca, the Cuban Communist leader, said, the Cuban Revolution is the "first socialist revolution

---

[1] Sigmund, Paul E. The USSR, Cuba, and the Revolution in Chile. In, Donaldson, The Soviet Union in the Third World, chapt. 2, p. 27.
[2] Blasier, The Giant's Rival, p. 99–102.
[3] Sigmund, The USSR, Cuba, and the Revolution in Chile, p. 27.

that was not made by the Communist Party." [4] In the words of Blasier, "Castro took over the Communists, not the reverse." [5]

c. Embracing Moscow and communism in self-protection

Castro, responding to the allure of socialist solutions and reacting at least in part against U.S. political counterpressures and economic sanctions intended to isolate Cuba and topple his nascent regime, found an alternative in a willing and able Soviet Union.[6] But he moved slowly before embracing his new mentor and its ideology. Ideologically, Castro was a latecomer to Communism. The chronology of events bears this out.

On January 1, 1959, Castro seized power; on the 11th, Moscow extended recognition. From October 1959, he actively sought Soviet economic assistance but had not made a substantial contact with Moscow until the Mikoyan visit in February 1960, at which time trade and credit agreements were concluded. Agreement was reached in May 1960 on exchanging ambassadors. In July 1960, the Soviets escalated their commitment with Khrushchev's promise of Soviet rocket support "figuratively speaking" and conclusion of a military and economic aid agreement. In early 1961, Castro proclaimed the Cuban Revolution "Socialist," and by the end of the year, he pronounced himself a Marxist-Leninist, vowing to remain one until the end of his life.[7]

d. The Soviets' strained justification

Thus Castro's journey to Communism, taking some 24 months, began from a political reality unassociated with Communist ideology, the Communist Party, or the Soviet Union. Castro was a revolutionary "primitive" who in the early years of the Cuban Revolution used Marxism-Leninism to insure the protection of Moscow [8] and later to provide the organizing principle for his regime.

The Soviets have been hard pressed ever since to expunge this defect in Castroism and to claim a positive contribution by the Soviet Union. In contradiction to historical truth, they insist that the Communists made a "large contribution" to the victory of the revolution and the building of Socialism in Cuba. Revolutionary conditions produced the environment for Socialism: This is acknowledged. As O.T. Darusenkov explains in his recent review of Castro's published works:

> The Cuban Revolution was able to achieve victory and survive precisely because within it, although in a unique form, the proletariat had hegemony; for the revolutionary process *moved in accordance with the interests and the ideology of the proletariat, which was reflected and expressed by the revolutionary vanguard headed by Fidel Castro.*

According to Darusenkov, ideology followed the reality of revolution and was adapted accordingly; he insists that the revolution had some of the essentials for the eventual rise of Socialism. Thus he explains:

---

[4] The Giant's Rival, p. 102.
[5] Ibid.
[6] Ibid., p. 101–103.
[7] Sigmund, The USSR, Cuba, and the Revolution in Chile, p. 28.
[8] Ibid.

First socialism was accepted, and later Marxism-Leninism began to be accepted. In other words, here the facts preceded the theoretical explanation. And later the time came for theoretical explanations as well.[9]

3. NASCENT IMPERFECTIONS AND THE CUBAN MODEL FOR REVOLUTIONARIES

Notwithstanding ideological imperfections, Castro's revolution did complete its course, carrying Cuba eventually along the road to Socialism, with substantial Soviet help. In this experience lay the seeds of the idea that makes Cuba a viable model for other Latin American revolutionaries.

By and large Latin American Communist Parties, as in the case of Cuba before the Castro era, have neither been strong nor effective. But existing deplorable conditions in many regions, as in Central America today, have nourished genuine revolutionary movements that can be exploited by indigenous "leftists" who like Castro, though not initially Communists, often look to Moscow (and now Havana) for assistance and support. Linkage of Soviet power directly or indirectly through Cuba to these ideologically imperfect revolutionary movements increases the chances of their success and the possibility of future alignment with the Soviet Union. Thus the danger is not so much in Communism as such but rather in the conditions that produce revolution and invite Soviet intervention and the introduction of its power.

B. SOVIET MILITARIZATION OF SOCIALIST CUBA

1. CUBAN ARMED FORCES: "ONE OF THE LARGEST AND BEST EQUIPPED" IN LATIN AMERICA

The second point that emerges in the Soviet-Cuban relationship is the Soviet militarization of Socialist Cuba. (See Figures 2 and 3.) The military buildup which began in earnest in the late 1960's and early 1970's accelerated during the next decade, making Cuba's military forces one of the most powerful in all Latin America.[10] The following data suggests the size of the Soviet military investment in Cuba and the extent to which it has militarized Socialist Cuba.

---

[9] Darusenkov, O.T. The Cuban Revolution: From the People's Democratic to the Socialist Stage. Voprosy Istorii Kpss, no. 2, Feb. 1984, translated in USSR Report, Political and Sociological Affairs, Apr. 11, 1984, p. 13–14 (JPRS–UPS–84–034).

[10] For a detailed description of this buildup and its effects of Cuba, see, Leiken, Soviet Strategy in Latin America, p. 53–60.

308

FIGURE 2

U.S.S.R. Seaborne Military Deliveries to Cuba

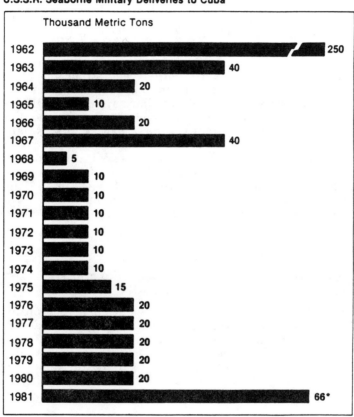

*Approximate figure

Source: U.S. Dept. of State. Bureau of Public Affairs. Cuban Armed Forces and the Soviet Military Presence, August 1982, p. 3. (Special Report No. 103.)

FIGURE 3

Relative Military Strength

For Selected Caribbean Countries

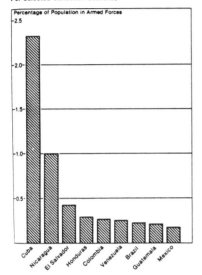

For Selected Latin American Countries

Country	Population (thousands)	People in Military (thousands)	% of Population in Military
Cuba	9,800	227.0	2.32
Argentina	28,000	185.5	.66
Bolivia	5,500	26.6	.48
Brazil	124,780	272.6	.22
Chile	11,180	92.0	.82
Colombia	27,310	70.0	.26
Ecuador	8,250	38.8	.47
Paraguay	3,270	16.0	.49
Peru	18,075	130.0	.72
Uruguay	2,945	29.7	1.01
Venezuela	16,459	40.8	.25
Dominican Republic	5,835	22.5	.39
Guatemala	7,200	15.1	.21
Honduras	3,900	11.2	.29
Mexico	69,000	119.5	.17

Source: *Military Balance, 1981–1982.*

Source: U.S. Dept. of State. Bureau of Public Affairs. Cuban Armed Forces
and the Soviet Military Presence, August 1982, p. 2.   (Special
Report No. 103.)

FIGURE 4

Strength and Missions of Cuba's Paramilitary Organizations

Organization	Subordination	Strength	Mission
Youth Labor Army	MINFAR (Ministry of the Revolutionary Armed Forces	100,000	Civic action force, receiving little military training in peacetime. One wartime mission would be to operate and protect the railroads.
Civil Defense Force	MINFAR	100,000	"Military" units would assist in providing local defense; non-military would provide first aid and disaster relief.
Territorial Troop Militia	MINFAR	More than 500,000 at present; still forming	Regional security/local defense.
Border Guard Troops	MININT (Ministry of the Interior)	3,000 full-time, plus unknown number of civilian auxiliaries	Help guard Cuban coastline.
National Revolutionary Police	MININT	10,000, plus 52,000 civilian auxiliaries	Responsible for public order in peacetime; could help provide rear area security during wartime.
Department of State Security	MININT	10,000–15,000	Counterintelligence and prevention of counter-revolutionary activities.

Source: U.S. Dept. of State. Bureau of Public Affairs. Cuban Armed Forces and the Soviet Military Presence, August 1982, p. 4. (Special Report No. 103.)

2. SOVIET MILITARY AID

As noted above, it is conservatively estimated that the Soviets gave $3.8 billion in military aid to Cuba during 1961-1979.[11] Jorge Dominguez, a seasoned, moderate scholar of Cuban affairs residing in the United States, placed the figure at $4.5 billion to 1975, which increased substantially since Cuba's involvement in Africa.[12]

In 1984, Kenneth Skoug, a ranking official of the State Department, placed the total amount of annual outlays in Soviet military aid to Cuba at $950 million.[13]

In November 1984, Nestor D. Sanchez, Deputy Assistant Secretary of Defense for Inter-American Affairs, gave more recent figures on Soviet military aid to Cuba in a speech at the First Annual Latin American Symposium meeting in Montgomery, Alabama. "Soviet presence and influence in the Western Hemisphere is expanding," he said. Soviet military advisors in Cuba have increased to 2,800, in addition to a Soviet brigade of 3,000 troops and 8,000 civilian advisors. Soviet economic aid has increased to about $5 billion annually, a quarter of the Cuban GNP. According to Sanchez, Soviet military equipment deliveries have averaged in excess of 60,000 metric tons annually over the past three years, and a large number of modern Soviet weapons have given Cuba a capability "far in excess of defensive needs." And he lists: 270 jet combat aircraft, 90 helicopters; 208 surface to air missile launchers; 950 tanks; 700 artillery pieces; 2 Koni-class frigates; 3 attack submarines; amphibious landing craft and over 50 torpedo and missile attack boats.

"It is this excess," Sanchez declared, "which concerns U.S. and Cuba's neighbors." For Cuba's equipment, combat experience, and extensive training, including joint exercises with the Soviet Navy and amphibious exercises, "give Cuba, with Soviet assistance, a capability to project its power in the Caribbean and elsewhere."[14]

Thus there can be no doubt that the Soviet Union has invested a great deal of their resources in Cuba, and that Cuba has become a dependency of Moscow as a partial price for its continuing support.

3. CUBAN MILITARY ESTABLISHMENT

Estimates vary on the size of the Cuban armed forces. In 1983, Blasier wrote that "Cuba now has one of the largest and best equipped armed forces in Latin America." He estimated that there were about 227,000 men in 1981, up from 117,000 before the Angolan War.[15]

The authoritative International Institute for Strategic Studies reported in its Military Balance, 1983-1984 that Cuba had total armed forces numbering some 153,000. The Army was believed to

---

[11] Blasier, The Giant's Rival, p. 100.

[12] Sigmund, The Soviet Union in the Third World, p. 29. On estimates of total Soviet aid, Sigmund writes: "If one includes the forgiven interest, military aid . . ., and the subsidized prices, Soviet aid to Cuba may be as high as $4 million a day, and total assistance to Cuba over the last 20 years in excess of $12 billion."

[13] Rand, Robert. Soviet Union Said to be Forcing Allies to Aid Cuba. RFE-RL. Radio Liberty Dispatch, RL 35/84, Jan. 18, 1984, p. 2.

[14] Sanchez, Nestor D. Deputy Assistant Secretary of Defense for Inter-American Affairs. U.S. Security Interests in Central America and the Caribbean. Nov. 16, 1984, p. 7-8.

[15] Blasier, The Giant's Rival, p. 125-126.

constitute 125,000 men with 190,000 in Ready Reserves; the Navy 12,000; and the Air Force 16,000. The Institute listed all types of weaponry, presumably Soviet supplied. A true indicator of Cuba's investment in defense is their defense budget. IISS estimated its defense expenditures for 1981 at $1.3 billion from a GNP estimated at $16 billion.[16]

According to Thomas O. Enders, Assistant Secretary for Inter-American Affairs, the Soviets play "an active military role in Cuba itself." They maintain a 2,600 man combat brigade, some 2,000 military advisers, 6,000–8,000 civilian advisers, and a major tele-communications and intelligence facility that, he says, "monitors wide spectrums of U.S. civilian and military telecommunications and conducts periodic air and naval visits directed against the United States and NATO."[17]

From even this fragmentary data it is apparent that the Cuban military establishment is impressive by any standard for a nation of ten million people. It plays a major role as an instrument of in-ternal control and external adventure.

C. Use of Socialist Cuba in Soviet Strategy

1. SERVING COMMON INTERESTS IN A DEPENDENCY RELATIONSHIP

Having built this formidable military establishment, the Soviet Union has used it to pursue its goals as a superpower in interna-tional politics and as a contender for influence and power in the Third World.[18] Conversely, Castro also used this power-in-being and the political leverage of the Soviet connection to achieve Cuba's goals regionally and internationally. Common interests of both sides, symbolized by a growing integration of controlling bu-reaucracies, have been served in this relationship.[19]

---

[16] The International Institute for Strategic Studies. The Military Balance, 1983–1984. London, 1983, p. 108–109.

[17] U.S. Dept. of State. Bureau of Public Affairs. Dealing with the Reality of Cuba, Dec. 14, 1982, p. 4. (Current Policy No. 443). Enders notes that since 1975 more significant Soviet weapons have been delivered to Cuba, including "approximately 150 jet fighters—a considerable number of these are MiG-21s and Mig-23/FLOGGERS, AN-26 troop/cargo transports, Foxtrot subma-rines, a Koni-class frigate, T-62 tanks, MI-8 and MI-24 helicopters, Osa-class guided-missile attack boats, minesweepers, and Turya-class hydrofoil torpedo boats." It has been reported that Cuba would double the strength of its 500,000 strong militia. "Since its creation in 1980," the report says, "it has become an instrument for the militarisation of Cuban society." (The Econo-mist Foreign Report, no. 1822, May 10, 1984, p.4.)

[18] Valenta writes of the evolving Soviet-Cuban relationship: "By the 1970s, the Soviet Union and Cuba had formulated a coherent strategic vision with regard to the Third World in general and the Caribbean basin in particular. After the discord of the 1960s there was an integrated, flexible and long-term plan of action designed to achieve specific ideological, political, security and economic objectives." (Soviet Policy in Central America, p. 290.) In stressing the advantages to the Soviets from this relationship, Luers notes that, "Without the Cuban fighting force and without the Cubans ready access to and knowledge of Third World countries, the Soviets would be a less adventurous and a less successful competitor with the United States." And then he ventures this judgement on the closeness of the relationship: "Cuba is probably the closest, most dependable, and most effective ally the Soviet Union has not excepting even East Germany and Bulgaria." Luers explains how Cuba is used as an instrument of Soviet Third World policy, con-cluding: "Cuba in 1982 had 70,000 military troops and advisors as well as civilian advisors in 23 countries worldwide—in most cases enhancing Soviet political influence in those countries." (The Soviets and Latin America, p. 20–21.)

[19] For a commentary on the integration of Soviet-Cuban bureaucracies, see, Blasier, The Giant's Rival, p. 9–11. "Latin America is no longer just a concern of the [Soviet] Party; there are vested interests of the government as well." (p. 10) Writing of the pro-Soviet lobby among Soviet-trained technicians and military officers and sympathetic state and party officials, Leiken con-cludes: "Together with the bonds of economic dependency these measures constitute an elabo-rate neocolonial relationship designed to assure Soviet predominance immune to ch.nges in the present leadership." (Leiken, Soviet Strategy in Latin America, p. 51.)

Differences do occur between Castro and his mentors in Moscow but never to the point of threatening the alliance. Still, total Cuban reliance on Soviet political, economic and military support makes this an uneven relationship, one of patron to client.[20] It is generally maintained that Cuba's dependency on the Soviet Union is so complete that Castro's regime could not pursue an aggressive Third World policy without Soviet support.

2. SERVING SOVIET PURPOSES IN CENTRAL AMERICA AND THE CARIBBEAN

a. On contesting U.S. hegemony

Cuba has served Soviet purposes in Central America and the Caribbean in two ways: to contest U.S. hegemony and establish the legitimacy of a Soviet presence; and to encourage and actively support "leftist" revolutions as a first step in the process of moving from the stage of "national liberation" towards the ultimate goal of the Marxist-Leninist brand of Socialism.

Contesting U.S. hegemony and establishing the legitimacy of a Soviet presence are different sides of the same coin. Cuba has played a major role in this Soviet effort. Cuban bases are used to service Soviet warships. Port calls by naval vessels have occurred with such increasing frequency—and in size and numbers—that they now seem to have become customary. Cuban air bases serve as platforms for Soviet air reconnaissance along the U.S. coastline and over the vital Atlantic sea lanes of communications. Cuban and Soviet naval forces, including the 20,000 ton Soviet helicopter cruiser *Lenin,* have joined in recent maneuvers off the southern coast of the United States.[21]

Military strategists express concern for the presumptive political purpose underlying Soviet activity; namely, to establish the legitimate "right" of a Soviet presence. But many also believe that such

---

[20] For discussions of Cuban dependency and vulnerability, see, Luers, The Soviets and Latin America, p. 21-22; Leiken, Soviet Strategy in Latin America, p. 44 ("The current relationship . . . is much more like clientage than partnership . . .); Enders, Dealing with the Reality of Cuba, p. 4 ("Cuba is a Soviet surrogate, heavily dependent on Soviet assistance to avoid economic collapse and obliged to support Soviet foreign policy."); Valenta, Soviet policy in Central America, p. 288 ("Cuba is not entirely subservient to the Soviet Union in Africa and the Caribbean and at times appears even more assertive. Castro undoubtedly exercises some autonomy in formulating policy towards other countries and influences Soviet policy-making."); Smith, Wayne S. Cuba: Time for a Thaw. The New York Times Magazine, July 29, 1984, p. 54 (Writing about a conversation "with an old Cuban friend, a writer" on a recent visit to Havana, Wayne S. Smith quotes him as saying "No, . . . this is not the same Cuba, or the same Castro you had to deal with 20 years ago. Both have matured and become more pragmatic. We hold to our revolutionary principles, but interpret and implement them in a different way. We will not sever our ties with the Soviet Union. At the same time, however, we certainly understand that our interests and Moscow's don't always coincide—perhaps not even usually.")

[21] For commentaries on the Soviet-Cuban offensive in the Caribbean and Central America, see, Blasier, The Giant's Rival, p. 139-141; Leiken, Soviet Strategy in Latin America, p. 53-56, 61-72; Leiken, Central America: Anatomy of Conflict, p. 17; Cirincione, Joseph and Leslie C. Hunter. Military Threats, Actual and Potential. In, Anatomy of Conflict, chapt. 8; and Andrews, Walter. Cuba Joins Soviets in Exercise Off U.S. Coast. The Washington Times, April 10, 1984, p. 2A. President Reagan said in a speech on U.S. security in the Caribbean in March 1983: "As the Soviets have increased their military power, they have been emboldened to extend that power. They are spreading their military influence in ways that can directly challenge our vital interests and those of our allies." (Congressional Record, March 24, 1983, p. S3910.)

presence in time of war would be a wasting asset given the proximity and magnitude of U.S. naval power.[22]

For example, Luers writes: "The Cubans know that in case of a threat of superpower conflict they would be the target of swift U.S. military action. The defense of Cuba would be a low priority for the Soviet Union in such a situation. Cuba's distance from the Soviet motherland imposes critical limits on a response, even if the Soviets were inclined to make one. This ambiguous Soviet commitment to the defense of Cuba must rankle Castro and the Cuban leadership."

Nonetheless, there is potential danger in the Soviet-Cuban connection, one that stems mainly from the tactic of military incrementalism. The sudden escalation of a Soviet military presence in the Caribbean does not seem likely. The cautious Soviet leaders appreciate too well U.S. strategic sensitivities having learned that lesson from the missile crisis of 1962. Rather the real danger lies in the gradual, incremental, virtually unnoticed military buildup that can take place over a period of time with American acquiescence and the use of this power-in-being for political purposes. Power-in-being is essential for purposes of political expansion within the evolving process of incrementalism that plays for time, gradualism and acquiesence by the adversary. Since 1962, Cuba has developed into a formidable power base for the projection of Soviet-Cuban influence in Latin America, a reality not likely to be reversed in the near or perhaps even distant future.[23]

b. Supporting revolutions

Upsurging revolution in the Caribbean Basin and Central America has been an open invitation for Soviet intervention directly or indirectly through its client Cuba. In Grenada, the Soviet Union and Cuba, as will be shown below, participated in a mutual effort to build and consolidate the leftist Bishop regime.

In Nicaragua, the Soviets, conscious of U.S. strategic sensitivities and wishing to conceal their surreptitious involvement, have used Cuba along with Algeria, Libya and its East European Allies as surrogates or conduits for transshipping military supplies. For example, Soviet MIG fighters are believed to be in Cuba, waiting for transshipment to the new airfield at Punta Huete near Managua. This new air facility has the longest runway in Central America with a capability of handling any aircraft in the Soviet inventory. Soviet concern for a sharply critical U.S. reaction to this deep Soviet involvement is believed to be the reason for holding up de-

---

[22] The Soviets and Latin America, p. 21. Blasier makes this judgment: "Cuba also is a military strategic liability for the USSR although rarely viewed as such in the West." (The Giant's Rival, p. 99–100).

[23] Christopher A. Abel provides this description of incrementalism at work that includes: "the elements of a gradual, purposeful buildup . . . as well as the strategic use of favorable opportunities when presented . . . Inherently low-risk in nature, this strategy seeks steady success in the long run at the expense of larger triumphs . . . [The] plan calls for the setting of an initial precedent which is followed by desensitizing regional powers to that action's significance. Once accomplished, another precedent is set and the process begins over again." (A Breach in the Ramparts. The Proceedings of the U.S. Naval Institute, July 1980: 47, quoted in Leiken, Soviet Strategy in Latin America, p. 54.)

livery. For more than three years Nicaraguan pilots have been receiving flight training in the Soviet Union, Bulgaria and Cuba.[24]

3. ADVANCING SOVIET EXPANSIONIST GOALS IN AFRICA

In Africa, the Soviets have effectively used Cuban troops, again to conceal involvement, in the pursuit of their Third World goals. The significance of this action was underscored by Leiken when he wrote, "The intervention in Angola marked the beginning of a Soviet global, strategic offensive." [25]

Cuba was a willing participant in this offensive, and the degree of its commitment can be measured by the size of its troops dispatched to Africa. In the mid-1970's, some 20,000-25,000 Cuban troops were directly engaged in the Angolan civil war. Subsequent accumulated evidence placed the figure at 19,000-20,000, augmented by some 4,000 civilian technicians. In 1980, some 19,000-21,000 Cuban military personnel and over 7,000 civilians were stationed in Angola.[26] In 1983, the rebel UNITA forces in Angola estimated Cuban combat troops and civilian advisers at 30,000-40,000.[27]

When Soviet involvement in Africa expanded in 1977 to the Horn where Ethiopia and Somalia were at war over the disputed territory of Ogaden, the Cubans followed in lockstep, lending their military support to the Ethiopian Marxist regime and accordingly binding themselves closer to Moscow. An estimated 16,000 to 17,000 Cuban troops were eventually sent to Ethiopia.[28] The figure peaked at 17,000 in the spring of 1978. After the defeat of the Somali Army in Ogaden, the Cuban forces were gradually reduced to about 12,000. According to U.S. intelligence sources in 1980,

---

[24] The caution with which the Soviets escalate their military presence in this region, in keeping with the tactic of incrementalism, is demonstrated by their hesitancy to transship advanced MIG fighters to Nicaragua for use in the new and expanded air field at Punto Huete. The United States warned Moscow against taking such action. (Murphy, Bill. Nicaragua to Receive MIG Fighters? RFE-RL, Radio Liberty Research, RL 361/84, Sept. 24, 1984, p. 1-4. For CIA Director William Casey's observations, see, U.S. News & World Report, Apr. 23, 1984: 27. See also, Volman, Dennis. Cuba Reportedly Holds up Delivery of MIGs for Nicaragua. The Christian Science Monitor, July 6, 1984, p. 7; for the U.S. warning on the MIG delivery, see, The New York Times, Aug. 18, 1984, p. 4.)

[25] Leiken, Soviet Strategy in Latin America, p. 102.

[26] HFAC, Soviet Policy and United States Response in the Third World, p. 61.

[27] Girardet, Edward. Angolan Rebels Go on Offensive Against Soviet-backed Regime. The Christian Science Monitor, May 31, 1983, p. 1. For a discussion of the Soviet-Cuban relationship in the Angolan civil war, see, Valenta, Soviet and Cuban Responses in Central America, p. 139-141. According to Valenta, Castro's foreign policy cannot be viewed as "totally subservient" to Moscow, but he adds that "it would be far-fetched to think of Cuba as an independent or even semi-independent actor." Cuba's dependence on the Soviet Union in carrying out military and security operations in Africa was first demonstrated in the Angolan crisis of 1975-1976. He notes Soviet caution initially owing to uncertainty about the U.S. response. But in early November 1975, the Soviets "took over the Cuban air- and sea-lift, transforming the Angolan campaign into a massive operation during which both the Soviet air force and the Soviet Navy were operationally active. A small yet effective Soviet naval task force provided physical and psychological support to the Cuban combat troops, protected the Cuban staging areas against local threats, served as a strategic cover for established sea and air communications, and worked as a deterrent against possible U.S. naval deployment." (p. 141)

[28] HFAC, Soviet Policy and United States Response in the Third World, p. 61. On this campaign Valenta writes: "The alliance between the Soviets and Cubans was even tighter in the case of the intervention in Ethiopia in 1977, where four Soviet generals ran the entire operation from start to finish. While during the original stage of the operation in Angola the Cubans temporarily functioned independently, in the case of Ethiopia Cuba functioned as a very subordinate actor, if not a Soviet proxy, during the conflict in the Ogaden between Somalia and Ethiopia. Clearly the Soviet leadership determines the limits of Cuban options in Africa." (Soviet and Cuban Responses in Central America, p. 141.)

Cuba still maintained combat troops in Ethiopia, but the official estimate was classified.[29]

During 1979–1980, Cuba had approximately 35,000 military personnel stationed in sub-Sahara Africa. The total number of Cubans overseas approached 50,000. In addition to those in Angola and Ethiopia, they maintained, as of May 1980, a military force in Third World regions closely associated with Soviet activity: 100 to 650 in Mozambique, 200 in Guinea and from 100 to 200 in Sierra Leone. Cuba was also said to have some 13,000 civilians overseas, 7,000 of whom served in Angola alone.[30]

Apparently, Cuban forces abroad have been sustained at a fairly high number in areas where the Soviets have been deeply involved as in Angola where in early 1983 Western diplomats reported that Cuban reinforcements of 5,000 to 10,000 troops had arrived in the previous two months.[31] According to the IISS report for 1983–1984, Cuba had 25,000 troops in Angola; 750 in the Congo; 11,000 in Ethiopia, now declared a Socialist Republic; 750 in Mozambique; 500 in other parts of Africa; 300 in South Yemen, a Soviet stronghold; 1,000 in Nicaragua and 30 in Grenada.[32]

The Cuban presence in Africa has thus been very real, and for them and the Soviets this military presence has served their mutual interests, both collectively and individually. For the Soviets, the Cubans have proven to be useful instruments in projecting their power in this Third World region.

4. AS A SOVIET SURROGATE IN THE NAM

Finally, the Soviets have used Cuba as a surrogate within the Non-Alignment Movement (NAM). As Blasier states, Castro "has become the champion of the USSR in the Third World, most particularly in the nonaligned movement"[33] where "Cuba has been working hand-in-glove with Soviet leaders . . . for years."[34]

At the 6th summit meeting of NAM leaders in Havana during 1979, Castro, the host and president for the next three years, effectively outmaneuvered Yugoslavia and other moderates in the movement, giving the conference, as one report said, "clear indications of a tilt in the movement's orientation toward the U.S.S.R." Moderates led by President Tito of Yugoslavia were overshadowed by Castro who gave the meeting "a decidedly pro-Soviet cast." In his opening address Castro proclaimed his friendship for the Soviet Union, sharply criticized the United States and in general hued to foreign policy positions in line with Moscow. Thus the conference received such accolades of the Soviet Union as firmly rebuffing "provocative sallies" and insisting that the countries of the NAM "do not want any longer to sing to the tune called by imperialism."[35]

[29] HFAC, Soviet Policy and United States Response in the Third World, p. 61.
[30] Ibid., p. 61–62.
[31] The New York Times, Jan. 18, 1983, p. A27.
[32] IISS, Military Balance, 1983–1984, p. 109.
[33] Blasier, The Giant's Rival, p. 137.
[34] Ibid., p. 114.
[35] Facts-on-File, 1979, p. 674B2–675C2; Kessing's Contemporary Archives, 1980, p. 30038–30039; and Duncan, Soviet Power in Latin America, p. 16. Duncan writes: "Havana . . . is a visible regional supporter of pro-Soviet Communist parties, through its hosting of regional Communist party meetings. It also plays a vital role in the nonaligned movement, drawing Latin American countries into common alliances against the developed world, led by the United States, as in its role of host to the September 1979 meeting of nonaligned countries in Havana."

But Castro failed in his efforts to get the conference to accept the "radical thesis" he espoused that identified the Soviet Union as a "natural ally" of the NAM against "imperialism." The Soviets had aggressively supported this move which for them has been a central propaganda theme in their approach to the Third World. But India, Yugoslavia and other moderate member states successfully resisted pressure from Cuba, Ethiopia and Vietnam.[36]

Castro has thus been a useful, but not always effective, tool for Moscow in the NAM. Nonetheless, the NAM has enabled Castro to make his case for Socialism before the Third World in periodic collective conclaves and to act as a broker, as Duncan suggests, "drawing Latin American countries into common alliances against the developed world, led by the United States. . . ."[37]

D. Cuba, a Client State in the Service of Its Patron, the U.S.S.R.

Thus, the Soviets have sought to use Cuba as an instrument of their foreign policy, particularly in the Third World. In rhetorical statements of policy, they have gradually escalated their support for Cuba in its struggle with the United States; but in practice, this support has been cautious and carefully measured in a calculus of risk and gain.[38]

With Castro's experience as a model, the Soviets seem to have found the formula, having made the proper ideological adjustments, for allowing the transition of revolutionary-prone Third

---

[36] Soviet Union in the Third World, 1980–1982, Part II, p. 149. For a strong Yugoslav defense of the principle of nonalignment in opposition to the "natural ally" thesis of the Soviet Union, see, Decermic, Bogdan. On the Eve of the Summit. Belgrade Borba in Serbo-Croatian, Feb. 6, 1983, p. 8, in FBIS Daily Report, Eastern Europe, v. 2, Feb. 10, 1983, p. 14. Decermic explained the divisive effects of adopting the "natural ally" thesis and quoted approvingly the definition by Indian leader Rao: "The essence of nonalignment is not in being aligned with or leaning toward one or another direction, but in a positive role in international affairs, a role devoid of any *a priori* obligations toward any side." And, of course, Castro has never concealed Cuba's clear alignment with the Soviet Union and its Communist allies within the NAM. For a vigorous Soviet statement giving its perspective on the NAM, see, Bandura, Yu. An Important Factor in World Politics. On the Movement of Nonaligned Countries. Izvestiya. Sept. 30, 1982, Morning Edition, p. 5, in, FBIS Daily Report, Soviet Union, v. 3, Oct. 18, 1982, p. CC12–CC13.

[37] Duncan, Soviet Power in Latin America, p. 16.

[38] For a listing of Soviet statements of support for Cuba, see Rothenberg, Latin America in Soviet Eyes, p. 3–5. Moscow has been forthright, but still cautious, in its declarations of support. And though Soviet leaders have avoided giving Castro the formal treaty he seemed to have wanted, their commitment has increased "several notches in the early 1970's," as Rothenberg puts it. In June 1972, Brezhnev declared that "Socialist Cuba is not alone. It is a strong constituent part of the world system of socialism." Shortly thereafter Cuba was admitted to the Council for Mutual Economic Assistance, their closest legal tie. In January 1975, Brezhnev visited Cuba, "another important step in Cuban integration with the Soviet world," writes Rothenberg. On September 11, 1979, an authoritative editorial in Pravda asserted the "inalienable right" of the Soviet Union and Cuba to establish any military relationship they pleased. The bond with the Socialist world was more closely established with the conclusion of the Treaty of Friendship and Cooperation between Cuba and the German Democratic Republic in May 1980, the only political-military treaty between Cuba and a member of the Warsaw Pact. Rothenberg noted that the treaty terms were "relatively weak, but its symbolic importance is considerable." In February 1981, against a background of U.S.-Cuban tension, Brezhnev raised the Soviet commitment another degree by listing Cuba among the members of the "socialist community" for the first time. The importance of this action was underscored by the Soviet-Polish joint declaration in March 1981: "The socialist community is indissoluble; defense of it is the cause not only of each state but of the entire socialist coalition." And a few weeks later Brezhnev declared in Prague: "The glorious Republic of Cuba, an inseparable part of the community of socialist states, is fulfilling the task of its development under difficult conditions. The Soviet Union firmly and invariably supports and will continue to support the fraternal Cuban people." Rothenberg cites other examples of the escalation of the Soviet commitment. Under Andropov the commitment was reaffirmed. (p. 5–6) Chernenko also reaffirmed Soviet policy as in his election speech of March 2,

Continued

World countries from the inchoate stage of "national liberation" to the rigidly structured Socialism of the Soviet brand.[39] Valenta gives this apt description of revolutionary regimes in the Caribbean and Central America in their ideological rite of passage from "national liberation" to Leninism:

This first class of [revolutionary] regimes consists of Soviet clients such as Cuba, Nicaragua and Grenada (before October 1983). These regimes are either developing along Leninist lines or, in the case of Cuba, have already achieved a Leninist identity. The Soviets support these regimes by giving political, economic, and military aid, and advisory assistance. The Soviet Union's political and economic support and arms transfers to Nicaragua and Grenada (before October 1983) are patterned after its relationship with Cuba and indicate the Soviets' faith in the eventual Leninist transformation of these countries.[40]

The Soviets have also succeeded in militarizing Socialist Cuba, re-making it in their own image as a regional military power. And finally, they have used Cuba, with mixed results, in pursuit of their policy goals in relations with the United States, in Latin America, Africa and elsewhere in the Third World.

Castro has gained from this relationship, as Cuba's prominence internationally today attests. But this prominence is somewhat unreal, a fiction, because it is due wholly to Cuba's linkage with Soviet power and not something gained on its own. Moreover, Cuban dependence upon Moscow for its survival constricts its room for maneuver, making this an uneven relationship between a powerful patron and a willing but essentially weak client state. For Cuban dependency has become so entrenched that whatever the relative importance of emerging differences in matters of time, place and resources, the Soviet Union still has the last word.[41]

1984, when he pledged that the Soviet Union, "was, is, and will remain on Cuba's side in fair weather and storm" as it confronts an "economic blockade and military threats" from the United States. "The Cuban people are resolutely supported by the fraternal socialist countries," he said. (Moscow Tass in English, 1510, GMT, Mar. 2, 1984, in FBIS Daily Report, Soviet Union, v. 3, Mar. 5, 1984, p. R16.) The Cubans reminded Chernenko of this commitment when in an article recently published in Pravda Jose Ramon Machado, top-ranking Cuban Communist official, wrote: "The assistance given by the Soviet Union to Cuba in all our efforts aimed at transforming the island of freedom into an unconquerable bastion of socialism, a bastion of such strength and firmness that the U.S. imperialists would meet the resolute resistance of an armed people were they to attack our republic, may be called truly exemplary. K.U. Chernenko, . . . provided evidence of the great support for our just cause when he said that the USSR 'has been, is, and will remain with Cuba through thick and thin.'" ("Comrades-in-Arms, Like-Minded People." Jose Ramon Machado Ventura. Pravda, Sept. 19, 1984, 1st ed., p. 4, in FBIS Daily Report," Soviet Union, v. 3, Oct. 1984, p. K5.)

[39] On the transition to totalitarianism, the Kissinger Commission's Report (p. 88) states:

The Totalitarian Outcome. Because the Marxist-Leninist insurgents appeal to often legitimate grievances, a popular school of thought holds that guerrilla leaders are the engines of reform. They characteristically reinforce this by inviting well-meaning democratic leaders to participate in a Popular Front, taking care, however, to retain in their own hands a monopoly of the instruments of force. If the insurgents were in fact the vehicles for democratic and social progress, the entire security issue would be moot; they would no longer be the problem, but rather the solution.

Unfortunately, history offers no basis for such optimism. No Marxist-Leninist "popular front" insurgency has ever turned democratic after its victory. Cuba and Nicaragua are striking examples. Regimes created by the victory of Marxist-Leninist guerrillas become totalitarian. That is their purpose, their nature, their doctrine and their record.

[40] Valenta, Soviet Policy in Central America, p. 292.

[41] Scholars writing on Soviet-Cuban relations debate the degree of autonomy the Cubans may or may not have in their dependence upon Moscow, but there seems to be general agreement that Moscow is the final arbiter. Valenta writes: "Cuba is . . . highly vulnerable to Soviet politico-economic coercion, which the Soviet leaders used to their advantage in the late 1960s, when they slowed down the supply of oil and arms to Cuba to make Castro more amenable to the subtleties of Soviet 'anti-imperialist' strategy." The Soviets are likely to use this leverage again should the need arise." (Soviet and Cuban Responses in Central America, p. 141.)

III. CENTRAL AMERICA AND THE CARIBBEAN: UPHEAVAL AND OPPORTUNITY

A. QUALIFIED SUCCESS IN NICARAGUA

1. FROM INDIFFERENCE TO INVOLVEMENT

a. Contrasting outcomes in Nicaragua and Grenada

Political upheaval in Central America and the Caribbean in the 1970's created new, but initially unperceived, opportunities for Moscow in this Third World region considered by 1979–1980 to be "ripe for revolution." Cuba, a militarily strengthened regional power acting unilaterally and in concert with the Soviets, was to become both the point man and instrument for Soviet policy; for both had common interests to be served. Qualified success thus far seems to have been achieved in Nicaragua, though the ruling Sandinista regime faces serious economic problems and may have a long way to go to establish any form of legitimacy for their rule, even Socialist legitimacy. But failure in Grenada was assured when U.S. troops intervened in October 1983.

b. Soviet failure to perceive opportunity

The Soviets were slow to perceive emerging revolutionary possibilities in Central America, moving cautiously from a position of indifference to one of deep and later measured involvement. Adhering to the Khrushchevian principle of peaceful transition to Socialism that had been reinforced by Allende's momentary success in Chile, the Soviets had rejected guerrilla warfare, though they have always regarded it as a "possible" tactic, never as "necessary" *a priori.* Conditions in a specific country, they argue, have to be "ripe for revolution" in order to succeed, and it was not judged to be so in Central America.[1] As one Soviet analyst affirmed before 1978, "none of us would utter an optimistic phrase about the future of that struggle" in Central America.[2] The Soviets were thus admittedly taken by surprise when the Sandinistas overthrew Somoza.

Early in the revolutionary drive of the Sandinistas the traditionally Soviet backed Socialist Party of Nicaragua (PSN) followed the prevailing Soviet line opposing armed struggle. Not at all political-

---

[1] Ramet and Lopez-Alves, Moscow and the Revolutionary Left in Latin America, p. 259–260. See also, Blasier, The Giant's Rivals, p. 95–98.

[2] Leiken Robert S. Fantasies and Facts: The Soviet Union and Nicaragua. Current History, Oct. 1984: 316. Luers writes of the Soviet Cuban relationship: "The largely restrained Soviet foreign policy of the 1960s and early 1970s has been changed by the relationship with Castro. Cuba has given the Soviets the tools and the rationale for extending their power into the developing world at low risk. Now in Central America and the Caribbean, where Castro has again challenged the role of the communist parties and threatened to take charge of a growing revolutionary situation, the Soviets must engage the issues or be left behind. Central America does indeed appear ripe for revolutionary change and the Soviets, therefore, must be involved." (The Soviets and Latin America, p. 25.)

ly important, never numbering more than 250, the PSN maintained only meager relations with Nicaragua's leftist organizations, and its policy towards the Sandinista guerrillas, the leading revolutionary force in Nicaragua, was, as Pedro Ramet and Fernando Lopez-Alves, U.S. specialists in Latin American affairs, state, "one of lukewarm self-restraint and general cautiousness."[3] Not until 1978, after the first insurrection against the Somoza regime took place, was an armed wing of the PSN created.[4]

---

[3] Ramet and Lopez-Alves, Moscow and the Revolutionary Left in Latin America, p. 351. According to these scholars, the PSN's abstention from armed struggle had created distrust within the Sandinistas so that by the time the PSN finally joined the struggle against Somoza in late 1977, the break between the PSN and Sandinistas was already well established.

[4] Leiken, Fantasies and Facts: The Soviet Union and Ncaragua, p. 316.

Map 6

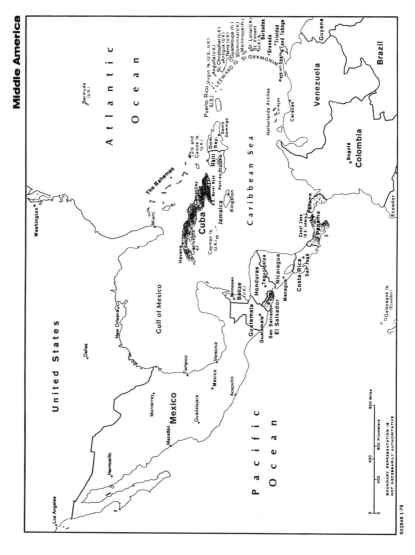

Central America and the Caribbean

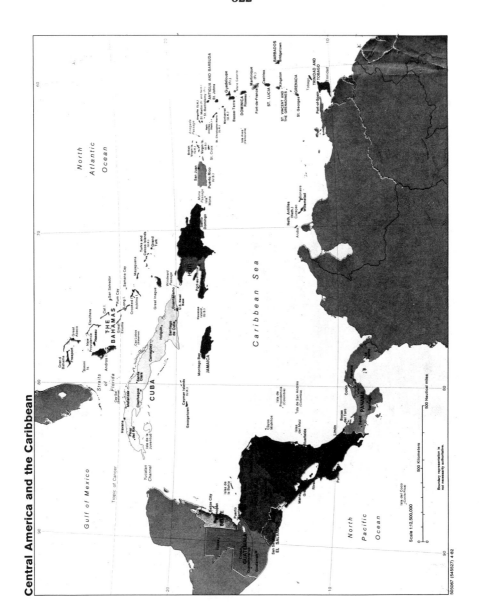

c. Cuba, the catalyst for success

By and large the Soviets remained indifferent to events in Nicaragua during this period, apparently failing to see the potential political benefits to be gained. Not so the Cubans who in general proved to be the catalyst for success. In sharp contrast to Moscow, they supported the Sandinstas at the outset, though urging caution in September 1978 in the wake of the first insurrection against Somoza.[5] They assumed the burden of training and supplying the Sandinistas, albeit with weapons furnished them by the Soviet Union.[6] In addition, they acted as a broker for the Sandinistas within the Socialist bloc.[7] In March 1979, the Cubans succeeded in reuniting the competing factions within the Sandinistas, giving hegemony to the pro-Cuban elements. They actively participated in the approaching 1979 uprising, increasing arms deliveries, organizing and arming an "internationalist brigade" to fight with the guerrillas, and sending military specialists into the field. For their active support the Cubans were rewarded after victory with key military advisory and intelligence positions in the Sandinistas regime.[8]

Beyond building Cuba's military strength and improving its interventionist capabilities, the Soviets seem to have played no direct role. Only after the victory of the Sandinistas in July 1979 did they move from indifference to involvement—and they did so with great speed, believing, as Valenta notes, that Central America is "the 'weakest link' in the chain of 'imperialist domination'" in Latin America.[9] For the Soviets the Sandinista victory signalled a new revolutionary upsurge in Latin America and an historic watershed reversing the downturn in Communist fortunes since Allende's overthrow in Chile.

2. SEIZING AN OPPORTUNITY WITH SANDINISTA VICTORY, JULY 1979

The Sandinista victory in July 1979 created an opportunity that the Soviets could not long resist: a chance to erode the U.S. position regionally; to expand its influence in the Americas; to reinforce their claims to the Third World that Socialism is the wave of the future; and to demonstrate again the value of the National Lib-

---

[5] Ramet and Lopez-Alves, Moscow and the Revolutionary Left in Latin America, p. 360. Valenta writes with respect to both the Soviet and Cuban commitment to revolution: "It is misleading to suggest, because of these trends [towards normalization with many Latin American countries in the 1970's] that the USSR and Cuba had given up the notion of supporting revolutionary movements in the region. Although their posture was realistic, it was not one of acquiescence. Neither the Soviets nor the Cubans entirely renounced the efficacy of revolution as a means for overthrowing unfriendly, anticommunist governments. In the mid-1970s, when conditions were not ripe for revolution in Latin America, the Soviets and Cubans were busy supporting their allies elsewhere, particularly Africa. This situation changed dramatically with the successful revolution in Nicaragua in 1979, and the unswing in guerrilla warfare in El Salvador in 1980." (Soviet and Cuban Responses in Central America, p. 133.)
[6] Valenta explains the Soviet connection: "Although Cuba is apparently an autonomous actor in the coordination and support of armed insurgency, such activity is not possible without continuous Soviet economic and military aid to Cuba and its new clients in Nicaragua and Grenada, as well as Soviet strategic coordination through local communist parties." (Soviet Policy in Central America, p. 293.)
[7] Ramet and Lopez-Alves, Moscow and the Revolutionary Left in Latin America, p. 351.
[8] Leiken, Fantasies and Facts: The Soviet Union and Nicaragua, p. 316. For a commentary on the movement of military-political fronts like the July 26th Movement in Cuba and the Sandinistas in Nicaragua replacing the proletariat parties as a revolutionary vanguard, see Blasier, The Giant's Rival, p. 95–98.
[9] Valenta, Soviet Policy in Central America, p. 296.

:ration Movement (in this case, the Sandinista variety) as a spawning ground for Socialism without benefit of a proletarian party, and for the transition in the Cuban manner from an amorphous Marxist oriented mass movement, to the state of a "vanguard party" and on to the formation of a Marxist-Leninist system.[10]

The Sandinista triumph stirred expectations in Moscow for further successes and the impending Havana meeting of the NAM summit in September with Nicaragua added to the role of member states provided a sufficient platform for Moscow's alleged "natural allies" to extoll the praises of Socialism.[11] The Soviet media and academic circles hailed the revolution as an event of "colossal international importance." The revolution was to mark a dramatic long-term departure in Soviet relations with Central America.[12] As Rothenberg explains its meaning:

> The victory of the Sandinista revolution in Nicaragua heightened Soviet hopes for increased influence in Latin America. The Kremlin sought to make this hope a reality through intensifying ties to the new Nicaraguan regime and by encouraging the emulation of the Nicaraguan experience elsewhere in the region. Nicaragua was particularly important for Moscow because it raised the possibility of widening Cuba's breach in the doctrine of "geographic fatalism"—which had held that the U.S. would not permit leftist governments or strong Soviet influence close to the United States.[13]

3. ADJUSTMENT IN TACTICS: SANCTIONING ARMED STRUGGLE AND EXPANDING THE REVOLUTION

a. Belated triumph for Che Guevara

Success of the Sandinistas generated a reversal of Soviet tactics from advocacy of peaceful transition to acceptance of armed struggle. According to Ramet and Lopez-Alves, the Sandinista triumph proved "pivotal" in changing Soviet thinking about Latin America: "the Soviets now admitted that the Sandinista revolution constituted a vindication of the old Castroism of Che Guevara."[14]

This dramatic shift in Soviet tactics was reflected in the advocacy and explanations by Soviet scholars in their journal, Latinskaya Amerika. In the March 1980 issue, taking stock of the Sandinista success, Boris Koval wrote in what was described as "a stunning passage" that,

> the Nicaraguan experience [has] demolished the previous simplistic interpretation of guerrilla actions, confirmed the justice of many of the Che Guevara's strategic principles, and crystallized his idea of creating a powerful popular guerrilla movement.[15]

---

[10] Ramet and Lopez-Alves write: "The Soviets will support any leftist group and back any insurrectionary movement which promises to erode the U.S. position and to open new opportunities to the Soviets. The Soviets are not gripped by an obsession with absolute control; they play a cautious game and have been quite satisfied to make small gains in sundry locales. In this context, it is perhaps not so surprising that some of Moscow's biggest Third World successes (Cuba, India, Libya, Nicaragua, Syria, and South Yemen) have been gained without the traditional Communist parties (CPs) playing any major role." (Moscow and the Revolutionary Left in Latin America, p. 342.) Blasier makes this same point in The Giant's Rival, p. 95–98.

[11] Kessing's Contemporary Archives, 1980, p. 30037–38.

[12] Leiken, Fantasies and Facts: The Soviet Union and Nicaragua, p. 314.

[13] Rothenberg, The Soviets and Central America, in, Leiken, Central America: Anatomy of Conflict, p. 131.

[14] Ramet and Lopez-Alves, Moscow and the Revolutionary Left in Latin America, p. 357.

[15] Quoted in, Ramet and Lopez-Alves, Moscow and the Revolutionary Left in Latin America, p. 351.

Mikoyan, editor of the journal, offered a posthumous rehabilitation of Che Guevara, pointing out that "up to now only the armed path has led to revolutionary victory in Latin America." And N. Leonov added his authoritative voice to the conclusion that "the armed road . . . is the most promising in the specific conditions of most of the Latin American countries."[16]

Later in the year the authoritative CPSU journal Kommunist published a speech by Shafik Handal, leader of the Salvadoran Communist Party, in which he declared that proletarian revolution could succeed in El Salvador only through guerrilla warfare. Publication in Kommunist suggests the imprimatur of Moscow's highest authority sanctioning armed struggle as a road to power. By 1982, the Soviets concluded that not only El Salvador and Guatemala but also Chile, Uruguay, Colombia, Costa Rica and Bolivia were "ripe for revolution."[17]

b. Expanding the revolution in Central America

Soviet attitudes toward Central America initially seem to have been marked by two stages: in late 1979, they perceived violent revolutionary change to be imminent; in mid-1981, they decided to give their full support to the Sandinista revolution.[18]

Riding the crest of the Sandinista wave of success, the Soviets and their Cuban allies accelerated the momentum of revolution towards new targets in Central America, notably El Salvador.[19] Cuba served as a pipeline for Soviet military aid to leftist guerrillas, and in what was termed a "precedent-breaking move" the Salvadoran Communist Party announced in January 1980 that armed struggle was the only path to power, the first absolute endorsement by any Latin American party.[20] Shortly thereafter, the party

---

[16] Ibid., p. 352.

[17] Ibid.

[18] Ibid., p. 358.

[19] On the expansion of the revolution in Central America and the matter of economic cost Luers writes: "The Soviets believe that where their political and military influence expands is where regional strife is high. Central America seems now to be ripe for greatly expanded Soviet influence over the next few years as long as the Soviets can control and establish a military-security presence. The eventual financial cost of expanded influence and involvement in the region is not likely to be high even if it should eventually involve another client state. The current costs are low." (The Soviets and Latin America, p. 25.)

[20] The matter of military aid to the Salvadoran guerrillas through Nicaragua has been disputed. The Reagan Administration has contended that these arms transfers—smuggling—have taken place as a matter of course. In a conversation with Soviet Ambassador Anatoly F. Dobrynin on January 29, 1981, Secretary of State Alexander Haig raised the issue of Soviet weapons which he said were being supplied to the Communist-led insurgents in El Salvador through Nicaragua. "All lies," said Dobrynin. Haig retorted: "Photographs don't lie." Dobrynin noted that it would be unfortunate if Moscow got the impression that the Reagan Adminsitration was hostile to the Soviet Union since first impressions often last. Haig insisted that the United States was not hostile but "offended by Soviet excesses," particularly regarding Cuba. Dobrynin retorted: "All I ever hear from you is Cuba, Cuba, Cuba." (Kalb, Madeleine G. The Dobrynin Factor. The New York Times Magazine, May 13, 1984: 69.) For other commentaries on this matter, see, Taubman, Philip. U.S. Said to Have Large Spy Network in Latin America, Mar. 20, 1983, p. 16; Taubman, Philip. The C.I.A.: In From the Cold and Hot for Truth. The New York Times, June 11, 1984, p. B6 (former CIA operative disputes Adminsitration's claims that Salvadoran insurgents are supplied by the Sandinistas); McCartney, Robert J. Search for Arms: Proof of Source Elusive in El Salvador. The Washington Post, July 8, 1984, p. A1; Smith, Hedrick. A Former Salvadoran Rebel Chief Tells of Arms from Nicaragua. The New York Times, July 12, 1984, p. A10; Omang, Joanne, Nicaraguan Aid to Guerrillas Cited: Administration Reveals New Documents, Film as It Presses Case. The Washington Post, Aug. 9, 1984, p. A31; Mohr, Charles. Salvador Arms-Aid Charges Detailed. The New York Times, Aug. 9, 1984, p. A3.

adopted a ten-point program advocating the forcible overthrow of the government and the introduction of "profound social transformations" on the Leninist model.[21]

Developments suggest a Soviet determination to expand the Central American beachhead from Nicaragua. Large quantities of military equipment poured into El Salvador early in 1981 from Vietnam. The GDR gave military assistance. By early 1982, the Soviet Union expressly endorsed the guerrilla movement in El Salvador and pressed for the unification of guerrilla forces in Guatemala. By 1983, Soviet and Cuban military advisers in Nicaragua were conducting advanced guerrilla training courses for Salvadoran guerrillas and leftist guerrillas from other countries in the region. Nicaragua was also instrumental in transshipping Soviet and Cuban arms to El Salvador. By early 1982, if not before, Nicaragua was supplying arms to leftist guerrillas in Guatemala and Costa Rica, while Cuba undertook the training of Colombian and Bolivian guerrillas.[22]

Thus, the Sandinista victory provided a new and important target of opportunity for the Soviet Union, and it moved quickly to seize every advantage. For Nicaragua offered a distinct geopolitical prize by its strategic positioning on both the Caribbean and Pacific and its potentiality for another competing isthmian canal.[23] Seasoned observers of the Latin American scene may well have experienced a sense of deja vu as they saw the replication of the Soviet-Cuban experience in the 1960's and 1970's now being played out in Nicaragua and the adjoining countries.[24]

---

[21] Ramet and Lopez-Alves, Moscow and the Revolutionary Left in Latin America, p. 358. Valenta passes this judgement on Soviet expectations in Central America: Soviet clients such as Cuba, Nicaragua and Grenada (before October 1983) are regimes that are "either developing along Leninist lines or, in the case of Cuba, have already achieved a Leninist identity. The Soviets support these regimes by giving political, economic, and military aid, and advisory assistance. The Soviet Union's political and economic support and arms transfers to Nicaragua and Grenada (before October 1983) are patterned after its relationship with Cuba and indicate the Soviets' faith in the eventual Leninist transformation of these countries." (Soviet Policy in Central America, p. 292.) Wayne Smith expresses a contrary view in his review of Blasier's, "The Giant's Rival." Noting that Blasier points out that "far from following an aggressive blueprint, the Russians have usually been exceedingly cautious in Latin America. Their approach is characterized more by opportunism than by audacity. Nor does the evidence suggest they are pushing to turn other Latin American states into new Cubas. Given their own economic limitations and competing priorities, one Cuba may be quite enough. If they had as a first priority turning Nicaragua into a full-fledged Marxist-Leninist state, for example, one would expect them to pick up the tab for the hardpressed Sandinista Government. But they have refused. Thus, even if the Sandinista commanders wished to do so, they could not nationalize everything and set up a state economy. At least in part because of Moscow's unwillingness to open the purse strings, the Sandinistas are stuck with a mixed economy." (The New York Times Book Review, Dec. 25, 1983, p. 10.)

[22] Ramet and Lopez-Alves, Moscow and the Revolutionary Left in Latin America, p. 358–359.

[23] According to U.N. Ambassador Jeane Kirkpatrick, the Soviet Union has held secret discussions about the feasibility of building a sea-level canal linking the Caribbean with the Pacific. Kirkpatrick said the canal, which she characterized as part of a Soviet master plan to move "as rapidly as possible for the projection of their military power in the western Hemisphere," would follow the San Juan River which forms Nicaragua's southern frontier with Costa Rica, to its source in Lake Nicaragua; a second canal would link the western shore of Lake Nicaragua with the Pacific near the town of San Juan del Sur. This route had been under consideration at the turn of the century but the United States selected Panama. (Hempstone, Smith. Soviets, Nicaragua Air Construction of Canal. The Washington Times, April 29, 1983, p. 1A.) Scholars have emphasized the strategic importance of the Isthmus and its vulnerability to the Soviets under certain adverse conditions. See, Cirincione, Joseph and Leslie C. Hunter, Military Treats, Actual and Potential, in, Leiken, ed., Central America: Anatomy of Conflict, chapt. 8.

[24] On the matter of expanding the revolution in Central America, President Reagan said in a speech on May 10, 1984: "Shortly after taking power, the Sandinistas—in partnership with Cuba and the Soviet Union—began supporting aggression and terrorism against El Salvador, Hondu-

4. BUILDING "MULTIFACETED TIES" WITH MOSCOW

a. In the political sphere

(1) Establishing an integrated relationship

After the Sandinista triumph, the Soviets lost little time in seeking to build an enduring relationship. They did this using customary Soviet devices: establishing party-to-party and state-to-state ties; extending political support, along with military and economic aid; creating opportunities for cultural exchanges; and building an integrated infrastructure as a guarantee of continuing influence.

The Soviet Union greeted the Sandinista regime with an expressed interest, as Brezhnev said, in building "multi-faceted ties." Party and state relations were established forthwith between Moscow and Managua, and with countries of the Eastern bloc. By 1980, the Sandinistas had signed economic, scientific, technical, cultural accords with the Soviet Union, Cuba, East Germany, Bulgaria and Czechoslovakia. The consensus of various sources suggest that the Cubans provided doctors, teachers, construction workers, military specialists, intelligence operatives and advisers to the Sandinista party and various government ministries; the Soviets concentrated on state security along with the Cubans, East Germans and Bulgarians; the East Germans also assisted in intelligence and communications; the Bulgarians managed finance, economic planning and construction; and the Czechoslovaks provided some military advisers.[25]

(2) Intention of building a Marxist-Leninist system

On numerous occasions in the immediate wake of the revolution to as recently as September 1984, Sandinista officials visited the Soviet Union and Eastern Europe. These visits were intended to

---

ras, Costa Rica and Guatemala . . . The role that Cuba has long performed for the Soviet Union is now being played by the Sandinistas. They have become Cuba's Cubans. Weapons, supplies and funds are shipped from the Soviet bloc to Cuba, from Cuba to Nicaragua, from Nicaragua to the Salvadoran Guerrillas." (The New York Times, May 10, 1984, p. A16.) According to Rothenberg, "The Soviets saw the Sandinista victory as producing a domino effect in Central America. Operating mainly through Cuba and local communists, Moscow sought to duplicate the Nicaragua experience in El Salvador." (Rothenberg, The Soviets and Central America, in, Leiken, ed., Central America: Anatomy of Crisis, p. 136-137.) Cirincione and Hunter tend to downgrade Nicaragua as a direct military regional threat. Its military capabilities, they say, "are still largely defensive," and "their forces are not sufficient to invade even the relatively lightly-armed Honduras, let alone conquer an alliance of Honduras, El Salvador and Guatemala, backed by the United States." They conclude that, "Whether Nicaragua can become the 'mainland platform' for Soviet-Cuban expansionism depends in part on future shipments of arms." (Military Threats, Actual and Potential, in, Leiken, ed., Central America: Anatomy of Crisis, p. 177-178.) Leiken comments on the spread of insurgency in Guatemala and the Soviet-Cuban-Sandinista role, in, Soviet Strategy in Latin America, p. 81-83. For a commentary by the Soviets on U.S. policy in El Salvador, see, Krest' Yaninov, V.N. The Zigzags of Washington's Policy in El Salvador. Latinskaya Americaka (Moscow) in Russian, No. 1, Jan. 1984: 13-22, translated in, USSR Report, Political and Sociological Affairs, Apr. 12, 1984, p. 77-83 (JPRS-UPS-84-035). In a sharply critical commentary on U.S. policy in Central America, the writer charges that the "civil war" in El Salvador "was depicted by American diplomacy almost as if it were a central bridgehead in the struggle between East and West."

[25] Leiken, Fantasies and Facts: The Soviet Union and Nicaragua, p. 316. Within hours after the Sandinista seizure of power, Brezhnev sent a message congratulating the Nicaraguan people on their victory. Kommunist quoted Brezhnev as reaffirming the "sacred rights of each nation and of each country to select its own development path." Kommunist's treatment of the revolution revealed that the Nicaraguan Communists were regarded as only one element of many in the Somoza overthrow. At that time Brezhnev expressed Russia's readiness to normalize relations. The Soviet leadership moved more rapidly, Blasier notes, to establish ties with the Sandinistas than they had with Cuba. (The Giant's Rival, p. 44.)

gain Soviet military and economic support and to maintain the Soviet-Sandinista political relationship.[26]

No doubt the Soviets were encouraged by the so-called "72-Hour Document," alleged to be a record of a special three-day presentation by the Sandinista Directorate to its Sandinista National Liberation Front (FSLN) cadres during September 21–23, 1979. At this meeting the Sandinistas expressed their intention of removing their non-Marxist allies at a suitable opportunity and building a Marxist-Leninist system under Soviet protection.[27] The same theme was expressed in a secret speech by Bayardo Arce, one of nine Sandinista Commandantes, to the Central Committee of the pro-Soviet PSN in June 1984. Arce told a PSN gathering that the objective of Nicaragua's revolution was to establish a one-party state along orthodox Marxist-Leninist lines. Speaking of the November 4 election, Arce, considered to be the most radical of the nine Commandantes and without a cabinet post, said:

> We believe that the election must be used to secure a vote for Sandinism, which is being questioned and stigmatised by imperialism, in order to demonstrate that the Nicaraguan people . . . are for Marxism-Leninism. They will not overturn this vote by force, as they did in Chile.
>
> If it were not for the state of war forced on us . . . the electoral problem would be something completely out of step in terms of usefulness. What the revolution truly needs is the power to take action. And this power to take action is what constitutes the essence of the dictatorship of the proletariat . . . So the election is, from this point of view, a hindrance, like a number of other things . . . But, from a realistic point of view, these things are weapons of the revolution in forwarding the building of socialism.[28]

---

[26] According to Rothenberg, the Soviet Union "worked assiduously" to strengthen its ties with the entire ruling junta, particularly the military, intelligence and security apparatuses. On March 17, 1980, the first major Sandinista delegation arrived in Moscow and later went on to Bulgaria, East Germany, and Czechoslovakia. The delegation included Minister of Interior Tomas Borge, Minister of Economic Planning Henry Ruiz, and Minister of Defense Humberto Ortega. Between May 1982 and mid-1983 Sandinista leaders made, in Rothenberg's words, "a remarkable number of trips" to the Soviet Union. In May 1982, Daniel Ortega concluded a series of economic agreements. In September, Borge visited Moscow to discuss bilateral relations, a visit publicized by Managua but not by Moscow. Daniel Ortega represented the Sandinistas at Brezhnev's funeral in November and Minister of Agriculture Jaime Wheelock at the 60th anniversary of the USSR in December. In February 1983, Planning Minister Ruiz met with his Soviet counterpart. In March 1983, Daniel Ortega passed through Moscow en route home from the NAM conference in New Delhi and was received by Andropov. In June, Political Coordinator Bayardo Arce visited to carry out the 1980 party-to-party agreement, and in July Wheelock returned to sign an agricultural agreement. Perhaps most significant were the military relationships that were established by Humberto Ortega's visit in March 1980, and a return visit in November 1981. During the latter visit Ortega conferred with three leading Soviet military officials, Defense Minister Ustinov, Chief of Staff Nikolai Ogarkov, and General Yepishev, head of the Armed Forces' Main Political Administration. (Rothenberg, The Soviets and Central America, in, Leiken, Central America: Anatomy of Conflict, p. 133–134.) At a meeting with Daniel Ortega on February 15, 1983, Chernenko reaffirmed the Soviet pledge of support for Third World Countries shattering "the fetters of colonial dependence" and "especially" with those who "have to repel the attacks of the aggressive forces of imperialism." According to Tass, "both sides strongly denounced Washington's intention to whip up tension, to interfere in the internal affairs" of Central America and Chernenko "reiterated the Soviet people's firm support for the just cause of the Nicaraguan people." (Soviet World Outlook, v. 9, Feb. 15, 1984: 3.)

[27] Ramet and Lopez-Alves, Moscow and the Revolutionary Left in Latin America, p. 353. According to another interpretation, the document tells how to coopt some and isolate others.

[28] A Secret Sandinista Speech. The Economist Foreign Report, no. 1837, Aug. 23, 1984: 4–5, and no. 1838, Sept. 6, 1984: 3–4. The Sandinista regime was said to be "seriously embarrassed" by the disclosure of this speech in the Barcelona newspaper, La Vanguardia. For a discussion of the movement of the Sandinista Front towards a Marxist-Leninist one-party regime, see, Leiken, Soviet Strategy in Latin America, p. 83–88. For a penetrating analysis of the radicalization of the Sandinistas, see Cruz, Arturo Sequeira. The Origins of Sandinista Foreign Policy, in, Leiken, Central America; Anatomy of Conflict, Chapt. 4. Ambassdor Otto Reich, a special adviser to the Secretary of State on Latin America, and especially Central American affairs, gave the following assessment of whether the Sandinistas have moved closer to the Cubans and the Soviets: "It

By mid-November, many specialists agreed that the so-called "hard-line," doctrinaire Sandinistas had abandoned the early promises of their revolution and, in the words of the press report, "are steering the country down a leftist path inimical both to the Nicaraguan people and to Nicaragua's neighbors."[29]

(3) Accruing mutual benefits

In reciprocation for Soviet good works, the Sandinistas have supported Soviet positions in foreign policy, for example, on such important occasions as at the Havana meeting of the NAM leaders in September 1979 and in the United Nations where they abstained from the balloting that condemned the Soviet invasion of Afghanistan.[30]

The Soviets have also extended their gestures of support for the Sandinista regime. During the winter of 1980–81, when their optimism towards the regime's future peaked, Boris Ponomarev, the leading Soviet Central Committee authority on the Third World, referred to Central America as being a region where "socialist-oriented" states were emerging; he later alluded to Nicaragua's "taking the road of transition to socialism."[31] In addition, in May 1983, the Soviets admitted Nicaragua to the Soviet-sponsored Intersputnik Telecommunications Consortium, its first accession to a multilateral Communist organization, and in September admitted Nicaragua to CMEA as an observer.[32]

Finally, the Soviet Union is progressing along the cultural and informational front. It is reportedly building a ground station to tie in Nicaragua with the Soviet bloc television network. Soviet bloc literature is also widely featured in some Nicaraguan bookstores and news stands; Soviet manuals predominate in Nicaraguan schools and universities; and about a thousand Nicaraguan students are studying in the Soviet Union.[33]

b. Estimates of Soviet military assistance

(1) Transforming a guerrilla force into an army

The Soviets have also been forthcoming with military equipment for the Sandinista regime, assisting in transforming their guerrilla force of about 6,000 into a conventional army and in developing concurrently large militia and reserve forces. After nearly five

---

is apparent to me that they are basing their model on the Soviet and Cuban model. The political model is the one they are following based on a police state terrorism. Although they have announced elections, one has to be skeptical about elections when the ruling party controls all elements of national life, and when the people in power have said elections will be held only to ratify the revolution, to ratify the power of the revolution, and not to raffle off power." (Interview with Ambassador Otto Reich. U.S. Policy Toward Central America is Working. The Washington Times, July 9, p. 4C.) For other commentaries on the FSLN and its relationship with the Soviet Union, see, Cruz, Arturo Sequeira. The Origins of Sandinista Foreign Policy. In, Leiken, ed. Central America: Anatomy of Crisis, p. 99–104; Leiken, Soviet Strategy in Latin America, p. 83–88; and Valenta, Soviet and Cuban Responses in Central America, p. 145–148.

[29] U.S. Power Struggle Over Nicaragua. The Christain Science Monitor, Nov. 15, 1984, p. 1. The report continues: "Yet many US observers believe the US should not be trying to subvert a government with which it had diplomatic relations."

[30] Leiken, Fantasies and Facts: The Soviet Union and Nicaragua, p. 316.

[31] Ibid., p. 317.

[32] Ibid., p. 344, and Ramet and Lopez-Alves, Moscow and the Revolutionary Left in Latin America, p. 344.

[33] Leiken, Fantasies and Facts: The Soviet Union and Nicaragua, p. 344. For more detailed data on Soviet cultural and educational ties to Latin America, see, Jacobsen Report, p. 29–30.

years, the Sandinistas have increased their entire active duty military forces to some 48,800, in addition to expanding the militia, having enacted a universal military training law, which all told, if fully mobilized and including reserves, would number over 100,000.[34]

An array of Soviet bloc equipment was displayed during the first anniversary victory parade on July 19, 1980, that included 96 East German trucks, 18 Soviet light anti-aircraft guns, 6 SAM-7 surface-to-air missiles and other weaponry. Soviet bloc weapons known to be in the Nicaraguan arsenal by the end of 1980 included more than 50 Soviet T-54/55 tanks, at least eight 122mm and 12 155mm howitzers, more than 800 military supply trucks, 12 mobile missile launchers, and since the end of 1982, electronic radar equipment.[35]

In 1981, the Soviet bloc shipped some 66,000 tons of military hardware to Cuba, the greatest amount since the missile crisis of 1962. Much of this hardware was said to have been transshipped to Nicaragua. In addition, the Sandinista regime received from the Soviet Union between 1981 and 1983 five helicopters, patrol boats, armored personnel carriers, transport aircraft, spare parts for AN-26 transport aircraft and other equipment. Some 70 additional MIG fighters were said to be waiting in Cuba for transshipment to Nicaragua when the Nicaraguan pilots completed training in Bulgaria. Between 1979 and 1982, Nicaragua received an estimated $125 million in military equipment and supplies from the Soviet Union alone. During 1983 another 15,000 tons of Soviet bloc arms and equipment were given to the Sandinistas.[36]

In 1984, official U.S. estimates placed Nicaraguan armor units and artillery at about 100 Soviet medium tanks (T-54/T-55), over 20 light amphibious tanks (PT-76) and 120 other armored vehicles. During the first six months of 1984, U.S. sources noted the arrival of over 200 military trucks, about 300 jeeps, in addition to small numbers of other vehicles and spare parts. In 1983, the Sandinistas received nearly 500 trucks, over 500 jeeps and about 100 other vehicles. The GDR alone provided more than 1,000 trucks since 1980. Deployment of almost 50 Soviet 152mm and 122mm howitzers has also been confirmed. The Soviet bloc also supplied the Sandinistas with at least 24 122mm multiple rocket launchers. "The rocket launchers and howitzers, in addition to the 240 tanks and armored vehicles," notes the official U.S. report on the Nicaraguan military buildup, "give Nicaragua a firepower and mobility unmatched in the region, and the amphibious ferries provide a water-crossing capability for the armor force." [37]

(2) Building the foundations of an air force

Augmenting the buildup of land forces, the Sandinistas have created the foundation for a strong air defense and air force with Soviet and East European help. According to the U.S. report on the Nicaraguan military buildup, the Sandinistas now have about 120 Soviet-made anti-aircraft guns and at least 700 SA-7 surface-to-air

[34] U.S. Dept. of State and Dept. of Defense. Background Paper: Nicaragua's Military Build-up and Support for Central American Subversion. Washington, July 18, 1984, p. 8.
[35] Ramet and Lopez-Alves, Moscow and the Revolutionary Left in Latin America, p. 356.
[36] Ibid., p. 356-57.
[37] Nicaragua's Military Buildup, p. 9.

missiles, about ten MI–8 helicopters and six AN–2 light transport aircraft.[38]

Preparations for using Soviet advanced fighter aircraft in Nicaragua have been taking place for more than three years. In 1981, Nicaraguan pilots were sent to Cuba and Bulgaria for training to fly Soviet built MIGs. As late as 1983, some 70 additional MIGs were reportedly waiting in Cuba for transshipment to Nicaragua where the pilots completed their training.[39] As noted above, the Sandinistas have been building a military airfield at Punta Huete that when completed will have the longest runway in Central America (3,200 meters) and, as the U.S. report on the Nicaraguan buildup notes, will have the capability of receiving any aircraft in the Soviet inventory. Hence the report concludes:

. . . a basis has been laid for the receipt of modern [high performance advanced] jet fighters and for accommodating large military planes, such as heavy transport planes and Soviet "Backfire" bombers. If Nicaragua were to receive MIG fighters, the Sandinistas could rapidly develop a formidable air force.[40]

(3) Influx of military advisers from the Soviet bloc, Cuba, and North Korea

The Soviet bloc along with Cuba have also furnished military advisers for the Sandinistas. Presumably within a few weeks after the Sandinista victory, five Soviet generals secretly visited Nicaragua.[41] In March 1983, some 70 Soviet military advisers were reportedly on duty in Nicaragua; by early 1983, some 6,000 Cubans (2,000 of them military and security personnel) were reported to be present along with 100 East German advisors and some 100 Bulgarians. In June 1983, Cuba sent General Arnaldo Ochoa Sanchez, a veteran of the African wars, to Nicaragua. North Korean military advisers have also assisted the Sandinistas.[42] In 1984, the Cuban presence was estimated by U.S. official sources to be 9,000, of which 3,000 are military and security personnel attached to "the armed forces and to internal security and intelligence organizations, from the general staff down to individual batallions." [43] General Paul F. Gorman, head of the U.S. Southern Command based in Panama, told Congress in August that, "The Cuban presence is all pervasive, with upwards of 10,000 personnel spread throughout all levels of both military and governmental organizations." [44]

(4) Downgrading military assistance; a qualification: "The "MIG Scare"

Some sources tend to downgrade the size of Soviet military assistance to the Sandinistas. Leiken notes that Soviet deliveries of

---

[38] Ibid., p. 9–11.
[39] Ramet and Lopez, Alves, Moscow and the Revolutionary Left in Latin America, p. 356–57.
[40] Nicaragua's Military Buildup, p. 10. For other commentaries and estimates of Soviet bloc assistance to the Sandinistas, see, Jacobsen Report, p. 15–16 and 18; Rothenberg, The Soviets and Central America, in, Leiken, Central America: Anatomy of Crisis, p. 134–35; Middleton, Drew. Latin Issue: A Well-Armed Nicaragua. The New York Times, May 6, 1984, p. 12; Mallin, Jay Sr. Soviets Bolstering Military Presence in Latin America. The Washington Times, April 17, 1984, p. 1A and 12A; and Blasier, The Giant's Rival, p. 115–17.
[41] Leiken, Fantasies and Facts: The Soviet Union and Nicaragua, p. 315.
[42] Ramet and Lopez-Alves, Moscow and the Revolutionary Left in Latin America, p. 355.
[43] Nicaragua's Military Buildup, p. 11.
[44] Knickerbocker, Brad. The Military Balance in Central America. The Christian Science Monitor, Nov. 13, 1984, p. 3.

military equipment to Nicaragua increased "substantially" since 1981.[45] However, he concludes that "the total volume of Soviet bloc military equipment remains low, about 17,500 metric tons from 1981 through early 1984." By comparison, in 1962 the Soviets delivered 250,000 metric tons of arms to Cuba; in 1963, 40,000; in 1964, 20,000.[46] Ramet and Lopez-Alves describe the Soviet shipments as "modest."[47] Joseph Cirincione, a staff member of the Central American Project of the Carnegie Endowment for International Peace, and Leslie C. Hunter, a Latin American specialist with the U.S. Department of the Navy, conclude that "Nicaragua's military capabilities are still largely defensive," and its four-year arms buildup has made it "unlikely that the country could be successfully invaded by any combination of Central American countries. . . ." And whether Nicaragua can become the "mainland platform" for Soviet-Cuban expansionism, they assert, "depends in part on future shipments of arms."[48]

However "modest" in relative terms the amount of Soviet bloc and Cuban military aid going to the Sandinistas and whatever its capabilities as a regional military force at this juncture, the important point to be borne in mind is the Sovet commitment to the Sandinistas, their demonstrated intention of protecting their revolution, albeit it cautiously, and under proper conditions perhaps even extending it, and the erosive effects of incrementalism on the U.S. power position as it has been applied in Soviet-Cuban policy in the Caribbean.

Moreover, it is difficult to determine at least at this juncture just how open-ended the military pipeline is from Moscow and Havana to Nicaragua and whether Nicaragua will indeed become a "second Cuba" as many Administration officials fear. The so-called "MIG scare" in mid-November 1984 aroused deep concerns within the Administration and the press about Soviet-Cuban intentions in Nicaragua. The issue arose directly from an Administrtion "leak" that advanced MIG fighters were on their way to Nicaragua from the Soviet Union, an allegation the Soviets and Nicaraguans denied. Though the threat of delivering MIGs had been made before, the actual press report of a possible shipment on the way created a crisis atmosphere.

The incident, though transitory in its gravity, nonetheless, gave the United States the opportunity to lay down the limits of its tolerance with respect to Soviet arms shipments to Managua. MIG fighters, as noted elsewhere in this study, would qualitatively change the character of Soviet involvement in Nicaragua, trans-

---

[45] Leiken, Fantasies and Facts: The Soviet Union and Nicaragua, p. 344.
[46] Ibid.
[47] Ramet and Lopez-Alves, Moscow and the Revolutionary Left in Latin America, p. 356.
[48] Cirincione and Hunter, Military Threats, Actual and Potential, in, Leiken, Central America; Anatomy of Crisis, p. 176–78. Administration sources have contended that Nicaragua is a military threat to other nations in the region because of its military buildup. But John H. Buchanan, a retired Marine Corps lieutenant colonel and the only American known to have been allowed access to the Nicaraguan military said, "I don't think the army is yet designed for offensive purposes." It was Buchanan's "impression" that Nicaragua is "developing an army very loyal to the Sandinistas, an army that will become like the army in Poland, be used to control the people." Buchanan described the "might" of the Nicaraguan air force as "infinitesimal" and that the country lacked the oil refineries and other facilities necessary to support a large air force. (Bonner, Raymond. Behind Nicaraguan Buildup: Soviet-Bloc Aid Cited. The New York Times, April 27, 1983, p. A17.) For other judgments on Soviet-Cuban military aid to the Sandinistas, see, Jacobsen Report, p. 15–18.

forming it from the regional to the strategic level of concern. As one official said with respect to Soviet efforts to turn Nicaragua into a "second Cuba," giving it another base of operations and influence in the hemisphere: "If it comes down to that, you can bet this Administration won't sit still."[49]

Furthermore, delivery of the MIGs would have significant political implications: It would signal to the Soviets another degree of U.S. acquiesence in their pressure and accordingly imply a lowering of the threshold of U.S. tolerance and acceptance of a further strengthening of the Soviet position in Central America. Such a qualitative and quantitative change could adversely affect the U.S. position regionally and eventually even globally if the trend continued. For U.S. Administration officials, therefore, the MIGs had both a real and symbolic significance. They responded quickly and vigorously to what they perceived to be a serious challenge.

Secretary of Defense Caspar W. Weinberger expressed deep concern about the "tremendously increased flow of offensive weaponry" into Nicaragua. Some observers likened it to the Soviet shipments to Cuba prior to the missile crisis. Weinberger said that the United States "is prepared for a number of contingencies that may have to be taken." He disclosed that "the Soviets are supplying a great deal of heavy offensive arms to Nicaragua" for the purpose of intimidating Nicaragua's neighbors.[50]

Secretary of State George P. Shultz added his authoritative voice to others in the Administration expressing their public concern. Speaking to the press on his way to a meeting of the Organization of American States in Brazil, he said:

The Nicaraguans seem intent on militarizing their society and accumulating a level of weapons and armed capability that is entirely outside the standpoint of any conceivable defensive mission.[51]

But others expressed deeper concern about the shipment of Mi24 Hind helicopter gunships than the MIGs, having in mind their regional significance, that is, their effectiveness in guerrilla warfare. Adolfo Calero, a leader of the Contra forces, said they are more dangerous for them than MIGs. Hinds, used by the Soviets in Afghanistan, are capable of "saturation attacks" against large areas, he said, and they "can obliterate entire villages." With this weaponry in their armory, the "Sandinistas could polish us off between now and February", the terminating date of Congress' suspension of funds for the Contras.[52]

Thus the sudden upgrading and increase in Soviet military shipments to the Sandinistas in mid-November argues for caution in prejudging the extent of Soviet assistance. For this episode suggests not only the strength of the Soviet commitment but the open-endedness of their military pipeline to Nicaragua.[53]

---

[49] Taubman, Philip. Policy Rift on Nicaragua. The New York Times, Nov. 12, 1984, p. A8.
[50] Hiatt, Fred. Nicaragua Buildup Called Defensive. The Washington Post, Nov. 13, 1984, p. A1 and The New York Times, Nov. 12, 1984, p. A8.
[51] Taubman, Philip. U.S. is Said to Be Studying Ways to Increase Pressure on Nicaragua. The New York Times, Nov. 11, 1984, p. A16.
[52] The Washington Post, Nov. 13, 1984, p. A19.
[53] Another significant indication of the Soviet commitment to the Sandinistas is the report that according to U.S. intelligence sources there is some $300 million in ongoing military construction in Nicaragua funded by the Soviet Union and Cuba. (The Christian Science Monitor, Nov. 13, 1984, p. 3.)

c. Economic assistance to the Sandinista regime

(1) Not overly generous

The Soviets have not been overly generous in their economic aid to Nicaragua.[54] According to Ramet and Lopez-Alves, the Russians were "slow to extend concrete material aid," and in fact rebuffed the Sandinistas in March 1980 when they sought economic assistance.[55] Leiken writes that despite Sandinista efforts to ingratiate themselves with the Soviet leaders, sometimes excessively, the Russians have been "exceedingly chary," especially in economic assistance.[56]

Statistics bear this out. Between 1981 and 1984, Soviet economic aid fluctuated between $75 million and $150 million. Total bloc aid was estimated between $200 million and $250 million, a "strikingly low" figure, according to most observers in view of the continuing deterioration of the Nicaraguan economy.[57]

Nor have the Soviets been forthcoming in the Sandinista's "desperate" requests for foreign exchange. At best, the Soviets have preferred to grant emergency assistance when propaganda dividends were conspicuous, as in the case of the shipment of 20,000 tons of wheat in 1981 (the first tangible Soviet contribution to the Nicaraguan revolution in 1981), another 7,000 tons of "scarce" wheat in November 1983, and oil in 1984.[58]

Nor did the Soviets come to the rescue when the United States reduced the Nicaraguan sugar quota in the spring of 1983 further deepening the country's economic distress.[59]

Most Soviet bloc economic assistance has been in long-term development aid in the medical, hydroelectric and agricultural areas.[60] In January 1982, the Soviet extended some $220 million in credits to Nicaragua, and in March 1983, Nicaragua signed a trade agreement with Poland, and a three-year $170 million aid and trade agreement with Bulgaria. The Sandinista regime concluded additional economic agreements with Bulgaria, Czechoslovakia and East Germany in 1983.[61]

(2) Not a "primary client" in trade

Nor has trade figured significantly in the Soviet-Nicaraguan relationship. A little more than 10 percent of total Nicaraguan imports and exports is carried on with the Soviet bloc, placing it behind the United States, EEC countries, Central America and the rest of Latin America. The Soviet bloc purchases moderate amounts of traditional Nicaraguan exports, but, as Leiken ob-

---

[54] See Jacobsen Report, p. 18–25.
[55] Ramet and Lopez-Alves, Moscow and the Revolutionary Left in Latin America, p. 353.
[56] Leiken, Fantasies and Facts: The Soviet Union and Nicaragua, p. 344.
[57] Ibid. See also, Cody, Edward. Dissatisfaction Spreads in Nicaragua: Many Blame Sandinistas for Economic and Political Difficulties. The Washington Post, Oct. 21, 1984, p. Al, and Despite Problems, Many Support Sandinistas, The Washington Post, Oct. 22, 1984, p. Al; Kinzer, Stephen. With Economic Woes Deepening, Managua Sees Years of Shortages. The New York Times, Oct. 22, 1984, p. A1. For a recent assessment of the Sandinista regime by Leiken, see his, Nicaragua's Untold Stories: Sandinista Corruption and Violence Breed Bitter Opposition. The New Republic, v. 191, Oct. 8, 1984: 16–22.
[58] Ramet and Lopez-Alves, Moscow and the Revolutionary Left in Latin America, p. 354.
[59] Leiken. Fantasies and Facts: The Soviet Union and Nicaragua, p. 344.
[60] Ibid.
[61] Ramet and Lopez-Alves, Moscow and the Revolutionary Left in Latin America, p. 354.

serves, "it has not become Nicaragua's primary client as it is in Argentina and Cuba." [62]

(3) No blank check for Nicaragua

Thus Nicaragua is not the beneficiary of any economic largesse from Moscow. Pressed by serious problems in its own economy, the Soviet Union can little afford to add another client state to its long list of economic liabilities—Cuba, Afghanistan and Vietnam. A Latin American diplomat seems to have captured the essence of the Soviet attitude when he recently said:

> If the Sandinistas ever hoped the Soviets would give them a blank check, they don't any more. The Soviets have made clear that they can't afford to underwrite another Cuba, and besides they are not so taken by the Sandinistas. [63]

There seems little doubt, therefore, that the potential danger of increasing the imperial burden goes far to explain why the Soviets are "exceedingly chary" in their economic commitment to the Sandinistas.

5. SOVIET CAUTION AND RESTRAINT

a. Contrasting perspectives

Early in 1981, according to Leiken, the Soviet seemed to have backed off somewhat from any deep involvement in Nicaragua and Central America. Caution and restraint appeared to characterize their attitude and behavior. [64] One of the main reasons for this change in emphasis was the failure of the 1980–1981 "final offensive" in El Salvador. Another was the apparent growing Soviet uncertainty about the political maturity of the Sandinistas and the U.S. response to their involvement. Hence the judgment of one Latin American diplomat in March 1984 that the Soviets "are not so taken by the Sandinistas" and the conclusion of another:

> The Russians are very big on objective conditions, and they don't see in Nicaragua the objective conditions for a transition to socialism. They don't seem to be pushing the Sandinistas to greater radicalization. [65]

However, some time in the course of 1981, according to Ramet and Lopez-Alves, the Soviets seemed to have decided to commit themselves "more explicitly" to Nicaragua, at least politically. [66]

These contrasting perspectives suggest important nuances in the Soviet approach to this Third World region.

b. Tending toward caution and restraint

Soviet optimism about the continuing success of the Sandinistas seemed to peak in the winter of 1980–1981. This optimism was re-

---

[62] Leiken, Fantasies and Facts: The Soviet Union and Nicaragua, p. 344.

[63] Kinser, Stephen. Soviet Help to Sandinistas: No Blank Check. The New York Times, March 28, 1984, p. A1 and A4. Rothenberg flatly states: "Moscow has been reluctant to take on the economic burden of Nicaraguan as it did in Cuba." He also notes that Nicaraguan trade with the Soviet bloc remains "limited." Rothenberg quotes Andropov's comments before the Central Committee plenum in June 1983 (cited in Part I of this study) cautioning countries with which it has close political sympathies as with Nicaragua not to pin excessive hopes on economic support from the Soviet Union. The theme of Andropov's message was "self-help." (The Soviet and Central America, in, Leiken, Central America: Anatomy of Crisis, p. 141.)

[64] Leiken, Fantasies and Facts: The Soviet Union and Nicaragua, p. 317.

[65] The New York Times, March 28, 1984, p. A4.

[66] Ramet and Lopez-Alves, Moscow and the Revolutionary Left in Latin America, p. 354.

flected in Ponomarev's statement designating Nicaragua a "socialist-oriented" state.[67] Viktor Volski, President of the Soviet Association of Friendship with Latin American countries, reflected this same confidence when he termed the Sandinista victory in Nicaragua as a "model" to be followed elsewhere in Latin America.[68] Both Pravda and Tass featured what Leiken called "triumphal reports" on the Salvadoran guerrillas' "final offensive."[69]

But in a retrospective glance, Leiken suggests in 1984 that failure of the offensive may have provoked a reassessment of Moscow's Central American policy. After the defeat of the "final offensive," Leiken notes, "optimism disappeared from the Soviet bloc media and a curtain descended on El Salvador."[70]

Indications of Soviet disenchantment with Central America are numerous and are recorded in many sources:

—Brezhnev's failure to mention El Salvador or Central America in assessing global affairs in his speech at the 26th Party Congress in February 1981.[71]

—Brezhnev's cautious rejoinder to a pledge of "full support" for Soviet positions on the arms race, detente, the proposed Soviet "unilateral" moratorium on deploying nuclear weapons in European Russia, by Nicaragua's Head of State Daniel Ortega during a visit to Moscow in May 1982. Brezhnev emphasized the "vast oceanic expanses separating Nicaragua from the Soviet Union", suggesting some disinterest.[72]

—The failure of Moscow to be more forthcoming in economic assistance to the depressed and floundering Nicaraguan economy and their urging upon Nicaragua, as with other Third World countries, economic diversification in relations with the world economy, the value of maintaining a mixed economy, and the virtues of self-help.[73] According to one Sandinista observer "with excellent government contacts," some Soviet leaders gave the Sandinistas hope that after Brezhnev's death, aid would increase. However, when high-ranking Sandinista leaders attended Brezhnev's funeral in November 1982, it became clear that neither Andropov, Brezhnev's successor, nor any other Soviet leader wanted to increase aid substantially.[74]

—Soviet rejection of Nicaragua's application for full membership in CMEA and admission only as an observer, implying a Soviet economic commitment less than it is willing or able to give.[75]

—The widely circulated report in diplomatic circles in 1984 that CMEA had turned down a Nicaraguan request for a loan.

—The "recent and graphic illustration," as Leiken put it, of Ortega's "dismal" trip to Moscow in June 1984, returning "empty-handed from his latest effort to upgrade Soviet com-

[67] Leiken, Fantasies and Facts: The Soviet Union and Nicaragua, p. 317.
[68] Kissinger Commission's Report, p. 89.
[69] Leiken, Fantasies and Facts: The Soviet Union and Nicaragua, p. 317.
[70] Ibid.
[71] Ibid.
[72] Ibid., p. 344.
[73] Ibid. and Rothenberg, The Soviets and Central America, in, Leiken, Central America: Anatomy of Crisis, p. 141.
[74] Volman, Dennis. Nicaragua's Marxist Leaders May Stick to Mixed Economy. The Christian Science Monitor, April 19, 1984, p. 9.
[75] Leiken, Fantasies and Facts: The Soviet Union and Nicaragua, p. 344.

mitments to Nicaragua's staggering economy and hard-pressed defense." [76]

—The absence of a communique, a departure from customary Soviet protocol, suggesting "sharp differences" between Chernenko and Ortega during his June 1984 visit to Moscow.[77]

—The lack of intimacy between the Sandinista leaders and Soviet Ambassador German Y. Shyapnikov who, as recently reported, prefers to make only occasional public appearances and then to donate grains or medicine.[78] And finally,

—The apparent Soviet hesitation in transshipping advanced, high performance MIG figher-bombers for use at the new military airfield at Punta Huete. Defense Minister Humberto Ortega said on September 18, 1984 that Nicaragua would soon acquire this advanced aircraft. The United States looks upon such a transfer as a serious provocation.[79]

By early 1982, Leiken notes, both the Soviet Union and Cuba "were anxious to appear as peacemakers in the Caribbean basin." [80] The heady optimism evident in the wake of the July 1979 Sandinista victory gave way to "a more guarded view of revolutionary possibilities in Central America." Expressions such as "regional upsurge" to describe conditions in the Central American area gave way to stress on the "ebb and flow" of specific situations in specific countries.[81]

Hence Leiken's conclusion that "over the last three years, more often than not, Moscow has disappointed fond Sandinista expectations" by its apparently carefully measured support.[82] And the observation of a senior Western diplomat in Managua:

---

[76] Ibid., p. 314. Commentaries in 1984 clearly portray the dismal state of the Nicaraguan economy. Edward Cody writes from Managua: "The most common complaints long have revolved around the faltering economy, starved for foreign exchange because of low prices for Nicaraguan exports, such as sugar and coffee, and U.S. pressure to block loans in international financial institutions. In addition, hard currency and agricultural manpower have been diverted to the military to meet the guerrilla threat, depleting the treasury and blunting production." (Dissatisfaction Spreads in Nicaragua. The Washington Post, Oct. 21, 1984, p. A22.) Jay Mallin, Sr. corroborates this judgment in his report from Managua: "From top to bottom, the Nicaraguan economy is a near-disaster, Pedro Joaquin Chamorro, the editor of the embattled opposition daily La Prensa, says. 'The Sandinistas are suicidal. They are going to take the people to chaos.'" (Nicaragua's Economy Appears on the Brink of Disaster. The Washington Times, Sept. 25, 1984, p. 6A.) Daniel Ortega defended the Sandinistas in the Soviet media by placing the blame for the economic crisis that has "hit the countries in the region" on the "hegemonist and predatory policy of imperialism, mainly U.S. imperialism." Their economic crisis, he says, has been aggravated "by the growing aggression of the United States." (Revolution on the March, New Times, no. 27, 1984: 6.) For other analyses of Nicaragua's economic condition, see the reports by Dennis Volman: Nicaragua's Marxist Leaders May Stick to Mixed Economy. The Christian Science Monitor, April 19, 1984, p. 9; Difficult Years Ahead for Sandinistas. The Christian Science Monitor, July 17, 1984, p. 9; and, Will Sandinistas Loosen Their Rule or Face More U.S. Pressure? The Christian Science Monitor, July 18, 1984, p. 11.

[77] Leiken, Fantasies and Facts: The Soviet Union and Nicaragua, p. 314.

[78] The New York Times, Mar. 28, 1984, p. A4.

[79] Murphy, Bill. Nicaragua to Receive MIG Fighters? RFE–RL. Radio Liberty Research, RL361/84, Sept. 24, 1984, p. 1–4. Visiting Soviet leader Ivan Kapitonov denied in Mexico City that the Soviet Union sells weapons to Nicaragua and that it had any airplanes in Nicaragua, but he insisted that "in view of the imperialist aggression to which it is subject, Nicaragua has the right to arm itself." Humberto Ortega, also in Mexico City, said that Nicaragua's purchase of aircraft depended to some degree on economic issues; he hinted that they might be donated. (Madrid EFE in Spanish, 0430 GMT, Sept. 21, 1984, in FBIS Daily Report, Soviet Union, v. 3, Sept. 21, 1984, p. K.)

[80] Leiken, Fantasies and Facts: The Soviet Union and Nicaragua, p. 317.

[81] Ibid.

[82] Ibid., p. 314.

I don't think the Russians want Central America to be high on the U.S.-Soviet bilateral agenda. They don't want to be seen as abandoning a country struggling for revolution, but overall, they have been pretty cautious here.[83]

c. Reconciling contrasting points of view: Constraint with commitment

Differences between these points of view seem more apparent than real; for the main thrust of Soviet policy in Nicaragua and Central America, particularly since the U.S. invasion of Grenada in October 1983, seems to be marked by caution and restraint, but without any diminution of commitment.

The initial momentum of the Sandinista revolution appears at this juncture to have been spent. The downward turn of Communist fortunes in El Salvador and Grenada and the growing economic problems in Nicaragua seem to have coverged to impose reassessment. For the Soviets, long experienced with the vagaries of politics in the Third World, are reluctant to back losers. They "are not so taken by the Sandinistas" and they "don't seem to be pushing the Sandinistas to greater radicalization," as the foreign diplomats in Managua only recently observed.[84] And as Leiken recently writes in his summary of the Sandinista experience after four years in power portraying a reality hardly appealing to Moscow:

From the standpoints of the development of the "productive forces" and of "mass participation," the Nicaraguan revolution seems to contradict its own rhetoric. Nor has it provided the "pluralistic, democratic, non-aligned model" that the revolutionary leadership promised the Nicaraguan people and their international supporters. That leadership has earned a reputation for post-revolutionary conspicuous consumption and corruption.[85]

In brief, the "correlation of forces" appears to have changed, at least momentarily. Accordingly, the Soviet leadership, assessing the "ebb and flow" of developments in Central America and the Caribbean, may have judged that the time has come to consolidate their gains before moving out on another offensive when conditions are "ripe"—that is, a policy of opportunism carried forth in the tested mode of incrementalism.[86]

---

[83] The New York Times, Mar. 28, 1984, p. A4. In an analysis of Soviet reaction to developments in Central America during mid-1983, Robert Rand, a Soviet specialist at Radio Liberty's Research Department, cited two major constraints on the Soviets: geographical distance from the Soviet Union and proximity to the United States. These factors compel the Soviets to approach the region "with some caution." American officials believe, therefore, that "the Kremlin's willingness to assist pro-Communist movements there has its limits." Few believe the Soviets would risk "a direct military confrontation with the United States by aiding Cuba or Nicaragua with Soviet personnel in the event of a war in Central America." (The Soviet Reaction to Recent Developments in Central America, RFE-RL, Radio Liberty Research, RL 292/83, July 29, 1983, p. 2.) In a subsequent RL interview with State Department officials, one analyst defined the limits of Soviet restraint this way: "The Soviets are not willing to get into any conflict with the US over Central America. They are certainly willing to continue arms shipments to the region as long as by doing so they don't face any direct confrontation with Washington—a blockade, for instance, or a quarantine. I think that is the threshold at which they might say, O.K., we've done what we can, and our interests are no longer to antagonize the situation." Another official concerned with Soviet affairs stated that the Soviets do not want a confrontation with the United States because "it would be a fundamental departure from their principal tactic, which is to engage in a strategy of attrition and gradualism." (Rand, Robert. USSR Said to Gain Benefits in Central American Crisis. RFE-RL, Radio Liberty Research, RL 311/83, Aug. 17, 1983, p. 3.)

[84] The New York Times, Mar. 28, 1984, p. A1 and A4.

[85] Leiken, Robert S. Overview: Can the Cycle be Broken? in, Leiken, ed., Central America: Anatomy of Crisis, p. 12.

[86] The Soviet political commitment and its policy of caution and restraint in Central America, particularly its sensitivity towards the U.S. reaction to Soviet-Cuban involvement in the region,

Yet this judgment, tentative at best, must be weighed against the perceptible increase in Soviet military deliveries to Nicaragua in mid-November 1984. For Nicaragua is a moving target, and the tactic of incrementalism requires not only vigilance but persistent monitoring and reassessing of forward movement.

B. FAILURE IN GRENADA

1. EVOLVING SECURITY PROBLEM; A U.S. MILITARY SOLUTION

In contrast to their qualified success in Nicaragua, the Soviet Union and its Cuban ally suffered a sharp setback in Grenada in October 1983, when U.S. forces along with contingents from the Organization of East Caribbean States (OECS) intervened ostensibly to protect "innocent lives, including up to 1,000 Americans," to forestall "further chaos," and to assist in restoring "law and order" and "governmental institutions on the Island." A deeper concern was the belief that the Soviets and Cubans were establishing what some claimed to be the beginnings of a military base in the Caribbean.[87]

A former colony of Great Britain, Grenada was granted independence on February 7, 1974. Prior to the revolutionary crisis, Grenada had a population of approximately 110,000, inhabiting 133 sq. miles, twice the area of Washington, D.C. On March 13, 1979, the leftist New Jewel Movement (NJM)—Jewel, the acronym for Joint Endeavor for Welfare, Education and Liberation—overthrew the government of Prime Minister Eric Gairy known for its oppressive, "bizarre behavior," and established a People's Revolutionary

---

seems reflected in the press briefing given by Zamyatin, head of the International Information Department of the CPSU Central Committee, on the occasion of the visit by Francois Mitterrand, President of France, to the Soviet Union. L.M. Zamyatin said: "On our initiative, the issue of the situation in Central America was touched upon. Comrade Chernenko particularly stressed the danger of the situation that has come about in the region during June 1984. In this connection, it was stated that Washington's attempts to destroy a political system that does not suit it, one chosen by the people of Nicaragua, are dangerous. The danger of the armed intervention in that country and of the blockade and blackmail being conducted against that independent state was pointed out. It was plainly stated that this is dangerous for general peace. We expressed ourselves in favor of the achievement of a political settlement to the conflict situation in Central America on the basis of respect for the sovereignty of the countries of that region and noninterference in their internal affairs." (Moscow Domestic Service in Russian, 1230 GMT, June 21, 1984, in FBIS Daily Report, Soviet Union, v. 3, June 22, 1984, p. G3.)

The Soviet commitment to Nicaragua is also evident in the Central Committee slogans for the coming 67th anniversary of the Bolshevik Revolution. Such slogans, traditionally issued on major Soviet holidays, suggest the priority of Soviet political concerns, domestically and internationally. The slogan for Latin America is number 54 in a total of 63, but it is listed after Africa, but before the Middle East, Western Europe, and Asia, a ranking that suggests the seriousness of the Soviet commitment. It says: "Warm greetings to the peoples of Latin America who are fighting against imperialism and reaction and for peace and democratic development of their countries! Peoples of the world! Demand an end to the aggressive actions of the United States against Nicaragua! Strive for the liberation of Grenada from American occupation!" (Pravda, Oct. 11, 1984, 1st ed., p. 1, in FBIS Daily report, Soviet Union, v. 3, Oct. 12, 1984, p. R4.)

[87] Text of Reagan's Announcement of Invasion, The New York Times, Oct. 26, 1983, p. A16. A statement issued by Tass declared that "the Soviet Union firmly condemns the United States aggression against Grenada and stigmatizes it as a crime against peace and humanity. It is the duty of all states and peoples firmly to come out against Washington's arbitrariness and lawlessness, in defense of the Grenadian people." (Pravda, Oct. 27, 1983, 1st ed., p. 4., in FBIS Daily Report, Soviet Union, v. 3, Oct. 27, 1983, p. K.1.) For a sharp condemnation of the U.S. action, see Murav'yev, D. Grenada—Victim of U.S. Imperialist Aggression. Kommunist, no. 16, Nov. 1983, p. 109–111, Translated in, USSR Report, Translations from Kommunist, Jan. 23, 1984, p. 125–129 (JPRS–UKO–84–004). The writer refers to this episode as the "latest gangsterly attack" by American "imperialism." "The entire world condemned the barbaric aggression against Grenada," he said, "as a violation of the UN Charter and the universally accepted norms of international law . . . No justification whatsoever exists for such an aggression."

Government with strong ties to the Soviet Union and Cuba. Modelling their revolution along lines of other Communist countries, notably Cuba in the late 1960's and 1970's which by then had successfully established a Communist regime (and encouraged to do so by the Soviets and Cubans), the leaders of the NJM, Prime Minister Maurice Bishop and Deputy Prime Minister Bernard Coard, proceeded in the next four years to transform Grenada into what some have claimed to be an incipient Soviet-Cuban military base in the Caribbean.[88]

Factional disputes between the Bishop and Coard forces, the latter urging a quickened pace of socialist transformation and the former a more gradualist approach, erupted in 1982–83, creating acute instability within the Grenada Government. On October 15, 1983, the issue was resolved temporarily with Bishop's removal from power and his execution four days later.[89]

For apparent security reasons and in response to a call for assistance from the OECS, U.S. military forces invaded Grenada on October 25, 1983, deposing the ultra leftist government of Coard and preventing what was claimed to be the establishment of another Socialist enclave in the Caribbean region.[90]

2. SOVIET ROLE IN GRENADA

a. Building an ideological and political infrastructure [91]

(1) The Valentas and the Grenada documents

Grenada is a unique case of Soviet expansionism in the Third World. What makes it unique is the availability of official documents captured in Grenada by the American forces that reveal Soviet actions from an authentic primary historical source as reported by Grenadian officials. For the Grenada documents consist of NJM Political Bureau and Central Committee minutes; secret agreements with the Soviet Union, Cuba and other countries; letters, diaries, personal papers and diplomatic correspondence from the Grenadian Embassy in Moscow. Only in the case of German captured Soviet documents in World War II and those available during the Czechoslovak crisis of 1968 has the West been provided such insights, however indirect, into the Soviet decision-making process and inter-Communist relations.

The Grenada documents, while revealing only the Grenada side of the relationship, contain, nonetheless, authentic reportage and assessments of Soviet thoughts, actions and reactions at a critical

---

[88] Valenta, Jiri and Virginia. Leninism In Grenada. Probems of Communism, v. 23, July–Aug. 1984: 1–23; and The New York Times, Oct. 26, 1983, p. A21.

[89] Valenta, Leninism in Granda, p. 19.

[90] The New York Times, Oct. 26, 1983, p. 1 and 16–22. See also, Rand, Robert. Grenada's Links with the USSR and Cuba. RFE–RL, Radio Liberty Research, RL 401/83, Oct. 26, 1983, p. 1–3. In an extensive commentary on revolution and the historical inevitably of Communist success, Boris Ponomarev, a leading Soviet authority on the Third World, included Grenada in the context of U.S. support of "counter-revolution": "The imperialists need the anti-communist proposition of 'export of revolution' in order to try to substantiate their policy of export of counter-revolution. There are ample proofs of that: the aggression against freedom-loving Grenada, the undeclared war against Nicaragua, the encouragement of the counter-revolutionary forces in the African countries, support for counter-revolution in Afghanistan, anti-socialist acts of subversion against Central and Eastern Europe and many other things." Such actions, he says, "are historically doomed to a failure." (Kommunist, Tass, Nov. 5, 1984, in FBIS 059, Take 2-3.)

[91] The Valentas analyze this process in detail in their "Leninism in Grenada," p. 2–8.

time during the Socialist transformation of this Third World country. As the Valentas observe:

> Regardless of one's opinion about that invasion [of which there has been much criticism], these documents are a windfall for scholars in providing an unprecedented glimpse into the inner workings of an aspiring Third World Leninist regime and its relations with more established such regimes elsewhere.[92]

Jiri and Virginia Valenta, collectively seasoned scholars in Soviet, East European and Latin American affairs, have recently published an article in USIA's much respected scholarly journal, Problems of Communism, giving a detailed description and analysis of the Soviet and Cuban role in the attempted Communization of Grenada.[93] Their study is based on the Grenada documents and on interviews in Grenada and Barbados with business and labor leaders, journalists and political leaders, including former NJM officials. It is the first published extensive commentary and analysis of these documents. Special attention is given to inter-Communist relations, and it is from this part of their study that much of the data below is drawn in order to suggest the Soviet role in Grenada and their use of Cuba as an instrument of Soviet Third World policy in Latin America. Because the Valentas' article is the principal source, quoted material in the text is not always identified as the source.[94]

(2) Soviet personnel in Grenada

In pursuit of its expansionist objectives in the Caribbean, the Soviet Union extended the "most vigorous forms of support" (except economic) to Grenada, according to the Valentas. Political and ideological ties were strengthened between Grenada, the Soviet Union, its allies in Eastern Europe and Cuba by the "relatively large number of officials," notably intelligence operatives, posted on the island.[95] The Soviets alone had about 47 officials, judged to be a considerable number considering the embassy had only been established in November 1981 and considering also the small size of the country. Gennadiy Sazhenev, the first Soviet Ambassador, has been identi-

---

[92] Valentas, Leninism in Grenada, p. 1.

[93] For another view of this episode, see Duncan, Soviet Interests in Latin America, p. 168–175, 193–194. Deputy Secretary of State Kenneth W. Dam reviewed the contents of some of the documents noting that the Soviet Union, North Korea and Cuba had agreed in secret agreements to provide $37.8 million in military equipment. (The Washington Times, Nov. 3, 1983, p. 6A, and The Washington Post, Nov. 3, 1983, p. A1 and A28.)

[94] The Soviets place their own interpretation of the Grenada documents. Vitaliy Korionov, a Soviet political observer, wrote on the anniversary of the invasion: "The International Association of Democratic Lawyers stated with good reason: 'The U.S. armed intervention in Grenada does not fit within any juridical framework and is therefore an illegal and immoral act of aggression which no arguments can justify.' And quite recently, the experts of the Council on Hemispheric Affairs, a research organization operating in Washington, who spent a year studying all the documents relating to that aggression, arrived at the unambiguous conclusion that not one of the assertions used by the Reagan administration to justify the invasion is corroborated by facts." (Grenada Calls Us to the Struggle. Pravda, Oct. 25, 1984, 1st ed., p. 4., in FBIS Daily Report, Soviet Union, v. 3, Oct. 30, 1984, p. K1.)

A selection of "a few hundred pages out of tens of thousands" of the captured documents has been published by the U.S. Government. The documents reproduced are photographic copies of the original. The volume is very large and while unpaged it measures 8½" by 11" and over 2" thick, roughly the size of a Manhattan phone book. See, U.S. Department of State and Department of Defense. Grenada Documents: An Overview and Selection. with introduction by Michel Ledeen, a State Department Consultant, and Herbert Romerstein, an official with USIA. Washington, U.S. Govt. Print. Off., Sept. 1984, Ca. 820 p. Apparently, the entire collection is now unclassified and made available to the public.

[95] Valentas, Leninism in Grenada, p. 8.

fied as a four-star KGB general, the ambassador to Argentina during 1975–78 when Communists and other guerrillas were staging major operations, and one of the KGB's foremost experts on political conquest.[96] Tass, the official Soviet news agency, also installed its wire service.[97]

(3) "Progressive Social Transformation" of Grenada

The Soviets lost little time placing their imprimatur of approval on a grateful NJM Socialist regime. As Michael Ledeen and Herbert Romerstein note in their introduction to "Grenada Documents: an Overview and Selection,"

From the beginning, Bishop and other NJM leaders sought to bring Grenada into the Soviet orbit, and there are thousands of documents showing the intimate relationship that developed between the USSR and Grenada.[98]

As early as 1981, the Soviet press spoke of Grenada's "progressive social transformation" and described the NJM as the "political vanguard." Cautious Soviet spokesmen referred to the NJM, as they did to Nicaragua, Angola, Ethiopia and Afghanistan, as "progressive," "anti-imperialist," "national-democratic" or at most "on the path towards socialist orientation," meaning not yet "Leninist," a term preferred by the Valentas rather than "Marxist-Leninist" presumably to differentiate the corruption of the former by the latter. One analyst referred to Grenada and Nicaragua as having achieved "new . . . popular-democratic statehood," a term describing the East European satellites in the late 1940's before they became fully Socialist regimes.[99]

Such political terminology is important because it designates the degree of progress towards full Socialism, that is, "developed socialism" as in the case of the Soviet Union, Eastern Europe, Mongolia, Vietnam and Cuba. And Moscow, having experienced reversals in the Third World, seemed particularly cautious in officially categorizing Grenada.[100]

Nonetheless, Grenada was singled out by some Soviet officials for high favor, treating the NJM by 1982 as a "fraternal," that is, a Marxist-Leninist party. In Moscow, some lower ranking officials in conversation with Grenadian Embassy officials even called the

---

[96] Possony, Stefan, Associate Editor. USSR: Leadership Analysis. Defense & Foreign Affairs Daily, Dec. 8, 1983, p. 2, in, Supplemental Clips: Thursday, Dec. 15, 1983, p. 64.

[97] An extensive report from St. George's, Grenada on August 7, 1983 recorded the influx of Communist officials into the island, amid growing concern by the Grenadians. When asked about the growing number of Russians and Cubans in Grenada, Bishop said in their economic state they needed help from any quarter. It was estimated that a dozen Soviet science teachers would be arriving in September to complement the Soviet advisers in other fields and 400–600 Cuban workers and technicians. Cubans were reported by diplomatic sources to be present at every level and in virtually every meeting of the Government. "It is pretty humiliating," said one diplomat. Grenadians in service industries reported that the Soviet staff has grown considerably over the last year, but no reliable figures were available. (Crossette, Barbara. Grenadians Anxious Over New Influence of Soviet and Cuba. The New York Times, Aug. 7, 1983, p. 1 and 12.)

[98] Grenada Documents: An Overview and Selection, p. 5. Blasier writes: "Soviet relations with Grenada are probably more cordial than with any other nation in the hemisphere except Cuba and Nicaragua. . . . Bishop and his associates grew up under the influence of radical thinkers like Frantz Fanon, Malcolm X, Fidel Castro, and Lenin and naturally took their place among the pro-Soviet governments in the Third World." Grenada's visible support of the Soviet Union was demonstrated in the U.N. when it voted against the resolution condemning the Soviet invasion of Afghanistan. (Giant's Rival, p. 46–47.)

[99] Valentas, Leninism in Grenada, p. 8–9.

[100] Ibid., p. 8.

NJM a "Communist Party."[101] By and large the Soviets adopted a "protective" attitude towards Grenadian diplomats in Moscow, tending to downgrade the level of the relationship partly to avoid giving any pretext to the United States, in the words of one Grenadian diplomat, to "further squeeze Grenada."[102]

(4) Establishing formal party ties

In May-June 1980, the Soviet Union initiated formal relations between the CPSU and NJM during a visit by Deputy Prime Minister Coard to Moscow. In July 1982, the Soviets, having concluded on the basis of "considerable information" that the Socialist revolution was taking hold in Grenada, decided to make a formal commitment, this time during a visit to Moscow by Prime Minister Bishop.[103]

An important agreement was concluded on July 27, 1982 in which the CPSU and NJM laid out the terms of their relationship among which were the following:

—Both parties would cooperate in ways similar to those pursued by the Soviets in dealing with other "anti-imperialist," "socialist-oriented" countries in the Third World. Inter-party cooperation was said to be "a most important basis" for developing relations between both countries in line with their "common commitment . . . to scientific socialism," meaning the Soviet brand of "socialism."

—Soviet-Grenadian relations were to be handled mainly through party channels augmenting inter-state relations and mass organizational ties.

—They pledged to "extend and deepen" cooperation "at all levels," to "exchange experience in party work and party guidance" in the social, economic, and cultural development of the respective countries, "including regular exchange of information," and to have consultations and exchanges of opinion on international matters.

—Cooperation was called for in "training party and government cadres" and developing contacts between the party presses and other mass media.

—The Soviets pledged to assist in building a party headquarters for the NJM.

—The Soviets "pressed" the NJM into accepting scholarships for Grenadian party officials, 15 in 1982 alone. Other NJM members were to study at the Higher Party School of the CPSU along with counterparts from other revolutionary parties in the Third World. Fourteen Grenadians were enrolled in May 1983. The NJM was encouraged to establish its own party

---

[101] Ibid.
[102] Ibid. What Leiken describes in 1981 suggests the validity of these Soviet designations. The new radical government had won a following among urban youth by certain short-term redistribution policies. However, "the political methods of the new Grenadian regime are disquieting. It has suppressed the only opposition newspaper, suspended habeas corpus and elections, and rationalized these measures with Soviet-style slogans attacking bourgeois democracy. The Cubans have uniformed, armed and trained a Grenadian army of 2,000 out of a population of 120,000." (Eastern Winds in Latin America, p. 100–101).
[103] Valentas, Leninism in Grenada, p. 9.

school as a "top priority" and urged to start sending teacher trainees to the Soviet Union.[104]

(5) Preparation in propaganda; membership in World Peace Council

Ledeen and Romerstein write in their introduction to the Grenada Documents:

> Perhaps the most intensive Soviet assistance to Grenada was in the field of indoctrination, for it was necessary to train a new Communist generation on the island. The Soviets participated in some of the "ideological crash courses."[105]

Both the Soviets and Cubans played a major role in the political indoctrination of Grenada. Arrangements were made for Grenadians to train party cadres in Cuba where their studies included propaganda and foreign relations, particularly applicable to the Caribbean region. In 1983, 18 were scheduled for study and training in political indoctrination and propaganda techniques; a "small fraction of dozens," according to the Valentas, were said to be studying in Cuba at the time of the U.S.-OECS invasion. Provisions were also made for cadres to study in East Germany and Bulgaria.[106] Conceivably, the Communist instructors faced many difficulties in training the raw Grenadian cadres.

In keeping with plans of the NJM's propaganda department, the propaganda organs of the Soviet Union and other Communist countries distributed "progressive materials" in Grenada for "deepening the internationalist spirit and socialist consciousness of the Grenadian masses." A number of Soviet consultants and advisors were also attached to the various Grenadian ministries (Ministry of Education, for example), and other agencies. As customary, a Soviet-Grenadian Friendship Society was formed.[107]

Finally, the Soviets established further organizational ties with the NJM through the newly created Grenada Peace Council, an affiliate of the World Peace Council (WPC) supervised by the International Department of the Central Committee, CPSU. In 1982–83, Grenadians participated in a number of WPC meetings relating to Nicaragua and the anti-nuclear movement.[108]

(6) Secret agreements with Cuba

In 1983, the NJM concluded various new agreements with the Communist Party of Cuba (PCC). These accords provided for closer and more regular cooperation between the two parties, including, one agreement reads, "regular meetings and exchange of experience between the different departments and secretaries of both parties." One secret agreement pledged the PCC and NJM to "coordinate the positions of the governments of Cuba and Grenada at international events, conferences, and agencies where they participate in attention to the political, economic and social interests of both parties."[109]

---

[104] Valentas, Leninism in Grenada, p. 10. For a copy of the agreement, see Grenada Documents: An Overview and Selection.

[105] Ibid., p. 7.

[106] Valentas, Leninism in Grenada, p. 10.

[107] Ibid.

[108] Ibid.

[109] Ibid., p. 11. Documents in Grenadian-Cuban relations are reproduced in, Grenada Documents: An Overview and Selection.

The NJM perceived itself as a bridge between the PCC and the leftist parties in the English-speaking Caribbean. It also participated in other "anti-imperialist" projects with Cuban party leaders, such as, meetings in Grenada of representatives of the NJM using funds partly furnished by the PCC. A Cuban-Grenadian Friendship Society also served bilateral relations between both countries. In addition, the NJM participated in the Libyan General Congress of the World Center for Resistance against Imperialism, Zionism, Racism and Reaction, and its representative was appointed to the secretariat.[110]

b. Establishing a Soviet military presence

(1) Ogarkov on favorable conditions in Caribbean region

The evolving political-ideological infrastructure under Soviet and Cuban guidance was underpinned by a series of security arrangements that seemed intended to strengthen Grenada militarily and eventually even to provide facilities for the continuing projection of Soviet-Cuban military and political power in Latin America. For the Grenadians saw themselves as Soviet proxies. W. Richard Jacobs, the Grenadian Ambassador to Moscow, reminded his NJM colleagues that their importance to the Soviets would eventually depend on their success in exporting revolution. As he put it, "To the extent that we can take credit for bringing any other country into the progressive fold, our prestige and influence would be greatly enhanced [sic]." Jacobs had in mind Suriname as the first such project.[111]

In 1983, Chief of the Soviet General Staff Marshal Ogarkov set forth Soviet security objectives in the Caribbean, particularly the Soviet desire to develop military ties with revolutionary regimes in the area; he also defined Moscow's military relationship with Grenada. In a conversation on March 10, 1983 with his Grenadian counterpart Major Einstein Louison who was then training in Moscow, Ogarkov, in the words of Louison, spoke of "raising the combat readiness and preparedness" of progressive forces facing a threat from imperialism, that is, the United States and its allies. The Marshal felt that "United States imperialism would try to prevent progress but that there were no prospects for imperialism to turn back history." In what amounts to a Soviet version of the "domino theory," Ogarkov went on to specify conditions and trends favorable to Soviet goals: "Over two decades ago there was only Cuba in Latin America; today there are Nicaragua and Grenada, and a serious battle is going on in El Salvador."[112]

(2) Soviet-Grenadian "top secret" military aid agreement, October 27, 1980

The captured Grenada documents reveal that the Soviet Union gradually upgraded military aid to Grenada, for Soviet aid had preceded ideological recognition of the NJM. Before concluding the

---

[110] Valentas, Leninism in Grenada, p. 11.
[111] Grenada Documents: An Overview and Selection, p. 6.
[112] Meeting Between Chiefs of General Staff of Soviet Armed Forces and People's Revolutionary Armed Forces of Grenada, Thursday, Mar. 10, 1983 (4 p.m.), in Grenada Documents: An Overview and Selection, Doc. 24, 1-5.

formal agreement, the Soviet Union and Cuba had already provided 1,000 automatic rifles, and Nicaragua 2,000 uniforms.[113]

The "top secret" agreement of October 27, 1980 between the
Soviet Union and Grenada, signed in Havana, covered military assistance during the year 1980–1981. It provided for deliveries for
"special and other equipment" free-of-charge, as with two subsequent agreements, valued at 4.4 million rubles. Cuba was to act as
the go-between for the transfer of Soviet arms. All Soviet weapons
and ammunition were sent "almost exclusively," according to the
Valentas, through Cuba, except for two Soviet coast guard boats
sent directly to Grenada in 1983. Thus, the Soviets delivered their
military cargo by sea to Cuban ports, where it was transshiped on
Cuban ships to Grenada. From there, as the Valentas note, the
arms were transported "in the darkness of night to hidden depots
throughout the island." [114]

The "special equipment" cited in the first agreement included 12
mortars, 24 anti-tank grenade launchers, 54 machine guns, 1,000
submachine guns, 18 anti-aircraft mounts, and other weapons, communication devices, ammunition, logistical equipment and spare
parts. The agreement provided for training Grenadian forces in the
Soviet Union to ensure mastery of the equipment; it prohibited the
sale or transfer of the arms to third parties without Moscow's consent; and it pledged Grenada to secrecy with respect to the terms
and execution of the agreement.[115]

(3) Second Soviet military aid agreement, February 9, 1981

The second major Soviet military aid agreement with Grenada
was signed in Havana on February 9, 1981. It covered arms shipments between 1981 and 1983. Again the Soviets resorted to the eu-
phemism of "special and other equipment"; the value of the shipment increased to 5 million rubles.[116]

This new agreement provided for the delivery of eight armored
personnel carriers, two armored reconnaissance and patrol vehicles, 1,000 submachine guns, and other armaments and munitions;
engineering, communications, and transport equipment; along with
other materials. The agreement provided for 12,000 complete sets
of uniforms, apparently intended for an army of 6,300 men; spare
parts and training; and auxiliary equipment amounting to nearly
one million rubles.[117]

(4) The third Soviet military aid agreement, July 27, 1982

On July 27, 1982, the Soviet Union and Grenada concluded in
Moscow a third "top secret" military aid agreement valued at 10
million rubles, covering the period 1982–1985. Included in this
agreement were an additional 50 armored personnel carriers, 60
mortars, 60 anti-tank and other heavy guns, 50 portable rocket
launchers, 50 light anti-tank grenade launchers, 2,000 submachine

---

[113] Valenta, Leninism in Grenada, p. 11.
[114] Ibid.
[115] Ibid.
[116] Ibid.
[117] Ibid., p. 11–12.

guns, and small arms, communications and engineering facilities and other equipment.[118]

For the first time, the 1982 agreement included "civilian" equipment for Grenada's expanding Ministry of the Interior. The Ministry and the People's Militia were to receive 20 light anti-tank rocket launchers and 50 submachine guns, plus "special instruments" such as infrared viewers, videotape recorders, tape recorders, cameras, "PTU-47" television systems, and other equipment intended for clandestine intelligence operations. In the package was also mini-microphones and accessories for bugging requested by the Grenadians.[119]

The agreement provided for the training of Grenadian servicemen in Soviet military schools and their training in Granada by Soviet military and security "specialists and interpreters." Special privileges were also provided for the Soviets, in the words of the agreement, such as, "comfortable living accommodation" municipal utilities, medical services, transport facilities, meals at reasonable prices—all without "any taxes and duties."

Article 4 of the new agreement suggests plans for greater Soviet military involvement in the future. This section directed that the Soviet Union would periodically send a group of advisers to Grenada to plan technical assistance for an equipment and vehicle repair shop, a command staff school, and storage facilities and roads. By the terms of an additional agreement in November 1982, the Soviets would send a team of specialists to Grenada for 15 days to assist in these tasks. According to Ogarkov, the Soviet Union was going to send a team of military experts to Grenada in 1983 to "conduct studies related to the construction of military projects." He also noted that requests for military aid beyond the 1982 agreement was handled officially by the Soviet Ministry of Foreign Affairs, but that the Ministry of Defense "would exercise some control of the solution." [120]

Another secret agreement, unsigned and dated 1983, called for the delivery of "special and other equipment" valued at 5.4 million rubles, covering the period 1983–1986. Included in this transaction were two patrol gunboats, spare parts, tools and accessories, 3,000 more uniforms, and 12,000 rounds of ammunition.[121]

(5) Other aspects of Communist military aid to Grenada

The Valentas catalogued other forms of Communist military aid to Grenada, including the following:

—Grenadian officers were sent to the Soviet Union for training. In late 1982, 15 were studying at Soviet military schools and an additional 20 were expected to arrive in 1983. Some officials from the Interior Ministry were trained in Soviet intelligence and counterintelligence facilities.[122]

---

[118] Ibid., p. 12.
[119] Ibid.
[120] Ibid., p. 12–13.
[121] Ibid., p. 13.
[122] Ibid. According to Ledeen and Romerstein, "There was no lack of Soviet support for Grenadian intelligence and counterintelligence operations. A draft letter dated February 17, 1982, from General Hudson Austin to Yuri Andropov, then the chief of the KGB, requested training courses for three Grenadians in counterintelligence and one in intelligence work. Austin

—Cuba granted training scholarships to Grenadian military, 12 for 1982. Cuba maintained 27 permanent military advisers in Grenada, supervised by a Cuban working in the Ministry of Defense, in addition to approximately a dozen advisers sent for terms of two to four months. By 1982, Cuba had in Grenada a small contingent of military advisers, a number of overt and covert agents and civilian workers, and several hundred construction workers, many armed, building an airport runway at Point Salines.[123]

—The airport, initially designed mainly for tourism, appeared to have "some military purpose" after its opening scheduled in March 1984, according to the Valentas. It "probably would have served as a facility for Soviet reconnaissance aircraft and as a refueling stop for Soviet and Cuban transports bound for Angola," the Valentas speculate.[124]

—Division of labor in Communist security assistance followed this pattern: Cubans provided manpower; East Germans, technical and military or internal security equipment and highly qualified technicians; and the Czechoslovaks, explosives, ammunition, and automatic rifles.

—After Bishop's visit to Pyongyang in April 1983, North Korea agreed to supply arms worth $12 million, including thousands of rifles and 50 rocket launchers, two coast guard boats, and uniforms.

—Bulgaria concluded a military agreement. Vietnam agreed to train 20 military officers.

Thus, the captured Grenada documents disclosed heretofore secret plans for an important role to be played by this little Caribbean island in Soviet-Cuban strategy in the region. The Valentas conclude:

> The document suggest that all this security aid to Grenada was designed, in addition to the potential access to Grenadian officers and facilities it provided the donors, for a more immediate military purpose: to build by 1985 a sizable Grenadian armed force of four regular and 14 reservist battalions. Since arms transfers were scheduled through 1986, US forces recovered fewer arms than indicated in the agreements. The weapons recovered in Grenada, however, were already sufficient to equip about 10,000 men.[125]

---

thanked Andropov for the 'tremendous assistance which our armed forces have received from your party and government in the past.'" (Grenada Documents: An Overview and Selection, p. 7.)

[123] Valentas, Leninism in Grenada, p. 13.

[124] For a commentary on the airport's potential use, see, Rand, Grenada's Links with the USSR and Cuba, p. 1-2.

[125] Valentas, Leninism in Grenada, p. 14. In an aggregate statement on Communist military aid to Grenada, Ledeen and Romerstein write: "Overall, the documents . . . showed that the Soviet, Cuban, North Korean, and Czechoslovakian agreements included the following items, which were to have been delivered by 1986:

—Approximately 10,000 assault and other rifles;
—More than 4,500 submachine guns and machine guns;
—More than 11.5 million rounds of 7.62 mm ammunition;
—294 portable rocket launchers with more than 16,000 rockets;
—84 82 mm mortars with more than 4,800 mortar shells;
—12 75 mm cannon with 600 cannon shells;
—15,000 hand grenades, 7,000 land mines, 60 armored personnel carriers and patrol vehicles;
—More than 150 radio transmitters, 160 field telephone sets, approximately 23,000 uniforms, and tents for about 7,700 persons."

The Defense Department estimates that the equipment found on the island (and not all have arrived) would have equipped a fighting force of roughly 10,000 men. Evidence revealed that

c. Contributing to Grenada's economy

(1) "Minor role" of Soviet economic assistance

The low priority given to Soviet economic objectives in the Caribbean and their current downgrading of economic assistance to the Third World is reflected in the "minor role" economic aid played in Soviet policy towards Grenada. Between 1979 and 1983 progress had been achieved in Soviet-Grenadian economic cooperation, but not on the scale of military and security assistance. As the Valentas concluded, "Economic aid to Grenada was clearly not proportionate to the aid given Cuba, and was aimed primarily at reinforcing Soviet political objectives." [126]

(2) Limited economic assistance

Grenada sought and received some economic assistance from Moscow and its Communist allies. Officials in the State Planning Committee (Gosplan) and CMEA were consulted by Grenadian officials on various aspect of economic cooperation. Gosplan offered a training course to several NJM officials, including the permanent secretary of the Ministry of Construction, Michael Prime.[127]

CMEA markets were opened to Grenada, and the Soviet Union, East Germany and Bulgaria agreed to purchase such vital Grenadian exports as cocoa, nutmeg and bananas. The Grenadians also received several million dollars in foodstuffs and construction materials from the Soviets, in addition to dozens of vehicles and machines negotiated on the basis of deferred payments. Other forms of assistance were granted, for example: miscellaneous credits and grants; and upgrading of Radio Grenada, giving it the capability of broadcasting to foreign audiences; and an An–26 transport plane for use by the leadership.

Assistance came from other Communist and non-Communist sources. The East Germans delivered trucks and other vehicles. The North Koreans agreed to provide assistance in agriculture and fishing and to construct a 15,000 capacity national sport stadium. Grants and loans for public works, including the Port Salines airport, came from Libya, Cuba and countries of the Middle East and Western Europe. Poor quality, mismanagement or both, however, reduced the value of some of the equipment and material coming from Communist sources.[128]

In general, the Soviets could hardly be called generous. There was no full financing of projects recommended by Soviet technicians, such as, water supply and seaport development. Nor were the Soviets committed to supply 20,000 tons of fertilizer free-of-charge that was requested by Grenada. Thus with respect to economic assistance the Valentas rightly conclude: ". . . the USSR was unable or unwilling to provide much help in transforming Grenada into a socialist paradise in the Caribbean." And Grenada, it must be remembered, was in great need of economic assistance.

---

there may have been plans for special forces since the Soviets promised to send an aircraft capable of transporting 39 paratroopers as well as other special equipment. (Grenada Documents: An Overview and Selection, p. 5–6.)

[126] Valentas, Leninism in Grenada, p. 14.
[127] Ibid.
[128] Ibid., p. 14–15.

d. Backing the Leninist faction in internal power struggle

(1) Emerging Bishop-Coard power struggle

By mid-1983, the Soviet Union and its Communist allies had accumulated, if not an economic investment, then a "substantial" political and security investment in Grenada. An internal power struggle, however, surfaced in September 1983 that threatened to jeopardize this investment. The Soviets, though apparently not the Cubans, maneuvered to protect their position, but the record on their role is far from complete. For a while the violent outcome favored Moscow's side; but U.S.-OECS military intervention brought an end to this significant but transitory episode.[129]

Briefly, no single issue precipitated the power struggle in the NJM leadership. Rather, the Grenada documents suggest that the causes were a generally shared feeling in the NJM Politburo that the revolution was failing, and the personal ambition of one of the major protagonists, Bernard Coard.

The dispute between the Bishop and Coard factions was on two levels: one, a conflict of personalities; the other ideological and political differences over the pace of the revolution. Coard's faction, impatient and deeply ideological, wanted to quicken the pace of Socialist transformation, strengthen Leninism, and deepen the connections with Moscow and its Communist allies. Bishop's faction seems to have favored gradualism and even entertained a rapprochement with the United States.[130]

---

[129] Idid.

[130] According to a secret speech published in the Grenada Documents, Bishop had an elaborate plan to gain economic assistance from the United States and the "bourgeoisie" of Grenada, while moving the country more decidedly towards Marxism-Leninism. The speech, entitled, "Line of March for the Party," was delivered at a general meeting of the NJM on Sept. 13, 1982. Bishop expressed his fear of a U.S. military intervention if his true Marxist-Lininist position were revealed. In setting forth the tasks "for the present period" as "seen by the Central Committee," Bishop said: "The first task is sinking the ideas of Marxism/Leninism among the working class and the working people." He then proceeded to cite four other tasks for building Marxism-Leninism in Grenada. In this first stage of the National Democratic Revolution, Bishop insisted that "the leading role of the working class through its Marxist/Leninist Party backed by some form of the dictatorship of the proletariat" had to be insured. Yet he stressed the importance of maintaining an alliance "firstly, with the peasantry and other elements of the petty-bourgeoisie, and secondly with sections of the upper petty-bourgeoisie and the national bourgeoisie." In a retrospective commentary on the make-up of the ruling council of the People's Revolutionary Government, Bishop explained why various members of the bourgeoisie were brought into the leadership: ". . . this was done deliberately so that imperialism [meaning the United States] won't get too excited and would say 'well they have some nice fellas in that thing; everything alright.' And as a result wouldn't think about sending in troops." In justifying the alliance with the non-Communist elements, Bishop explained that it was necessary in order "to hold power in the first few days and weeks"; "to consolidate and build the revolution and to ensure the defeat of imperialism"; and "because we don't have enough managers, because we don't have enough capital, because we don't have enough international contacts, because we don't have enough markets." Bishop's speech was highly ideological and stressed many times his commitment to Marxism-Leninism, developing "proletarian internationalism," and building "rapidly our links with the Socialist World, especially the Soviet Union." But it was highly pragmatic in his analysis of Grenada's status as a "National Democratic Revolution" in the stage of "socialist of orientation," and particularly pragmatic in his justification for alliance with the bourgeoisie and search for assistance from the United States. Bishop failed to get any assistance during his visit to the United States during the summer before his death, but, as one report noted, "in his own party and within the Marxist-Leninist community, he was perceived as being too soft with capitalists. His trip to the United Nations and appeals to U.S. businessmen to drum up travel business for the island were looked upon with suspicion by his fellow communists." (Bishop's "Line of March" speech is reproduced in the Grenada Documents as Document 1. See also the commentary on the speech by Stephanie L. Nall in, Bishop Hoped to Hide Marxism, Trick U.S. into Aiding Grenada. The Washington Times, Sept. 18, 1984, p. 2A.)

The showdown came on October 15, when at a meeting of the NJM's Central Committee the Coard faction, representing a majority, pressed for a collective leadership that would effectively reduce Bishop's power base. Coard partisans attacked Bishop, accusing him of "rightist opportunism," failing to build a "Marxist-Leninist vanguard," and charging him with failure to "tighten" relations "with the World Socialist Movement, especially Cuba, the USSR and the GDR." [131]

Bishop was expelled from the NJM, disarmed, and placed under house arrest. On October 19, "Bloody Wednesday" as it came to be called, some 10,000 Grenadians sympathetic to the charismatic Bishop took power into their own hands and attempted to free the imprisoned Bishop in a peaceful demonstration. They were fired on by NJM troops—about 40 were killed; Bishop and his immediate followers were executed; the stage was set for the U.S.-OECS military intervention on October 25. [132]

(2) The Soviet role in the factional struggle

No clear evidence exists to categorically determine the extent of Soviet or Cuban involvement in the Bishop-Coard power struggle during September-October 1983. Most likely they were willing to take advantage of the deteriorating situation, but apparently did not plot it. On the basis of evidence from the Grenada Documents (none are obviously available from CPSU and PCC archives), the Valentas advance the thesis that Soviet officials knew about the struggle, and, unlike the Cubans, "very likely sought to aid the anti-Bishop conspirators in their efforts to demote him." "At any rate", they conclude with some restraint, that the Soviets "made no move to help the embattled Bishop." [133]

In constructing their case for Soviet involvement, the Valentas make the following points:

—Soviet suspicion of Bishop's independence and his poor Leninist credentials. Bishop's independence was evident in his belated attempt, apparently not coordinated with an irritated Moscow, to establish a rapprochement during a visit to the United States in June 1983. [134] Bishop's unwillingness to accept the NJM Central Committee's decision to establish a collective leadership, thus rejecting the basic management principle in the Soviet system, "democratic centralism," would have revealed to the Soviets an unacceptable lack of discipline and systemic commitment. In general, Coard's position was more ideologically in line with that of Moscow's.

—Soviet awareness of the intensifying struggle in late summer of 1983. Given their long experience in factional politics (it is a way of life within the Soviet political system), and their preference to deal with competing cliques in a collective, playing one off against the other rather than dealing with a charismatic, headstrong leader like Bishop, the Soviets were probably well

---

[131] Valentas, Leninism in Grenada, p. 17.
[132] Ibid., p. 15–20.
[133] Ibid., p. 20, and Steven R. Harper, Analyst in Latin American Affairs, Congressional Research Service.
[134] Explained in detail by the Valentas on Page 21.

aware of trouble on the island and the opportunities for manipulation it presented to them.

—The early establishment of a "back channel" to Coard's faction. Coard had a personal relationship with the Soviet leadership: He led two high level NJM delegations to Moscow in 1979 and 1980; he attended the 26th Party Congress in 1981 and Brezhnev's funeral in 1982; his family apparently vacationed in Russia, at the request of the leadership, during the summer of 1983; his wife Phyllis reportedly had friendly relationships with the wives of the Soviet advisers in Grenada. Members of the anti-Bishop conspiracy also had close ties with the Soviets, some having studied in the U.S.S.R. and having continued to maintain contacts there. Moreover, as the Valentas suggest, "The Soviets most probably shared this faction's hostile attitude toward 'right opportunistic' trends in the NJM." [135]

—Soviet reservations about Bishop. These were clearly revealed during his last stop-over visit at Vnukovo airport in Moscow, a month before the coup. No official visit was arranged which would have been the case had the Soviets really supported Bishop. Rather by staging a brief meeting at the airport, they clearly gave Bishop the "cold shoulder." [136]

—Soviet failure to eulogize Bishop and his supporters in the final violent outcome of the coup. The Soviets neither admonished Coard nor admitted that Bishop's death was the result of a conspiracy. They glossed over his death, referring to the entire episode in Kommunist only as a "tragis turn of events." In contrast, Castro tried to build up Bishop's prestige and morale after returning from his foreign tour in September 1983, and once the coup had succeeded he tried to save Bishop's life. But, according to the Valentas:

. . . it would be wrong to exaggerate Soviet-Cuban tactical differences over the handling of the October 1983 crisis in Grenada. There is no record of a sustained Cuban attempt to intervene on behalf of Bishop's political standing during the final phase of the coup.[137]

By no means, therefore, did the Soviets stay on the sidelines as dispassionate observers of this power struggle. Their interests and investments had to be protected, and, as the Valentas suggest, they appear to have skillfully maneuvered to apply their pressure and support in favor of the Coard faction.[138]

---

[135] Ibid., p. 21.

[136] Ibid.

[137] Ibid., p. 22.

[138] For Duncan's analysis of the coup, see his Soviet Interest in Latin America, p. 168–173. Duncan notes that Cuba was "long a Bishop ally" and "denounced his overthrow in no uncertain terms." Far from playing a direct role in Bishop's downfall, Duncan writes, "the Cubans condemned it." But once military intervention was underway both Cuba and Grenada sought to forestall it (p. 172). The picture of Soviet involvement, he states, "is less clear." In the days before the coup there was a "flurry of activity" between the Soviet Embassy and Bishop's radical enemies. A planned trip to the Soviet Union by the conspirators was called off three weeks before the coup, indicating, according to Duncan, "that the Soviets may have known what was happening to Prime Minister Bishop." Soviet official media clearly denounced the United States over Grenada, but its "formal position was made at a relatively low level." Bishop was considered a "friend" by the Soviets, but, Duncan notes, "it is known that a majority of Soviet leaders did not have great confidence in him, even though they publicly defended his policy." (p. 172.)

3. SIGNIFICANCE OF THE GRENADIAN EPISODE

a. A case study in Soviet expansion by incrementalism

The Grenada episode is a revealing and instructive case study of Soviet expansion by incrementalism in the Latin American sector of the Third World. The episode reveals through authentic documentation, albeit it largely from the Grenadian perspective, Soviet efforts to establish control over Grenada.[139] It demonstrated not only Moscow's use of Cuba in its expansionist policy but also Soviet skill in applying the tactic of incrementalism in preparing an emerging revolutionary regime for a larger role in its Third World policy. Gradualism, dictated by a desire not to provoke a U.S. counteraction, determined the influx of Soviet military equipment going into Grenada and the visibility of Soviet support.

b. Grenada: A staging area for exporting revolution?

Where the Soviet foray into the Caribbean would have led had not the United States intervened can only be a matter of speculation. Conclusive evidence is lacking to prove that Grenada had actually become a staging area for exporting Communist revolution. But plans in the offing, sketched out in numerous secret military assistance agreements, tend to corroborate the cautious, but essentially accusatory, judgment of the Valentas:

. . . though Genada did not have Soviet military bases at the time of the U.S.-led invasion, one cannot exclude the possibility that it might have become a component of Soviet military planning and a bridge to revolutionary forces elsewhere in the region, as Cuba has in the last quarter-century.[140]

c. The limits of Soviet and Cuban power and influence

Finally, the episode reveals the limits of Soviet and Cuban power when their thrusts, particularly in the U.S. "strategic backyard," are challenged by American military power. Conversely, the episode demonstrates also the limits of Soviet support and protection for dependent Third World countries and their leaders when the consequences of direct Soviet involvement risks confrontation with the United States. In brief, the Soviets are wary about dispensing blank checks to their clients in the Third World. Expanding on this theme, the Valentas conclude:

---

[139] Duncan concludes: "The October 1983 crisis in Grenada left little doubt that the Soviet and Cuban presence has been expanding in the Caribbean basin." (Ibid., p. 163.); and, "Ever resourceful, the Soviet Union quickly perceived these [revolutionary] developments [in the Caribbean Basin countries] as opportunities with the potential to advance their interests there, and moved to insert or to increase its presence either directly or through its Cuban ally" (168); and "In the Grenadian situation then, both the Soviet Union and Cuba utilized the political change as an opportunity to insert their presence through trade, aid, and advisors,and with it their influence" (170). For a postmortem of the Soviet experience in Grenada by a specialist in the Soviet Latin American Institute, see Lunin, V.N. Grenada: The Logic of Imperial Force. Latinskaya Amerika (Moscow), no. 2, Feb. 84, p. 134–144, translated in USSR Report, Political and Sociological Affairs, June 14 1984, p. 26–38 (JPRS-UPS-84-053). On the durability of the "Grenada Revolution," Lunin writes: "Also obvious is the entire absurdity of the imaginings of Washington's Caribbean satellites concerning the supposed 'Grenadian menace' hanging over them. For them the real menace consisted, of course, not in the military threat on the part of Grenada's government but rather in the magnetic force of a revolutionary break-through, capable of inspiring the peoples of the region's other states. And this magnetic force did not disappear with the demise of the Grenadian Revolution; it will remain—and not only in the memory of Grenadians. . . ." (p. 27).
[140] Valentas, Leninism in Cuba, p. 23.

What happened in Grenada thus has troubling implications for the Nicaraguan and even for the Cuban governments. Castro, in the final analysis, could count only on his own forces to defend revolutionaries elsewhere in the Caribbean Basin; he may now be wondering about Soviet backing for Nicaragua, or for Cuba itself in case of a direct conflict with the United States. Unlike its behavior at its own periphery or in remote regions of Africa, the Soviet Union is much less able and willing to support pro-Soviet regimes in the Americas "backyard"—particularly when Washington is willing to protect its interests there with military force.[141]

Thus the real significance of the Grenadian episode: It demonstrates the limits of Soviet power and influence in the Latin American sector of the Third World, particularly when the United States resorts to military force to protect its interests.[142]

C. SOVIET INVOLVEMENT IN CENTRAL AMERICA AND THE CARIBBEAN: ITS MEANING

1. KEY TARGET OF OPPORTUNITY

Soviet involvement in Central America and the Caribbean during the past half decade clearly indicates that this Third World region presents another opportunity for Soviet expansionism. Revolutionary upheavals, with all their deep-rooted causes, have created the opportunity; Soviet arms transfers and political support for leftist revolutionary regimes and a working alliance with Cuba have created the means. In Soviet eyes the region's vulnerability makes it the "weakest link" in "imperialism's" chain of control, meaning U.S. regional hegemony. Of all Latin America, this area alone has been historically the most strategically important for the United States.

2. CONVERGING SOVIET INTERESTS: EXPLOIT VULNERABILITY AND ERODE U.S. POWER

Thus both lines of Soviet interest converge, for the vulnerability of the region creates conditions for the expansion of their influence and power, while its importance to the United States and the consequent erosion of its hemispheric position in failures to respond to Soviet challenges is proportionately measured by the degree of Soviet success.

As for Central America, the final verdict has yet to be rendered. But such is not the case with Grenada. For the Soviets, Grenada may have been a setback, but given the vulnerability of the region as a whole, the Soviets can, and do, adjust to the "ebb and flow" of

---

[141] Ibid., p. 23. Duncan makes this final observation in his detailed and perceptive article on, Soviet Interests in Latin America (p. 194): "Western journalists in Havana came away with the impression that the Grenadian setback was unlikely to alter Cuba's well-known commitment to 'internationalist solidarity,' which will continue to benefit the Soviet Union. This assumption means that we are left with uncertainty about which long-range lessons the Soviets and Cubans will draw from their Grenadian setback and how they may seek to exploit future opportunities. Of one thing we can be certain: The Soviet quest for new footholds will be offset by the continuing limits to Moscow's influence."

[142] For a comprehensive analysis and commentary (with policy recommendations) on Soviet/Cuban Third World policy in the context of Grenada, see Soviet/Cuban Strategy in the Third World After Grenada: Toward Prevention of Future Grenadas. A Conference Report. Washington, The Woodrow Wilson International Center for Scholars, 1984, 79 p. This conference was held by the Kennan Institute for Advanced Russian Studies and the Soviet and East European Studies Program, Department of National Security Affairs, Naval Postgraduate School, Monterey, Calif. Some of the Nation's leading specialists in Soviet and Latin American affairs attended this conference.

history, waiting for the proper "correlation of forces" before advancing again.

3. DANGER OF CONFRONTATION AND CRISIS

The essence of the problem is, therefore, reduced to this simple proposition: Nowhere in Latin America is Soviet and American policy more deeply engaged in potential conflict and on a collision course than in Central America and the Caribbean. American interests in the region are vital in the same way areas close to the Soviet Union are vital to them. The Soviets, despite earlier evidence of caution, thus appear to have accepted greater risks of confrontation. Soviet insensitivity to U.S. interests and reckless, irresponsible behavior as in the Cuban missile crisis of 1962 could lead to an international crisis.[143]

---

[143] In Third World areas such as the Middle East and Persian Gulf the pattern of Soviet-American actions and counteractions over recent years suggest implicit acceptance of certain "rules and the game" that imply limits of involvement and provocation. From the American perspective, this pattern seems absent in the current Soviet approach to Central America and the Caribbean as it had been absent in the Cuban missile crisis. Thus, the Soviets are either ignorant of American vital interests in the region (which seems clearly not the case) or they are determined to make a geopolitical point with all its negative implications for the United States; namely, that the United States must accept a Soviet presence in its "strategic backyard."

IV. SOVIET UNION AND ARGENTINA: EMPHASIS ON TRADITIONALISM

A. DIVERSITY IN EXPANDING RELATIONSHIPS

Traditionalism in the conduct of diplomatic relations—insofar as it is possible for an essentially revolutionary power to conduct diplomacy in the traditions of universally accepted Western diplomacy—is the third major category in the Soviet approach to Latin America. Pragmatism and expediency are the predominating characteristics. Though fully cognizant of the various revolutionary movements that have existed in the region, the Soviets have, nonetheless, placed greater importance in recent years on state-to-state relations than on revolutionary relationships, at least in this third sector of their tripartite approach to Latin America.[1] Thus Soviet behavior in this Third World area, in contrast to its unique, near-alliance relationship with Socialist Cuba and its policy of revolutionary opportunism in Central America and the Caribbean, can perhaps be generally likened to the expected "normal" behavior of a modern nation-state, bearing in mind, however, the qualification that a revolutionary elan drives the Soviet Union towards its unchanging theoretically ultimate goal of establishing a global Socialist international system.

Accordingly, the Soviets have expanded their physical presence in Latin America over the past two decades impressively and in concert with the globalization of their foreign policy. Rothenberg speaks of Soviet success in establishing a multifaceted network of "routine" contacts throughout the region.[2] By the end of 1950, for example, the Soviets had diplomatic relations only with Argentina, Brazil and Uruguay. By 1983, this had increased to 19 countries, that is, all of Latin America except Chile and Paraguay. Trade has expanded rapidly, though it still remains a small percentage of total Soviet foreign trade, and decidedly to the Latin American advantage.[3] Except for Peru, military aid programs, a principal instrument of Soviet policy in the Third World, have not been a major factor in this sector of Soviet-Latin American policy. Cultural diplomacy, albeit from the uniquely Socialist perspective, has also expanded with growing Soviet interest in the region.[4]

---

[1] The cautious Soviet approach to revolutionary movements in Latin America, according to Wayne Smith, has its roots in the "disasters of 1928 to 1935." He writes that as a result of these disasters, "the Latin American Communist Parties remain exceedingly dubious about armed struggle as a tactic and are usually reluctant to be in the forefront of a revolutionary movement." He notes that a conference of Communist and left-wing theoreticians in Havana in 1981 "acknowledged that national liberation movements rather than Communist Parties might represent the vanguard in certain revolutionary situations—a tacit admission of the parties' failure to play the role." (The New York Times Book Review, Dec. 25, 1983, p. 15.) As a principle, the Soviets have rarely if ever placed the interests of foreign Communist Parties above Soviet state interests.

[2] Rothenberg, Latin America in Soviet Eyes, p. 15.

[3] Blasier, The Giant's Rival, p. 50–54.

[4] Rothenberg, Latin America in Soviet Eyes, p. 15.

In sum, the Soviets have built multifaceted linkages to Latin America, but linkages, at least in this third sector, generally characteristic of "normal" relations between nation-states in the world community.

B. ARGENTINA: A CASE STUDY OF TRADITIONALISM IN SOVIET DIPLOMACY

1. FAVORABLE ECONOMIC AND POLITICAL RELATIONS

a. Emerging relations

The complexity of Latin American politics, notably the many diverse revolutionary movements, and its sheer size geographically virtually defy simple generalization, even within the restricted context of this study on Soviet Third World policy. For simplicity's sake, therefore, Soviet-Argentine relations have been selected as an instructive case study to illustrate the traditional great power behavior of the Soviets in much of Latin America, though Argentina is, to an extent, exceptional.

As long ago as the early 1920's, the Soviet Union and Argentina explored the possibilities of bilateral relations. In 1946, diplomatic relations were finally established, and in 1953, the Soviets negotiated with Argentina the first bilateral treaty to be concluded with any Latin American country. Upon Peron's return to power in 1973, both countries, as Luers observes, "began to take their mutuality of interests seriously." [5]

b. Mutuality of interests

In 1984, Luers referred to the Soviet-Argentine connection as an "increasingly pragmatic, close, but not intimate, relationship," one that reflects "mutual convenience." [6] And so it has evolved over recent years on the basis of firmly established and mutually recognized self-interest.

The Soviets have looked upon Argentina as a logical partner for a long-term state-to-state relationship. For Argentina has many attributes that are appealing to Moscow: It is the second largest country in South America; it commands a strategic position along the sea lanes of the South Atlantic; traditionally, it has been the most independent-minded state in Latin America, and thus a prospect for political influence; it has had a consistently adversarial relationship with the United States, a value not lost to the Soviets; and finally it has been a rich source for much needed grain, meat, wool and other consumer goods, and a viable market for Soviet machinery, generators, and other heavy equipment, especially for energy producing projects.

On their side, the Argentines have come to value the Soviet Union as a major dependable market for their exports and also as a great power alternative to the United States in world and hemispheric politics.

---

[5] Luers, The Soviets and Latin America, p. 12–13.
[6] Ibid.

c. Fruitful economic relations

Accordingly, Argentina has enjoyed a fruitful economic relationship with Moscow—a relationship, Blasier notes, built upon "a remarkable coincidence of economic interests." The Soviets urgently need grain, meat, consumer materials and goods; the Argentines benefit from these purchases and are a good prospect for Soviet exports of thermal, hydro, and nuclear power equipment.[7]

Since 1979, the Argentines have looked upon the Soviet Union as a major dependable market for their exports. In 1980, the Soviets imported 33.7 percent of Argentine exports for a total value of $2.9 billion; Argentina purchased less than 3 percent of its imports from the Soviet Union.[8] By 1980, grain shipments to the Soviets constituted 60 percent of Argentina's grain exports and 22 percent of its total exports. (Recall that Argentina defied the U.S. grain embargo following the Soviet invasion of Afghanistan, picking up most of the slack in what was probably a critically important act to the Soviets.) Soviet purchases of fresh meat equaled 50 percent of frozen meat exports and 25 percent of total meat exports in 1980. As Blasier observes, "The USSR became Argentina's greatest single foreign customer."[9]

Argentina, like other South American countries, has also benefited from Soviet technical assistance, scientific cooperation and the availability of heavy equipment in developing their large hydroelectric energy projects, such as those at Rio Parama Medio, Salto Grande, Costanera, Bahia Blanca and Yacireta.[10] Argentina also receives from the Soviets the heavy water, enriched uranium, and technological assistance under a bilateral nuclear energy agreement, thus enabling it to have the most advanced nuclear program in Latin America.[11]

The wide range of Soviet assistance to Argentina is readily apparent in the stipulations in past economic agreements that have included Soviet participation in the construction and training for Argentine industrial projects in the fields of energy, chemical industry, shipbuilding, and the construction of ports.[12] As recently as June 14, 1984, respresentatives from the Soviet Union and Argentina meeting in Buenos Aires explored the possibility of establishing joint ventures for exploitation and research in fishing. The Soviets offered full support in training specialized personnel for scientific research in fishing and even for joint production through the creation of joint ventures.[13]

Soviet-Argentine economic relations have thus been mutually advantageous, though the Soviets have suffered from a serious imbalance of payment in their trade. Nonetheless, this interaction reveals a "normal" traditional relationship that has flourished in

---

[7] Blasier, The Giant's Rival, p. 31.
[8] Luers, The Soviets and Latin America, p. 13.
[9] Blasier, The Giant's Rival, p. 31. Blasier notes that Argentina supplied one-fifth of Soviet imports from the LDCs in 1980.
[10] Varas, Ideology and Politics in Latin American-USSR Relations, p. 44.
[11] Luers, The Soviets and Latin America, p. 13.
[12] Blasier, The Giant's Rival, p. 30.
[13] Buenos Aires TELAM in Spanish, 0217 GMT, June 15, 1984, in FBIS, Daily Report, Soviet Union, v. 3, June 19, 1984, p. K7.

recent years, in somewhat the manner of that existing with Mexico and other countries of South America.

d. Mutual support in politics, defense, and foreign policy

Despite strong ideological and political differences, the Soviet-Argentine relationship has been established on firm grounds of mutual interests. This close, but pragmatic, relationship survived the 1976 coup in Argentina and the past seven years of repressive military rule. The Soviets have downplayed the repressive character of the regime and have refrained from interfering in internal Argentine affairs.[14]

The former Argentine military government, deeply anti-Communist and anti-Socialist and replaced by an elected President in 1983, believed that it could manage the Soviets internally. Leftist parties were formally outlawed, but the Argentine Communist Party, like those of the right and center, was allowed to retain offices and equipment and to function in a semilegal status.[15]

Relations in the military sphere, though modest, have taken root and apparently have thrived. Military attaches have been exchanged, and frequent visits have taken place by military delegations from both countries. High ranking Argentine military officers have studied in Leningrad's military college.[16] The military relationship could become closer should the Soviets achieve their goal of being the major arms supplier to the Argentines as an alternative to arms markets in the West.[17] The Argentines have indicated an interest in purchasing weapons.[18]

Internationally, the Soviets and Argentines have displayed mutual concern for each other's interests and have taken action accordingly. At the 26th Party Congress Brezhnev gave official sanctions to the doctrine advanced by his specialists that "the states of Latin America, including Mexico, Brazil, Argentina, Venezuela, are playing a more important role" in international affairs. He pledged continued development of their expanding "mutually beneficial relations." [19] In the United Nations the Soviets abstained from votes on resolutions criticizing Argentine violations of human rights.[20] They have also supported Argentina in its dispute with Chile over the Beagle Channel.[21]

In reciprocation, Argentina has softened its criticism of Soviet repressive measures in Afghanistan and Poland and ignored the U.S. grain embargo of 1979–80, though it supported the boycott of the Moscow Olympics.

Symbolic of this evolving traditional relationship is the recent visit of Argentine parliamentarians to Moscow. Representatives

---

[14] Ramet and Lopez-Alves, Moscow and the Revolutionary Left in Latin America, p. 359. They note: "The Soviet-guerrilla symbiosis is pragmatic, unstable, and contingent on variations in Soviet diplomacy. Hence, as Soviet-Argentine relations have warmed up in the past few years, terrorism in Argentina has withered away as Libya, Cuba and other pro-Soviet actors have cut off aid to the Montoneros and other similar groups in Argentina."
[15] Blasier, The Giant's Rival, p. 31.
[16] Leiken, Soviet Strategy in Latin America, p. 101.
[17] Luers, The Soviets and Latin America, p. 13.
[18] Varas, Ideology and Politics in Latin American-USSR Relations, p. 45.
[19] Rothenberg, Latin America in Soviet Eyes, p. 14.
[20] Blasier, The Giant's Rival, p. 31.
[21] Luers, The Soviets and Latin America, p. 13.4

from Argentina's National Congress conferred on October 9, 1984, with top ranking Soviet officials. They exchanged information on their respective legislative activity, discussed matters of bilateral cooperation, and reviewed a number of topical international problems. The Soviets put a propaganda slant to the visit for the benefit of their Russian audience with this Vremya television newscast:

Serious concern was expressed at the increase in tension in Central America. The need was stressed for activization of the activity of parliamentarians of all countries in the struggle for a lasting peace on the planet, for the liquidation of the threat of nuclear catastrophe.[22]

e. A pattern of traditional diplomacy

All of the foregoing suggests a pattern of traditional diplomatic behavior in Soviet relations with Argentina. As Varas notes in reviewing recent aspects of Soviet-Argentine relations, the Soviets have not "aggressively pursued what appeared to be a promising opening for enhancing its influence in South America at Washington's expense." They did not exercise a veto on behalf of Argentina in the U.N. Security Council's deliberations on the Falkland War. Nor have they sold weapons to Argentina, despite high level Argentine interest. Instead, Varas concludes:

Moscow appears to be more interested in the quiet but steady expansion of normal diplomatic, cultural, and economic ties—as evidenced by continuing grain purchases from Buenos Aires, even after the signing of a new, long-term grain agreement with the United States. Indeed, the Argentine case typifies a generally cautious Soviet approach to South America in recent years.[23]

2. SOVIET SUPPORT FOR ARGENTINA IN THE FALKLANDS CRISIS

a. Official Soviet backing: Cautious and nonmilitary

Perhaps the most compelling example of Soviet traditionalism in its diplomacy with Argentina is its support for Argentina against Great Britain during the Falklands crisis in the spring of 1982. In this episode the Soviets had their own hidden agenda, but their conduct during the crisis was, nonetheless, not exceptional from that of any great power seeking to achieve such responsible foreign policy goals as expanding influence and politically solidifying a relationship with another friendly country at least superficially sharing common interests.

The Falklands crisis, provoked by Argentina's seizure of the British owned but disputed Falkland Islands (Malvinas Islands to the Argentines and the rest of Latin America), provided an opportunity for the Soviet Union, through its political and diplomatic support, to draw closer to Argentina and broaden its influence through out Latin America.[24] Though military aid was not forthcoming, it was believed that the Soviets used surveillance satellites to deliver intelligence to the Argentines on the British Navy's movements in the area.[25] However, American officials were concerned that this

[22] Moscow Television Service, 1530 GMT, Oct. 9, 1984, in FBIS, Daily Report, Soviet Union, v. 3, Oct. 11, 1984, p. K2.
[23] Varas, Ideology and Politics in Latin American-USSR Relations, p. 45.
[24] Southerland, Daniel. Global Isolation Prods Argentina Closer to USSR. The Christian Science Monitor, April 13, 1982, p. 1.
[25] Rand, Robert. The Falklands crisis and the USSR: An Update. RFE–RL. Radio Liberty Research, RL 234/82, June 8, 1982, p. 1.

crisis could pave the way for the development of a Soviet military assistance program to Argentina. As Admiral Bobby Inman, the outgoing deputy director of the Central Intelligence Agency, said, the possibility of Soviet arms sales to Argentina "is a major cause for worry in the months ahead." [26]

In general, the Soviet media, sympathetic to Argentina in its treatment of the issue, criticized the British use of force in the dispute and attacked the Reagan Administration's decision to support Britain in what they referred to as an attempt to restore the "vestiges of the era of colonial brigandage." [27] Yet officially the Soviets treaded a very careful line during the crisis, measuring their support with circumspection. On the propaganda media level they sharply criticized the British, the United States and its sympathetic allies; but formally and officially they advocated a peaceful solution of the dispute, exercising great care not to endorse Argentina's seizure of the islands. Soviet caution in the diplomacy of this crisis was revealed in April when they abstained from a U.N. Security Council resolution calling for the withdrawal of British troops. Apparently, Moscow would go no further than to officially warn Britain that the Soviet Union regarded the imposition of the naval exclusion zone around the disputed Falklands as "unlawful." [28]

In May, at a dinner honoring the visiting Sandinista leader Daniel Ortega, Brezhnev criticized unnamed "forces" (that is, Britain and the United States) for trying to "preserve or restore" positions of dominance by means of "blackmail, threats, the use of arms, blockade, and resort to actions reminiscent of the time of colonial brigandage." His recommended solution was a negotiated peace. [29]

What this statement reveals, the first by a high-ranking Soviet official, is the difficulty the Soviets had in maintaining their position of trying to exploit the anti-colonial theme detrimental to Britain, the United States and its other supporters, without endorsing the use of force to solve an irredentist claim. Soviet commentators finessed the problem by deploring Britain's use of force to "restore" colonial rule, while avoiding a statement of Moscow's position on the sovereignty question.

In a further display of non-military support, the Soviets announced at a critical moment in the crisis during June an increase in their purchase of grain from Argentina by several million tons in excess of the amounts already contracted for. [30] Coincidentally, this announcement was made against the background of completed negotiations for various economic agreements. At the beginning of the crisis in April, Soviet Deputy Foreign Minister Aleksei N. Manzhulo was in Buenos Aires to sign additional accords solidifying the Soviet-Argentine economic relationship. These new accords provided for the establishment of mixed companies for fishing off

[26] Rand, Robert. Soviet Response to Falklands Crisis Reflects Moscow's Growing Interest in Latin America. RFE–RL, Radio Liberty Research, RL 211/82, May 24, 1982, p. 3–4.
[27] Ponomarev, M. Col. Conflict in the South Atlantic. Krasnaya Zvezda, Apr. 7, 1982, p. 3, in FBIS Daily Report, Soviet Union, V. 3, Apr. 12, 1982, p. DD10.
[28] Rand, Robert. Soviet Response to Falklands Crisis Reflects Moscow's Growing Interest in Latin America. RFE–RL, Radio Liberty Research, RL 211/82, May 24, 1982, p.1.
[29] FBIS 81, May 5, 1982.
[30] Rand, The Falklands Crisis and the USSR: An Update, p. 1–2.

the southern coast of Argentina and for Soviet enrichment of uranium for an Argentine nuclear power station.[31]

b. Moscow's "hidden agenda": Rationale for support

Soviet motivations for supporting Argentina during the Falkland crisis beyond propaganda declarations and superficial acts of support can only be inferred and deduced from their conduct and pronouncements at the time, and from the subsequent positive effects they could have derived in the aftermath.[32]

There can be little doubt that the crisis opened up many opportunities to expand Soviet influence throughout Latin America. In particular, it enabled Moscow to expand and solidify its total relationship with the then isolated Argentines—a warning the Argentines themselves issued in private to Western officials in Buenos Aires—and to create anxiety in the United States over the posssible inclusion of military assistance in this relationship.[33] Similarly, the crisis enhanced Soviet prestige in other Latin American countries sympathetic to Argentina and created a wave of anti-American sentiment throughout Latin America undoubtedly contributing to altering the image of the Soviet Union as a promoter of internal revolution.[34] It is possible that the timely visit by Ortega to Moscow during the unfolding crisis strengthened Moscow's position in Nicaragua considerably.

Simultaneously, the crisis enabled Moscow to stress more convincingly its persistent and familiar propaganda theme of condemning "U.S. imperialism in Latin America." Such attacks, re-invigorated by more compelling evidence, could appeal to deep-rooted anti-American prejudices and contribute to the further weakening of the inter-American system.[35] Familiar themes attacking U.S. "imperialism," citing this crisis as a current example, have been recurring in Soviet literature ever since the Falklands crisis.[36] NATO also became a renewed and viable target for Soviet propaganda assaults and open to familiar Soviet accusations of its "aggressive" purposes.[37]

---

[31] Shabad, Theodore. Argentine-Russian Trade is Surging as Soviet Takes 77% of Crop Exports. The New York Times, April 18, 1982, p. 18.

[32] For a comprehensive commentary on Soviet benefits from the crisis, see Seib, Gerald F. Falklands Fallout: Soviet Union is Seen the Real Victor in War in the South Atlantic. The Wall Street Journal, May, 14, 1982, p. 1.

[33] Ibid. One American official said of this point: "Of all the opportunities the Soviets have, that one is the most real." See also, Markham, James M. Argentines Warn of New Soviet Influence. The New York Times, Apr. 17, 1982, p. 3.

[34] Doder, Dusko. Soviets Expect Gains from Falklands Crisis. The Washington Post, Apr. 19, 1982, p. A16. Robert Rand, a Soviet specialist at Radio Liberty, writes: "Whether or not the USSR ultimately assumes a military role in Argentina, Moscow's political standing in that country has already grown significantly as a result of the Falklands war. Moscow doubtless hopes that it can achieve similar gains elsewhere in Latin America by riding the wave of anti-American sentiment that the Anglo-Argentinian conflict has produced among the states of the Western Hemisphere." (Rand, The Falklands Crisis and the USSR: An Update, p. 2.)

[35] Duncan, Soviet Interests in Latin America, p. 182.

[36] See for example, Volskyl, Dmitry. South Atlantic: The Mainsprings of the Conflict, New Times, no. 20, May 1982: 8-9; Volskiy, V.V. Interview on Regional Developments in Latin America: "The Difficult Path of Freedom." Komsomolskaya Pravda, March 30, 1983, p. 3, Translated in, USSR Report, Political and Sociological Affairs, No. 1411, May 24, 1983, p. 4-5 (JPRS 83532); and Dmitriyev, V. The Crisis of Imperialists' Colonial Policy in Latin America. International affairs (Moscow), no. 10, Oct. 1982: 33-42.

[37] Moscow Exploits the Falklands War. Soviet Analyst, v. 11, May 5, 1980, p.3.

Finally, the crisis gave the Soviets the opportunity to reassert their claim to being a "natural ally" of the Third World. And equally important it enabled the Soviets to divert world attention from their own imperial-colonial struggles in Afghanistan and Poland.[38]

C. A MATTER OF PRIORITIES

Many aspects of traditional diplomacy are, therefore, apparent in Soviet relations with Argentina. State interests intersect at many points, and both countries, notwithstanding fundamental differences in social systems, have responded accordingly. The same may be said of Brazil, perhaps Russia's second largest trading partner in Latin America next to Argentina.

Deeper motives, however, could lie beneath Soviet willingness to accept what seems to be intolerable trade deficits with Argentina and elsewhere in Latin America.[39] Some observers may see in this Soviet acquiesence to indebtedness a willingness to pay the price for the long range benefits to be accrued from the political penetration of the country. Leiken concludes his study on Soviet strategy in Latin America, "In the southern cone Moscow continues to favor peaceful penetration." [40] He explains by citing the cases of Brazil, Argentina and Peru.

In observations on trade as a "political instrument of the Soviet state" and as a means of "penetration," Blasier acknowledges that one of the reasons for accepting high trade deficits may be a long range Soviet determination to "expand economic and political influence in the region." But he disputes this "penetrationist" argument. He suggests rather that Soviet resources are "still so limited as to discourage purely political use." So great are their domestic needs for resources, he further argues, that the Soviets "cannot afford to take many losses in Latin America for purely political purposes." Other geographic areas closer to the Soviet Union, moreover, "take priority." "In any case," Blasier concludes, "Soviets trade and influence in the area (except Argentina) to date are low both in absolute and relative terms." [41]

Whatever the validity of either argument, it is, nonetheless, significant that one of the Soviet Union's leading foreign policy journals has suggested (seemingly by implication), in the words of Rothenberg, that "the main arena of struggle in the hemisphere will not be in Central America or the Caribbean, but on the Latin American mainland." According to these specialists, A. Glinkin and P. Yakovlev,

The US ruling calculates that however important in strategic or political relations the individual small countries of the region are, the outcome of the opposition between the forces of progress and reaction on the soil of Latin America is being decided in key countries—Brazil, Mexico, Argentina.

[38] Duncan, Soviet interests in Latin America, p. 181.
[39] Blasier writes: "The most significant aspect of Soviet economic relations with Latin America (except Cuba) is the large continuing trade deficit . . . In recent years Soviet trade deficits with Latin America have fluctuated between 200 and 1,400 million rubles a year, and the Soviet global balance has been between 4 billion rubles plus and 2 billion minus. Thus Latin America has contributed heavily to the negative side of the Soviet balance of payments." (The Giant's Rival, p. 50.)
[40] Leiken, Soviet Strategy in Latin America, p. 100–101.
[41] Blaiser, The Giant's Rival, p. 54.

Next in importance, they note, are "the countries of the so-called 'second echelon': Colombia, Venezuela, Peru." [42]

On the basis of resources, strategic location and political importance, Brazil, Mexico and Argentina may rightly rank high in Soviet and American priorities of importance with Colombia, Venezuela and Peru being assigned to the "second echelon." But the critical hemispheric problems of the moment are in Central America and the Caribbean; for it is there where revolution is rife, instability rampant, U.S. interests most deeply engaged and most seriously threatened, and the ingredients for a Soviet-American confrontation most troublesome.

---

[42] Glinkin A. and P. Yakovlev. Latin America in the Global Strategy of Imperialism. Mirovaya Ekonomika i Mezhdunardonyye Otnosheniya (Moscow), Oct. 1982, p. 79, quoted in Rothenberg, Latin America in Soviet Eyes, p. 14.

V. SOVIET THIRD WORLD POLICY IN LATIN AMERICA: OPPORTUNITIES, RISKS, CONSTRAINTS, AND THE FUTURE

A. DOMINANT CHARACTERISTICS OF SOVIET THIRD WORLD POLICY IN LATIN AMERICA

1. AN INTEGRATED THIRD WORLD POLICY

Soviet Third World policy in Latin America is an integral part of its total Third World policy. The purposes and goals are the same since Soviet expectations are cast on a global scale within the vast panorama of history. When Moscow's New Times extolled the virtues of the Great October Revolution on its 1984 anniversary as generating and indeed being the wave of the future for all mankind, its editors had Latin America as much in mind as any other part of the world. For them the future of humanity belongs to Socialism: The same prophetic vision encompasses Latin America.[1]

The instrumentalities for advancing Soviet Third World policy are as visible in Latin America as in any other part of the Third World. Polarizing the political environment into adversaries and advocates, the Soviets lend their political support when an advantage is to be gained whether it be to a leftist Cuba in 1959–1960, seeking a political alternative to an antagonistic United States, or an Argentina in 1982, governed by a rightist military oligarchy, also seeking a political alternative in its war with Britian over the Falkland Islands.

Military assistance in the form of arms transfers, training, reorganizing the defense infrastructure along Soviet lines, and direct use of military power for political purposes is the primary instrument of influence and sometimes control. In Latin America, Cuba is the model and Nicaragua and Grenada the examples of an approach that has worked well elsewhere in the Third World—Ethiopia, for example. Use of military power for political purposes has been dramatically demonstrated by combined Soviet-Cuban naval maneuvers and other Soviet naval and air force operations in the Gulf of Mexico and the Caribbean.

Economic assistance continues to be a useful device, but downgraded to a lower priority to fit the drastic needs of a much troubled Soviet economy. For Moscow is unwilling to underwrite another client state like Cuba whose enormous burden it now seeks to spread among its East European allies.

State-to-state relations formally define Soviet ties with its Third World constituents, providing the necessary veneer of diplomatic

---

[1] The Future Belongs to Socialism. New Times (Moscow), no. 45, Nov. 1984: 1. The editorial concluded: "The future belongs to socialism with its concern for the material and spiritual well-being of the popular masses, with its faith in the radiant ideals humanity has cherished and suffered for throughout its history. The future belongs to socialism, whose triumphal march on our planet began in Russia in October 1917."

traditionalism, while creating the deeper and more meaningful political connection for influence. In Socialist Cuba, the Soviets have used this connection to gain considerable control over the regime, to influence and in some instances direct its economy and internal political affairs, and to exert political pressure internationally as in the NAM and the U.N.[2] In Grenada, the Soviets were establishing the foundations of a similarly formal state-to-state connection. How far, if even at all, the Soviets have progressed in Nicaragua can only be a matter of conjecture. But in this case, as with Cuba and Grenada, the leftist revolutionary leaders have reached out to Moscow and found a willing but sometimes cautious and slow-reacting Soviet ally in support of a common Socialist cause.

Party-to-party relations serve a similar purpose of reinforcing the political relationship in the case of governing leftist regimes and to an undetermined extent in non-ruling leftist parties. A striking, but admittedly superficial, illustration is the congratulatory letters of praise and adulation from Ortega and Arce to the Soviet leadership on the celebration of the 67th anniversary of the Bolshevik Revolution in November 1984. An objective reader would find little difference in the content of those letters from the Nicaraguan leaders from those of the Communist leaders in established regimes and non-ruling parties.[3] Yet in non-ruling Communist parties the connection of the CPSU is less clear, particularly in the multi-varied Latin American revolutionary environment. The situation calls for tactical diversity, a virtue never wanting in the Soviets as shown in their acceptance of a "tolerated" position of the Argentine Communist Party by a rightist military regime when the Soviets seek to maintain a close political and expanding economic relationship.[4]

Other points can be noted to show the integration of Soviet policy in Latin America with its larger Third World policy: the expansion of cultural diplomacy with its emphasis on international exchange and student education; the expanding use of radio broad-

---

[2] Jose Luis Llovio Menendez, a top ranking Cuban official who had defected to the United States, cited in a press interview in November 1984 aspects of the Soviet presence in Cuba. Llovio said that when he was appointed chief adviser to Finance Minister Francisco Garcia Valls in early 1977, he was assisted by 12 Soviet officials. "They [the Soviets] handle all the budget, all the money," he said. (Lardner, George Jr. Cuban Defector Says Castro Finances 'Salvadoran Rebels' Arms Purchases. The Washington Post, Nov. 19, 1984, p. A10.)

[3] Daniel Ortega wrote: "We Nicaraguans join today in the fraternal Soviet people's festivities since we are guided by the same desire to be free and independent and to struggle for peace, equality and solidarity among the world's peoples. That is why our two countries are united by ties of brotherhood and solidarity." And Bayardo Arce wrote in part: "Progressive mankind and all honest people in the world today acknowledge the immense gains in the spheres of politics economy well-being that were achieved in the course of the military battles, struggles, and labor of the Soviet people led by Lenin and his outstanding party of Bolsheviks." (Izvestiya, Nov. 10, 1984, p. 4, and Nov. 12, 1984, p. 4., in FBIS Daily Report, Soviet Union, v. 3, Nov. 15, 1984, p. 06–07.) The Laotian Communist leaders wrote: "With the victory of the October Revolution, the world's first socialist state was born and a new epoch ushered in: the epoch of transition from capitalism to socialism on a worldwide scale. That victory showed the oppressed peoples the way and raised them to the struggle for national independence, freedom, and social progress. Under the very difficult conditions of the struggle against counterrevolution and intervention, and encircled by enemies who were seeking to destroy the October Revolution's gains, the Soviet people, under the leadership of Lenin's party, the vanguard of the working class, implemented socialist transformations for the first time." (Pravda, Nov. 9, 1984, p. 4, Ibid., p. 04.)

[4] For insights into the commonality of views between Moscow and the Latin American Communist Parties, see, Statement by a Meeting of the Communist Parties of South America. Information Bulletin, Oct. 1984, p. 29–32. This is a report on their meeting in Buenos Aires from July 5 to 7, 1984. Representatives from the Communist Party of Cuba and "a specially invited delegation" from Nicaragua's FSLN attended as observers.

casting for disseminating Soviet propaganda; and the establishment of serious minded research institutes in the Soviet Academy of Sciences to backup policymakers in the CPSU and Soviet Government.

In brief, Soviet Third World policy is a whole with many parts, and the principles and policies, the instrumentalities and goals, institutional connections and an enduring commitment appear to be only superficially different in Latin America from that of other Third World areas in Asia, Africa and the Middle East.

2. REVOLUTIONARY OPPORTUNISM IS SOVIET THIRD WORLD POLICY

Revolutionary opportunism is the second dominant characteristic in Soviet Third World policy in Latin America. By a remarkable historical coincidence Castro's revolution in Cuba erupted only four years after Khrushchev had launched his out-reaching policy of globalism. This policy, asserting its principle of "peaceful coexistence," had revolutionary pretentions that encompassed the Third World and frontily contested the prevailing international order. Though belatedly, Khrushchev seized upon Castro's success as an opportunity to downgrade U.S. predominance in the Western Hemisphere, placing it within the global context of an asserted claim that the balance of world forces had shifted against the United States and the capitalist world and in favor of the Soviet Union and the Socialist world.

Even after the withdrawal of the missiles from Cuba in the crisis of 1962, provoked largely by this power-seeking policy, the Soviets, driven by a clear opportunity to expand their presence in the Western Hemisphere, broadened their base in Cuba incrementally within limits tolerated by the United States. Thus by taking advantage of an opportunity that opened up a quarter century ago, the Soviets were able to create for themselves a position in the Western Hemisphere that has both profound regional and geopolitical implications.

In Grenada and Nicaragua, similar opportunities opened up for Moscow, and again, though belatedly, the Soviets moved in to take advantage. Judging from the military materiel found in Grenada after the invasion and the military assistance agreements in force or awaiting final signature, the Soviets and their Cuban allies clearly had other revolutionary adventures in mind, if not actually planned, using Grenada as a staging area. And as for Nicaragua, there seems little doubt that Soviet and Cuban aspirations extend beyond that Sandinista stronghold to El Salvador and perhaps other Central American neighbors. Only recently Castro's former top aid, Jose Luis Llovio Menendez, one of the highest-ranking members of the Castro regime to defect, said that the goal of Cuban foreign policy (read also Soviet) is "to make a lot of Cubas everywhere." "They want Nicaragua and El Salvador," he said. "After that, Honduras and Guatemala, you can be sure." [5]

What all this suggests is simply this: The Soviets seek to exploit revolutionary opportunity whether it be one arising from a natural

---

[5] Maitland-Werner, Leslie. High Cuban Defector Speaks Out, Denouncing Castro as "Impulsive." The New York Times, Nov. 19, 1984, p. A6. Llovio served as chief adviser to the head of the Cuban State Committee for Finance from 1977 to 1980 and as chief adviser to the Minister of Culture from 1980 to 1982.

environment breeding revolution as in Nicaragua or an unnatural one created by themselves as in the military conquest of Eastern Europe and their military invasion and occupation of Afghanistan. Because of the policy-conditions created by Marxism-Leninism, they naturally search for targets of opportunity in an ever-changing world. Nowhere has this reality been more forcefully and convincingly shown than recently in Latin America.

3. RESORT OF DIPLOMATIC TRADITIONALISM

The third characteristic of Soviet Third World policy in Latin America is their tactical use of diplomatic traditionalism when the occasion demands it. A patina of diplomatic tradition rooted in the customs of the West and imperial Russia coexists with revolutionary impulses in Soviet foreign policy. In many respects, therefore, Soviet behavior in foreign relations is not what it seems. For their diplomacy functions on two seemingly irreconcilable levels: one that seeks to transform the world order mainly through the use of force, military power, and subversion; the other that seeks to maintain the niceties of international comity, abiding by the customs of international diplomacy and conducting the affairs of state according to rules of universally accepted diplomatic practice.[6]

Thus the Soviets can aid and abet on-going revolution in Cuba, Grenada and Nicaragua while simultaneously carrying on normal relations with neighboring Mexico and with other non-communist states in Central America, the Caribbean Basin and South America. The Soviets can give support for an Allende in Chile whose aspirations of establishing Socialism they shared; they can lend support to like-minded Communist and leftist parties in furthering their revolutionary purposes. At the same time they can carry on normal diplomatic relations as a nation-state, closely associating themselves with an Argentina fighting a regional war with Britain as nations customarily do when in distress and interests converge, or maintaining extensive economic programs which is universally accepted as legitimately advancing international development in areas that need it.

Thus Soviet policy in the Third World is revolutionary in that it seeks to transform established order; but it is also traditional in its resort to accepted norms of diplomacy often as a tactical means to achieve essentially revolutionary purposes. What distinguished Soviet diplomacy from that of the West making it fundamentally irreconcilable, as Western scholars of diplomacy have emphasized, is its enduring commitment to revolution.[7]

---

[6] Harold Nicolson, a leading British authority on diplomatic practice, asserted that Soviet diplomacy was not diplomacy but rather "something else," meaning that there is a valid distinction between it and that of the West. It is a diplomacy with a difference, and that difference is a fundamental, ideological, and political commitment to revolution in the Third World. It is this difference that makes Soviet diplomacy "socialist diplomacy," as the Soviets themselves would be the first to acknowledge, and gives it that essential element of incompatibility with the United States and the other liberal democracies in the world. (HFAC, Soviet Diplomacy and Negotiating Behavior, p. 541.)

[7] Ibid.

4. DANGER OF SOVIET-AMERICAN CONFRONTATION

The inherent danger of future Soviet-American confrontations in the manner of the Cuban missile crisis is the fourth and final dominant characteristic of Soviet Third World policy in Latin America.

The Cuban missile crisis is perhaps the most accurate benchmark against which to measure American tolerance of Soviet military activities in Latin America, particularly in the strategically important Caribbean Basin. President Kennedy accepted the Soviet challenge to U.S. hemispheric predominance and its world position as a superpower at the risk of thermonuclear war. Congress and the American people supported him. The agreement that dissolved the crisis and subsequent exchanges in the Nixon Administration restricting the basing of Soviet submarines in Cuba established the general parameters of acceptability, but seemingly left open any precise definition of terms. Accordingly, the area has been vulnerable to the Soviet tactic of incrementalism. Witness the Soviet militarization of Cuba and Soviet-Cuban expansionist schemes in Grenada, and the "unprecedented" arms buildup in Nicaragua.[8]

Grenada is a more recent benchmark against which to measure U.S. tolerance of Soviet military probes in this vulnerable region. A Soviet presence was ended by the U.S.-OECS invasion. In all probability the Soviets were taken aback by this counterthrust and accordingly have been compelled to reassess their policy of expansionism in the region and reassess also their estimates of U.S. acquiescence in the projection of their power.

The expected delivery of Soviet MIGs to Nicaragua and the upgrading of its military assistance in the fall of 1984 aroused anew the anxiety of the Administration and a large sector of American opinion in what appeared to be a new test of American tolerance. Official statements by the Administration made clear that the United States would not accept any drastic change in the military balance in Central America and threat to hemispheric security that delivery of the MIGs would entail.

In a sort of cat-and-mouse game the Soviets have been testing American resolve to resist their pressures in this area. This is a dangerous course that opens up the possibility of a serious Soviet-American military confrontation down the road. In 1962, the Soviets misjudged the degree of U.S. tolerance of their military buildup in Cuba; in 1983, they misjudged again in Grenada; in the future, they could misjudge still again and invite another vigorous U.S. riposte.

An aroused democracy responding to perceived threats to its vital interests creates a deep-seated crisis situation not easily managed much less dissolved without seriously impairing the foreign policy positions of the contending sides. In the Caribbean region the danger of a serious Soviet-American confrontation, should the Soviets continue the projection of their power in this "strategic backyard" of the United States, cannot be exaggerated and its like-

---

[8] Secretary of Defense Weinberger dramatized the effects of Soviet incrementalism when in a speech to the National Press Club on November 28, 1984 he condemned an "unprecedented" arms buildup in Nicaragua, saying 15,000 tons of weapons will have been delivered from Soviet-bloc countries by the end of 1984. Arms imports in 1981, he said, were 790 tons. (Omang, Joanne. Managua Gets New Warning. The Washington Post, Nov. 29, 1984, p. A31.)

lihood ruled out: Its effects would extend beyond the regional to the global level. Two factors magnify the gravity of any such confrontation: one, the existence of strategic parity, which the Soviets had not yet achieved in 1962, and the exponential improvement in arms technology on both sides; and the other, a Soviet determination not to back down in another showdown. The words of Vasily Kuznetsov, a top ranking Soviet official, to John McCloy as the Soviet missiles were being withdrawn from Cuba have a special meaning today: "You Americans will never be able to do this to us again." [9]

B. Gains and Losses, Advantages and Constraints

1. apparent gains and losses

a. A foothold in Nicaragua

The Soviets seem to have made many gains in Latin America during the past five years. The collapse of Allende's Socialist regime in Chile had dealt a serious blow to the Soviet leadership that apparently had great expectations for its future. But this loss, an object lesson in failing to sufficiently value the military dimension of maintaining political power, was recouped in 1979 by the Sandinistas' success in Nicaragua.

The continuing Soviet-Cuban military buildup, intended, they say, to stabilize the regime and to protect it against hostile neighbors and the threat of U.S. intervention, has strengthened the Communist position in Central America, and, along with generous political support and some economic assistance, has enabled the Sandinistas to strengthen their base of power and radicalize their policy. However, a competing view from another perspective suggests that the Sandinistas have expansionist designs on their Central American neighbors, notably El Salvador, and that the failure of the 1980 offensive and the subsequent strengthening of the democratic forces led by President Jose Napoleon Duarte have been measurable setbacks for them and their leftist allies in El Salvador. At this juncture the issue remains open.

Whatever the nuances of interpretation, the political reality is an entrenched Sandinista regime in Nicaragua, backed by Soviet power and consolidating its position and having at least the potentiality of transforming Nicaragua into a Socialist state with Cuba and their Cuban mentors as models. This is a clear gain for the Soviets.

b. Setback in Grenada

An equally clear loss for the Soviets is their setback in Grenada. Analysts will never know "what might have been" had not the invasion taken place. But evidence of military weaponry found on the island and plans for the future documented by military assistance agreements, minutes of meetings, diplomatic correspondence and diaries, suggest that both the Soviet Union and Cuba had under-

---

[9] HFAC, Soviet Diplomacy and Negotiating Behavior, p. 395.

way plans for extended political and military activities in the Caribbean Basin and perhaps even beyond.

c. A stronghold in Cuba

However, the negative effects of this setback have been softened by Russia's continuing ability to rely on a loyal and militarized Cuba. For the Soviets, the cost in economic resources has been high. Economic aid has increased to about $5 billion annually, a quarter of the Cuban GNP; military aid has been estimated conservatively at $3.8 billion during 1961-1979 and increasing. But in return they have at their disposal a base for the projection of their power and influence both regionally and geopolitically on a scale never before achieved by an adversary of the United States.

Moreover, the Cubans, while serving themselves, have also served the Soviet well in common expansionist enterprises in Africa and in their political activity within the NAM. Assets and liabilities in such international undertakings may be diffcult, if not impossible, to measure precisely; but the fact of a viable Soviet presence directly in Africa and indirectly in the NAM through Cuba and other Communist allies, places the Soviet Union at the center of two important areas in Third World politics—hardly a wasting asset.[10]

d. A plus in Argentina

Much the same can be said for Argentina in the aftermath of the Falklands War. Soviet support at a crucial moment had given an isolated Argentina a counterweight in the international politics of the war, and at little or no cost to the Soviet Union. For the war had conveniently served many Soviet regional, hemispheric and international purposes.

Recent exchanges of high-level delegations and the expansion of economic relations (even though suffering a trade deficit) suggest that Moscow's resort to diplomatic traditionalism has been an asset in its Third World policy in Latin America, particularly in further opening up the vital South American continent to Soviet influence. Recent discussions of further arms sales to a politically troubled Peru suggests the value of the same traditional approach and the further opening up of this area to a resourceful Soviet Union.

2. ADVANTAGES, DISADVANTAGES, AND CONSTRAINTS

a. Some advantages for the Soviets in Latin America

(1) Managing foreign policy more effectively

The Soviets have had advantages, disadvantages and constraints in Latin America. Advantages have had both internal and international aspects: the internal, strict control over their foreign policy

---

[10] One of the most recent and authoritative statements on the Soviet attitude towards the Third World was made by Foreign Minister Gromyko in his speech at the U.N. in November 1984: "We regard the countries of Asia, Africa and Latin America that make up the majority of the non-aligned movement—an influential force of today—as our fellow-fighters in the struggle between those who work for peace and those who work against it. It is the intention of the Soviet Union to continue to do all in its power to deepen and develop friendly ties with these countries." (FBIS 089, Moscow Tass in English, 154 GMT, Sept. 27 1984, Take 12.)

process, and the positive value of ideology; the international, advantages that come from not sharing like the United States some responsibility for past inequities in Latin America whether real or imagined.

States under rigid political control have not been faultless in managing foreign policy without the institutional constraints existing in democracies. They have made more than their share of serious mistakes.[11] Nonetheless, the Soviets do function with certain institutional and organizational advantages. Without a constituency to justify policy beyond the nucleus of power concentrated in the Politburo and Secretariat, and other official institutions, the Soviet leadership is free to function in the Third World as it sees fit in order to achieve its self-designated policy goals. Self-justification by and accountability to the leadership elite, was all that was needed for them to move into Nicaragua and Grenada and also to continue underwriting their client, Cuba.

Contrast this freedom of action to take initiatives in foreign policy and freedom from accountability with efforts in the Reagan Administration to strengthen the Contra forces fighting against the Sandinistas and to shore up the Duarte regime against the internal revolutionary leftists said to be supported from Nicaragua. The point being made here is not to pass judgment on policy but rather to indicate the institutional constraints that constitutionally limit freedom of action by democracies in foreign policy.

(2) The positive value of ideology

The Soviets also have certain advantages that derives their revolutionary ideology. Marxism-Leninism gives the Soviet foreign policy planner and executor an ultimate theoretical design, an eschatological scheme, so to speak, of where he is going and how he can get there. In this scheme, power, notably military power, is the most important element. However wrong the assumptions of this ideology, the Soviet believer, nonetheless, has implanted in his mind through years of politization a design for international life to guide him and a mechanism for assessing the correlating of forces that determine advance, withdrawal or temporizing in harmony with the ebb and flow of history and of Soviet fortunes. In retrospect, removal of the missiles from Cuba in 1962 was only a temporary retreat graphically demonstrated subsequently by the Soviet resort to other strategies and tactics to militarily strengthen their position in Cuba.

Ideology also gives the Soviets the driving elan that characterizes the aggressive element of their foreign policy. It provides the inner impulse to value, build and expand power. As Walter Lippmann discovered in his interview with Khrushchev in the early 1960's, genuine "peaceful coexistence," as democracies understand it, is impossible to the Soviets and acquiesence in what democracies would term the status quo, unthinkable. To Khrushchev (and his successors) "peaceful coexistence" is in reality a form of advance;

---

[11] Dexter Perkins has written on this point. See, The American Approach to Foreign Policy. Cambridge, Harvard University Press, 1962, chapter 8 and 9; and Foreign Policy and the American Spirit. Ithaca, Cornell University Press, 1957, chapters 4 and 10.

and the status quo, as he told Lippmann, means simply the unimpeded progress of the march of Communism.[12]

Cuba, Nicaragua and Grenada are not territories vital to Soviet security in the sense that they are to the United States or that Poland and the Kuriles and Sakhalin in the Soviet Far East are to the Soviet Union. Yet the unimpeded progress of world Socialism as a universal idea is very important to them, even vital; for it gives legitimacy to their own governance and that of other Communist states, and justification for their beliefs and political existence. Thus support for Cuba and Nicaragua takes on an important value for the Soviets, worthy of running the risks of confrontation with the United States.

In brief, ideology, reinforced by a deep appreciation and the reality of power, gives the Soviets that aggressive edge in foreign policy. Establishing an acceptable harmony of interests with adversaries in the mode of the 19th Century balance of power system is alien to Soviet ideology. Detente and agreements may be reached on strategic weapons as in SALT I and SALT II in 1972 and 1979 respectively as a matter of self-interest. But as the Soviets contended when they were seizing new targets of opportunity in Angola and Ethiopia in the mid-1970's and as they responded to complaints by Secretary of State Kissinger that detente could not take any more Angolas, detente cannot arrest the historical forces at work in the Third World, they said, nor can it arrest the deeper Soviet ideological impulses to seize these opportunities in order to advance the cause of Socialism globally.

(3) Unburdened by historic injustices in Latin America; a message of "hope"

Finally, the Soviets do not share the burden of responsibility, as does the United States, for historic inequities and injustices in Latin America, whether real or imagined. The lingering effects of these inequities and injustices, apparently still very real in large parts of Latin America, have been to contribute to those objectives conditions that have made areas of Latin America "ripe for revolution," vulnerable to Soviet exploitation, and fertile soil receptive to its message of "hope" in Marxism-Leninism.

The United States carries a heavy burden of responsibility for the past and many Latin Americans, with historical memories deeply imbedded in their political culture, have been unforgiving. The cry of "Yankee imperialism" still stirs deep feelings of anti-Americanism in many quarters; and often acts by the United States, justifiable from its perspective, can regenerate old historic hatreds.

The Soviets share no such burden. Latin Americans have never felt the cruelty of Soviet imperialism and colonialism, as have the Baltic peoples during and since World War II, East Europeans since 1944–1945, and particularly the Hungarians in 1956, the Czechoslovaks in 1968, the Poles and the Afghans since 1979. "Geographic fatalism" has served the Soviets well, protecting their reputation by concealing the harsher side of life under Soviet Commu-

---

[12] U.S. Congress. Senate. Committee on Foreign Relations. Khrushchev and the Balance of World Power. 87th Cong., 1st sess. Wash., U.S. Govt. Print. Off., 1962, p. 15–16. (Doc. 66)

nism and allowing their propaganda to perpetuate and preserve long held anti-American prejudices. Appeals to these prejudices have become standard procedure and a common theme in Moscow's Latin American propaganda. The lingering effects of these real inequities and injustices so much a part of Latin American life have been to create objective conditions in many parts of Latin America "ripe for revolution" and vulnerable for Soviet exploitation. Organized Communism has never been strong and appealing in Latin America; only the conditions in which its message can thrive. Communists played no effective role in the Cuban revolution; they remained on the sidelines, hostile and uncooperative in Castro's revolutionary strategy. Their role was after the fact, and then not so much as a party but the organizing appeal of their ideology, Marxism-Leninism. The Soviets still are hard pressed to justify this inaction by their "vanguard" party. Rather it was the socioeconomic and political conditions in Cuba that insured Castro's initial success, and later Soviet support and the organizing prinicple of Marxism-Leninism that insured the consolidation of his regime. Hence, Socialist Cuba, successful in its revolution, holds itself up as the ideal model for the transition from a "national liberation movement" to Marxism-Leninism.

The same is true in the Sandinista revolution and the guerrilla rebellion in El Salvador. The traditional Communist Parties have been minor actors; the ingredients for success lay elsewhere: in existing conditions, the appeal of Marxism-Leninism as an organizing principle, and the proffered power of the Soviet Union as a supporter and mentor. Hence a perceivable pattern in the revolutionary politics of Latin America: indigenous conditions create the revolutionary milieu; the revolutionary leaders, initially perhaps more nationalist than Socialist, reach out for an alternative and find an organizing principle for national development in Marxism-Leninism and support from the Soviet Union. The promise of Marxism-Leninism, however fallacious to those who know its false message and many failures, can, nonetheless, be appealing to the uninitiated among the downtrodden and oppressed. It is such conditions existing in large parts of Latin America and elsewhere in the Third World that gives the Soviets an undeserved advantage.

b. Disadvantages and constraints

(1) Constraints on foreign policy resources

The obverse side of assets enjoyed by the Soviets in their Third World policy towards Latin America are the serious disadvantages and constraints that adversely affect performance, effectiveness and results. The greatest constraint are the serious limitations on Soviet foreign policy resources all across-the-board.

By all accounts the Soviet Union continues to be beset by serious political, economic, social and foreign policy problems—"deeply troubled," as William G. Hyland, a leading American authority on the Soviet Union, put it.[13] It has become commonplace in commentaries on the Soviet Union of today and assessments of its future to cite such shortcomings and problems as:

[13] Hyland, William G. Brezhnev: A Pre-Postmortem. The New Republic, May 19, 1982: 21.

—The piling up of serious economic problems which the Soviet system appears incapable of dealing with effectively, largely, perhaps, because of the strictures of ideology and the fear of losing legitimacy (and political control) by bending ideology sufficiently to solve the accumulating problems—including, irrationalities of allocation in central planning, low labor productivity, a shrinking labor force, overemphasis on defense production at the expense of the civilian, inability to cope satisfactorily with modernization, a resistance to reform, the need for Western technology and credit: an economy, in short, like Soviet society itself plagued by corruption, that in the future faces prospects of increased demands amid deteriorating economic performance; [14]

—The overextension of the Soviet Union's imperial domain and possible weakening of its home base, creating such problem as, increased doubts about the loyalty of its Socialist allies as demonstrated by the upheaval in Poland and even doubts about the effectiveness of Soviet military power used both for conquest and political purposes and seen in the failure to pacify backward Afghanistan now going into its sixth year of war, the increased burden of empire caused by the global expansion of Soviet power and the costly Soviet involvement in the Third World from Vietnam in Southeast Asia to Nicaragua in Latin America, problems compounded by the failure to reconcile differences with China and reconstitute the unity of the world Communist community, and the failure also to come to terms with the West and thus ease the heavy burden of arms, armaments, and empire;

—A demographic problem of declining birthrates, especially among the more advanced Slavic and other European peoples but not the backward Muslims of Central Asia, and the rising mortality rates, poor health care and rampant alcoholism that potentially threaten all aspects of Soviet society, particularly in providing much needed manpower for the economy and defense; [15]

—Inter-ethnic tensions in this vast multinational state of over a hundred different peoples and cultures, along with the revival of religious feelings, that have created increasing anxiety among the leadership and raise the question of the primacy and perhaps even the legitimacy of Great Russian predominance in the USSR; and finally,

---

[14] A recent report from Moscow gave this picture of Soviet society: "Crime, divorce and alcoholism are on the rise. And the gap between the demands of the new class and the sluggish pace of the economy, burdened by enormous military outlays, has bred corruption and the growth of a second, black-market economy. A new breed of economists point out that the large investment capital and expanding labor force that fueled the economic boom of the 1960's and 1970's no longer exists. Economic growth, they argue, must come from greater productivity and new forms of management and organization." The writer continues: "Against these demands, the traditional publicity about World War II, Marxist ideology, grand achievements or the superiority of the Soviet way of life no longer has much affect." (Schmemann, Serge. Chernenko's Control Seems Firm; Nostalgia for Andropov Endures. The New York Times. Nov. 21, 1984, p. A6.)

[15] Dr. Murray Feshbach, a Senior Research Scholar at Georgetown University's Center for Population Research, Kennedy Institute for Ethics, and leading specialist in the West on Soviet demography, has written widely on the demographic problems facing the Soviet Union. See, Social Maintenance in the U.S.S.R.: Demographic Morass. The Washington Quarterly, v. 5, Summer 1982: 92–98, and, The Soviet Union: Population Trends and Dilemmas. Population Bulletin, v. 37, no. 3, Aug. 1982. 44 p.

—Widespread popular apathy and alienation from an ideology that promises much but delivers little, creating what a recent observer reported "a loss of ideological faith," the rise of a debilitating "malaise," and "a feeling that the Soviet Union has lost its sense of purpose." [16]

Shortcomings in such vital areas upon which a successful and viable foreign policy depends put serious, though not necessarily crippling, constraints on performance, effectiveness and results in the Soviet Union's Third World policy. Thus it is reasonable to conclude that Soviet expansionism, like expansionism in all other empires in past history, has its limitations, though a view of its recent activities in Asia, Latin America, the Middle East and Africa could rightly raise the question just what those limitations may be. [17] Nonetheless, the Soviet cup "runneth over" with problems so fundamental to the sustained strength of its imperial base that Soviet leaders cannot fail to take them into account when seeking new and costly targets of opportunity and political and military conquests in the Third World. [18]

(2) Validity of "geographic fatalism"

The continuing validity of "geographic fatalism" acts as a further constraint upon any deep Soviet involvement in Latin America.

Sources suggest the weakening of this exclusionary Soviet principle in the two decades after the successful Cuban revolution. This apparent change in perceptions may be true on the Soviet side, but hardly on the American and perhaps not even really on the Soviet. For the geographic reality that places Latin America physically far from the Soviet homeland has not changed; nor has there been any change in the geopolitical reality that places Latin America clearly within the parameters of U.S. vital security interests. That the Soviet Union has moved cautiously in escalating its probes into Nicaragua suggests their awareness of U.S. concerns and the con-

---

[16] The New York Times, Nov. 21, 1984, p. A6.

[17] The Falklands War and its aftermath, for example, had shown the limits of Soviet influence and power in that they could not decisively determine the outcome; Argentina remains anti-Communist and suspicious of the Soviet Union; and Argentine-U.S. relations have been strengthened.

[18] With respect to the Soviet economy, Western economic specialists continue to make "gloomy" forecasts. At a NATO-sponsored symposium in April 1984, Jiri Slama of the Osteuropa-Institut in Munich, said: "There is no evidence that the slowdown in Soviet growth will be reversed." The general conclusion of the participants was the same, according to the press report: "The Soviet leadership will be faced with an agonizing choice between bolstering the civilian economy and expanding the ever-growing military machine for some time to come." (Yerkey, Gary. Gloomy Forecast for Soviet Economy. The Christian Science Monitor, April 17, 1984, p. 11.)

The Valentas stress many of the points made above and conclude:

> The cumulative effect of all these conditions may be forced Soviet constraint in the Caribbean basin, for at least a few years. To be sure, it would be overly optimistic to conclude that the Soviets will cease the arms transfer and economic support necessary for the survival of existing revolutionary regimes in the region. Their support for Cuba, Nicaragua, and Grenada, in fact, intensified in the early 1980s. Yet in several years to come they will very likely be more cautious about giving new or significant support to struggling revolutionaries because of necessarily increasing preoccupation with their own domestic problems and problems at their periphery. The Soviets, who determine the limits of Cuban assertiveness, may likewise moderate future Cuban activities while waiting for new, low-risk opportunities.

(Valenta, Jiri and Virginia. Soviet Strategy and Policies in the Caribbean Basin. in, Wiarda, Howard J., ed. Rift and Revolution: The Central American Imbroglio. Washington, American Enterprise Institute, 1984, chapt. 8, p. 242.)

tinuing validity of "geographic fatalism." A measure of Soviet caution (in addition to their resort of incrementalism as a tactic) is seen by the fact that the arrival of the *Bakuriani* in Nicaragua, the ship that was supposed to have delivered the MIG fighters, marked the first time that the Soviets had sent weapons to Nicaragua under their own flag, rather than through its surrogates, Cuba or Bulgaria.[19]

Reports of the alleged MIG shipments to Nicaragua may have proved to be false (Jane's Defense Weekly reported that they were believed to have been unloaded in Libya). But statements by official Administration spokesmen, reasserting U.S. intentions of preserving its vital interests in Central America in what momentarily appeared to be an incipient crisis, have no doubt reinforced a more conservative interpretation of "geographic fatalism," particularly if it is true, as speculated, that the MIG incident was intended to test the limits of U.S. tolerance.[20]

(3) Geography and economics, political philosophy and culture as deterrents to Soviet influence

Finally, the sheer geographic size of Latin America (it is larger than a continent), its deep philosophical roots in Western traditions of political democracy, the predominance of Western culture with all its material, spiritual and intellectual values, along with the vast economic interconnections with the West through foreign trade, economic assistance and international investment—all act as a deterrent to Soviet influence.

It is important to recall that direct Soviet political influence and control has not extended much beyond its own geographical borders. Eastern Europe remains defiant, though quiescent, in its forced submission to Moscow. Elsewhere Soviet influence and its presence have been bought cheaply with arms and military equipment; and even in these instances, as in the case of India, its influence has been nominal at best, and in Indonesia and Egypt, to name only two Third World countries who once had close ties with Moscow, vaporous and transitory. Soviet ideology and the Soviet model of development have lost whatever appeal they may have once had in much of the Third World. Even in the Soviet Union ideology is losing its appeal, according to qualified observers. Eastern Europe, no longer looking to Moscow as a model, has turned to the West to stave off the decline of its living standards because the Soviets cannot sustain their economic subsidies.[21]

The Soviets cannot even command the attention much less the loyalty of the Chinese who in their modernization program look to Japan and the industrialized West, not to the failing Soviet economy. And in Southeast Asia, the Soviet Union has had little appeal much less making any noticeable progress among the non-Communist Pacific community of nations who are entering a new era of economic prosperity in unity with Japan and the United States.

[19] Time, Nov. 27, 1984: 73.
[20] The New York Times, Nov. 22, 1984, p. A3.
[21] Markham, James M. East Bloc Sees Chernenko's Rule as an Era of Transition and Drift. The New York Times, Nov. 22, 1984, p. A10.

All of this suggests the limited appeal the Soviets actually have in Third World areas. It suggests also that given its foreign policy failures, including failures within its own economy and polity as whole, how much more difficult it would be for the Soviets to fundamentally affect the destiny of such a vast continental area as Latin America where the traditions of political democracy remain strong and are expanding, and where the ties with Western culture and the Western economies remain vigorous and self-reinforcing. Moreover, the growing strength of the middle class and left of center political forces in Latin America suggests that indigenous Communists may be compelled to moderate their radicalism; but it suggests also that strong political forces are taking shape that could act as a further deterrent to Soviet influence.

Moreover, the transcending historical trend now enveloping Latin America, as Varas notes, is towards independence and non-intervention by great powers, not dependency and submission. In brief, Latin America has been moving towards a higher stage of maturity in the community of nations, and this progress is graphically portrayed in Map 8 that shows the continuing surge of Latin American states towards democracy. As the Kissinger Commission's Report states, "democracy is becoming the rule rather than the exception" in Latin America.[22] And this reality, despite known difficulties in establishing democracy in Latin America, stands as another deterrent, perhaps the most improtant, to Soviet ambitions.

Undoubtedly the supreme irony of Castro's revolution is that it may have won the complete independence of Cuba from the United States, but just as surely it has made Cuba not only a client but a dependency of the Soviet Union upon which it must rely for its economic life, its political existence, and its military support. Cuba is out of step with the rest of Latin America; or in Communist terminology, it is in "contradiction" to the main trend in Latin American life; namely, towards democracy.

---

[22] Kissinger Commission's Report, p 11. In an address to the First Annual Latin American Symposium meeting in Montgomery, Alabama on Nov. 16, 1984, Deputy assistant Secretary of Defense for Inter-American Affairs Nestor D. Sanchez gave the following appraisal of the surge towards democracy in Latin America:

"Many of the countries of this hemisphere continue to face serious problems. But we need to put these problems into perspective by comparing the situation today to 1980, when 16 of the 35 states of the hemisphere were ruled by dictatorships.

"Today, only ten are under dictatorial rule, and four are planning elections in the near future. Over the past four years, our southern neighbors have cast some 150 million votes in 34 elections in 25 countries. This number of voters is about 2 and ½ times greater than the number voting 20 years ago.

"In 1983, more than 15 million Argentine voters went to the polls, ending nearly a decade of military rule. This was the largest turnout in Argentina's history.

"In Brazil's 1982 congressional and municipal elections, 48 million voted, more than triple the number in the 1962 legislative elections.

"In May of this year, 1.5 million Salvadorans elected Jose Napoleon duarte President, and in July, 1.8 million voted in the Constituent Assembly elections in Guatemala."

"Sanchez added the following qualification respecting elections in Nicaragua:

"The numbers of voters participating in elections of course in not the sole measure of whether real democracy is exercised. In Nicaragua in 1974, Anastasio Somoza received 95 percent of the votes, and ten years later—less than two weeks ago—the Sandinistas did what they were expected to, proving again to the people of Nicaragua that elections alone do not make democracy." Nonetheless, elections, carried out in freedom, are a key criterion for democracy, and the achievements in Latin America are impressive. (Text of Sanchez speech, p. 1-2.)

C. A SUMMING UP

To sum up, the Soviets have advantages, disadvantages and constraints in pursuing their Third World policy in Latin America. Soviet propaganda, the aggressive and military character of their foreign policy, and the certainty of the message inherent in their ideological beliefs—all tend to portray the image of the Soviet Union as a superpower on the offensive, seeking new targets of opportunity and having the power to achieve their historic goals. But even a cursory review, such as this of the disadvantages they face in Latin America and the constraints on their use of power, suggests that, despite certain vulnerabilities, Latin America, formidable in its search for a free and independent place in the society of nations, constitutes a problem of the first magnitude for Soviet policy planners.

Map 8

Democratic Trend in Latin America

Source: Goodsell, James Nelson. Latin America to Get Another Democracy.
The Christian Science Monitor, Dec. 26, 1984, p. 1 and 28. Goodsell
reports that Brazil's presidential election of January 15, 1985 is
expected "to nudge Latin America's largest nation toward civilian
rule...." and that "re-democratization" is perhaps a "more important
hemisphere trend" than turmoil in Central America and the foreign
debt problem. According to Venezuelan President Jamie Lusinchi,
"This return to democracy probably will have more impact on Latin
America than any other issue. It is one of the most exciting developments of our times." However, some Latin American specialists caution
against too much optimism about the current trend, noting that there
is a cyclical tradition of democratic rule and dictatorial rule in
Latin America. Only a few Latin American democracies today, they say,
have established democratic traditions. Goodsell concludes: "For
Latin American democrats, the challenge at this juncture is to build
on the current democratic trend and to implant democracy's roots more
firmly."

C. IMPLICATIONS OF SOVIET THIRD WORLD POLICY FOR LATIN AMERICA

1. SOCIALIST CUBA: MODEL FOR LATIN AMERICA?

Soviet Third World policy has far-reaching implications for both Latin America and the United States. In Socialist Cuba, the Soviets have found a willing instrument for advancing their Third World goals in Latin America and within the NAM. But the arrangement is not wholly one-sided; the Cubans see many of their own interests being achieved and goals advanced possible only in alliance with Moscow.

Nonetheless, Cuba has paid a high price: its complete independence.[23] As a dependency of the Soviet Union, the Cubans, judging by assessments of the Soviet Union by qualified observers, have hitched their wagon if not to a falling then to a faltering star. Having made its choice, Cuba carries the message of revolution, subversion and the Communist brand of Socialism, projecting itself as a model for Latin America to follow, and serving as an advanced base in the geopolitics of East-West relations in the Western Hemisphere.

The high risk role that Cuba has taken on for itself has created a challenge of the first order for Latin Americans who are advancing towards fuller democracy and economic development and who want a Western Hemisphere free from the dangers of nuclear war, a potentiality always possible in a Soviet-American confrontation that the Soviet-Cuban connection could create.

2. CENTRAL AMERICA AND CARIBBEAN: VULNERABILITY AND POWER OF CHOICE

For the vulnerable Central American and Caribbean region, Soviet Third World policy has the greatest significance, but the power of choice of which direction their national development will take remains with the countries of the region, perhaps even in Nicaragua.

Soviet military intervention in Grenada and Nicaragua, directly and through its surrogates, is a fact of international life. The Grenada Documents substantiate Soviet purposes beyond doubt, suggesting some variation on a modus operandi remarkably resem-

---

[23] A study prepared by Lawrence H. Theriot, Office of East-West Policy and Planning, Department of Commerce, for the Joint Economic Committee describes Cuba's "overwhelming" dependence on the Soviet Union in these words: "The Cuban client role is reflected in its dependence on massive Soviet assistance to meet its basic consumption and investment needs. Cuba's general lack of exploitable natural resources, its semi-developed status, and its controversial foreign policies have combined to hamper Havana's ability to generate domestic investment capital or attract Western foreign investment. In recent years, Soviet support has been greater, and perhaps more crucial than ever, because of Cuba's deteriorating foreign payments situation and its ambitious foreign policy intitiatives." Theriot gives the following examples for 1979: the $3 billion in Soviet economic assistance equaled about one-quarter of Cuba's GNP; the Soviets purchased 72 percent of Cuba's $4.5 billion of exports, including 55 percent of Cuba's sugar exports and 50 percent of Cuba's nickel exports; the Soviet Union "accounted for three-fifths of Cuba's $4.7 billion of imports, including all of Cuba's petroleum imports, the bulk of its imported foodstuffs, and a major portion of its capital goods;" and finally, "The $125 million Soviet hard currency purchase of Cuban sugar accounted for about one-sixth of Cuba's hard currency export earnings." (U.S. Congress, Joint Economic Committee. Cuba Faces the Economic Realities of the 1980s. 97th Cong., 2d Sess. Washington, U.S. Govt. Print Off., 1982 p. 17–18.)

bling Soviet political-military conquests elsewhere, as in Eastern Europe and now Afghanistan.

Grenada is a closed case; Nicaragua remains open and perhaps undecided.

With Soviet and Cuban assistance, the Sandinistas in Nicaragua have succeeded in establishing what appears to be a transition regime; but one that looks to Moscow and Havana, not only for protection, but for support, sustenance and guidance. Whether the regime will run the full course of Castroism in Cuba seems an open question at this juncture, according to some observers.

But the Sandinistas' closely established relations with Moscow and Havana, their growing reliance on their military and political support (for bigger and more advanced weapons said to be beyond defensive needs), their harassment of the opposition and constriction of freedom after the November election, professed unwillingness to share political power, suggest to other observers that Nicaragua may be well into the early stages of a transition to Communism reminiscent of the Cubans in the early 1960's and those regions in Eastern Europe before their Communization in 1947–1949.[24] One high-ranking American official described Nicaragua and its Sandinista regime as a country "where the consolidation of a heavily armed totalitarian regime is underway." [25]

The mechanism enabling this transition is a nominal coalition government of leftist to centrist forces varying in shades of political beliefs from Communism to democratic liberalism. For example, the Polish Provisional Government, recognized by the Great Powers in July 1945, had no less than five parties in this nominal coalition--Polish Workers' Party (Communist), Polish Socialist Party, Democratic Party, Labor Party and the People's Party (Peasant). The hard-core radicals—in Eastern Europe, it was the Communists—maintain a monopoly on the enforcement powers of the state by taking control of the police and the military, essentially deny any genuine and meaningful power sharing with their other associates in the coalition, and in the course of time through pressure, harassment and even terror as in Eastern Europe, dispose of their opposition and establish complete control. It is this radical nucleus—the Communists in Eastern Europe and the Castroites in Cuba, supported by the Soviet Union—that ultimately determines the direction and pace of the revolution.[26]

---

[24] For a report on post-election harassment of the opposition in Nicaragua, see McCartney, Robert J. Nicaragua Steps Up Harassment of the Opposition. The Washington Post, Dec. 3, 1984, p. A1.

[25] Sanchez, Nestor D., Deputy Assistant Secretary of Defense for Inter-American Affairs. U.S. Security Interests in Central America and the Caribbean. Speech before the First Annual Latin American Symposium, Montgomery, Alabama, Nov. 16, 1984, p. 3. For a perceptive analysis of the evolution of revolution, especially in Latin America, see Lewis, Flora. The Roots of Revolution: Resistance to a Perceived Tyranny is the Thread Common to All Such Uprisings, Present and Past. The New York Times Magazine, Nov. 11, 1984: 70–78, 82–86.

[26] For a commentary on power sharing in Nicaragua, see Volman, Dennis. A Top Sandinista Commandante Says Nicaragua Cannot Turn into "Another Cuba," The Christian Science Monitor, Nov. 21, 1984, p. 13. This article is based on an interview with Commandante Carlos Nunez, the Sandinista leader in charge of negotiating Nicaragua's political future with opposition leaders. Most revealing of Nunez's thinking is his comment on one sector of the opposition. Asked what they wanted, he replied: "I think they want to force the Sandinistas from power . . . They want to change the revolutionary road for a process which is essentially reformist, like Social Christian political processes throughout Latin America. Basically, they want the disappearance of *Sandisimo* as a real force." He said the Sandinistas would never agree to this because "this

Should a genuine democratic Socialist government evolve in Nicaragua like those existing in Western Europe and elsewhere in the non-Communist world that divests itself of the Soviet connection (for here is the heart of the matter that arouses U.S. security concerns), it is conceivable that the danger and fear of converting Nicaragua into another Cuba would subside. However, if indeed Nicaragua continues along the Cuban course and is converted into another Soviet military stronghold in Latin America, with all its attendant threats to American security, then the ingredients are present for a possible Soviet-American confrontation down the road. At this juncture the choice of which course Nicaragua will take seems to rest largely with the ruling Sandinistas.[27]

The essential point being made here is the dangerous implications of Soviet policy in this Third World area, not only for Nicaragua and its neighbors, but more importantly, for Soviet-American relations. For the issue is regional in only a narrow sense; its primary importance is geopolitical, and it is the Soviet presence that makes it so.

---

would mean the sacrifice of the process, the suicide of the revolution." For insights into the functioning of coalition governments and the transition to Communism, see U.S. Congress. Senate. Committee on the Judiciary. A Study of the Communist Party and Coalition Governments in the Soviet Union and in Eastern Europe. By Joseph G. Whelan, Legislative Reference Service, Library of Congress. 89th Cong., 2d sess. Washington, U.S. Govt. Print. Off., 1966, 33 p.

[27] For an analysis of the November 4 election, see Moore, Patrick. The Nicaragua Elections: Pluralism or Salami Tactics? RFE–RL. Radio Free Europe Research. RAD Background Report/ 197 (Latin America), Oct. 29, 1984, 7 p. This article "exar-ines the political landscape in which voting will take place and concludes that the opposition CDN has good grounds for being wary of the Sandinistas' intentions." According to Moore, the Nicaraguan Democratic Coordinating Council, or Coordinadora (CDN) "in its size and program constitutes the main serious alternative to the FSLN." The Social Christian Party (PSC), the Social Democratic Party (PSD), and the Independent Liberal Party (PLI) had joined with two labor federations and the business and professional organization COSEP to form the CDN. Moore described those three parties as being "liberals to three main centrist parties."

A report by Dennis Volman from Managua on November 6 began, "The election here is over, and no one has been holding his breath as to whether the Sandinistas won." However, he continued, "hopes for a continued political dialogue between the ruling Sandinistas and the political opposition have not been abandoned. And both Nicaraguan opposition leaders and watching diplomats say that a Cuban-type clampdown on political activity is not expected." Volman noted that two main opposition leaders withdrew from the election charging, as he said, that "they were harassed and prevented from making their case during the early stages of the campaign." Foreign electoral observers stressed that the non-participation of the two major opposition parties "robbed the election of much of its importance," but, nonetheless, "the process did have some significance," namely, the opening up of the political system "which occurred during the latter part of the campaign, they say, has been an important one." Hopes for "anything positive" coming out of the electoral process, Volman writes, "rests in the dialogue" which the Sandinistas began a week ago. (Volman, Dennis. After election, Sandinistas Remain Under Pressure to Keep Talking with Opposition. The Christian Science Monitor, Nov. 6, 1984, p. 1.)

However, Arturo Jose Cruz, former Nicaraguan Ambassador to the United States, an opposition leader, and member of the Sandinista Junta, expressed his disillusionment with the Sandinistas whom he expected would "move in a totalitarian direction" but feared that "hasty criticism" might make things worse "by strengthening its stand against the Sandinistas before the people of Cental America were sure of their own attitudes." But Cruz confessed, "Alas, I badly underestimted the vigor with which the newly elected Nicaraguan Government would proceed to repress its opponents and militarize the state." According to Cruz, "The Sandinistas are evidently determined to ignore the democratic yearnings of the Nicaraguan people. They have staged an electoral charade and refused to allow serious opponents to participate. They have begun an open buildup of Soviet arms, pressed ahead with the militarization of Nicaraguan life and resumed their censorship of the country's only free newspaper." (Cruz, Arturo Jose. Managua's Central Problem. The New York Times, Dec. 6, 1984, p. A31.)

For an assessment of political conditions in Nicaragua late in the fall—the continuing shift to the left towards a Marxist-Leninist regime, the strengthening of the Sandinistas, the constriction of liberties and disaffection of Mexico, Venezuela and other Latin American countries along with the Social Democrats of Western Europe—see Chase, James. In Search of a Central American Policy. The New York Times Magazine, Nov. 25, 1984, p. 49–51 and 62.

3. STABILITY IN AREAS OF DIPLOMATIC TRADITIONALISM

In areas where Soviet Third World policy has functioned in the accepted norms of diplomatic traditionalism (as in Mexico and South America, for example), stability has been the prevailing characteristic of the relationship. Accordingly, the implications of Soviet policy appear to be benign compared to the other two regions. The leadership, though distrustful of the Soviets, seems content to maintain normal diplomatic relations, use Soviet political influence when necessary (for example, Argentina in the Falkland War), exploit the Soviet market for their products much needed by the Russians, enlist Soviet assistance mainly in large industrial and energy producing enterprises, and in the case of Peru consider the resumption of arms purchases.

Whatever negative implications there may be, such as, an expanding Soviet presence and influence, would seem to lie in the distant future and probably be determined in large measure by the outcomes of revolutionary developments now enveloping the Central American and Caribbean regions.

4. HEMISPHERIC SOLIDARITY IN A DEMOCRATIC FUTURE

But this absence of a deep revolutionary involvement does not mean that the Soviet Union has written off these stabler areas of Latin America. As noted above, Soviet Third World policy represents an enduring commitment by leaders who, unlike their disillusioned citizenry, are firm believers of Marxism-Leninism. Theirs is a policy geared to the future. It takes into account the correlation of forces, the ebb and flow of history, and the deep-rooted socio-economic and political forces at work in the area that, unless rectified, can make it "ripe for revolution" at some future time.

Effective counteraction to Soviet purposes would seem to lie in the reconstitution of hemispheric solidarity in every respect, accepting the responsibility of a mature community of nations, setting aside historic grievances of the distant past, and building on shared common interests in security and aspiring democratic values.

D. IMPLICATIONS OF SOVIET THIRD WORLD POLICY FOR THE UNITED STATES

1. CONTAINING SOVIET POWER IN CUBA; DIPLOMACY IN CONVERGING INTERESTS

What implications Soviet Third World policy in Latin America has for the United States center mainly on the Caribbean and Central American region. This is the area most vulnerable to revolution, most inviting for Soviet involvement, and important for U.S. national security. Primary U.S. concern is in containing Soviet power in Socialist Cuba and in preventing its spread to Central America.

Socialist Cuba has not only become a Soviet dependency; it has become a formidable base of Soviet power in the Western Hemisphere. The threat to U.S. security stems not from Cuba or its Socialist system per se but from the Soviet connection. The threat lies primarily in the potential challenge this connection represents to vital U.S. sea lanes and to the further projection of Soviet power and influence in Latin America on its own and through Socialist Cuba. This incipient challenge was demonstrated in Grenada and presently seems to be underway in Nicaragua.

U.S. observers of the Latin American scene seem to uniformly agree that protecting these strategic interests requires careful U.S. monitoring of the Russian presence in Cuba, insuring particularly that it not exceed tolerable limits. The inherent dangers of incrementalism, that is, seizing opportunities and employing a tactic of calculated ambiguity ("salami tactics," it was once called in Eastern Europe), complicates the response, places heavy demands on monitoring procedures, and makes the decision to act difficult and uncertain.[28] Implied in this approach is a readiness to use military power as a last resort to check encroachments upon those interests.

Some observers place equal stress on the role of diplomacy in reducing the Soviet connection with Cuba and in attempting to build a new relationship with the United States. Given the depth of Cuban dependency on the Soviet Union today and the likelihood of its continuation, perhaps even being broadened and deepened, prospects seem dim for any diplomatic rapprochement in the near future. Nonetheless, it is conceivable that hemispheric solidarity, reconstituted on a basis of equality and reinforced by a vision of economic progress and improving social conditions, could attract leaders of a post-Castro Cuba. Some influential Latin Americans apparently place considerable stock in this possibility.[29]

Under such conditions, within an evolving convergence of interests, diplomacy and negotiations might finally have their day in reestablishing U.S.-Cuban relations and returning Cuba to its proper place in the hemispheric community of nations. Continuing decline of the Soviet economy, the deterioration of its society under a failing Socialist system, and accumulating Soviet failures in the Third World and in foreign policy generally, could conceivably diminish the appeal of Moscow to a post-Castro generation. And the case of China, seeking modernization in a renewal of ties with the United States, the industrial West and Japan and turning away from their once respected Soviet mentors, indicates that this development is not necessarily utopian.[30]

---

[28] On this matter the Kissinger Commission's Report says: "At the other extreme, clearly any Soviet involvement in the region that poses a strategic threat to the United States is unacceptable. The policy questions are, first, to decide at what point between these two extremes of Soviet involvement [the first being the exclusion of Soviet involvement in Central America altogether which it says "is no doubt impossible"] the balance point of U.S. interests lies; and second, to take those actions necessary to preserve those interests." The Commission established this criterion of acceptability: "The United States cannot accept Soviet military engagement in Central America and the Caribbean beyond what we reluctantly tolerate in Cuba." (p. 122)

[29] Nina M. Serafino, Analyst in Latin American Affairs, Congressional Research Service.

[30] For a critique of current U.S. policy towards Cuba and considerations on the diplomatic option, see Smith, Dateline Havana: Myopic Diplomacy, p. 157-174; LeoGrande, William M. Cuba Policy Recycled. Foreign Policy, no. 46, Spring 1982: 105-119; and Smith, Cuba: Time for a Thaw?, p. 21-25, 54 and 56. For a statement on the Administration's views, see U.S. Rules Out Broader Talks with Cuba for Now. The New York Times, July 28, 1984, p. 3.

2. CHALLENGE OF SOVIET POWER IN NICARAGUA

For the United States, the implications of Soviet involvement in Nicaragua are probably more serious than in the case of Cuba.[31] Bordering on the Caribbean, a Nicaragua with a formidable Soviet presence could jeopardize the security of vital U.S. sea lanes in that region. It could be argued that along the Pacific Ocean and in proximity to the Panama Canal, a Soviet presence could place in double jeopardy vital sea lanes in that area and water passages. The possibility of building a competing Nicaraguan canal (rejected by the United States at the turn of the century in favor of Panama), though apparently remote, underscores still further the gravity of what appears to be a developing Soviet challenge in Nicaragua. (See maps 2, 3, 4, 5 and figure 1.)

On numerous occasions the United States has reaffirmed its historic security interests in Central America. During the recent agitation over the MIG issue, Administration spokesmen emphatically declared that delivery of the MIGs would be unacceptable. Before this incident the United States seemed to pursue a policy of creative ambiguity regarding the level of acceptability in arms shipments. In a press interview on November 27, 1984, his first since re-election, President Reagan, however, restated the principle of unacceptability when commenting on the disclosure of six Soviet ships ladened with arms then en route to Nicaragua:

Well, we have let them [the Nicaraguans] and we have let the Soviet Union know that this is something we cannot sit back and just take, if they do that, because that is so obviously, then, a threat to the area. . . .

And that would be just the crowning thing to have those high-performance planes representing a threat to the area and to the hemisphere. We've made it plain that we're not going to sit by quietly and accept that.[32]

Nestor Sanchez, a high ranking U.S. Defense Department official and authority on Latin America, summed up the rationale behind the President's statement in a speech on November 16, 1984, explaining U.S. security interests in Central America and the Caribbean. On the vital importance of the sea lines of communications in the region of the Caribbean and Gulf of Mexico, he said:

To make Central America and the Caribbean secure, it is necessary to counter and reduce Soviet and Cuban presence and influence. We must maintain the security of the Caribbean trade and sea lines of communication. These are essential to our economic prosperity and national security, and to the well-being and security of our neighbors to the south, and our allies in Europe. We should not forget that in an emergency 95 percent of our reinforcements and supplies will travel by surface ship.[33]

Whether the Soviets are just "testing" the limits of U.S. tolerance can only be speculated. What those limits are, except for the

---

[31] The State and Defense Department's report on the military buildup in Nicaragua concluded: "The Sandinista government represents the first triumph of the generation of Latin American guerrilla fighters trained and unified by Fidel Castro. The ideological orientation and backgrounds of key Sandinista leaders have no question as to why the ideals of Lenin are a 'guiding star' in their struggle.'" The report noted further: "In the opinion of at least two Sovietologists [Jiri and Virginia Valenta], the triumph of the Sandinistas in Nicaragua signaled a milestone in what Moscow considered the progressive transformation of the Caribbean basin, perhaps equal in importance to the victory of Castro in Cuba. In both cases, according to the same analysts, the United States was perceived by the Soviets as suffering humiliating political defeat." (Nicaragua's Military Buildup, p. 12-13.)

[32] Interview. The Washington Times, Nov. 29, 1984, p. 4A.

[33] Sanchez, U.S. Security Interests in Central America and the Caribbean, p. 12.

MIGs, seem at this juncture to be undetermined—at least not publicly announced, particularly when delivery of the MI-24 Hind helicopter gunships, said to be very effective against guerrilla forces, had not been protested. Nonetheless, the Soviets have clearly placed themselves on a collision course that has many of the ingredients for the making of a first class confrontation.[34]

American policymakers, therefore, seem to be facing in the near future a critical moment on a policy that has hemispheric ramifications—indeed, global ramifications in East-West relations—namely, to determine what are the *real* limits of U.S. tolerance as Soviet military supplies continue to pour into Nicaragua, if indeed they do, (as they did in Cuba during the critical months of August and September 1962 before the October crisis), and what is to be done if the Soviets exceed those limits and thus challenge the U.S. position in its own "strategic backyard." Clearly, the Soviets could draw "potentially dangerous conclusions" from the MIG controversy, as one analyst put it, if the United States is construed in Moscow as accepting as criteria for permissible escalation the military cargo actually delivered in the *Bakuriani*. That cargo has given the Sandinistas a "significant new source of firepower" particularly with delivery of the Hind MI-24 helicopter gunships and the Czech-built L-39Z jet trainer whose fighting characteristics for a "trainer" are considerable. In brief, the *Bakuriani* has raised the ante.[35]

---

[34] The speech by Deputy Assistant Secretary of Defense for Inter-American Affairs Sanchez before the First Annual Latin American Symposium on Nov. 16, 1984, provides significant insights into the official U.S. perception of the Soviet buildup in Nicaragua. He described Nicaragua as a country where "the consolidation of a heavily armed totalitarian regime is underway," and "with the support of Cuba and the Soviet Union, is serving as a base for terror and subversion in other countries of the region." Sanchez explained that the "threat in Central America is not *to* Nicaragua. It is *from* the Sandinista regime, and behind it, Cuba and the Soviet Union. The countinuing delivery of arms to Nicaragua, its constant military buildup, and its support for guerrillas and subversion throughout the region threaten not only its neighbors, but challenges U.S. security on our southern and Caribbean flank," Sanchez stated that "Nicaragua's arms inventory is totally out of proportion to anything possessed by any combination of its neighbors." He proceeded to list some of the weapons being delivered. In an effort to draw a comparison to show the stepping up of deliveries, Sanchez noted that, "In 1982, Soviet bloc ships made five military deliveries to Nicaragua. In 1983, they made 20. And so far this year, they have exceeded the 20 of 1983." (U.S. Security Interests in Central America and the Caribbean, p. 3-5.)

For an assessment of Soviet policy in Central America as seen in Moscow during mid-December 1984, see Thatcher, Gary. Soviets Justify Central America Policy. The Christian Science Monitor, Dec. 14, 1984, p. 18. Thatcher begins: "The conflict in Central America may be simmering now, but Soviet experts predict it will be boiling again soon." The "Soviet experts"—all members of the Latin American Institute—are Anatoly Yeletentsev, Ilya Bulichev and Marina Chumakova. In an interview with Thatcher they justify the Soviet position in Central America in line with much of the commentary and analysis presented in this study. For example, they "hotly deny" that Nicaragua has attempted to export revolution to neighboring states; they deny that Cuba is acting as a Soviet military surrogate and insist that "Cuba is a sovereign state and we have no control over what they do"; they deny that the Soviet Union is secretly funneling arms shipments to the Sandinistas through third-party states like Libya and North Korea; and they place the burden of blame on the United States for revolution and disorder in Central America. Thatcher writes: Soviet "Central American policy is no exception [to the rule that it adheres to "Leninist" principles]. Soviet policy in the region is, in effect, self-justifying. The argument goes like this: Revolution is natural and inevitable phenomenon. Those who impede it are involved in a futile exercise. Why not, then, accept the inevitable?" He continues: "That sums up the Soviet view of the Central American conflict, and helps to explain why it is unalterably at odds with US policy in the region."

[35] For a further discussion of the MIG controversy stressing the Soviet reaction and future prospects, see Murphy, Bill. Low-Key Soviet Reaction to Tensions in Nicaragua. RFE-RL. Radio Liberty Research. RL 458/84, Nov. 25, 1984, 4 p. Murphy notes "the caution exhibited by the Soviet Union" that "masked a low-risk strategy of ambiguity and 'gradualism' in the region." The aim of the strategy, he continues, "appears to be to use military assistance to consolidate the regime in Managua and to establish a center of Soviet influence in Central America." The

Continued

By the spring of 1985, evidence suggests an apparent reduction in direct large-scale deliveries of major Soviet military weapons systems to Nicaragua. The report by the Departments of State and Defense published in May 1985 entitled, "The Sandinista Military Buildup," records the last deliveries of MI–24 helicopter gunships and K–8 minesweepers in late 1984. Press coverage of deliveries on the scale of *Bakuriani* episode were notably absent. While this evidence seems to indicate a certain "backing off" by the Soviets in their direct military support to Nicaragua, perhaps in response to expressed U.S. official concern, still it is important to note that Soviet political support remains vigorous and vocal and deliveries in Soviet ships currently run at about the same rate as in 1984. The overall scale of Soviet bloc deliveries of military equipment can be roughly measured by the rise from 6 deliveries (6,700 metric tons) in 1982, to 25 (14,000 metric tons) in 1983, to 37 (18,000 metric tons) in 1984. The State-DOD report concludes that "the total value of the tanks, helicopters, and other material shipped to Nicaragua was approaching $500 million by early 1985." [36]

The gravity of this matter is evident by the fact that, what is being challenged here is not just a simple variation on a policy, but rather the historic tradition of U.S. primacy in an area vital to its security, a tradition that was first established at the founding of the American Republic and rigorously adhered to ever since, particularly in times of great national peril. [37]

---

strategy also "supports Sandinista efforts to stock offensive weapons before a regional arms freeze can be achieved." Murphy observes that the Soviet leadership has probably concluded that Administration officials "have undermined their own credibility as a result of their disjointed handling of recent events. They probably expect that US officials will in the future find it difficult to prevent the Sandinistas acquiring Czech-built L–39Z jet trainers. If this is the Soviet line of thought, it virtually guarantees that MIGs will follow the jet trainers, probably early next year." Murphy believes further that the Soviets could "draw potentially dangerous conclusions" from the fact that in the MIG controversy the U.S. leaders "appeared to be accepting delivery of the military cargo that the *Bakuriani* is reported to have actually delivered": MI–24 helicopter gunships, giving the Sandinistas a "significant new source of firepower" against the Contras and back-up equipment for the Czech-built L–39Z jet trainer. This aircraft, long believed destined for Nicaragua, can carry bombs, rockets and guns and has a combat radius of about 300 miles. (p.4) See also, The Washington Times, August 27, 1985, p. 2A and footnote 48 below on page 437.

[36] Department of State and Department of Defense. The Sandinista Military Build-up. Washington, May 1985, p. 29. (Department of State Publication 9432. Inter-American Series 119.)

[37] Perhaps one of the most visionary American statesmen in the 19th Century who understood the geopolitics of 20th Century America was William Henry Seward, Secretary of State in the Lincoln and Johnson Administrations (1861-1869) and an ardent expansionist. In mid-century Seward foresaw the role that the United States was to play as a great future world power and established the pattern of national expansion that others were subsequently to follow.

A critical aspect of Seward's expansionist efforts was to acquire naval bases and possessions in the Caribbean, Gulf of Mexico and the Central American region. His rationale was strategic necessity and continental expansion. The Civil War experience had particularly spurred Seward in this effort. Successful Confederate blockade runners and the shipment of arms and supplies to European possessions in the West Indies for further trans-shipment to the Confederacy, in defiance of the Federal blockade, exposed a serious vulnerability in the Caribbean, Gulf of Mexico and Central American region and revealed a potential future danger to American security. But Seward's views on the geopolitics of U.S. security extended beyond this region to embrace a much larger strategic conception, one that was evident in his expansionist philosophy and in his efforts as Secretary of State to acquire, among other expansionist enterprises, Hawaii and to build a canal across the Isthmus of Darien in Central America. To further this latter design he concluded a treaty with Nicaragua in 1867, giving the United States canal rights using the Nicaraguan route.

Seward failed in all of his expansionist efforts, except for Alaska. A significant factor in propelling his drive for national expansion in a larger sense was the vision of a great American empire in North America built upon the principles of democracy and the necessity of global commerce. To build and maintain this empire he envisioned required protecting vital sea lines

Adding to the gravity is the lack of a national consensus on policy, indeed, on whether a threat exists at all. Serious minded observers argue forcefully for a political solution through diplomatic negotiations; others with equal force and conviction, but less publicly vocal, tend to stress the military option; while still others emphasize the combination of force and diplomacy.[38]

Uncertainty prevails in many quarters of the Nation on whether U.S. vital interests are really at stake in Central America. Lingering fear of "another Vietnam" in Nicaragua and uncertainty as to the true character of the Sandinista regime and the extent of Soviet-Cuban influence within it seems to hover over this troubling matter, perhaps not paralyzing policy, but making it very difficult, nonetheless, to clearly state American vital interests and have it believed. It is this uncertainty and doubt that has created an opportunity for the Soviets, and they seem to be exploiting it to the fullest measure.[39]

3. DIPLOMACY IN BUILDING HEMISPHERIC SOLIDARITY

The potentially serious consequences of Soviet Third World policy in Central America could compel the United States to rethink its relationship with the whole of Latin America.[40] Whether the Soviets would ever provoke a U.S. military intervention in Nicaragua remains an open question. Arguments have been made by responsible observers that Soviet provocations in Nicaragua are

---

of communications which in turn required possessions in the surrounding oceans and seas as well as an Isthmian canal.

But Seward's extensive design for expanding American power came to naught. A Nation, exhausted by four years of Civil War, was not ready to take on his agenda: It had to await another generation. Near the close of his administration of the State Department, Seward told his hometown friends in Auburn, New York: "Certainly the country is not less now, but is larger than I found it when I entered my last public office." America had "already begun to enjoy the wealth of polar seas," he said, continuing, exclaimed, "I am sure it is not my fault if the flag is still jealously excluded by European nations from the ever verdant islands of the Caribbean sea." (Seward, Works, vol, 5, p. 557. Quoted in, Whelan, Joseph G. William Henry Seward, Expansionist. Rochester, NY, University of Rochester, 1959, p. 214. Unpublished Doctoral Thesis.)

[38] For a comprehensive analysis (with recommendations) of the U.S. response to Soviet Third World Policy particularly in Latin America, see Soviet/Cuban Strategy in the Third World After Grenada: Toward Prevention of Future Grenadas. A Conference Report. Washington, The Woodrow Wilson International Center for Scholars, 1984, 79 p. On the matter of force and diplomacy, the Conference recommended that "The U.S. must continue to be prepared to combine diplomacy and force (direct and indirect) to further foreign policy objectives and to insure security of the United States in the Caribbean Basin." (p. 8) For emphasis on the political solution to problems on Central America, see Chace, In Search of a Central American Policy, p. 49-51 and 62. "The only way to reduce tension in the region, "the author argues," is through demilitarization and encouragement of democracy."

[39] For a commentary and analysis of U.S. security interests in Central America, see the Kissinger Commission's Report, chapter 6 entitled, "Central American Security Issues," For a view from the perspective of the U.S. Navy and the implications of the Soviet-Cuban naval activity in the Caribbean and Gulf of Mexico, see Middleton, Drew. U.S. Officers Report a Buildup by Cuba. The New York Times, March 28, 1983, p. A3.

For a critique of U.S. policy by one of the Soviet Union's leading Latin Americanists, see Mikoyan, S. The Policy of Recklessness. Pravda, June 9, 1984, p. 4, in USSR Report. Political and Sociological Affairs, Nov. 16, 1984, p. 2-6 (JPRS-UPS-84-099). Mikoyan writes that the approach of the Reagan Administration to events in Central America is "amazing in its primitiveness (which, of course, does not make it less dangerous). All revolutions and crises in the world are attributed to 'the mischief of the Soviets.' " Mikoyan asserts, in conclusion, that "The peoples of Central America have understood that their destiny can only be changed by resistance to imperialism and reaction [that is, the United States], by revolutionary actions and unity in their struggle [that is, behind the Sandinistas supported by the Soviet Union and Cuba]."

[40] For a statement on U.S. policy toward Latin America combining all political, economic, national security, diplomatic and social elements, see Sanchez, U.S. Security Interests in Central America and the Caribbena Basin, p. 10-15. See also, Valentas, Soviet Strategy and Policies in the Caribean Basin, p. 244-249. Under a section entitled, "Toward a New U.S. Strategy," the writers examine various options and scenarios as a guide to future policy.

intended to divert U.S. attention and resources from other trouble-some global fronts. Still, if the United States sees its interests seri-ously jeopardized, it may act with the same decisiveness and dis-patch that it had in Grenada, notwithstanding the increased diffi-culty of the mission.

This criteria for the use of U.S. military combat forces to protect vital U.S. interests was officially laid down by Secretary of Defense Weinberger on November 28, 1984 in a speech at the National Press Club that was discussed with the President and cleared by the National Security Council. The first of six criteria, or "tests," was, "the United States should not commit forces to combat over-seas unless the particular engagement or occasion is deemed vital to our national interest or that of our allies." Earlier in his address Weinberger said: "In those cases where our national interest re-quire us to commit combat forces, we must never let there be doubt of our resolution." But he also said that, "The commitment of U.S. forces to combat should be a last resort, and to be used only when other means have failed." [41] This speech was described as "the clearest enunciation of military policy" since the President was elected in 1980. [42]

Nonetheless, diplomacy has a role to play in this prolonged crisis, and it has been recognized by the Administration, particularly the State Department. One aspect of this diplomatic approach is in per-suading the Soviets to desist from their course. Exchanges that occur in normal diplomatic relations and particularly the negotia-tions in Geneva in 1985 on resuming arms control negotiations pro-vide channels to communicate this message. [43] Attempts had been made in the past, notably at the Brezhnev-Nixon summit of 1972, unsuccessfully it turned out, to establish a set of "rules of the game" where risks of confrontation and possible war were readily recognized by both sides.

The other role for diplomacy is in rebuilding hemispheric solidar-ity. What this requires of the United States is a determination, beyond creative participation with the Contadora Group now seek-ing a negotiated peace in Nicaragua, to return to the basic princi-ples of the Clark Memorandum of 1928, the Good Neighbor Policy of the 1930's and 1940's, and the collective security arrangements during World War II and the Cold War. Underlying these princi-ples are assumptions that respect the maturity, independence, sov-ereignty and equality of Latin American nations. Movement to-wards restoring hemispheric solidarity, particularly with a reaffir-mation of these principles, could provide a strong base for dealing with the Soviet threat, not just as an American problem but what it really is, an hemispheric problem.

Reversal of the trend towards a weakening of the inter-American system could serve to focus greater attention on the troublesome

---

[41] The New York Times, Nov. 29, 1984, p. Al, A4–A5.

[42] The New York Times, Nov. 29, 1984, p. Al, A4–A5. With respect to the military buildup in Nicaragua, Michael Burch, a spokesman for the Defense Department, said that the United States would "provide whatever assistance is necessary" to protect its hemispheric interests. Asked if it would include military intervention, he said: "I'm not willing to include or exclude anything." (Time, Nov. 26, 1984: 72.)

[43] Robert C. McFarlane, national security adviser to the President, said that negotiations in Geneva should include also regional issues from Afghanistan to Central America. (The New York Times, Nov. 23, 1984, p. A12.)

economic and social problems in the hemisphere. Manifestations of this changing attitude can be seen in two recent developments. The appeal of the United States among Latin Americans, notwithstanding historic feelings of distrust and often disaffection, remains vigorous. (Latin Americans are the most numerous among recent immigrants to the United States, and their Spanish language second only to native American English.) American economic strength and its political ideals that together command respect and attention in the world are realities that properly managed in a revived inter-American system could constitute a formidable collective deterent to harmful Soviet encroachments in the Western Hemisphere.[44]

But reverting to the positive values and policies of past U.S. diplomacy would not seem to be sufficient. For rebuilding a strong inter-American system requires more than the United States recognizing and accepting the trend towards Latin American independence. It requires Latin America on its part to share a common concern about the long-term Soviet threat in a spirit of interdependence. In the mid-1980's this potential threat seems to be minimized by an attitude in important quarters that invites Soviet participation in their economic progress through trade and technical assistance, and rightly so; but fostering at the same time an attitude that: focuses on the present at the expense of the future; downgrades the darker side of Soviet policy; encourages individual security, while minimizing collective security; fails to address the danger of Soviet involvement in Central America and the Caribbean to hemispheric security; and finally diminishes the importance of a shared responsibility for the safety of the Western Hemisphere.

E. FUTURE TRENDS IN SOVIET POLICY IN LATIN AMERICA

1. PERMANENT OPERATING PRINCIPLES

Future trends in Soviet Third World policy in Latin America will in all probability continue to be shaped by the following perma-

---

[44] In his work on Soviet strategy in Latin America, Leiken concludes with the following prescriptions for policy: "As in the 1930s when another power sought world dominance, the United States must recognize once again the strategic imperative of a Good Neighbor policy. A Good Neighbor policy today must proceed from changed Latin American realities, especially its increased economic and political independence. . . .

"The prospect of new Soviet bases in the Western hemisphere should be of concern to the United States because they would endanger the political independence of Latin America and the logistical support system of the Western alliance. To meet this challenge, the United States must learn to listen carefully to Latin Americans and develop a policy that takes into account local and regional as well as global realities." (Soviet Strategy in Latin America, p. 103.)

The Kissinger Commission stressed the importance of hemispheric cooperation in "meeting threats to the security of the region." The report explained: "The present international framework for dealing with challenges to the mutual security of the Americas is weak. With respect to Central America, the Inter-American system has failed to yield a coordinated response to the threat of subversion and the use of Soviet and Cuban proxies, which have become endemic since the day when the instruments of Inter-American cooperation were first drawn up.

"A modernizing of the regional security system is imperative. Just as there can be no real security without economic growth and social justice, so there can be no prosperity without security. The Soviet and Cuban threat is real. No nation is immune from terrorism and the threat of armed revolution supported by Moscow and Havana with imported arms and imported ideology. The nations of Latin America—and of each of its regions, as is being demonstrated in Central America—have authentic local collective security interests. These should be expressed in new mechanisms for regional cooperation and consultation, and in a commitment to common action in defense of democracy adapted to the special circumstances and interests of the nations affected. Otherwise the temptations of unilateralism will become overwhelming." (p.14)

ment operating principles in Soviet foreign policy touched on in this study but deserving of reemphasis:

— Marxism-Leninism provides the driving energy, goals and purposes, direction and design of Soviet policy. It is the essence of the Soviet commitment whose ultimate purpose, at least theoretically, is the establishment of a future Communist world system.

— Khrushchev's doctrine of peaceful coexistence, laid down in the mid-1950's and radically different from the Western interpretation of the term, provides the rationale, the strategy and tactics for achieving Soviet foreign policy goals in the Nuclear Age. It represents a commitment to globalism, but seeks to avoid nuclear war through diplomacy and negotiations; it calls for concentration on the vulnerabilities of the Third World, and sanctions multiple means for achieving access to power, peacefully or by subversion and revolution. Thus "peaceful coexistence" is not really peaceful, nor is it a pledge to coexist as democracies would understand the term. Rather it is a controversial policy for advancing Soviet purposes in the Nuclear Age.

— The United States, as the leading capitalist power in the world, is Russia's major, indeed "natural," adversary, given their ideology, whose right to life is theoretically untenable and in fact is doomed by the forces of history. Continuous rivalry is insured by the power realities of international life and in the preserving quality of Marxist-Leninist ideology.

— The Soviets have maintained a firm commitment to Cuba for a quarter century, despite a brief period of dispute over tactics, and this relationship has been strengthened by far-reaching military and political arrangements, economic relations that has reduced Cuba to a dependency status, and common action in Third World enterprises including Latin America, Africa and the NAM.

2. PRESENT REALITIES AND FUTURE POSSIBILITIES

All of these Soviet operating principles remain in place at this juncture in the mid-1980's; they constitute the essence of Soviet policy in Latin America; and they are not likely to change radically in the foreseeable future.[45]

There is no available evidence to indicate any serious break in Soviet-Cuban relations for the near term. Continuity in Moscow's

---

[45] The Soviets project an optimistic picture of their prospects in Latin America for the future. In a speech on December 4, 1984 in Prague at a meeting to discuss the work of the international Communist journal, Problems of Peace and Socialism, Boris Ponomarev, top ranking Soviet official and head of international Communist affairs within the CPSU, made this appraisal: "In Latin America a new upsurge in the liberation movement is in evidence, connected with Nicaragua's selfless struggle for independence and the right to free, autonomous development, with the struggle of the Chilean, Uruguayan, and Salvadoran patriots for democracy, with the stepping up of the activity of revolutionary democratic forces, and with progressive development in a number of other countries. Socialist Cuba was and is the bulwark of social progress and anti-imperialist resistance in this part of the Western Hemisphere." (Pravda, Dec. 6, 1984, 1st ed., p. 4, in FBIS 054, take 3.)

reliance on Cuba as an instrument of its Latin American policy seems to be the more likely trend for sometime to come.[46]

Nor does it seem likely that the Soviets will break off their offensive in Central America, the region they have judged to be most "ripe for revolution" and most vulnerable to diminish U.S. influence and power regionally and globally.[47] Incrementalism has served the Soviets well in Cuba over the past quarter century. Using this tactic of stealth and subterfuge, they have escalated their presence and built Cuba into a Socialist stronghold from a small ill-equipped guerrilla force to one of the strongest military regional powers in Latin America. And thus far this tactic of gradualism has proven to be successful in Nicaragua.

Diplomatic traditionalism in the stabler countries of Latin America, from all appearances a reasonable success, seems not likely to change.

Thus, developments in Soviet policy in the near future suggest possibly little variation from its tripartite direction described in this study. Any change in course would seem to depend upon the impact of serious constraints and limitations on Soviet Third World policy noted above, particularly the heavy demands on Soviet foreign policy resources and the overall burden of maintaining an empire stetching from Eastern Europe to Afghanistan and Cuba; the continuing loyalty of Socialist Cuba; the extent, intensity and effectiveness of U.S. counteraction against Soviet thrusts into Central America and the Caribbean; and the strength and effectiveness of a reconstituted inter-American system that is intended to collectively protect and preserve hemispheric interests and deter unacceptable and harmful Soviet encroachments into the Western Hemisphere.[48]

---

[46] For an assessment of Soviet-Cuban relations in the 1980's, see Valentas, Soviet Strategy and Policies in the Caribbean Basin, p. 241. The authors explain the multuality of interests and conclude: "Short of a very unlikely anti-Castro coup, in the 1980s there is probably very little possibility for polarizing change in the Soviet-Cuban alliance. Even Castro's death would not likely lead to profound changes in Cuban policy. His replacement by the number two man, who is Fidel's brother, Raul Castro, would result in Cuba's becoming even more subservient to the Soviet Union."

[47] Secretary Weinberger gave this appraisal in his Press Club speech: "The possibility of more extensive Soviet and Soviet-proxy penetration into this hemisphere in months ahead is something we should recognize." Should this happen, "we will clearly need more economic and military assistance and training to help those who want democracy." (The New York Times, Nov. 29, 1984, p. A4.)

[48] For a commentary on future Soviet policy in Latin America, particularly their caution in dealing with the United States, see Rothenberg, Latin America in Soviet Eyes, p. 17–18.

PART VI—AND THE FUTURE? [1]

The Soviet Union has always supported the struggle of peoples for liberation from colonial oppression. And today our sympathies go out to the countries of Asia, Africa and Latin America which are following the road of consolidating independence and social renovation. For us they are friends and partners in the struggle for a durable peace, for better and just relations between peoples.

—Gorbachev before the Central Committee,
March 11, 1985.

The future belongs to socialism with its concern for the material and spiritual well-being of the popular masses, with its faith in the radiant ideals humanity has cherished and suffered for throughout its history. The future belongs to socialism, whose triumphal march on our planet began in Russia in October 1917.

—New Times editorial, Nov. 1984.

I. DURABLE COMMITMENT TO A VITAL PURPOSE

A. A FIRM COMMITMENT TO THE THIRD WORLD

1. AFFIRMATION OF THE HFAC STUDIES OF 1977 AND 1981

Examination of Soviet involvement in the Third World since 1980, as recorded in the preceding five parts of this study, confirms the correctness of the generalizations set forth in the 1977 and 1981 studies published by the House Foreign Affairs Committee; namely, (1) that the Soviet Union maintains a firm and active commitment to the developing countries of the Third World; and (2) that the Third World holds an important, perhaps even vital, place in the Soviet worldview of contemporary international relations.

2. AFFIRMED IN WORDS AND ACTIONS

The Soviet commitment to the Third World has been an enduring fact of international life affirmed by their words and their actions. As a matter of national policy, this commitment has been affirmed in the words of Soviet political and military leaders and in the writings of Soviet Third World scholars, ideologists and international relations specialists.

It has been affirmed concretely by such activities as,
—The expanding Soviet presence in Asia;
—The deepening Soviet involvement in the wars and politics of the Middle East where they have staked out impressive strategic positions in such critical areas as South Yemen and Ethiopia, areas that oversee crucial sea lines of communications (SLOC) in the Middle East;

---

[1] Prepared by Joseph G. Whelan, Senior Specialist in International Affairs, Congressional Research Service.

—Soviet actions in Latin America, threatening and challenging in Central America and the Caribbean Basin, and only potentially so in their resort to norms of traditional dipolomacy elsewhere in Mexico and the Southern Cone of the Western Hemisphere; and finally,

—Soviet efforts to consolidate their extensive gains in Africa after a decade of political, military and economic expansion in such critical areas as Angola, Mozambique and the Horn of Africa.

The line of commitment is straight, and it is directed toward an ultimate ideological and political purpose; namely, the building of a Socialist international system. Variations occur only in time and place according to the correlation of regional forces within the ebb and flow of history.

What is recorded in this study thus represents an unrelenting Soviet effort to expand from a continental power to one with influence throughout the globe that began with Khrushchev in the mid-1950's and continues 30 years later with Gorbachev in the mid-1980's: Its prime target, the Third World.

B. The Third World in the Soviet Worldview: An Essential Ingredient

1. SOVIET WORLDVIEW, TWO-DIMENSIONAL

The Third World holds a central place in the Soviet view of contemporary international relations. Two elements, affecting Soviet-Third World relations, make up this worldview: the ideological connection between the Soviet Union and the Third World; and the underlying great power dynamics that normally operate in relations between nation-states without regard for time, place, or ideology.

2. THE IDEOLOGICAL ELEMENT

The Soviet worldview is based on the Marxist-Leninist ideological assumption that a symbiotic relationship exists between the Soviet Union and the Third World, a "natural alliance", as the Soviets say, that links both to a common Socialist destiny.

Ideology also establishes a context for policy, as described in Part V of this study. It projects a grand schematic design in which a set of dogmatic beliefs are integrated into a body of time-tested strategies and tactics and into policy analysis and execution.

Moreover, ideology infuses policy with a spirit of elan that can give it staying power after commitment, a cutting edge against adversaries, a cohesiveness binding real and imagined allies, and a tactical flexibility in pursuing established goals.

This ideology assumes a fundamentally uncompromising adversarial relationship with the Capitalist world led by the United States that the Soviets claim is irreconcilable. The concept "Who-Whom?"—that is, "Who will conquer whom?"—reinforces what they presume to be an enduring conflict between Communism and capitalism until the final victory of Communism.

As a central tenet, Marxist-Leninist ideology links Soviet purposes to the historical process. As Soviet Foreign Minister Gromyko said recently, "Socialism is not begging for a place in history. It is history itself. We regret it if someone does not understand this."[2] This is an important concept, for Marxism-Leninism is perceived by believers such as Gromyko to be at once an instrumentality for fulfilling and completing history, and a secular faith which, like ancient Judaism and Christianity, is identified with the fulfillment of man's destiny within the historical process. This idea of mission, expectation, and fulfillment, even though applied within the Communist setting and judged to be erroneous by the democratic West, gives Marxism-Leninism a powerful sustaining force and a unique vitality which past experience with Soviet expansionism attests is hardly a wasting asset. This idea endows Marxism-Leninism with an uncommon preserving quality for it is upon this eschatological belief that rests the legitimacy of the system, the integrity of the institutions upon which it is built, and the vision of a perfected future. In the strength of this idea lies the inner dynamic that gives force and direction, cohesion and durability to the Soviet system and to the pursuit of its presumed shared destiny with the Third World.

And finally there is another aspect to the ideological element; namely, justification of the internal empire. For if Moscow abandons its ideological rationale, it surrenders legitimacy in maintaining the multi-national empire of the continental U.S.S.R.[3]

Thus to the outsider Marxist-Leninist ideology may have serious limitations and may have lost much of its attraction to the Soviet man-in-the-street; but for the ruling elite in the Kremlin it has provided, despite its errors, the essential ingredients for pursuing a vigorous and expanding policy in the Third World.[4]

3. GREAT POWER DYNAMIC

a. The Soviet Union as a great power

The other essential element in the Soviet worldview is the great power dynamic.

The Soviet Union is a great power. As in the case of any great power, it has established major foreign policy goals, and with available resources on hand, though often limited, it has sought to achieve those goals (for example, in the Middle East, to reduce the U.S. presence.) Much of the dynamic energy in Soviet foreign policy issues from its attributes as a great power (geographic size, resources, population, etc.) and its rivalry with the United States, the capitalist West, Japan and other competitors for power like China. The source of this dynamism—the inner kinetic energy that drives Soviet ambitions—lies in the Soviet compulsion to expand its power on the one hand and the determination of its adversaries, in the Toynbeean mode of challenge and response, to resist and contain that expansion on the other.

This interacting dialectic among the great powers can be described in terms of old-fashioned geopolitics. In the global context

---

[2] FBIS 071, Nov. 6, 1984, Take 10.
[3] Stuart D. Goldman, Analyst in Soviet Affairs, CRS.
[4] For a discussion of the uses of history, see, Plumb, John H. The Death of the Past. Boston, Houghton Mifflin, 1970. 153 p.

the United States and its associates seek to maintain an international status quo that permits orderly change without dangerously altering the balance of power and within an acceptable harmony of interests, particularly among the leading great powers. The Soviets seek a directed change, minimally through political action and the proxy use of or intimidation by military power (that is, military assistance, the use of military power for political purposes as in the Berlin crises), and maximally through revolution ("wars of national liberation", for example), if necessary. The ultimate Soviet goal, so they themselves infer as an historical inevitably, is to create a new international Socialist system.[5]

The principal area in contention between the competing East-West powers is the Third World because, as noted in Part I, it is, among other reasons the most politically volatile area in the world and thus the most amenable to revolutionary change. Accordingly, the Third World has attracted the East-West great power competitors as it had in another context, and in another era, during the Age of Discovery and in the subsequent Age of European Imperialism.

What has been taking place on the international scene, therefore, is a great power conflict, not markedly different in essential ingredients from that exsiting is such conflicts of the past as: the rivalry of the emerging nation-states (France, Sweden, the Hapsburg Monarchy of Austria) that brought on the prolonged Thirty Years' War (1618–1648) in Germany; the contests for power among Britain and France, Russia, Prussia and Austria in the 18th Century through the Napoleonic Wars in early 19th Century; the rivalry between the Triple Entente (Britain, France and Russia) and the Triple Alliance (Germany, Austria-Hungary, and Italy) prior to World War I; and the Japanese-American competition for power during the 1930's and early 1940's that finally led to the Pacific War.

Without the element of ideology, the Soviet Union is thus no different from any other great power, (though many observers argue that ideology is central to Soviet policy.) Seemingly, a natural law of international politics imparts to great powers competing values and interests that frequently conflict in an often puzzling, but nonetheless real, dialectic of historical forces.

b. Traditional power-seeking instrumentalities

As a principal actor on the international stage, the Soviet Union, like any other great power, uses traditional power-seeking instrumentalities in achieving its foreign policy goals. However, it uses them in a distinctly Soviet manner, as explained in Part V, that often distinguishes its particular Communist style from that of the West.

Thus the Soviets have built a formidable alliance system constituting Eastern Europe, Communist Southeast Asia, Cuba and certain client states like Iraq and Syria in the Middle East and Ethiopia in Africa. As this study indicates, the Soviets have also tried to

---

[5] For a concrete diplomatic example of conceptual differences between the Soviets and the Americans, see the discussion of the Kennedy-Khrushchev Vienna meeting in 1961, in, HFAC, Soviet Diplomacy and Negotiating Behavior, p. 329–330.

establish a network of friendly associates and clients in the non-Communist Third World. India holds a special place of preference. Political support, military assistance and economic aid have proved to be useful instruments of policy. Afghanistan, Ethiopia and Angola are examples of the Soviet use of military power directly and indirectly for conquest or the expansion of their power and influence.

As skilled goepoliticians, the Soviets highly value mineral resources in the Third World, particularly in Africa, the denial of which to the West could inflict serious economic, and thus political, injury. Accordingly, the acquisition of mineral resources and their denial to the West enter into their calculatiions of Third World policy.

As a naval power with an increasing global reach, the Soviet Union places a high value on crucial sea lines of communications (SLOCs) that transit critical Third World areas. In pursuing a strategy of sea denial, their naval strategy, they have concentrated limited military and naval force projection resources on critical choke-points and passageways in such vital areas as that near the Strait of Malacca in Southeast Asia and the strategically important Tsushima, Tsugaru and Soya Straits in Northeast Asia constricting vital Soviet access through waters surrounding Japan to the open seas (See Part II). They have concentrated on building a strong military presence in Ethiopia and South Yemen both of which hold commanding positions over the Bab-el-Mandeb that connects the vital line of sea communications from Russia proper to the Mediterranean through the Suez Canal to the Red Sea, the Gulf of Aden and on to the Indian Ocean in South Asia, and terminating in the Soviet Far East in the North Pacific.

Thus, the Soviets have taken full advantage of the traditional power-seeking instrumentalities that other great powers have used to expand their power and influence in the world. Indeed, given the largely one-dimensional aspect of Soviet power; namely, military power, and given the freedom of the ruling elite to exercise that power to advance their foreign policy goals, often ruthlessly as in Afghanistan, Hungary, Czechoslovakia and Poland, the Soviet Union may be said to have even improved on those instrumentalities.

But the point being made here is simply this: The Soviet Union is a great power, and it employs the traditional instrumentalities of great powers to attain its ends.

4. IDEOLOGY + THE GREAT POWER DYNAMIC = CONFLICT

The fusion of ideology with the great power dynamic that create the Soviet worldview is a formula for unresolved conflict with the West. For this worldview is a unity of ideas and physical power in which the transending purpose is an irrepressible drive for power and ultimately the conquest of power. The Soviets have said all along, particularly during detente in the 1970's, there can be no "peaceful coexistence" in ideology, meaning that the dialectic of struggle with capitalism goes on as an historical inevitability until the predestined victory of Communism.

The expansion of Russian power is a reality of contemporary international life.[6] As noted in Part V, Dimitri Simes finds the roots of Soviet expansionism largely in Russian history. Marshall D. Shulman, Director of the Harriman Institute at Columbia University, explains Soviet expansion as essentially a behavior normal in all great powers; that is, a belief in the notion that power begets power in an expanding cycle of growth.[7] Brzezinski, as explained in Parts II and V, stresses the one-dimensional aspect of Soviet power; namely, military power, a point of view shared by Simes.

However rationalized and whatever their origins, the fact remains that efforts to expand—physical, political, economic, military or a combination of all—appear to be the driving force in the Soviet worldview; it is *the* engine of Soviet power in which the rational search for a long-term harmony of great power interests often seems to be foreign.

This study of the Soviets in the Third World tends to confirm a view of continued global pretentions. Where efforts to build political, economic and security ties in the Third World have failed, the Soviets have resorted to military power projection. The expanding Soviet presence in Asia is a complex of contradictions that to the outsider does not make sense, except in these terms. In pursuit of a clearly militarized and aggressive foreign policy, the Soviets have in the 80's alienated the Third World nations of Southeast Asia; pushed Japan, a potential asset in the crucial economic development of the Soviet Far East, into a closer alliance with the United States and China; angered Peking, making reconciliation of their conflict, despite some movement in that direction, virtually impossible at this point; encouraged the building of an "anti-Soviet coalition" in the Pacific community; regenerated a U.S. return to Asia; and brought on serious strains with their favorite Third World country, India. In the Middle East and Africa, the Soviets have expanded their influence and power to an impressive degree and now seem to be protecting their investment. And in Latin America, Soviet policy is directed toward expanding its power and influence from what is now a firm base in Socialist Cuba to a Central America they claim to be, "ripe for revolution."

Taking a retrospective glance at Soviet policy toward the Third World during the past 30 years, there is little doubt that the Soviets though they have experienced numerous reverses have indeed made significant strides in their efforts to become a global power. (See map 1 prepared by the Department of Defense, and map 2, prepared by the Congressional Research Service.) And at this juncture in the mid-1980's, they seem firmly committed to staying the course, notwithstanding certain tactical variations here and there.

Yet, Soviet expansionism has provoked opposition among many nations of the world, particularly the United States, which see their interests being threatened. Hence the formula: Soviet ideology plus great power dynamics = Soviet expansionism = conflict with the West.

---

[6] For an explanation of this phenomenon in the context of recent Soviet-American relations, see, Ulam, Adam B. Dangerous Relations: The Soviet Union in World Politics, 1970–1982. New York, Oxford University Press, 1983, 325 p.

[7] Shulman, Marshall D. What the Russians Really Want. Harper's, v. 268, April 1984: 63–71.

400

Map 1

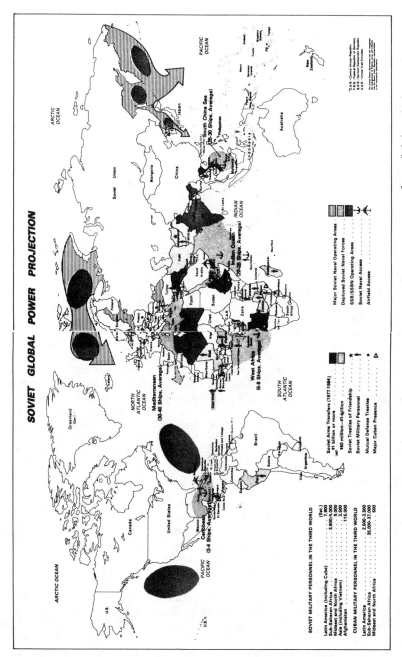

SOVIET GLOBAL POWER PROJECTION

ARCTIC OCEAN

ARCTIC OCEAN

NORTH ATLANTIC OCEAN

SOUTH ATLANTIC OCEAN

PACIFIC OCEAN

PACIFIC OCEAN

INDIAN OCEAN

Soviet Union

China

Mongolia

Japan

Australia

New Zealand

Canada

United States

Greenland (Den.)

Brazil

Argentina

Bolivia

Mediterranean
(30-40 Ships, Average)

West Africa
(5-8 Ships, Average)

Indian Ocean
(20-25 Ships, Average)

South China Sea
(25-30 Ships, Average)

Caribbean
(3-4 Ships, Average)

SOVIET MILITARY PERSONNEL IN THE THIRD WORLD

	(Est.)
Latin America (including Cuba)	7,900
Sub-Saharan Africa	3,800/4,000
Mideast and North Africa	9,000
Asia (including Vietnam)	3,500
Afghanistan	115,000

CUBAN MILITARY PERSONNEL IN THE THIRD WORLD

Latin America	2,500-3,500
Sub-Saharan Africa	35,000-37,000
Mideast and North Africa	500

Soviet Arms Transfers (1977-1984)
≥ $1 billion or more
$50 million—$1-billion

Soviet Treaties of Friendship ★

Soviet Military Personnel ●

Mutual Defense Treaties ●

Major Cuban Presence △

Major Soviet Naval Operating Areas

Deployed Soviet Naval Forces

SSB/SSBN Operating Areas

Soviet Naval Access

Airfield Access

Source: U. S. Dept. of Defense, Soviet Military Power, 4th Edition, 1985, p. 116-117.

Map 2

TERRITORIAL GROWTH OF THE RUSSIAN EMPIRE
AND THE SOVIET UNION, 1261 TO 1964

II. AN IMPERIAL BURDEN OR POLITICAL ASSET?

A. As an Imperial Burden

1. PATTERN OF EMPIRES

Great empires of the past have generally passed through various stages, from their inception and subsequent growth and expansion, to a period of success and prosperity, followed by decline and in some cases total disintegration and even extinction as with Carthage. Such was the general pattern of the Roman Empire, the Frankish, Napoleonic, Austro-Hungarian, Russian, the German Empire of Kaiser Wilhelm and the Third Reich of Hitler, the Japanese, British and the French.

Various causes have been attributed to imperial development in the Modern Age. The rise of nationalism and the emergence of the nation-state combined with the Age of Discovery and the expansion of Europe to set the stage for imperial growth within the European continent and abroad in Asia, Africa and the Americas. In the 19th Century, the impulse for empire, particularly in the United States, was often stimulated and rationalized by the theoretical application of the Newtonian law of gravitation and the Darwinian biological law of growth and decline, and by the Christian principle of "bearing the White man's burden" for bringing backward areas of the world into civilization.

Later on, the Marxist-Leninist synthesis attributed deeper economic forces within world capitalism as the cause of modern capitalist imperialism and colonial expansion. Militarism, nationalism and notions of racial superiority were causes attributed to the rapidly built and short-lived fascist empires of the 1930's and 1940's.

And in the post World War II era a new Socialist imperial system emerged amid the collapse of the old imperial systems of Europe and Japan, driven by the impulse to achieve Marxist-Leninist ideological goals and the great power ambitions of the Russian nation-state. In responding to this challenge, Soviet international relations specialists argue, the United States, as leader of world capitalism, has itself devised an imperial system that has sought to maintain the monopoly of world capitalism over the international economy and to thwart the expansion of world Socialism.

By and large empires have taken on three forms, according to a recent study by Rand: [1]

— "Internal empires," such as the multi-national Russian and Soviet Empires that were built on the conquest of contiguous territories and peoples (see map 2);

---

[1] Wolf, Charles, Jr., K.C. Yeh, Edmund Brunner, Jr., Aaron Gurwitz, and Marilee Lawrence. The Costs of Empire. Prepared for the Director of Net Assessment, Office of the Secretary of Defense. Santa Monica, Calif., The Rand Corporation, Sept. 1983. 66 p. See also, Wolf's article, "Costs of the Soviet Empire," in The Wall Street Journal, Jan. 30, 1984, p. 32.

—"Contiguous empires," as in the 19th Century territorial expansion of the United States and in Russia's present hegemony over Eastern Europe and its efforts to establish control over Afghanistan; and finally,

—"Empires abroad," represented in the Rand definition by varying degrees of control and influence as in the Soviet Union's relationship with Cuba, Vietnam, Angola, South Yemen, Ethiopia, Mozambique, Libya, Syria, Nicaragua and North Korea. A better example of overseas empires in the classic sense are the British and French Empires whose rule and control had embraced many parts of Asia, Africa and the Western Hemisphere.

Certain characteristics have been associated with empire building and empire maintenance. The most important is the use of military power, for the great empires of history were built and often maintained by military power.[2] Costs of empire building have not been especially great in the initial stage and even in periods of quiesence after control had been established as in Pax Britannica of the 19th Century. But the rise of competing external powers, as for example in the rivalry between Wilheminian Germany, Britain and France in Asia and Africa prior to World War I, and the emergence of distintegrative forces within the imperial system, as in the American War of Independence, 1776–1783 and the collapse of the European imperial systems after World War II, increase the costs for the metropolitan power sometimes to the point of unacceptability.[3]

2. BURDEN OF EMPIRE

a. Negative appraisals

The question arises as to whether the imperial burden has become too heavy for the Soviet Union to bear. It is now commonplace in the press, among Western government officials and scholars to consign the U.S.S.R. to Toynbee's degenerative stage of imperial "breakdown."

Herbert E. Meyer, Vice Chairman of the National Intelligence Council, described the Soviet Union in a CIA document prepared for its Director as being "the world's last empire" which after 67 years of Communism "has entered its terminal phase." [4]

Lord Carrington, former Foreign Secretary in the Thatcher Government and presently Secretary General of NATO, spoke of the

---

[2] In his extensive study on technology, armed force and society since 1000 A.D., William H. McNeill, Professor of History at the University of Chicago, explains that armed actions along the periphery of the British, French and Russian Empires "cost them next to nothing." "An amazing fact of world history," he observes, "is that in the nineteenth century even small detachments of troops, equipped in up-to-date European fashion, could defeat African and Asian states with ease." With the development of steamships and railroads supplementing animal packtrains, "natural obstacles of geography and distance became increasingly trival." Accordingly, European armies and navies "acquired the capacity to bring their resources to bear at will even in remote and previously impenetrable places." "As this occurred," NcNeill concludes, "the drastic discrepancy between European and local organization for war became apparent in one part of the world after another." (McNeill, William H. The Pursuit of Power. Chicago, Ill. The University of Chicago Press, 1982, p. 257.)

[3] Rand, Costs of the Soviet Empire, p. 9–12.

[4] Bonafield, Michael J. CIA Says Soviets in "Terminal" Phase. The Washington Times, Sept. 21, 1984, p. 1A.

Russians as "subsiding into a slow crisis because of their system." "The economy and the ideology of communism are moribund," he said, adding,

What we are witnessing in Poland, and imperceptibly in the corpulent body politic of the Soviet Union, is the onset of rigor mortis in a whole system—limb by limb.[5]

Less graphic but nonetheless telling is the assessment by Brzezinski, who in an appraisal of the Soviets in the 1980's writes:

Today the Soviet economy is widely perceived as being, if not in crisis, then at least noninnovative and confronting increasingly difficult Trade-offs. Soviet agriculture is an undisputed failure. The Soviet system generally has lost its ideological appeal, and that, too, detracts from Soviet influence.[6]

In brief, the opinion is widely held, with varying degrees of intensity, that the Soviets are in a stage of systemic crisis, one that begins within the Soviet Union itself—its "internal empire"—as summarized in Part V of this study, and extends to the outer reaches of its "geographically contiguous empire" and beyond to its "empire abroad." Perhaps the only bright sign from Moscow's perspective is its "awesome military machine," as Lord Carrington termed it.[7] Brzezinski corroborates this view in his assertion that "the Soviet Union is a global power only in the military dimension". He maintains that by the 1980's, Soviet military power "had acquired, for the first time, genuine global reach, thus compensating for the lack of systemic appeal." But he cautions, "global reach is not the same thing as global grasp." [8]

Hence the basic question of overcommitment and cost.[9]

b. Rand on cost of Soviet empire

In a complicated economic analysis, the Rand study, an objective weighing of costs and benefits, attempts to estimate the economic costs of the Soviet empire. However, there is this caveat. The Rand analysis tends to accept the cost-benefit assessment of a Western measurement which may not necessarily be that of the Soviet Union. The Soviets view their problems, possibilities and prospects in quite a different context than do the Americans. What may be an unbearable burden to the American, for example, is not necessarily so to the Russian.[10] Readers interested in its details, particu-

[5] Carrington, Peter, the Rt. Hon. Lord Carrington. Look Again: It's the West That's Strong, Moscow That's Weak. Article adapted from the Alastair Buchan Memorial Lecture. In, Congressional Record, May 17, 1983: 3026–3027 (Daily edition).
[6] Brzezinski, Zbigniew. The Soviet Union: World Power of a New Type. In, Hoffmann, Erik P. The Soviet Union in the 1980s. Proceedings of The Academy of Political Science. Montpelier, Vt., Capital City Press, 1984, p. 155.
[7] Carrington, Buchan Lecture, p. 3026.
[8] Brzezinski, World Power of a New Type, p. 151 and 155.
[9] See, Sestanovich, Stephen. Do the Soviets Feel Pinched by Third World Adventures? The Washington Post, May 20, 1984, p. B1. The author is a member of the National Security Council staff. In this article Sestanovich catalogs Soviet Third World commitments and some of their costs. For other commentaries on Soviet weakness, especially in its economy, see, Bialer, Sweryn. Socialist Stagnation and Communist Encirclement. In, Hoffman, Soviet Union in the 1980s, p. 161–176. See also his, "A Wounded Russian Bear is Dangerous," in, The Washington Post, Jan. 22, 1984, p. C1–C2. For other appraisals, see, Dobbs, Michael. The Soviet Empire: Reform or Revolt. The Washington Post, Sept. 12, 1982, p. A1, Dec. 13, 1982, p. A1, and Dec. 14, 1982, p. A1; Kaiser, Robert G. The U.S.S.R.: The Generation That Failed. The Washington Post, Sept. 23, 1984, p. A1, Sept. 24, 1984, p. A1, and Sept. 25, 1984, p. A1; and Chernenko's Nightmare: An Empire in Turmoil. U.S. News & World Report, Sept. 24, 1984: 28–31.
[10] John P. Hardt, Senior Specialist in Soviet Economics, CRS.

larly its complex methodology and criteria, are directed to the full report. However, Charles Wolf, Jr., director of Rand's research program in international economics, dean of the graduate school and participant in the project, summed up Rand's findings in The Wall Street Journal:

Clearly, enormous data problems bedevil these estimates. But the bottom line, even if blurred, is interesting and substantial. In constant 1981 dollars, using official exchange rates, costs of the Soviet empire rose from about $18 billion in 1971 to $24 billion in 1976 and about $41 billion in 1980, an annual growth rate of nearly 9% for the decade. As a proportion of published CIA estimates of Soviet GNP, the costs of empire rose from about 1.1% in 1971 to about 2.7% at the end of the decade, averaging 1.6% over the period. As a ratio to Soviet military spending, they rose from 9% to 19% during the decade, averaging almost 13%.

The picture is even more striking if these data are expressed in rubles rather than dollars. The ruble figures are relatively much larger than the dollar figures when the hard currency parts of empire costs are converted to rubles at realistic, rather than official, exchange rates. (Realistic rates represent the ratios between internal ruble prices and external dollar prices of Soviet hard-currency imports during each year of the past decade.) Expressed thus in rubles, which the Soviets use for the bulk of their economic activity, the costs of empire rose from 1.8% of Soviet ruble GNP in 1971 to 3.6% in 1976 and 6.6% in 1980, averaging 3.5% for the decade. As a ratio to Soviet military spending, in rubles the costs rose from 14% in 1971 to 28% in 1976 and 50% in 1980, averaging 28%. The annual average growth rate of the ruble costs of empire was more than 16% for the decade.[11]

Whether the costs of the Soviet empire are large or small depends upon the criterion adopted, according to Wolf. But the ultimate criterion, he notes, is not economic, but political and strategic. Unfortunately, this criterion is "the least measurable." It encompasses both tangible elements such as bases in Cuba, Vietnam and elsewhere, that increase Soviet military effectiveness, and the less tangible, but perhaps more important elements such as international political prestige, Russian national pride, intimidation/deterrence value and the quest for systemic and political legitimacy.[12]

c. Noneconomic costs of empire

Afghanistan is perhaps the most serious case to illustrate what Wolf calls the non-economic costs of empire. The Soviet invasion and subsequent efforts to conquer Afghanistan, it will be recalled from Part II, have had a multidimensional effect in which the Soviets have had to pay a heavy but immeasurable political price. In response to the invasion, the United States reversed its policy of essentially global retrenchment after Vietnam. It reassessed its global position; undertook a deeper commitment in the Middle East, Asia and the Western Pacific; expanded its military budget at a progressively accelerated rate since 1981; and shelved SALT II and other agreements that issued from the period of detente. In the prolonged aftermath of Afghanistan, Soviet-American relations worsened, and the Soviet world position suffered a serious setback. Afghanistan also cost the Soviets substantially in Western Europe.

The invasion and the continuing protracted Soviet attempt to subdue the Afghan guerrillas alienated most of the Muslim world, placed further strains on Sino-Soviet relations, antagonized a usu-

---

[11] The Wall Street Journal, Jan. 30, 1984, p. 32.
[12] Ibid.

ally friendly India, and pushed Japan and the ASEAN nations of Southeast Asia into a closer relationship with the United States and China. The overall effect of Soviet policy in Asia—for the invasion of Afghanistan was only one aspect of a larger militarization of Soviet policy—was to accelerate formation of an anti-Soviet coalition in Asia and seriously dampen any Soviet hopes for expanding its influence in this Third World area.

Examination of this entire study will reveal other non-economic costs to the Soviets, perhaps not so burdensome as that in Asia, but costs, nonetheless.

3. EFFECTS OF THE IMPERIAL BURDEN

a. The reality of a heavy burden

Thus there are weighty economic costs imposed upon the Soviet Union in their pursuit of empire. The burden of its "internal empire" can be inferred from the general assessments by specialists on the weakened state of the Soviet economy and the need for reform particularly when facing, as it now does, prospects for a renewal of the arms race with the possible result of further spiralling arms costs.[13] The burden of its "contiguous empire" in Eastern Europe can be inferred similarly by the negative appraisals of specialists who uniformly report on the declining state of the East European economies and the erosion of their loyalties to Moscow.[14] And then the burden of the "empire abroad," estimated by Rand's scholars, adds to the total imperial burden.

Specific costs of Soviet involvement in Afghanistan, Vietnam and Cuba, variously estimated and recorded in this study, suggest at least in a very general way the heavy burden the Soviets are bearing. Economists have argued that the Soviets can, for example, bear the economic burden of supporting Cuba. This may be true of Cuba, and perhaps even of Afghanistan and Vietnam. But these enterprises have demonstrated that they are not, thus far, economically cost-effective, and over a prolonged period of continuing stress (for there seems to be no light at the end of these tunnels), the burden could be too much, particularly if economic stress in the "internal empire" goes unrelieved without reform. Historical anal-

---

[13] Observes have speculated that Soviet willingness to engage in current arms negotiations with the United States is largely due to the cost of a continuing arms race, especially in space. Negative appraisals of the Soviet economy have been fairly consistent. For example, Bialer writes: "The profound economic, social, and political problems that Brezhnev bequeathed to Andropov and Chernenko represent the cumulative effects of the inherent weaknesses in the basic Soviet structures. The most immediate problems facing the Soviet Union are in its economic structure. Without decisive action by Chernenko (and now Gorbachev), the situation promises to become even more acute as the 1980s progress." Bialer later concludes: "Internal decline will surely continue or even accelerate during the remainder of the 1980s." (Socialist Stagnation and Communist Encirclement, p. 160-161 and 175.)

[14] For a commentary and analysis of the current state of Soviet-East European relations, see, Gati, Charles. East Europe's Communists Are Tugging at Russia's Leash. The Washington Post, July 8, 1984, p. D1 and D2. Gati, a specialist in Soviet and East European affairs at Union College and Columbia University, writes: for the East European countries "the continuation of European detente—regardless of the climate of U.S.-Soviet relations—is essential to political stability, and perhaps even to their political survival. With drastic cutbacks in Soviet economic subsidies already underway, these countries desperately need close economic relations with the West to avoid lowering living standards and risking domestic unrest." He concludes: "The political winds appear favorable for gaining a measure of independence." Brezezinski develops the same theme in, The Soviet Union: World Power of a New Type, p. 158, and Ulam in, Dangerous Relations, p. 310.

ogies such as, the costly French commitment in the American Revolutionary War that contributed to the economic forces bringing on the French Revolution, British support with limited resources for its weakened imperial system in the post World War II era, and the social, political and economic cost of U.S. involvement in Vietnam, suggest that there are limits of tolerance even among great powers: sometimes the price can be too high, especially when the commitments provoke opposition within the metropolitan base.

At this juncture in the mid-1980's there seems to be no easing of the Soviet imperial burden; it may even be increasing. Soviet specialists, aware of this pressing burden, have indicated an unwillingness to take on "another Cuba" in Central America. And the thrust of thinking among Soviet Third World specialists, as noted in Part I and treated in detail by Valkenier, suggest an awareness at least among some Soviet scholars, of economic limitations on Soviet involvement in the Third World. Recent Soviet leadership appears to have accepted their arguments but the degree to which they have been acted upon seems to be only selectively recorded.[15]

And then there are the non-economic costs to the Soviets. While these costs cannot be quantified in any measurable way, still data presented in this study suggest that the Soviets have had to pay a high price for whatever success they may have already achieved in the Third World.

b. Imperial burden as a limitation on expansionism

There seems little doubt, therefore, that expansionism has imposed a heavy cost on the Soviet Union. Hence it is reasonable to conclude that the cost of empire can impose constraints on the Soviet commitment to and involvement in the Third World, particularly for the remainder of the 1980's, in light of the serious state of the Soviet economy and the extensive Soviet commitment to the Third World. Again, it is worthwhile underscoring Valkenier's observations and those Soviet sources cited in Part I along with Hough's that suggest a Soviet awareness of these economic constraints and their search for burden-sharing options. Though the Soviets extend much largesse in military assistance to the Third

---

[15] Jerry Hough, a close observer of debate within the Soviet scholarly community on Third World matters, writes: "In the Third World, the Soviet Union has suffered a series of defeats. Countries far behind in industrialization have proven susceptible to very radical revolution, but those countries that have begun to industrialize seriously have all been moving to the center or the right, including India, Egypt, the major countries of Latin America, and even Iran. These countries need Western investment, and economies with strong markets have by and large proven more successful in industrializing than countries without them. The Soviet scholarly literature over the last twenty years has featured a major debate on the course of Third World development. Those scholars and officials who have been pessimistic (from the Soviet point of view) gradually have been becoming more dominant in the debate, and in the Andropov period the leadership essentially accepted their arguments. In a series of ways it signalled its willingness to cut back commitments." (Rethinking the Soviet-American Relationship, in, U.S.-Soviet Relations: Perspectives for the Future. Washington, Center for National Policy, Sept. 1984, p. 32.) Further insight into Soviet concern for the Third World burden was revealed in an interview with an unnamed Soviet Colonel by an unnamed correspondent in Moscow that was published in a British journal. In reply to the interviewer's statement that "The Soviet Union does at least seek to expand its influence in the Third World," Colonel "X" stated: "We still feel alone in a hostile world, and naturally we look for allies. But these allies, or clients, are extremely expensive for us to maintain. If detente is made secure, I do not think we shall be so keen to collect new clients." (Leeds Detente in English No. 1, Oct. 1984, p. 2-3, in, FBIS 052.)

World where they are strongest, they are far more constrained in economic assistance where they are weakest.[16]

Accordingly, the burden of empire can be added to other constraints on Soviet expansionism, many of which are noted in this study.[17] Geography imposes limitations on the extent of their involvement in Latin America and the degree to which they can be a prime actor in the Pacific, at least in extremis, owing to distances from their European base of power. It is important to recall also the constraints on the global reach of the Soviet Navy that for all its significant achievements in the past three decades still faces such operational limitations as a need for bases.[18]

[16] In discussing Soviet military assistance to the Third World, CIA Director William J. Casey said that "the Soviets have become the world's leading supplier of arms. Over recent years, their arms shipments to the Third World have been four times greater than their economic assistance. Casey continues: "Yet the Soviet Union is crippled. It is crippled in having only a military dimension. It has not been able to deliver economic, political or cultural benefits at home or abroad. Without exception, the economic record of the countries which have come under Soviet influence has ranged from poor to very poor." (What We Face. 40th John Findley Green Foundation Lecture, Westminister College, Fulton, Missouri, Oct. 29, 1983, p. 10.)

With respect to Latin America, Duncan writes: "In assessing the overall limit to Soviet influence in Latin America, a simple but major point needs to be made: The Soviets are constrained greatly in how far they are willing to go in supporting revolutionary regimes in Latin America in both economic and military terms. In light of their past economic record (Chile under Marxist-Leninist president Salvador Allende; Nicaragua to date), the Soviet are quite unprepared to engage in 'another Cuba.' They cannot afford it, and the record of economic and political 'payoffs' for them in terms of past aid recipients has been marginal at best." (Soviet Interests in Latin America, p. 184.)

[17] Brzezinski writes: "The Soviet Union is a new type of world power in that its might is one-dimensional; thus it is essentially incapable of sustaining effective global dominance. The fact of the matter is that the Soviet Union is a global power only in the military dimension. It is neither a genuine economic rival to the United States nor—as once was the case—a source of a globally interesting ideological experiment. This condition imposes a *decisive limitation* on the Soviet capability to act in a manner traditional to world powers or claimants to the status of world power." (Underlining added. The Soviet Union: World Power of a New Type, p. 151.)

Hough writes: "Economic power has become progressively more important . . . In the Third World . . . the industrializing countries have a need for foreign investment and a private sector if they are to prosper economically, and these two factors severely limit the ability of Third World countries to follow a radical or totally pro-Soviet path. The Soviet Union simply cannot afford to bankroll many more Cubas or Vietnams." (Re-thinking the Soviet-American Relationship, p. 38.)

With respect to Latin America, Duncan states that the Soviet Union is "substantially constrained in the actual influence that it exerts in Latin America." He believes that "The Soviets appear careful about where and how they become involved and under what conditions. They seem to be aware of limitations and constraints to their power in Latin America. And the limits to Soviet power are there." (Donaldson, ed., Soviets in the Third World, p. 17 and 13.) The Grenada episode dramatized the limits on Soviet power in the Western Hemisphere. Gromyko seemed to underscore this point in a meeting with Maurice Bishop, Prime Minister of Grenada at the time. The meeting took place in April 1983. According to a Grenadian document recently released, Gromyko "warned the Grenadians to move carefully in their revolutionary expansionism so as not to signal their plans to the 'imperialists' ", seeming to imply that the Grenadians were on their own. (Brinkley, Joel. U.S. Says Russians Try to Make Satellite of Central America. The New York Times, Feb. 10, 1985, p. 1 and 11.).

[18] For an examination of the role of the Soviet Navy in foreign affairs, see, U.S. Congress. Senate. Committee on Commerce. Soviet Oceans Development. 94th Cong., 2d sess., Washington, U.S. Govt. Print. Off., 1976. "Political-Strategic Framework for Soviet Oceanic Policy" by Dr. John R. Thomas (pp. 23–46), and "Historical Continuity in Russian Soviet Oceans Policy" by Nicholas G. Shadrin pp. 47–182). Other chapters in this document provide insights into Soviet oceans policy particularly as it relates to foreign policy. See, for example, Michael MccGwire's chapter entitled, "Naval Power and Soviet Oceans Policy," (pp. 79–182). With respect to constraints on the Soviet Navy, MccGwire writes: "In 1973, Admiral Sergeev, Chief of Naval Staff, was asked by a Western naval attache what his greatest problem was as the result of the shift to forward deployment. He replied without hesitation: 'Bases'." (p. 146) Thomas points out "political dilemmas and strategic dangers which may limit the benefit the U.S.S.R. may derive from new status as an oceanic power." For example, as a seapower the Soviets have developed a vested interest on oceanic issues such as preserving unrestricted passage of straits and limiting the expansion of territorial water claims, a posture that could put them in conflict with some LDC's. Strategic dilemmas arise from ambiguities inherent in the "two-front threat": that is, the threat from Germany in Western Europe and China in the Far East which could also have a constraining effect. For these reasons, Thomas concludes: "It would seem appropriate for the

Continued

To this constraint can be added the fact that nations of the Third World, as noted in this study and the two preceding ones, seek their own interests and not those of the Soviet Union (or the United States). And, as in the case of Indonesia, Egypt and Somalia, and even India, they will forsake the Soviets when their interests require it.[19] Added to such uncertainties and the sheer magnitude of the problems facing the Third World are the declining appeal of Marxist-Leninist ideology and the Soviet model of economic development in the Third World, and in contrast the growing attraction of adaptations of Western and Japanese capitalism as seen, for example, in the dramatic economic success of South Korea, Taiwan and the ASEAN countries.[20] Nor can the Soviets depend upon the unquestioned loyalty of ruling and non-ruling parties within the international Communist movement. Moscow continues to press for greater international Communist cohesion in some form giving increasing Soviet control either organizationally or through the holding of an international conference such as the

---

United States to take note of both the Soviet achievements and constraints so that it neither underestimates nor overestimates Soviet capabilities on the oceans to the detriment of its own interests." (p. 22, 32 and 36–37).

Recent studies on Soviet naval power have stressed their efforts to overcome constraints imposed upon them. John M. Collins, Senior Specialist in National Defense, CRS, writes in his 1980 study on the U.S.-Soviet military balance, "Stress on conventional power projection and sea control seems to be increasing, but current capabilities are most suitable for small-scale activities in lightly-contested areas. The Soviet Navy has not yet produced credible wartime capabilities to protect its own sea lines of communication against attack by a first-class power. Underway replenishment capabilities to offset the shortage of secure overseas bases are still insufficient to support sustained combat operations in remote regions." (Collins, John M. U.S.-Soviet Military Balance: Concepts and Capabilities, 1969–1980. New York, McGraw-Hill, 1980, p. 251.) In his most recent appraisal of the military balance, Collins notes Soviet emphasis on limited sea control applied to the Arctic Sea and the Sea Okhotsk in contrast to previous concerns for sea denial. On the improvements in the Soviet Navy Collins states: "Qualitative progress presently is more evident than quantitative expansion." (Collins, John M. The U.S.-Soviet Military Balance, 1980–1985. New York, Pergamon-Brassey's, 1985, Mss.)

In an over-all appraisal of constraints on the Soviet Navy, John Allen Williams, Loyola University of Chicago, writes: "An overriding constraint . . . when considering Soviet naval missions concerns geography. The Soviet navy is divided into four fleets; they can reinforce each other only with great difficulty, and all must pass through areas controlled by the United States or its allies to reach the open sea. These geographical restrictions are compounded by several facts: Soviet ships have had limited endurance and weapons reload capabilities, the resupply system is inadequate for a long war, and currently no high performance aircraft are available to naval forces once they are beyond the (considerable) range of land-based Soviet naval aviation—itself subject to interdiction by allied forces." For these reasons a former commander of the U.S. Sixth Fleet observed that it was this dependence on shore bases close to home that causes Western analysts to describe the Soviet navy as "defensive" in nature. "It has limited capability," he said, "to project its influence and power over long distances or for long periods of time, and to truly control the sea." (Williams, John Allen. The U.S. and Soviet Navies: Missions and Forces. Armed Forces & Society, Summer 1984: 517.)

[19] For a discussion of such limitations on Soviet policy in the Third World, see, HFAC, Soviet Union and the Third World, 1977, p. 148–154, and HFAC, Soviet Policy and United States Response in the Third World, 1981, p. 123–132.

[20] This idea has virtually become a commonplace in the literature on Soviet activities in the Third World. For example, Donald Southerland wrote in 1983: "The Soviet economic model, whose failings are now obvious to all, fails to inspire. In the third world, any number of nations have turned quietly to the U.S. for investment and economic cooperation, having failed to see any economic payoff from close relations with the Soviet Union. The small West African nation of Guinea, which ended up getting Soviet tractors more suited to Siberia than to the African heat, is a prime example." (US Approaches Limits of Superpower Clout. The Christian Science Monitor, April 27, 1983, p. 18.) This matter was extensively discussed at the Stanley Foundation's 25 Annual U.S. Foreign Policy Conference, Oct. 11–13, 1984, by specialists on Soviet Third World affairs. The conference report states: "The Soviet economic model . . . has been largely discredited by most of the Third World . . . it has great short- and long-term costs, and does not always work." (Strategy for Peace. 25th Annual U.S. Foreign Policy Conference Report, Oct. 11–13, 1984. Sponsored by The Stanley Foundation, Muscatine, Iowa, p. 23.)

last one in 1969. But it continues to meet resistance.[21] Correlated with this rejectionist view is the further reality that the transcending historical trend in the Third World since 1945 has been towards independence and not re-submission to imperial control.

A final constraint is the growing strength of the United States and its willingness to contest Soviet power and become involved in the Third World as the Nation's interests require. The United States has been playing an active role in the politics of southern Africa; it has remained firm in its deep commitments to the Middle East; it has revealed a clear desire to take a forward position among the Pacific community of nations in a return to Asia after suffering a serious setback in Vietnam; and it has left no doubt in Moscow's mind of its vital interests in Central America and the Caribbean region.

There seems little doubt, therefore, that the Soviets bear a heavy imperial burden and face formidable obstacles in the pursuit of their Third World policy.

B. As a Political Asset

1. REASONABLE JUDGMENTS

There are, nonetheless, political assets accrued by the Soviets from their expansion into the Third World that may offset certain aspects of the imperial burden. For as Wolf notes, the ultimate criterion is not economic but political and strategic. Clearly, this criterion, as Wolf adds, is not "measurable" as in the case of the economic, but such imprecision would not seem to rule out reasonable judgments that can be deduced from given realities. Still, it must be borne in mind that international politics is subject to constant change, in varying degrees of magnitude: What seems to be a liability or cost one day can be an asset or gain the next.

2. EXPANDING SOVIET PRESENCE IN ASIA

a. Military assets in Northeast Asia

More than any place else, it could be argued that the Soviets have traded off political, economic, and diplomatic advantages in return for strategic benefits of their expanding military presence in Northeast Asia (See Part II). Never in Soviet history have the Russians achieved such a presence in Asia as they have by the 1980's. By their extensive military buildup in Northeast Asia—the driving force of their expansionism—they have appreciably strengthened their position against China, giving Moscow greater intimidating and deterrent capability against Peking (and military resources in place should an attack come from that quarter), and improving its negotiating position in the on-going talks ostensibly intended to "normalize" relations. Furthermore, the buildup of strategic and

---

[21] The Soviet World Outlook, v. 9, Oct. 15, 1984, p. 6-7. For a report of the 91-party Prague meeting to discuss the work of the World Marxist Review in which opposition to a world conference was apparent, see, Devlin, Kevin. New Moves for a World Communist Conference. RFE-RL. Radio Free Europe Research. RAD Background Report/221 (World Communist Movement), Dec. 20, 1984, 13 p. Devlin notes that the Italian, Yugoslav, Japanese and French Communist Parties have already made it clear that they would boycott such a world conference.

naval forces around Japan and the North Pacific has enhanced Soviet ability to intimidate Japan politically and contain the potential expansion of Japanese power militarily, while simultaneously acting both as a deterrent and a threat to the United States in the Western Pacific.

b. Benefits accrued in Southeast Asia

Deep Soviet involvement in Indochina, notably in Vietnam, has also had its political and strategic payoffs. From this position the Soviets have been able to "round out" their efforts to contain China in the south, clearly a target in its broader Asian strategy. But equally important, it has given the Soviets a potentially significant position near the strategically vital SLOCs around Southeast Asia through which courses the main sea traffic from the Middle East to Northeast Asia. Granted ASEAN has achieved great economic success, to the embarrassment of Russia's Indochinese allies, and it also has in the making an "anti-Soviet coalition." But there are soft spots in Southeast Asia, notably in the Philippines where internal disorders could create future opportunities for Soviet mischief and potential political and strategic gains.

c. Political yield in South Asia

In South Asia, India remains a close associate and continuing useful political instrument as leader of the Non-Alignment Movement (NAM), despite New Delhi's visible but momentary irritation over Afghanistan. The Soviets remain firmly in place in the subcontinent. And while the issue of Afghanistan remains unresolved to Moscow's disadvantage, the Soviets have adjusted to a long-term strategy that could eventually wear down the guerrillas and lead to a pacified Afghanistan firmly under Soviet control. (Clearly, Afghanistan no longer prevents improvement in Soviet-American relations or even Sino-Soviet relations. Hence, this liability has been lessened, though complete "normalization" has not yet been achieved.)

Military success in Afghanistan could give the Soviets a secure southern border, insulating their own Soviet Muslims from an intruding and potentially disruptive Muslim Fundamentalism. It could also improve the possibility of annexing like ethnic territories adjoining the Soviet border, thus reducing any potential threat from Afghanistan in the future. And finally it could strengthen Moscow's political and strategic position in dealing with Iran and in penetrating the oil-rich Middle East.

In brief, the Soviets may have paid a high price for expanding their presence in Asia through direct and indirect application of military power. But there appear to have been important political and strategic compensations.

3. BENEFITS FROM THE MIDDLE EAST

a. On being an active participant

In the Middle East certain notable political and strategic benefits continue to flow in the direction of the Soviet Union, though they have experienced some setbacks. (See Part III). As a principal great power competitor, the Soviet Union has played the role of an active participant and a spoiler in the politics of the region. By pursuing an essentially cautious policy, carefully avoiding confrontation with its chief adversary, the United States, the Soviet Union has succeeded in maintaining, perhaps even expanding, its power position and drawing accordingly substantial political and strategic dividends as a result.

b. Evidence of political assets: Syria, Iraq, Libya

In bordering Iran, the Soviets realized substantial political and strategic gains after the fall of the Shah and the victory of Khomeini in 1979. These gains were brought about not necessarily by their own actions, but rather by being the beneficiary of events beyond their control that led to the virtual elimination of the U.S. presence and influence in Iran. Continuing instability in Iran, moreover, increases the potentiality for further Soviet gains. To date, however, the Soviets have been unable to increase their influence in Iran.

Stresses and strains have characterized recent Soviet-Iraqi relations. They issued from the debilitating and indecisive Iraqi-Iranian War and from Iraqi efforts to lessen its dependency on Moscow by turning to the West for arms. Nonetheless, the Soviets continue to maintain their essentially privileged position in the country. Moreover, they remain firmly ensconced in Syria, despite the momentary Syrian setback in the Lebanese war of 1982. Renewed material and diplomatic support along with expanded arms transfers and military commitments, particularly delivery of the sophisticated high-altitude SA–5 missile with Russian crews, amounted to a clear declaration of intention that the Soviet Union is in Syria to stay.

Soviet relations with Libya remain closely bound in arms sales that benefits the Soviet Union considerably, particularly in gaining much needed hard currency and in furthering their long-term aspirations for bases in the Mediterranean. Libya's persistent anti-American and anti-Western posture, along with its vigorous role in the NAM, have been proven assets for the Soviet Union in international politics.[22]

c. Geopolitical gains in South Yemen

Geopolitics has been the principal driving force behind Soviet policy in the Middle East, and the benefits derived have been geopolitical. Nowhere has this been better demonstrated than in South Yemen, formally called the People's Democratic Republic of Yemen (PDRY). For the Soviet Union, South Yemen is undoubtedly its most valued political and strategic asset in the Middle East, well worth the expenditure of its limited resources. Consider the following. The PDRY:

---

[22] Egypt, once a close ally before the Soviet expulsion, has in the post-Sadat period broadened its foreign contacts, including with Moscow. The latter effort was designed primarily to ease its reintegration into the Arab world. Egypt remains resolutely pro-United States and sees its interests tied with it. (Michael J. Dixon, Research Analyst in Soviet and East European Affairs, CRS.)

—Serves as a bridgehead for Soviet involvement in northwest Africa and the Arabia Peninsula;

—Acts as the principal staging area for Soviet military penetration in the Horn of Africa and the northwest quadrant of the Indian Ocean since the loss of Berbera in Somalia; and

—Provides port facilities for the Soviets at Aden, a base at Khormaksar (used as staging areas for Soviet and Cuban troops dispatched to Ethiopia), anchorages at Socotra in the Gulf of Aden and at the island of Perim in the Bab el-Mandeb strait (a vital chokepoint in the traffic from the Mediterranean, through the Suez canal, down the Red Sea, and on the seas and oceans to the East), and numerous airfields for reconnaisance over the Indian Ocean and the Horn of Africa. These privileges and facilities enabled the Soviets to successfully support Ethiopia in its war with Somalia during 1977–78. Their value has been further enhanced by the increased attention given to the Arabian Peninsula and Persian Gulf region.

The large Soviet presence in North Yemen (Yemen Arab Republic) is further evidence of a successfully unfolding policy. The North Yemenis have seen their interests served by maintaining a security relationship with Moscow. The USSR supplies a large portion of the North's arms supplies and military training. In October 1984, the U.S.S.R. renewed a 1964 Treaty of Friendship and Cooperation with North Yemen, a development that ensures the continuation of the Soviet presence.[23]

In this resource-rich Middle-East region of the Third World, intersected by strategic crossroads vital to world communications, the Soviets have thus gained considerable political and strategic assets. These assets do not appear to be wasting at this juncture in the 1980's; but rather they seem to be building blocks for a much larger inter-related regional structure designed for projecting Soviet power and influence in the Middle East, Asia and Africa.

4. CONSOLIDATING GAINS IN AFRICA

a. Geopolitical focus

Africa is an important segment of the larger Soviet geopolitical design for the Third World, and their concentration on the Horn of Africa and activity in such resource-rich and strategically important countries as Angola, Mozambique and Namibia, suggest clear geopolitical purposes (See Part IV). Soviet interests in Africa are principally geostrategic; they are determined by efforts to overcome limited access to the oceans and a long-term denial of valuable mineral resources to the West.

b. Ethiopia: A major geopolitical gain

Soviet success in winning and now consolidating their position in Ethiopia can be regarded as a political and strategic gain of the first magnitude. South Yemen and Ethiopia bestride the critically important chokepoint at the Bab el Mandeb strait which courses the sea routes from the Black and Mediterranean Seas, through

---

[23] Michael J. Dixon, Research Analyst in Soviet and East European Affairs, CRS.

the Suez Canal, the Red Sea, the Indian Ocean and on to Asia. This is a vital Soviet SLOC, connecting European Russia with their accessibly limited Soviet Far East. From its position in Ethiopia, the Soviets can also build political pressures against pro-Western Saudi Arabia, the Sudan, Oman and even Kenya. Close proximity to the Persian Gulf could enable the Soviets in Ethiopia, moreover, to interdict oil shipments in the event of hostilities, at least initially. Ethiopia's strategic value was clearly proven when the Soviets used it as a base for ferrying weapons to Angola during its on-going civil war and in its conflict with South Africa.

Thus Ethiopia serves both Soviet regional and global interests. The political and strategic payoff represents an unmeasurable value to Moscow for which it seems all too willing to pay the price of underwriting the Mengistu regime in this impoverished Third World country.

c. Naval assets in South Atlantic

Much the same can be said for such benefits the Soviets gain by their presence in West Africa. With their naval assets in the South Atlantic, for example, they could in the short term threaten the sea routes around the Cape of Good Hope, an important commercial link and SLOC uniting the West to allies in the Persian Gulf region and the Far East. The Cape SLOC is the most heavily trafficked sea route, particularly for supertankers delivering oil from the Middle East to the West.

In brief, involvement in Africa represents a sizable investment of Soviet resources. But what the Soviets have achieved thus far in the Horn and elsewhere suggests that benefits to Soviet global strategy are significant and the cost presumably worth it.

5. PROBING FOR OPPORTUNITIES IN LATIN AMERICA

a. Tangible political and strategic assets

The political and strategic benefits accruable from Soviet involvement in Latin America are very tangible because in large part they impinge directly on important U.S. interests. For Americans, the Soviet presence in Cuba and their attempt to establish what is believed to be a similar presence in Central America are not abstractions but geographic realities that challenge historic U.S. vital interests. Thus the benefits potentially accruable to the Soviets offer the greatest political and strategic reward: But they also carry with them the greatest risk for Soviet-American confrontation as in the Cuban missile crisis of 1962.

b. Building assets in Socialist Cuba

The Soviets highly value Socialist Cuba for political and strategic reasons spelled out in Part V.[24] What the Soviets have achieved in

---

[24] For the most recent appraisal by the Administration of Soviet and Cuban involvement in Central America and the Caribbean, see, U.S. Department of Defense and Department of State. The Soviet-Cuban Connection in Central America and the Caribbean. Washington, March 1985, 45 p.

Cuba in the last quarter century is by any measure remarkable. No other great power competitor of the United States in its entire diplomatic history has successfully challenged U.S. security interests to the extent that the Soviets have. Granted in the event of outright Soviet-American hostilities, U.S. power could quickly dispatch the Castro regime. But it is the grey area of neither war nor peace, as Trotsky would have described it, when the Cuban asset takes on a special value to the Soviets and conceivably is well worth the cost of underwriting the Cuban economy.

As masters in the use of military power for political purposes, the Soviets, using Cuba as their instrumentality for the most part, have in effect challenged U.S. predominance in what could be called the Nation's most sensitive "national security zone"—a term used by Michael McGwire in his writings on naval matters to designate vital national interests. In a skillful application of the tactic of incrementalism, the Soviets have succeeded in emphatically making a geopolitical point; namely, that they have a right to have a military presence at what is more the American doorstep than what is usually termed the American "strategic backyard." And their success thus far in Socialist Cuba may only be the beginning, or it may mark the high point in an evolving venture.

c. Expectations in Central America

In Central America, notably in Nicaragua, where they pursue a policy of revolutionary opportunism, the Soviets have expanded their Caribbean strategy, targeting what is clearly a most vital security interest of the United States; naɪ ̣ely, SLOCs upon which depend not only the defense but the livelihood of the Nation. Through a tactic of incrementalism, the Soviets have established the beginnings of what some observers call (but others deny) "another Cuba." Where this will end can only be speculated, but the example of the military buildup in Socialist Cuba since the missile crisis of 1962 provides an historical benchmark, so to speak, against which to measure the degree and seriousness of the Soviet threat.

Generally, Americans seem to agree that the United States has a vital interest in Nicaragua and in Central America as a whole. But they are deeply divided on the degree of the threat and more importantly on how to deal with the Soviet-and Cuban-backed Sandinista regime. The Soviets have been able to exploit this uncertainty and the resulting confusion in the Nation, thus buying time to deepen the Sandinista hold on the country. Pursuing the tactic of ambiguous gradualism (which seems to be the preferred Soviet modus operandi in sensitive parts of the Third World that bear on U.S. interests), the Soviets could reduce the risk of a forceful U.S. reaction and accordingly permit the unimpeded consolidation of the second Marxist-Leninist regime in the Central American-Caribbean region. Success in this effort could give the Soviets practical advantages in expanding their revolution throughout Latin America and substantial political assets in dealing with the United States as a global competitor.

d. Yield from traditional diplomacy

The pursuit of traditional diplomacy in Mexico and the cone of South America also produces important political assets for the Soviets, but on a far smaller scale than that of Socialist Cuba and in revolutionary Central America and the Caribbean. There seems little doubt that the Soviets have gained many political benefits throughout Latin America by supporting Argentina in the Falklands War. There are also political benefits from trade (often at an economic cost to themselves) in the agricultural goods they need in exchange for types of technical assistance, such as, building hydroelectric complexes, that many Latin American countries need.

What the Soviets have succeeded in doing through diplomatic traditionalism is to give Latin America an alternative to the United States in its search for an independent role in world and Hemispheric politics. Unmeasurable as it may be, the Soviet Union has in this way built up important political assets in this third area of Latin America upon which they can draw.

C. ON BALANCE

1. IMPRESSIONISTIC JUDGMENTS AND RAND'S ANALYSIS

Thus the Soviets have secured many political and strategic benefits from their Third World policy, notwithstanding the burden of empire that they have assumed. It is impossible to balance total benefits and costs in such a global undertaking with anything but "impressionistic" judgments, particularly in measuring political assets, for in international politics there are political costs as well as assets, equally unquantifiable. Somewhat more precise judgments are possible from economic analyses and analogical comparison with empires of the past as the Rand study had done.

2. SOVIET AWARENESS OF COSTS

Surely the Soviets are aware that they are paying a high price for expansion into the Third World, particularly in light of the added cost-producing economic problems besetting their "internal" empire at home and those troubling the "contiguous" empire in Eastern Europe. Some Soviet economists and Third World specialists have urged in their published works an easing of the economic burden and burden-sharing measures in the Third World. Soviet hesitancy thus far to fully underwrite Nicaragua and their apparent intention of making economic relations with Cuba more cost-effective suggest an awareness of this burden, beyond the scholarly community to the mid and upper echleons of the Soviet ruling elite.[25] Significantly, in their public pronouncements on the Third

---

[25] According to U.S. intelligence sources, heavy Soviet pressure and mounting economic difficulties are responsible for the changing direction of the troubled Cuban economy. New measures call for "a dramatic increase in exports to the West, belt-tightening at home, and lessened tensions with the United States," the press account said. Analysts do not expect Castro's growing economic difficulties to lead him to break with Moscow or cut off assistance to revolutionary movements. According to intelligence sources, Soviet officials attacked the Cuban economic policy last summer, in the words of the press account, "as wasteful and unrealistic." Soviet officials were reported to have been especially increased at "Havana's continued waste in imported and, increasingly expensive, Russian oil." According to American intelligence sources, the Sovi-

World, Brezhnev and Andropov stressed the importance of a lower economic profile in the Third World, seeming to imply the virtues of self-help. Under Chernenko and thus far under Gorbachev, this policy of apparent economic retrenchment seems not to have been changed.

3. POLITICAL AND STRATEGIC BENEFITS WORTH THE COST

What this review suggests is that the political and strategic benefits to be accrued in the Third World may well be worth the cost in the Kremlin assessment, and what the Soviets appear to be seeking in the economic rationalization of their Third World policy is a more economically cost-effective imperial system. For the Soviets have continued to seize "targets of opportunity" and expand upon them, as in upgrading military assistance to Nicaragua in the fall of 1984. Nor have they appeared to reduce but rather have continued to expand their political and military commitments in the Third World. In brief, political and strategic benefits, expected or in potential, have a high value in Moscow, apparently, well worth the economic costs of empire.

Thus Wolf concludes:

In the aggregate, these benefits of empire may, from the Politburo's viewpoint, amply justify the costs. They suggest that Soviet efforts to expand the empire are likely to continue.[26]

In a more comprehensive statement, the Rand study concludes:

. . . it is probably a reasonable presumption that the total costs—both noneconomic and economic—of the Soviet empire, at the levels they have reached in recent years, are likely to appear to the Soviet leadership to be quite reasonable, if not modest, in relation to this formidable package of benefits ascribed to the empire. Finally, our dollar estimates of CSE [Cost of Soviet Empire] seem to be well within the bounds that have been acceptable to imperial powers in the past, whereas the ruble estimates toward the end of the 1970s had reached levels that seemed to be transcending those bounds.[27]

Thus at this juncture in the mid-1980's the Soviets give the impression of having an empire in place and of pursuing a role in the Third World that is both an economic burden—but thus far not an unbearable one—and a political and strategic asset, the benefits of which are coming under serious question by some Soviet government officials and Third World specialists.

---

ets have in recent years displayed their displeasure over Cuba's poor economic performance by leveling off aid. In 1982, total Soviet economic assistance peaked at nearly $4.7 billion; in 1983, the figure dropped to $4.2 billion; a preliminary estimate for 1984 (that did not factor in cheap oil exports to Cuba) showed Soviet aid amounting to less than $3.8 billion. (Fontaine, Roger. Soviets Turn Stingy: Cubans Reap Woes. The Washington Times, April 16, 1985, p. 1A and 6A.)

[26] Wolf, Costs of the Soviet Empire, Wall Street Journal.

[27] Rand, Costs of the Soviet Empire, p. 50.

III. IMPLICATIONS FOR U.S. FOREIGN POLICY

A. CHALLENGE TO THE U.S. WORLD POSITION

1. RUSSIA'S "POSSESSIVE DEFENSIVENESS AND DISRUPTIVE OFFENSIVENESS"

By a combination of military strength and the projection of its power into the Third World, both Socialist and non-Socialist, the Soviet Union has established a global presence. Brezhnev's often-made claim that no major international problem could be solved without Soviet participation contains more than a grain of truth. But Soviet power, as Brzezinski observes, is one-dimensional. It is largely military and accordingly lacks the sort of systemic, ideological and socio-economic appeal that could broaden and deepen its hold on allies and clients, making their relationship more lasting.[1] In brief, it lacks certain ingredients of imperial cohesiveness that insures unity, strength and durability.

Moreover, as explained elsewhere in this study, the Soviets do not accept the status quo in international affairs. They reject the notion of orderly changes toward their goal. They adhere to the principle of continuing "struggle" as the norm of international life until, at least theoretically, their global ambition of establishing a Socialist international system has been established.

But this global effort is constrained by fear of nuclear war and risk of confrontation with the United States. Accordingly, these characteristics produce a world outlook that is a combination of what Brzezinski calls "possessive defensiveness and disruptive offensiveness,"[2] meaning excessive concern for their defense and security and a durable commitment to disrupting the prevailing international order. Thus Brzezinski concludes:

> The Soviet Union is . . . condemned to seeking global status neither by direct nuclear collision nor by peaceful socioeconomic competition. The only way open to global status is that of attrition and gradual disruption of stable international arrangements so that the United States suffers directly and indirectly.[3]

In brief, the one-dimensional military character of Soviet power and the adversarial philosophy underpinning and driving its foreign policy pose a challenge of the first magnitude to the U.S. world position.

2. SOVIET GEOPOLITICAL TARGETS

The Soviets have pursued their "strategy of disruption" by building sufficient, and in some instances excessive, military power to deter U.S. responses to the projection of their power in many parts

---

[1] Brzezinski, World Power of a New Type, p. 141 and 151.
[2] Ibid., p. 156.
[3] Ibid.

of the world, as in Ethiopia, and to intimidate its allies, as in the Brezhnev-Andropov anti-nuclear campaign in Western Europe. The Soviets have also sought to encourage trends hostile to U.S. interests in strategically vital areas of the Third World that have the greatest potential for affecting a shift in the global political-economic balance as in the Caribbean region and Central America.

In brief, the Soviets have targeted strategically and geopolitically significant, often vital, areas in the Third World that could determine the future direction of Soviet-American relations and define the Soviet global role.[4]

The general pattern of Moscow's disruptive strategy is clearly visible in this study:

—Their expanding presence in Asia, particularly their impressive and threatening military buildup in Northeast Asia, and the staking out of strategically important positions in Southeast Asia, formerly held by the United States, overseeing vital SLOCs connecting Northeast Asia and the Western Pacific with the Middle East;

—Their deep involvement in the strategically important Middle East, gaining access, for example, to military bases along vital chokepoints overseeing traffic in the Middle East;

—Their military presence in the strategically crucial Horn of Africa and the South Atlantic; and

—Their provocative, challenging military and political actions in Central America and the Caribbean region where lie historically important life-lines of sea communications.

In sum, the Soviets have targeted areas in the Third World where U.S. interests and those of its allies are very important, in many instances, vital. Hence the magnitude of the Soviet challenge to the United States in the Third World.

B. U.S. RESPONSE TO THE SOVIET CHALLENGE

1. TURNING FULL CYCLE

The U.S. response to Soviet policy in the Third World has turned full cycle since the publication of the first House Foreign Affairs Committee study on this subject in 1977. Then, the United States was caught up in the so-called "Vietnam syndrome" that virtually paralyzed policy, making difficult, if not impossible, a forceful military response to Soviet and Cuban machinations in Angola and Ethiopia. Restricted by this national mood of withdrawal from military and sometimes political involvement in far off regions of the Third World, American policymakers seemed hard-pressed to counter this and other Soviet challenges in the Third World. This did not mean, however, that the United States had reverted to isolationism. On the contrary, it did pursue an activist, internationalist policy as in concluding the Panama Treaty and Camp David Accords, and mounting a forthright human rights campaign internationally. Military intervention, as in Vietnam, was, however, out

---

[4] Ibid., p. 156–157.

of the question and in contradiction to the prevailing national mood.[5]

In a reversal of policy, brought on by the Soviet invasion of Afghanistan in 1979—truly a "watershed event," as Brzezinski correctly termed it—the United States finds itself in the mid-1980's again on the political frontiers of the Third World, forcefully reasserting its policy of global containment. James R. Schlesinger, former high-ranking U.S. national security official, contends that "in much of the Third World . . . our power is certainly commensurate with our commitments." [6] And Lord Carrington gives the further assurance that the West, particularly in its contest with Soviet power, is entitled to approach its problems "with more self-confidence. We are now in a position of considerable strength not only militarily, but economically and politically, too." [7]

Notwithstanding these assurances, the reality of the mid-1980's, as this study illustrates, is that the Soviet Union by its global military power has broken through the American policy of geographic containment first proclaimed in the Truman Doctrine of 1947. In this progressive process, covering three decades, Soviet strategic and political purposes in the Third World have been clear; namely, to build an infrastructure to buttress its policy of expanding globalism. And for the West at this historical stage of transition from colonialism to moderated interdependence in the Third World, the problem it faces has become equally clear; namely, how to reconstitute its position in the Third World and adapt it to new conditions doing so patiently and in a sustained incremental adjustment in order to preserve its vital interests now in contention with the Soviet Union.

2. GLOBAL CONTAINMENT IN THE REAGAN ADMINISTRATION

a. Third World vying for attention

Since its beginning in 1981, the Reagan Administration has vigorously pursued a policy of global containment of Soviet power. Vying for equal attention with the Administration's major focus on the buildup of the Nation's military forces, particularly in strategic weapons, Third World problems, nonetheless, appear to have consumed perhaps a disproportionate amount of the Administration's time. Central America, Cuba and continuing crises in the Middle East have dominated the array of Third World problems facing the Administration, including coping with Argentina and the Falklands War and giving concrete military support to the Afghan guerrillas.

---

[5] This distinction was made by George D. Holliday, an economist and specialist in Soviet affairs in CRS.

[6] Schlesinger continues cautioning that "there is simply no domestic consensus regarding the prospective use of force. Thus, overall, in all parts of the world we are likely to have to contend with at least one of the two gaps. Such is the penalty for the loss of our postwar pre-eminence." Excerpts from Schlesinger's testimony before the Senate Foreign Relations Committee, New York Times, Feb. 7, 1985, p. A14.

[7] Carrington, It's the West That's Strong, Moscow That's Weak, p. H3027.

b. Characteristics of administration Third World policy

A review of major policy statements by Administration leaders, such as, posture statements by the Secretary of Defense and the Joint Chiefs of Staff, frequent pronouncements by the President on the Soviet Union and world Communism, and commentaries on defence guidance, 1985–89, suggest the following descriptive characteristics with respect to the Administration's response to the Soviet challenge in the Third World:

—The response is highly ideological, encouraging, some critics would say, perhaps a less subtle distinction among Third World revolutionary forces;

—It is global in its commitment of American policy and military power;

—It places great reliance on the buildup of U.S. military forces, particularly of its naval power needed to protect vital SLOCs and natural resources overseas;

—It stresses the use of military power in countering the projection of Soviet and Cuban power in Central America (for example, Nicaragua) and the Caribbean region (for example, the invasion of Grenada); and finally

—It views the Third World more strictly in the geopolitical context of the East-West conflict and places great importance on an active U.S. role.

c. Casey's Fulton, Missouri, speech, October 29, 1983

Perhaps more than any other Administration official, CIA Director William J. Casey has been a spokesman for U.S. policy in countering the Soviets in the Third World. In what was described as a "remarkable" speech on October 29, 1983 at Westminster College, Fulton, Missouri, the site of Churchill's "Iron Curtain Speech" in 1946, Casey laid out a U.S. strategy for blunting the Soviet offensive.[8]

Casey explained Soviet policy, emphasizing: its military character; the extent of Soviet expansion thus far; the "growing ability of the Soviet Union to project power over long distances"; Moscow's resort to techniques of "creeping imperialism" to extend Soviet influence and control; and their effective use of proxies.

Casey elaborated on a "realistic counter-strategy" for the United States in pursuit of its Third World goals whether or not the Soviets were involved. He made four proposals as a guide to policy and action:

1. We have too often neglected our friends and neutrals in Africa, the Middle East, Latin America and Asia until they became a problem or were threatened by developments hostile to our interests. These countries now buy 40% of our exports; that alone is reason enough to pay greater attention to their problems before our attention is commanded by coups, insurgencies or instability. The priority of less developed countries in our overall foreign policy needs to be raised and sustained.

2. We must be prepared to demand firmly but tactfully and privately that our friends observe certain standards of behavior with regard to basic human rights. It

---

[8] Lardner, George, Jr. Third World Strategy Offered. The Washington Post, Oct. 30, 1983, p. A5. For the text of the speech, see, Casey, William J. Director, CIA. What We Face. Remarks at Westminster College, Fulton, Missouri, Oct. 29, 1983. (Central Intelligence Agency, Public Affairs). The essence of this speech appears in an article by Casey entitled, "Regroup to Check the Soviet Thrust," and published in The Wall Street Journal, April 22, 1983, p. 29.

is required by our own principles and essential to political support in the U.S. Moreover, we have to be willing to talk straight to those we would help about issues they must address to block foreign exploitation of their problems—issues such as land reform, corruption and the like. We need to show how the Soviets have exploited such vulnerabilities elsewhere to make clear that we aren't preaching out of cultural arrogance but are making recommendations based on experience.

3. We need to be ready to help our friends defend themselves. We can train them in counterinsurgency tactics and upgrade their communications, mobility, police and intelligence capabilities. We need changes in our foreign-military-sales laws to permit the U.S. to provide arms for self-defense more quickly. We also need to change our military procurement policies so as to have stocks of certain basic kinds of weapons more readily available.

4. We must find a way to mobilize and use our greatest asset in the Third World—private business. Few in the Third World wish to adopt the Soviet economic system. Neither we nor the Soviets can offer unlimited or even large-scale economic assistance to the less developed countries. Investment is the key to economic success in the Third World and we, our NATO allies and Japan need to develop a common strategy to promote investment and support it with know how in the Third World. The Soviets are helpless to compete with private capital in these countries.[9]

Casey cautioned that without a "sustained, constant policy applied over a number of years, we cannot counter the relentless pressure of the USSR in the Third World." He strongly urged both the Executive Branch and the Congress "to take the Soviet challenge in the Third World seriously and to develop a broad, integrated strategy for countering it."

Casey concluded with this prophecy: "The less-developed nations of the world will be the principal US-Soviet battleground for many years to come."[10]

3. FACTORS AFFECTING THE U.S. RESPONSE

a. A sense of deja vu

At this juncture in the mid-1980's, students of Soviet-American relations could experience a sense of deja vu. Presently, the United States and the U.S.S.R. have undertaken possibly far-reaching arms control negotiations in Geneva. The declared goals of these negotiations, formally entitled, "Negotiations on Nuclear and Space Arms," are to establish some form of stability on earth and in space acceptable to both sides, specifically as it affects their relationship, the regime in space and European security. During much of the Reagan administration's first term, negotiations were carried forth—unsuccessfully as it turned out—on control of strategic and intermediate nuclear weapons. Despite U.S. efforts to reach agreement in this critical arms control area through negotiations, the Soviet Union, while negotiating, continued to test and probe for opportunities in the Third World and intervene if necessary. The Caribbean and Central America were prime target areas.

In the mid-1970's, a comparable general situation had existed: The Soviet Union and the United States were negotiating SALT II that was finally concluded in June 1979; simultaneously the Soviet Union intervened in Angola, Ethiopia and elsewhere in the Third World, and gave full support to Vietnam's invasion of Kampuchea.

---

[9] Casey, What We Face, Westminster College Speech, p. 13–14.
[10] Ibid., p. 14. For recent references on the United States in the Third World, see, Hansen, Roger D. U.S. Foreign Policy and the Third World: Agenda 1982. New York, Praeger (for the Overseas Development Council), 1982. 249 p., the Feinberg, Richard E. The Intemperate Zone: The Third World Challenge to U.S. Foreign Policy. New York, W.W. Norton, 1983. 229 p.

Brezhnev perceived no contradiction between detente based on arms control in Soviet-American relations with Soviet support for "wars of national liberation" in the Third World. Believing that the "correlation of forces" is in their favor over the long-run, he argued that the Soviet Union could not arrest the forces of history that have preordained the creation of a world Socialist system.

In brief, the Soviets then as now seem to want it both ways; that is, nuclear stability in Europe and in East-West relations generally, but freedom to pursue Communist revolutionary goals in the Third World.

Hence, the United States and its Western allies face the same dilemma that perplexed them a decade ago; namely, how to resist mutidirectional Soviet expansionism, particularly now in Central America and the Caribbean Basin, while simultaneously negotiating honest and much needed agreements to minimize the chances of nuclear war.[11] Western democracies tend to view the search for peace and stability in its totality; the Soviets see it as divisible in order to achieve maximum tactical flexibility. Herein lay the danger of confrontation in the Third World between the Soviet Union and the United States, for support for wars of national liberation, as shown particularly in the Cuban missile crisis of 1962, can create conditions for confrontation and war.

b. Limits of power

(1) A "Forward Strategy" of global containment

Reagan Administration attempts to pursue a policy of global containment create another dilemma; namely, What are the limits of power?

The American "forward strategy" was laid out at the beginning of the Reagan Administration, incorporated into its national security doctrine, concretely expressed in its extensive military buildup and raised most recently in the declaration of the Strategic Defense Initiative. This strategy has reglobalized American commitments and power, as if in response to and in corroboration of the idea recently expressed by Arkady N. Shevchenko, the former top-ranking Soviet diplomat now living in the United States. To the Soviet leaders in the Kremlin, he said, American military power "is the main, if not only barrier to their plans for world domination."[12]

A basic geographic asymmetry differentiates Soviet-American national security requirements. The Soviet Union is continentalist; its base is firmly fixed in the Eurasian continent; and from there projects its power outward. In contrast, the United States is something of an "hemispheric island," requiring networks of SLOCs in its defense and the projection of its power outward. Emphasis on sea power and "freedom of the seas" is historically the first principle of its foreign policy.

Accordingly, soon after taking office, President Reagan laid out U.S. maritime strategy in terms that conformed to the Administra-

---

[11] Seweryn Bialer discusses this dilemma in his, The U.S.S.R. After Brezhnev. New York, Foreign Policy Association, 1983, p. 59. (Headline Series No. 265)
[12] The New York Times Book Review, Feb. 17, 1985, p. 3.

tion's determination to contest Soviet global initiatives and protect the Nation's security across a global front. This maritime strategy is a major component in the projection of American power abroad and in the containment of Soviet expansion. "'Maritime superiority for us is a necessity," the President said. "We must be able in time of emergency to venture in harm's way, controling air, surface and subsurface areas to assure access to all the oceans of the world." [13]

Admiral Harry D. Train, Supreme Allied Commander Atlantic, expressed the same idea. "The projection of naval forces," he said, "is essential to ensure a maritime balance is achieved in the forward littoral regions of the world." Train continued: "We are all highly dependent . . . [upon] the free flow of vital resources—this demands that we maintain control of the sea lines of communication—this, in turn, requires maritime superiority." [14]

General John Vessey, Jr., Chairman of the Joint Chiefs of Staff, was equally expansive in his statement on U.S. global responsibilities. When asked about the problem of maintaining a high level of military spending over a long period and whether it would make sense to cut back some U.S. global commitments, for example, in the Persian Gulf or the Far East or even Europe, the General replied in a manner suggesting an open-ended commitment of the type first expressed in the Truman Doctrine and reaffirmed by President Kennedy:

We've given a lot of thought to that. I don't see that you can do that in this world today.

There are two great military powers—the U.S. and the Soviet Union. We have economic, social and political connections with the rest of the free world, all of which are important to our society today. I don't believe we can abdicate those responsibilities even if we wanted to. The chances are that we would find out later that we made a mistake, and we'll pay a much higher price than we are being asked to pay today, and the coin in which we pay may well be the blood of our people or the loss of our freedom rather than simply dollars. [15]

(2) Awareness of the limits of power

But, what are the limits of American power in a competitive world shared with the Soviet Union?

Brzezinski acknowledges the limits of Soviet power, given its singular military dimension. But he warns that "American passivity in the Middle East and American overengagement in Central America are the most immediate geopolitical dangers" in countering Soviet expansionism. Brzezinski believes that Western, and especially American, efforts "to maintain and promote regional stability . . . will be decisive in determining whether Soviet global influence expands to the detriment of international stability." [16]

What Brzezinski seems to be calling for is a proper balance between commitment and resources in areas crucial to thwarting Russian power, implying, therefore, limitations on U.S. power to respond.

---

[13] Quoted in, Hiatt, Fred. Revived Battleship Flies Reagan's Defense Banner. The Washington Post, April 29, 1985, p. Al.

[14] Train, The Growing Soviet Naval Menace, p. 62.

[15] Why the U.S. Must Stay in the Arms Race. Interview with Gen. John Vessey, Jr., Chairman of the Joint Chiefs of Staff. U.S. News & World Report, Mar. 28, 1983: 27.

[16] Brzezinski, World Power of a New Type, p. 151 and 158.

Awareness of the limits of U.S. power was similarly implied in Secretary of Defense Weinberger's proclaimed criteria for U.S. military intervention abroad. During rising tensions in Nicaragua in the fall of 1984, sparked by reports of Soviet delivery of MIG fighter aircraft, Weinberger carefully set forth guidelines for the commitment of U.S. military power. The first of six criteria, or "tests", for the use of U.S. military combat forces was, "the United States should not commit forces to combat overseas unless the particular engagement or occasion is deemed vital to our national interest or that of our allies." "In those cases where our national interest require us to commit combat forces," he said, "we must never let there be doubt of our resolution." But he also said that, "The commitment of U.S. forces to combat should be a last resort, and to be used only when other means have failed," presumably meaning diplomacy. Weinberger's statement, discussed with the President and cleared by the National Security Council, was described as "the clearest enunciation of military policy" since the President was elected in 1980.[17]

(3) Weighing interests and measuring distances

Thus there are limits to American power in responding to Soviet threats in the Third World. And awareness of these limits creates a dilemma for a nation whose power does not always match its commitments abroad, whose people are not always sure of where their interests lie, and whose resolve, as in Vietnam, can be unpredictable. Failure to understand the limits of power could lead to a waste of national security resources and *in extremis* lead to national disaster. Responsible critics of U.S. defense policy complain of an absence of an integrated global military strategy, one that is designed to cope with challenges on a global front in a manner that carefully calculates what national interests are really *vital*—in brief, a strategy that rationally matches global foreign policy commitments with national security resources in a carefully structured hierarchy of interests.

Americans could, therefore, be guided by the wisdom of King Louis Philippe of France. On the occasion of the Polish revolt against Russian rule in 1830, Lafayette proclaimed enthusiastically, "All France is Polish." But the King had second thoughts and cautiously responded, "We must weight interests and measure distances."[18]

c. Establishing a code of conduct in the Third World

(1) Consequences of colliding policies

The global projection of Soviet power and the U.S. policy of global containment, particularly the securing and maintaining of

[17] The New York Times, Nov. 29, 1984, p. A1, A4–A5.

[18] Quoted in, The Washington Post, Feb. 12, 1985, p. A21. For a commentary on questioning among U.S. national security specialists of costs, benefits and rationale of far flung U.S. military deployments, see, The Christian Science Monitor, Aug. 1, 1984, p. 17. Prof. Eliot Cohen of Harvard University likens the United States these days to the British Empire in its waning days, overcommitted around the world and forced to restructure its forces and reexamine its foreign policy goals. For a conservative critique of Administration national security policy and its failure to match foreign policy commitments with resources in an integrared design, see, The Defense Budget: A Conservative Debate. Policy Review, Summar 1985:13–27.

SLOCs in a strategy of maritime supremacy, create a potential situation for collision and in all probability somewhere in the gray areas of the Third World. The consequences could be confrontation and even war. Arbatov explains this likelihood simply and logically from a Soviet perspective:

> The notion that the United States can have a dialogue with the Soviet Union only when the latter comes to realize it cannot catch up with the United States stems from the design to achieve military supremacy over the Soviet Union. This is the real design hidden in his [President Reagan's] remarks [before the Japanese Diet].
>
> The United States considers that there are 16 transport routes, which are necessary to obtain resources, across the world. It believes that these 16 transport routes must be kept under its control. The United States takes it for granted that it will keep under its control whatever places it deemed necessary. This stand is typically imperialistic. Should this stand prevail, we will have to kill one another to secure resources.[19]

Conflict is not, however, inevitable, even in the case of ostensibly colliding policies. The solution lies in establishing and abiding by a mutually acceptable "Code of Conduct" in the Third World, or as it is often referred to as, "Rules of the Game." In a word, permit diplomacy to function as an assuaging force in an otherwise sharply adversarial relationship. Such a code, written or unwritten, offers a viable alternative to conflict by opening up the possibility of achieving a mutually agreed "plateau of security."[20]

(2) Efforts in the past

(a) Kennedy-Khrushchev meeting at Vienna, June 1961

Efforts had been made in the past to establish a Code of Conduct in Soviet-American relations generally and specifically in the Third World. They failed.

At Vienna in June 1961, President Kennedy tried to reach an accommodation with Khrushchev that would satisfy the vital national interests of both sides. The key element was a mutual acceptance of the existing equilibrium of power and thus a common per-

---

[19] Arbatov Interview. Mainichi Shimbun (Tokyo), Nov. 13, 1983, morning edition, p. 1, E.

[20] Instructive insights into this problem of establishing a Code of Conduct in the Third World are provided by Charles S. Maier, a professor of history at Harvard University, in a commentary on the coming of World War I. Maier writes: "The difficulty was that a country could be powerful and vulnerable at the same time. Thus Germany—far and away the greatest industrial power in Europe and the most efficient mobilizer of armed strength—remained preoccupied with Russian power; for Russia, which had taken off at a very rapid rate of development, though from a more primitive level of economy and society, threatened to complete key military reforms and strategic railroad links by 1916. Conversely, Russian statesman felt that they must surrender all claims to being a great power unless they acted to reverse the checks that Vienna and Berlin were repeatedly inflicting. Here is one of the most disturbing analogies for today— the inability to find any *plateau of security* on which both sides might feel relatively secure at the same time. There were few to suggest in 1914 that vulnerability was a fact of international life and did not in itself negate deterrent strength." (August 1914: The Whys of War. The New York Times Book Review, July 29, 1984, p. 23. Italics added.)

This idea of establishing a mutually acceptable "plateau of security" has a special relevance to Soviet-American rivalry in the Third World. The expansion of Soviet power and the competing efforts by the United States and its allies to contain it by their own counter-thrusts of power have characterized the behavior of both superpowers since the end of World War II. This has been particularly the case in the Third World in the past three decades. The Third World seems to be the great gray area of unpredictability where the elements of control are weakened and where a Code of Conduct seems minimal. It is this unpredictability that makes the Third World so vulnerable to superpower conflict. The parallel of today is strikingly familiar with the picture Maier draws of 1914 and the onset of World War I when the competing alliances had failed to find what Maier calls a "plateau of security" on which both sides could simultaneously feel secure. Today the task is very difficult considering the volatility of the Third World, the magnitude of the stakes to be won and the inability of the superpowers to establish a mutually agreed upon "plateau of security."

ception of the status quo. Kennedy did not seek a freeze in the international status quo, for he recognized that political and institutional change were both inevitable and desirable. What he sought was a process of change that would not entail the transfer of power from one bloc to the other and would not make either side feel threatened and therefore obliged to resist change by force.

Khrushchev rejected Kennedy's perception of the balance of power concept, arguing the thesis set forth in his January 6, 1961 speech; namely, that social revolution as a global phenomenon was preordained by history; that such revolutions, that is "wars of national liberation," were "sacred"; and that the Soviet Union had an obligation to assist them whenever possible. For Khrushchev, the status quo, in the Third World, for example, meant the continued process of the conquest of power by Communist revolution on a global scale. Kennedy's conception of a global standstill was in his view an attempt to alter the status quo, not support it; it was an attempt to press evolutionary development and arrest the revolutionary process.

Thus the conflicting perception of the balance of power concept and its implications for the status quo became entangled in Soviet-American relations, dangerously so because it meant that Soviet support for global revolutions (as then taking place in Cuba, Vietnam, Laos, Burma, Malaya, etc.) and refusal to recognize an acceptable balance of power (as was evolving in Berlin and Europe) would expose the great powers to the very miscalculations and confrontations that Kennedy sought to avoid. Out of this essentially ideological conflict of worldviews emerged the dynamic forces that produced the crisis in Berlin in 1961, and one year later, the Cuban missile crisis.[21]

(b) Nixon and Brezhnev: Establishing and Soviet reneging on code of conduct, 1970's

At the high point of detente in the early 1970's, President Nixon and General Secretary Brezhnev endorsed the idea of a Code of Conduct. In a formal document entitled, "Basic Principles of Relations Between the Union of Soviet Socialist Republics and the United States of America," and signed, along with other documents, at the Moscow summit conferences in May 1972, both leaders pledged that their respective countries would not seek "unilateral advantage" in the conduct of foreign affairs.[22]

Soviet intentions in signing this document and their interpretations of it became clear when the question of Soviet-American collaboration, implied in the Basic Principles, became controversial in the Communist world and had to be rebutted by Moscow. In a clarification, Nikolay Inozemtsev, head of the Institute of World Economics and International Relations and thus Moscow's leading academic spokesman on foreign policy, wrote in Pravda two weeks after the summit that although anyone with "common sense" could see the benefits of East-West accord, "attempts are being made . . . to replace common sense by unscrupulous speculation about some

[21] HFAC, Soviet Diplomacy and Negotiating Behavior, 1979, p. 229–30.
[22] This section is based upon, FBIS. Analysis Report. Soviet-America Competition in the Third World: Moscow's Evolving Views on a "Code of Conduct." Jan. 17, 1983, p. 4–8.

'conspiracy between the two superpowers' to the effect that the Soviet-American agreements are allegedly detrimental to some third countries." The Soviet Union, Inozemtsev declared, "has been, is, and will always remain a loyal friend of peoples struggling for national independence and freedom against imperialism and colonialism." In endorsing a posture of "maximum flexibility" in dealing with the West, Inozemtsev recalled Lenin's entreaty to his contemporaries to "make use of agreements and compromises with other parties and states" in order to advance the Communist revolutionary cause.

The arguments presented here, in effect, established Moscow's line of defense against critics of detente within the Communist world as Soviet-American collaboration expanded in subsequent months.

Soviet defenders of detente countered critics with the further argument that relaxation of Soviet-American tensions would actually enhance prospects for "progressive" change in the Third World rather than impede it. This thesis gained wide circulation after the second Nixon-Brezhnev summit a year later in June 1973 which produced the "Agreement on the Prevention of Nuclear War." Both parties again pledged a policy of restraint in the conduct of foreign policy.

As the decade of the 1970's wore on, the Soviets intervened in the Angolan civil war (1975–76) and in the Ethiopia-Somalia conflict over Ogaden in 1977–78. Western critics of detente charged that the Soviets had reneged on their pledges of restraint and exploited Third World conflicts to their own advantage.

In response, the Soviets contended that detente established rules for East-West relations, but did not affect the differing approaches of each side to revolutionary change in the Third World. In his speech to the 25th CPSU Congress in February 1976, Brezhnev singled out the Angolan issue in defending Soviet Third World policies. He depicted the revolutionary MPLA as a victim of "foreign intervention" and declared that Moscow would always give support to "peoples who are fighting for their freedom." Brezhnev argued further that detente "does not in the slightest way" abolish the "laws of class struggle" but actually creates "more favorable conditions for peaceful socialist and communist construction." In a charge that recalled the Kennedy-Khrushchev exchange at Vienna in 1961, Brezhnev scored capitalists and "leftists" alike for viewing detente as a "freezing of the social and political status quo."

In brief, the Soviets, when pressed to the test of compliance in an agreement, would not accept the idea of establishing a Code of Conduct that in any way would place them in the position of rejecting the ideological principle of "class struggle" and reversing their approval of Communist "revolutionary change."

(c) Brezhnev's proposal for code of conduct, 1981

In the spring of 1981, the Soviets had directed their peace offensive, then underway, at a special target, the Third World.[23] The oc-

---

[23] For a study on Brezhnev's peace offensive, see, Whelan, Joseph G. Brezhnev's Peace Offensive, 1981: Propaganda Ploy or U.S. Negotiating Opportunity? Washington, Library of Congress, Congressional Research Service, May 17, 1981, 129 p. (Report No. 82–96S)

casion for broadening the offensive was Brezhnev's speech at a Kremlin dinner on April 27, honoring the visiting Libyan leader, Muammar Qaddafi. Addressing the need for regulating great power relationships in the Third World, Brezhnev laid down the following principles as a "code of conduct":

—The recognition of the right of each people to decide its domestic affairs without outside interference, renunciation of attempts to establish any forms of domination or hegemony over them or to include them in the "sphere of interests" of any power.

—Strict respect for territorial integrity of these countries, inviolability of their frontiers. No outside support for any separatist movements aimed at partitioning those countries.

—Unconditional recognition of the right of each African, Asian and Latin American state to equal participation in international life, to the development of relations with any countries of the world.

—Complete and unconditional recognition of sovereignty of those states over their natural resources and also de facto recognition of their complete equality in international economic relations, the support of their efforts aimed at the liquidation of the vestiges of colonialism, at the eradication of racism and apartheid in accordance with the well-known decisions of the United Nations.

—Respect of the status of non-alignment chosen by the majority of African, Asian and Latin American states. Renunciation of the attempts to draw them into military-political blocs of big powers.[24]

Brezhnev's speech and particularly, as he said, his "roughly" stated principles on behavior in the Third World, are significant for two reasons: first, they broadened the peace offensive to include the conduct of the great powers in the Third World; and, second, they signaled Soviet recognition that such a Code of Conduct was necessary.

With respect to the first point, Brezhnev broadened his peace offensive, apparently, to embrace the enduring problem of averting an East-West confrontation in the Third World, but also to place an aura of peaceful intent on Soviet policy in that much contested area of world politics.

On the second point, establishing a Code of Conduct, the Soviets had in the past rejected U.S. efforts to establish what American foreign policy specialists call "rules of the game." As noted above, the Soviets consistently responded that such rules would perpetuate Western dominance in Third World areas, and that they were in contradiction to Soviet political and ideological support for "wars of national liberation."[25]

---

[24] Moscow Tass in English, 1653 GMT, April 27, 1981. In, FBIS Daily Report: Soviet Union, v. 3, April 28, 1981, p. H3–H4.
[25] Dr. Robert Legvold of Columbia University has written on this matter of "rules of the game." See his articles The Nature of Soviet Power, Foreign Affairs, v. 56, October 1977, p. 49–71, and The Super Rivals: Conflict in the Third World, Foreign Affairs, v. 57, Spring 1979, p. 755–778. For a discussion of the application of this idea to arms sales in the Third World, see, Pierre, Andrew. Arm Sales: The New Diplomacy. Foreign Affairs, Winter 1981/82: 282.

Thus, Brezhnev seemed to have made a qualitative change in Soviet Third World policy—"a bow toward the American position," as William G. Hyland, an American specialist in Soviet affairs, termed it.[26]

The purpose of this change could have been to open the dialogue with the United States that Brezhnev had proposed in his report to the 26th CPSU Congress in February 1981 and ultimately through negotiations to establish some rules of international conduct in the Third World for avoiding superpower confrontations. Or it may have been proposed strictly as a propaganda "cover" for what Hyland referred to as "an aggressive, exploitative Soviet offensive elsewhere." [27]

Whatever the purpose, the effect seemed to serve the larger objective in the Soviet peace offensive; namely, of deflecting world criticism of its conduct in Afghanistan and Poland (then under severe Soviet pressure) and place the burden of responsibility for world tensions on the United States. Only in this instance the focus shifted from arms control in Europe, then the principal target of the offensive, to peaceful accommodation of interests in the Third World. To emphasize the point, Soviet officials and political observers repeated Brezhnev's proposal throughout the Soviet media.[28]

(d) Revival of the code of conduct, January 1983

The idea of a Code of Conduct for superpower behavior in the Third World lay somewhat dormant in Brezhnev's declining years and during the Andropov-Chernenko succession regimes. The Third World had been given "short shrift" as attention focused mainly on East-West relations and arms control.[29]

However, on January 6, 1983, the Warsaw Pact leaders issued a Political Declaration in which the Code of Conduct idea surfaced briefly. That document differed from previous declarations, in keeping with Moscow's fairly low-profile policy, in that it downplayed proclamations of support for Third World clients and emphasized concern over the broader international consequences of regional wars. The Declaration warned that such local conflict could develop into "armed confrontation on a worldwide scale," and it linked improvement in world affairs to the "elimination" of current conflicts in Asia, Africa and Latin America and to the "prevention of new conflicts." [30]

The Warsaw Pact's solution to the problem was to revive the principles set forth in Brezhnev's Code of Conduct that had dropped from public discussion during the General Secretary's last year in power. The Declaration also reiterated Brezhnev's "peace proposals" regarding the Third World and called on the United States to return to the suspended talks on limiting Soviet and American arms transfers to foreign countries.[31]

---

[26] Hyland, William G. The Soviet Union and the United States. Current History, October 1981: 344.

[27] Ibid.

[28] See, for example, Kudryavtsev, V. Voice of Reason and Justice, Izvestiya, April 30, 1981, Morning Edition, p. 5. In, FBIS Daily Report: Soviet Union, v. 3, May 6, 1981, p. A6–A8, and Ovchinnokov, V. For Equal Rights, Against Arbitrariness. Pravda, May 5, 1981, p. 4. In, FBIS Daily Report: Soviet Union, v. 3, May 6, 1981, p. CC4–CC6.

[29] FBIS, Soviet-American Competition in the Third World, p. 11-13.

[30] Ibid., p. 113.

[31] Ibid.

Nothing came of the Warsaw Pact proposal given the deteriorating state of Soviet-American relations particularly after the KAL incident in September 1983. But its resurrection in early 1983 suggests that the idea of a Code of Conduct and the necessity for avoiding confrontation in Third World areas remain a reasonably high priority in the post-Brezhnev years.

(3) A code of conduct for the mid-1980's

(a) Changing political environment, 1984–85

Whether or not the Soviet Union and the United States can establish a Code of Conduct in the Third World for the mid-1980's is a major, and open, question, particularly in light of Mikhail S. Gorbachev's accession to power in March 1985 with the passing of Chernenko.

Since the fall of 1984, the political environment in Soviet-American relations has changed appreciably. Having failed in Geneva and in their peace offensive to thwart U.S. efforts to counterbalance Soviet SS–20's by installing Pershing II and cruise missiles in Western Europe, and alarmed by the negative strategic implications for them of the Strategic Defense Initiative (SDI), the Soviets reversed their policy of calculated antagonism, initiated a new peace offensive directed at SDI, and agreed to return to the conference table.

On the American side, the overwhelming victory of President Reagan at the polls, a professed determination to resume constructive negotiations with the Soviet Union having achieved the goals of the military buildup, and the presumed desire of Reagan to go down in U.S. history as a "peace" President, created new and favorable conditions for a reversal of policy. Accordingly, the Administration initiated a 180 degree turn from the posture it had maintained consistently during the President's first term.

Thus, the political climate has improved considerably with actions taken by both countries, preparing the way for the resumption of arms control negotiations at Geneva and as both sides, on the occasion of Gorbachev's taking over the Soviet leadership, voiced agreement to negotiate on a wide range of problems. By mid-March 1985, the President, in still another reversal of previous policy, invited the new Soviet leader to a summit meeting in the United States; the invitation has been accepted in principle but specific details have yet to be worked out.

Many serious problems divide Moscow and Washington as they enter the mid-1980's but at least the improved atmospherics of the relationship seem to have reconstituted the mood of hopeful expectation prevailing in the pre-Afghanistan and SALT II days of 1979. Accordingly, a Code of Conduct could be appropriately and reasonably placed on the superpower agenda of things to be done.

(b) Diplomacy and power: The credo of Secretary Shultz

Secretary of State Shultz welcomes the re-opening of negotiations with the Soviet Union as a beginning in "eventually forging a more constructive relationship." In recent speeches he placed great emphasis on diplomacy as a vital instrument in maintaining peaceful relations with the Soviet Union, though not to the detriment of physical power. To some observers this accent on diplomacy has no doubt been viewed as a positive turn away from what some critics have perceived as a persistent "hardline" and "over-militarized" U.S. approach to Soviet relations.

Last October, Shultz delivered a speech before the Rand/UCLA Center for the Study of Soviet International Behavior entitled, "Managing the U.S.-Soviet International Relationship Over the Long Term." In the speech the Secretary set forth his credo on the proper balance between diplomacy and physical power for establishing the basis for a good relationship:

We have tended all too often to focus either on increasing our stength or on pursuing a course of negotiations. We have found it difficult to pursue both simultaneously. In the long run, the absence of a consistent, coherent American strategy can only play to the advantage of the Soviet Union.

Therefore, we must come to grips with the more complex reality of our situation. A sustainable strategy must include all the elements essential to a more advantageous U.S.-Soviet relationship. We need to be strong, we must be ready to confront Soviet challenges, *and* we should negotiate when there are realistic prospects for success.[32]

With respect to the Third World, the Secretary stated categorically that, "If the Soviet Union pursues aggressive policies in the Third World, and not least in our own hemisphere, that threaten us and our friends, then we will respond equally strongly." And then he asks, "Isn't the level of armed conflict in the Third World too high already?"—seeming to imply that conflict should not be proliferated by great powers but rather controlled and reduced.

The Secretary reiterated the President's approval of a statement the day before by Chernenko saying that the Soviets "are ready to pursue a constructive dialogue with us." He concluded with his assessment of long-term Soviet-American relations and the role of diplomacy in what he termed "forging a more constructive relationship":

What we have begun to do over the past 4 years, and can continue to do in the future, is to persuade Soviet leaders that continued adventurism and intransigence offer no rewards. We have provided persuasive reasons for the Soviets to choose, instead, a policy of greater restraint and reciprocity. We must be comfortable with the requirements of such a strategy, including its price, its risks, and its predictable periodic setbacks. *We must be able to deter Soviet expansionsim at the same time as we seek to negotiate areas of cooperation and lower levels of armaments.*

These are the essential elements of our long-term policy. If we pursue such a strategy with wisdom and dedication, we have a much better prospect for achieving our goals: countering the Soviet challenge, directing the competition into less dangerous channels, and eventually forging a more constructive relationship.[33]

Thus for the American side the ingredients are present in the Shultz credo on diplomacy and power for constructing a Code of Conduct in the Third World: the necessity of "greater restraint and

[32] Shultz, George. Secretary of State. Managing the U.S.-Soviet International Relationship Over the Long Term. Speech delivered to the Rand/UCLA Center for the Study of Soviet International Behavior. Inserted in, The Congressional Record, Jan. 22, 1985: S458 (Daily edition). Shultz clarified still further the relationship between diplomacy and power in a speech at Yeshiva University in New York on Dec. 9, 1984. He said: "Americans have sometimes tended to think that power and diplomacy are two distinct alternatives. This reflects a fundamental misunderstanding. The truth is, power and diplomacy must always go together, or we will accomplish very little in this world. Power must always be guided by purpose. At the same time, the hard reality is that diplomacy not backed by strength will always be ineffectual at best, dangerous at worst." (U.S. Dept. of State. Bulletin, v. 85, Feb. 1985, p. 2. The speech was entitled, "The Ethics of Power.").

[33] Shultz, Managing the U.S.-Soviet International Relationship, p. S459. Underlining added.

reciprocity" by the Soviets, a determination to deter Soviet expansionism, and a willingness to negotiate.[34]

(c) Gorbachev's views on the Third World

By and large Gorbachev's views on the Third World, and particularly on establishing a Code of Conduct, can only be inferred and deduced from his general association with recent Soviet foreign policy as a full member of the Politburo since 1980, and more explicitly from comments made at the Chernenko funeral and on other occasions thereafter. Gorbachev is a product of the Soviet system and its unique political culture. Accordingly, his comments thus far as General Secretary amount to a reassertion of known Soviet foreign policy positions. Gorbachev's concentration on domestic economic issues during his career as a party apparatchik and his junior status in the leadership no doubt account for the absence of an historical record and any recent extensive commentaries on foreign policy.[35]

The theme of the pronouncements since Chernenko's passing is continuity. As one press account put it, "Continuity . . . remains a central element in Soviet foreign policy." [36] Suggestive of the idea that Gorbachev will probably be locked in for some time on the general thrust of Soviet policy is the comment by one analyst who said, "Gorbachev will inherit a 'legacy' of previous foreign policy moves that cannot easily be undone—chief among them the substantial commitment of money, men and resources in Afghanistan."[37]

Gorbachev's declared attitude towards the Third World as Secretary General of the CPSU first appeared in his speech before the Central Committee on March 11 in which he reiterated the stock (and bland) Soviet formulation:

The Soviet Union has always supported the struggle of peoples for liberation from colonial oppression. And today our sympathies go out to the countries of Asia, Africa and Latin America which are following the road of consolidating independ-

---

[34] In a press conference on March 15, Secretary Shultz said that Gorbachev's succession, coupled with other factors, created "a moment of opportunity" for across-the-board improvement in Soviet-American relations, including in the Third World. The President, he said, "firmly intends" to seize the moment for high-level dialogue and improvement of relations. In a statement approved by the President before the press conference, Shultz listed four areas for potential improvement. One was the Third World where he called for better understanding on solutions "in regions of crisis and potential confrontation." The President has proposal periodic consultations at "policy level" to discuss areas of regional conflict. Such talks had already taken place of Feb. 19–20 in Vienna on the Middle East. Shultz stressed the importance of optimism tempered by realism in dealing with the Soviets—"a realism based upon a history which has not always fulfilled our expectations." (Oberdorfer, Don. Shultz Sees Hope for Better Relations. The Washington Post, p. A1 and A29.)

[35] Since Brezhnev's death in November 1982, Gorbachev has gained limited foreign policy experience outside the narrow confines of party-to-party relations. In May 1983, he led a Supreme Soviet delegation to Canada where he had reportedly made a favorable impression. In December 1984, he visited England where he had conducted himself with equal deftness. On these occasions he held discussions with political leaders and fielded questions from the Western press. In April 1984, he was nominated to succeed Chernenko as Chairman of the Foreign Affairs Commission of the Supreme Soviet and in that capacity addressed joint meetings of the foreign affairs commissions of both Supreme Soviet Chambers in June on training of foreign cadres in the USSR and in November on Soviet economic relations with the Third World. Owing to his limited experience in foreign affairs, Gorbachev's statements on international issues have closely hewed to established Soviet positions. (FBIS, Gorbachev: A Political Profile. March 11, 1985, Take 7.)

[36] The Christian Science Monitor, March 14, 1985, p. 1.

[37] Ibid. Soviet troops were said to be massing for a spring offensive against the Afghan guerrillas.

ence and social renovation. For us they are friends and partners in the struggle for a durable peace, for better and just relations between peoples.[38]

However, a more specific clue of Gorbachev's attitudes appeared in his comments to Third World leaders that he conferred with during the Chernenko funeral, particularly those made to Daniel Ortega, a Sandinista leader and President of Nicaragua. The Tass report of the meeting with Ortega contained a reassertion of the Soviet commitment to support the Sandinista regime against the United States. Tass stated:

> There was an exchange of opinions about the situation in Central America. Mikhail Gorbachev confirmed solidarity of the Soviet people with the Nicaraguan people heriocally upholding its right to free independent development. Both sides condemned resolutely the course of the U.S. Administration aimed at interference in the affairs of countries of the region, at the creation of a dangerous seat of tension there. At the same time, the sides confirmed the need of further intensification of international efforts, including the activity of the "Contadora Group" in the interests of a just political settlement in Central America. In this connection the Soviet side highly assessed Nicaragua's new constructive initiative advanced recently.[39]

On March 14, Moscow Radio carried a report to its Soviet audience on Gorbachev's meeting with Ortega, thus singling out the Nicaraguans among other Third World leaders for special attention:

> The Soviet has always supported the struggle of the peoples for liberation from colonial oppression. Our sympathy is still on the side of the countries of Asia, Africa and Latin America which are struggling to strengthen their independence, for their social renewal. Mikhail Sergeyevich Gorbachev's meetings with the leaders of a number of states of these regions were a visible manifestation of the solidarity of the land of the Soviets with this hard, persistent struggle. Thus, for example, during his meeting with Daniel Ortega, President of Nicaragua, Comrade Gorbachev confirmed the solidarity of Soviet people with the Nicaraguan people, which is heroically defending its right to a free and independent development.[40]

Western diplomats in Moscow took note of the special treatment accorded Ortega, possibly signaling that Nicaragua may be given a higher priority of Soviet concern. On the first day Gorbachev conferred with Ortega along with Haile Mariam Mengistu of Ethiopia, another favored Socialist ally. At Andropov's funeral a year ago, Ortega was given less favorable treatment, and the Ethiopians were not received at all, suggesting by comparison that the Third World is very much on Gorbachev's mind.[41]

From all outward appearances, therefore, Soviet policy under the new Gorbachev leadership remains consistent with the past. It openly and boldly asserts "full support" for the Sandinista regime, charges the United States with "aggression and intervention" in Nicaragua's internal affairs, but cautiously commits itself only to "contribute energetically" to finding a "political" settlement of differences.[42]

---

[38] The New York Times, March 12, 1985, p. A16.
[39] FBIS 105. Moscow Tass in English, 1723 GMT, March 13, 1985.
[40] FBIS 073. Moscow Radio. Moscow Domestic Service in Russian, 0900 GMT, March 14, 1985.
[41] Bohlen, Celestine. Gorbachev Impresses in Talks with Visitors. The Washington Post, March 15, 1985, p. A29.
[42] In what was termed a "sharply-worded" and "authoritative" statement timed to coincide with Congressional debate on Nicaragua, the Soviets adhered to their "usual cautious public approach of reaffirming political support for Managua but stopping short of any commitment of concrete assistance." The Tass statement of April 14 depicted the United States of embarking on

Castro's failure to attend Chernenko's funeral, or even sign the condolence book at the Soviet Embassy in Havana as protocol requires, was interpreted as a sign of his displeasure with Moscow, signaling to the new Soviet leader that all is not well with his Cuban ally. Castro had attended the funeral of Andropov and Brezhnev; for Chernenko's he sent his brother Raul, Cuba's Vice President and Defense Minister.

East European sources revealed that Castro felt frustrated and annoyed by Chernenko's conciliatory approach towards the United States and apparently a less than forceful Soviet policy towards Nicaragua. Castro was said to have been profoundly annoyed with Chernenko last March when he refused to allow a Soviet naval flotilla to approach Nicaraguan waters. At the time a Soviet tanker had been severely damaged by a mine at the entrance to Nicaragua's Pacific harbor of Puerto Sandino. Castro urged that the flotilla proceed to Nicaragua to demonstrate Soviet military support for the Sandinistas.

Gorbachev met with Raul Castro, and according to the communique, the meeting conveyed a spirit of "fraternal friendship, cordiality and full mutual understanding." Earlier Castro had conferred with Soviet Defense Minister Marshal Sergei Sokolov and other senior Soviet officials.[43]

Perhaps the most revealing, and ominous, public sign of Gorbachev's views on Third World problems was Tass' account of his meeting on March 14 with President Mohammed zia ul-Haq and Foreign Minister Sahabzada yaqub Khan of Pakistan. In contrast to the conciliatory tone in which he received other leaders, Gorbachev, according to Dusko Doder's report from Moscow in The Washington Post, issued the Soviet's "sternest warning to date" to Pakistan for supporting the Afghan guerrillas. Briefly, Gorbachev's message was strongly accusatory in tone and substance.

---

a campaign to destabilize the Sandinista government. It declared Moscow's "resolute opposition to imperialist diktat and rude pressure" against Nicaragua and registered its "categorical rejection" of what it termed a U.S. policy of "aggression and intervention" in Nicaragua's internal affairs. Calling for an end to such actions, the statement warned that they "are fraught with serious consequences" for international peace. Presumably having in mind the beginning of Congressional debate on aid to the anti-Sandinista forces, the statement accused the United States of blocking a peaceful settlement in Central America, chided the United States for unilaterally suspending the U.S.-Nicaraguan talks and for rejecting Managua's "constructive" proposals for resolving differences, and professed to see "mounting concern" in the American public that the Reagan Administration's policy toward Nicaragua "may result in a repetition of the errors of the past," (a clear reference to the Vietnam experience.) In keeping with the other Soviet media comment, the statement ridiculed President Reagan's proposal of April 4 for church-mediated discussions between the Sandinistas and Contras as "deliberately unacceptable." Consistent with its past caution, the Soviet statement went no further than to express "full support" for the Sandinista approach to resolving U.S.-Nicaraguan and regional differences. Moscow was committed only to "contribute energetically" to finding a "political" settlement, specifying "the only possible way" to do so is through discussions between "relevant" states, (FBIS 004. Moscow Hits "Aggressive" U.S. Policy in Nicaragua, April 17, 1985.)

In what appeared to be a clear and perhaps decisive turn towards the Soviets on April 27, President Daniel Ortega and other officials departed for Moscow to seek aid for Nicaragua's failing economy. A government source said that Ortega planned to ask the Soviets for $200 million in emergency cash assistance to buy food and other essential products. While providing Nicaragua with millions of dollars worth of military weapons, it rarely has provided cash aid to other countries. The Ortega trip followed U.S. Congressional rejection on April 23 of President Reagon's request for $14 million to assist the Contra rebels fighting the Sandinista government. (The Washington Post, April 28, 1985, p. A29.)

[43] Doder, Dusko. Castro Faults Soviets on Managua Aid. The Washington Post, March 24, 1985, p. A1 and A33.

According to "well-informed circles," Doder writes, the Kremlin was considering "unspecified actions" against Pakistan if President Reagan "continues his military pressure on Nicaragua." A Tass report of the Gorbachev-Zia meeting, he notes, included "extraordinarily harsh language." According to Tass, Gorbachev and Gromyko gave the Pakistani leaders "a frank, principled assessment of the policy conducted" by the Zia government, code words for tough talking. "Aggressive actions" against Afghanistan are being carried out from Pakistani territory, the Tass report continued. Such actions, according to Tass, "cannot but affect in the most negative way Soviet-Pakistani relations." [44]

Doder suggests that by associating himself in a face-to-face meeting with Zia with charges against Pakistan and warnings of dire consequences made in Soviet media in the past, Gorbachev "appeared to be taking an entirely new and tougher approach toward the Afghanistan issue."

Moscow sources hinted that the intensified pressure on Zia was not only linked to Russia's growing frustration over the five-year military stalemate in Afghanistan but also to President Reagan's increased pressure on the Sandinistas in Nicaragua. These sources added that any U.S. military action against Nicaragua would, in Doder's words, "provoke a serious effort to topple the Zia government."[44a]

Diplomatic observers in Moscow noted that by linking Afghan insurgency with U.S. pressure on Nicaragua, the Soviets may be sending a signal that they are capable of "inflicting real damage on U.S. interests in an area close to the Soviet borders."[45] It could also indicate that Gorbachev intends to keep Nicaragua in the forefront not only as a way of underscoring possible Soviet intentions of establishing "another Cuba" in the Caribbean region and thus making the geopolitical point of a permanent Soviet presence, but also as a means of pressuring the United States against giving further aid to the Afghan guerrillas through Pakistan.

Whether these signals from Gorbachev suggest any prospects for possible tradeoffs seems unclear. But they, along with the reception

---

[44] According to a report from Islamabad, Zia was "badly shaken" by his meeting with Gorbachev. He came away with the impression that the Soviets, who already have 115,000 troops in Afghanistan, would be prepared to commit up to 500,000 men. The increasingly heavy concentration of Soviet forces on the border has led Western and Pakistani officials to conclude that the Soviets may be embarking on what the press report termed "its most serious campaign so far to totally cut the flow of Western weapons to the mujahideen." On March 18, a Soviet armored personnel carrier, filled with Soviet troops and flying a white flag, crossed the Pakistani border and demanded that three Afghan Army defectors be returned. For three days the border post of Tor Kham where the transaction was taking place was bombarded by 125 rounds of heavy artillery and fire from Soviet T-55 tanks. By noon on March 20, the Pakistanis returned the three Afghans. (Weaver, Mary Anne. Soviets Twist Pakistan's Arm Over Aid to Afghan Guerrillas. The Christian Science Monitor, April 22, 1985, p. 1 and 36.)

[44a] Indian Prime Minister Rajiv Gandhi's visit to Moscow in May 1985 provided Gorbachev the opportunity to reassure India of his continuing patronage. In contrast to his harsh treatment of Zia, Gorbachev went out of his way to reaffirm Moscow's commitment to India. On the occasion of their meeting, Gorbachev appeared in person at the door of Gandhi's Kremlin apartment ten minutes before they were to begin talks in another part of the Kremlin. Throwing his arm around Gandhi, Gorbachev said in a friendly and jocular manner: "Spring is here. I suggest we skip the limousines and walk to our meeting. You and I can take care of the protocol boys." Later Gorbachev and Gandhi signed economic agreements providing an immediate Soviet credit of $1.2 billion to India and paving the way for scientific and technical cooperation through the year 2000. (Time, September 9, 1985:21)

[45] Doder, Dusko. Gorbachev Warns on Afghan Aid. The Washington Post, March 16, 1985, p. A1 and A28.

extended to Ortega and Mengistu, suggest that Gorbachev may be determined to seek a solution of the Afghan issue; that Nicaragua may hold a position of growing importance in Soviet councils;[46] and that the new leadership has no intention of lowering the Soviet profile in the Third World. For Gorbachev's views on the Third World are fixed in traditional Soviet attitudes toward the Third World recorded throughout this study. His view are a lineal descendant of those held by Khrushchev, Brezhnev, their successors and others in the ruling elite.

This connection with past Soviet Third World policy was reaffirmed on April 29 when Ortega met with Gorbachev and other Soviet leaders in Moscow. Among the top leaders at the meeting were Geydar Aliyev, member of the Politburo, Foreign Minister and Politburo member Andrei Gromyko, Boris Ponomarev, an alternative Politburo member and in command of international Communism, and Nikolay Baybakov, Chairman of the State Planning Committee of the USSR. In addition to Ortega, Nicaragua was represented by Henri Ruiz, Minister of Foreign Economic Cooperation and member of the FSLN national leadership, Miguel D'Escoto, Minister of Foreign Affairs and Sandinista official, Jacinto Suarez, Nicaragua's Ambassador to the Soviet Union and member of the Sandinista Assembly, and by Julio Lopez, head of the FSLN International Department and member of the Sandinista Assembly.

According to the Tass report, the meeting passed "in an atmosphere of friendship and complete mutual understanding." Both sides expressed "satisfaction with expanding cooperation" and "reiterated their desire to continue developing relations of friendship on the basis of equality, mutual respect and non-intervention in each other's internal affairs." Ortega "spoke highly of the consistent and principled policy of the CPSU and the Soviet state, aimed at strengthening world peace and defending the sovereign rights of the peoples." Tass noted that he also "described the struggle waged by the Nicaraguan people to defend their freedom, independence and right to unhindered development against incessant acts of hostility" by the United States. Ortega pledged the "resolve of the Nicaraguan people to defend the achievements of the Sandinista Revolution." He also reiterated Nicaragua's "readiness" to negotiate "a fair political settlement" in Central America.

The participants at the meeting, according to Tass, "strongly denounced the escalation of U.S. intervention in Central America and the expansion of U.S. military presence there." Such action "poses

---

[46] An indication of Moscow's determination to render vigorous verbal support to the Sandinistas and use this issue to attack the United States is the Soviet response to President Reagan's charge that Soviet military personnel were engaged in Nicaragua.

In his weekly radio address on April 20, President Reagan said that the Soviet Union had "military personnel" in the battle zones of northern Nicaragua near the Honduran border. A White House official later said the number was small and had been sighted near Cotal where a Sandinista military garrison is located. According to the official, the Soviet personnel was probably there as "military advisers rather than involved in actual combat." (The New York Times, April 21, 1985, pl 1 and 17). On April 23, Pravda ridiculed the President's charge as "unsubstantiated" and "absurd fabrications" intended to "disguise the real reasons for tension in Central America." According to Pravda, the "original cause of the critical situation is Washington's interference in the internal affairs of the countries of the region and the policy of imperialist diktat being conducted there." Red Star referred to the "liars from Washington" and their charge of a Soviet military presence as "a raving piece of sensationalism unique in its impudence." The charge was "a crude provocation." (FBIS 022. Moscow Tass International Service in Russian, 0330 GMT, April 23, 1985.)

a threat to the security of Latin Ameican countries and turns that area into a dangerous seat of tension." Not through pressure from "strength, imperial ultimatums and diktat" would the Central Ameican problems be resolved but rather "through peaceful settlement on the basis of talks with respect for the legitimate interests and sovereignty of all the countries in the region." Both sides advocated support for the Contadora group.

Tass noted that the Soviet Union voiced "complete support" for the Sandinista's initiatives for relieving tension in Central America and "ensuring for all the peoples in the region the right to live in peace and good-neighborliness." Gorbachev emphasized that the Soviet Union, in the words of Tass, was "resolutely coming out in defense of the inalienable right of the Nicaraguan people to free, democratic and independent development and was in solidarity with the struggle waged by Nicaragua against the aggressive intrigues of imperialism." The Soviets pledged to give "friendly Nicaragua assistance in resolving urgent problems of economic development, and also, political and diplomatic support in its efforts to uphold its sovereignty." Tass continued:

> The Soviet leadership proceeds from the assumption that in the present-day situation broad international solidarity with Nicaragua is an inalienable part of the common struggle for peace and for the right of all the peoples to freedom and independences.[47]

Soviet pledges of support for Nicaragua, concretely demonstrated by stepped up Soviet military aid that coincided with the Ortega visit, were confirmed by the conclusion of an economic cooperation agreement. By the terms of the agreement, a Soviet-Nicaraguan inter-governmental commission on economic, trade and scientific-technical cooperation was established. It was described as "a new step" for a "further development and deepening of mutually beneficial and equal trade and economic relations" between the Soviet Union and Nicaragua. Milhail Sergeychik, Chairman of the USSR State Committee for Foreign Economic Relations, representing the Soviet, said that the agreement, in the words of Tass,

> will make it possible to realise the great potentialities of the USSR and Nicaragua in the field of economic, trade and scientific-technical cooperation and will serve towards the cause of strengthening friendship between the peoples of the two countries.[48]

(d) Prospects for a code of conduct

What, then, are the prospects for establishing a Code of Conduct in the Third World? Is it at all possible to set down "rules of the

---

[47] FBIS 022. Moscow Tass in English, 1141 GMT, April 29, 1985.

[48] FBIS 018. Moscow Tass in English, 0942 GMT, April 29, 1985. Ortega's visit to Moscow coincided with stepped up Soviet military aid to Nicaragua. Since the beginning of 1985 shipments of arms from the Soviet Union appeared to taper off. However, on April 26, U.S. intelligence sources reported that Soviet arms were unloaded at the port of Corinto by the Soviet freighter *Novo Moskovesk*. These sources noted that the Soviets unloaded at least two MI8-17 "Hip" helicopters used as gunships and troop-carriers (and less threatening than the MI-24 "Hind), along with other arms, ammunition and equipment. The net value of the Soviet shipment was placed at more than $14 million. (O'Leary, Jeremiah. Russians Maneuver After Reagan Defeat: Soviets Ship Arms to the Sandinistas. The Washington Times, April 26, 1985, p. 1A and 8A.)

In Moscow, Ortega termed Nicaragua's relations with the Soviet Union as "exemplary" while those with the United States were marked by open attacks on the Nicaraguan people, "terrorism, destruction and death to Nicaragua." He reiterated Soviet support for Nicaragua against "the U.S. policy of aggression." (FBIS 060. Madrid EFE in Spanish, 0904 GMT, April 30, 1985.)

game," so to speak, that would minimize superpower confrontation and maximize peaceful cooperation?

The answer: Prospects and possibilities seem not to be very good, except in the long-term and through what Bialer suggests the pursuit by the West of a policy of containment, detente *and* confrontation with the Soviet Union.

The fundamental problem in establishing such a code was recently posed by a "ranking" Soviet official in Moscow who has known and worked with Gorbachev within the CPSU for a number of years and is conversant on arms control matters. "The basis, the main thing behind [U.S–Soviet] disagreements," he said, "is a different perception of the realities of the world and the possibilities of peace." [49] Though this statement was made in the context of arms control, it still applies with equal relevance to solving regional problems at least by initially setting down some Code of Conduct.

The historical record does not encourage much hope for success. The power dynamics of the Soviet-American rivalry, the incompatibility of worldviews, underlying political philosophies and modes of life produced persistent failures at Vienna in 1961, during detente of the 1970's and since Brezhnev's peace offensive of 1981. The structure of detente that emerged from the Nixon-Brezhnev summit of 1972 appeared to offer the best chance for laying down some acceptable principles for behavior in the Third World. The document, "Basic Principles of Relations,' concluded after agreement on arms control, provided the first step towards accommodation in the Third World.

But this proved unsuccessful as new revolutionary opportunities opened up in Africa, and the Soviets responded enthusiastically (and naturally, given their ideology) to the pull of their own political and ideological interests. American weakness and its policy of global retrenchment, due notably to its defeat in Vietnam, minimized, indeed ruled out, any meaningful counteraction the United States would take to ensure Soviet adherence to the "Basic Principles." Brezhnev could act with impunity, and he did, ignoring the protest by Kissinger that detente could not stand another Angola.

Thus, the lesson of the 1970's seems to be that mutual interests must by the natural law of international politics dictate the requirements of a viable Code of Conduct. Clearly, this was the case when rules of behavior were established by mutual consent when both sides said they would abide by the terms of SALT I, though the pact expired, and by SALT II, though it had never been ratified. Efforts have been made, apparently with some success, to work out mutually agreeable "rules of the road" to prevent naval collisions at sea. The same can be said about confidence-building measures agreed upon in the Helsinki Accords, such as, notifications of troop maneuvers. Unstated "rules of the game" seem to have prevented the explosive Middle East from enveloping the Soviets and Americans into an irretrievable crisis, confrontation and conflict. Finally, until the shooting of U.S. Army Major Arthur D. Nicholson, Jr. in East Germany on March 24, 1985, the prevailing

---

[49] Thatcher, Gary. Gorbachev Wants "real results" at Geneva, Says Soviet Official. The Christian Science Monitor, March 15, 1985, p. 14.

"rules" for close-in reconnoitering of each other's military forces stationed near East Berlin in administering their vestigal occupation rights in Germany had worked successfully. Both sides moved quickly to preserve the arrangement and to avoid future spoiling incidents.[50]

In brief, mutual interests, often reflecting an agreed strategic balance of power, lay at the center of an effort to establish a code of behavior whether it be on arms control, space exploitation or conduct in the Third World.

Perhaps, the growth of U.S. and Western power all across-the-board and equalizing that of the Soviet Union and its allies offers the best change to ensure Soviet good conduct in the Third World, at least those parts that encompass vital U.S. interests (for example, in Nicaragua). Having available power to counterbalance that of a challenger provides both the substance and leverage to encourage Soviet adherence to peaceful behavior. And in the Nuclear Age where the dangers of war are readily recognized, the choice of a peaceful course has its own built-in appeal for both sides; namely, survival.

Thus, given the power dynamics driving the Soviet-American rivalry and their incompatability opposite ideological worldviews, the chances of establishing a workable Code of Conduct in the Third World seems very slight, except perhaps for selected areas of common interest and except in the long-term. Perhaps the most that can be said is that negotiations on strategic and space weapons now taking place in Geneva could at some point in the future create an acceptable balance of power upon which an agreement could be concluded. And, as in SALT I, an arms control agreement negotiated on an agreed basis of equal strength and security could enhance prospects for establishing a Code of Conduct in the Third World.

Bialer suggests a long-term solution, applying Toynbee's principle of "Challenge and Response." He perceives East-West relations in the context of Soviet expansionism versus Western containment. He argues that only by pursuing a combined and well orchestrated

---

[50] The Washington Post, March 31, 1985, p. A1. Ambassador Dobrynin and Secretary Shultz conferred on this matter, and talks were arranged between military commanders from both sides. Red Star, the organ of the Soviet military forces, sharply rebuked the commanders of a Soviet regiment in East Germany on April 3 for failing to properly train infantry units. This was the second such criticism in many days. (The New York Times, April 4, 1985, p. A10.) Informed Soviet block sources said on April 10 that the Soviet sentry who had killed Nicholson is facing disciplinary measures and may be courtmartialed. These sources, whose information came form Soviet military officers, reported that the sentry was under arrest and was likely to be charged with violating guard duty regulations by using excessive force. (The Washington Post, April 11, 1985, p. A28.) In meetings between top Soviet and American military commanders, the Soviets agreed on April 16 that they would not permit the use of force or weapons against members of the American liaison mission in the future. They also agreed to refer the American demand for an apology and for compensation to the Nicholson family to higher authority. (The New York Times, April 17, 1985, p. A1.)

Differences arose, however, when the issue was referred to higher Soviet authority. In a statement issued on April 22 by the Soviet Embassy in Washington, the Soviet Government regretted the "tragic outcome" of the incident but placed "entire responsibility for what happened . . . wholly on the appropriate U.S. authorities." (The New York Times, April 23, 1985, p. A1 and A6, and April 24, 1985, p. A6.) Nonetheless, the agreement worked out in 1947 permitting surveillance by all sides of the military liaison missions in the other's half of Germany to observe military activities remains unimpaired, underscoring the point being made here that even in the most tense area in Soviet-American relations, on the borders between East and West in Europe, "rules of the game" do exist and while they may break down as in the Nicholsoin case, still they serve the interests of both sides and accordingly are respected by all sides.

policy of containment, detente *and* confrontation towards the Soviet Union will the expansionist stage of Soviet national life pass away and thereupon open up real possibilities not only for improving East-West relations specifically but generally for creating a reasonably stable international order through mutual recognition of a harmony of interests. On such a basis of East-West accord a Code of Conduct could conceivably be established.[51]

---

[51] Bialer, the U.S.S.R. After Brezhnev, p. 60.

IV. THE THIRD WORLD IN THE SOVIET AND AMERICAN FUTURE

A. SOVIET EXPANSIONISM: PERMANENT OR TRANSITORY?

1. HISTORICAL COMMITMENT TO EXPANSION

a. A question with future implications

Perhaps the most important point in considering the Third World in the Soviet-American future is whether Soviet expansionism is a permanent or transitory feature of Soviet foreign policy. If it is permanent, then the Third World, as the area most vulnerable to Soviet penetration, will become, as Casey predicts, "the principal US-Soviet battleground for many years to come." [1] If it is transitory, then it will no doubt cease to spur forceful counteraction by the United States and its allies, opening up thereby the opportunity to establish a harmony of interests in a mutually recognized interdependent world.

b. Russian expansion: An historical reality

Maps 1 and 2 demonstrate graphically and conclusively the expansionist nature of Imperial Russia and its successor state, the U.S.S.R. For students of Russia, like Ulam, Bialer, Brzezinski, Simes, Shulman and Laqueur, expansionism is an historical reality—a fact of history that was given renewed stimulus in the Soviet period by its ideological and systemic commitment to global aggrandizement. [2] Thus, when Secretary Shultz was recently asked whether he believed the Soviet Union was primarily "an inherently militarist and expansionist regime" or was "just another great power," he answered quite naturally, "you have to assume the former, because that's basically the way they have always described themselves and always behaved." [3]

c. Soviet expansion since Stalin

In the lifetime of most Americans today, the Russians have expanded territorially and politically from a continental great power to a global superpower. As a result of territorial conquests in

---

[1] Casey, What We Face, p. 14.

[2] In his recent book on Socialism as a world system, Butenko portrays the Soviet self-perception of the expanding Socialist system: "Whereas at the start of the century socialism had taken only its first steps in post-October Russia, it now exists and is developing as a powerful world system of socialist states of Europe, Asia and Latin America, a system with which countries of a socialist orientation are joining up and with which revolutionary detachments of the nonsocialist world are interacting increasingly closely, multiplying the impact of socialism and gradually turning it into a force capable of exerting a decisive influence on all world politics." (Socialism as a World System, p. 238.)

[3] Gwertzman, Bernard. Russian's Statement Worries Shultz, The New York Times, March 18, 1985, p. A3.

World War II, Stalin extended Russia's imperial domain to Eastern Europe and territorial acquisitions in the Far East (see map 1). Stalin later agreed with Soviet Central Committee Secretary Andrei Zhdanov's statement of regret at not occupying Finland, commenting, "We were too concerned with the Americans, and they wouldn't have lifted a finger." [4]

In early 1946, Stalin hinted at the "limits" of Moscow's imperial reach. It was during the emerging crises in Iran and Turkey and on the occasion of U.S. Ambassador Walter Bedell Smith's first audience with the Soviet leader. Smith probed deeply Soviet intentions and goals. "How far is Russia going to go?" he asked. Stalin replied, "We're not going much further," and then proceeded to explain the Soviet demand for a base in the Dardanelles as "a matter of our security." [5]

Khrushchev, building on the Stalin legacy, extended Russia's reach to the Third World where Soviet influence was henceforth to take on a global character, Shevchenko best describes Krushchev's ambitions when he recently wrote in his diplomatic memoir, "He understood the danger of nuclear war, but aggressive expansionism was irresistible to him" [6]

Brezhnev expanded still further on the Khrushchev legacy to include other areas in Asia and Africa and to impose the principle of non-reversibility, at least within Russia's contiguous empire, in the declaration of the "Brezhnev Doctrine." Afghanistan has proved to be Moscow's nemesis. Though Andropov's and Chernenko's terms of leadership were cut short by illness and early death, still, as this study illustrates, they not only maintained the Soviet commitment to expansion but, as seen in Nicaragua and elsewhere, they have improved upon it (See Map 1).

As the inheritor of this collective imperial legacy reaching back to Stalin, Gorbachev has thus far said and done nothing to alter the expansionist course of Soviet foreign policy. With Boris Ponomarev, Party Secretary and candidate member of the Politburo since 1972, at his as head of the International Department, Gorbachev has a formidable advisor and advocate of deep Soviet involvement in the Third World. The International Department guides and instructs Communist parties abroad and oversees political activities within the National Liberation Movement and the Third World. "As the upholder of a militant internationalist faith, committed to the evantual triumph of Communism in the world," writes Shevchenko, "the department is the justifier of Soviet expansionism." [7]

---

[4] Quoted in, Djilas, Milovan. Rise and Fall. New York, Harcourt Brace Jovanovich, 1985, 424 p., and Robert Conquest's review in, The New York Times Book Review, Feb. 24, 1985. p. 6.

[5] HFAC, Soviet Diplomacy and Negotiating Behavior, p. 222.

[6] Shevchenko, Breaking With Moscow, p. 127.

[7] Shevchenko continues: "In its role as liaison with extremist movements and an instrument to influence public opinion in the West, it is also the inspirer of much of the disorder which threatens stability and Western interests in the Third World." He describes Ponomarev as a "vigorous and determined disciple of Mikhail Suslov and his doctrinal rigidity." (Breaking with Moscow, p. 188–190.)

2. DIFFERENTIATION IN SOVIET EXPANSIONISM

a. "Internal" and "contiguous" empires

Soviet expansion seems to have differentiated characteristics. The internal and continguous Soviet empire, as shown in map 2, has the dominating characteristic of direct territorial and political control in the case of the former and indirect in the case of the latter. The relationship is strictly imperial in the sense of traditional continental empires of the past, such as, the Austro-Hungarian and Napoleonic Empires. Thus in Russia's "internal empire" of over 271 million, some 45 million Muslims, to name only one of over a hundred non-Russian nationalities, have been politicized into accepting what objectively is an imperial relationship in the classic sense. And with respect to the "contiguous empire" of Eastern Europe, Soviet military intervention in Hungary in 1956, Czechoslovakia in 1968 and indirectly in Poland in 1980-81 were clear attempts to maintain imperial control akin to the European suppression of the liberal revolutions of 1848.

b. "Empires abroad" in the Third World

What the Soviets seem to have in mind, however, for a world Socialist system does not seem to be this type which realistically seems unatainable—it defies history—but rather one that has the characteristics of what the Rand study would term an "empire abroad." Competition for and ultimately gaining influence over Third World countries rather than direct physical control seems to be the principal characteristic of this relationship as, for example, that existing with such Third World countries as India and Syria. Though the Soviets have had visions of a world state, at least theoretically, perhaps as a practical matter they seek this sort of arrangement as an interim if not a final goal.

In brief, the Soviet approach to the Third World suggests the creation of an "empire abroad" based more upon an ability to influence through all the instrumentalities described in this study rather than to control directly. Hence prestige, meaning a "reputation for power," as Hans Morgenthau defined it, takes on a high value for the Soviets. For prestige is power; it exemplifies a presence that can command attention, respect and even emulation. As power increases, it attracts other nations like a magnet and can in some instances (for example, Ethiopia) generate a willingness to comply with Soviet forms and wishes.

Conceivably, India could be that type of Third World ally practically evisioned by the Soviets on a larger scale for the distant future. Soviet efforts to grade the level of Socialism among Third World states, described in Part I, establishes criteria for acceptability. It suggests an evolving Soviet relationship with Third World countries according to varying degrees of adherence to Moscow's definition of Socialism and thus acceptability.

c. Cuba, a case in point

Cuba is a case in point to show the evolution of a Third World country from the stage of "national liberation" to that of a Socialist ally. When Khrushchev came to America to speak at the United Nations in the fall of 1960, the Soviet relationship with Cuba was just taking shape. At the time Khrushchev told Shevchenko who accompanied the Soviet leader abroad the *Baltika*: "I hope that Cuba will become a beacon of socialism in Latin America." Castro, he said, "offers that hope," and he added that "the Americans are helping us" by driving Castro into the Socialist camp. Instead of establishing normal relations with Cuba, he said, the United States was doing everything to drive Castro to the wall, as paraphrased by Shevchenko, "by organizing a campaign against him, stirring up the Latin American countries against him, and establishing an economic blocade against Cuba." "That's stupid," Khrushchev said, and he predicted: "Castro will have to gravitate to us like an iron filing to a magnet."[8]

Part V of this study describes Cuba's transformation in the next twenty years into an important, but often troublesome, Socialist ally of Moscow in which over time the interests of both countries have coalesced.

Thus, if Soviet expansion leads to some form of world Socialist system allying the Soviet Union with the Third World, as they claim, it would seem more likely to be one that has evolved out of a coalescing of political interests among like-minded Third World Socialists states rather than a form of physical "domination" in the classic imperial sense.

3. CONTINUING SOVIET EXPANSION?

Whether Soviet expansion will continue can only be a matter of speculation. The historical record suggests the likelihood of continuing expansion of Soviet power, despite known costs. Expansion has been a powerful, irrepressible dynamic in Russian history, one not likely to be arrested and reversed in the near term and perhaps not even the long term. For the concept of expansionism has been deeply engrained in the Soviet political culture as a tenet of faith fortified by the protecting and proselytizing commitment of a powerful self-perpetuating bureaucracy.

Wolf concludes, on the basis of his anlysis of the Cost of Empire, that in the aggregate the benefits of empire "may, from the Politburo's viewpoint, amply justify the costs. They suggest that Soviet efforts to expand the empire are likely to continue."[9]

Casey quotes from Churchill's " Iron Curtain" speech at Westminster College in 1946:

Nobody knows what Soviet Russia and its Communist international organization intends to do in the immediate future, or what are the limits, if any, to their expansive and proselytizing tendencies.

---

[8] Shevchenko, Breaking with Moscow, p. 105.
[9] Wolf, Costs of the Soviet Empire, p. 32. In a more comprehensive statement, the Rand study concludes: ". . . it is probably a resonable presumption that the total costs—both noneconomic and economic—of the Soviet empire, at the levels they have reached in recent years, are likely to appear to the Soviet leadership to be quite reasonable, if not modest, in relation to this formidable package of benefits ascribed to the empire. Finally, our dollar estimates of CSE [Cost of Soviet Empire] seem to be well within the bounds that have been acceptable to imperial powers in the past, whereas the ruble estimates toward the end of the 1970s had reached levels that seemed to be transcending those bounds." (Rand, Costs of the Soviet Empire, p. 50.)

Casey then proceeds to record Soviet expansionism in the Third World since the 1970's, implying by the tone and substance of his speech that unless counteraction is taken Soviet expansion will indeed continue.[10] Unless forced out as in the case of Egypt, it is not likely that the Soviets by their own volition would soon withdraw from such important geopolitical strongholds as the Horn of Africa, South Yemen, Cuba or Da Nang and Cam Ranh Bay in Vietnam.

B. POLAR ALTERNATIVES: MILITARISM OR GLOBAL INTERDEPENDENCE

1. THE PATH OF MILITARISM

a. Brzezinski's thesis: The USSR as a one-dimensional military power

Assuming that Soviet expansion into the Third World will continue at its present pace, the question arises as to which direction it may take. For the sake of analysis two possible directions, radically different, are projected: one towards continuing militarization; the other towards achieving global interdependence.

Brzezinski has advanced the thesis that for the first time Soviet military power has acquired a genuine global reach. But, he cautions, "global reach is not the same as global grasp."[11] For he contends that Soviet power is only one-dimensional, that is, military; that it lacks systemic appeal; that it "cannot be the point of departure either for comprehensive global leadership or for an enduring global partnership with the United States"; that its world outlook is a "combination of possessive defensiveness and distruptive offensiveness"; and accordingly that the only course open to achieving global status, given the closing of the nuclear option, is that of attrition and disruption of a stable international order.[12] In brief, Brzezinski maintains that one-dimensional Soviet power is "essentially incapable of sustaining global dominance."[13] In other words, it cannot do what Britain did for perhaps two centuries before the final collapse of its empire after World War II.

Whatever the merit of Brzezinski's thesis (and there is much to be said for it), there can be little doubt that the Soviets have indeed been pursuing the path of militarism in attempting to build a world Socialist system by creating a symbiotic relationship with the Third World. This fact is amply deomonstrated in this study.

The Soviets *have* built up "an awesome military machine," as Lord Carrington notes; they *have* shown that they are prepared to use it; and they *have* "the means and the motivation to project" their power "into large areas of the world."[14]

Soviet expansion into the Third World *is* essentially military, and it has been achieved either directly through the use of their military power, as in Asia, or indirectly with the transfer of arms, military equipment and other forms of military assistance as in Cuba, Syria and Africa.

---

[10] Casey, What We Face, Westiminster College Speech, p. 7.
[11] Brzezinski, World Power of a New Type, p. 155.
[12] Ibid., p. 155–156.
[13] Ibid., p. 151.
[14] Carrington, It's the West That's Strong, Moscow That's Weak, p. H3027.

Soviet expansion is also built upon Marxism-Leninist ideology. These principles may have only limited appeal to Third World nations who seek economic development from the West and who value not only the markets and technology of the industrialized non-Communist world but also freedom of political choice in organizing their own societies. Nonetheless, these principles endow Soviet expansionism, through their unique ideological and organizational characteristics, with unusual staying power, a sense of mission and conviction in ultimate purposes, and protection against imperial fatigue that plagued other imperial systems of the past that had failed. The political elite that inspires and directs Soviet expansionism is held captive by its own restrictive ideology; it is impervious to the need for fundamental systemic reforms, dedicated to essentially unchanging means and ends, and both isolated and insulated by a self-perpetuating bureaucracy. Because of its closed political system, the Soviet Union is, politically speaking, an island unto itself.

The effect of these influences on Soviet expansion apparently is to strengthen the conviction of the political leadership that the path of giving pre-eminence to military power is the correct and perhaps the only one.[15]

b. Implications of Soviet militarism

(1) Lasting tensions; increasing risk of conflict

The Soviet choice of militarism appears to have twofold implications: first, it could, if unrestrained, create a dangerous world political environment in which tensions between the superpowers could continue to increase, and increase accordingly the risk of conflict, even nuclear war; and second, it could also expose the Soviet Union to the serious consequences of overmilitarization.

Lasting tensions and increased risks of conflict appear to arise from three elements; namely, the great power dynamic, conflicting ideological beliefs and the militarization of foreign policy. The center of gravity of international politics appears to have shifted largely to the Third World where all three elements converge.

As this study suggests, Soviet expansionism has provoked formidable opposition among many nations around the globe, particularly the United States, Japan, NATO Europe and even China, which see their interests being threatened. It creates an international problem because Soviet ideology, plus the presence of the great power dynamic, produces conflict, and conflict, in a setting of unrestrained arms race, can place all mankind in jeopardy.

Theoretically, the Soviet elite conceives world politics as a vortex of dynamic human struggle where force is exaulted and power sanctified. Adhering to a conception alien to Western diplomatic traditions, this elite perceives power relationships among nations inherently conflicting, not adjustable, and thus impervious to rational solutions that would respect or maintain the status quo or a particular harmony of interests. This idea is a basic premise of Brzezinski's thesis.

---

[15] For a commentary on just how closed Soviet society is, see, Shevchenko, Breaking With Moscow, p. 180–81.

For the Soviets, the drive for power is a continuous factor in foreign relations and thus genuine peace between capitalism and Communism is unthinkable. International politics, even in times of peace, is a continuation of war by other means. To this ruling elite, therefore, genuine "peaceful coexistence" as understood by Western democracies is imposcible and acquiesence in what the West would term the status quo unthinkable. Peaceful coexistence is in reality a form of advance; and the status quo, as Khrushchev told Walter Lippmann in the early 1960's and President Kennedy at Vienna in 1961, means simply the unimpeded progress of the march of Communism.

The military ingredient, when added to this unresolved ideological conflict and the interacting dynamics of great power relationships, has the effect of catalyzing the conflict, virtually insuring increased tensions as a "normal" state of relations, and, accordingly, increasing the risk of conflict and war.[16]

A distinctive characteristic in Soviet behavior could contribute to a worsening of relations with the West; namely, an inclination toward external aggressiveness during a period of internal weakness as a way of concealing vulnerabilities and as a defense mechanism for counteracting the "machinations" of external "enemies." Stalin's aggressive behavior in the Cold War has been attributed to this characteristic. At the time Russia was recovering from an exhausting world war in which it suffered some 20 million fatalities, and Stalin was preoccupied with fears of a new "capitalist encirclement." Current Soviet internal failings could conceivably inspire a similiar posture of calculated hostility in order to counteract outside perceptions of internal weakness.[17]

(2) Consequences of militarism and overmilitarization

Choosing this singular path of militarism (against Engels' advice, it might be emphasized) poses three potential problems for the Soviet Union; namely, the difficulty of maintaining an empire; the serious consequences of exceeding its imperial grasp; and, similarly, the serious consequences of over-militarizing the Soviet state.

At this juncture in the mid-1980's, the cost of empire may be acceptable to the Soviet leadership as the Rand study suggests, but the problem of empire maintenance could increase with each outward imperial thrust. Afghanistan, Cuba and Vietnam are case

---

[16] Scholars sometimes differ on the impact of ideology on Soviet foreign policy, but the practical judgment of Max M. Kampelman gives some idea of the extent that leading Soviet negotiators are guided by Marxism-Leninism. Kampelman, presently head of the U.S. arms control delegation in Geneva, gave this account of his experience negotiating with the Soviets on the Commission on Security and Cooperation in Europe: ". . . I had not expected to find the degree of commitment to Leninism that I actually did find in the heads of the Soviet delegation. I am not prepared to generalize and to say that that degree of commitment went through the whole delegation. I didn't meet every member, or at least didn't have intensive conversations with every member of the Soviet delegation. Nor am I prepared to say this necessarily means that Leninism has deep roots within the Soviet society. I do not know. What I can say, however, is that I was surprised by the degree of commitment to Leninism that existed in the leadership of that delegation. When you are spending 400 hours in conversations, and particularly if you feel you are a little bit familiar with the concepts of Marxism-Leninism, it isn't difficult to find yourself involved in conversations about Marxism-Leninism. I expected to find a more pragmatic view, maybe a more cynical view." (Madrid Conference: How to Negotiate with the Soviets. American Bar Association. Standing Committee on Law and National Security. Intelligence Report, v. 7, no. 2, Feb. 1985, p. 3.)

[17] For a discussion of Stalin's behavior in the postwar era, see HFAC, Soviet Diplomacy and Negotiating Behavior, p. 220-221.

studies in the cost of empire to the U.S.S.R. These costs are increasing, not decreasing. A point of diminishing returns could be reached when the cost of empire maintenance exceeds the resources needed to safely sustain the Soviet's own home base of power. The serious economic and social problems facing the Soviet Union, summarized in Part V of this study, suggest the magnitude of the demands being placed upon the new leadership now and perhaps for some time to come.

As this study shows, there are limits to Soviet expansion in the Third World through the use of military power. Lacking the essential ingredients for creating imperial cohesion as the British had successfully done, Soviet influence has lacked staying power in its overseas empire, as for example in countries like Egypt where they were forced out.[18] Even in areas where they are now deeply involved, as in Ethiopia, their influence is judged to be superficial and its durability transitory.[19]

Secondly, over-commitment and over-extension have been critical to empires of the past, leading to decline, as in the case of the Roman Empire. The same risk applies to the Soviet Union, only with the added risk that over-expansion could lead to a "disastrous" outcome. Brzezinski gives this explanation:

> By having become a global military power, the Soviet Union has broken through the United States' policy of geographic containment. At the same time, by expanding its exposure when its own capacities are still very one-dimensional, the Soviet Union is exposing itself to the possibility of over-extension and eventually to a major external misfortune, because of some protracted military-political misadventure. And in that respect Moscow's strategy of deliberate exploitation of global turbulence could turn out to be historically disastrous.[20]

---

[18] James P. Wootten, a specialist in Middle East and defense affairs in the Congressional Research Service, noted in conversation that one of the most important observations to be made during his many travels in the Middle East, especially in Egypt, is the absence of a deep Soviet influence in the area. In Egypt, he said, "you would never know that they had been there. This cannot be said of the British who during their imperial days did indeed make an impact."

[19] Michael J. Dixon, a senior research analyst in Soviet and East European Affairs, CRS, and author of Parts III and IV of this study.

Luers gives the following explanation of Soviet aims in the Third World that bears on this point: "Whether or not the Soviet have a global strategy, they most certainly are determined to increase their political influence in the world. Since they find it difficult or impossible to exercise that influence through international economic, financial or trading bodies or through regional groups, they seek instead to build military-political clients. The evolution of Soviet involvement in Africa, Southeast Asia, the Middle East and the Caribbean Basin attest to this Soviet desire for influence through close alliances with willing or threatened nation states. The Soviets in this way seek to establish parity with the United States as a superpower, not only in the military but also in the political sphere." (The Soviets and Latin America, p. 25.)

In what he terms a "strategy of disruption," Casey gives this explanation of Soviet reliance on military power to expand its presence in the Third World instead of relying on the creative instrumentalities of development: "Military support can establish a relationship between a superpower and a small country. But in the long run it is economic, financial, scientific, technical and cultural exchanges which attract, deliver benefits, and maintain close relationships with Thrid World countries. The Soviet Union cannot compete in these areas. This forces the Soviets to rely on subversion and disruption of stable political and economic relationships to weaken Western relationship and create a condition of chaos in which their surrogates and internal allies can seize power." (What We Face, p. 11.)

[20] Brzezinski, World Power of a New Type, p. 158. The best case study to demonstrate the outcome that Brzezinski describes is the Cuban missile crisis. In his diplomatic memoir, Shevchenko records how Khrushchev initiated the crisis and what he hoped to gain: "The idea to deploy nuclear missiles in Cuba was Khrushchev's own; many years later he admitted as much in his memoir. Beyond a defense for Cuba, the more important gain would be a better balance of power between the United States and the U.S.S.R. [then inferior to the United States in strategic nuclear weapons]. Khrushchev's plan was to create a nuclear 'fist' in close proximity to the United States, and at first glance it seemed seductive. The Soviet Union could get a 'cheap' nuclear rocket deterrent, and accomplish much with very little." In the process Khrushchev brought the world close to the brink of nuclear war. (Breaking With Moscow, p. 116–18.)

Continued

Finally, over-militarization of society could have serious consequences for the health of a nation. Milovan Djilas, a former Yugoslav leader, long experienced with Communism in the Soviet Union and Yugoslavia, explains one side of Soviet military expansion. He writes:

> Soviet communism . . . is a military empire. It was transformed into a military empire in Stalin's time. Internally, such structures usually rot; . . . but to avoid internal problems, they may go for expansion . . . if it is stopped, the process of rotting will go faster.[21]

But in the long-term military expansion can at best be only a temporary palliative. More serious is over-militarization that can consume the creative energies of a people, bringing their nation to a point of exhaustion by conflicts and wars. In his massive historical study of world civilizations, the British historian Arnold Toynbee concludes that militarism is symptomatic of "breakdown" in civilization. His explanation, though cast in the larger context of civilizations, nonetheless, has particular relevance to the potential danger the Soviet Union could face sometime in the future should it continue along the path of militarism:

> Militarism . . . has been by far the commonest cause of the breakdowns of civilizations during the last four or five millennia which have witnessed the score or so of breakdowns that are on record up to the present date. Militarism breaks a civilization down by causing the local states into which the society is articulated to collide with one another in destructive fracticidal conflicts. In this suicidal process the entire social fabric becomes fuel to feed the devouring flame in the brazen bosom of Moloch. This single art of war makes progress at the expense of the divers arts of peace; and before this deadly ritual has completed the destruction of all its votaries, they may have become so expert in the use of their implements of slaughter that, if they happen for a moment to pause from their orgy of mutual destruction and to turn their weapons for a season against the breasts of strangers, they are apt to carry all before them.[22]

2. THE PATH OF "GLOBAL INTERDEPENDENCE"

a. The meaning of interdependence

Global interdependence offers the Soviet Union a conceptual, polar alternative in the Third World that could reduce the negative

---

On the occasion of the 50th anniversary of establishing Soviet-American diplomatic relations, Soviet Ambassador Dobrynin alluded to the Cuban missile crisis and the great danger both nations faced. Noting the expansion of nuclear weapons and the need for understanding each other, he cautioned: "We should keep 1962 in mind." (Kennan Institute for Advanced Russian Studies. Fifty Years of Diplomatic Relations Between the United States and the Union of Soviet Socialist Republics. Washington, 1983, p. 14. Occasional Paper, Number 189.)

[21] Quoted in, Wolf, Costs of the Soviet Empire, p. 32.

[22] Toynbee, Arnold J. A study of History. Abridgement of Volumes I-VI by D.C. Somervell. New York, Oxford University Press, 1947, p. 190.

Bialer points out the Soviet dilemma in their reliance on military power in the Third World: "It is likely that the pattern of acquiring power through military intervention will prove very temporary in the final analysis, yet the danger that it will be repeated in the 1980s is quite high.

"But if it was possible in the 1970s for the Soviet leadership to engage in foreign military actions without recognizing what effect this would have on the behavior of the United States, today this is impossible. A decision to risk inevitable American reaction with more Angolas or Ethiopias would have to be carefully premeditated. It would signify a Soviet decision that relations with the United States cannot improve in the foreseeable future, and a willingness by the Soviet leadership to take much higher risks than in the late 1970s.

"In the Third World, the use of military might has become the Soviets' only alternative to an effective foreign policy. Naturally, any Soviet leader is likely to consider ineffectiveness unacceptable. But military intervention will prove very dangerous in the 1980s." (Bialer, Seweryn. Soviet-American Conflict: From the Past to the Future. In U.S.-Soviet Relations: Perspectives for the Future. Washington, Center for National Policy, Sept. 1984, p. 17.)

consequences of militarism, contribute to solving troubling global problems that affect all mankind, give greater assurance of world peace, and ultimately allow the Soviet Union to turn its creative energies inward and improve its own failing Socialist system.

Interdependence is a term used to describe what is perceived by some to be a new cycle of change in international politics. Regarded as a conceptualization of the world in transition, it has been variously presented as a workable rationale for assuring safety and continuity in a time of change.

The idea of interdependence is not new, but its realization on a global scale is without precedent. Centuries ago John Donne expressed it in his phrase, "No man is an island." In recent years interdependence has been given currency and momentum by the search for accommodation in East-West relations; by the emergence of the Third World, especially those countries resource rich, as a power factor in international relations; by the global nature of some of today's problems, such as, over-population, environmental pollution, scarcity of resources in great demand, notably energy and food, arms control, international development, equitable use of oceans and seabeds, establishment of a fair and just international economic system, to name some of the most important. The appeal of interdependence arises from the belief that it can offer a route for common survival. In brief, it offers a conceptual alternative to the path of militarism.

In practical terms interdependence requires renewed emphasis on functional diplomacy, a type of conduct in international relations that places a high premium on international cooperation. Diplomacy, in short, is given a new lease on life. Its advocates assume that through cooperative interaction of nations international relations will become infused with a moderating and conciliatory spirit. Solutions to common problems can issue from this new spirit, it is argued; peace and security for all may be achieved. The binding force of this new diplomatic functionalism, in contrast to the international rivalry generated by militarism, is the common desire to survive. Mankind has no other choice, it is said; interdependence offers a path towards common survival.[23] For the Soviet Union it arguably offers an opportunity for systematic renewal and a regeneration of the positive values of Russian civilization.

b. Soviet views on interdependence

In official position statements the Soviet Union has defined interdependence as an ideological weapon in the service of Western "neocolonialism" and directed against the Third World. But some serious Soviet scholars, and even Soviet political leaders, look upon certain aspects of interdependence as a necessity for continuing life in the Nuclear Age.[24]

---

[23] For a discussion of interdependence in the Third World context, see, HFAC, Soviet Union and the Third World, 1977, p. 167–171.

[24] See the section on "Global Interdependence" in, Jamgotch, Nish, Jr. Soviet Security in Flux. Muscatine, Iowa, The Stanley Foundation, May 1983, p. 19–23. (Occasional Paper 33). See also, Butenko, Socialism as a World System, p. 241. Butenko lists an array of problems facing mankind, for example, overpopulation, scarce raw materials, maintaining the planet's ecological balance, the solutions of which are becoming "increasingly urgent," and decalres: "All these and other global problems today demand the unification of the efforts of all people of good will and the joint actions of states with different social systems."

Part I of this study summarizes the views of the "globalists" among Soviet Third World scholars who share many of the concerns expressed by Western advocates of interdependence. Arbatov has been a persistent supporter of this view. In an extensive interview in Le Matin of Paris on March 29, 1984, for example, he expressed views that have virtually become commonplace. Speculating on the solution to problems over the next fifty years, he said:

I believe that we are entering particularly difficult decades and that we will no longer be able to afford to indulge in the activities which we are currently pursuing, such as the arms race. The problems of a global and national nature will assume such proportions that we really will have to tackle the realities. In 50 years' time, we will perhaps find ourselves laughing at what our anxieties in the seventies or eighties were. The problems of resources will become very difficult; those of ecology and of the Third World could become terrible. Consider the increase in population. Feeding all those people! It is the equivalent of another globe. In 50 years' time, we will have to have built and created as much as we have done throughout our history . . . that will require terribly rational conduct, a great deal of cooperation, a sharing of borders. . . .

Asked specifically about East-West cooperation, Arbatov said:

If we wish to survive, it is not only the danger of war—even if it is the most urgent—that must be disspelled. We must change a host of things of quite a different kind which detente cannot in itself resolve. But without detente, without stopping the arms race, without cooperation, there will be no question of even approaching the solutions.[25]

Judging by past comments, Gorbachev seems to be sympathetic with many of the tenets of interdependence. In a speech to the British Parliament in December 1984, he used the occasion primarily to make a strong case for East-West accommodation. Extolling the virtues of cooperation during the 1970's, he urged East and West to "learn to live together, proceeding from the realities of the modern world." "We live in a vulnerable, fairly fragile, but interconnected world," he said, where, "whether you like it or not, it is essential to coexist with each other." Gorbachev added that "there is always room for reasonable compromises" in international relations and urged that East and West take advantage of their "vast" potential for building on "close or coinciding interests."[26]

c. Factors encouraging interdependence

Many factors could encourage greater attention to the value of interdependence in the Soviet approach not only to the Third World but to East-West relations as well. Conceivably, increased costs of empire, particularly for a country plagued by economic problems for many decades, could force a reassessment of policy

---

[25] FBIS 065. Paris Le Matin in French, March 29, 1985, p. 12–13. Arbatov interview with Jean-Louis Arnaud. On March 6, 1985, Arbatov appeared on Channel 17 Cable TV in a program moderated by the Rev. Theodore M. Hesburgh, President of Notre Dame University. Other panelists were Dr. Carl Sagan of Cornell University, Admiral Noel Gaylor, USN (Ret.), and Dr. Rauld Sadeev of the Soviet Institute of Space Research. The thrust of the entire program was towards an understanding of interdependence and its importance today. Both Arbatov and Sadeev concurred with the American panelists in virtually every aspect of the discussion. Particular emphasis was placed on the importance of space cooperation and generally on maintaining an active Soviet-American dialogue.

[26] FBIS 018. Gorbachev, March 11, 1985, Take 8. For a discussion of the Soviet view of North-South problems and interdependence, see Laird, Robbin F. and Erik P. Hoffmann. Soviet Perspectives on North-South Relations in the Era of "The Scientific-Technological Revolution," in, Hoffmann, Erik P. and Frederic J. Fleron, Jr. The Conduct of Soviet Foreign Policy. New York, Aldine Publishing Co., 1980, chapter 24.

and possibly encourage retrenchment abroad. (Recall that Russia did withdraw from Russian-America by selling Alaska in order to reduce its imperial commitments, and that the Soviet Union also withdrew from Austria in 1955, apparently, for political reasons. Historically, then, Russian expansion is not irreversible.) As Walter C. Clemens, Jr., a specialist in Soviet Third World affairs at Boston University, recently wrote, "Empire-building is a showy but expensive business."[27]

Such a reassessment had begun in the last years of Brezhnev's rule and continued under Andropov. Economic reform has been placed high on the new leadership's agenda. In a speech to an ideological conference on December 10, 1984, Gorbachev, aligning himself with the Andropov legacy, quoted the same Leninist formula in Andropov's speech in November 1982: "Socialism has exerted and continues to exert its main influence on world development through its economic policy and its successes in the socioeconomic field." Like Andropov, Gorbachev seemed to be cautioning his audience that the lagging Soviet economy was preventing the Soviet Union from exercising the influence it wishes in global affairs and that until the economy functioned efficiently, then, as Elizabeth Teague, a Soviet specialist at Radio Liberty, suggests, "the USSR will remain a second-class, one-dimensional power." To correct these economic deficiencies, Gorbachev went on, "profound transformations" will have to be made not only in the economy but "in the entire sphere of social relations." He called for "truly revolutionary solutions" to quicken the application of new scientific and technological discoveries in the production process.[28]

Indeed, Gorbachev's election speech in February 1985 amounted to an agenda for economic reform.[29] And in a secret speech to a limited Moscow audience three months before becoming General Secretary, parts of which were published in the West on March 27, Gorbachev lays out in almost painful detail and in dramatic and forceful language the necessity of reform and the heavy burden that the Soviet people will have to bear to achieve "the highest standards of Socialism." What he seems to envision is not only economic reform but social, and, apparently, even political reform as well. In brief, a deep systemic reform.[30] Preoccupation with eco-

[27] Clemens, Walter C. Jr. US and USSR: An Agenda for a New Detente. The Christian Science Monitor, March 21, 1985, p. 16.

[28] Teague, Elizabeth. Gorbachev Picks Up Where Andropov Left Off. RFE-RL. Radio Liberty Research. RL 78/85, March 14, 1985, p. 4. For the text of Gorbachev's speech, see, Moscow Pravda in Russian, Dec. 11, 1984, 1st ed, p. 2, in FBIS Daily Report, Soviet Union, v. 3, Dec. 11, 1984, p. R2–R9. For other commentary on Gorbachev's views, see, Nahaylo, Bohdan. Gorbachev and Foreign Policy—More of the Same, At Least for Now. RFE-RL. Radio Liberty Research, RL 79/85, March 19, 1985, 6 p., and Hanson, Philip. Mikhail Gorbachev and the Soviet Economy. RFE-RL. Radio Liberty Research, RL 80/85, March 14, 1985, 3 p.

Bialer states that Gorbachev inherited a non-competitive Soviet economy "that is in a terrible state. A cumbersome system of central planning produces shoddy goods, and discourages any sort of creativity or technological innovation. The Soviet economy is simply incapable of participating in the high-tech, electronic age." Bialer notes that the economic crisis is compounded by a social crisis and a political crisis and analyzes the prospects for "radical reform" under an innovative, forceful Gorbachev regime. (Bialer, Sweryn. Will Russia Dare Clean Up its Economic Mess? The Washington Post, Outlook, April 21, 1985, p. K1–K2.)

[29] FBIS 052. Pravda, Feb. 21, 1985, 1st ed.

[30] FBIS 031. USSR: Gorbachev's "Secret Report" to Moscow Conference, by Rudolfo Brancoli, Rome La Republica in Italian, March 27, 1985, p. 1 and 9.

nomic reform could encourage a redirection inward of Soviet policy, particularly if the costs of empire were judged to outweigh benefits.

Time will also be needed for Gorbachev to establish his "Socialist legitimacy"; that is, not only the right to rule by virtue of investiture of office, but the power to direct, to control and most importantly to be obeyed. It took Stalin 10 years, Khrushchev four and Brezhnev six years to achieve this degree of authority.[31] In all probability Gorbachev will not have an easy time bringing an ossified bureaucracy into a new economic order. Deeply entrenched bureaucratic interests and old habits are difficult to change. Success will require a strong leadership to get the economy moving in the direction some reformers foresee. Accordingly, economic reform will no doubt require time, a period of tranquility and the tapping of resources and scientific-technological know-how in the industrialized non-Communist developed world to re-vitalize and modernize the backward Soviet economy. Such a development could open the possibilities for easy international tensions and expanding cooperation internationally.[32] Yet, give the magnitude of the tasks ahead and the systemic constrictions on an ambitious, innovative leader such as Gorbachev, it is more likely that improved relations leading towards detene and possibly even interdependence, if it does take place, would be very gradual.

Moreover, it is entirely possible that a re-vitalized Soviet economy could encourage the Soviet leaders to assume greater burdens in the Third World to the detriment of the United States. This study indicates that the weak Soviet economy has largely prevented them from acquiring far greater influence in the Third World states.[33]

A new generation of leaders more pragmatic and less ideological than its predecessors could conceivably see more clearly differing Soviet interests as well as their limitations in the Third World and accordingly scale down its costly involvement.[34] Ironically, Foreign Minister Gromyko, cautious by nature (according to Shevchenko) and whose tenure as a diplomat exceeds 40 years and spans two generations, has apparently been indifferent perhaps even skeptical about the value of the Third World to Soviet foreign policy. Shevchenko, his close adviser in the Foreign Ministry, not only substantiates this view but also emphasizes Gromyko's preference for detente and a pragmatic approach to foreign policy.[35]

---

[31] Whelan, Joseph G. Soviet Successions from Lenin to Brezhnev: The Troubled Search for Legitimacy. Washington, Congressional Research Service, The Library of Congress, Sept. 20, 1982, p. 81–82 (Report No. 82–152 S).

[32] For a reasonably optimistic appraisal of Soviet-American relations in the Gorbachev succession, see, Hyland, William G. The Gorbachev Succession. Foreign Affairs, v. 63, Spring 1985: 800–809.

[33] Michael J. Dixon, Research Analyst in Soviet and east European Affairs, CRS.

[34] Hough points out the growing skepticism in the Soviet scholarly literature on Third World development and its impact on the leadership, noting that in the Andropov period the leadership essentially accepted their arguments. (Rethinking the Soviet-American Relationship, p. 32.)

[35] Shevchenko, Breaking With Moscow, p. 190, 151, 152, 157–159. He notes that despite countless invitations, Gromyko had never visited any black African nation. Except for Cuba, he has never visited any Latin American country. Shevchenko also felt that Gromyko was "simply bored with persistent challenge to Soviet domination in Eastern Europe and viewed these countries as a burden to us." He also believed that Gromyko looked upon dealing with their leaders and visiting the bloc countries as a "nuisance." Gromyko was openly criticized by orthodox

Whatever the truth of Shevchenko's revelation, the fact remains that Gromyko has for a long time been a principal actor in the Soviet foreign policy process that has been directing the Soviet thrust into the Third World since the mid-1950's. Whatever his personal preference as a foreign policy theorist, he has been, nonetheless, part of a foreign policy collective distinguished more for strict adherence to established policy line than for deviation.

Still, should Gromyko's influence remain strong in the new leadership, which thus far seems to be the case, conceivably Soviet priorities could in a calculated short-term maneuver shift away from the more ideological extremes of the past (recall Brezhnev's shift to realism after Khrushchev's extremism) towards a harder, more realistic appraisal of Soviet interests and concrete possibilities. Such a tactical shift need not sacrifice long-term Soviet goals in the Third World that have become so deeply imbedded in the Soviet political culture nor sacrifice gains already achieved in the Third World.

As pointed out in this study, Brezhnev in his declining years and Andropov his immediate successor had themselves attempted this shift in policy. They had lowered Soviet priorities in the Third World, particularly in economic matters, but without sacrificing either long-term Soviet goals or on-going advances in geopolitically crucial Third World areas. At that time East-West problems rather than North-South problems seemed to be given greater priority as the arms race appeared to enter a new cycle of escalation. Conceivably, Gorbachev, acting under the same pressure, could similarly shift priorities as a timely tactic, particularly during a period of much needed economic reform at home and a dangerous escalation of the arms race abroad, but like his predecessors doing so without sacrificing desirable forward positions already achieved in the Third World or long-held Soviet policy goals.

It is thus possible that more pragmatic, problem-solving leaders like Gorbachev and presumably Gromyko, with attention fixed on the necessity of economic reform at home and aware of rising costs of empire abroad in an East-West environment of escalating arms race, could opt for a more cautious, cost-effective Third World policy. Such a policy could dictate a continuing lower profile in the Third World, at least in the economic realm, and accordingly open the door, however slight, to the concerns of global interdependence.[36]

Finally, the resumption of arms control negotiations could be the first major step towards achieving other forms of cooperation that ultimately could lead to a fuller awareness of the need for global interdependence. According to Secretary Shultz, President Reagan "firmly intends" to seize this "moment of opportunity" for high-level dialogue and across-the-board improvement in Soviet-Ameri-

---

hard-liners as "becoming too keen on Realpolitik in dealing with the Americans." Among the hawks in the Central Committee, he had earned the reputation for being "ideologically soft." The comparison of Gromyko to Talleyrand, perhaps the master of realpolitik, was, he said, "not too farfetched."

[36] George Holliday of CRS provided valuable insights into the development of the points made here. On July 2, 1985, Gromyko was replaced as Foreign Minister by Eduard Shevardnadze and elected to the post of President. His continuing influence on foreign policy remains a matter of speculation.

can relations.[37] Shultz realistically recognizes that the United States and the Soviet Union have incompatible ideologies. Therefore, "we have to expect competition," but, he contends, "that doesn't mean in this world that we have to resign ourselves to a nuclear holocaust or anything of that kind." [38]

The Soviets, too, have declared their intention of moving forward on an agreement in arms control. Neither side minimizes their differences nor the gravity of the problems at hand; but negotiations have begun, and that is significant.[39]

It is conceivable, therefore, but not especially probable, that the climate of relations could improve to the point where in a "spillover" effect the problems of global interdependence would be given a higher priority.[40]

3. WHITHER THE SUPERPOWERS?

The probability is that the Soviets will take neither the path of militarism nor global interdependence [41] but in the near term will

---

[37] Oberdorfer, Don. Shultz Sees Hope for Better Relations. The Washington Post, March 16, 1985, p. A1 and A29.

[38] The New York Times, March 18, 1985, p. A3.

[39] One senior Soviet official explained Soviet-American differences simply: "The problem involves the size of the planet. It is too small. You Americans think you can be secure at our expense. That is impossible. We both can only be secure when we both feel secure." (The Washington Post, Sept. 25, 1984, p. A16.)

[40] An article in Moscow's foreign policy weekly New Times of March 1985 made a strong case for global interdependence. The writers equated the burden of the arms race with the pressing global problems mankind faces, such as, the growing food problem that is becoming "increasingly acute"; the problem of adequate raw materials and energy for production; and the "destruction of the natural environment" that is "assuming menacing proportions." The writters acknowledge the different perspective of Socialism and capitalism but add that the "world system of economic, political and ecological ties and relationships" make these problems "a factor of truly global dimensions affecting mankind's development as a whole." If the solution of these problems is pigeonhold," they caution, "this could have destructive, perhaps irreversible consequences for the present and especially for future generations." According to these writers, the arms race is "one of the most formidable obstacles to the solution of global problems," and they urge that the solution of these global problems "calls for enormous material outlays comparable in size to world military spending." Furthermore, they warn that "time for the solution of global problems is running out," measured at best in decades. Accordingly, mankind is faced with a choice between continuing the arms race and "vigorous joint actions to avert a global crisis such as the world has never yet known." They conclude on this hopeful note: "In these circumstances the Soviet-American talks just opened in Geneva are of special importance. They open a real possibility, even though distant and requiring no little effort, of saving mankind from the oppressive burden of the arms race." (Kapitsa, L. and Y. Fyodorov, Missile-Age Alternative. New Times, no. 12, March 1985: 15.)

[41] Simes gives the following mid-April assessment of expected Soviet Third World policy under Gorbachev: "In the third world, the Russians feel over-extended. But their reluctance to make new costly commitments does not amount to packing their bags and abandoning places where they have already invested resources and prestige. Moscow's attitude might best be called assertive retrenchment': from Nicaragua to Angola, from Syria to Afghanistan, the Kremlin shows no willingness to seek a graceful exit. On the contrary, as Mr. Gorbachev warned Pakistan, Soviet patience with hostile guerrilla movements and their foreign supporters is wearing increasingly thin. If he puts his money where his mouth is, a new superpower crisis may be around the corner in the third world." (Simes, Dimitri K. Gorbachev's Hardball with a Soft Touch. The New Times, April 19, 1985, p. A31.)

Dr. Alvin Z. Rubinstein, a specialist in Soviet Third World policy and Professor of Political Science at the University of Pennsylvania, analyzed aspects of the strategic balance and Soviet risk-taking in the Third World. Rubinstein concludes that the strategic balance "is not apt to affect Soviet risk-taking, because both superpowers seem to share the conviction that a nuclear war is too high a price for marginal real estate; and because essential equivalence at the nuclear level seems destined to persist for the foreseeable future. If these assumptions are accurate, the Soviet Union will accordingly, neither resort to its nuclear power to acquire some mere local advantage nor precipitate a nuclear confrontation by doing anything as rash as choking off Persian Gulf oil from the West and Japan." Nonetheless, Rubinstein foresees an increase in Soviet risk-taking in the Third World "in the years ahead." Three factors strengthen this assumption, he says: "the USSR's enormously enhanced capability to project miltiary power beyond the conopt for a mix of the two. This suggests an extension, more or less, of current Soviet policy with emphasis on maintaining their military strength in order to preserve "equal security" with the United States, retain a hedge against U.S. superiority and protect the Soviet Union against perceived threats stemming therefrom. Sustained military strength provides the Soviets also with an instrument, albeit limited, for maintaining and, when possible, expanding their influence in the Third World. This does no preclude pursuit of elements of global interdependence, but only at a minimum level of activity as Soviet national interests may dictate.

What the United States does in the realm of international security will no doubt impact considerably upon the Soviet choice. The main focus of this study is on the Soviet Union, but the hypothetical construct of alternative paths of militarism and global interdependence, presented here for analytical purposes, applies also to the United States.[42] The serious consequences of militarism and the postive value of global interdependence have universal application.

The Soviets accent the military side of the American approach to international affairs, while ignoring U.S. concerns for troubling global issues. Whether a misperception, a propaganda ploy or a mix of both, the Soviet view is instructive, as is their critical view of U.S. foreign policy toward the U.S.S.R. itself. When asked by Shevchenko what he saw was the "greatest weakness" of the U.S. foreign policy towards the Soviet Union, Gromyko responded "promptly":

> They don't comprehend our final goals. And they mistake tactics for strategy. Besides, they have too many doctrines and concepts proclaimed at different times, but the absence of a solid, coherent, and consistent policy is their big flaw.[43]

---

fines of the Soviet bloc; its perception that the United States, notwithstanding greater spending, is inceasingly constrained or unwilling to use its power for the promotion and defense of political strategic objectives in the Third World (arms sales are no substitute for a coherent policy); and an increase in the opportunity factor, which derives from local and regional instability and the alacrity with which local actors turn to the Soviet Union in order to advance their own ambitions and acquire added leverage over the United States. This situation is unfolding concomitant with, yet independent of, the nuclear relationship between the superpowers." (Rubinstein, Alvin Z. The Changing Strategic Balance and Soviet Third World Risk-Taking. Naval War College Review, March/April 1985: 17.

Dr. Francis Fukuyama, a senior analyst at Rand Corp. specializing in Soviet Third World affairs, concludes a recent study with this projection: "The Soviet Union will continue to exploit opportunities to expand its influence in the Third World as they arise in the future. However, as a result of its past successes, the new issues for future Soviet policy are likely to revolve increasingly around the question of managing the burden of empire in established positions." In the political sphere, Fukuyama notes, "the Soviets will have to seek ways to improve the staying power and reliability of their clients." In the military sphere, "the Soviets and Cubans will face a number of unpleasant and unfamiliar choices" with respect to the large-scale counterinsurgency wars in Afghanistan, Angola, Ethiopia, and Kampuchea. Beyond continuing peacetime force deployments, Fukuyama writes, "the Soviets and Cubans may be forced to take more drastic decisions to intervene on behalf of certain clients to keep them in power," as in the case of Afghanistan in 1979. Citing economic costs of empire, Fukuyama concludes finally that given the high cost of maintaining an empire already in place and the declining growth rate of the Soviet economy, "Soviet economic planners must question the rationale behind some of Moscow's Third World commitments." Some voices in the Soviet leadership "have been urging retrenchment and greater selectivity in Moscow's Third World commitments." (Fukuyama, Francis. U.S.-Soviet Interactions in the Thrid World. RAND/UCLA Center for the Study of Soviet International Behavior. Santa Monica, Calif., March 1985 p. 26-29. Occasional Paper OPS-004.)

[42] For examination of the U.S. side of the Soviet challenge in the Third World, see, HFAC, Soviet Policy and United States Response in the Third World, 1981, chapts. I, II, IV-VI.

[43] Shevchenko, Breaking With Moscow, p. 279.

Shevchenko offered his own criticism; namely, that the United States does not understand the Soviet "voracious appetite for expansion."[44]

There seems little doubt that the United States and the Soviet Union have reached a crucial point in their relationship. Both sides perceive this development. In March 1985, Arbatov explained to his Moscow readers that the United States and the Soviet Union have reached "a Rubicon." At this point in the history of their relations "it is clear, more than ever before, that a resolute turn must be taken towards normalization, towards stopping the arms race and easing tensions." According to Arbatov, a "great danger" exists that should such a turn not take place, then "a serious threat to the international situation will arise." Thus he concludes that the superpowers have arrived at their "Rubicon": Decisions have to be made; and if the moment is not seized, arms limitations may become "practically impossible," implying the outbreak of an uncontrollable arms race with all its dangerous and negative consequences.[45]

Developments in both Soviet-American relations and internationally appear to be converging in the mid-1980's, making imperative a choice of direction by both superpowers. The first step has already been taken with resumption of arms control negotiations in Geneva. Whether this first step will lead to consideration of larger issues of interdependence on the global agenda—establishing, for example, a "Code of Conduct" for the superpowers in the Third World—can at this juncture only be a hopeful expectation and not an assured reality.[46]

C. THE THIRD WORLD IN THE CONTEST FOR CIVILIZATION

1. THE THIRD WORLD: PERMANENT AREA OF CONFLICT

A review of the Soviet role in the Third World such as presented in this study reinforces the prediction of CIA Director Casey that,

---

[44] Ibid., p. 283.

[45] The New York Times, March 11, 1985, p. A6.

[46] For insights into the problem of the Soviets and global interdependence, see the works of Walter C. Clemens, Jr., a Soviet specialist at Boston University. On Feb. 6, 1985, for example, he published an article in The Christian Science Monitor (p. 15) entitled, "USSR May be Willing to Work with the West on Global Problems." See also, his chapter entitled, "Interdependence and/ or Security: Soviet Dilemma", in, Duncan, W. Raymond, ed. Soviet Policy in the Third World. New York, Pergamon, 1980, p. 295-312. Writing in 1980, Clemens believes that prospects are not particularly bright for a prominent Soviet role in the next decade. He notes that there is "little domestic support—elite or mass—for globalist policies implying further economic sacrifice for the long-suffering Soviet consumer." Moreover, "the Kremlin and Soviet society as a whole are less empathetic to global needs than Western governments and peoples." Clemens continues: "The Politburo may also fear that it could not hold its own in cooperative programs with the West, because of technological backwardness, less experience, and a clumsier human touch in dealing with Third World peoples. Such considerations will not necessarily lead Moscow to attempt to sabotage global cooperation, but they set stiff barriers to Soviet leadership and participation in such efforts." (p. 308-09).

In his more recent appraisal in The Christian Science Monitor article, Clemens concludes: "Euphoria over the latest moves in Moscow or Washington is premature. Cold winds from either capital could kill the seeds of detente before spring. In any case the harvest is far off. Still, more attention to global problems could take the superpowers' attentions away from potential space wars and down to earth, where the challenges of feeding, housing, and educating the globe's billions demand a synthesis of the best insights from Novosibirsk to Palo Alto to Ibadan and Hyderadad, and where none of us stand immune from the quirks of nature which, combined with those of man, can suddenly transform abundance to shortfall."

"The less-developed nations of the world will be the principal US-Soviet battleground for many years to come."[47]

Chronic instability generated by underdevelopment, poverty and political immaturity; great power competition for minerals and natural resources in short supply; competing geopolitical interests, such as critical straits, communications networks and potential political alliances to be gained, protected and denied to others; the natural desire of great nations to expand their power and restrict that of their competitors; conflicting ideological beliefs that lift otherwise manageable rivalries to a moral level of doctrinal certainty that defies reconciliation; the catalytic effect of a seemingly uncontrollable arms race—all of these powerful human and political, material and intellectual elements seem to converge in the Third World and conspire to make it a bear pit of international disorder and potential conflict.

What makes this so dangerous is the potential for superpower conflict. Recognition of the inviolability of State borders in Europe, formally confirmed in the Helsinki Accords, has appreciably stabilized the East-West conflict in that vital and dangerous region. The search for a mutually acceptable formula to control the nuclear arms race, though far from successful, nonetheless, still continues and accordingly has had a somewhat stabilizing effect, as does the balance of terror in strategic confrontations.

Not so in the Third World, where regional volatility and Soviet-American geopolitical rivalry have created conditions that invite conflict. Thus there seems little doubt that, as Casey predicts, the Third World will, indeed, be "the principal US-Soviet battleground for many years to come" or as the Soviet Third World authority K. Brutents writes, the "liberated countries" of the Third World including Central America "are and for a long time will remain an undampened hotbed of anti-imperialist sentiments and actions,"[48] meaning undiminished conflict between the Soviet Union and the West with their respective friends and proxies in the Third World.

---

[47] Casey, What We Face, Westminster College Speech, p. 14. Brzezinski suggests the permanency of conflict when he writes: "The positive task of shaping a wider international system that genuinely embraces the newly emancipated Third World, and thus replaces the narrower European world order that collapsed during the course of World War II, will have to be pursued for some time without constructive Soviet involvement. The Soviet Union—too strong not to be a rival, yet feeling itself too weak to be a partner cannot be counted on to become a true participant in the constructive global process, since its systemic interests are diametrically opposed to the preservation of the status quo in a world that Moscow can disrupt but not dominate." (Brzezinski, World Power of a New Type, p. 158-159).

Serge Schmemann, chief of the New York Times Moscow bureau, gives this appraisal of Soviet foreign policy as it is likely to take shape under Gorbachev: "Foreign affairs is the field of Soviet endeavor least likely to change under a new generation. Gorbachev's public statements on foreign issues have demonstrated no marked originality, and his ideological discourses on differences between Communist and democratic systems have been dull and standard. He would likely favor detente, if only to give breathing space to domestic programs. But nothing suggests that he or any of his peers would react any differently from their predecessors to the insecurities, expansionist forces or sensitivity to loss of face that govern so much of Soviet behavior abroad." Hence, continuity can be expected in Soviet Third World policy under Gorbachev if Schmemann's analysis is correct. (Schmemann, Serge. The Emergence of Gorbachev. The New York Times Magazine, March 3, 1985: 57.)

[48] Brutents, K. The Liberated Countries at the Beginning of the 1980's. Moscow Kommunist in Russian, No. 3, Feb. 1984: 102-113, translated in, USSR Report, Translations from Kommunist, May 11, 1984, p. 121, (JPRS-UKO-84-009).

2. COMPETING IDEAS ON SOCIAL ORGANIZATION OF THE THIRD WORLD

a. Limited appeal of Soviet communism

A central idea, indeed the driving force, in the Soviet-American rivalry in the Third World is the matter of its future social organization in the broadest meaning of the term. Apart from the power factor, the key issue here is the ideological struggle between the priniciples of Communism as interpreted and proselytized by the Soviet Union pitted against the principles of democratic capitalism advocated by the United States and democratic socialism, an acceptable variant of Marxism based on political pluralism prevalent in Western Europe.[49] Such is how the superpowers perceive their rivalry. Still, it must be recognized that neither the U.S nor Soviet forms of social organization and ideology may be acceptable to the nations of the Third World who have their own self-interests to satisfy.

As this study shows, the Soviets enjoy certain advantages in the advocacy of their Marxist-Leninist brand of Socialism. For the most part, the Third World had experienced West European imperialism and colonialism, never the Soviet variety as it exists in Eastern Europe and Afghanistan. Accordingly, their animus has been directed against the West, though even this has been losing its force with passing generations.

In matters of intra-regional rivalries, the Soviets have also given "leftists" and "home-grown" Socialists, as in Cuba and Nicaragua, an alternative. Using arms transfers as both a political weapon and lever, the Soviets have been a solidifying force for these leftist regimes which have placed themselves under Soviet tutelage and protection. Soviet and East European guidance in maintaining elite control through political police and surveillance also has some appeal in various countries.

Despite these advantages, Soviet influence has been superficial and their presence in many instances transitory. Beyond offering its design for economic development and mobilizing anger in anti-imperialism, Soviet ideology has made little headway in the non-Communist Third World. The Soviet model of economic development and societal organization, perhaps the most measureable criteria of influence, has been largely discredited and its appeal diminished over recent decades. Hard pressed in making their own economy work, the Soviets have proven to be better arms dealers than economic developers. Cognizant of these serious shortcomings, Soviet Third World specialists have urged diversity in matters of trade and economic assistance among their leftist clients in the

[49] The U.S. view was sharply defined by President Reagan in a speech to the British Parliament in June 1982. He detailed Soviet shortcomings and failures and then proclaimed: "What I am describing now is a plan and a hope for the long term—the march of freedom and democracy which will leave Marxism-Leninism on the ash-heap of history, as it has left other tyrannies which stifle the freedom and muzzle the self-expression of the poeple." He concluded: "Let us now begin a major effort to secure the best—a crusade for freedom that will engage the faith and fortitude of the next generation. For the sake of peace and justice, let us move toward a world in which all people are at last free to determine their own destiny." (Keesing's Contemporary Archives, August 13, 1982, p. 31639.) Much the same idea of the democratic struggle against Communism appears in the statements and speeches by Secretary Shultz. See, for example, his statement before the Senate Foreign Relations Committee on Jan. 31, 1985, in, Congressional Record, Feb. 5, 1985: S1059–S1063 (Daily edition).

Third World. Economic development and investment capital is the first priority in the Third World, and it is to the West, not to the Soviet Union, that these countries turn for assistance.

Thus Soviet Communism has little to offer in the social organization of the Third World, beyond what its military power and military assistance can give, and beyond providing an alternative source of political support in international politics.

b. Appeal of scientific-technological civilization of the West

In contrast, the United States, NATO Europe, and Japan—in brief, the industrialized democracies of the world—have much more to offer the Third World, not only in the material and intellectual resources of their Scientific-Technological Civilization, but, equally important as they see it, in the organizing principles of pluralistic democracy. So great is the attraction of America to Third World students and scholars that the United States has become known as "the Graduate School of the Third World."[50] It is not surprising, therefore, that Third World countries turn to the West for support, trade, investment and ideas: Except for the Philippines, they have in the prospering ASEAN countries of Southeast Asia, South Korea and Taiwan, whose prosperity rests on Western trade and market economies, promising economic models adaptable for success in the modern world.[51]

---

[50] For a study on the implications of this attraction, see, U.S. Congress. Subcommittee on National Security Policy and Scientific Developments of the Committee on Foreign Affairs. Brain Drain: A Study of the Persistent Issue of International Scientific Mobility. Prepared by Joseph G. Whelan, Congressional Research Service, Library of Congress. Washington, U.S. Govt. Print. Off., 1974, 272 p. (Part 13 in the series on "Science, Technology, and American Diplomacy.")

[51] John Hughes, former Assistant Secretary of State for Public Affairs, expressed a commonly held view when he wrote describing Malaysian electronic technology and how in some respects it has overtaken the United States: "This is an indication of one of the most remarkable shifts of power in recent times: the evolution of Asia as a manufacturing, trading, and economic power that has outstripped Europe in importance to the United States." (Hughes, John. The Future of Asia. The Christian Science Monitor, March 20, 1985, p. 13.) Observers have written of a new frontier opening up in Asia along a "vast rim of the far Pacific, stretching from South Korea in the north to New Zealand in the south." One account states: "Dynamic growth is the hallmark of most of the countries in this sweeping Pacific arc, in contrast with the stagnation that plagues America's traditional partners in Western Europe." Some observers speak of the "Pacific century." (U.S. News & World Report, Aug. 20, 1985: 45.)

A case in point to demonstrate the shift in attitudes in some Third World countries from political-ideological concerns to economic development is that of Algeria. In mid-April 1985, President Chadli Benjedid signaled his intention to use his first official visit to the United States by an Algerian head of State to purchase American military equipment in an effort to lessen Algeria's dependence on the Soviet Union and to seek American assistance in the economic development of his country. According to Michael Dobbs and Jonathan C. Randal of the Washington Post Foreign Service, Benjedid seemed at pains during an extensive interview "to draw attention to his pragmatic stance at home and abroad." His low-key presentation, the correspondents note, provide a "dramatic contrast with the espousal of dogmatic socialism at home and militant Third World causes abroad" for which Algeria was known since gaining independence from France in 1962. Western diplomats in Algiers view the five-day visit, in the words of the press report, as a "symbolic milestone" in Algeria's "gradual transition from a revolutionary socialist state to a nation seeking to redirect its primary energies to tackling long-neglected economic and social problems." Among the points made in the interview was Algeria's need for economic development. Algeria, along with other Third World countries, Benjedid said, has in the past devoted too much attention to political and ideolgcial questions at the expense of economic development. He acknowledged that Algeria had much to learn from the United States in what have now become priority areas in the economy, noting particularly agriculture, irrigation and housing construction. "My policy is based on pragmatism rather than dogmatism," he said. "I want to be close to the needs of our people, their basic aspirations," adding that the "happiness of the individual" had now become the watchword in Algeria. Benjedid cited as "a very positive development" a decision by the Organization of African Unity to devote its July summit tackling what the press report termed "the continent's staggering economic problems, such as famine and drought." In Benjedid's view, "This shows that Africa is more interested in economic

Continued

What these Third World countries have seemingly done is to compress centuries of historical development in the West into one generation. The results have been extraordinary. Advanced Third World countries, such as India, having gone beyond the initial stage of economic development, now look to Japan and other industrialized democracies of the world, not to the Soviet Union, for the much needed products of scientific and technological civilization.[52] In sum, the West and the ideas it represents along with its range of political organizations and designs for economic development offer the more attractive models for countries of the Third World to achieve modernization than the Socialist bloc.[53] Ironically, but realistically, even China now looks to Japan and the industrialized West, more than to Moscow, for technological and economic assistance in its current modernization drive.[54]

---

problems than ideological and political problems. . ." Benjedid is spending part of his American tour examining modern irrigation techniques in California's San Joaquin Valley. (Dobbs, Michael and Jonathan C. Randal. Algerian to Seek Arms in Visit Here. The Washington Post, April 14, 1985, p. A1 and A30.)

[52] Prime Minister Rajiv Gandhi clearly laid out India's choice of close association with the industrialized democracies. Speaking at a roundtable conference of industrialists on April 15, 1985, sponsored by the European Management Forum, Gandhi invited collaborative economic projects in order to make India competitive with the developed world. According to government officials and industrialists, a technology transfer agreement reached between the United States and India in March is expected to be a major benefit to India's planned technology boom. Included in the agreement was reportedly an arrangement for "high-tech parks" to be established in India which will receive high-technology data from the United States and distribute it to Indian companies. (Claiborne, William. Gandhi Solicits Foreign Investment in India. The Washington Post, April 16, 1985, p. D3.)

[53] The report of the Stanley Foundation on U.S.-Soviet competition in the Third World states: "The attractiveness of the Soviet and US (Western) models to Third World leaders was an issue given particular emphasis by the discussants. In general, most felt that over the last twenty years, the development of the Third World could more appropriately be characterized as 'Westernization' than as 'Sovietization.' Despite much policy mismanagement (as noted earlier), not to mention the potential for anti-Western sentiment during a period of active decolonization, the United States and the West have maintained and even increased their military, political, and economic influence in much of the Third World. As one participant noted, evidence as obvious as the dramatic cultural dominance of the West and the increasing prevalence of the English language are indicators of how unsuccessful the Soviets have been." (Stanley Foundation, Strategy for Peace, 1984, p. 22-23.)

In his commentary on the appeals of the Western economies to the Third World, Hough writes: "In the Third World . . . the industrializing countries have a need for foreign investment and a private sector if they are to prosper economically, and these two factors severely limit the ability of Third World countries to follow a radical or totally pro-Soviet path. The Soviet Union simply cannot afford to bankroll many more Cubas or Vietnams. Moreover, the incentive system of capitalism is vastly superior to that of socialism with respect to foreign relations. Capitalism gives economic managers the incentive to invest abroad, while the incentive structure of Soviet-type socialism gives its managers a disincentive." (Hough, Rethinking the Soviet-American Relationship, p. 38.)

[54] For a commentary on Soviet deficiencies in "information technology" and the use of the computer, see, Harvey, David S. Advanced Technology: Is the USSR Missing the Real Revolution? Defense & Foreign Affairs, March 1985: 31. Harvey concludes: "The explosion in 'knowledge-engineering' and the technology to go with it is potentially so huge that the Soviet Union will soon slip irrevocably behind what the rest of the world is planning. It is a new type of challenge, which up to now has only presented itself in theoretical terms. Now, though, a lot of it is fact. The USSR could be missing out on a revolution far more important to it—ultimately—than its own."

In April, it was reported that the Soviets have decreed that in September computer classes will begin "on a large scale" for the 8 million ninth and tenth grade students in the Soviet Union's 60,000 high schools. "All-round and profound mastering by young people of computers," the decree said, "must become an important factor in speeding up the scientific and technological progress in the country." Technological progress and strong economic growth in such industrial countries as the United States and Japan have been stimulated by the rapid spread of information made possible by the computer. However, progress, especially in the use of personal computers, can be restricted in the U.S.S.R. because of Moscow's tight control over information. Olin Robinson, President of Middlebury College in Vermont and a Soviet specialist, observes: "The Russians can't easily accommodate computer technology because it gives too many people too much information" in a country where secrecy and control of information are vital. Accord-

c. Ideas and systems in conflict

This appeal of the West to the Third World seems to represent perhaps another stage in the globalization of the ideas, values and knowledge of Western Civilization. During the centuries from the fall of the Roman Empire to the Age of Discovery, Western Civilization, only a seedling of what was to come, had been confined essentially to the Mediterranean Basin, sealed off, except for southern Spain, from the leavening culture of the Arab World and from the creative influence of the far more culturally and technologically advanced ancient civilizations of China and India, and nourished only in Christian monasteries of Western Europe and the Celtic Fringe in Ireland.[55] The West was part of the Third World of that era.

The Age of Discovery globalized Western Civilization, spreading to the farthest reaches of the world not only its problems, wars and afflictions, but more importantly the creativity, the liberating ideas and the learning of the Renaissance, Reformation, Counter-Reformation, Enlightenment, the Industrial Revoluton and finally the Scientific-Technological Revolution of the 19th and 20th centuries.[56]

By the 19th century, after throwing off the Mongol yoke and breaking through the restrictive, inner-directed influence of Byzantium, Russia, too, shared in these benefits by its association with Western Europe, though only superficially, expanding its empire to the borders of Central Europe, southern Asia, into the Far East and even to the Americas. Marxism had its roots in the West, but was altered by the Leninist interpretation and put into practice in Russia after the Bolshevik Revolution as Marxism-Leninism. This mixture of traditional Russian authoritarianism with Lenin's radical variant of Marxism was globalized and given wide currency as a dynamic, revolutionary force, especially in the Comintern era of the 1920's and 1930's, and during the post-colonial era of "national liberation" after World War II. Socialism, though not necessarily of the totalitarian Soviet Marxist-Leninist variety, became a competing principle for organizing society in the post-colonial Third World. It was in this politically volatile environment that Khrushchev challenged the West in the mid-1950's to a contest for influence and power in the Third World—a contest that "would determine the character" of future civilization in the Third World. For what the Soviets offer is not only collectivist principles for organiz-

---

ing to Time's analysts, "If the Soviet Union maintains restrictions on their use, it might not come close to realizing the full economic potential of the computers." Loren Graham, a professor of the history of science and a Soviet specialist at M.I.T. writes: "We may be about to learn that the Soviet system is not designed for the information age. If that is the case, it is going to be increasingly difficult for the U.S.S.R. to maintain its pretensions as the world's second superpower in the decades ahead." (Time, April 14, 1985: 84–85.)

In his report to the plenum of the Central Committee on April 23, Gorbachev called attention to the fact that scientific and technological progress in most economic sectors is sluggish. "Revolutionary changes are needed," he said. "What is at issue in actual fact is the re-tooling of all sectors of the national economy on the basis of latest scientific and technological advances." Inferred in Gorbachev's speech was an open admission of severe Soviet shortcomings in science and technology and their adaptation to the Soviet economy. (FBIS 072. Gorbachev CPSU CC Plenum Report. Moscow Tass in English, 1341 GMT, April 23, 1985, Take 5.)

[55] Toynbee, A Study of History, p. 155–156.

[56] For a comprehensive treatment of the Age of Discovery and its impact on world civilization, see, Boorstin, Daniel J. The Discoverers. New York, Random House, 1983. 745 p.

ing society but an "attractive" exportable characteristic; namely, the offer of totalitarian mechanisms of domestic control to authoritarian Third World elites.[57]

At present, the industrialized democracies, having achieved great things in the course of the evolving Scientific-Technological Revolution, clearly have the upper hand over the Soviets for reasons already explained in this study. Widespread Soviet scientific and technological espionage in the West and Japan attests to the extent of Soviet deficiencies. Nonetheless, the struggle to influence the shape of future civilization in the Third World continues,[58] and Soviet military power, Marxist-Leninist ideology aside, still remains a powerful force to reckon with. Were the ideological struggle resolved, the contest for power would still continue in a way that such contests have historically occurred between competing great powers.[59]

3. DIPLOMACY AND NEGOTIATIONS: PROVIDING A MARGIN OF SURVIVAL

a. De Toqueville's prophecy

The future holds the answer to the final outcome of this contest, and if history "teaches us anything," as Arthur Schesinger, Jr., the American historian, suggests, the outcome "will be full of surprises and will outwit all our present certitudes."[60] Perhaps all that can be certain in this relationship of uncertainties is the generally accepted dictum that only through diplomacy and negotiations will it be possible for the United States and the Soviet Union to manage their rivalry without placing mankind in jeopardy.

Ironically, Alexis de Toqueville, a French political philosopher, predicted this Russian-American contest 150 years ago. In his classic work, "Democracy in America," written at the age of 26 following an extensive tour of the United States, De Toqueville prophesied that Russia and America were heading towards a conflict apparently to take place at some time in the distant future. What he described in 1835 has finally come to pass today:

---

[57] Stuart D. Goldman, Analyst in Soviet Affairs, CRS.

[58] In a speech on April 22, 1985, commemorating Lenin Day, G.A. Aliyev, member of the CPSU's Politburo, spoke of the Communist mission in terms of saving civilization. "The framework of the historic mission of Communists has also been extended," he said, "It today bears responsibility for saving civilization and man's primary right, the right to live." (FBIS 090. Aliyev Lenin Day Speech. Moscow Television Service in Russian, 1255 GMT, April 22, 1985, Take 10.)

[59] Shulman places greater emphasis on the power factor over ideology in the Soviet-American rivalry, implying that competing great power interests are, therefore, negotiable. Long-term U.S. policy, he writes, "should have an evolutionary purpose: it should be designed to encourage future generations of Soviet leaders to see that acting with restraint and enlarging the area of genuine cooperation between the United States and the Soviet Union serve their own self-interest. The main objective of our policy should therefore be to respond to the Soviet challenge in ways that will protect our security, our interest, and our values, rather than to try to force changes in the Soviet Union or to bring about changes in its foreign policy indirectly by seeking to undermine the Soviet system." The best that can be hoped for, he writes, appraising Soviet-American relations in the future, is a "Cold Truce, an improvement in the climate of confrontation that is now patently leading toward greater military competition and a greater risk of misperception and miscalculation in responses to local crises." With respect to the Third World, Shulman makes a case for global interdependence and the peaceful solution of issues that impact upon the interests of both powers. (Shulman, Marshall D. What the Russians Really Want: A Rational Response to the Soviet Challenge. Harpers, v. 268, April 1984: 70–71.) For other views, see, Simes, The New Soviet Challenge, p. 128–131, Ford, The Soviet Union: The Next Decade, p. 1143–1144.)

[60] Schlesinger, Arthur, Jr. The Futility of Futurism. The Wall Street Journal, Dec. 12, 1977, p.16.

—America and Russia started from "different points" but tended "towards the same end": global power.
—Their growth continues "along a path to which no limit can be perceived."
—The "conquests of the American" have been achieved largely and figuratively "by the plowshare" of peace; that of the Russian "by the sword" of militarism.
—The principal instrument of government and society for the American is freedom; for the Russian, "servitude" and the concentration of "all the authority of society in a single arm."
—Both nations began from a different "starting-point"; their courses of development have not been "the same"; yet each in fact now has the power "to sway the destinies" not just of "half the globe", as De Toqueville predicts, but that of the entire world.[61]

b. Importance of diplomacy and negotiations in the nuclear age

Whether the Russians and Americans can shift their rivalry in the Third World from its increasingly conflictual and militarized direction back toward less confrontational and more political and economic competition is a question of the greatest significance for all mankind; the latter course, as both recognize, improves prospects for world peace and survival.[62] Power, properly and acceptably balanced, can offer at least some assurance of peace, but only when it is integrated into the process of diplomacy and negotiations. In such a unity, this assurance can be reasonably complete; for it is diplomacy and negotiations, properly used, that can provide the vital margin of survival. The resumption of negotiations in Geneva could be the first step in that direction.[63]

American statesmen, reflecting a broad spectrum of political views, have held to the first principle of diplomacy in their dealings with the Soviets since the establishing of diplomatic relations in 1933. Over a century and a half ago Talleyrand, a master of the diplomatic art, defined this principle as simple, "One must negotiate, negotiate, and always negotiate." This principle could be taken one step further: The necessity and thus the value of negotiations can be measured in proportion to the intensity, the potentiality, and the expected destructive outcome of failure and conflict.[64]

[61] De Tocqueville, Alexis. Democracy in America. New York, Alfred A. Knopf, 1951, p. 434.
[62] Peter Jay, former British Ambassador to the United States, wrote pessimistically about the disappointment in store for those who envision an end to the Soviet-American nuclear rivalry: "The United States and the U.S.S.R. are doomed to watch one another like hawks, to negotiate constantly by day for strategic parity and to plot ceasely by night for strategic advantage. Since neither can or will feel fully confident unless its parity is more equal than the other side's parity, dynamic instability is inherent in the very static stability they seek." (Quoted in, Marder, Murrey, U.S., Soviets Still Search for Stability. The Washington Post, Jan. 3, 1985, p. A22.)
[63] In a speech at Yeshiva University on Dec. 9, 1984, Secretary Shultz explained the relationship between power and diplomacy: "The truth is, power and diplomacy must always go together, or we will accomplish very little in this world. Power must always be guided by purpose. At the same time, the hard reality is that diplomacy not backed by strength will always be ineffectual at best, dangerous at worst." (Shultz, George P. The Ethics of Power. State Department Bulletin, v. 85, Feb. 1985, p. 2.)
[64] Paul H. Nitze, the veteran U.S. negotiator, stresses the importance of establishing Soviet-American relations on the basis of a "live and let live" policy through negotiations. He explains his prescription for dealing with the Soviets in, Living with the Soviets, p. 371–374. Brzezinski

Continued

Diplomacy and negotiations give nations great and small what Geroge Kennan once termed a vital "cushion of safety" between peace and war. Negotiations give time: time for reflection; time to weigh interests more carefully; time to reach solutions through the exercise of reason; time to let the historical process work so that shared interests might become more clearly perceived. In contemporary world politics where the volatile Third World has the combustible materials to ignite a wider conflagration, the danger of nuclear war is a reality. Time (Ambassador Dobrynin spoke of only 8 minutes for the triggering of a nuclear exchange) may provide the only margin of safety, indeed the only margin of survival.[65]

It is for these and other reasons that Sir Robert Peel said over a century ago, diplomacy is "the great engine used by civilized society for the purpose of maintaining peace."

c. Dobrynin and Shultz on the value of diplomacy and negotiations

Ambassador Dobrynin revealed his understanding of this political truth when he explained the value of the diplomatic process on the 50th anniversary of establishing Soviet-American relations. The anniversary was commemorated against a background of deteriorating relations brought on by the KAL incident and the impending breakdown in arms control negotiations:

In olden times, the important part of any diplomatic success was the ability to keep an opponent in the fog, mystified about one's real intentions. In times like ours, when humanity lives under the constant danger of a nuclear conflict, the clarity of one's intentions becomes a necessary axiom for survival, based upon at least minimal mutual trust.

A continuous, rather than episodic dialogue of substance between our two countries is yet to be established. Without it, nothing at all will come out. The aim of diplomacy is to keep things moving, to generate compromises, to look for alternatives, opportunities, and possibilities. Should we pronounce them as an anathema to Soviet-American relations now and think that the complex international problems are best solved by military force or by trying to turn a threat of nuclear war into an instrument of diplomacy?[66]

Secretary Shultz answered this question in a statement before the Senate Foreign Relations Committee on June 15, 1983, and in so doing he reaffirmed the traditional American commitment to negotiations: "Strength and realism can deter war, but only direct dialogue and negotiation can open the path toward lasting peace."[67]

---

foresees the relationship in very realistic terms: "Historical coexistence with the Soviet Union will remain dominated by the largely negative task of avoiding a nuclear catastrophe. Western acts of commission or omission will ultimately determine whether that historical coexistence—a precariously peaceful coexistence at best for a long time to come—will eventually produce a more harmonious relationship or deteriorate into wider global anarchy." (Brzezinski, World Power of a New Type. p. 159).

[65] Dobrynin, Fifty Years of Soviet-American Diplomatic Relations, p. 13.

[66] Ibid. For an insider's assessment of Dobrynin as a diplomat, see Shevchenko, Breaking With Moscow, p. 194. "Dobrynin is an exceptional Soviet diplomat," he writes, "not just because of his unusually long service in Washington or his access to and influence in Moscow's highest political circles. His personality also sets him apart from most Soviet diplomats, who dogmatically follow instructions, concerned above all with securing their careers." Shevchenko, as others in the United States, in brief, assess Dobrynin favorably, giving him perhaps the highest compliment by referring to him as a real professional diplomat. For other appraisals of Dobrynin, see, HFAC, Soviet Diplomacy and Negotiating Behavior, p. 415-417. What these favorable assessments suggest is that Dobrynin's observations such as those cited here deserve respectful and thoughtful attention.

[67] Shultz, George P. U.S.-Soviet Relations in the Context of U.S. Foreign Policy. Text of Statement. June 15, 1983, p. 21.

Yet diplomats, like Gromyko and his successor Shevardnadze, Dobrynin and Shultz, are only the craftsmen of diplomacy and their diplomacy but a reflection of deeper and oftentimes conflicting national interests and national policy. Whether the issue of competing Soviet and American interests in the Third World can ever be resolved is the question of questions. For its resolution probably depends more upon the underlying forces of history, often in collision and characteristically unfathomable, than upon the skill of the diplomats engaging in their craft. Still, as principal actors on the international scene the task is theirs, and success or failure in whatever measure could be profoundly affected by their efforts.

A SELECTED BIBLIOGRAPHY [1]

I. INTRODUCTION TO THE BIBLIOGRAPHY

The purpose of this bibliography is to provide researchers with a guide to literature and research tools on Soviet policy in the Third World. The bibliography is organized into five subject areas: a section on general works on Soviet policy toward the entire Third World and four additional sections on Soviet relations with individual Third World regions—the Middle East, the Far East and South Asia, Sub-Saharan Africa, and Latin America. The entries are grouped into two categories: (a) books and (b) articles and documents. With few exceptions, only materials published since 1980 are included.

A. THE STRUCTURE OF THE BIBLIOGRAPHY

The bibliography was largely compiled by including materials that viewed Soviet relations with the Third World from the Soviet perspective. For a more complete appreciation of Soviet-Third World relations, the reader may wish to consult materials that examine the foreign policies and histories of individual Third World nations. Additionally, works on U.S. foreign policy toward and security interests in Third World regions commonly include aspects of Soviet foreign policy interests and superpower rivalry. For a fuller perspective the researcher may wish to look at East European and Cuban foreign policies in the Third World. These states often pursue policies in Africa, the Middle East, and Latin America that complement Soviet interests.

The first section of the bibliography, "General Works on Soviet-Third World Relations," includes books, articles, and documents that view Soviet policies toward the Third World as a whole. These include anthologies examining Soviet relations with multiple regions and countries of the world as well as articles that evaluate Soviet policies toward the entire Third World. Thus, the reader should consult the individual regional sections as well as the general section for materials on Soviet regional policies.

The bibliography is almost entirely comprised of books, journal articles, and U.S. government documents. It does not list newspaper articles and only a few items appearing in newsletters. A limited number of Soviet materials (books and journal articles) are cited. With the exception of Russian language materials, all the entries are in English. Most, if not all, of the Soviet entries are available in translation in the U.S. Joint Publication Research Service (JPRS) publications.

B. SOURCES OF INFORMATION ON U.S.S.R.-THIRD WORLD RELATIONS

The periodicals used in compiling the bibliography include major U.S. and British journals on foreign and communist affairs, such as Foreign Affairs, Foreign Policy, World Politics, International Security, Orbis, Current History, The Washington Quarterly, Journal of International Affairs, International Affairs (London), The World Today, Survival, and others. Important journals of communist affairs include Problems of Communism, Survey, and Soviet Union, from which a number of articles were selected. Sources from West Germany include the English-language version of Aussenpolitik and the English-language papers of Berichte des Bundesinstituts fur Ostwissenschaftliche and Internationale Studien in Cologne.

In addition to the standard foreign policy journals, the researcher should consult periodicals and documents specializing in the Soviet Union. These include, for example, the Radio Liberty research papers published weekly in Munich, West Germany, the bi-weekly Soviet Analyst, the weekly Current Digest of the Soviet Press, the monthly Soviet World Outlook, the bimonthly USSR and Third World, and U.S. Foreign Broadcast Information Service (F.B.I.S.) monitorings of Soviet and East Europe-

[1] Prepared by Michael J. Dixon, Research Analyst in Soviet and East European Affairs, Congressional Research Service. First published in May 1985 as CRS Report No. 58–113 S.

an media, published daily. F.B.I.S. also publishes daily monitorings of the Third World media.

There are a large number of defense-related magazines that frequently examine Soviet military affairs, such as Jane's Defense Weekly, the U.S. Naval Institute Proceedings, Air University Review, Parameters, Strategic Review, and Defense and Foreign Affairs Daily (and Monthly), to name just a few.

The many journals of regional affairs such as the Middle East Review, American Arab Affairs, Journal of Modern African Studies, African Affairs, Africa Confidential, Asian Survey, and Asia Pacific Community, Journal of Inter-American Studies and World Affairs, and Cuban Studies/Estudios Cubanos are useful resources for analyses of Soviet regional policies.

Soviet writings are an indispensable tool for interpreting the USSR's policies. International Affairs (Moscow), a monthly review, the weekly New Times, with an emphasis on world affairs, and World Marxist Review provide the official Soviet perspective. Other Soviet periodicals relating to Third World affairs (often available in translation from JPRS) are Kommunist (the party's theoretical journal, published eighteen times a year), Aziya I Afrika Segodnia (Asia and Africa Today), Narody Azia i Afriki (bimonthly), Latinskaya Amerika (monthly), and MEMO (Mirovaya Ekonomika i Mezhdunaronya Otnosheniya, or World Economics and International Relations, a monthly). JPRS publications are listed in the Monthly Catalog of U.S. Government Publications.

The researcher may wish to pay special attention to the many Soviet spokesmen with particular responsibilities in Soviet-Third World affairs. They include—with their offices and specialties:

Igor Belyayev, an editor with Literaturnaya Gazeta, Middle East.

Karen Brutents, deputy chief of the CPSU Central Committee International Department, Middle East.

Pavel Demchenko, Pravda editor, Middle East.

Anatoliy Gromyko, director of the Africa Institute, son of the foreign minister.

Konstantin Geyvandov, Izvestiya political observer, Middle East.

Georgiy Kim, deputy director of the Oriental Institute of the Academy of Sciences, Asia.

Boris I. Koval, deputy director of the Institute of the International Workers Movement of the Academy of Sciences.

Sergo Mikoyan, chief editor of Latinskaya Amerika.

Yu. S. Novopashin, Institute of Economics of the World Socialist System, Third World.

Yevgeniy Primakov, director of the Oriental Institute, Middle East.

Boris Rudenko, chief of Communist, Workers, and National Liberation Movements Department in CPSU Social Sciences Institute.

Rostislav Ulyanovskiy, deputy chief of the CPSU Central Committee International Department, Africa and the Middle East.

Aleksey Vasilyev, deputy director of Africa Institute.

Victor Volskiy, director of Latin America Institute.

Since no bibliography can claim to be complete, the reader should consult other bibliographies on Soviet-Third World relations, occasionally available in other works. Of particular value on the Soviet economic experience in the Third World is the bibliography found in Elizabeth Kridl Valkenier's The Soviet Union and the Third World: An Economic Bind (pp. 161–176). On the Soviet military and the Third World, see Mark Katz's bibliography in The Third World in Soviet Military Thought (pp. 168–183). Most books and articles provide sources, either in the footnotes or in bibliographic form.

Other sources of information are the publications of the U.S. Government. Reports and hearings of Congressional committees dealing with communist affairs, U.S. national security, and regional developments along with the Congressional Record are often valuable resources. State and Defense Department officials testifying before Congress often provide testimony representing the thinking of the Administration on U.S. national security and Soviet intervention and policies abroad. The U.S. Department of Defense recently began publishing an annual review, Soviet Military Power, which represents the Pentagon's evaluation of the Soviet threat in certain regions of the world. Researchers should also consult the annual "posture statements" of the Secretary of Defense and Joint Chiefs of Staff for valuable official appraisals of Third World problems in Soviet-American relations. The Central Intelligence Agency and the State Department approximately every year publish a survey of Soviet and East European economic and military aid to the Third World. The Arms Control and Disarmament Agency publishes annually a review of world arms transfers by supplier and recipient.

The researcher might wish to consult general reference works for another perspective on Soviet-Third World relations. These include The Military Balance, published annually by the London-based International Institute for Strategic Studies; the International Security Handbook (by the Georgetown Center for Strategic and International Studies); Africa Contemporary Record, an annual review of African affairs (by issue and by country), by African Publishing Co., New York, and edited by Colin Legum. Europa Publications of London prepares annually Africa South of the Sahara and The Middle East and North Africa, two volumes with a regional perspective. The Foreign Area Studies of the American University in Washington produces handbooks periodically profiling the economic, political, historical, military, and foreign policy practices of various countries.

II. The Soviet Union and the Third World: General Works

A. BOOKS

1. Butenko, Anatoly P. Socialism as a world system. (in Russian) [Sotsializm kak mirovaya systema], Moscow, Politizdat, 1984. 320 p. (Translated in, USSR Report. Political and Sociological Affairs. August 27, 1984. Joint Publications Research Service. JPRS–UPS–84–032–L)
2. Copper, John F. and Daniel S. Papp, eds. Communist nations' military Assistance. Boulder, Co., Westview Press, 1983. 201 p. UA12 .C64 1983
    Partial contents.—Communist military assistance: an overview, by Papp.—Soviet military assistance to the Third World, by Roger E. Kanet.—Eastern European military assistance to the Third World, by Trond Gilberg.—China's military assistance, by Copper.—Cuban military assistance to the Third World, by W. Raymond Duncan.
3. Dismukes, Bradford and James M. McConell, eds. Soviet naval diplomacy. New York, Pergamon Press, 1979. 409 p. DK66. S63 1979
4. Donaldson, Robert H., ed. The Soviet Union in the Third World: Successes and Failures. Boulder, Colorado, Westview Press, 1981. DK274 .S651965
5. Duncan, W. Raymond. Soviet policy in the Third World. New York, Pergamon Press, 1980. 322 p. DK274 .S6515 1980
    Partial contents.—Soviet environmental policy toward the Third World, by Barbara Jancar.—The Soviet Union and the world food system, Robert L. Paarlberg.—The Soviet perception of military intervention in Third World countries, Carol R. Saivetz.—Soviet policy toward Africa: impact of the Angolan war, by Arthur Jay Klinghoffer.—Soviet policy in South Asia, by Robert H. Donaldson.—Southeast Asia in Soviet perspective, by Simon W. Sheldon.—Moscow and Latin America: objectives, constraints and implications, by Duncan.—Interdependence and/or security: Soviet dilemma, Walter C. Clemens, Jr.
6. Duncan, W. Raymond, ed. Soviet Policy in Developing Countries. Huntington, New York, Krieger Publishing Co., 1981. 254 p. DK274 .D8 1981
    Contents.—Soviet policy in the developing countries, by Duncan. Soviet economic and military aid to the less-developed countries, 1954–78, by Orah Cooper and Carol Fogarty.—Eastern Europe and the developing countries, by Roger Kanet.—The Soviet Union and the wars in Indochina, by Allan W. Cameron.—Moscow and Havana in the Third World, by Duncan.—Oil and Soviet policy in the Persian Gulf, by David Lynn Price.—Military elites in Soviet perspective, by Charles G. Petersen.—Trends in Soviet research on the developing countries, by Elizabeth Kridl Valkenier.—Detente and American-Soviet competition in developing countries, by Fred Warner Neal.
7. Feuchtwanger, E.J. and Peter Nailor, eds. The Soviet Union and the Third World. New York, St. Martin's Press, 1981. 229 p. DK274.S651963 1981
    Contents.—Introduction: political and ideological aspects, by Otto Pick.—The new military instruments, by Jonathan Alford.—Soviet trade with the Third World, by Brian Pockney.—The commercial policies of the communist Third World: Mozambique, Angola, Ethiopia, Somalia, the People's Democratic Republic of Yemen, (various authors).—The Soviet Union in the Middle East: great power in search of a leading role, by Karen Dawisha.—Colossus or humbug? the Soviet Union and its southern neighbors, by Malcolm Yapp.—The Soviet Union in South-East Asia, by Mark Leifer.—The Soviet Union and Africa: how great a change?, James Mayall.—The Soviet experience in the Horn of Africa, by Christopher Clapham.

8. Hosmer, Stephen T. and Thomas W. Wolfe. Soviet policy and practice toward Third World conflicts. Lexington, Mass., Lexington Books, 1983. 318 p. DK274.H67 1982

9. Imam, Zafar. Towards a model relationship: a study of Soviet treaties with India and other Third World countries. New Delhi, ABC Pub. House, 1983. 193 p. JX1555.Z5 1983

10. Jackson, Richard L. The non-aligned, the U.N., and the superpowers. New York, Praeger, 1983. 315 p. JX1395.J314 1983

11. Kanet, Rober E., ed. Soviet foreign policy in the 1980s. New York, Praeger, 1982. 360 p. DK274.S6513

   Partial contents.—The Soviet Union as a global power, by Kanet.—The nationality factor in Soviet foreign policy, by Rasman Karklins.—China and the Soviet Union in Asia: the dynamics of unequal competition, by Rajan Menon.—The Soviet-Cuban relationship, Merritt Robbins.—The Soviet threat and the security of Japan, Hiroshi Kimura.—Military power, intervention, and Soviet policy in the Third World, by Rajan Menon.—The Middle East and Africa in recent Soviet policy, by David E. Albright.— Soviet policies in West Asia and the Persian Gulf, by Zalmay Khalilzad.— Soviet involvement in South Asia and the Indian Ocean region, by Robert H. Donaldson.

12. Kaplan, Stephen S., ed. Diplomacy of Power: Soviet Armed Forces as a Political Instrument. Washington, D.C., The Brookings Institution, 1981. 733 p. UA770.K28

13. Katsikas, Suzanne Jolicoeur. The arc of socialist revolutions. Cambridge, Mass., Schenkman Pub. Co., 1982. 332 p. HX44.K354 1982

14. Katz. Mark. The Third World in Soviet Military Thought. Baltimore, Maryland, Johns Hopkins University Press, 1982. 188 p. UA770.K345 1982

15. Laqueur, Walter, ed. The pattern of Soviet conduct in the Third World. New York, Praeger, 1983. 250 p. D888.S65P37

   Contents. Soviet diplomacy in the Third World, by Aryeh Eilan.—The Soviet Union in India, by Robert H. Donaldson.—Soviet influence in contemporary Iran, by Muriel Atkin.—Libya and the Soviet Union: alliance at arms length, by Ellen Laipson.—Getting a grip on the Horn: the emergence of the Soviet presence and future propects, by Paul B. Henze.—The Soviet Union in Africa: an assessment, by Raymond W. Copson.—Vanguard parties in the Third World, by David E. Albright.—Aid and trade: Soviet attitudes toward African client economies, by Herbert Block.

16. Pierre, Andrew J. The global politics of arms sales. Princeton, N.J., Princeton University Press, 1982. 352 p. HD9743.A2P5

17. Radu, Michael, ed. Eastern Europe and the Third World: East vs. South. New York, Praeger, 1981. 356 p. DJK50.E16

   Contents. East vs. South: the neglected side of the international system, by Radu.—Albania and the Third World, by Elez Biberaj.—Czechoslovakia and the Third World, Vratislav Pechota.—The GDR and the Third World: supplicant and surrogate, by Michael Sodaro.—East German security policies in Africa, by Jiri Valenta and Shannon Butler.—Hungary and the Third World: an analysis of East-South trade, Scott Blau.—Poland and the Third World: the primacy of economic relations, Howard Frost.—Romania and the Third World: the dilemmas of a "free rider," by Radu.—Yugoslavia and the Third World, by Michael M. Milenkovitch.—Patterns of Eastern European economic involvement in the Third World, by Roger Kanet.— Policy patterns of Eastern European socialist countries toward the Third World, by Janos Radvanyi.

18. Soviet military power. 4th ed. Washington, U.S. Dept. of Defense, Govt. Print. Office, 1985. 143 p.

19. Ulam, Adam B. Dangerous relations: The Soviet Union in world politics, 1970– 1982. New York, Oxford University Press, 1983. 325 p. DK274.U4 1983

20. U.S.-Soviet relations: perspectives for the future. Washington, Center for National Policy, September 1984. 55 p.

   Contents.—Introduction by W. Averell Harriman.—Soviet-America conflict: from the past to the future, by Seweryn Bialer.—Competition and dialogue, by Lee H. Hamilton.—Rethinking the Soviet-American relationship, by Jerry Hough.—The security aspect of U.S.-Soviet relations, by John Steinbruner.

21. Valkenier, Elizabeth Kridl. The Soviet Union and the Third World: an economic bind. New York, Praeger Publishers, 1983. 188 p. HF1557.V34 1983

22. Wiles, Peter, ed. The new communist Third World. New York, St. Martin's Press, 1982. 392p.   HF1413.N495 1982
      Partial contents.—The general view, especially from Moscow, by Wiles and Alan Smith.—Angola: Soviet-type economy in the making, by Nicos Zafiris.—Ethiopia, by Barry Lynch.—Mozambique: pragmatic socialism, by Zafiris.—The People's Democratic Republic of Yemen: scientific socialism on trial in an Arab country, by Moshe Efrat.—The People's Republic of Benin, by Andrew Racine.—The People's Republic of the Congo, by Racine.—Democratic Republic of Madagascar, by Racine.—Somalia: the one that got away, by Barry Lynch.—The Socialist Republic of Vietnam, by Adi Schnytzer.

B. ARTICLES AND DOCUMENTS

23. Bialer, Seweryn. Socialist stagnation and communist encirclement. In, The Soviet Union in the 1980s. New York, The Academy of Political Science. (Proceedings, v. 35, no. 3, 1984). p. 160-176.
24. Brzezinski, Zbigniew. The Soviet Union: world power of a new type. In The Soviet Union in the 1980s. New York, Academy of Political Science, 1984. (Proceedings, v. 35, no. 3, 1984). p. 147-159.
25. Casey, William J. Director of CIA. What we face. 40th John Findley Green Foundation Lecture, Westminster College, Fulton, Missouri, October 29, 1983. 18 p.
26. Copper, John F. China and the Third World. Current history, v. 82, Sept. 1983: 245-248, 278-279.
27. Developments in Soviet arms exports and imports, 1980-1983. Wharton Econometric Forecasting Associates. Centrally Planned Economies Current Analysis. v. 4, no. 62, Aug. 15, 1984. 4 p.
28. Donaldson, Robert H. The Soviet Union in the Third World. Current history, v. 81, Oct. 1982: 313-317, 339.
29. Economic assistance by CMEA countries. Organization for economic co-operation and development, Paris, 1983. 14 p.
30. Edgington, Sylvia Woodby. The state of socialist orientation: a Soviet model for political development. Soviet Union, v. 8, no. 2., 1981: 223-251.
31. Etzold, Thomas H. Responding to Soviet intervention in the Third World. Naval War College review, v. 35, May–June 1982: 25-35.
32. Ford, Robert A.D. The Soviet Union: the next decade. Foreign affairs, v. 62, summer 1984: 1132-1144.
33. Fukuyama, Francis. U.S. Soviet interactions in the Third World. RAND/UCLA Center for the Study of Soviet International Behavior. Santa Monica, CA., March 1985. 35 p. (Occasional Paper OPS-004)
34. Gavriilov, Y.N. Problems of the formation of vanguard parties in countries of socialist orientation. Narody Azii i Afriki, no., 6, 1980.
35. Grinter, Lawrence, E. Checkmate in the Third World? Soviet intervention and American response. International Security Review, v. 6, spring 1981: 35-56.
36. Gu, Guan-fu. Soviet aid to the Third World, an analysis of its strategy. Soviet Studies, v. 35, Jan. 1983: 71-89.
37. Harris, Lilian Craig. China's Third World courtship. Washington quarterly, v. 5, no. 3, summer 1982: 128-136.
38. Hyland, William G. The Gorbachev succession. Foreign affairs, v. 63, spring 1985: 800-809.
39. Imam, Zafar. Soviet treaties with Third World countries. Soviet studies, v. 35, Jan. 1983: 53-70.
40. Jamgotch, Nish, Jr. Soviet security in flux. Muscatine, Iowa, The Stanley Foundation, May 1983. 31 p. (Occasional Paper 33)
41. Khrishtich, E. The program of 'collective self-reliance:' a critical analysis. Mirovaya ekonomika i mezhdunarodnaya otnosheniya, n. 6, June 1982: 120-128.
42. Kim, G. The national liberation movement today. International affairs (Moscow), no. 4, April 1981.
43.———The Soviet Union and the national liberation movement. Mirovaya ekonomika i mezhdunarodnaya otnosheniya, no. 9, Sept. 1982: 19-33.
44.———The USSR and national-state construction in developing countries. International affairs (Moscow), no. 1, Jan. 1983.
45. Krause, Joachim. Soviet military aid to the Third World. Aussenpolitik, v. 34, no. 4, 1983: 392-403.
46. Laird, Robbin F. Soviet arms trade with the noncommunist Third World. In The Soviet Union in the 1980s. New York, Academy of Political science, 1984. (Proceedings, v. 35, no. 3, 1984). p. 196-213.

47. Laird, Robbin F. and Erik P. Hoffmann. Soviet perspectives on North-South relations in the era of 'the scientific-technical revolution.' In, Hoffmann, Erik P. and Frederic J. Fleron, Jr. The Conduct of Soviet Foreign Policy. New York, Aldine Publishing Co., 1980, Chapter 24.
48. Lebidinskaya, L.N. Peoples of the former colonial world and real socialism. Rabochiy klass i sovremenny mir, no. 4, July–Aug. 1982: 16–26.
49. Legvold, Robert. The super rivals: conflict in the Third World. Foreign affairs, v. 57, spring 1979: 755–778.
50. Macfarlane, Neil. Intervention and regional security. Adelphi papers, no. 196, spring 1985. 66 p.
51. Menon, Rajan. The Soviet Union, the arms trade and the Third World. Soviet studies, v. 34, July 1982: 377–396.
52. Nitze, Paul H. Living with the Soviets. Foreign affairs, v. 63, winter 1984/85: 360–374.
53. Pajak, Roger F. Soviet arms transfers as an instrument of influence. Survival, v. 23, July–Aug. 1981: 165–173.
54. Pineye, Daniel. The bases of Soviet power in the Third World. World development, v. 11, no. 12, 1983: 1083–1095.
55. Primakov, Evgeni M. USSR and the developing countries. Journal of international affairs, v. 34, fall-winter 1980–81: 269–281.
56. ——— Countries of socialist orientation: the difficult but real possibility of the transition to socialism. Mirovaya ekonomika i mezhdunarodnaya otnosheniya, July 1981: 3–16.
57. Reichel, Hans-Christian. The CMEA states and the developing countries. Aussenpolitik, v. 32, no. 4, 1981: 386–392.
58. Rubinstein, Alvin Z. The changing strategic balance and Soviet Third World risk-taking. Naval War College review, March/April 1985: 5–17.
59. Schultz, Siegfried and Heinrich Machowski. U.S. and Soviet trade and aid relations with the Third World. Berichte des Budesinstituts fur Ostwissenschaftliche und internationale studien. Cologne, West Germany. August 1983. 73 p.
60. Shulman, Marchall D. What the Russians really want. Harper's, v. 268, April 1984: 63–71.
61. Shultz, George P. Secretary of State. The future of American foreign policy: new realities and new ways of thinking. Testimony before the Committee on Foreign Relations, U.S. Senate, Jan. 31, 1985. Inserted in, The Congressional Record, Feb. 5, 1985: S1059–S1063. (Daily edition.)
62. ——— Managing the U.S.-Soviet international relationship over the long term. Speech delivered to the Rand/UCLA Center for the Study of Soviet International Behavior. Inserted in, The Congressional Record, Jan. 22, 1985: S457–S459. (Daily edition.)
63. Singleton, Seth. 'Defense of the gains of socialism:' Soviet Third World policy in the mid-1980s. Washington quarterly, v. 7, no. 1, winter 1984: 102–115.
64. Soviet, East European and Western development aid, 1976–83. [London, H.M. Stationery Office 1984?] 24, [15] 1. (Foreign policy document, no. 108)
65. Trofimenko, Henry. The Third World and the U.S.-Soviet competition: a Soviet view. Foreign Affairs, v. 59, summer 1981: 1021–1040.
66. Ulam, Adam. The world outside. In, Robert F. Byrnes, ed. After Brezhnev: sources of Soviet conduct in the 1980s. Bloomington, In., Indiana University Press, 1983: 345–423.
67. Ulyanovsky, R.A. The twentieth century and the national liberation movement. Narody Azii i Afriki, March-April 1980: 2–9.
68. U.S. Central Intelligence Agency. Communist aid activities in non-communist less developed countries, 1979 and 1954–1979, Oct. 1980. 45 p. ER 80–10318U.
69. U.S. Congress. House. Committee on International Relations. The Soviet Union and the Third World: a watershed in great power policy? Prepared by Joseph G. Whelan and William B. Inglee, Congressional Research Service, Library of Congress. 95th Congress, 1st sess. Wash., U.S. G.P.O., 1977. 186 p.
70. U.S. Congress. House. Committee on Foreign Affairs. Soviet policy and U.S. response in the Third World. Prepared by the Congressional Research Service, Library of Congress. 97th Congress, 1st session. Wash., G.P.O., 1981. 323 p.
71. U.S. Dept. of State. Soviet and East European aid to the Third World, 1981. Feb. 1983. 23 p. Publication no. 9345.
72. U.S. Information Agency. Office of Research. Communist international radio broadcasting in 1982. Dec. 6, 1983. 9 p. (Research memorandum)
73. U.S. International Communication Agency. Office of Research. Soviet cultural and information activities, 1981. Feb. 9, 1982. (Publication no. R-3-82)

74. U.S. Library of Congress. Congressional Research Service. Trends in conventional arms transfers to the Third World, 1976–1983. Report no. 84–82 F, by Richard F. Grimmett. 35 p.
75. U.S.-Soviet competition in the Third World: strategy for peace. Twenty-Fifth Annual U.S. Foreign Policy Conference Report, October 11–13, 1984, p. 14–26. Sponsored by The Stanley Foundation, Muscatine, Iowa. Reproduced in appendix of Part VI of this study.
76. Valkenier, Elizabeth Kridl. The USSR, the Third World, and the global economy. Problems of communism, v. 28, no. 4, July-Aug. 1979: 17–33.
77. ——— Development issues in recent Soviet scholarship. World politics, v. 32, no. 4, July 1980: 485–508.
78. Wolf, Charles, Jr., K. C. Yeh, Edmund Brunner, Jr., Aaron Gurwitz and Marilee Lawrence. The costs of the Soviet empire. Rand Corporation, Santa Monica, Ca., September 1983. 66 p.
79. Worden, Robert L. China's balancing act: Cancun, the Third World, Latin America. Asian survey, v. 23, May 1983: 619–636.
80. Yashkin, V.A. Liberated countries in the system of world socialist relations. Narody Azii i Afriki, no. 6, 1980.
81. Zafar, Imam. Soviet treaties with Third World countries. Soviet studies, v. 35, no. 1, Jan. 1983: 53–70.
82. Zamostny, Thomas J. Moscow and the Third World: recent trends in Soviet thinking. Soviet studies, v. 36, Apr. 1984: 223–235.
83. Zorin, I. The developing countries in the political structure of today's world. Mirovaya ekonomika i mezhdunarodnaya otnosheniye, no. 8, August 1982: 80–91.

III. The Soviet Union and the Middle East

A. Books

84. Bennigsen, Alexandre and Marie Broxup. The Islamic threat to the Soviet state. New York, St. Martin's Press, 1983. 170 p.   DK855.5 .M8 B45 1983
85. Chubin, Shahram. Security in the Persian Gulf: the role of outside powers. London, International Institute for Strategic Studies, 1982. 180 p.   DS326 .S43 1981b
86. Dawisha, Adeed and Karen, eds. The Soviet Union in the Middle East: Policies and perspectives. London, Holmes and Meier, 1982. 172 p.   DS63.2 .S65S67 1982
    Partial contents.—The Soviet Union in the Arab world: the limits to superpower influence, by Adeed Dawisha.—Soviet relations with the northern tier, by Malcolm Yapp.—The East Europeans and the Cubans in the Middle East: surrogates or allies?, by Edwina Moreton.—Energy as a factor in Soviet relations with the Middle East, by Anthony Stacpoole.—The influence of trade on Soviet relations with the Middle East, by Alan H. Smith.—Soviet-American rivalry in the Middle East: the military dimensions, Jonathan Alford.—The correlation of forces and Soviet policy in the Middle East, by Karen Dawisha.
87. Freedman, Robert O. Soviet policy toward the Middle East since 1970. New York, Praeger, 1982. 485 p.   DS63.2 .S65 F73 1982
88. Golan, Galia. The Soviet Union and the Palestine Liberation Organization: an uneasy alliance. New York, Praeger, 1980. 289 p.   DS1119.7 .G623
89. Halliday, Fred. Soviet policy in the arc of crisis. Washington, Institute for policy studies, 1981.
90. Kauppi, Mark V. and R. Craig Nation, eds. The Soviet Union and the Middle East in the 1980s. Lexington, Mass., D.C. Heath, 1983. 292. p.   DS63.2 .S65 S66 1983
    Contents.—The interplay of superpower and regional dynamics, by J.C. Hurewitz.—The sources of Soviet involvement in the Middle East: threat or opportunity?, by Nation.—The Soviet reaction to the Reagan Middle East policy: from the inauguration to the Arab summit at Fez, by Robert O. Freedman.—Socialism, communism, and Islam: Soviet ideological appeal in the Middle East, by Udo Steinbach.—Perspectives on Arabian Gulf security, by Mamoun Kurdi.—The Soviet Union and Egypt after Sadat: premises, prospects, and problems, by Mohammed Anis Salem.—The Soviet Union and the Palestine Liberation Organization, by Galia Golan.—Politics in the Yemens and the Horn of Africa: constraints on a superpower, Paul R. Viotti.—The Soviet Union and Iran since 1978, by Malcolm Yapp.—The Soviet occupation of Afghanistan, by Henning Behrens.—The superpowers in the Middle East: the dynamics of involvement, by Richard Ned Lebow.

91. Novik, Nimrod and Joyce Starr, eds. Challenges in the Middle East. New York, Praeger, 1981. 133 p. DS63.1 .C5
92. Rabinovich, Itanar. The Soviet Union and Syria in the 1970's. New York, Praeger, 1982.
93. Roi, Yaacov, ed. The USSR and the Muslim world; issues in domestic and foreign policy. London, Allen & Unwin, 1984. 298 p. DK855.5 .M8 U85 1984
94. ——— The feasibility of a Soviet-Israeli dialogue: an analysis of the Soviet position. Tel Aviv, Tel-Aviv University, 1981. 26 p. DS63.2 .S65 R64 1981
95. Rubinstein, Alvin Z. Soviet policy toward Turkey, Iran and Afghanistan. New York, Praeger, 1982. 200 p. DK68.7 .T9 R83 1982
96. ——— ed. The great game: rivalry in the Persian Gulf and South Asia. New York, Praeger, 1983. 275 p. DS326 .G66 1983
    Partial contents.—Perceptions and policies of the Gulf states toward regional security and the superpower rivalry, by Michael Sterner.—Soviet policy toward south and southwest Asia: strategic and political aspects, by Rubinstein.—The impact of arms transfers on recipient countries, by Shirin Tahir-Kheli.—Regional security as a policy objective: the case of south and Southwest Asia, by Barry Buzan.
97. Sella, Amnon. Soviet political and military conduct in the Middle East. New York, St. Martin's Press, 1981. 211 p. DS63.2 R9 .S376 1981
98. Smolansky, Oles M. The Soviet Union and Iraq, 1968–1979. New York, Praeger, 1982.
99. Stookey, Robert W. South Yemen: a Marxist state in Arabia. Boulder, Colo. Westview Press, 1982. 124 p. DS247 .A28 S83 1982
100. Tahir-Kheli Shirin, ed. U.S. strategic interests in Southwest Asia. New York, Praeger, 1982. 229 p. UA830 .U19 1982
    Partial contents.—The strategic process: considerations for policy and strategy in Southwest Asia, William O. Staudenmeier.—Soviet interests, objectives, and policy options in Southwest Asia, by Jiri Valenta and Shannon R. Butler.—Soviet constraints in Southwest Asia: a military analysis, by Keith A. Dunn.—Nonregional impacts of Southwest Asian policy: the U.S.-Soviet-OECD triangle, George E. Hudson.—Pakistan since the Soviet invasion of Afghanistan, by Francis Fukuyama.
101. Wohlstetter, Albert, et al: Interests and power in the Persian Gulf. Marina del Ray, Calif., Pan Heuristics. 1981.
102. Yodfat, Aryeh. The Soviet Union and the Arabian Peninsula. New York, St Martin's Press, 1983. 191 p. DS228 .S65 Y53 1983
103. ———The Soviet Union and revolutionary Iran. New York, St. Martin's Press, 1984. 168 p. DS274.2 .S65 Y62 1984
104. Zabeh, Sepehr. Iran since the revolution. Baltimore, Johns Hopkins University Press, 1982.

B. ARTICLES AND DOCUMENTS

105. Alexander, Yonah. Some Soviet-PLO linkages. Middle East review, v. 14, no. 3–4, spring-summer 1982: 64–69.
106. Andelman, David A. Andropov's Middle East. Washington quarterly, v. 6, spring 1983: 110–114.
107. Atkin, Muriel. Soviet relations with the Islamic Republic. SAIS review, v. 3, no. 1, winter-spring 1983: 183–194.
108. ——— Moscow's disenchantment with Iran. Survey, v. 27, autumn-winter 1983: 247–260.
109. Bennigsen, Alexandre. Soviet muslims and the world of Islam. Problems of communism, v. 29, Mar.-April 1980: 38–51.
110. Braker, Hans. The implications of the Islam question for Soviet domestic and foreign policy. Berichte des Bundesinstituts fur ostwissenschaftliche und international sutdien. Cologne, West Germany, April 1983. 34 p.
111. Breslauer, George W. The dynamics of Soviet policy toward the Arab-Israeli conflict: lessons of the Brezhnev era. Center for Foreign Policy Development, Brown University. Oct. 1983. 34 p. (Working paper no. 8)
112. Campbell, John C. Soviet strategy in the Middle East. American Arab affairs, no. 8, spring 1984: 74–82.
113. ——— Soviet policy in the Middle East. Current history, v. 80, Jan. 1981: 1–4, 42–43.
114. Chubin, Shahram. Gains for Soviet policy in the Middle East. International security, v. 6, spring 1982: 122–152.

115. ——— The Soviet Union and Iran. Foreign affairs, vol. 61, no. 4, spring 1983: 921–949.
116. Dawisha, Karen. Soviet decision-making in the Middle East: the 1973 October war and the 1980 Gulf war. International affairs, v. 57, winter 1980–81: 43–59.
117. ——— Moscow's moves in the direction of the Gulf—so near and yet so far. Journal of international affairs, vol. 34, no. 2, fall/winter 1980–81: 219–234.
118. ——— The USSR in the Middle East: superpower in eclipse? Foreign affairs, vol. 61, no. 2, winter 1982/83: 438–452.
119. Dixon, Michael J. Soviet policy in the Persian Gulf. Journal of defense and diplomacy, v. 3, no. 2, Feb. 1985: 23–28.
120. Dunn, Keith A. Soviet strategy, opportunities and constraints in Southwestern Asia. Soviet Union, v. 11, no. 2, 1984: 182–211.
121. ——— Constraints on the USSR in Southwest Asia; a Military analysis. Orbis, v. 25, no. 3, fall 1981: 606–629.
122. Dunn, Michael Collins. Soviet interests in the Arabian Peninsula: the Aden Pact and other paper tigers. American Arab affairs, no. 8, spring 1984: 92–98.
123. Epstein, Joshua M. Soviet vulnerabilities in Iran and the RDF deterrent. International security, v. 6, no. 2, fall 1981: 126–158.
124. Freedman, Robert O. Soviet policy towards the Middle East since the invasion of Afghanistan. Journal of International Affairs, vol. 34, no. 2, fall/winter 1980–81: 283–310.
125. ——— Soviet policy toward Syria since Camp David. Middle East review, v. 14, no. 1–2, fall-winter 1981–82: 31–42.
126. ——— Moscow, Damascus and the Lebanese crisis of 1982–1984. Middle East review, v. 17, no. 1, fall 1984: 22–39.
127. Golan, Galia. The Soviet Union and the Israeli action in Lebanon. International affairs (London), v. 59, winter 1982–83: 7–16.
128. Grayson, Benson Lee. Soviet intentions and American options in the Middle East. Washington, National Defense University Press, 1982. 67 p. (National Security Affairs monograph series 82–3).
129. Halliday, Fred. Current Soviet policy and the Middle East: a report. Merip [Middle East research and Information Project] reports, no. 111, Jan. 1983: 18–22.
130. ——— The Middle East, Afghanistan and the Gulf in Soviet perception. RUSI [Journal of the Royal United Services Institute for Defense Studies], v. 129, Dec. 1984: 13–18.
131. Hannigan, J.B. and C.H. McMillan. The Soviet-Iranian gas agreement: nexus of energy politics, East-West relations, and Middle East politics. Soviet Union, vol. 9, no. 2, 1982: 131–153.
132. Hottinger, Arnold. Arab communism at low ebb. Problems of communism, v. 30, July–Aug. 1981: 17–32.
133. Karsh, Efraim. Soviet arms transfers to the Middle East in the 1970s. Tel Aviv, Tel Aviv University, Jaffee Center for Strategic Studies, 1983. 47 p. (Paper no. 22).
134. Kashkett, Steven B. Iraq and the pursuit of nonalignment. Orbis, v. 26, summer 1982: 477–494.
135. Katz, Mark N. Soviet policy in the Gulf states. Current history, v. 84, Jan. 1985: 25–28, 41.
136. ——— Sanaa and the Soviets. Problems of communism, v. 33, Jan.-Feb. 1984: 21–34.
137. Khalilzad, Zalmay. Islamic Iran: Soviet Dilemma. Problems of communism, v. 33, Jan.-Feb. 1984: 1–20.
138. Lenczowski, George. The Soviet Union and the Persian Gulf: an encircling strategy. International journal, v. 37, no. 2, spring 1982: 307–327.
139. Makinda, Samuel M. Soviet policy in the Red Sea region. Australian National University, Strategic and Defense Studies Centre. August 1984. 28 p. (Working paper no. 82)
140. McNaugher, Thomas L. Balancing Soviet power in the Persian Gulf. Brookings review, summer 1983: 20–24.
141. The Middle East in the 1980s: Problems and prospects: proceedings of a conference. Washington, Middle East Institute, 1983. 189 p.
    Partial contents.—Prospects for Soviet influence in the Middle East: Moscow's supplementary strategy, by M. Lenker.—Soviet policy toward the Arabian Peninsula, by Stephen Page.
142. Ofer, Gur. Economic aspects of Soviet involvement in the Middle East. Soviet and East European Research Center, Hebrew University of Jerusalem, July 1977. 50 p. (Research paper no. 23.)

143. Olcott, Martha Brill. Soviet Islam and world revolution. World politics, v. 34, no. 4, July 1982: 487–504.
144. Page, Stephen. Moscow and the Arabian Peninsula. American Arab affairs, no. 8, spring 1984: 83–91.
145. Phillips, James A. As Israel and the Arabs battle, Moscow collects the dividends. Washington, Heritage Foundation, 1983. 14 p. (Backgrounder no. 291)
146. Quandt, William. Riyadh between the superpowers. Foreign policy, no. 44, fall 1981: 37–56.
147. Rabinovich, Itamar. The foreign policy of Syria: goals, capabilities, constraints, and options. Survival, v. 24, July-Aug. 1982: 175–183.
148. Roberts, Cynthia A. Soviet arms-transfer policy and the decision to upgrade Syrian air defences. Survival, v. 25, July-Aug. 1983: 154–164.
149. Ross, Dennis. Considering Soviet threats to the Persian Gulf. International security, v. 6, fall 1981: 159–180.
150. ——— Soviet views toward the Gulf war. Orbis, fall 1984: 437–447.
151. ——— The Soviet Union and the Persian Gulf. Political science quarterly, v. 99, winter 1984-85: 615–635.
152. Rubin, Barry. Iran, the Ayatollah, and U.S. options. Washington quarterly, v. 6, no. 3, summer 1983: 142–161.
153. Rubinstein, Alvin Z. The Soviet Union and Iran under Khomeini. International affairs, vol. 57, autumn 1981: 599–617.
154. ——— The Soviet presence in the Arab world. Current history, v. 80, Oct. 1981: 313–316, 338–339.
155. Selim, Mohammed el-Sayed. The Soviet role: conceptions, constraints, prospects. In Michael C. Hudson, ed. Alternative approaches to the Arab-Israeli conflict: a comparative analysis of the principal actors. Washington, D.C., Georgetown University Center for Contemporary Arab Studies, 1984. 217 p. DS119.7. A654 1984
156. Sella, Amnon. The USSR and the war in Lebanon: mid-1982. RUSI [Journal of the Royal United Service Institute for Defence Studies], v. 128, June 1983: 35–41.
157. Simes, Dimitri K. The Soviet approach to conflict. In Michael C. Hudson, ed. Alternative approaches to the Arab-Israeli conflict: a comparative analysis of the principal actors. Washington, D.C., Georgetown University Center for Contemporary Arab Studies, 1984. 217 p. DS119.7 .A654 1984
158. Smolansky, Oles M. The Kremlin and the Iraqi Ba'th, 1968–1982: an influence relationship. Middle East review, v. 15, no. 3–4, spring-summer 1983.
159. ——— and Bettie M. Smolansky. The Sino-Soviet interaction in the Middle East. In Herbert J. Ellison, ed. The Sino-Soviet conflict: a global perspective. Seattle, University Press, 1982. 240–267.
160. Soviet and East European trade and financial relations with the Middle East. Washington, Wharton Econometric Forecasting Associates, v. 3, nos. 76–77–78, Oct. 11, 1983. 18 p.
161. Spulber, Nicolas. Israel's war in Lebanon through the Soviet looking glass. Middle East review, v. 15, spring-summer 1983: 18–24.
162. St. John, Ronald Bruce. The Soviet penetration of Libya. World today, v. 38, April 1982: 131–138.
163. Thompson, W. Scott. The Persian Gulf and the correlation of forces. International security, v. 7, no. 1, summer 1982: 157–180.
164. Turner, Arthur Campbell. Iraq: pragmatic radicalism in the fertile crescent. Current history, v. 81, Jan. 1982: 14–17.
165. U.S. Congress. Senate. Committee on Energy and Natural Resources. 96th Congress, 2d session. The geopolitics of oil. Dec.1980. Publication no. 96–119. 89 p. Washington, G.P.O.
166. Van Hollen, Christopher. North Yemen: a dangerous pentagonal game. Washington quarterly, v. 5, no. 3, summer 1982: 137–142.

IV. THE SOVIET UNION AND ASIA

A. BOOKS

167. Asian security 1982. Tokyo, Research Institute for Peace and Security, 1982. 183 p.
168. Bradsher, Henry S. Afghanistan and the Soviet Union. Durham, N.C., Duke University Press, 1983. 324 p. DS357.6. S65 1983
169. Gelman, Harry. The Soviet Far East buildup and Soviet risk-taking against China. Santa Monica, Ca., Rand, 1982. 138 p. UA770.G33 1982

170. Gidadhubli, R.G. Indo-Soviet trade. Bombay, Somaiya Publications, 1983, 246 p. HF3788.S65 G53 1983
171. Hammond, Thomas, T. Red flag over Afghanistan: the communist coup, the Soviet invasion, and the consequences. Boulder, Colorado, Westview, Press, 1983. 262 p. DS371.2. H35 1984
172. Horn, Robert C. Soviet-Indian relations: issues and influence. New York, Praeger, 1982. 231 p. DK68.7 .I5 H67 1982
173. Kapur, K.D. Soviet strategy in South Asia. New Delhi, Young Asia Publications, 1983. 548 p. DS341.3 .S65 K37 1983
174. Mishara, Girish. Relevance of Indo-Soviet economic relations. New Delhi, Allied Publishers, 1983. 89 p. HC435.2 .M528 1983
175. Park, Jae Kyu and Joseph M. Ha, eds. The Soviet Union and East Asia in the 1980s. Seoul, South Korea, Institute for Far Eastern Studies, Kyungnam University, 1983. 284 p. DS518.7 .S69 1983
176. Ram, Raghunath. Soviet policy towards Pakistan. New Delhi, S. Chand, 1983. DK68.7.P3 236p. R8 1983
177. Roy, A. India and the Soviet Union. Calcutta, Firma KLM, 1982. 194 p. DS450.R63 1982
178. Segal, Gerald, ed. The Soviet Union in East Asia. Boulder, Colorado, Westview Press, 1983. 150 p.
        Contents.—Soviet attitudes towards East Asia, by Malcolm Mackintosh.— The Soviet Union and China, by Christina Holmes.—The Soviet Union and the United States, by J. David Armstrong.—The Soviet Union and Japan, Wolf Mendl.—The Soviet Union and Korea, Segal.—The military dimension of Soviet policy, by Lawrence Freedman. The economic dimension of Soviet policy, by Kazuyuki Kinbara.—Soviet policy in East Asia: the certainty of uncertainty, by Segal.
179. Zagoria, Donald S., ed. Soviet policy in East Asia. New Haven, Conn., Yale University Press, 1982. 360 p. DS518.7.S68 1982
        Partial contents.—The strategic environment in East Asia, by Zagoria.— Asia in the Soviet conception, by John J. Stephen.—The political influence of the USSR in Asia, Robert A. Scalapino.—The Sino-Soviet conflict: the Soviet dimension, by Seweryn Bialer.—Soviet policy in southeast Asia, by Zagoria and Sheldon W. Simon.—The Soviet Union and the two Koreas, by Ralph N. Clough.—The Soviet Union's economic relations in Asia, by Ed. A. Hewett and Herbert S. Levine.—Soviet military power in Asia, by Paul F. Langer.—Coalition building or condominium? The Soviet presence in Asia and American policy alternatives, by Richard H. Solomon.

B. ARTICLES AND DOCUMENTS

180. Ali, Mehrunnisa. Soviet-Pakistan ties since the Afghanistan crisis. Asian survey, v. 23, Sept. 1983: 1025–1042.
181. Barnds, William J. The impact of the Sino-Soviet dispute on South Asia. In Herbert J. Ellison, ed. The Sino-Soviet conflict. Seattle, University of Washington Press, 1982. p. 206–239.
182. Bradsher, Henry S. Afghanistan. Washington quarterly, v. 7, summer 1984: 42–55.
183. Canfield, Robert L. Soviet gambit in Central Asia. Journal of South Asia and Middle Eastern studies, v. 5, fall 1981: 10–30
184. Chang, Pao-min. The Sino-Vietnamese conflict over Kampuchea. Survey, v. 27, autumn-winter 1983: 175–206.
185. Dibb, Paul. Soviet capabilities, interests and strategies in East Asia in the 1980s. Survival, v. 24, July–Aug. 1982: 155–162.
186. ——— The Soviet Union as a Pacific power. International journal, v. 38, spring 1983: 234–250.
187. ——— Soviet strategy towards Australia, New Zealand and Oceania. Canberra, Australiam National University, 1984. 34, 4 p. (Working paper no. 90)
188. Donaldson, Robert H. The Soviet Union in South Asia: a friend to rely on? Journal of internation affairs, v. 34, no. 2, fall-winter 1980–81: 235–258.
189. Feeney, William R. U.S. strategic interests in the Pacific. Current history, v. 81, Apr. 1982: 145–149, 183–185.
190. Gelman, Harry. Andropov's policy toward Asia. Journal of northeast Asian studies, v. 2, no. 2, June 1983: 3–12.
191. Ghosh, Partha S. and Rajaram Panda. Domestic support for Mrs. Gandhi's Afghan policy: the Soviet factor in Indian politics. Asian survey, v. 23, March 1983: 261–279.

192. Griffith, William E. The USSR and Pakistan. Problems of communism, v. 31, Jan.-Feb. 1982: 38–44.
193. Heinzig, Dieter. Russia and the Soviet Union in Asia: aspects of colonialism and expansionism. Cologne, West Germany, Berichte des Bundesinstituts fur Ostwissenschaftliche und Internationale Studien, v. 48, 1982.
194. Hammond, Thomas T. Will the Soviets pull out of Afghanistan? Survey, v. 27, autumn-winter 1983: 232–246.
195. Harrison, Selig S. A breakthrough in Afghanistan? Foreign policy, no. 51, summer 1983: 3–26.
196. ——— Afghanistan stalemate: "self-determination" and a Soviet force withdrawal. Parameters, v. 14, no. 4, winter 1984: 34–39.
197. Hinton, Harold C. The United States and extended security commitments: East Asia. In National security policy for the 1980s. Philadelphia, American Academy of Political and Social Sciences, 1981. (Annals, v. 457, Sept. 1981) p. 88–108.
198. Horn, Robert C. Afghanistan and the Soviet-Indian influence relationship. Asian survey, v. 23, March 1983: 244–260.
199. Khalid, Zulfikar A. What went wrong with Pakistan-Soviet relations? Asia Pacific community, no. 22, fall 1983: 74–95.
200. Khalilzad, Zalmay. The struggle for Afghanistan. Survey, v. 25, spring 1981: 189–216.
201. ——— The strategic significance of south Asia. Current history, v. 81, May 1982: 193–196, 228–230.
202. ——— Soviet-occupied Afghanistan. Problems of communism, Nov.-Dec. 1980: 23–40.
203. Kimura, Hiroshi. Soviet policy toward Japan. Working paper no. 6. Providence, R.I., Center for Foreign Policy Development, Brown University, Aug. 1983. 51 p.
204. ——— Recent Japan-Soviet relations: from clouded to "somewhat crystal." Journal of Northeast Asian Studies, v. 1, Mar. 1983: 3–22.
205. ——— The love-hate relationship with the polar bear: Japanese feeling toward the Soviet Union. Japan quarterly, v. 28, Jan.-Mar. 1981: 39–44.
206. Ladozhsky, A. India: a path of peace and cooperation. International affairs (Moscow), no. 10, Oct. 1983: 24–31.
207. Latyshev, I. Soviet-Japanese relations at the present stage. Mirovaya ekonomika i mezhdunarodnaya otnosheniya, in Russian, no. 2, Feb. 1983: 27–36.
208. Lee, Deng-ker. Soviet foreign policy in Southeast Asia—an analysis of the Moscow-Hanoi alliance. Issues & studies, v. 19, July 1983: 50–67.
209. Leifer, Michael. The security of sea-lanes in South-East Asia. Survival, v. 25, Jan.-Feb. 1983: 16–24.
210. Magnus, Ralph H. Tribal Marxism: the Soviet encounter with Afghanistan. Conflict, v. 4, no. 2–4, 1983: 339–368.
211. Mahbubani, Kishore. The Kampuchean problem: a Southeast Asian perception. Foreign affairs, winter 1983–84: 407–425.
212. Malhuret, Claude. Report from Afghanistan. Foreign affairs, v. 62, winter 1983–84: 426–435.
213. Mediansky, F.A. and Diane Court. The Soviet Union in Southeast Asia. London, Strategic and Defence Studies Centre, Australian National University, 1984. 77 p. (Canberra papers on strategy and defense no. 29)
214. Menon, Rajan. The Soviet Union in East Asia. Current History, v. 82, Oct. 1983: 313–317, 339–343.
215. Modenov, S. Tokyo's militaristic syndrome. International affairs (Moscow), no. 12, Dec. 1983: 83–87, 117.
216. Palmer, Norman D. Soviet perspectives on peace and security in Asia. Asian affairs, v. 9, Sept.-Oct. 1981: 1–19.
217. Pike, Douglas. Southeast Asia and the superpowers: the dust settles. Current history, v. 82, April 1983: 145–148, 179–180.
218. ——— The impact of the Sino-Soviet dispute on Southeast Asia. In Herbert J. Ellison, ed. The Sino-Soviet dispute. Seattle, University of Washington Press, 1982. p. 185–205.
219. Pope, Ronald R. Moscow's potential for miscalculation in Asia. Asia Pacific community, fall 1981: 93–102.
220. Radtke, Kurt W. Global strategy and Northeast Asia. Journal of Northeast Asian studies, v. 2, no. 1, Mar. 1983: 59–76.
221. Riencourt, Amaury de. India and Pakistan in the shadow of Afghanistan. Foreign affairs, v. 61, winter 1982–83: 416–437.

481

222. Robinson, Thomas W. The Soviet Union and Asia in 1981. Asian survey, v. 22, Jan. 1982: 13-32.
223. Rosenberger, Leif. The Soviet-Vietnamese alliance and Kampuchea. Survey, v. 27, autumn-winter 1983: 207-231.
224. Rubinstein, Alvin Z. The Soviet Union and Afghanistan. Current history, v. 82, Oct. 1983: 318-321, 337-338.
225. ――― Afghanistan: embraced by the bear. Orbis, v. 26, spring 1982: 135-153.
226. Sagar, Imroze. Indo-Soviet strategic interests and collaboration. Naval War College review, v. 34, Jan.-Feb. 1981: 13-33.
227. Scalapino, Robert A. The U.S. and East Asia: views and policies in a changing era. Survival, v. 24, July-Aug. 1982: 146-155.
228. ――― Pacific prospects. Washington quarterly, v. 4, spring 1981: 3-16.
229. Simon, Sheldon W. Davids and Goliaths: small power—great power security relations in Southeast Asia, v. 23, no. 3, Mar. 1983: 302-315.
230. ――― The Soviet Union and Southeast Asia: interests, goals, and constraints. Orbis, v. 25, spring 1981: 53-88.
231. Singh, S. Nihal. Why India goes to Moscow for arms. Asian survey, v. 24, July 1984: 707-720.
232. Solarz, Stephen J. The Soviet challenge in Asia. Asia Pacific community, no. 25, summer 1984: 1-27.
233. Solomon, Richard H. Choices for coalition-building: the Soviet presence in Asia and American policy alternatives. [Santa Monica, Calif., Rand Corporation] 1981. 88 p. (Paper P-6572)
234. Solution in Afghanistan: from Swedenization to Finlandization. Washington, Kennan Institute for Advanced Russian Studies, Wilson Center, 1982. 51 p.
235. A Soviet symposium on Pacific-Asian issues. Asian survey, v. 24, Nov. 1984: whole issue (1099-1181 p.)
    Partial contents.—Arms limitation and the situation in the Asian-Pacific and Indian Ocean regions, by A. Arbatov.—Five years of the People's revolutionary power in Kampuchea: results and conclusions, by G. Chufrin.—Soviet-U.S. differences in their approaches to Japan, by I. Latyshev.
236. Thomas, Gerry S. Their Pacific fleet. U.S. Naval Institute proceedings, v. 108, no. 10, Oct. 1982: 82-87.
237. Thornton, Thomas Perry. The USSR and Asia in 1982: the end of the Brezhnev era. Asian survey, v. 23, Jan. 1983: 11-25.
238. ――― The USSR and Asia in 1983. Asian Survey, v. 24, Jan. 1984: 1-16.
239. Trottier, Paul and Craig Karp. Afghanistan: five years of occupation. Dept. of State bulletin, v. 85, Feb. 1985: 28-35.
240. U.S. Congress. House. Committee on Foreign Affairs. Subcommittee on Europe and the Middle East. The Soviet role in Asia. Hearings before the Subcommittee on Europe and the Middle East and on Asian and Pacific Affairs of the Committee on Foreign Affairs, House of Representatives, 98th Congress, 1st session. Washington, G.P.O., 1983. 576 p.
241. U.S. Congress. Senate. Committee on Foreign Relations. Hidden war: The struggle for Afghanistan. 98th Congress, 2d session. Washington, G.P.O., April 1984 55 p. (Committee print, S. Prt. 98-181.)
    Hearings held July 19- Oct. 19, 1983
242. ――― Committee on Foreign Relations Situation in Afghanistan 97th Congress, 2d session. Washington, G.P.O., 1982. Hearings a held March 8, 1982.
243. U.S. Library of Congress. Congressional Research Service. Soviet policy toward Japan and the strategic balance in northeast Asia. Report no. 84-64 F, by Stuart D. Goldman. Washington, Feb. 27, 1984.
244. VanderKroef, Justus M. From Phnom Penh to Kabul: the Soviets' new Asian gambit. International security review, v. 6, spring 1981: 13-34.
245. Vertzberger Yaacov. The Malacca/Singapore straits: the Suez of South-East Asia. London, Institute for the Study of Conflict, 1982. 28 p.
246. Westwood, James T. Japan and Soviet power in the Pacific. Strategic review, v. 11, fall 1983: 27-35.
247. Wriggins, W. Howard, Pakistan's search for a foreign policy after the invasion of Afghanistan. Pacific affairs, v. 57, summer 1984: 284-303.
248. Yong, Mun Cheong. Singapore and the Soviet challenge. In, Northeast Asian and European relations: new dimensions and strategies. Taipei, Taiwan, Asia Institute, 1984. p. 95-105.
249. Zagoria, Donald. Soviet policy and prospects in East Asia. International security, v. 5, fall 1980: 66-78.
250. ――― The Moscow-Beijing detente. Foreign affairs, v, 61, spring 1983: 853-873.

482

V. The Soviet Union in Africa

A. BOOKS

251. Arlinghaus, Bruce E., ed. Arms for Africa. Lexington, Mass., D. C. Heath, 1983. 229 p. HD9743. A4382 A75 1983
   Partial contents.—Linkage and leverage in African arms transfers, by Arlinghaus.—Overview of communist arms transfers to Sub-Saharan Africa, by David E. Albright.—Soviet arms transfers in the 1980s: declining influence in sub-Saharan Africa, Edward J. Laurance.—Military relations between Eastern Europe and Africa, by Roger E. Kanet.—Chinese arms transfers to Africa, by George T. Yu.—Western approaches to military assistance to sub-Saharan Africa: an overview, by Cynthia A. Cannizzo.
252. Charles, Milene. The Soviet Union and Africa: the history of the involvement. [Washington] University Press of America [1980] 237 p. DT38.9 .R8 C46
253. Clough, Michael, ed. Changing realities in southern Africa: implications for America policy. Berkeley, Ca., Institute of International Studies, 1982. Research series, no. 47. 318 p. DT747 .U6 C47 1982
   Partial contents.—The natural ally: Soviet policy in southern Africa, by Seth Singleton.
254. Hanks, Robert J. Southern Africa and western security. Cambridge, Mass., Institute for Foreign Policy Analysis, August 1983. 71 p. UA855.6 .H36 1983
255. Henriksen, Thomas H., ed. Communist powers and sub-Saharan Africa. Stanford, Ca., Hoover Institution Press, Stanford University. [1981] 137 p. (Publication no. 252) HX438.5 .C65
   Contents.—Union of Soviet Socialist Republics, Richard E. Bissell.—East European states, by Roger E. Kanet.—Cuba, Goerge Volsky.—People's Republic of China, William E. Ratliff.—Communism, communist states, and Africa, by Henriksen.
256. Isaacman, Allen and Barbara Isaacman. Mozambique: from colonialism to revolution, 1900-1982. Boulder, Co., Westview Press, 1983. 235 p. DT463 .I82 1983
257. Gann, L.H. and Peter Duignan. Africa south of the Sahara: the challenge to western security. Stanford, Ca. Hoover Institution Press, 1981. 114p. (Publication no. 238) UA855.7 .G36
258. Nation, R. Craig and Mark V. Kauppi. Lexington, Mass., D.C. Heath, 1984. 274 p. DT38.9 .S65S68 1984
   Contents.—Introduction: the Soviet impact in Africa, by Nation.—The Soviet Union's encounter with Africa, by Colin Legum.—The Soviet Union and Eastern Europe: patterns of competition and collaboration in southern Africa, by Christopher Coker.—Revolutionary change in Africa: some implications for East German policy behavior, by Bernard von Plate.—From intervention to consolidation: the Soviet Union and southern Africa, by Seth Singleton.—Soviet arms transfers to sub-Saharan Africa, by Joachim Krause.—The significance of Soviet strategic military interests in sub-Saharan Africa, by Richard B. Remnek.—Superpower competiton and regional conflicts in the Horn of Africa, by Marina Ottaway.—The Soviet Union and Zimbabwe: the liberation struggle and after, by Keith Somerville.—The Soviet Union and Africa: the dynamics and dilemmas of involvement, by Mark V. Kauppi.
259. Ottaway, David and Marina. Afrocommunism. New York, Africana Publishing Co., 1980. 237 p. HX438.5 .O87 1980
260. Ottaway, Marina. Soviet and American influence in the Horn of Africa. New York, Praeger, 1982. 187 p. DT367.63 .S65 O87

B. ARTICLES AND DOCUMENTS

261. Albright, David E. The USSR and Sub-Saharan Africa in the 1980s. Washington, Center for Strategic and International Studies, 1983. 129 p. (Washington papers, v. 11, no. 101)
262.——New trends in Soviet policy toward Africa. C.S.I.S. Africa notes, no. 27, April 29, 1984. 10 p. (A publication of the African studies program of the Georgetown University Center for Strategic and International Studies)
263. Bienen, Henry. Perspectives on Soviet intervention in Africa. Political science quarterly, v. 95, spring 1980: 29-42.
264.——Soviet political relations with Africa. International security, v. 6, spring 1982: 153-173.
265. Bissell, Richard E. Soviet activity in Africa: should the West care? South Africa international, v. 10, Apr. 1980: 199-210.

266. Bowman, Larry W. The strategic importance of South Africa to the United States: an appraisal and policy analysis. African affairs, v. 81, Apr. 1982: 159–191.

267. Brind, Harry. Soviet policy in the Horn of Africa. International affairs (London), v. 60, winter 1983–84; 75–95.

268. Bukarambe, Bukar. The Indian Ocean: a zone of peace or strategic primacy. Horn of Africa, v. 6, no. 1, 1983: 21–28.

269. Chiteji, Frank M. Superpower diplomacy: arming Africa. Current history, v. 83, Mar. 1984: 125–128, 138.

270. Clement, Peter. Moscow and Southern Africa. Problems of communism, v. 34, Mar.-Apr. 1985: 29–50.

271. Coker, Christopher. Adventurism and pragmatism: the Soviet Union, Comecon, and relations with African states. International affairs (London), autumn 1981: 618–633.

272. Desfosses, Helen. North-South or East-West? constructs for superpower African policy in the eighties. Journal of international affairs, v. 34, no. 2, fall-winter 1980–81: 369–394.

273. de St. Jorre, John. Destabilization and dialogue: South Africa's emergence as a regional superpower. C.S.I.S. Africa notes, no. 26, April 17, 1984. 7 p. (A publication of the Georgetown Center for Strategic and International Studies)

274. Gorman, Robert F. Soviet perspectives on the prospects for socialist development in Africa. African affairs, v. 83, April 1984: 163–187.

275. Grey, Robert D. The Soviet presence in Africa: an analysis of goals. Journal of modern African studies, v. 22, Sept. 1984: 511–527.

276. Gromyko, Anatoliy. Soviet foreign policy and Africa. International affairs (Moscow), no. 2, Feb. 1982: 30–35.

277. ——— Socioeconomic development of Africa and prospects of Soviet-African relations. Vestnik adademii nauk SSR, no. 10, Oct. 1983: 32–41.

278. Henriksen, Thomas H. The USSR and Africa: challenge and prospects. Survey, v. 27, autumn-winter 1983: 261–272.

279. Henze, Paul B. Communism and Ethiopia. Problems of communism, v. 30, no. 3, May-June 1981: 55–74.

280. ——— Arming the Horn, 1960–1980. Wilson Center, Smithsonian Institution, Working Paper no. 42, July 28, 1982. 34 p.

281. Knight, Virginia Curtin. Political consolidation in Zimbabwe. Current history, v. 83, Mar. 1984: 109–112, 135.

282. ——— The social and economic transformation of Zimbabwe. Current history, v. 82, Mar. 1983: 106–109, 129–130.

283. Laidi, Zaki. Soviet-African relations after the signing of the Nkomati Accord. Communist affairs, no. 3, 1984: 461–466.

284. Larus, Joel. The end of naval detente in the Indian Ocean. The world today, v. 36, Apr. 1980: 126–132.

285. Latham, S. F. About-turn in Mozambique? World today, v. 37, Feb. 1981: 69–73.

286. MacFarlane, S. N. Intervention and security in Africa. International affairs (London), v. 60, winter 1983–84: 53–67.

287. ——— Africa's decaying security system and the rise of intervention. International security, v. 8, spring 1984: 127–151.

288. Nolutshungu, Sam C. African interests and Soviet power: the local context of Soviet policy. Soviet studies, v. 34, July 1982: 397–417.

289. Ogunbadejo, Oye. Soviet policies in Africa. African affairs, v. 79, July 1980: 297–325.

290. Phillips, James A. Ethiopia's Kremlin connection. Washington, Heritage Foundation, 1985. 11 p. (Backgrounder no. 404)

291. Potts, James. Angola and the U.S.: the shape of a prudent compromise. Washington, Heritage Foundation, 1984. 10 p. (Backgrounder no. 347)

292. Remnek, Richard B. Soviet military interests in Africa. Orbis, v. 28, spring 1984: 123–143.

293. Rothenberg, Morris. The USSR and Africa: new dimensions of Soviet global power. Washington, D.C., Advanced International Studies Institute. Monographs in international affairs, 1980. 280 p.

294. Serfaty, Simon. The Soviet Union in Africa: realities and limits. South Africa international, v. 14, July 1983: 311–319.

295. Shaw, Timothy M. The future of the great powers in Africa: towards a political economy of intervention. Journal of modern African studies, v. 21, no. 4, 1983: 555–586.

296. Singleton, Seth. Soviet policy and socialist expansion in Asia and Africa. Armed forces and society, v. 6, spring 1980: 339–369.

297. —— The shared tactical goals of South Africa and the Soviet Union. C.S.I.S. Africa notes, no. 12, April 26, 1983. 6 p. (A publication of the Georgetown Center for Strategic and International Studies)

298. Smock, David R. and Norman N. Miller. Soviet designs in Africa. [Hanover, N.H.] American Universities Field Staff, 1980. 17 p. (Fieldstaff reports, 1980/ no. 17 [Africa])

299. Somerville, Keith. The USSR and southern Africa since 1976. Journal of modern African studies, v. 22, no. 1, 1984: 73–108.

300. Tarabrin, Y. Africa in confrontation with U.S. imperialism. International affairs (Moscow), no. 6, June 1984: 33–42.

301. U.S. Congress. Senate. Committee on the Judiciary. Subcommittee on Security and Terrorism. The role of the Soviet Union, Cuba, and East Germany in fomenting terrorism in Southern Africa. Hearings, 97th Congress, 2d session. Mar. 22–31, 1982. Washington, G.P.O. 2 v. "Serial no. J-97-101"

302. —— Soviet, East German and Cuban involvement in fomenting terrorism in Southern Africa; report. Washington, G.P.O., 1982. 28 p. At head of title: 97th Congress, 2nd session. Committee print.

303. Valenta, Jiri. Soviet-Cuban intervention in the Horn of Africa: impact and lessons. Journal of international affairs, v. 34, no. 2, fall-winter 1980–81: 353–368.

304. Valkenier, Elizabeth Kridl. Great power economic competition in Africa: Soviet progress and problems. Journal of international affairs, v. 34, no. 2, fall-winter 1980–81: 259–268.

305. Westwood, James T., Lt. Cdr USN. The Soviet Union and the southern sea route. Naval War College review, v. 35, Jan.-Feb. 1982: 54–64.

306. Zartman, I. William. Issues of African diplomacy in the 1980s. Orbis, v. 25, winter 1982: 1025–1043.

VI. The Soviet Union and Latin America

A. BOOKS

307. Blasier Cole. The giant's rival: the USSR the Latin America. Pittsburgh, University of Pittsburgh Press, 1983, 213 p. F1416 .S65 B57 1983

308. Falcoff, Mark and Robert Royal, eds. Crisis and opportunity: U.S. policy in Central America and the Caribbean, Washington, Ethics and Public Policy Center, 1984. 491 p. F1439.5 .C73 1984

309. Feinberg, Richard E., ed. Central America: international dimensions of the crisis. New York, Holmes and Meier, 1982. 280 p. F1436.7 .C46 1982
    Partial contents.—U.S. interests and practices, by James Kurth.—The recent rapid redefinitions of U.S. interests and diplomacy in Central America, by Feinberg.—U.S. security interests in Central America in global perspective, by Margaret Daly Hayes.—Soviet and Cuban responses to new opportunities in Central America, by Jiri Valenta.

310. Grabendorff, Wolf, and Heinrich—W. Krumwiede and Jorg Todt. Political change in Central America: internal and external dimensions. Boulder, Colo., Westview Press, 1984. 312 p. F1439.5 .P65 1984

311. Hayes, Margaret Daly. Latin America and the U.S. national interest. Boulder, Colo., Westview Press, 1984. 295 p. HF1456.5 .L3H38 1984

312. Leiken, Roberts S., ed. Central America: anatomy of conflict. New York, Pergamon Press, 1984. 354. p. F1439.5 .C45 1984
    Partial contents.—The origins of Sandinista foreign policy, by Arturo Cruz Sequeira.—The Salvadoran left, by Leiken.—The Soviets and Central America, by Morris Rothenberg.

313. —— Soviet strategy in Latin America. New York Praeger, 1982. 124 p. (The Washington papers, v. 10, no. 93) Published with the Center for Strategic and International Studies, Georgetown University, Washington, D.C. UA602.3 .L44 1982

314. Levine, Barry B., ed. The new Cuban presence in the Caribbean. Boulder, Co., Westview Press, 1983. 274 p. F2178 .C9 N48 1983

315. Wesson, Robert, ed. Communism in Central America and the Caribbean. Stanford, Ca., Stanford University Press, 1982. 177p. HX118.5 .C65 1982
    Contents.—Moscow, the Caribbean, and Central America, by W. Raymond Duncan.—Cuba, by William LeoGrande.—Nicaragua, by James Nelson Goodsell. El Salvador, by Thomas P. Anderson.—Guatemala, by Daniel L. Premo.—Costa Rica, Honduras, and Panama, by Neale J. Pearson.—Jamai-

ca, by W. Raymond Duncan.—Eastern Caribbean, by George Volsky.—Guyana, by William E. Ratliff.—Conclusion, by Wesson.

316. Wiarda, Howard J., ed. Rift and Revolution. Washington, American Enterprise Institute, 1984. 392 p.   F1439.5 .R53 1984
    Partial contents.—The origins of the crisis in Central America, by Wiard.—The roots of revolution in Central America, by Thomas P. Anderson.—Revolutionary movements in Central America: the development of a new strategy, by Ernest Evans.—Soviet strategy and policies in the Caribbean basin, by Jiri Valenta and Virginia Valenta.—U.S. security in Latin America, by Jeane J. Kirkpatrick.

317. ———— In search of policy: the United States and Latin America. Washington, American Enterprise Institute, 1984. 147 p.

B. ARTICLES AND DOCUMENTS

318. Ashby, Timothy. Nicaragua: Soviet satrapy. U.S. Naval Institute proceedings, v. 110, July 194: 48–56.

319. Blasier, Cole. The Soviet Latin Americanists. Latin American research review, v. 16, no. 1, 1981: 107–123

320. ———— Soviet relations with Latin America in the 1970s. Washington, National Council for Soviet and East European Research, 1980.

321. Bulychev, I. The Contadora group and the search for peace in Central America. Mirovays ekonomika i mezhdunarodnaya otnosheniya, no. 2, Feb. 1984: 95–99.

322. Clement, Peter. Moscow and Nicaragua: two sides of Soviet policy. Comparative strategy, v. 5, no. 1, 1985: 75–92.

323. Di Giovanni, C., Jr. U.S. policy and the Marxist threat to Central America. Washington, Heritage Foundation, 1980. 16 p. Backgrounder no. 128.

324. Dmitriyev, V. The crisis of imperialists' colonial policy in Latin America. International affairs (Moscow), no. 10, Oct. 1982: 33–41.

325. Dominguez, Jorge I. Cuba's relations with Caribbean and Central American countries. Cuban studies, v. 13, summer 1983: 79–120.

326. ———— U.S. interests and policies in the Caribbean and Central America. Washington, American Enterprise Institute [c1982] 55 p. Special analysis no. 81–9.

327. Duncan, W. Raymond. Soviet interests in Latin America. Journal of Inter-American studies and world affairs, v. 26, May 1984: 163–198.

328. Feinberg, Richard E. Central America: the view from Moscow. Washington quarterly, v. 5, no. 2, spring 1982: 171–175.

329. Gershman, Carl. Soviet power in Central America and the Caribbean: the growing threat to American security. AEI foreign policy and defense review, v. 5, no. 1, 1984: 37–46.

330. Hough, Jerry F. The evolving Soviet debate on Latin American. Latin America Research review, v. 16, no. 1, 1981: 124–143.

331. Ikle, Fred C. A security policy for America's 'fourth border.' Defense, July 1983, 2–7.

332. Jacobsen, C. G. Soviet attitudes towards, aid to, and contacts with Central American revolutionaries. Prepared by C. G. Jacobsen in association with David R. Jones, Mohiaddin Mesbahi, and Robin Rosenberg for the State Department. April 10, 1984. 31 p.

333. Katz, Mark N. The Soviet-Cuban connection. International security, v. 8, no. 1, summer 1983: 88–112.

334. Kiracofe, Clifford A. The Soviet network in Central America. Midstream, v. 27, May 1981: 3–6.

335. Leiken, Robet S. Fantasies and facts: the Soviet Union and Nicaragua. Current history, v. 83, Oct. 1984: 314–317, 344–345.

336. ———— Eastern winds in Latin America. Foreign policy, no. 42, spring 1981: 94–113.

337. LeoGrande, William M. Through the looking glass: the Kissinger report on Central America. World policy journal, v. 1, winter 1984: 251–284.

338. ———— Cuban-Soviet relations and Cuban policy in Africa. Cuban studies, v. 10, Jan. 1980: 1–48.

339. Luers, William H. The Soviets and Latin America: a three decade U.S. policy triangle. Washington quarterly, v. 7, winter 1984: 3–32.

340. ———— U.S. interests in Central America. AEI foreign policy and defense review, v. 5, no. 1, 1984: 26–37.

341. Lunin, V.N. Grenada: the logic of imperial force. Latinskaya Amerika, no. 2. Feb. 1984: 134–144.

342. Mastny, Vojtech. The Soviet Union and the Falklands war. Naval War College review, v. 36, May–June 1983: 46–55.
343. McClintock, Cynthia. Democracies and guerrillas: the Peruvian experience. International policy report. Washington, Center for International Policy, 1983.
344. McColm, R. Bruce. Central America and the Caribbean: the larger scenario. Strategic review, v. 11, summer 1983: 28–42.
345. Moore, Patrick. The Soviet threat to Western interests in Central America. Radio Free Europe research, RAD background report/163, Aug. 30, 1984. 9 p.
346. Moorer, Thomas H. and Georges A. Fauriol. Caribbean basin security. New York, Praeger, 1984. 108 p. (Washington papers, v. 11, no. 104) Published for the Georgetown Center for Strategic and International Studies.
347. Pushkov, A.K. The ideological factor in the Latin American policy of the Reagan administration. Latinskaya Amerika, no. 11, Nov. 1983: 14–27
348. Radvanyi, Miklos K. Soviet leaders and the Americas. [Washington] Council for Inter-American Security [c1980] 24 p. (Special report)
349. Ramet, Pedro and Fernando Lopez-Alves. Moscow and the revolutionary left in Latin America. Orbis, v. 28, summer 1984: 341–363.
350. Rebkin, Rhoda Pearl. U.S.-Soviet rivalry in Central America and the Caribbean. Journal of international affairs, v. 34, no. 2, fall-winter 1980–81: 329–352.
351. Rosenberg, Robin. "Soviet support for Central American guerrilla movements as a strategic initiative." In, David R. Jones, (ed.). Soviet armed forces review annual, volume 8, 1983-1984. Gulf Breeze, FL., Academic International Press, 1985, pp. 348–389.
352. Rothenberg, Morris. Latin America in Soviet eyes. Problems of communism, v. 32, Sept.-Oct. 1983: 1–18.
353. ――― Since Reagan: the Soviets and Latin America. Washington quarterly, v. 5, no. 2, spring 1982: 175–179.
354. Sanchez, Nestor D. Regional security: United States security interests and concerns in Latin America. California Western international law journal, v. 12, summer 1982: 434–446.
355. Schwab, Theodore and Harold Sims. Revolutionary Nicaragua's relations with the European communist states, 1979-1983. Conflict quarterly, v. 5, no. 1, winter 1985: 5–14.
356. The Soviet challenge in Central America and the Caribbean. New York, CAUSA International, 1985. 16 p.
357. Soviet/Cuban strategy in the Third World after Grenada: toward prevention of future Grenadas: a conference report. Washington, Woodrow Wilson International Center for Scholars, 1984. 79 p.
358. U.S. Dept. of State. Soviet activities in Latin America and the Caribbean. February 28, 1985. Current policy no. 669. 6 p.
359. U.S. Dept. of State and Dept. of Defense. Background paper: Nicaragua's military build-up and support for Central American subversion. Washington, July 18, 1984.
360. ――― Grenada documents: overview and selection. Washington, G.P.O., Sept. 1984. 820 p.
361. ――― The Soviet-Cuban connection in Central America and the Caribbean. Washington, D.C., U.S. G.P.O., March 1985, 45 p.
362. U.S. National Bipartisan Commission on Central America. Report. Washington, The Commission, Jan. 1984. 134 p. Popularly known as the Kissinger Commission report. Also published by Macmillan.
363. Valenta, Jiri. The USSR, Cuba, and the crisis in Central America. Orbis, v. 25, fall 1981: 715–746.
364. ――― Soviet strategy in the Caribbean Basin. United States Naval Institute proceedings, v. 108, May 1982: 169–181.
365. ――― Soviet policy in Central America. Survey, v. 27, autumn-winter 1983: 287–303.
366. Valenta, Jiri and Virginia Valenta. Leninism in Grenada. Problems of communism, v. 23, July-Aug. 1984: 1–23.
367. Varas, Augusto. Ideology and politics in Latin American—USSR relations. Problems of communism, v. 33, Jan.-Feb. 1984: 35–47.
368. ――― Soviet-Latin American relations under United States regional hegemony. Washington, the Wilson Center, Smithsonian Institution, 1984. no. 140.
369. ――― "The Soviet Union in the foreign relations of the Southern Cone." In, Heraldo Munoz and Joseph S. Tulchin (eds.). Latin American nations in world politics. Boulder, Co., Westview Press, 1984. p. 243–259.

DATE DUE